HAMBURGERS IN PARADISE

HAMBURGERS
IN
Paradise

THE STORIES BEHIND
THE FOOD WE EAT

LOUISE O. FRESCO

Translated by Liz Waters

PRINCETON UNIVERSITY PRESS

Princeton & Oxford

Requests for permission to reproduce material from this work should be sent to Permissions, Princeton University Press

Published by Princeton University Press, 41 William Street, Princeton, New Jersey 08540 In the United Kingdom: Princeton University Press, 6 Oxford Street, Woodstock, Oxfordshire OX20 1TW

press.princeton.edu

THE HOLY BIBLE, NEW INTERNATIONAL VERSION®, NIV® Copyright © 1973, 1978, 1984, 2011 by Biblica, Inc.® Used by permission. All rights reserved worldwide.

Jacket art: Detail from Luis Meléndez, *Still Life with Bread, Ham, Cheese and Vegetables,* about 1772. Photograph © 2015 Museum of Fine Arts, Boston.

Library of Congress Cataloging-in-Publication Data

Fresco, Louise O., author.
    [Hamburgers in het paradijs. English]
    Hamburgers in paradise : the stories behind the food we eat / Louise O. Fresco ; translated by Liz Waters.
        pages   cm
    Includes bibliographical references and index.
    ISBN 978-0-691-16387-1 (hardcover : alk. paper)
    1. Food supply—Social aspects.   2. Food supply—History.   3. Food consumption.
4. Food security.   I. Waters, Liz, translator.   II. Fresco, Louise O. Hamburgers in het paradijs. Translation of (work):   III. Title.
HD9000.5.F73513   2015
338.1′9—dc23   2015013030

British Library Cataloging-in-Publication Data is available

N ederlands letterenfonds
dutch foundation
for literature

This book was published with the support of the Dutch Foundation for Literature.

This book has been composed in Sabon Next LT Pro with Montserrat and Bickham Script display by Princeton Editorial Associates Inc., Scottsdale, Arizona.

Printed on acid-free paper. ∞

Printed in the United States of America

10 9 8 7 6 5 4 3 2 1

CONTENTS

Color plates follow pages 174 and 270.

Food–A Voyage of Discovery

Food is a source of intense confusion these days. Can we justify continuing to eat steak when every cow emits greenhouse gases of the worst kind? How can we opt for cereals instead, if a bowl of muesli entails carbon emissions equivalent to a drive to the supermarket in the next village? Is it really sensible to eat more fruit if it has to be flown in from distant places, where it may have been picked in unhygienic conditions by underpaid workers, simply because the choice of seasonal fruit is inevitably limited in winter in northern latitudes? Is sugar ultimately to blame for all our health problems, and should we switch to honey? Or does honey contain the same molecules? Ought sugar to be banned altogether, or is it a cheap source of calories and a source of employment in poor countries? Anyhow, we can make biofuel from sugar, which is surely good for the environment. Or is it? Perhaps the government ought to regulate and tax the consumption of food as it does tobacco. Except that if fat is rationed or made relatively expensive, then just about everything that tastes good will have a stigma attached to it. In any case, that degree of state interference is incompatible with our love of freedom. We have a right to say what goes on in our own kitchens, at the very least, you might think. All right, so we need better information, and a ban on advertisements aimed at young children. And shouldn't we immediately stop subsidizing farmers, given that it causes poverty in the rest of the world? Or is that not how the world market works? Do we want to buy tomatoes from low-wage countries because that will help to create jobs, or from our own efficient greenhouses? Or from Spain or Italy for solidarity's sake, in light of the economic crisis in member states of the European Union? Should we cease producing meat altogether? Those horrifyingly vast milking parlors, those factory-farmed chickens.... Or is large-scale food production a blessing for humanity? And what about the dangers of genetically modified food? Might it soon prove to be our salvation? A small risk is acceptable, isn't it? Are we being manipulated by big business and advertising, or have the food industry and the supermarkets made our food safer and healthier? Speaking of health, how can we live with the knowledge that there are now twice as many overweight people as undernourished people in the world?

This book looks at all these questions and more. Few subjects give rise to such contrasting visions, such uncertainty and fierce emotion. Everyone has an opinion about what we eat and how our food is produced and prepared. No one can remain indifferent to food, not a French housewife or an African politician, a farmer or a baker, a gourmet or a chef, and passions are easily roused by questions about which foods are good or bad. Food evokes profound feelings and old memories. Of course that's because food is essential; eating is something we do every day. We can't survive without it, as individuals or as a species, so it's only logical that in all ages food has been subject to value judgments and taboos, and that rulers of the past, like governments today, have always wanted to keep control of food resources, waging war over them if necessary. None of this is new.

Dis-moi ce que tu manges, et je te dirai ce que tu es. ("Tell me what you eat and I'll tell you what you are"—not "who you are," as the expression is sometimes wrongly translated.) Those oft-quoted words were first spoken in 1825 by a French chef named Jean Anthelme Brillat-Savarin, and they have lost none of their relevance. But whereas he focused on a gastronomic code and the pleasures of eating, our concerns about food are now largely a matter of ethics and of knowledge about how the world works. Agriculture and food are bound up with culture and history, wherever and whoever we may be, and therefore with issues of equality and development. It makes no sense to look at our own food choices in isolation.

In the past decade or so, confusion over food has only increased. Who in the past ever asked where their broad beans came from, or what kind of milk they were drinking? Those who worried about hunger in the world were mainly concerned about starving children and drought-ravaged harvests. Today, everything that has to do with food—from seed grain and agriculture to food manufacture, supermarkets, and home cookery—is complex and riddled with ambiguities. Behind every peanut butter sandwich lies a long story of prices and feed stocks, climate and politics, big business and small farmers, tradition and scientific innovation, touching on everything from hidden ingredients to thoughtless consumption. Knowledge about that proverbial sandwich reaches the consumer in dribs and drabs, and knowledge only adds to our confusion. After all, what is "good," whether for the environment, for our health, for those malnourished children, or for the animals? In this climate of confusion, modern social media provide a platform for everything and everyone: miracle diets and slimming pills, alternative fertilizers for the vegetable plot, traditional recipes for suet pudding, criticism of Europe for its E-numbers policy and its tight regulations, revelations about scientific conspiracies, moving stories by farmer's wives, gruesome photographs of battery chickens alongside idyllic shots of cows in flowery meadows. Anyone who feels the urge can have their say.

Food has gained an additional moral charge in recent years. Agriculture and edible produce have become the touchstone of responsible citizenship among those concerned about the state of the world. If you eat well in an ethical sense, then your heart is in the right place. Conversely, if you care about the environment and about animals, it will show through in your eating habits: seasonal vegetables and cheese from the farmers' market, perhaps, and no cheap meat or imported fruit. Anyone who eats differently from us fails to measure up. Hamburgers? Dreadful. Or perfectly fine. Everything about food has acquired a moral dimension. Like it or not, every food choice we make has global ramifications.

We have lost our naïveté, our ability to respond naturally to food, which once demanded a great deal of hard work and absorbed a large part of our income, but about which we asked few questions other than what time the next meal would be ready and whether it tasted good. These days we're confronted with an overwhelming number of relatively cheap options, each with ethical and political consequences that are almost impossible to assess. Every day the media tell us new stories about agriculture and food, reflecting the complexity of both. Environmentalists berate us, saying our eating patterns are costing the earth, and social activists explain how hamburgers contribute to poverty. Doctors warn of the dangers of consuming certain foods and the beneficial effects of others, and everyone worries about everyone's weight. Scientists reassure us with promises of breakthroughs in the battle against cancer and obesity. Eat a pineapple a day and everything will be all right. And above all avoid fish 'n' chips (or no, that's a pretty healthy meal).

This new complexity has to do with the globalization of the production and processing of food, today's worldwide food network with all its positive and negative impacts. The spread of new means of production, foods, and dietary habits is as old as human migration, but the sheer scale on which food has been arriving from all parts of the world over the past ten to fifteen years and the diversity presented to us as a result are unprecedented. As a major trading nation, my own country, the Netherlands, is an important intersection for the food chains that span the world. In our politics and in our personal choices, many of the dilemmas felt across the globe come together here.

———————

The disappearance of a purely instinctive attitude to food creates uncertainty, but it also encourages us to try to find out what food means to us, the urban generations. Interest is growing everywhere, and it's not just a matter of politics, morality, or medicine. Food is increasingly an aspect of outlook and lifestyle. Every TV station offers a range of programs that visit farms, bakeries, and restaurants. Intimate revelations in the kitchen under the all-seeing eye of the TV camera have proven a successful formula. Stars big and small describe their favorite recipes. A newspaper or magazine without a cookery and wine section is unthinkable. Chefs with strong foreign accents perform conjuring tricks with oysters and truffles; in fact, cooks are well on their way to becoming the gurus of our day and restaurants the temples of the new food religion. Expensive delicatessens are flourishing, and even the most basic of supermarkets sells scallops, mozzarella, seaweed, and avocados. Food is now an aspect of our lifestyle that bridges the old divide between the sexes; men are just as fanatical as women (if not more so) when it comes to the culinary arts—on weekends, at least. Cooking has become a pastime for yuppies. These trends are both high-tech, with liquid nitrogen used to make all kinds of foam, and calculatedly simple, with a return to old recipes and techniques, such as the haybox. Algal foam versus stuffed tripe. So no wonder artists, architects, directors, and writers have become interested in entirely new ways in the countryside, in food and agriculture, and in cooking and eating. Writers are discovering the lamb and the pig and the enticements of making their own wine. We see film festivals devoted exclusively to documentaries and feature films about food and agriculture, about traditions preserved and lost. Gastronomic explorers recount their experiences in the farthest reaches of Macao and Marrakesh as if talking of freshly discovered continents, while architects and town planners dream of new, organic communes where gardening, eating, and work all converge.

This mass of culinary trends and obsessions does not make our decisions any easier. We remain confused about what good food is, in the sense of both healthy—for people, animals, and the environment—and morally acceptable. The more we think we know, the less clear it all becomes. Knowledge, far from breeding acceptance, makes us want to give things up. Confusion often leads to a kind of paralysis, a sense that in the end it doesn't matter what we choose as individuals, that we can never get it right whatever we do, because it's impossible to predict all the consequences of our actions. There's a temptation to seize on one simple guideline that makes everything black-and-white: we glorify vegetarianism, believe in organic apples and tomatoes, or swear by keeping our own chickens; we extol the virtues of Buddhist bread making, or propose that nursery schools start teaching children about vegetables. Better a few rules of our own, even superstitions, than disorder or dilution.

The tragedy of our time—and I do not use the word lightly—is that most people in the rich and emerging economies, even in the countryside, are barely conscious any longer of how their daily food actually reaches their plates. Food demands both consciousness and a conscience. We can't discuss or judge food without knowing its story, a tale of origins and production, of ancient traditions and modern science and technology, of values and taboos, of sharing meals, and of eating alone. With food, the personal is always political, to use an old slogan of the feminist movement. But we can only make genuinely personal choices if we have some understanding of how it all works, nationally and internationally, technically, economically, and socially. We struggle to find our way out of a maze of facts and opinions, knowledge and ignorance, values and traditions, because wherever we may have our origins, food connects us with rest of the globe. In fact food is all about connections, among farmers, manufacturers, retailers, and consumers: from farm to fork, as the saying goes.

Hamburgers in Paradise arose from a desire to do something about the disparity between scientific advance and social insecurity in relation to farming and food, a disparity made all the more stark by our tendency to adopt black-and-white attitudes and simple slogans. I have described this tendency as shadow thinking. The gloom of the shadow thinkers can be found everywhere, but the two best examples are Thomas Malthus and Lester Brown. Malthus claimed at the start of the nineteenth century that the growth of the human population would be limited by a shortage of land, forgetting that yields can increase. In our own era, Lester Brown predicted that China would fall prey to widespread famine by 2000, and he still makes a similar claim, in a variety of new ways. Shadow thinkers often voice perfectly justified concerns, but they extrapolate problems without seeing that circumstances, morality, knowledge, policy, and much else can change. They are to be found in the media, inside and outside government, and in science. As an academic researcher or as an essayist, you'll be far more popular if you come out with supposedly hard facts about aggression in meat eaters and butterfly deaths caused by pesticides than with cautious and nuanced conclusions. Unfortunately, there are no cut-and-dried, universally valid guidelines. We need to understand all the devilish details and subtle distinctions and to accept that sometimes no perfect solution exists, that everything comes at a price.

There's no single good way of dealing with food responsibly. If only there were. Then I could write out a list of ingredients for a twenty-first-century diet. If life were that simple, I'd be able to design the agriculture and food industry of the future. What counts in the end, as ever, is full awareness when dealing with choices, based on insights into how food supply chains work. Hardly any food or agriculture is inherently bad—apart from rotting or contaminated produce and farming that requires the felling of rainforests, the mistreatment of workers and animals, or the excessive use of chemicals. Which is why it makes no sense to forbid specific food items. It would be nonsense, for example, to place a total ban on fast foods, because in some situations they may be a sensible option for a family or an individual, and moderate consumption need not be a problem. Nor does it make sense to stick rigidly to a vegetarian diet. Nonetheless, there are undoubtedly some irresponsible and unhealthy eating habits and production methods, and we should find out which they are and put a stop to them, or at least reduce their prevalence. This book offers ingredients for a fully conscious way of thinking about farming and food, about shopping and cooking, for all of us, as both citizens and consumers.

My ultimate message is optimistic: even though we have much to worry about, there's also a great deal that's going well or could yet change for the better. In the end, barring disaster on a global scale, we will be able to feed present and future generations in ways that are sustainable and healthy as well as balanced and equitable. There's no justification for the doom-mongering so popular with some, or for disaster scenarios or draconian laws. There is certainly a need—and potential—for many improvements, and they will require a combination of modern science and valuable tradition, but more than anything this book is an ode to human progress. The majority of human beings today have enough food, and it's safe and varied. My main concern is to offer an unprejudiced view—whether of artificial fertilizer, biotechnology, organic farming, or meat—and where necessary some criticism of recent developments, such as the dominance of supermarkets and the effects of large-scale farming. Science in the broad, interdisciplinary sense, rather than ideology, forms the first pillar on which this book rests. But although I have tried to give a scientific grounding to every assertion, this is not an academic book, because another, equally important pillar is the evolutionary, historical, and cultural context of farming and food. Which is not to suggest this is a historical cookery book, or an encyclopedia of foodstuffs, or a textbook on the philosophy of food, or a guide for allotment holders.

I'm fascinated by the evolution of farming and the food supply, by how humanity in an evolutionary blink of an eye has built up a complex and generally efficient food network after hundreds of thousands of years of scarcity. To this day an important part is played by culture and religion, and especially the three main monotheistic religions. It may not seem obvious that agricultural science should include culture as part of its field of study, but I've become convinced that no better way exists to understand the current confusion surrounding food.

The title *Hamburgers in Paradise* points to the archetype of carefree abundance and to a product that symbolizes contemporary culinary transgression. Paradise is among other things a metaphor for our planet's landscapes, for the loss of innocence and a pre-industrial past that seems so much more attractive than the confusion we find ourselves in today. Although paradise is primarily associated with Judaism, Christianity, and Islam, the concept exists in almost all cultures. My thesis is that, implicitly or explicitly, we are deeply influenced by it as a metaphor, in both a positive and a negative sense. Paradise still resounds through art, and art is perhaps better than science at revealing those things that give shape to our thoughts. Art sometimes has other, allegorical dimensions, and they don't make it any less pertinent, which is why I've included a number of pictures of artworks that portray the essence of paradise, farming, food, and landscape, and have started each chapter with literary quotations. I've treated some of the sources fairly freely, especially the Book of Genesis, by reading them selectively and as far as possible with an open mind. Although some of the stories in this book may be anecdotal or, as befits stories, contain contradictory and speculative elements, the value, pleasure, and opportunities for reflection lie in the quest itself. I have therefore attempted to make the chapters more or less self-contained, so that each can be read independently. We do not live by knowledge alone. Knowledge cannot always provide an explanation, nor can it answer ethical questions, which arise time and again in matters of food.

The world's food production, processing, and consumption add up to such a broad subject, about which so much has been written, that I was continually forced to make choices and impose constraints. To judge from the piles of unused material I've collected over the years, each chapter could easily have grown into a book in its own right. This is the kind of book that can never really be finished. Every day, further books, articles, and research results are published that ought to be given a place in it. I've selected what I see as relevant right now, but I'm more aware than anyone of the lacunas and of the eclectic nature of the subjects I've chosen. There is plenty of room for debate over the selection of artworks. I realize that the liberties I've taken will not sit well with everybody.

This book is a personal account of the many years I have devoted to farming and food, sometimes in my own country, the Netherlands, but mainly beyond. I regard my many travels and the unique observations and extraordinary meetings that have arisen from them as a privilege. They have enriched my life. This experience is reflected in the personal style of the book, in which I do all I can to avoid jargon. I've been forced to compromise by using such terms as "developed," "Western," "OECD countries versus developing countries," "rich versus poor and emerging economies," or "middle classes and the poorer classes," all of which I use rather loosely, as there are no unambiguous distinctions. I didn't want to downplay the pleasure I take in looking at landscapes, in cooking, and in food as a cultural expression, nor my admiration for and interest in farming life and the kitchen, wherever in the world they may be.

Hamburgers in Paradise has turned into a voyage of discovery, with the aim of finding the meaning of farming and food, and therefore it is a search for the stories behind what ends up on our plates. Those stories sometimes emerge from science, sometimes they are cultural or historical in nature, and often they are personal. For the sake of readability I decided in the end against using footnotes, but the book includes an extensive bibliography as well as the acknowledgments at the end of this introduction. Above all, I wanted this to be a book for anyone looking for nuanced reflection, anyone genuinely interested in farming and food, anyone who understands that the food they eat is not self-explanatory.

In 2006 I published a collection of pieces under the title *Nieuwe spijswetten* (New Dietary Laws). It prompted reactions from many quarters, from chefs and housewives, from environmentalists and nature lovers, farmers, clergymen, bureaucrats, and urban activists. Readers of *Nieuwe spijswetten* will see that several points I touched on in that book are dealt with again here, if at greater length and with updated knowledge. My curiosity as to the meaning of food and the gaping chasm between what we find on our plates and how it got there has only grown since then. This book was written over a long period, so I've taken up some themes from my earlier work, including my inaugural lecture for the Cleveringa chair in Leiden, where I built on the image of Eve and paradise; my Huizinga lecture; the Groeneveld lecture; the Kohnstamm lecture; my TED talk in Long Beach; countless lectures to more academic audiences; and several columns originally written for the Dutch daily newspaper *NRC Handelsblad*. (See www.louiseofresco.com for work of mine not mentioned in the Bibliography.)

Acknowledgments

I'm extremely grateful to many people for their inspiration and for the debates we've had, some over many years, others limited to specific occasions but nevertheless crucial. They will not always have realized how much they meant to me. There are many I won't name here but will instead thank in person when the opportunity arises. Over the years I've met students, young farmers, and chefs, all of whom set me thinking. Along with the continually stimulating interaction I've enjoyed with countless colleagues and former colleagues in Amsterdam, Stanford, and Wageningen, and at the Food and Agriculture Organization of the United Nations, the Consultative Group on International Agricultural Research, the Social and Economic Council of the Netherlands, Rabobank, and Unilever, I would like to mention in particular conversations with Bruce Ames, Joachim von Braun, Joy Burrough, Roel Coutinho, Wout Dekker,

Marcel Dicke, Robbert Dijkgraaf, Sam Dryden, Shenggen Fan, Elias Fereres Castiel, Anna Ferro-Luzzi, Claude Fischler, Joop Goudsblom, Louise Gunning, Martijn Katan, Frans Kok, Salomon Kroonenberg, Fouad Laroui, Rachel Laudan, Samuel Levi, Sijbolt Noorda, Frits van Oostrom, Henk van Os, Dick Plukker, Rudy Rabbinge, Prakash Shetty, Mahmoud Solh, Loretta Sonn, Bram de Swaan, Bonno Thoden van Velzen, Kraisid Tontisirin, Cees Veerman, Pamela Watson, Mieke van der Weij, Peter Westbroek, and Helen Westerik. Each of them has helped distill my thinking, although they are not responsible for any shortcomings of the final result. Like all contemporary works, this book was made possible in part by the existence of that inexhaustible, almost paradisiacal abundance of information available to us on the Internet, especially in the form of Wikipedia, Google Scholar, and Wikicommons. The infectious enthusiasm of Marjoleine Boonstra and Lies Janssen, with whom I saw all manner of things during the making of our TV documentary, was a pleasant distraction during the many months of writing. At the University of Amsterdam, Renée Bakkerus, Simonetta Gerritsen, Pauline van der Hoeven, Anna Holland, and Yvonne Sanders all patiently supported me, each in their own way, especially with regard to the source material, the Bibliography, and the illustrations. As a critical reader of the manuscript, Joost van Kasteren helped guard me against imbalance. Lodewijk Brunt, partly inspired by his knowledge of India, supplied critical commentary and over the years repeatedly brought interesting points to my attention. I thank Liz Waters for her excellent translation and many suggestions. I am also grateful to the staff of Princeton University Press for their great support for the English version of the book and its launch. I'm extremely grateful to the University of Amsterdam for the space my position as university professor there gave me to write this book. Cuban painter Julio Breff Guilarte, whom I first discovered at the time of my Huizinga lecture and quoted in it, was kind enough to allow me to use a picture of his painting, as was Berend Strik. Without the encouragement of Mai Spijkers, more than twenty years my publisher, and the patience of Job Lisman, who greeted each chapter with joy, all the material for this book would have been put out with the waste paper long ago, where perhaps it might have been of more use as part of the eternal ecological cycle.

ONE

Paradise: An Exceptional Ecology

Now the Lord God had planted a garden in the east, in Eden; and there he put the man he had formed. The Lord God made all kinds of trees grow out of the ground—trees that were pleasing to the eye and good for food. In the middle of the garden were the tree of life and the tree of the knowledge of good and evil.   *Genesis 2: 8–9*

The exhaustive description and study of Paradise, with detailed bits about its location and inner structure, ended melancholically with: "The precise location of paradise is not known." And, at tea, at dinner, and during my walks, I repeated this sentence: "Regarding the geographical longitude of the felicitous paradise, there is no precise information."   Leon Trotsky, *My Life*

Pictures of Paradise

A slender minaret and an arched arcade on the market square next to the mosque were the only interruptions to the flat rectangular rooftops. Here and there, shadows colored the white walls pale blue or purple. In the deep, zigzagging alleyways with their steep steps, the walls gleamed in the sun. On the horizon I saw nothing but the exposed edge of a chalk plateau that, seen from the air, forms a barely perceptible scar in an endless expanse of sand and rock stretching to the far side of the Sahara.

Years ago, in Algeria, I visited Ghardaïa, a town that lies amid a complex of oases in the M'zab Valley, some 600 kilometers south of the capital Algiers. The unique cubic houses of the town, founded in the eleventh century, were the inspiration for the French architect Le Corbusier. In the desolation of the midday heat, I walked down more than a hundred steps to the *wadi*, the oasis. A shady forest of date palms with dry rustling leaves and heavy clusters of dates awaited me. In between were low orange trees and red-blossomed pomegranate bushes, and beneath them bright-green clover and fodder grasses. From all sides I heard the splash of invisible water, channeled from more than 800 wells through a complex network of narrow, overgrown, and in some cases subterranean irrigation ditches. An ingenious use of date pits as stoppers regulated the water levels and the flow to the farthest gardens. The planting was in three layers, to make optimum use of the water and at the same time to minimize evaporation. In one area, golden wheat was ripening in fields edged with young palms. Insects buzzed around me, and close to a young apricot tree I spotted two beehives. Beside the path, a few fat-tailed sheep were grazing, tied to a rope. Each garden led to the next, ten of them in total, separated by earthen embankments designed to keep out the drifting desert sand. The scent of orange blossom mingled with smells of fresh grass and mint. After the dusty emptiness of the high plateau and the blinding light of the white village, the impact of coolness and greenery was breathtaking.

It struck me immediately: this must be where the tradition of paradise comes from. In the dry, inhospitable landscape of the Middle East, as in North Africa, the sight of a garden with water sources and green plants is so unexpected and at the same time so welcome that the notion of a supernatural creative hand is impossible to resist. Conversely, in such a barren environment, a garden is virtually the only way in which God's creative powers could manifest themselves, since water, shade, and food are the ingredients that make the difference between habitable and uninhabitable, survival and death. The image of a creative hand needs to be taken literally, if only as a reference to the hand of humankind. In Ghardaïa the oasis has been carefully tended for centuries by semi-nomadic tribes. Water management and the planting of trees close to the naturally occurring palms have created a microclimate where other plants and insects can become established. The work is not without its dangers. Sudden floods in the narrow *wadi* at times of excessive rainfall, such as occurred as recently as 2008, can cost many lives and ruin the planting for decades.

———

The sight of a green, lush idyll in a dry climate has stayed with me through all the years since then. A second revelation soon joined it. Just as the discovery of an oasis in a dry region has something miraculous about it, so, historically speaking, does the invention of agriculture: that unexpected abundance, greenery in the midst of dry plains; the water, fruits, and grains that refresh and feed us. Slowly it began to dawn on me that in the oasis of Ghardaïa I could see a dual archetype: paradise and agriculture. The former is a mythical garden where human beings were created and for which they will always yearn. The latter, agriculture, is an attempt by human beings to replicate paradise by their own means.

———

I did not grow up with paradise in the religious sense, but ever since childhood I have come upon it repeatedly, first in painting and the architecture of churches and their stained-glass windows, later in literature. Sometimes paradise was the final resting place after death, a reward, the antithesis of hell. The distinction between a future heaven and an earthly paradise that forms the background to creation—the Garden of Eden—was less than clear in my mind for a long time, but after my visit to Ghardaïa I realized that paradise in the afterlife is in fact a continuation of the paradise of creation. Now I see paradise pop up at the most unexpected places as the epitome of bliss, in classical and modern art, in literature, and of course in advertising, sometimes as an actual portrayal, sometimes as a metaphor or figure of speech. The Italian coffee brand Lavazza, for example, describes its delicious brew as *"una offerta direttamente del paradiso."* You could interpret the work of Danish artist Olafur Eliasson as a variation on the theme of paradise. That certainly applies to his most famous work, "The Weather Project," at Tate Modern, London, with its giant sun and ceiling mirrors, in which humanity can bask as if face-to-face with a god, and to his "Beauty," a garden hose linked to drip irrigation, in which the viewer sees a rainbow.

In Western art, paradise turns up all over the place. In the Museo Nacional del Prado in Madrid I encountered the brightly colored "Garden of Earthly Delights" by Hieronymus Bosch, which I'd seen long before in a retrospective in the Dutch city of Den Bosch. After moving to Italy I started to see paradise everywhere. The painter Masaccio, in his horrifying "Expulsion from the Garden of Eden," depicts the desolate world outside paradise: colorless, without plants or animals—almost a moonscape. He portrays paradise through its negation, and all the more vividly for that. Again in Florence, again in the fifteenth century, Lorenzo Ghiberti created the gilded bronze doors to the Baptistery opposite the Duomo, with a depiction of Adam and Eve at the top left. In the reliefs on those panels you can follow, from left to right, top to bottom, Adam's creation from clay, his temptation by Eve, and the expulsion from paradise. The temptation takes place beside a sturdy date palm, under trees heavy with fruit, their lush crowns extending their branches over Eve. The leaves are depicted down to the tiniest detail. With their beauty and realism, the doors quickly became known as "Porta del Paradiso," the doors (or door) to paradise.

My personal favorite is the famous 1530 painting "Adam and Eve" by Lucas Cranach the Elder, in which, as if foreshadowing the modern comic strip, Adam and Eve are shown several times in successive frames. At the top right we see the temptation scene, set in a thick forest of fruit trees that look very much like apples and pears, and bushes resembling medlars and oranges. The trees are unnaturally laden with fruit, and their leaves are as abundant and shiny dark green as holly. In the background is what might be a field of grain with geese, and elsewhere sheep and a white horse. A circular painting by Henri met de Bles (also known as Henri de Dinant) depicts a bird's-eye view of paradise as a clearing in a dense forest. Beyond the trees we see flatter land with open meadows bounded by hedgerows, and beyond it a number of steep, karst-like rocks rising out of water. It's an extremely improbable combination geologically, but it emphasizes the green intimacy of the forest with its multitude of animals.

Ever since the Renaissance, our image of paradise has largely coincided with the landscape of Tuscany, around cities such as Siena and Florence, but the theme of paradise is not limited to the West or to Christian culture. It turns up everywhere. When leafing through a book about early Islamic art, I discovered the most beautiful pictures of garden paradises. In a much copied book of miniatures from thirteenth-century Baghdad, about the characteristics and uses of the animals (*Manafi' al-Hayawan*), based on work by the Persian scholar Abu Sa'id Ibn Bakhtishu, I came upon a portrayal of Adam and Eve surrounded by blossoming shrubs and flowering grass. Clearly recognizable are pomegranate bushes with their red flowers, in which two colorful birds are nesting. Elsewhere are figs and grapes, fountains and irrigation. The pomegranate, a symbol of paradisiacal plenty, is ubiquitous, as at any contemporary oasis.

Anyone who has grown up in a society with Jewish, Christian, or Islamic cultural roots or influences (even if very recent, as in Africa) will be familiar with the concept of paradise. That accounts for roughly half the world's population. But even outside those three monotheistic religions we find the theme of a proverbial garden full of happiness, abundance, and peace. Almost all cultures on earth feature an image of a place where food is plentiful. This is particularly true of the peoples and cultures of the Middle East, including the Ancient Egyptians and the Phoenicians, and of Zoroastrianism, which has its own myths of a heavenly place. The Gilgamesh epic includes descriptions that could easily have been derived from paradise: trees heavy with foliage, streams, and a tree of life. Elsewhere, too—in Hinduism, for example—we find the concept of an ideal earth created out of chaos and darkness, where food is suddenly abundant.

From childhood I recall that classical antiquity featured a series of idyllic gardens, beginning with the parklike Arcadia, the gods' place of delights. This was virgin land that needed no cultivation, closely resembling the paradise of monotheism. In the garden of the Hesperides, the daughters of Atlas guard Hera's golden apples (which may have been the inspiration for the golden apples in Christian paintings). These divine and mythical gardens contrast with the hard reality of dry, rocky Greece, which lacks both major rivers and the tradition of irrigation and oases. In Greece the green garden must have delighted the eye and the soul in a way comparable to the gardens and oases of the Middle East and North Africa. In a rocky landscape, where people struggled mightily to tend their arid grain fields and olive groves, the gods played amid flowering meadows and shady copses. The enchantments of a life in paradise are described by Homer, who tells of the gardens of Alcinous that produce fruit all year round, even in winter. In the Greek Arcadia and its equivalents, nature is generous, there is no suffering, and humans and animals live together in peace. Hesiod writes that the fertile earth, without being worked, brings forth a profusion of fruit, a description repeated almost word for word by Plato in *The Republic*, with trees that bear crop after crop and plants that the earth generates all by itself, without the need for people to work the soil or even to sow seeds. Horace speaks of land that produces grain year after year without being ploughed and of grape vines that give fruit without ever being pruned. Comparable themes of a golden age can be found in the culture of the Roman Empire—in Ovid, for example, who in *Metamorphoses* writes that the earth brought forth food without ploughing, and the fields, never having lain fallow, "grew white with ripening grain."

The dreamed-of paradise that will welcome the virtuous after the last judgment has similar components: an abundance of water and food, and harmony between humans and nature. Over the centuries the earthly paradise of creation and the heavenly paradise of the afterlife merged into a pastoral utopia. Boccaccio, Torquato Tasso, and other poets in what is now Italy describe a place where nature is benevolent to humans, and there are no seasons, nor any struggle to survive—a place outside time and space, outside reality. It's no surprise to find that in Dante's *Divine Comedy,* paradise is the least interesting location, because it is unrealistic and lacks drama. Paradise is a dream, a myth, which is precisely the source of its power. From the time when European explorers first began bringing exotic animals back from their voyages in the sixteenth century, the most beautiful, most colorful, and most extraordinary of them were given names that referred to paradise: the birds of paradise of New Guinea (such as *Lophorina superba* and *Seleucides alba,* which was believed to have no feet) the paradise fish (*Macropodus viridiauratus*) and the Brazilian paradise nut (*Lecythis zabucajo,* also known as the cream nut or *sapucaia*).

Gradually the utopian nature of paradise displaced its religious character in art and literature. Arcadia became synonymous with carefree shepherds and peasants playing innocently in the grass, never having experienced deprivation, scarcity, or violence. In the sixteenth-century *Utopia* by Thomas More we do find people working the land, but they represent an ideal of plenty, breeding countless chickens and tending gardens that produce more tasty fruit than anywhere in our world. People are allowed to take as much food home with them from the communal dining rooms as they can carry.

As urbanization increased in Europe in the sixteenth and seventeenth centuries, a sense arose that this idyllic place had been lost for good, that paradise was inaccessible not only during our lives but also perhaps for the rest of time. That thought bred a desire for innocent harmony between humans and nature, for the kind of abundance that nature freely provides. We see this emphasis on the lost idyll reflected in literature, in *Lucifer* by the Dutch poet Vondel, for example, or in *Paradise Lost* and *Paradise Regained* by the seventeenth-century English poet Milton. The expression *Et in Arcadia ego*—much used as a title for paintings (by Barbieri and Poussin, for instance), or in work by writers including Schiller, Goethe, and Nietzsche, and as the title of a brilliant play by our contemporary Tom Stoppard—refers both to the notion that everyone has once known paradise and to the sense of mortality that mars it. Literally translated the phrase means "Even in Arcadia, there am (or was) I," where "I" can refer either to humanity or to death.

In the eighteenth and nineteenth centuries this longing for the innocence and purity that only nature can offer increased. The city was the focus of industry and avarice, Arcadia was an idealized version of the countryside, and there alone nature and those close to nature—farmers, hunters, herdsmen, and villagers with their local stories and traditions—still formed a harmonious society in which, it was felt, equality and dignity prevailed. Marie Antoinette and her ladies-in-waiting at Versailles played at being shepherdesses and peasants to escape the suffocating life of the court. Composers, too, sought the romance of the countryside, of the natural world as a contrast to their own. We need only think of Beethoven's *Pastorale* or Smetana's *Die Moldau,* and of Dvořák, who took inspiration from folksongs. Arcadia may seem a long way from the original image of paradise, but the difference is superficial. The romanticized version remains very close to an outlook in which perfect nature is proof of a divine order, even if no such order is explicitly mentioned and nature itself is declared divine. The artist along with the citizen, who served as patron, could happily ignore the stark contrast between the bitter reality of peasant life in the midst of harsh nature and the ideal of paradise. Our image of a charming natural world is still very much alive, as demonstrated by the Walt Disney film *Snow White.* In the dark forest where Snow White is lost, nature greets her in the form of snuffling, smiling deer, frolicsome rabbits, and singing birds, all of them eager to play with her.

I've found only one story about the relationship between humans and nature that does not fit this long tradition of creation myths featuring paradise and Arcadia. In the creation story told by the Masai in Kenya, humanity has its origins in a tree, and each ancestor receives an appropriate instrument made of a tree branch. One is given a bow for firing arrows, the second a hoe to till the soil, and the third a stick for driving livestock. They become hunters, farmers, and herdsmen. It forms a striking contrast to the story of paradise in the three main monotheistic religions, because the Masai believe humans were furnished from the start with instruments for acquiring food; there is no reference to a mythical world in which sustenance was available without the requirement of effort. Yet even their story suggests that people were equipped from the start to deal with nature and did not have to learn to survive by trial and error.

Paradise as an Ecosystem

The popularity of paradise in so many eras and cultures is easy to understand, because it represents so much: innocence and temptation; freedom from care followed by sin and flight; abundance, peace, and stability. Creation begins with paradise. In the art and stories of Christianity, much attention is paid to the most dramatic moments, namely, the temptation of Eve by the snake, the concealing of Adam and Eve's nakedness, and their ultimate eviction from paradise. Chagall's wonderful lithographs of the story enable us to feel something of the loneliness that must have afflicted the fallen pair as they entered the insecure world outside paradise, and their shame and incomprehension in the face of sin.

The earthly paradise of creation, as it has come down to us in religion, literature, and art, is an ecological idyll, a myth, a utopia. Nothing limits the luxuriant growth of plants and animals, neither too much rain nor too little, neither heat nor cold, not floods, infertile rocky landscapes or diseases and infestations. Food is available in unlimited quantities for both humans and animals, which are not each other's enemies. All depictions of paradise have this abundance of nature in common. Painters, composers, and writers drew inspiration from earlier stories and interpretations. Although each constructed paradise in their own way, what they show is not simply wilful, arbitrary, or the product of chance. They belong to a long tradition, and their work reflects all kinds of ideas about paradise—moral ideas first of all, of course, but always including an implicit image of paradise as an ecosystem. That the emphasis is not on the latter only makes it all the more revealing.

Wondering what the ecology of paradise would have looked like may, on the face of it, seem absurd. Something that does not exist has no ecological characteristics. But the image of paradise is so powerful and we encounter it so often that it cannot be dismissed as an unscientific religious doctrine or naive mythology. Artists give shape to archetypes, so art enables us to trace the very oldest ideas people had about abundance, farming, and food. And as paradise is still present in everyday speech, we should not underestimate its continuing influence.

It goes without saying that paradise is not a reality and never has been. Paradise has no address and no era, even though for almost 3,000 years the Jews, and in their wake the Christians and Muslims, have had no doubt of its historical authenticity as described in the book of Bereshit or in Genesis. Paradise was located in the east (from the perspective of present-day Israel), in Mesopotamia, at the mouth of the Tigris and the Euphrates or indeed at their source in the far east of Turkey. Columbus thought he would find paradise in India, while others set their sights on Ethiopia, or on such islands as Ceylon (today's Sri Lanka).

Both the theory of evolution and the science of geology provide overwhelming evidence that a primeval paradise never existed in any place or time. All ecosystems on earth are the product of developments stretching back over hundreds of millions of years. Nor can there be any doubt that the human species originated in East Africa rather than the Middle East. The gradual evolution of primates into hominids and eventually *Homo sapiens* took many millions of years and a great deal of luck. It involved neither creation nor a primeval existence in paradise.

None of this detracts from the uninterrupted success of the image of paradise, even outside the harsh climate of the Middle East, where it originated. Paradise presents something lacking throughout the history of humankind in almost all times and places: an abundance of grain, fruit, and animals, a miraculous presence of water in all seasons, and food secured without any need to work. We see the same landscape elements in almost every description and depiction of paradise: water in the form of springs, fountains, or streams; cool shade; and a great array of plants and animals. They are the features of a fixed backdrop, as in a play or a film. Lush nature is symbolized by the countless seeds of the strawberry or the pomegranate (a visual reference as far back as Ovid to a mythical golden age); by the peacock with its impressive variegated tail, the diversity of flowering plants, the intense green of leaves and grass, and a wealth of other natural colors; and by those images that recur all over the world of rivers and streams branching out, sometimes toward the four points of the compass, even, as Milton claimed, defying gravity by flowing uphill.

The ecology of paradise is miraculous, as befits a divine creation. A garden or field that demands no effort is an ecological impossibility. Tamed nature assumes a god as the ultimate gardener, a being that has conquered chaos and the seasons and now ensures eternal fertility and endless harvests. Art extrapolates further from these ecological miracles. Whereas Genesis speaks only of fruit trees and seed plants (the latter a reference to cereals and pulses), artists of subsequent generations added twists of their own. Hieronymus Bosch created a climatological potpourri, a hilly landscape of deciduous trees from temperate climes inhabited by an elephant, a unicorn, deer, and a vast profusion of birds and cacti. Rubens introduced an apple tree, along with a red parrot, and Breughel included a multitude of exotic birds. In Cranach we see apple trees, which require frost, next to oranges, which cannot withstand temperatures under 10° Celsius. I suspect these painters knew perfectly well that those species do not occur in the same climatic zones, or in some cases do not exist at all (the unicorn), but they brought them together in their paintings as a way of maximizing the impact of their images of an idyll.

That idyll is a metaphor not just for abundance but for abundance without effort. No costs or losses are involved. True, Genesis 2 states that God put man in paradise to be its custodian, but as we see from all the descriptions in that same chapter, it is meant rather in the way one might be the custodian of a painting, without any real need for intervention or maintenance. The ideal character of paradise in ecological terms is confirmed elsewhere in the Bible, in Ezekiel 47:12, for example, where it is revealed to the Jews in exile in Babylon that close to the new temple will be trees whose leaves never dry out and that bear fresh fruit every month of the year. Virgil is in fact the first to acknowledge that people in paradise would have to work to make the plants thrive, but even he claims they are never tired by their efforts and are guaranteed to be able to harvest good food.

As an ecosystem, paradise never forces us to choose between incompatible goals. Arable fields do not entail the felling of forests; the diversion of watercourses does not necessitate depriving other areas of water; cows are not eaten by wild animals, nor do they contract mad cow disease. Food for human beings is not acquired at the expense of nature or other species, any more than it demands labor. In all those paintings there are no weeds, no trees that need pruning, no withered leaves, no dead animals or rotting fruit, only perfect lawns and harmonious park landscapes. Paradise exhibits a perfect ecological balance. Harvest after harvest can be brought in from fields where manure has never been applied. There are merely, here and there, a few good-natured pollinating insects.

Paradise Measured against an Ecological Yardstick

Nearly everyone understands that this ideal garden is an impossibility. Paradise as portrayed in the monotheistic religions sends us off, by its very definition, on completely the wrong track as far as the essence of food production is concerned. Ecosystems are always changing, even if they appear stable from the perspective of our human timescale. Chemical elements and compounds, such as nitrogen, potassium, and phosphate—important plant nutrients—are part of complex cycles originating in water, soil, or air and involving many species. Even in a seemingly eternal rainforest, changes occur—some rapid, some slow. Species find new niches and new species emerge, while others are lost. In ecology nothing is free of demands or obligations. With every process, some substances are released, some consumed, and all consumption is at the expense of other organisms. The basic principle of ecology is that everything has a price.

Food is the ultimate sign of life. Without the consumption of nutrients there can be no metabolism, growth, and reproduction, processes we regard as evidence of life. Food always comes from other organisms or materials, and ingesting it always takes energy. All life on earth is part of one great food chain. Initially, when it was formed 4.6 billion years ago, the earth was a hot, lifeless lump of rock. A billion years passed before the influence of life forms made itself felt. These forms arose from a combination of chemical reactions entered into by methane, sulfur, phosphate, and carbon, under the influence of sunlight and water. Carbon and amino acids (the building blocks of proteins, which in turn contain nitrogen) have an important part to play in the metabolisms of all organisms, partly as enzymes that speed up chemical reactions. Food for the first primitive life forms may have been the methane that rose through volcanic splits in the earth's crust. The earliest living organisms were heterotrophs that took their sustenance from organic elements and spontaneously occurring amino acids. Autotrophs, which developed from heterotrophs, can make their own food with the aid of sunlight, water, and carbon dioxide. Plants are autotrophs, and they form the basis of the human food chain, which means that photosynthesis is the foundation of our lives. Green plants on land developed in the early Cambrian period, less than 500 million years ago, quite late relative to the age of the earth. When we eat fish or meat, we are indirectly consuming grass and other plants or plankton that have been digested by animals. Through green plants and their photosynthesis, we are part of a continual recycling of the earth's chemical elements. In that fundamental sense, everything is food, and everything is always "natural."

We humans are the product of sunlight and a little stardust. That is not a literary metaphor but the plain fact of the case. We, and everything around us—our clothes, our houses, our books, our cars, our cities, not forgetting our energy—everything we know and possess, even our consciousness, can exist only as a result of photosynthesis, that very precise process by which a plant converts carbon dioxide and water into carbohydrates and oxygen under the influence of photons provided by sunlight. Photosynthesis requires light frequencies ranging from 400 to 700 nanometers. About half the sunlight that falls on the earth is within those frequencies. The process takes place in green plants, algae, and some types of bacteria, at a specific location in the cell, namely, the chlorophyll molecules or chloroplasts, which act like tiny solar panels with a magnesium atom inside a carbon-oxygen ring. At one time chloroplasts were themselves independent organisms. In deserts and high mountain ranges, where there is hardly any water, plants have developed a slightly different chemical route that makes photosynthesis possible even there.

So plants grow more or less on water and a dash of sunlight, along with a few minerals. The sun is the engine of the chemical conversion of air (or rather the carbon dioxide in the air) into carbohydrates, which we consume, and oxygen, which we breathe. The complex dynamics of our planet have caused the oxygen content of the atmosphere gradually to rise to its current 21 percent, and in that combination of processes, photosynthesis has an important place. The sun is a fantastic source of energy. In a single hour, more energy from sunlight reaches the earth than we use in a year. And sunlight is free. In a sense, what our lives depend on simply falls into our laps. Imagine if the sun stopped shining on our planet. Everything we think of as life on earth would disappear, then winds and ocean currents would stop, and only a few rare organisms would survive, those that draw their energy from volcanic fissures on the ocean bed. In the end, oxygen would also cease to exist.

The extraordinary nature of photosynthesis emerges from the first experiment ever to be staged with the aim of unraveling how the process of plant growth works. In the early seventeenth century, Flemish doctor and alchemist Jan Baptista van Helmont showed that a plant does not grow merely by converting nutrients in the soil. He put a small willow tree in a pot and carefully weighed it every few months. After five years the tree was 77 kilograms heavier, but the soil in the pot had lost only 57 grams.

Unfortunately Van Helmont drew the wrong conclusion. He thought the plant had grown purely from the water he had given it in those five years. We now know that although water provides the electrons that get the process of photosynthesis started, it also evaporates from the plant. The increase in weight results from the conversion of CO_2. The soil in the pot loses weight because of the uptake of other chemicals, such as nitrogen, potassium, and phosphate, which the plant needs in small amounts. These are the elements that need to be added in the form of fertilizer, unless a field is left to lie fallow for a long time, or the soil is so rich that nutrients are available in unlimited quantities from volcanic ash or river silt, as was once the case in the Nile delta and is still true at oases such as Ghardaïa.

The sun and photosynthesis are essential for the existence of ecosystems, those complex networks of organisms that depend on and compete with one another. In essence, life on earth comes down to eat or be eaten. In an ecosystem nothing is lost, because anything that dies is food for other organisms in an endless cycle.

The ecological cycle is best illustrated by an imaginary pond. Aquatic plants serve as food for plant-eating insects, which in turn are eaten by fish that are preyed on by birds. Dead birds sink into the mud of the pond or its banks, becoming food for small scavengers and for microorganisms that then determine the chemical environment of the pond—its salt and acid content, for example, and its nitrogen concentration. If plants are few, then the number of organisms further up in the food chain will be limited, so ultimately there will be few birds of prey. The food chain is a pyramid with an extremely broad base consisting of bacteria and vegetation, fueled by sunlight.

This imaginary, simplified pond also clearly shows that a disturbance to the prevalence of one species has consequences for the rest of the chain. Ecosystems in which species cannot easily take one another's places are therefore delicate.

Human evolution is nothing less than a successful appropriation of natural resources, such as water, land, and the products of other species, including seeds (grains), fruits, leaves (green vegetables), milk, and meat. In an ecosystem a species is successful, by definition, at the expense of other species. So in paradise, with its endless abundance and eternal balance, there is no evolution. Nor is there any nutritional cycle. The chemical elements absorbed by the fruits and grains Adam and Eve ate in paradise come from nowhere, and their waste goes nowhere, nor is there any place for the nutritional needs of other species, such as bacteria and insects.

Ecosystem Earth encompasses the entire planet, people just as much as fungi, giraffes, cactuses, viruses, and soybeans. We are always competing with other species for the food supplies we tap. As consumers of both plants and animals, we're at the top of the food chain, dependent on the sunlight it concentrates. Food is our most intimate way of interacting with nature. We eat things produced in part by sunlight. Not in the sense that sunlight becomes a solid in some poetic way but in the strict, literal sense of an ontological transformation. Our bodies, our very selves, are to some degree constructed out of sunlight acquired through the food chain. That which I am not becomes "me."

In the artistic representations of paradise that have entered our consciousness over the centuries, ecological cycles have settled into perpetual immobility. The seed-bearing plants and fruits that Adam and Eve are allowed to eat emerge from nowhere. There is nothing that points to a natural ecological cycle. As an impossible perpetual motion machine, without any supply of chemical elements or energy in the form of work, paradise exists outside nature. The sun doesn't even shine at full strength; in all images of paradise the light is shrouded, as if photosynthesis were irrelevant. This is an unchanging system, rather than a dynamic, ever-evolving food pyramid or cycle. In some depictions of paradise the chain of eat and be eaten is explicitly broken in the sense that wild animals live peacefully with their prey, as in a 1620 painting of paradise by Breughel the Younger, in which lions lie down next to deer and none of the fruit has been touched, despite the many birds on the canvas. It's an illusion of idyllic peace and the absence of anything to disturb that peace. In this paradise, humans are part of an immobile and impossible harmony.

Paradise as a Garden

Paradise is an invention, a metaphor, but it is rooted in reality. Not in ecological or scientific reality; rather it's drawn from familiar images that were experienced or idealized as real at the time it was first conceived. But why is carefree abundance always portrayed as a garden, not as a city, a fort, or a market, all of which developed in the same historical era? The garden provides an appropriate frame of reference for paradise because it represents the interaction between humans and nature in a concentrated form. To those without any understanding of gardening or biology, a well-tended garden is a miracle of spontaneous ecological harmony. The garden as it came into being in the Middle East, in Persia and Mesopotamia, and as it can still be seen at oases or in the Alhambra in Granada, is the perfect backdrop to a marked-off, self-absorbed universe detached from arid, ruthless nature.

The word "paradise" almost certainly comes from the Persian *pairi daiza,* meaning "walled space, garden." *Pairi* is related to the Greek for "around" (*peri*); *diz* to the Sanskrit for "robust" (*digen*), traces of which can be seen in the Greek word for "wall" (*teikhos*), the Latin for "forms" (*fingere*), and possibly the English word "dike." The *paradeisos* of classical Greek, derived from Persian, originally meant "garden" until, in New Testament Greek, it became the word for paradise. The Garden of Eden, another name for paradise, comes from the Arabic *janna 'adn.* Words derived from *pairi daiza,* like the Hebrew *pardes,* also refer to gardens, vegetable plots, or vineyards. In the Koran and in *One Thousand and One Nights* the garden appears time and again as the location of a better life, sometimes in Baghdad or Constantinople (present-day Istanbul). In Islam paradise is primarily an image of a future life, a prospect for the virtuous, a garden with fruit trees.

Gardens are, however, anything but spontaneously arising harmonious ecosystems. No garden will last long without continual intervention by people, however much it may be described as "wild." Without regular maintenance, every garden ends up dominated by a few species, in most cases eventually trees or, if the climatic zone is too cold, wet, or windy for trees, low bushes. Neglect a garden in northern Europe, and you will have only nettles, Himalayan balsam, elder, and ground elder. Even more than arable fields or forestry plantations, gardens, with their diversity of plants in a limited area, demand perfect control. In gardens exactly the same ecological processes are at work as in natural ecosystems: photosynthesis, competition, and death. The difference is purely that people take charge of those processes to produce the outcomes they desire, whether they be fruit, lawns, or rose beds.

Archaeological finds have shown that arable farming started with various kinds of horticulture, usually practiced beside or not far from domestic properties, and the growing of crops on a small scale. In contrast to an arable field, the domestic vegetable plot is a place where food is produced in small quantities, usually close to the home, often right outside the kitchen door. A garden is land used to grow plants that have been influenced and domesticated by humans but are not relied on directly as a source of basic foodstuffs. Arable farming was not practiced on a significant scale in the Middle East until draft animals were deployed, and it expanded when irrigation developed. Over the course of history the domestic garden became on the one hand the arable field and on the other the ornamental garden we know today, which is not intended for food production. The nineteenth-century allotment with vegetables and a few flowers is part of this tradition in Europe. Nowadays allotments often fall somewhere between the flower garden and the vegetable plot, but their original purpose was to supplement the diets of factory workers. From the very beginning, gardens were used for food production; later they acquired a recreational function as well. Its evolution explains why the garden is such an ancient and attractive image.

There is no hard and fast distinction between a garden and an arable field, only a complex continuum in the landscape, related in part to its distance from the dwelling and the degree to which it is influenced by untamed nature. A farmed field is land where people permit only one kind of plant or animal, removing all others and trying to ensure that the desired species grows as successfully as possible. The garden appears to stand halfway between nature and the farm in the sense that, although a wide variety of species can be found in it, each of the different plants and animals is cared for meticulously. With the exception of chickens and ducks, domestic gardens are not intended for animal husbandry. The small scale of the garden and its proximity to the home mean that people can have far more influence on it, especially if water and domestic waste (which serves as fertilizer) are brought in. Not all gardens are close to houses, however. The availability of water may mean that they lie quite a distance from domestic dwellings, like the oasis at Ghardaïa, while homes may sometimes be surrounded by farmland, as in the polders of the Netherlands. There are gardens that receive little attention, such as those along the Senegal River in Africa, far from the nearest village, and arable fields that are manicured like gardens, such as Japanese tea plantations or Balinese rice paddies. It has been argued that the whole of the Netherlands is a garden, given the degree of control exercised by the Dutch over land, plants, animals, and water.

The extent to which gardens represent paradise is strikingly illustrated by a fifteenth-century miniature from the *Antiquités judaïques* by Flavius Josephus (now in the Bibliothèque de l'Arsénal in Paris). Here paradise is a walled castle garden. In another illustration in the same work, depicting the marriage of Adam and Eve in paradise, we see a similar walled garden, surrounded by water, where the animals live next to one another in peace and the trees have as many fruits as leaves, epitomized by the orange tree, with its bright shiny fruit and its evergreen foliage. In monasteries, too, such as Clairvaux Abbey in France, the garden was an important symbol, not just the closed *hortus conclusus*, a place of contemplation, but the garden in the form of an arable field, where the monks achieved the approved degree of asceticism by tackling the thorns and the wilderness. Because of its gardens, the monastery became an earthly paradise from which sin was banished.

Ornamental gardens come into being only when there is sufficient space, water, and labor to grow things that have no direct use. This kind of gardening may have started when a few flowers popped up spontaneously on a dung heap, or after seed was collected from attractive plants in the wild. Perhaps fruit-bearing trees were planted to give shade and then came to be appreciated for their aesthetic value. But only with the rise of a rich, leisured class could the purely decorative garden emerge. It is no accident that the biblical towns of Babylon and Nineveh, the richest in the Middle East, became famous in their day for their gardens.

In the most ancient artworks, ornamental gardens and paradise go together. In a grave in Thebes in Egypt, an astonishing depiction has been found of a garden belonging to Sennefer, a noble in the time of Amenhotep III (1417–1379 BC). The plan shows a walled garden with its main entrance leading straight to the house. An avenue of trees runs around the periphery, and other avenues divide the garden into eight similarly planted areas of varying sizes. There are two square ponds with lotuses and ducks. At the center we see what is probably a vineyard. The geometrical layout is identical to that of the garden described in Genesis, where the river that waters paradise splits into four arms, a pattern found elsewhere in the Middle East and in the Islamic gardens of Andalusia.

After these and the closed monastic gardens of the Middle Ages, the garden as a status symbol for the rich emerged in Europe. There was less concern about paradise and the divine and more of a focus on the noble properties of the owners—their wealth and exquisite taste—as demonstrated by the presence of exotic varieties, such as tulips and azaleas. Eventually gardens largely ceased to symbolize divine generosity and became more about displaying the things money can buy. The same goes for the garden as a park in the romantic sense, in which wild nature is carefully reconstructed, or formal gardens like those of Versailles, with their orderly vegetation and high degree of control. Yet you only have to look at the front gardens of European and North American suburbs to see the extent to which abundant variety has remained a key ingredient since gardens became available to all social classes. The strength of the association between the garden and paradise even today is illustrated by the titles of many gardening books, and by the name of a popular summer course offered by the University of Oxford: "Paradise in an English Garden." Time and again, gardening turns out to be all about the illusion of a perfect ecosystem, of complete control over other species—and, in Mediterranean and other dry climates, over water. Seemingly effortless abundance finds an extreme form in the mythical Land of Cockaigne, where everything is possible, a place where the supply of food is unlimited, and doves fly straight into your mouth.

———————

Looking at depictions down through the centuries, we see that paradise with its multiplicity of species is neither an arable field nor an untamed wilderness but the archetype of the garden. As such it defines the relationship between humans and nature. Descriptions and pictures of gardens that do not explicitly refer to paradise often stress the garden's paradisiacal character, especially its peace, variety, and harmony. This is true even of cultures that do not have a paradise story, the culture of the Roman Empire, for example, as demonstrated by the fresco of the flower garden of Empress Livia of the second century AD. The garden is the primal image of almost every civilization and therefore of an idealized relationship between humans and nature; of uninterrupted security; of fertility and water; and of food, scents, and flowers.

The Paradise Theory

Only after my move from Italy back to the Netherlands did I realize that my professional life was made up of three periods, each lasting roughly a decade, in which I learned to think differently about farming and food. My early years in developing countries were marked by a sense of an acute scarcity of everything: of tools, vehicles, water, seed, and above all food. The markets stalls—there were generally no shops—consisted of a tarpaulin spread out in the mud or on sand, or a bit of cardboard on which were displayed a handful of peanuts or a bunch of bananas, a few cans of condensed milk, and sometimes a bowl of rice or (when in season) a couple of mangos. Once sold, the wares were wrapped in newspaper or in pages from old school exercise books. In retrospect I'm astonished that I didn't ask more questions in situations in which for months there was nothing to eat, even for me, apart from rice with the occasional cassava leaf—sometimes mixed with sardines but more often only with caterpillars—or dry bread with a banana and a little of the mustard I'd imported myself. It was a life without running water (and of course without bottled mineral water). In my kitchen—in the garden under a lean-to—I had to cook on charcoal over an open fire, which meant I needed to go in search of firewood. The only source of variety in my diet was my vegetable plot, plagued by insects and molds, which featured a few puny tomato plants and two rather unproductive papaya trees. From time to time my neighbors hunted antelope and small game, and I sometimes drove the huntsmen's Land Rover or stood on the hood with a lamp to attract prey. Despite my strong preference for vegetarianism, my knowledge of surgical dissection meant I had little choice but to help bone the meat. Feasts were occasionally held if the local missionaries or the doctors at the hospital had received a food parcel from abroad. At the same time I felt embarrassed by such exceptions and wanted to eat as far as possible according to local custom. In my youthful arrogance and eagerness to adjust, I never dared give the impression that I was affected by Western prejudice, so I ate everything that was offered to me, from roasted palm beetles and dried caterpillars with yellow and green stripes to python in tomato sauce.

———

Later, too, when I no longer lived for long periods in the tropics but returned there every year for a month or two at a time, I barely thought about my own food. Instead I contemplated how little was available to the world's population and the reasons for this scarcity, which included a lack of water, fertilizer, and seed. It became second nature to concentrate on scarcity, partly because my work took me mainly to remote and poor areas. The value of food seemed simpler there than elsewhere: it was above all a way to alleviate hunger, and issues of status or religion came a long way behind—or so I thought at the time.

As the years went by I started to understand that even, perhaps especially, when it is scarce, food is governed by norms and values. Even in situations of acute food shortage, despite a lack of choice, people who had little food talked frequently and at length about culinary dishes: the freshwater fish that were sometimes caught, the small antelope that were rarely spotted, the first unripe mangos, even if they were fibrous and tart. Looking back, it perhaps makes perfect sense that my doctoral thesis was about cassava, the most flavorless poor person's food in the world.

———

In the intervening periods, when I was in the Netherlands, food remained in the background, food preparation even more so. I concentrated on food production, and on the statistical abstractions that inevitably flow from a global, model-based approach to world food issues. Food was something to be relied on, and what mattered most were factors such as soil composition, temperature, water, plants, animals, labor, pesticides, and artificial fertilizers.

It was a long time before I started to understand the multifaceted nature of food. Its production, however complicated, is only one side of the coin. I began to realize that in our era the demand for food drives supply, rather than the other way around, as in most of human history. We no longer suffer scarcity and hunger as a result of an inadequate supply of food, rather it is variety, a degree of variety none of us can truly conceive, that determines what the vast majority of human beings today, all but the truly poor, can and want to eat. So I had to look beyond the poorest countries in the world, beyond the peasant farmer. Suddenly the entire food chain was relevant, along with what happened in shops, restaurants, and kitchens, up to and including what people think and feel about food.

Living for almost ten years in Italy, I discovered the culture of food in all its complex richness. That sounds like a cliché, but it really is what happened. In Rome I experienced how conditions in agriculture and food production develop with the seasons—and how difficult it is to form a value judgment about any of that. I saw it all: farmers in Umbria growing lentils and broccoli who barely earned enough to cover their costs because of the way they were locked into contracts with the food-processing industry; European support for olive groves that were not commercially viable but contributed to the beauty of the landscape; family meals in the countryside for which the stone oven was fired up two days in advance to cook the paschal lamb and the bread scattered with fresh thyme; simple trattorias that had no menus, where you were simply served the meal of the day and the wine from the village, dishes that were always delicious and cost next to nothing; and formal dinners with many courses and desserts of white chocolate resembling miniature termite nests. During all those meals I spoke with my Italian fellow diners about other dishes they had once eaten, or wanted to eat, or intended to cook, and about the cousin of the butcher's next-door neighbor who kept dairy goats high in the mountains, where he made the best cheese in the world. But I also noticed how, in my district in the historic center of Rome, the supermarkets were increasingly forcing the *alimentari,* the little shops selling vegetables and other foodstuffs, onto the defensive. Some of them closed, while others, more enterprising, started to concentrate on ready-made snacks for tourists and took on low-paid illegal immigrants to meet growing demand. At the same time, those much-maligned supermarkets had a fantastic supply of local produce, including the most diverse fish and seafood, countless different mushrooms, juicy figs, ten varieties of tomato, and a huge range of fresh pasta. Nothing is simple, I realized, when it comes to farming and food.

The extent to which food is bound up with social behavior became fully clear to me only when I returned to the Netherlands after those years in Rome. Aside from the major cities in the United States, I know of no place in the Western world where so much eating goes on in the street as in Amsterdam. I suddenly noticed how many people were obviously carrying too much weight. The statistics confirmed my impression; for the first time in human history, the number of people who were over-weight exceeded the number who were underweight. When I worked in Rome and we looked at those figures, around the turn of this century, the numbers were roughly equal (one billion). Now there are nearly twice as many overweight people as thin. People also eat on the streets in Asian cities, but consumption is far more concentrated around prescribed meal-times and small restaurants, although even there fast food is spreading rapidly. The contrast between Italy and the rest of Europe is skin deep. In the Mediterranean region you also see overweight children, even though their parents still sing the praises of farmland and tradition.

So my thoughts about food as a source of confusion slowly began to take shape. Our attitude to food does not originate in a vacuum; it reflects the past. In the great monotheistic religions the first human being walked in a garden of vegetables and flowers created by God, not in a natural wilderness. The creation of humankind is therefore not directly connected with the means of survival, such as agriculture and animal husbandry. In that mythical primal state before civilization developed, paradise meant there was an environment in which nature provided food. Death was unknown, whether of animals or of people, because there was no ecological cycle. In mythology, the garden that is paradise, ruled by a god or the gods, precedes farming. Paradise is the ideal static ecosystem, a state of unchanging harmony—all permanently curtailed by the expulsion of Adam and Eve.

However impossible paradise may be as an ecosystem, from a religious and cultural point of view the notion of stable abundance without effort represents an irresistibly successful formula. Although all of human evo-lution is marked by perpetual and often acute and fatal scarcity—and for every species, evolution is the story of a life-and-death struggle for food— religions have arisen that reflect the opposite: Judaism, Christianity, and Islam. All three have abundance as their starting point and only later, after the Fall of Man, is scarcity introduced. In contrast, in the Greek Arcadia, abundance in a garden-like landscape is reserved for the gods. What a revolution in thought that paradise of the Jews, Christians, and Muslims represents: instead of scarcity, an unbroken stream of the most delicious food without any need for people to do anything—except to refrain from eating the fruit of that one special tree.

It sounds too good to be true (and of course outside of the myth, it is). Indeed a sense that the biblical description of paradise is not to be taken literally but instead seen as a metaphor arose early on, at the start of the Christian era. Philo, a Jewish thinker in the Eastern Roman Empire, wrote that it was absurd to think God himself planted vines, apple trees, olive groves, and pomegranate bushes. Doubts also arose here and there regarding the complete absence of farming in paradise, so people struggled for centuries with the question of whether, and if so why, agricultural activities in paradise would have demanded real human effort. St. Augustine gave the clearest answer with his famous statement that working the land is *non laboriosa, sed delitiosa,* not an effort but a source of joy. Various commentators have developed this into the concept that every virtue requires a certain degree of effort and that farming in paradise cannot be a punishment. It became so only after the Fall; until then it was a pleasurable means of relaxation—you might even call it an early form of fitness training. Moreover, farming in paradise is a way for humankind to contribute to the further perfecting of nature. Moses Bar Cephas, a ninth-century Syrian bishop, claimed that Adam is not in paradise to sow or to prune, nor to use heavy gardening implements. His jobs are limited to the creation of clearings and avenues to open up the forests of paradise so that pleasant walks can be enjoyed.

Despite the efforts of philosophers to provide a commentary on our image of paradise, the irresistible idea of the impossible ecosystem continues to accompany us in many versions, in many cultures, even outside monotheism. Sometimes it takes the form of the ideal primeval garden, sometimes the "Land of Cockaigne," a paradise on earth. Pieter Breughel the Elder developed the Land of Cockaigne into a Never-Never Land, a place of unlimited food and outrageous blowouts. In documents from the late Middle Ages we read that in the Land of Cockaigne, exertion is forbidden by God. Food arrives by itself in prodigious quantities, sometimes in the form of animals who offer themselves for consumption, such as a pig that runs around with a knife stuck into its back. The happy inhabitant of Cockaigne is continually surrounded by food, which grows on the trees already boiled or baked. The roofs are made of fruit flans and the fences of sausages. Notably, game is almost entirely absent, which is logical enough, since in paradise wild animals are not wild. It also reflects the fact that in the sixteenth century, game was the food of the rich, whereas Cockaigne is all about food for the common people.

Breughel's painting shows paradise in overdrive, a psychedelic trip. The weirdness and exaggeration must surely be intended to ease the experience of drudgery, chronic food scarcity, and a monotonous diet characteristic of the late Middle Ages, and indeed many other periods. Such hardship is beautifully depicted in the painting "The Fall of Adam" by Hugo van der Goes from the second half of the fifteenth century, which shows a thin Adam and an equally thin but pregnant Eve standing under the apple tree. Adam is already stretching out his hand longingly for the apple that Eve has yet to pluck, in a gesture tellingly similar to the stance I have seen African children adopt when food is distributed in refugee camps.

Paradise remains far more present in our consciousness than we generally realize, usually in a tacit or indirect way. The Enlightenment, and especially modern science, with its geology and evolutionary theory, put an end to the literal belief in the historical existence of paradise, but not to images in the Bible, art, and literature that have been with us since the myth first arose. In today's depictions of paradise, the humor and ridicule typical of stories of Cockaigne have gone. What remains is the desire. "Paradise" has become a term found in advertisements and popular media, associated with carefree holidays, unspoilt beaches, and a perfect climate, unlimited idleness (preferably with a dash of eroticism), and for intellectuals a series of cultural delights. If food features at all in such a paradise, then it will be in the form of local, sun-drenched products made with love, or so it is claimed, and transported straight from the farm to the dining table. Paradise remains irresistible even to the richest, as demonstrated by the fact that the French jeweler Cleef & Arpels not long ago launched a collection called "Couleurs de Paradis."

From all this we can derive what I would like to call "paradise theory," according to which the idea of paradise as an impossibly stable, diverse, and productive ecosystem has had a profound effect on our thinking about nature, farming, and food and remains a powerful influence even today. So despite the secularization that followed the flourishing of the main monotheistic religions (a transition that has, as we know, taken place to a lesser extent in the Islamic world), paradise is a frame of reference for what we think and do in relation to food. Although in Islam paradise mainly represents the afterlife, I believe that there too it amounts to a guiding principle, representing the joys of effortless plenty. Associations with paradise mean that we are now almost defenseless in the face of the overwhelming volume of goods available, especially food, which is so abundant and cheap in our late-capitalist society. Conversely, paradise resonates in our criticism of that society, which has raised abundance and technology to the status of dogma, displacing the idealized harmonious past. In the Judeo-Christian tradition at least, paradise explicitly precedes creation, so it also offers a point of reference for what we believe nature was like before humanity existed: "untouched by humans" suggests plenty and harmony. People are seen as having caused the loss of this original, more generous natural world.

Paradise theory therefore embraces both the idyll and its opposite, both the longing for abundance and the discomfort that plenty evokes, along with our sense of guilt at the idyll's loss. Reflected in that discomfort is the discrepancy between our high-tech society and the archetype of intimate harmony. We see unproblematic plenty and carefree repose as our birthrights but sadly recognize that we have squandered them, which only increases our longing for the past. Paradise is the touchstone of our yearning for boundless abundance, for an idyllic way of life that we have lost and must somehow regain.

Paradise theory helps to explain why, all over the world, rich societies and the middle classes have such a complex relationship with food. It illuminates both our obsession with plenty and our alienation from and resistance to it, a result of the fact that our evolutionary development in times of scarcity has made us helpless in the face of the unlimited availability of food. Food is everywhere now, in shops that are always open and in our overstuffed fridges. Excess calories are available to all but the poorest. We are surrounded by images in which a rich supply of food is linked to the Old Testament idyll. Advertising perpetuates images of paradise in which growers pluck golden citrus fruit from a bough with no apparent effort, making no mention of laborious pruning or the miseries of fungal infections. Cows gambol in the fields, and in the very next shot chocolate milk pours into a cup. Anyone carrying paradise with them as part of their background will find it hard to know when to stop. They will either see only the harmonies of the food chain or only its tragedies. The media and dystopian documentaries reinforce the idea that something has gone badly wrong with our daily bread, both literally and metaphorically. In northern Europe all this is made all the more sombre by Calvinism, with its warnings against sinful pleasures. But elsewhere too, even in places where delicious food is not associated with sin and guilt—in southern Europe or India for instance—almost everyone finds it hard to eat with moderation.

So we tread a difficult path between our longing for the Garden of Eden as a metaphor of a peaceful life in harmony with nature and deep unease about our current food supply. As a counterpoint we have images of a new hell: the sheds and abattoirs of intensive livestock farming, or, to make matters even more unpleasant, the hell of liposuction, by which excessive fat consumed over the years is sucked out again. Our pleasure garden with its gleaming fruits seems a very long way away.

TWO

Eve's Temptation: Apple and Hamburger

> Forbidden Fruit a flavor has
> That lawful Orchards mocks—
> How luscious lies within the Pod
> The Pea that Duty locks—
> EMILY DICKINSON

Two Chinese men are walking out of Katz's Delicatessen. One says to the other, "The problem with Jewish food is that two weeks later you're hungry again." *Jewish-American joke*

Fall and Knowledge

In earthly paradise, that mythical place where humankind began, a beatific state of effortless nutritional plenty prevails against a decor of rich vegetation, mainly trees. An abrupt end to this *dolce far niente* is brought about by a series of dramatic events that destroy forever the equilibrium and ecological stasis that have always characterized paradise. The tragic developments begin with an apparently innocent warning by God never to eat the fruit of the tree of knowledge. Then Eve is tempted by the devil in the form of a snake, who offers her an apple from that tree. After partaking of the forbidden fruit, Adam and Eve become conscious of their nakedness, and as a result they hide from God, who cries out heartrendingly, "Adam, where art thou?" Finally they are punished with banishment from paradise. Humankind faces centuries of exile.

With its unity of time and place and its concentrated plot, this is a textbook example of effective drama, which helps to explain why the story has been told countless times, whether in the form of a play by Dutch seventeenth-century poet Joost van den Vondel, a poem by Milton, or a recent opera by Rob Zuidam titled *"Adam in ballingschap"* ("Adam in Exile"). In Vondel's version, the snake-devil, called "Belial," describes the tree as that "in which the prize / of all knowledge and wisdom lies," with apples "that afford / knowledge of the distinction between evil and good."

Afterward, all that remains to Adam and Eve is to set out for "an arid and thirsty land, in misery."

Much has been written about the forbidden fruit, the temptation of Eve, and the expulsion from paradise, and many interpretations are irrelevant in the context of a book about farming and food. Often the apple is seen as a symbol of sex, and the temptation is equated with the woman as such: the sin is her seductiveness. In the Zohar (the most important mystical commentary on the Torah, the five books of Moses) the story concerns the eternal distinction between man and woman. Eve undertakes something on her own account without Adam's permission, which naturally cannot end well.

There are, though, plenty of other things to be said about God's remarkable prohibition that do have a great deal to do with nutrition. After all, the story makes a connection between knowledge and abundance. The plenty so characteristic of paradise not only comes about without any effort, it also exists in the absence of any knowledge of photosynthesis, ecological cycles, natural selection, or techniques for the selective breeding of plants and animals. As the omniscient gardener, God is not in need of such knowledge, and as long as Adam and Eve are in paradise, it has no relevance for them. God bans only the produce of the tree of knowledge. It is the forbidden fruit. That is all they need to know.

It was the first food taboo. Food had become a danger, in a metaphorical sense at least. Not because the forbidden fruit was poisonous—the Bible confirms that Eve and Adam survive the eating of the apple without so much as a hint of indigestion—but because of the taboo itself. At the same time the apple represents knowledge; knowledge in itself is dangerous. The consequences make this plain. It is the fatal combination of food and knowledge that leads to banishment from the garden of plenty and a future of struggling to obtain sufficient food through lifelong effort. This is stressed in part by the fact that after eating the forbidden fruit, Eve and Adam become aware of their nakedness and in response they try to cover themselves and to hide. Their nakedness reflects not only their shame at having broken the taboo but also their vulnerability in the natural world, their dependence on a food supply they do not control. As they will soon discover, outside paradise not even God controls it.

This passage from Genesis is the first in which death occurs. God threatens Adam and Eve with a state as yet unknown in paradise, which will follow eating from the tree of knowledge. The threat is not carried out in full, as the fruits are not toxic and Adam and Eve do not die, although their punishment is harsh and applies to all the generations that come after them. Eve and her female descendants will bear children in pain, and for Adam and all those who follow him, the ground will henceforth be poor and bring forth little. The words of Genesis 3:17–19 are: "Because you listened to your wife and ate fruit from the tree about which I commanded you, 'You must not eat from it,' cursed is the ground because of you; through painful toil you will eat food from it all the days of your life. It will produce thorns and thistles for you, and you will eat the plants of the field. By the sweat of your brow you will eat your food until you return to the ground, since from it you were taken; for dust you are and to dust you will return."

From this we deduce that God, or at least the authors of Genesis, did have some awareness of ecological cycles; humans turn to dust and become a source of nutrients in the soil. The need for hard labor is likewise a recognition that there can be no food production without some input of energy, including human energy. This ecological knowledge, passed on by God to man as an incidental fact, applies only to the world outside paradise.

It is striking that God speaks of thistles and thorns, which in dry climates are generally a sign of poorly tended soil and overgrazing, and often of low soil fertility. Clearly God (or the authors of Genesis) understood that these are the ecological effects of farming. Remarkably, water is not explicitly mentioned, even though it is the main limiting factor in the Middle East. The perfect horticulturalist in the Garden of Eden, with his four rivers, says nothing about that aspect, even though it was to be so crucial for the food supply in the region.

This biblical passage is the first to describe the relationship between food, ecological cycles, labor, and the always meager yield of the land. Compared to paradise, most of the surface of the earth is "cursed" in this sense. Even in river deltas like that of the Nile (where until the building of the Aswan Dam, fertile silt was deposited naturally on the farmland every year), effort is required if we are to exploit that fertility, whether it be the building of dikes and drainage systems or ploughing, sowing, and weeding. The sweat of the brow is never far away.

Knowledge plays a dual role in this transaction between God, nature, and humankind. On the one hand, knowledge is essential, because it allows optimal use to be made of the opportunities afforded by soil and water for acquiring food outside paradise, even though it was knowledge that led to banishment from plenty in the first place and therefore to scarcity. Knowledge is both the cause of the Fall and essential for survival after the Fall. On the other hand, all kinds of interpretations equate knowledge with greed and human desire to dominate nature, even to dominate God. Consuming the products of nature is the most intimate and definitive form of domination, and after eating the forbidden fruit, humankind comes to realize just how abundant food was in paradise. We will always long to return. Knowledge also points to the consciousness of sin and to its opposite: arrogance and an overestimation of one's own power and worth. In the story of paradise, knowledge is the opposite of innocence. In acquiring knowledge of the world outside paradise—the real ecosystem—human beings lose their innocence, because the acquisition of food always involves disadvantaging other species, just as the use of technology, which arises from knowledge, always comes at an ecological and moral price.

Knowledge can also be seen as a metaphor for the consciousness of Adam and Eve, and indeed all humankind. By becoming aware of their humanity, of the fact that humans have evolved as part of the planet and therefore have a place in the earth's ecosystem, they realize that they are not a protected, unique, priceless species in a heavenly and unchanging parkland. After eating from the tree of knowledge, humans suddenly become aware that paradise is an artificial, closed garden and that existence outside it is trammeled by complex and unpredictable natural forces. This subversive interpretation, which in some ways is suggested in the Zohar as well, makes the snake/devil a clairvoyant that liberates human beings from the eternal, undemanding dullness of paradise, in which they could never have developed their true creativity. There is no freedom in paradise, no choice, and therefore no responsibility—these things exist only beyond it.

An indication of the liberating character of that all-too-tempting knowledge can be found in the most intriguing portrait of Eve that I know. It was created for the St. Lazarus Cathedral in Autun, a beautifully preserved historic town in Burgundy, France. It dates from 1130 and was originally mounted above the northern entrance. The oldest known Romanesque depiction of a female nude, it disappeared in the eighteenth century and was later rediscovered by chance as part of a half-ruined dwelling. The long relief is broken and incomplete, lacking the entire section showing the figures of Adam and the devil or snake, of which a fragment of tail or claw is still visible. The "Eve of Autun" is now in the Musée Rolin in Autun, and she is extraordinary above all for how self-aware she looks. She is stretched out in a sensual pose, supporting herself on her right elbow and her knees, her body turned toward us, amid flowering bushes and trees laden with fruit. She stretches out her left hand behind her, across her back, to a tree that hangs over her, grasping the fruit as she prepares to pull it free of the branch. Yet she is looking ahead, probably toward a now missing Adam, who, given the long, low shape of the relief, must have been lying or crouching in front of her. This is a woman fully conscious of what she is doing, in an almost erotically inviting pose, not someone tempted against her better judgment into a forbidden act. Although the position of her right hand with its extended fingers resting against her cheek has been interpreted as a sign of shame, her face suggests quite the opposite. We are able to look at it from different angles, and her expression seems to change depending on the position of the viewer in relation to the relief, from concentrated and self-assured to mournful, as if she is sad about something inevitable that is about to happen. Yet it is an outcome she favors; her gesture is voluntary and persuasive. Without falling back on a feminist interpretation, it is clear that the "Eve of Autun" suggests Eve was not merely a weak-willed victim of evil in the form of the devil and his tempting fruit. It appears she was herself keen to discover evil, or at the very least that she had a hand in her own temptation. This is surely not intended as a way of blaming the victim, although Adam does exactly that when he defends himself before God by saying Eve urged him to eat the apple. Here Eve is the prototype of the modern, inquisitive human being.

In no image of paradise, including "Eve of Autun," do we see Adam and Eve eating. The lush vegetation and laden trees are merely the promise of abundance as announced by God. Nowhere do we see how grain and fruit are actually harvested and consumed. There are no saucepans, cutlery, or plates, merely the temptation, the longing for the fruit. When Eve reaches out for the apple, in some depictions opening her mouth to take a bite in that magical moment of temptation, the stasis of the ideal, impossible ecosystem with its effortless plenty is about to be shattered. The eating of the forbidden fruit is not just a key scene that says something about the Fall, it is also symbolic of our attitude to food, making explicit the relationship between food and knowledge, and the desire for both. In that relationship lies the essence of what makes us human and distinguishes us from the animals: our perpetual curiosity; our longing for variety, in our diets as elsewhere; our desire to know more, even when we have no idea where knowledge will lead; the wish to understand and control our surroundings. This is not just daredevilry but the essence of science, which has helped us deal with the constraints of the world outside paradise.

Even more so than Adam, Eve is a symbol of curiosity and the desire to experiment. She gives in to the temptation that resides in not-knowing, in not-tasting, and she does so not out of frivolity or weakness, qualities older sources like to attribute to women, but because she is tempted by knowledge and by the thrill of the unknown. That is the first and ultimate sin that all the descendants of Eve and Adam inherit, the sin that leads both to the discovery of the world and to error. At a later stage it opens up opportunities to correct our mistakes.

The temptation of the unknown began, according to tradition, with the apple, that gleaming fruit, "mild with juices," in the words of Vondel, with its "heavenly qualities." Milton writes: "Fruit of fairest colours mixed / Ruddy and gold ... more pleased my sense / Than smell of sweetest fennel, or the teats / Of ewe or goat dropping with milk." Yet in most depictions of paradise, the fruit that Eve plucks resembles almost anything but an apple.

In the relief of Autun the bush that so neatly covers Eve's nakedness has the leaves of a stylized fig, though not its fruits. Elsewhere an orange rather than an apple is suggested. It seems probable that the "apple" of tradition was some other fruit, because in that period there were almost certainly no apples in the Middle East. They arrived only gradually from central Asia, along the Silk Road, and it took centuries for apple trees to emerge that could thrive in climates with a warm spring. The original fruit may have been a fig or a grape, or perhaps a date, a pomegranate, or a citrus fruit. Jewish, Christian, and Islamic sources usually simplify matters by speaking merely of the forbidden fruit, as if its precise identity is unimportant. One argument in favor of the fig is that in most depictions, Adam and Eve cover their nakedness with fig leaves. Occasionally scholars have claimed that the apple was introduced into the story later because of linguistic associations between the Latin word for apple (*Malus*) and the word for evil (*malum*), although the etymology of medieval Latin makes this less likely than it might at first appear. Some interpretations speak of a grapevine from which Eve pressed juice for Adam. It seems logical that fruits tend to be associated with temptation, given their juiciness and sugar content, so welcome in times of scarcity and drought.

Whatever the case may be, the temptation lies not merely in the abstract idea of knowledge, forbidden or not. The fruit itself is portrayed as irresistible—not because Eve and Adam are hungry, impossible by definition in paradise, but because the fruit is unknown, new, and, above all, forbidden. Its profuse character may be a factor too: the many seeds of the pomegranate or fig; the abundance of juice in the grape or orange. The nature of the forbidden fruit confirms, right from the very earliest representations, that we eat and desire food for reasons that go far beyond pure physiology. What makes the temptation so irresistible has to do with the attractiveness of that particular food along with the prohibition itself. The prohibition is a demonstration of power, that of God over Adam and Eve and later, in the form of dietary taboos, that of religious leaders over ordinary people.

Scarcity and Temptation

In stark contrast to the extraordinarily carefree start enjoyed by Adam and Eve, human evolution has been shaped by shortages and hunger. Until recently, almost without exception, food was for most people scarce; available only sporadically; frequently diseased, contaminated, or rotten; and of low nutritional value. Only the scarcest of foods—like meat, fish, nuts, and seeds—are highly nutritious, and partly for that reason they are particularly susceptible to decay. The need to resolve a chronic shortage of food lies at the heart of evolution and has made people all the more inquisitive and eager to learn. This remains true today, as even now much innovation is focused on land use for our basic needs. Think for example of the development of tractors with sophisticated satellite global positioning systems, or the genetic identification of pathogens. To find food, the human species has ventured beyond its places of origin, first to new hunting grounds outside Africa and then, after the invention of agriculture in the Middle East, in search of soils that could be cultivated and of pasture-land in all the climatological zones that lend themselves to it, on all continents except Antarctica. Scarcity has taught us to use fire to prepare food or to conserve it (by desiccation, for instance), to develop implements for hunting, to work the land, to use draft animals, and to invent methods of preservation and processing.

Chronic and often acute scarcity prevailed everywhere until about 250 years ago. The effects of its abolition are the clearest proof of how scarcity has marked our history and our biology. As soon as sufficient food began to become available to large numbers of Europeans, average life expectancy, height, and weight shot up. In most Western European countries, life expectancy tripled in the period 1750–2000.

This history of tens of thousands, if not hundreds of thousands, of years of food scarcity explains our preference for foods high in calories (fats and sugars), proteins, and other essential nutrients. It seems an obvious conclusion: at moments when food was in abundance, usually after a hunt or at harvest time, those who were able to eat and digest quickly and efficiently had an evolutionary advantage. In other words, we are programmed both genetically and socially to consume voraciously those things that give us energy and increase our resistance to disease. Such foodstuffs therefore soon acquired a special cultural and ethical status. Biological preferences reinforce themselves, since, as the term suggests, the satisfaction of hunger makes us feel content. Fats provide the most concentrated calories, more than twice as many by weight as carbothydrates or proteins. It's impossible to eat a large quantity of fat on its own, but combined with the right amount of carbohydrate or sugar, and possibly a pinch of salt, it suddenly becomes extremely easy to stomach, in fact almost irresistible. This seems to be true for everyone, irrespective of dietary habits and age, which explains why cakes and biscuits, chocolate, sugary pancakes, puddings, or strawberries and cream are so attractive, indeed addictive. Something similar applies to nuts, which don't contain much sugar but are an appealing source of calories because of their texture and taste. Even poor population groups in developing countries—people who have never eaten sweets or chocolate before—rapidly take to foodstuffs with high concentrations of sugar and fat. Most of us find the smell of seared meat mouthwatering, for the same reason. The Maillard reaction, which involves proteins and sugars, gives meat a stronger odor and taste when it's roasted, fried, or grilled. Perhaps an unconscious "memory" from the time of the hunter-gatherers may also be involved.

The combination of ingredients must be precisely right. Too much or too little sugar, salt, or fat is counterproductive. The texture of food has an effect, too, since the easier it is to chew and swallow, the more of it we will consume. This explains why liquid calories, found in sugary sauces, ice cream, and soft drinks, are such a hazard for those at risk of putting on too much weight. We barely notice we're consuming them. Experimental research shows, for example, that if you keep topping up bowls of soup through a tube under the table, people will keep on eating. It seems it's not the sense of having had enough that's decisive but availability. The food industry has made an art of increasing the attractions of snacks; the fat in chocolate or caramel melts in the mouth, releasing sugars, and the combination of this with something slightly crunchy (such as nuts or puffed rice) adds flavor, bite, and chewiness in precisely the right amounts. With clever packaging and advertising, food products have an even more irresistible appeal to senses sharpened by evolution.

————

There are convincing reasons for thinking that the brain is involved in all kinds of ways in the temptation to eat something or to enjoy eating something, quite independently of the normal physiological reaction to hunger. Temptation in this sense means being tempted to eat a product you would not otherwise desire and for which you have no pressing physical need. It is unclear precisely how such temptation works, but it's a powerful force, and hardly anyone is immune, as we see from studies of people who are addicted to food or who are trying to lose weight. In our brains, temptation is connected to centers implicated in addiction. The sense of fulfilment that food provides creates positive feedback, which only increases our desire to eat when we have really had enough. The impossibility of resisting certain foods for long, let alone forever, means we need to make an almost superhuman effort of a kind that even those with great willpower can hardly ever sustain for any length of time. The terms in which we speak of such difficulties refer directly to Eve and to paradise. When we talk about eating too much, we may say, even today: "I succumbed and had a biscuit this morning," "I fell for the chocolate cake," or "I couldn't resist the cheese platter." You'll never hear anyone say they couldn't resist the mixed lettuce. Our sense of having sinned is confined almost entirely to foods rich in sugar, proteins, or fats.

The connection between food and temptation is represented in an extreme form by *fugu*, a Japanese delicacy prepared from a fish that contains a toxin capable of killing a human being in four to six hours. The toxin is produced by algae eaten by the fish (which is itself resistant, of course) and is confined to certain organs that must be removed with great care by a cook trained to do so, in such a way that no trace remains. There is no antidote. *Fugu* illustrates another aspect of temptation: trust. Those who don't produce and prepare their own food—and in modern society that means almost all of us—deliver themselves up to a system that feeds them, on the basis of trust.

In modern food advertising we often see images of temptation and abundance, and the irresistible combination of the two. A famous brand of cream cheese is presented in an imagined paradise being enjoyed by angels on little creamy clouds. One British pub—Simpson's in the Strand—serves its large English breakfast under the heading "the ten deadly sins." It would be hard to make the connection between temptation, sin, and death any more explicit than that. Abundance and temptation are deliberately linked: oranges roll without any apparent effort from the tree into a carton of orange juice; coffee beans allow themselves to be roasted, dancing to a samba rhythm, into instant coffee that immediately foams in the cup. Perhaps the most explicit link between temptation, sin, and food is found in an advertisement for Magnum ice cream that begins by showing laden dining tables before moving on to erotic gestures and clothing, an abundance of jewelery and finally, at the *moment suprême*, the delicious choc-ice on a stick. There are seven of these short films for the seven deadly sins, including greed and gluttony. And as if all this were not enough, the Magnum range includes a Magnum Temptation.

To put it irreverently, paradise is the most penetrative and successful piece of advertising ever invented, and grateful use is still made of it. The garden as a safe, bounded space in which nature is tamed and offers its abundance to humankind free of charge amounts to a primal state in which we would all like to live; it therefore frequently serves as a backdrop against which manufacturers recommend their products. The three main monotheistic religions have produced an extremely powerful metaphor that points to an ideal relationship between humans and a divine being, among humans, and between humans and nature. Paradise has entered our languages. We speak of heavenly vacations and of tax havens, with the suggestion of an idyllic sanctuary, tempting us to transcend the limitations of human life. We have only to reach out and enjoy the delights of a perfect existence.

Rules and Taboos

Yet humankind's long exposure to scarcity does not mean that in the past we simply stuffed ourselves with food uninhibitedly and indiscriminately on occasions when it was available. On the contrary, in conditions of scarcity, societies need to impose constraints to avoid the social instability that can result from sudden excess. If they don't, violent conflict may result. Food is power. Anyone who regulates the quantity and type of food available to the general population is in a position of power. Religion and politics therefore join forces, combining the authority of priests, parents, and village and family elders to inculcate in people the notion that food is both a danger and a temptation. The upbringing we give our children is one way of internalizing that notion, which is then used to justify rules about who eats what, when, and how, and to sanction the punishments imposed when dietary rules are flouted.

This begins even in paradise, where God, the world's first nutritional advisor, tells Adam and Eve what they (and, by extension, their descendants) are and are not allowed to eat. This doubles the temptation of the forbidden food, because it is made attractive not just by its nature (flavor, origin, recommendation from a mysterious snake) but also by its being forbidden. The prohibition therefore contains its own antithesis: the stricter the ban, the greater the temptation will be. If the prohibition is weakened or removed, a brake is released, and we have a tendency to pounce on the tempting item in question. This tendency has always existed, as illustrated by unbridled behavior during the Carnival that precedes fasting in the Catholic and Orthodox Christian traditions, but today, especially in rich countries and in major cities, we see a lack of restraint that is not confined to a brief period once a year. Now that parents no longer tell their children they cannot have sweets, or only on special occasions, now that everyone with even a few coins to spend is almost continually exposed to an abundance of easily available food displayed in the most tempting manner, little stands between us and the overconsumption of calories. We are overwhelmed not just by the delicious composition (protein, sugars, and fats combined with all kinds of flavorings) or forbidden character of certain foods but also by abundance itself. Excess proves irresistible, an additional stimulus to temptation, not just because of easy availability but also because it appeals to our ancient and justified fear of scarcity and to our urge to eat as soon as it becomes possible and is allowed. Studies show that people eat more when food is visible, attractively packaged or displayed, and easy to obtain at home or in the supermarket. The more prominent the packaging, the easier it is to open, and the closer it is to a person's mouth, the greater the temptation will be. And the easier the calories are to take in, perhaps in a liquid or semi-liquid form, the more of them we consume. Temptation doesn't stop there, because if the packaging tells us we are looking at a low-fat or low-calorie version of a product, we will actually eat more of it. Somehow an authority is lodged inside our heads that tells us this kind of food is less "bad," and we immediately adjust our behavior in response. We are tempted even by knowledge itself.

———————

The story of Eve and the snake therefore contains a warning that goes far beyond the story of paradise: food is a danger that has to be kept in check by dietary rules and taboos. This requires a religious authority that sanctions food, or, as the literal meaning of the word "sanction" suggests, sanctifies it, makes it holy. The three main monotheistic religions, like practically all faiths, have elaborate dietary laws. A taboo on a specific food may be justified by all kinds of religious arguments, but it is scientifically inexplicable; there is no actual relationship between the forbidden item and the reasons given. Taboos concern not just consumption but also the way foods are prepared—perhaps the best-known example being the separation of meat and milk in the kosher kitchen—and indeed produced, as in the notion of a sabbatical year in which the land must rest and nothing may be gathered from the trees. The majority of rules of this kind relate to the most valuable foods: meat and fish. There are few restrictions on vegetables and fruit, except that most religions ban the harvesting of fruit from young trees (according to the Jewish dietary laws in the Kashrut, young trees are to be regarded as uncircumcised) and insist that the first fruits must be offered as a sacrifice.

The ultimate goal of dietary rules and taboos is the ordering of the world into edible and nonedible, dangerous and safe, and the guarding of group identity. Access to food is kept in check, and it can therefore be shared out as desired between rich and poor, men and women. The notion that what you eat is what you are becomes at the same time: what you don't eat distinguishes you from other people and creates a bond with those who eat similarly. The best-known example of a dietary taboo is the ban on eating pork. For Jewish and Muslim believers, the world is divided into those who adhere to that prohibition and those who do not.

The Jewish laws of the Kashrut and the Islamic ban on pork have the same source. Kosher and halal mean "that which is permitted" (often wrongly translated as "clean" or "pure"). The word "kosher" is not actually found in the Torah, the first five books of the Bible. People have sought long and hard for a medical rationale behind these laws, but we can be fairly certain that any positive effects on public health are merely coincidental. The explicit justification lay first of all in the call for self-control. Anyone who adhered to the rules was demonstrating submission to divine commands, even if the reasons for those commands were sometimes impossible to comprehend. The Jewish rabbis indicated that they knew the rules were not sufficient to guard against the tendency to eat too much, even if only kosher food were consumed. Later religious authorities, such as the medieval Jewish scholar Maimonides, advanced medical arguments for banning pork, but hygiene was not the main purpose of these laws. True, pigs appear obviously unclean because of their tendency to roll in the mud and eat refuse and dung, and in the nineteenth century a connection was made between the consumption of raw or undercooked pork and a disease caused by the roundworm (*Trichinella* ssp.) called "trichinosis." That discovery seemed initially to confirm the medical argument, but undercooked beef is just as dangerous as a source of diseases, including brucellosis and anthrax, and larvae of the roundworm are also frequently found in game, including deer.

A more convincing argument concerns the ecological effects of pigs. Although pigs are more efficient at transforming feed into meat than, say, cows or goats, in the Middle East they compete far more directly with people for food than do ruminants (which include goats, sheep, and cattle). Pigs don't eat grass, they need more water than other animals, and they cope poorly with high temperatures. Moreover, cows can be used as draft animals, and goats and sheep provide wool, whereas pigs are useful only for their flesh and their skin. Ecological factors may perhaps have played a part, if only implicitly, in the introduction of a ban on pork and therefore on pig-keeping.

Something similar may be at work in the Hindu taboo on the eating of cows, water buffalo, and horses, all of which are essential for ploughing the heavy clay of the rice paddies. They also provide the milk and butter that are used to produce ghee, the only source of fats for many people in the Indian subcontinent and therefore an essential supplement to a generally meager diet. These animals are kept but not eaten.

We should perhaps think along the same lines in attempting to understand the rules about cooking a kid in its mother's milk, a taboo referred to three times in the Torah. The Talmud interprets it as a general ban on preparing meat alongside dairy products, and therefore divides foods into three categories: meat, dairy, and *parve* (neutral). Fish is regarded as *parve*, poultry as meat. The ban on combining meat with milk and products derived from milk could be interpreted medically as a ban on consuming too much fat and running bacteriological risks, and ecologically as a taboo on wasting proteins, which are costly in ecological terms. Other common restrictions concern aquatic animals that have scales and fins, fish eggs, birds of prey, and bats (the latter two were also proscribed in the Christian Middle Ages) as well as sick animals. That final category does seem to have a certain logic because of the danger of infection, but even here the argument is less than convincing.

The importance of dietary laws lies not so much in any ecological or medical advantages as in the maintenance of the unity of the group and social order. At the same time these laws help regulate individual food consumption. Ideally, in Hinduism as in other religions, eating becomes a carefully considered and controlled act. The mind is focused on the holy, and eating is preceded by obedience to rules about the production, preparation, and storage of food. In this vision, fasting is the ultimate form of self-control. Even when the rules are relatively few, as in Christianity, they do moderate food intake. In the Middle Ages the Catholic Church had 166 fast days, on which the consumption of meat and sometimes fish and other products was curbed. As recently as a couple of decades ago, European Catholics did not generally eat meat on Fridays. It is intriguing that Protestantism has no dietary laws or taboos. Perhaps the moderation so important to the Lutherans and Calvinists, which led rich seventeenth-century Dutch merchants to dress in sober black with no outward show of wealth, made explicit restrictions on food consumption irrelevant.

All religions attribute moral and psychological properties to food. It can be bad, unclean, or a cause of restlessness (like caffeine), according to the extensive dietary teachings of the Ayurveda and the guidance given by some diet gurus. Creatures that were considered unclean—moles, for example—came to symbolize the evils of humankind, miserliness, for example. Conversely, the kingfisher was not to be eaten because it was a symbol of abundance and prosperity.

Alongside forbidden foods are others said to make people more pure or to reinforce their good characteristics. According to Ayurvedic medicine, the pomegranate strengthens the body's "wind" and thereby creativity, and reduces the "heat" of the metabolism. In many religions, fasting, which demonstrates the ability to withstand hunger, is regarded as the highest virtue or a route to greater religious insight. This applies to both Christian and Islamic mystics, and the same idea has a place in Hinduism and the animistic religions of hunter-gatherers, including some Native Americans. Even today, countless fruit juice cures and the like are advertised as "detox diets" or ways of making you feel lighter, terms that echo older religious beliefs about purity and detachment.

Like temptation, dietary laws have both a qualitative and a quantitative side. There are physiological, psychological, and economic reasons that it is difficult or impossible for us to consume with moderation those things that are attractive and plentiful, whatever the rules. Modern secular humans still apply an informal classification of good and bad: vegetables are good; sweets and salty snacks are bad. The most tempting foods are those we greatly enjoy eating and at the same time see as "bad." Those we label "good" are foods that raise our status, perhaps because they come from abroad and are eaten mainly by the rich (at one time cheese fondue, now crab). Quantity remains relevant here too, of course. It is hard to label a pancake as bad, but what about five pancakes in one day? This is a new problem in the secularized West of recent decades, where we conflate "bad for the figure," "bad for the health," "bad for the environment," and "bad for the soul." Foods that are particularly enjoyable because of all the added sugars, fats, and salt, which make us unable to moderate our appetites, cause us to feel guilty. In those who suffer from food addiction, a sense of guilt makes self-control all the harder. ("I've already sinned today, so that extra cookie won't make any difference." "Tomorrow I'll go on a diet.")

On the one hand dietary rules are no longer strictly enforced, so we happily let ourselves go. On the other hand, dispensing with rules is a way of being ourselves. Big is beautiful, some feminists say, and they ask why they shouldn't eat whatever they like. Just as taboos are a way of preserving a group identity, breaking taboos in modern times is a way of affirming individual identity. In the case of such Jewish-American authors as Philip Roth, eating ham is an act of provocation. Food, our first requirement in life, the basis of our existence and our culture, can be both a sin and a means of self-expression. In modern history, no food embodies this ambiguity better than the hamburger, which demonstrates the intrinsically complex character of modern food, combining as it does enjoyment and guilt, individual identity and self-loathing, freedom and transgression.

Eve's Hamburger

Eve's apple is no longer the symbol of evil. On the contrary, apples had their reputation salvaged long ago by the more recent habit of seeing them as healthy, even if that notion has recently become controversial because of their high sugar content. Apples no longer have the tempting character they once had for naughty children who cycled past orchards on their way home from school, and no one talks any longer of an apple-cheeked child. If Eve's perfidious apple has a present-day equivalent, then it is surely the disturbing image of a genetically manipulated apple, sprayed with chemicals and perfect in shape and complexion. Such a fruit is irresistibly appetizing while at the same time symbolizing our fear that arrogant human intervention in nature—by "uncontrollable" commercial firms and irresponsible researchers—will cause irrevocable harm to the earth and to humankind.

The ultimate metaphor of modern temptation and sin is the hamburger. No food product of the past half-century has been more admired or more maligned. Were a modern-day Eve to want to tempt her Adam, she would do so with a hamburger, and with a story to accompany it. That story would tell not just of good and evil but of the rise and fall of the hamburger and the revival of an icon. The iconic hamburger is not just a food but a superfood, larger than life. It has been presented as such by, for example, a gigantic work of pop art called "Floor Burger," made out of polystyrene foam by Swedish sculptor Claes Oldenburg in 1962. The hamburger stands accused of all the evils of the modern world: of causing obesity, cancer, and cardiovascular disease; infecting the food chain with bacteria; causing the deforestation of the Amazon basin; destroying local culinary cultures and small businesses; imposing the values and uniform eating patterns of Western capitalism; creating food addiction; and much more besides. It was inevitable that documentary filmmaker Morgan Spurlock would use the hamburger rather than any other food product in his film *Super Size Me* to demonstrate the perversity of American gastronomic culture. The hamburger as proof of the loneliness of the consumer was perhaps best expressed by Danish filmmaker Jørgen Leth, in a 1981 documentary made up of sixty-six scenes from American life, which includes a scene of just over four minutes showing Andy Warhol unwrapping a hamburger, lacing it with ketchup, and eating it, after which he looks at the camera with an impassive expression and tells viewers what they have just seen.

At the same time, for many people the hamburger is irresistible. It took the apple thousands of years to become the most widely distributed fruit tree in the world, whereas the hamburger established itself within half a century in almost every capital city. For many adults it may have become the symbol of unhealthy mass consumption of too much greasy food, but it was not always so, and even today this is not the case everywhere. The bun with meat filling was acclaimed as an American success story for many years. The precise origin of the hamburger is a matter of controversy, but around a century ago a product came on the market in America that closely resembled today's version. The history of the hamburger is the story of a continual quest to reinvent a food item by sophisticated means, leaving the end product apparently unchanged and therefore completely dependable for the consumer while almost invisibly introducing one innovation after another. What made McDonald's, Burger King, Jack in the Box, the once ubiquitous White Castle, and their like such successful companies was not the hamburger itself, nor the franchise system that has enabled it to penetrate all markets, but the systems and technology used to ensure that identical hamburgers would roll off production lines all over the world to be served to a public that knew exactly what to expect. Strict controls guarantee a standardized, flawless product that will appeal to vast numbers. Nowadays the hamburger is more relevant than ever to our increasingly mobile societies; meat wrapped neatly in bread, which you can eat with one hand without soiling your clothes.

Take the degree of thought that goes into the tasteless and squashable bun. It did not come into being because Americans were no good at baking bread but because a special consistency is needed to bring out to the full the juiciness of the meat. The bun is wrapping, plate, and napkin in one, and only after that a source of carbohydrates to accompany a product rich in protein and fat. The hamburger was invented to provide the most reliable, cheap, and quick way to enjoy meat (and from the start that was beef, a sign of quality, in contrast to supposedly inferior pork).

In the 1940s hamburger chains began to displace traditional restaurants in the United States. From a snack intended mainly for men, the hamburger grew into a family meal: a hamburger with French fries, a lettuce leaf, and a cold drink. At the root of the success of McDonald's lies the absolute predictability not just of the taste but also of the menu, the interiors of its restaurants, and the appearance of its drive-ins. They made consumers feel both at home and connected with people elsewhere who were eating hamburgers at the same time. Together they are all part of a universal hamburger culture carefully guarded by the McDonald's Hamburger University in Oakbrook, Illinois, where cookery and management classes are taught in more than twenty languages.

A fresh breakthrough came in the late 1950s, namely, the hamburger in an extra-large size (originally produced by Burger King), which only really started to take off in 1972, when McDonald's introduced its Quarter Pounder alongside its 1967 innovation, the Big Mac. It was a logical progression from the years after the Second World War, when everything grew inexorably: cars, houses, cities, even people. At the same time, life and therefore eating took on a faster, more hurried character. The production of a larger model of the hamburger was a new psychological step in the direction of food for the masses that was not simply as cheap as possible. The size of the portions became a goal in itself, reaffirming the identity of a generation that was "on top of the world." The speed of production made it possible to eat even more quickly. The concept of fast food was born, and it spread along the highways, across the suburbs, and into the inner cities, to commuters, families, and young people. Fast food meant rapidly getting a lot of calories inside you at an affordable price. It made the consumer feel part of a modern trend.

In the 1980s the hamburger began to find a market outside America and Europe, and after the fall of the Berlin Wall in 1989 its onward march met with an enthusiastic reception in Eastern Europe and the former Soviet Union. By 1990, the Moscow McDonald's was the busiest in the world. The hamburger had become a symbol of the triumph of the American capitalist model, along with blue jeans and Hollywood films. Partly thanks to the hamburger and the fast food culture it spawned, we are seeing increasing uniformity not only in the culinary and cultural fields but also in the shape of the human body, or rather its shapelessness.

The hamburger has been copied hundreds of times and adjusted to suit local conditions. In India a prototype of the vegetarian hamburger as street food has been invented. In Chengdu, China, in the early 1990s, I once stood in line at a hamburger joint, although that is perhaps a rather grand term for something that was little more than a grimy vegetable stall with a rudimentary bench out in front. The scent of burned meat in oil re-used rather too often rose from the pans. I asked for a vegetarian burger, but the soggy disc clamped between two bruised lettuce leaves in a bun tasted of nothing at all and had the fibrous texture of tough chicken. Nevertheless the place was popular, and a queue had formed. We ate our "hamburgers" as evening fell, and it occurred to me this would be the kiss of death to China's ancient and exquisite culinary tradition. I could not have been more wrong. Far from disappearing, that tradition has if anything strengthened as prosperity has increased. Chinese restaurants in China and elsewhere have been awarded Michelin stars, and elegant fusion cooking is the fashion among the rich. At the same time, the real American hamburger has become all-pervasive, despite or perhaps even because of high prices, which confirm its status. For the poor there is still the miserable Chinese hamburger, made of onions and meat scraps, which nevertheless signals that they aspire to the American lifestyle.

The iconic value of the hamburger and the McDonald's Corporation is so great that both have given rise to derivative terms meaning "bigger than big," especially through the use of the prefix "Mc." The label "McMansion" is applied to huge and ostentatious homes. "McWorld," a term invented by Benjamin Barber, is used to refer to the conglomerate of large industrial complexes that aims to globalize everything. Ever since 1986, the respected British periodical *The Economist* has published a more or less serious Big Mac Index, in which it uses the price of the Big Mac to indicate buying power in the world. This comparison is possible only because of the consistent combination of ingredients and the identical production methods used in every outlet. Something rather similar applies to "burger," which is both a generic term and the trademark of the main competitor of McDonald's: Burger King. Playful variations can be found on the Internet, such as the Porn Burger, which I will not attempt to describe here other than to say that it features a combination of spam, ham, and beef with generous lashings of mayonnaise.

———————

The antiestablishment protests of the 1960s and 1970s in America barely affected the hamburger at all, so closely bound up was it with the culture of the suburbs with its drive-ins and barbecues. Not until the 1980s and 1990s did resistance arise to the "McDonaldization" of the world. From India to Italy, protest was vehement on occasions, resulting in smashed windows, sit-ins, and even arson. In Italy the campaigners adopted the term "McCancro." In 1997 in Bangalore, the local hamburger joint was stormed by activists dressed in homespun cotton robes in the style of Gandhi, advocating a second struggle for Indian independence and to that end squirting tomato ketchup on checkout tills and smashing restaurant interiors. A similar fate had struck Pizza Hut a year before. For a long time now, the hamburger and McDonald's have been seen as typifying the kind of multinational undertakings that feel no sense of loyalty to any country or culture, evade all democratic controls, and show no concern for the environment or working conditions. Criticism is now directed less at the multinational itself and more at the attractiveness of the hamburger to children, at whom many of the advertisements, games, and special offers are aimed.

———————

Alongside the ambiguity of sin and attractiveness, and the appeal of abundance, there is another side to temptation: what you eat gives you status. It is a sign of your aspirations, in the way that good table manners or expensive chocolates can be. Anyone eating a hamburger is succumbing not just to laziness and poor taste but to the image of American modernity, the desire to belong to a new world. This is what makes the hamburger, despite all the criticism it inspires, so impossible to resist.

It is an aspect expressed beautifully in the work of Chinese artist Liao Yibai, who created the "Top Secret Hamburger," a 150-kilogram shiny steel hamburger that reflects the dream of the West and its addictive culture. In an interview, the artist, son of a military scientist, said that the first English word he learned at school was "hamburger." He knew nothing about the product itself, other than that it was a symbol of the evil and decadent West.

When the father of one of his classmates was sent to the United States on an official trip, the whole class begged him to bring back a sample of the mysterious hamburger. A few days after his return, the father called all the children to him, closed the curtains and showed them a thick envelope with the words "top secret" on it. Inside was a hamburger, an almost extraterrestrial green-brown thing with a terrible rotten smell and taste. They became convinced their teacher was right to say that capitalism was disgusting and perverse. Only much later did Liao Yibai understand that what he had experienced was not in fact the smell of the American system.

_____

But the story of the hamburger is not over yet. In another telling twist, the much-maligned McDonald's, which has seen its market share decline over the past ten years, is attempting to reinvent itself as a fast food chain concerned about health and sustainability: no more extra fat added during grilling, no more trans fats, far less salt, French fries made with real potatoes instead of potato flour, more vegetables, and even biological milk in the coffee (which now bears a stamp of approval from the Rainforest Alliance). In Britain, too, agreements have been made with local farmers, who provide most of the meat. In the Netherlands only dairy farmers with the most advanced, animal-friendly stalls, complete with music and waterbeds, are allowed to supply McDonald's. Standardization and adjustment to local conditions go hand in hand. Where necessary the menu is changed to suit the culinary traditions of the country, so in the United Kingdom it includes porridge and in Norway salmon. There are even special main-course salads and veggie burgers made with soy, so that vegetarians will have no reason to avoid the chain. In India the hamburgers, which go by the name Maharaja Mac, are made with lamb instead of beef (forbidden to Hindus). Since 2006 McDonald's has stated the nutritional value of its products on the packaging (now made of biodegradable plastic), and its used cooking oil is converted into biodiesel for its trucks. Even the interior design has been changed to provide more space for children to play. None of this has done the company any harm.

In several countries, McDonald's is managing to retain its position as one of the largest catering firms in a market that has shrunk since the economic crisis of 2007–2008. Partly stimulated by the national and international debate over sustainability and by such initiatives as those of the hamburger chains, other food-processing companies have made agreements about good practice, deciding for example that they will not use meat whose production involves deforestation, that waste and water usage must be strictly limited, and that carbon dioxide (CO_2) emissions per product unit will be reduced. The intention is that these practices will be monitored by independent organizations. Quality is still problematic in many of the smaller, local fast food companies, incidentally, although there are now some successful small chains that specialize in alternative, in some cases vegetarian, handmade burgers.

The hamburger tells a story of temptation and ambivalence, of sin, of abundance that nevertheless increases status, and ultimately of technological innovation and a new consciousness of responsibility for the earth. That you are what you eat was recognized by McDonald's, at least implicitly, in its most recent restyling in 2008. In its new restaurants the hamburger is promoted by means of realistic, artistic photographs of the product and by the slogan "What we are made of" (in Spanish-speaking countries "*Lo que estamos hecho de*"), which refers both to the hamburgers and, by extension, to those who eat them. Earlier, in Canada, a similar slogan was used: "There's a little McDonald's in everyone." This is not just an attractive metaphor; it is a scientific fact that we are made of the molecules we eat. The combination of hamburger, French fries, and Coca-Cola is known to its fans as the holy trinity.

Which brings us back to Eve and temptation. The apple has made way for the hamburger as a symbol of the food with which Adam could be tempted. Like the Eve of Autun, a contemporary Eve leads him astray not just by sinning or by being provocative but by allowing herself to long for something new, since by testing the boundaries we innovate and thereby reinforce our identities. The story of the hamburger is the story of an icon that is reinventing itself and at the same time prompting a radical change to the way we think about food, about production, and about consumption in general. We are shifting from outsized, standardized portions to the small-scale and unique. By its very success, highlighted in the film *Super Size Me*, the hamburger has brought about a countermovement of anti-fast food, anti-globalization, pro-vegetarian, and pro-local eating, a revival of concern about authenticity, diversity, health, and the relationship between farmers and consumers, as well as openness about the origins of ingredients. The hamburger brings together paradise and the Fall of Man, food, sin, arrogance and creativity, new knowledge and the willingness to learn from mistakes.

THREE

Agriculture: A Triumph of Hard Work

Continua messe senescit ager.
[A field becomes exhausted by constant tillage.]
PUBLIUS OVIDIUS NASO, *Artis Amatoriae* 3:82

I had never realized how all these problems were connected: energy,
nourishment, population growth, the scarcity of raw materials,
industrialization, the balance of nature, ecology. SICCO MANSHOLT

Agriculture as Myth

Expulsion from paradise means the end of a divine and automatic supply of food. From that point on, Adam and Eve have to fend for themselves. No more fruit plopping down out of the trees, no grassy fields full
of edible seeds. The transition from paradisiacal plenty to the frugality of
farming is hard. Hence those ominous predictions that from now on they
will eat their food by the sweat of their brow (Genesis 3:19).

The first concern of Adam and Eve and their descendants must have
been to care for the plants and animals that were of use to them. They
had to deal briskly with attacks by or competition from other organisms, such as insects, molds, weeds, and grazing animals, not to mention predators like lions or foxes that menaced the livestock. It was not
just a matter of limiting damage; they needed to ensure that useful
plants and animals could grow in the most favorable circumstances and
that seeds could germinate in well-tilled, fertile soil rather than falling on stony ground or coming to nothing for lack of water. The Bible
is full of such agricultural images, which are meant to be seen as fac-
tual representations but which also function as metaphors for how life
should be lived.

It is striking that the biblical God does not exhort Adam and Eve to go
hunting outside paradise or to gather berries and roots. Despite its osten-
sible chronology, the story of paradise doesn't precede the appearance
of humankind on earth and the long period of hunting and gathering;
rather it follows from them. The order of events is not first plenty in paradise, then hunting and gathering, then agriculture, but rather hunting

and gathering, the myth of paradise, then the growing of crops in fields and the keeping of herds and flocks. The book of Bereshit/Genesis has been dated to somewhere between the ninth and fifth centuries BC, and it points to events and locations of 2,000 years earlier. By that time, some 5,000 thousand years ago, farming had spread widely across the flood-plains of the Tigris and the Euphrates, and the first towns were emerging. The allegory of banishment from paradise arose as a way of looking back at the arrival of something new that would change human history fundamentally, the radical nature of which was recognized: the "taming" of plants and animals that was intended to put an end to scarcity. The process itself was accompanied by many uncertainties and failures, recounted in the Bible and many other sources. Existential angst about the availability of food lies at the heart of every civilization.

One of the most arresting expressions of that fear is Masaccio's "Expulsion from the Garden of Eden," a fresco of 1424–1425 in the Santa Maria del Carmine in Florence, created when the painter was twenty-three. It shows a sand-colored desert that begins just outside the high stone gates of paradise, with steep, eroded hills and not a trace of vegetation or human dwellings. Adam and Eve are naked, their bodies the same color as the sand, and they have left even their fig leaves behind in paradise. Churchmen later ordered garlands to be painted over their vital organs, but happily, those were removed when the work was cleaned in recent years, so that we can again experience in full the vulnerability of the unhappy first people amid the desolation of the landscape. Eve is weeping, and Adam has put his hands over his eyes on seeing the contrast between the desert and the—already invisible—fertile green garden they have left forever.

In Michelangelo's Sistine Chapel ceiling of around a century later, we see an almost identical image: the same sand-colored desert where nothing will grow, the same cloudless, glaring sky, those same utterly naked bodies in the color of the earth from which they are made and to which they shall return (Genesis 3:19, 23–24). Another three centuries later Romanticism adapted the image to match the dominant threat of the time: not the desert, which no longer existed in the collective memory, but the dark forest, that no man's land between cities. In the nineteenth-century engravings of Gustave Doré, an impenetrable European primeval forest with tangled roots begins right outside the door to paradise. Adam and Eve are properly clothed this time, and in that respect Doré adheres to Genesis 3:21, in which God covers human nakedness. In the series of drawings on biblical themes by Peter Vos of 1985, to take a modern-day example, Adam and Eve stand arm in arm like close friends in a mountainous landscape, looking out across an arid plain on which we see a few bushes and palm trees growing in a hollow almost like an oasis.

Despite the differences wrought by time, in all these images there is the same sense of desolation, the fear of a hostile environment that offers nothing to eat, where people have to provide for themselves for the first time. This is, I think, not just a reflection of the individual artist's fear of emptiness but the real fear of people emerging from centuries of hunger and of struggling with recalcitrant nature.

Agriculture means first of all the growing of crops, and it caused people to settle into more or less permanent homes. In Genesis, at the moment of the Fall, nothing is said about the keeping of livestock. It seems to me this is because the story was told by desert tribes constantly on the move, who were already herding animals. The keeping of livestock was far less epoch-making than the transition to the geographical permanence of agriculture. The expulsion from paradise is not a reference to a literal departure from a divine vegetable plot but to a process of social and technological adjustment to stable settlement, to the discipline of the seasons, and to work on the land. Much of the Old Testament, as well as the texts of the Tenach or the Koran, can be read as the sometimes painful documentation of economic and cultural conflicts between hunters, herdsmen, arable farmers, and emerging city-dwellers, conflicts that are still going on, in the Sahel, for example.

That the transition to agriculture was given a religious significance in retrospect flows from the far-reaching changes and risks it introduced. Anyone who farms permanent fields and settles near to them cannot simply flee to escape drought, storms, crop-destroying frosts, a failure of seed to germinate, or dying cattle. Anyone who settles down and no longer travels to pasture with the wild animals or livestock has time to make home more beautiful. Successful agriculture eventually leads to specialization and cooperation, and the number of people not employed in food production can gradually increase. But that freedom to do something else also entails dependence on others and therefore greater vulnerability and a need for collective trust, which must be addressed by all and given meaning.

———————

However far-reaching and positive the results of food production eventually became, seen from the perspective of human evolution, for more than 10,000 years agriculture was a source of great fear—of a lack of control and of bad harvests. Stories were needed to calm those fears, and rules had to be imposed. A divine authority was an essential ingredient, bound up with a concrete image of divine benevolence and rigor: the garden. What could be more reassuring than a place in which all the uncertainties and human impotence associated with agriculture are absent, where food can be taken for granted and people live in safety, protected by an omnipotent deity who bends nature to his will? In the ecology of western Asia it seems completely understandable that the divine has taken the form of an idealized garden, an eternal spontaneous oasis of lush greenery and unlimited water. There can be no greater contrast than between the peaceful garden and the primitive, labor-intensive, and insecure growing of crops or the cruelty of the hunt in regions with little rain. Those who leave the garden are at the mercy of the elements, dependent on their own skills. Images of a garden and of banishment from secure supplies of food and water were distilled into the allegory of paradise and the Fall.

———————

In almost all regions where hunter-gatherers eventually became farmers, agricultural gods and myths emerged. The discovery that plants can be grown as crops and animals tamed, instead of merely taken from the wild, was so extraordinary, and for a long time so uncertain, that it could only be attributed to divine intervention. The unpredictability of the weather and the harvest was interpreted to mean that people were in the hands of a god or gods, who must be placated year after year. Images of the divine serve not just to calm fears but also to explain how the world is ordered. The biblical Canaanites prayed to Ba'al, the god of fertility and also of rain and dew, essential ingredients of fertility. The Greeks had Demeter and the Romans Ceres, goddesses with a broad mandate that went beyond a narrow definition of agriculture, covering the fertility both of the soil and of humans, cereal crops, the seasons, and the harvest, and by extension marriage and the cycle of life and death. In pre-Columbian Peru, where the potato originates, the god of the potato, shown with a tuber in either hand, is the most important, a deity comparable to the rice goddess Inari in Japanese culture or India's Balram, god of agriculture, the plough, and the farmer. Rituals intended to ensure the success of the harvest usually include the crucial steps of preparing the land, sowing, and harvesting. They are almost always accompanied by sacrifice, sometimes of animals, often of plants, like the bowl of rice placed in the field at sowing time in many Southeast Asian villages. Some Protestant churches in northern Europe and North America still hold harvest festivals.

The ultimate symbol of abundance is the classical cornucopia, the horn filled with fruit, flowers, and grains, which according to myth came into being when young Zeus was fed by a goat and accidentally broke off one of its horns. As compensation, Zeus promised that the horn would always be filled with abundance, a myth developed further in the story of the Roman goddess Copia, from whose name is derived our word "copious," as in a copious meal. There is also a wonderful Attic vase, red on white, showing Hades carrying the horn of plenty for Persephone when she returns to Earth from the underworld to visit her mother—itself a story representing the start of spring. The filled horn belongs to agriculture, however, not to hunters and gatherers, because it holds grain grown as a crop and the keeping of goats dates back to a period several thousand years after agriculture began. Other cultures too, that of Japan, for example, have a horn of plenty, and it remains a popular metaphor for wealth. Agriculture promises abundance.

The Very Beginning

I can still recall the fascination I felt when, at twelve years old, I saw the first pictures of the excavation of cities in the fertile crescent, the area that connects the valleys of the Euphrates and the Tigris with the Jordan valley. The existence of many ancient cities in the region is revealed by innumerable little hillocks in the low landscape, called "*tels*," left over when clay walls collapsed. I saw those early black-and-white photographs of a desert region at a lecture, the first real lecture I ever attended, as far as I know. The moment that impressed me most was when the speaker, an archaeologist, described how, during a nocturnal flight in a small plane under the full moon, he could see from the shadow patterns made by irregularities on the ground how extensive the ruins were (this was of course long before satellite images and infrared cameras). Those cities, he said, were evidence of a wealthy period in a densely populated area that began seven thousand years ago, made possible by the fact that sufficient food could be brought in. Yet in his story I also discovered, even then, the dark side of agriculture. The shrivelled vegetation in the photographs was the result of mismanagement—of salinization, overgrazing, and erosion—and changes in rainfall and climate that mark the landscape to this day, fifty centuries later.

Food! Agriculture! It was at that moment that I became interested in a branch of human activity that seemed a world away from what I saw the adults around me doing, who were mainly occupied with books. Farming makes people sedentary. Instead of following wild animals, people could settle in one place and build something that would last for generations and be continually developed: a collective heritage of houses, barns, orchards, temples, and libraries. I realized for the first time at that lecture that the permanent and guaranteed availability of food is not self-explanatory but extraordinary, especially for those who are not farmers. That thought remained with me, if only on the verge of my consciousness, as such insights often are. My motivation to study agriculture at Wageningen University in the Netherlands had its origins elsewhere, in concern about underdevelopment and hunger, but over the years the historical dimension has unexpectedly come to the fore, and with it the relationship between farming, cities, language, and civilization.

———

We can define agriculture as the systematic use of sunlight and other resources (such as water and nutrients) for and by people, to produce feed for animals and plants, fibers like wool and flax, drinks, ingredients for pharmaceutical products, and building and packaging materials. As we make use of other species in these ways, they acquire different characteristics. The aurochs becomes the ox; the wild potato becomes edible. Agriculture encompasses the growing of crops, horticulture, and the breeding of livestock, including draft animals. By some definitions it also includes fish farming. Behind this relatively simple description lies a world of technological development and biological diversity, the result of 10,000 years of progress in many diverse climates. The use of sunlight for human nutrition ranges from the most primitive plantings of the Central African Bantu farmer, who merely makes a hole in the ashes after burning down a stretch of rainforest and plants a cutting there, to the vast combines that a Brazilian farmer uses to harvest hundreds of acres of zero-tillage fields, where the soil is no longer worked, and the farmer only has to spray herbicides across the genetically modified soybeans. In southern China, horticulture means growing leafy vegetables, beans, cabbages, and sweet potatoes that are draped over fences along and across the irrigation channels. In the Westland of the Netherlands, most horticulture is almost completely computerized, in closed greenhouses where insects are killed by natural enemies, such as parasitic wasps. In the United States, cows are kept in intensive feed lots. In Kenya, farmers have one or two cows at most, tended on an eroding hillside by a boy who really ought to be in school. Such is the diversity of farming.

Seen in the context of hundreds of thousands of years of human evolution, the transition to farming is without doubt the most far-reaching change in the existence of *Homo sapiens*. Without the Neolithic agricultural revolution, which itself arose from the Palaeolithic era (the stone age), the Industrial Revolution in which human and animal work was replaced by fossil fuels would be unthinkable, along with all the most recent developments in work and information technology that we also like to label as revolutions. Without farming there would be no cities or writing, because without the surpluses produced by farmers, people would not have been able to devote themselves in large numbers to anything other than meeting their daily food needs. There would be no writers, no artists, researchers, or technologists in a position to discover fossil fuels or silicon, or to invent the drilling rigs and computers that go with them.

We speak of revolutionary changes in the Neolithic period, but they should really be imagined as evolutionary, as gradual processes of adjustment and experimentation that took at least a hundred centuries. At a time when more than half the world's population lives in cities, it is almost impossible to imagine how world-shattering the gradual invention of farming was. We cannot comprehend such huge timescales as the first fifty or a hundred centuries before it began to arise, 15,000 or 20,000 years ago, when the first hesitant steps were taken toward making use of plants and animals, nor the gap of 10,000 years that separates us from the first real farmers. We ought to be continually amazed at having been born in the time after the invention of farming.

Agriculture's consequences for our food, health, and lifestyle are downright spectacular. In the 10,000 years since the start of farming, the human population has grown from an estimated 10 million to more than 7 billion. This was made possible by the availability of sufficient food, not by improved medical care. In fact medical care is an effect of population growth, not a cause; successful food production means we can afford to keep weaker people alive. The relationship between technical development and population growth works both ways: population pressure on the land leads to technical improvements (such as the invention of agriculture or the plough), but sometimes disaster strikes when overpopulation leads to ecological damage and depletion of the soil and the land has to be abandoned.

Because of agriculture, people learned to anticipate events systematically and to bend the ecosystem to their will, no longer simply waiting until circumstances are favorable for hunting or gathering. The invention of farming was an evolutionary masterstroke, because it involved turning to our advantage the only truly sustainable resource: sunlight, or at least concentrating on the photosynthesis that is of use to humankind— not nettles but oats; not only oak trees but olive trees too. Admittedly we weren't the first to replace hunting and gathering with cultivation. Fifty million years before us, termites and ants were exploiting molds and lice for their food and even selecting them, as we do with our crops and our cattle. We may have been late, but the sheer scale and speed with which we humans made countless species instrumental in satisfying our needs makes us unique.

Growing crops in preference to catching prey altered the food supply massively, because compared to grains, meat cannot be kept for long. Agriculture meant that food could be stored and people knew exactly where to find it, in fields that they tended themselves and in storage barns. It therefore seems probable that agriculture had a direct impact on the development of language and abstract thinking, by making it both possible and necessary to create long-term plans and the cooperative relationships that planning requires. Moreover, agriculture stimulated the development of science by creating a need to understand meteorology, hydrology, seasons, and time, and to organize food supplies.

If agriculture has such obvious advantages, why did humans not start growing cereals and keeping animals earlier in their evolution? Could it not have begun several hundred thousand years before, in the East African savannah, or at least immediately after people left Africa and moved to climates with a more obvious spring season? Theoretically it could have done, but there is no evidence that it did. No trace of the tentative beginnings of farming has ever been found, even in western Asia, dating from more than 20,000 or perhaps 15,000 years ago. There have been suggestions that in tectonically active regions, where more water can come to the surface and the soils are relatively young, the rise of agriculture was more likely. This applies to parts of the Middle East, China, India, Central America, and Ethiopia. The availability of fertile silt was of great importance in the phase during which agriculture expanded (in such places as the Fertile Crescent, the Nile, and the Indus), but not at the beginning. Farming originated because of a very special conjunction of circumstances. It is certainly not a Western or European invention.

Despite the evolutionary advantages of agriculture in the long term, it does not go without saying that eventually hunter-gatherers were bound to develop an alternative to their way of life. There must have been a good reason for the change. Our distant ancestors didn't always live in an ecological paradise; in fact they worked just as hard as farmers. Their life expectancy was fairly short, like that of the first people to farm the land. They usually had to invest a lot of energy in obtaining their food, although once killed or gathered it was generally in excess of their immediate needs. Their existence was precarious and turbulent. They could survive only in small groups, each living far from the next, which had its advantages, as it limited the spread of disease. The children of hunter-gatherers could not be fed by their parents alone but were dependent on other close relatives. When necessary, the population was regulated by infanticide and migration. In some climatic zones, such as tropical forests without large grazing animals, hunting was a marginal source of food. Studies of hunting populations of the twentieth century, in New Guinea, for example, show that hunting is so inefficient that only in combination with a field or a garden can it sustain life. Otherwise there is a net loss of calories.

So hunting and gathering made for a precarious existence, but not sufficiently so to prompt a radical change in the means of subsistence. In more than 2.5 million years after the date of the oldest known *Homo habilis*, it remained the only means of acquiring food. In other words, of all the hominids who ever lived, 90 percent were hunter-gatherers, 4 percent farmers, and 6 percent urban dwellers (that last percentage is now of course increasing rapidly). Until relatively recently, there was perhaps no need or no opportunity to approach food in a radically different manner. Possibly attempts were made but proved unsuccessful. We ought to stop and think about the fact that farming became the basis of our food supply only relatively recently.

————

So suddenly there was—what? A Neolithic woman who collected grass seeds, persuaded her husband to plough, planted the seed, and declared that it was good? No, of course it wasn't as simple as that. Agriculture didn't arise from a single breakthrough, a moment of brilliant insight, but from a gradual process of thousands of years of chance and experimentation, with many transitional stages between hunting and farming. Around 20,000 years ago the ice caps reached their maximum extent in Europe, and most of western Asia was covered with the kind of vegetation now found on the steppe, because water in the form of ice never becomes available as rain. When the ice melted, the land slowly grew wetter and the vegetation more diverse. Trees with edible seeds, such as almonds, pistachios, and acorns, were able to survive. All types of grasses profited from the increase in moisture, and perhaps higher rainfall meant there were more wild animals and therefore—because of more successful hunting—a growth in the human population. This may have produced local shortages as the number of humans increased more rapidly than that of animals, so dependence on grazing animals as food became too risky. This in turn may have encouraged experimentation with plants. Studies of native tribes living in the Amazon basin today provide indirect evidence for the theory that population pressure led to the development of farming. When populations decline, the tribespeople turn away from agriculture and become hunter-gatherers again.

Recent excavations indicate that before farming became established, people settled in semipermanent groups a few hundred strong. Such settlements are considerably larger in size than groups of hunter-gatherers, which are generally made up of a few dozen individuals. This may have led to increased pressure on the land, along with a deterioration in the ratio of people to wild animals, so that technological breakthroughs became more likely. Or it may have been the other way around, in that because of the beginnings of organized farming, people were able to live in larger groups. Perhaps the two processes reinforced each other.

————

The earliest traces of the use and possibly the protection of grasses (*Poaceae*) and pulses are from 19,000 years ago beside the Sea of Galilee. The oldest settlements are at oases, because water is always available there, even in dry seasons or periods of drought. Archaeological remains at oases are a strong indication of the importance of gardens in the development of early agriculture, and they help explain why the idealized garden with its water and green vegetation became so firmly anchored in our culture. For the Neolithic humans of western Asia who lived in the dry period at the end of the Ice Age, the garden would have been no less than a miracle, the stuff of dreams and myths.

So some 19,000 years ago, hunter-gatherers began to collect, protect, and perhaps even plant wild grasses near where they lived and to remove all other vegetation to keep away snakes and vermin. It may have been at this point that they began to develop pottery for the storing and cooking of food, although most pottery found by archaeologists dates from after the start of agriculture. Because after thousands of years animal bones are easier to find than plant remains or even seeds, too much attention was paid for too long to hunting as the dominant means of acquiring food in this period. Feminist researchers think that this notion arose partly because men are hunters, and men dominated the science of paleontology for many years. From observations of present-day hunter-gatherers, it is clear that not only would they have been familiar with a wide diversity of plant-based food, they would have protected certain wild species and even planted them, without engaging in any kind of systematic horticulture or agriculture. In New Guinea, hunter-gatherers have uprooted trees with stone tools to create open spaces where they can plant yams and the pandanus, a type of palm. We should therefore presume that for thousands of years people used wild grasses and a type of bean related to the lupine as food, without those plants ever evolving into agricultural varieties. Genetically their crops remained the same as the wild population, so there was as yet no farming as such.

Twelve thousand years ago, primitive forms of wheat and barley began to emerge, the remains of which have been found by archaeologists. They differ little from their wild relatives and weeds. From the same period, grain silos have been found near the Dead Sea, clearly dating back to before agriculture proper began. At more than thirty places in western Asia, traces have been found of the forerunners of agricultural species and varieties. Not all these places can claim to be where the growing of crops began, but there are clear indications that a proto-agriculture started more or less simultaneously, over a period of several millennia, at a number of different locations. It may be that as well as population pressure, fluctuations in rainfall had an effect. At least 300 millimeters needs to fall, spread over several months, before rain-dependent agriculture is viable. As well as the earlier oases, with their permanent water supply, we see areas emerging at the foot of the great mountain ranges of what are now Iran, Iraq, and southeastern Turkey, where sufficient rain falls. Of the mainly wooden tools from the beginnings of agriculture, little remains that could help us date this development accurately. Millstones and ovens with charred seeds have been found, but they prove little more than that wild grasses were used as food. We can speak of farming only when there is more going on than the protection and cultivation of a single type of plant. In fact, farming in the full sense of the word involves a combination of crops and animals, along with the use of tools and techniques over time, leading to genetic shifts in the species concerned. The earliest archaeological evidence of farming comes from around 9,500 years ago.

About 8,000 to 7,000 years ago, something else happened that was new, as a result of the melting of the ice caps. First the level of the Atlantic Ocean rose dramatically, because of the partial melting of the Laurentide ice sheet in North America. The water flowed into the Mediterranean and flooded the Black Sea (which until then had been a freshwater lake). In a very short time, just a few decades, as many as 100,000 people farming land on the coast must have been forced to move to higher ground. There they displaced hunter-gatherers, and farmland expanded dramatically. This extraordinary development finds an echo in the famous story of Noah and the flood. At the same time, but far less quickly and with less catastrophic results, the sea level rose in the Arabian Gulf, forming the delta of the Tigris and Euphrates. The higher sea level meant that the rivers dropped less steeply, flowed more slowly, and therefore provided more water for irrigation. Several thousand years later, agriculture moved to the floodplains, a shift possible only because there was more cooperation, aimed in particular at controlling water in times of flood and sharing it in times of drought. Almost always such cooperation requires some form of central authority, which indeed began to develop at the same time. With their great supply of sediment-rich and therefore nutrient-rich water from the hills, these plains were of decisive importance for population growth and the food supply. The combination of rich soils and water made possible the development of irrigation techniques, which reduced dependence on rainfall and extended the growing season. All this was further helped by improved tillage of the soil. The hoe was replaced by the stubble-clearing plough, which could tear the earth open, making sowing easier and uprooting weeds. The invention of the potter's wheel, in this same period, meant that pots could be produced on a large scale for the safe storage of food. The first complex civilizations therefore emerged, based on intensive and highly productive agriculture, controlled by a central authority. Far larger groups of people could now be fed. What happened in the Fertile Crescent was later repeated in other fertile river areas: the Nile, the Yellow River, the Yangtze, the Ganges, and the Indus. There we find the first large cities, and they are still inhabited: Erbil and Kirkuk in Iraq; Thebes (in modern-day Luxor), Giza, and Faiyum in Egypt; and Varanasi (also known as Benares) in India.

Domestication of Plants and Animals

So it was around 10,000 years ago that the step was taken from the collecting of grass seeds to the systematic planting of selected species. Water and nutrients were provided; such enemies as wild herbivores were kept at a distance; and weeds, infestations, and diseases were tackled by the removal of sick plants and of any insects visible to the naked eye. At harvest time the new horticulturalists consistently selected the plants that looked best, had the largest ears of grain, or bore fruits that kept longest. Because of selection, and because of improvements to cultivation—for example, the raking of the ground or the custom of sowing seed on heaps of manure (whether human or animal)—genetic shifts in plant populations gradually took place. Each plant reacts to its environment, and those that are not well adapted do not survive. Eventually, separate landraces or even species emerge. A new species is defined by its inability to cross with the original population from which it arose. This process, which distinguishes farming from the natural evolution of biodiversity, is called "domestication." Aside from most fish, seafood, and game, almost everything we eat today comes from organisms that are not only specially cultivated for that purpose but are also domesticated. Their reproduction and their environments, and therefore ultimately their genetic characteristics, have been partially influenced if not wholly determined by humans.

Archaeological finds suggest that the first domestication, that of the wild ancestors of wheat and barley, which were derived from grasses, took place in a number of stages. Einkorn wheat (*Triticum monococcum*, with a single grain per ear) and emmer wheat (*Triticum dicoccum*) are the oldest known precursors of today's barley, wheat, and spelt, all three of which are closely related. Both ancient types can still be found in the wild in Turkey, as can other ancestors of barley (with more or fewer grains per ear). The first farmers probably had a preference for plants with the largest grains. Perhaps they imagined that grain size was related to yield (although in reality this is doubtful), and larger grains certainly offer all kinds of advantages. They don't blow away and can more easily be planted as soon as the soil has been tilled by some means. From botanical remains we see two important characteristics emerge a few centuries later: ears whose grains do not easily separate from the central stem and the disappearance of hard husks. These evolutionary developments are the essential steps that prevent wheat that has been subject to selection by humans from being able to survive in the wild. Only plants that release their grains can spread with the help of the wind and wild animals. Domesticated wheat and its relatives are therefore dependent on humans for reproduction. For humans it is of course extremely handy if the wheat (the grain, that is) is easy to separate from the chaff. There are indications that the development of such varieties, and not long afterward edible beans, was hastened by the early use of the reaping hook or of harvesting knives. Cutting the wheat inevitably shakes the ear, and only an ear that does not lose its seeds can be of use. The tools also represent steps in the evolution of farming toward enhanced labor productivity.

If for generations those ears that lose their grains are avoided and only those that do not are sown for the next crop, a genetic shift will take place that favors plants that hold on to their grains but allow easy separation of the chaff. Something similar can be seen later with legumes, with selection for pods that don't burst open so often and eventually those that remain closed. This development is not a matter of chance. The logic of such biological selection criteria is obvious: if the grains were to fall more easily, they would have to be gathered one by one, and much of the harvest would be lost to birds and field mice. Searching for fallen grain on a harvested field is an image that occurs in the Bible, which shows that the crops then in use were less developed in this respect than those grown today. That wheat is generally self-pollinating helps with selection, because the desired qualities can be maintained more easily than with cross-pollination, which introduces new characteristics with every generation.

The earliest cultivation of crops emerged in southwest Asia (in what are now Iran, Israel, Turkmenistan, Syria, and Iraq) and in central Asia (Tajikistan and Uzbekistan) around 12,000 years ago. Relatively soon after that, about 10,000 years ago, entirely independently, rice cultivation began in China. Next, again completely independently, types of farming arose in the Indian subcontinent, in the Indus valley, in Malaysia, Ethiopia, and the Sahel, Central America, and the Andes. The first tree to be domesticated was the date palm, around 7,000 years ago. Europe's role in all this was late and extremely marginal. Only spelt may have early European origins (there are indications that it was domesticated independently in southern Europe). Genetic analysis shows that the first European farmers and herdsmen come from western Asia. They were therefore not related to the indigenous groups of European hunter-gatherers. The migration of farmers to Europe took 3,500 years, moving at an average of a kilometer per year.

It seems astonishing that none of the foods eaten today in northwestern Europe originally come from there. It is a similar story in Africa, even though Egypt and Ethiopia are among the places where early farming arose. The most important sources of calories in Africa are now corn (maize, referred to as "corn" throughout this book), rice, and peanuts, all of them domesticated elsewhere. Dependence on food introduced from other places is an ancient phenomenon, reflected in the names used and the confusion surrounding them. Often people did not know where a new kind of food had come from. In Italian, corn is called "*grano turco*" or "Turkish grain," the word "Turkish" signifying oriental or exotic. It is a common kind of confusion, and it has also occurred with what in English is called "turkey," in French "*dinde*" (*de Inde*) and in Turkish itself "*hindi*." In all these cases an exotic origin is attributed to the wrong country. Corn comes from Central America and turkeys from Madagascar (admittedly via Turkey). In Italian, turkey is "*faraona*," after the Egyptian pharaohs.

It is no accident that in each of the early farming areas, essential calories were provided by a combination of one or more grains and a legume. These two types of food combined, in a ratio of roughly 1:2, offer a range of amino acids that guarantee high-grade proteins. Some amino acids are absent in grains, such as lysine in the case of corn, and the gap can be filled by legumes. In western Asia the combination of barley and wheat with lentils, peas, or chickpeas emerged, in China rice with soy, in Central America corn with beans, and in West Africa sorghum and millet with other beans and peanuts. In Ethiopia we find teff (*Eragrostis tef*), a small grain crop, with beans and later ensete, a relative of the banana. There is some local variation. In China vegetables that can tolerate cold, especially cabbages, were domesticated at an early stage, as they were along the coast of the Mediterranean. They were also successful in central Asia and Eastern Europe. In other regions, humans domesticated sources of carbohydrates, such as cassava in Brazil; yams in Africa, Asia, and elsewhere; sweet potatoes in tropical regions of America; and potatoes in the Andes. These root vegetables were developed many centuries after grains and legumes were.

––––––––––

Almost everywhere, with the exception of the North American continent, farm animals gradually became important as producers of manure, wool, hides, meat, milk, eggs, and, several thousand years later, cheese. They were at least as important in their function as draft animals as they were as a source of food, both to work the land and to provide transportation. They also consumed such by-products as straw. The domestication of animals happened in parallel to that of plants, and it probably began with wild dogs, both as guard dogs and as pets. Grazing animals, such as cattle and sheep, evolved from wild herbivores that were at first simply herded. This explains why gazelles and deer, numerous in the Middle East and Africa, were never domesticated. They cannot be herded in the same way as goats and sheep (although admittedly rams and billy goats have horns), and they will not follow humans. So selection was initially a matter of finding the tamest mammals without horns, which were mainly sheep and goats, among the first animals to be domesticated. As cattle became more used to the presence of humans, possibly several centuries later, they were increasingly deployed as draft animals and as beasts of burden, thereby starting to become true farm animals. For humans the consequences were not purely advantageous, because they stood a greater chance of disease-causing microorganisms being passed on from animals to them.

As with plants, the selection process was intensive. Generation after generation, the strongest animals and those with the most wool or other desirable features were chosen for breeding purposes, causing a genetic shift until eventually the animals could no longer be crossed with the original species. Continual selection of offspring produced animals with lighter bones and more meat. The domestication of cattle first took place in western Asia some 8,000 years ago, then in the Indus valley and probably also in North Africa. The domestication of typical South American animals, such as llamas and alpacas, is far more recent, taking place some 5,000 years after that of cattle.

It seems remarkable that the development of agriculture and animal husbandry did not occur in those regions that have the greatest biological diversity. In the dry tropical forests of Australia and southern Africa, with their immense biodiversity, not a single plant was ever cultivated, let alone domesticated. In the tropical rainforests of the Amazon, Africa, and Asia—famous today as hotspots of biodiversity—wild plants and trees have been used for thousands of years as a source of food, fiber, building materials, and medicines, but hardly any crops have been domesticated, with the exception of cassava, pineapples, and peanuts, and a few species that have little nutritional value, such as coffee and cocoa. The wild relatives of the first three are actually from tropical areas on the boundary between forest and damp savannah, not from the rainforest itself. The use and planting of industrial crops from tropical ecosystems, such as rubber and oil palms, dates back only two centuries. Perhaps in a permanently humid tropical environment, people were never forced to discover farming because the absence of seasons meant food was available all year round. Moreover, these tropical ecosystems are well supplied with rivers rich in fish and other aquatic animals, which evened out the irregularities of the hunt. For whatever reason, the domestication of species to increase the food supply did not happen in equal measure across the earth but was confined to a fairly narrow strip between the thirtieth and forty-fifth parallel and was mainly concentrated in the northern hemisphere (where the surface area of the continents is greater).

This is contrary to expectations, because the tropics receive the most sunlight, although they are not the most densely populated or economically successful areas. The higher latitudes—the sparsely populated north and the smaller land masses of the far south—receive much less sunlight and have less vegetation. The area in between, beyond the tropics but outside the coldest latitudes, where Western Europe lies, as does the Indus valley, is the most successful from a human point of view. It is there that most farming takes place and the highest population density and economic productivity are now to be found. This was not always the case; 7,000 to 4,000 years ago the Indus valley in Pakistan was subject to periods of extreme drought, which severely limited human settlement.

Yet biodiversity did have a role to play in the emergence of farming. The first domestications all happened in hilly or mountainous regions, not on the plains, which is attributable to greater ecological variation on mountainsides than on flat land close to rivers. In hilly or mountainous areas, places can be found on the slopes at various altitudes that have their own microclimates, determined by small variations in temperature, sunlight, water infiltration, prevailing winds, soil structure, and erosion, so that plants and insects specific to them are able to develop. Grasses in particular profit from this kind of environment. In combination with the climatic requirements of early domestication (not too wet, nor too dry or too cold), this property led to remarkable similarities between the first grain crops and legumes to be domesticated on different continents. The same goes for rice, which we mostly know as wet rice, growing in water, but which also has a dry variety. Not only is a combination of grains and legumes optimal from a nutritional point of view, many leguminous plants are also capable of entering into a symbiosis with certain bacteria, thereby binding nitrogen from the air and improving the fertility of the soil. This further contributed to the success of the combination. If legumes are grown with or shortly before cereals, the survival chances and yield of the latter improve.

The domestication of crops is not merely a gradual historical process, it is still going on. During domestication, all kinds of intermediate forms of plants emerge that are protected but not genetically altered to the extent that they can no longer be crossed with their wild relatives. Good examples are the chestnut and oak forests in countries bordering the Mediterranean. They are an important part of the natural vegetation that in the course of history has been protected and sometimes planted. At the same time there have also been periods of large-scale deforestation and therefore of increased erosion—in Roman times, for example, when both cereals and timber for shipbuilding were much in demand. These have left traces that can be seen in fluvial deposits. To this day a sweet, high-quality flour is made in Italy from the protected but not domesticated chestnut, and it is added to the flour used in cakes. In the forests of Corsica, pigs still root for acorns and truffles. Given the value of the truffle, it seems likely that its domestication is not far away. Already the roots of wild oak seedlings are being inoculated with truffle spores.

One example of extremely recent domestication is the kiwi, originally a bitter kind of gooseberry from China. When grown by researchers in New Zealand, it achieved its present size and pleasantly sour-sweet taste. The kiwis of fifteen years ago were smaller, more fibrous and sour. Now we have sweeter, yellower fruit as the result of rapid refinement after initial domestication.

Domestication today mainly involves vegetables and fruit (and grasses and leguminous plants as feed for livestock), as at the moment there do not seem to be any new grains in prospect that will revolutionize our food supply. It seems probable to me that we will domesticate more and more algae and bacteria, to provide fuel, proteins, oils, and pharmaceuticals.

Over more than 10,000 years a complicated co-evolution has taken place between people and crops or, more broadly, among people, their environment, and their food. Without the influence of humans, neither wheat, corn, apples, nor lettuce would ever have evolved from their wild ancestors. They simply would not have their current characteristics. But without farming, humans would not be what they are either, a dominant species of strapping individuals nourished by a concentration of fats, carbohydrates, and proteins.

This co-evolution among people, food, and the environment can take even more complex forms. One extraordinary example is the consumption of the broad bean (*Vicia faba*) in the Mediterranean area. Sensitive individuals may develop an acute and potentially fatal form of anaemia after eating broad beans—in fact this response is quite common—yet the broad bean, one of the oldest crops from the early days of farming, has not disappeared from the menu. It is a popular food everywhere. The only possible explanation is that broad beans offer several evolutionary advantages: they confer a degree of protection against malaria, they bind nitrogen in the soil, and they contain a significant amount of protein.

Another case of co-evolution, in more recent times, is taking place in the wetter parts of West Africa, where farming is based on root crops, such as the yam (*Dioscorea*) and cassava (*Manihot esculenta*). The felling of the rainforests that farming entails improves the habitat for the malaria mosquito (*Anopheles* spp.), which by preference lives at the edges of forests. An increase in the number of such mosquitoes has caused them to concentrate more on people and in response, a special form of resistance has emerged, known as sickle-cell anemia, which represents an evolutionary handicap but makes it possible for malaria-infected people to continue farming. One might theoretically ask who is exploiting whom, the malaria mosquito the humans or humans the primeval forest?

Yet another form of co-evolution can be seen in the aversion to milk among the Chinese and many other Asians. It is explained by their inability to digest lactose (milk sugar) as a result of an absence or inefficiency of the enzyme lactase. The lack of this enzyme is a consequence of the fact that no dairy cows are kept in China, which in turn can be explained by a shortage of meadowland suitable for grazing cattle, sheep, and goats, or perhaps by the climate—most of the country is either too dry and cold or too damp for cows.

A symbiosis has developed between animals, grass, and pasture that benefits all parties. Humans cannot digest cellulose, but some animals can. Grazing promotes the growth of grasses, because shrubs and young trees are eaten by the animals, and grasses can colonize open areas more quickly than can other plants. So as long as there is no overgrazing, the animals actually help produce more grass. Furthermore, some of the digested grasses return to the meadow as manure, benefiting both grass and humans, since well-fed animals can be used to work the fields, where they also deposit their manure.

Farming as an Ecological Balancing Act

When Adam and Eve are banished from paradise, they do not immediately receive instructions as to how to farm the land, aside from a general encouragement to work hard (that famous sweat of the brow). The Jewish-Christian-Islamic God is clearly referring to an ecological principle best summarized in the saying "only sunlight is free." God, the first expert on the ecological cycle, is right. Food production without energy from outside is impossible. Green plants grow by converting sunlight, which costs us nothing. They form the basis of the food pyramid on which grazing animals live, who are themselves prey to predators. But the fruit of the trees doesn't fall into our laps, and grasses don't simply turn into wheat and wheat into bread. Ecologically speaking, only in paradise is there a free lunch, and this applies as much to parasites as to human beings. In every transformation, from grass into meat, from nitrogen into protein, from carbohydrates into sugars, small amounts of energy are lost. The same applies to all the transitions involved in taming the ecosystem, whether it's a matter of turning forests into fields, floodplains into polder by means of dikes, or a weed-ridden field into ploughed arable land. If people want to get food out of an ecosystem, they always have to add energy in the form of work. For many generations that meant the work of their hands, until it was largely replaced by the work of draft animals and finally, from the Industrial Revolution onward, fossil fuels.

But it is not sufficient for sunlight and rain to fall on the earth. If we are to be provided with food, then sunlight has to be guided to the species we can digest—and have learned to eat. Humans occupy a special niche in the food pyramid. We consume only a fraction of the available plants and animals. We hardly ever eat predators, such as lions or falcons, or the species that are most common: insects, bacteria, and molds. The vast majority of our calories come from around thirty species, from grains (such as wheat, rice, millet and corn), from root vegetables (such as potatoes, sweet potatoes, and cassava), from vegetable fats (including palm oil, coconut, and peanuts), and from a handful of animal species (mainly cows, pigs, and chickens). In most cases additional energy is needed to make these foods edible, by heating, drying, or fermenting them. Humans always protect certain species at the expense of others, in fact we deliberately eliminate many, which explains why farming systems are always much less diverse than natural ecosystems. Means of benefiting useful species include animal and industrial fertilizers, pesticides, herbicides, and fungicides, and all these have a further impact on the combination of species that makes up the field or meadow.

A farming system is by definition artificial. Even in its most primitive form, such as a few small fields between the trees of a primeval forest, it involves human intervention. Land is stripped of its original vegetation by fire and further worked or planted, all of which disturbs the natural balance of species. Nutrients in the form of wood, manure, straw, seed, and foods of all kinds are always removed from the fields and not returned to the ecosystem. They end up in homes and in cities, perhaps even in other parts of the world, like American corn, which is sent all over the globe.

Agriculture is based on a precarious balance. Favoring one kind of plant above others—wheat, for example—and harvesting its produce in the form of grains have a considerable ecological impact. Almost without exception, chemical substances have to be added to compensate, whether in the form of animal manure or artificial fertilizer, leaf mold, plaggen manure (fertile topsoil from other fields), or ash. Water—which transports the nutrients—comes from rain or from artificial irrigation. Usually the nutrients taken from the land have to be fairly quickly replaced, otherwise the soil becomes depleted and other less-demanding plants, often stubborn weeds, take over. Grazing by animals has the same effect, because even though the grasses that are eaten are to some degree converted into manure, the dung may end up elsewhere, while all the flesh and bones are taken away. Only if the soil is extraordinarily fertile, perhaps because of a natural supply of volcanic ash or river silt, can it produce a harvest year after year without any decline in productivity. This is the case in volcanic regions of Indonesia and the Philippines, where the system of rice terraces with their impermeable soil and dikes further limits erosion and the loss of nutrients. This helps explain the long, almost uninterrupted tradition of wet rice cultivation. In a few cases, with olive trees, for example, the yield is so minimal that the orchards can produce a harvest for up to 200 years without any fertilizer other than the droppings of grazing sheep.

The replacement of nutrients is the greatest challenge in farming, as even the Romans were aware. Without nutrients in the soil that feed the plants—primarily nitrogen, phosphate, and potassium—there will be no food for humans. As well as animal manure and artificial fertilizer, humus or layers of fresh soil may be brought in, or the land may be left to lie fallow and perhaps be sown with green manure, especially leguminous plants. The Bible commands humans to let the land lie fallow from time to time, allowing it to become covered in thorns and not sowing anything (Exodus 23:11 and Jeremiah 4:3). In that sabbatical year, poor people and animals are permitted to use the land. Such rest periods usually last far longer than the biblical one year in seven—as many as twenty or thirty years in the humid tropics—and they do make weeds less prevalent and soil more fertile in the long term. This, whether or not combined with the adding of humus and animal or human manure, was for thousands of years the most important way of maintaining soil fertility in regions with no recent supply of volcanic material or river silt.

The story is actually even more complicated. The growth of plants is limited by whichever nutritional element is in shortest supply. This limitation is known as the "law of the minimum." Plants cannot make up for a lack of, say, nitrogen by absorbing more potassium. They need both, in the right balance. Manure can be produced only by the digestive systems of animals that have eaten food (whether specially produced or naturally occurring) or grazed on grass, so land is needed for them too. Grazing brings risks of its own. Overgrazing causes a depletion of nutrients in the pastureland, and the animals can tread the almost-bare soil until, unable to absorb so much water, it is eroded by the rain running off it. Grazing also kills small shrubs and young trees, so meadows require fertilization. For centuries grassland was used as the source of nutrients for the fields, in the form of manure. This is a time-consuming and expensive process; an average of ten hectares of grassland are needed to produce sufficient nitrogen for a hectare of grain and at least two hectares for sufficient phosphate (a very rough estimate, as much depends on the quality of the grazing land and the nutritional requirements of the cereal crop), to say nothing of the need to transport all that manure.

Leaving fields to lie fallow is not a way of providing the kind of rest that enables a sick human to recover. The trees and bushes that grow up when no crops are planted and no grazing allowed put their roots down into lower soil layers, from which they bring nutrients to the surface. The burning of the vegetation at the end of the fallow period destroys weeds, harmful insects, and bacteria and makes the soil more fertile by releasing nutrients contained in the parts of the vegetation that stand above the surface. Fire is a quick way of mobilizing those substances; the ash is rich in potassium, although the nitrogen and some of the phosphorus will evaporate. Ash is slightly alkaline, too, so it will reduce the acidity of the soil, which is generally beneficial. This system is known as "slash and burn." Even with a fallow period followed by fire, soil fertility is a limiting factor, because it is impossible to return all chemical elements to it by burning. In some climatic zones, additional nutrients are brought in as wet or dry deposits, which is to say by flooding and winds. For 8,000 years Sudan "subsidized" Egyptian agriculture by means of the southerly wind and, before the building of the Aswan Dam, water from the Nile, both of which brought tiny soil particles to the land of Egypt.

The story of soil fertility and fallow land is so important because these factors determine how much land is needed and how much it will produce, and until recent centuries this defined how many people could live in a given region. The lower the yield was, the more land needed to be developed, and throughout history the key lay in the ability to raise the yield per unit of land by means of river silt, plaggen manure, cow dung, urban waste, or artificial fertilizer. High yields create wealth. Farming therefore often requires more land than is at first apparent, and it always requires more than for its arable fields alone. It would be more honest and accurate to measure yields per hectare based on the total amount of land needed to keep the fields viable, rather than per hectare of arable land. Theoretically this would have to include soil supplied in the form of river silt, as well as the grazing land needed for manure, fallow land, and the unused land or woodland that produces peat for plaggen manuring and humus. In many places the conversion of forest into pasture and arable land is reversed from time to time. The Amazon region, for example, turns out not to be made up entirely of virgin forest. Some areas have seen periods of intensive farming, as can be seen from charred remains, river silt, and the organic materials that make up the *terra preta* or "black earth." Land use, yield, and population growth are therefore closely connected, and they fluctuate through time.

There is just one source of nutrients that requires no land, or at least no land that is usable to humans. It is extremely rare. In South America the Incas discovered the rich properties of the layer of excrement from seabirds that lies meters thick on the bare cliffs of Peru. Guano is rare because only a few small islands feature large colonies of birds (mostly cormorants) in combination with a very dry climate. Rain quickly causes the guano to lose its beneficial properties. Guano, rich in nitrogen and phosphoric acid, became known in Europe only around 1800, and at about the same time Europeans began importing Chile saltpeter (sodium nitrate), from deposits in the deserts of northern Chile.

The Dominant Form of Land Use

After a hesitant beginning in western Asia, which took dozens of centuries, farming gradually conquered the rest of the world. For a very long time there were few means of structural improvement. The growing of barley, spelt, durum wheat for pasta, and wheat for bread-making spread to Egypt, and from Mesopotamia and Kurdistan via the Black Sea to Europe. During the Iron Age, around 1000 BC, cereal crops spread as far as southern England, but until the Middle Ages, farming in northwestern Europe was not particularly productive. Yields could sometimes reach 1,000 kilograms per hectare, but much of that, up to a third, was needed for seed. Furthermore, a three-field system was used, a form of crop rotation that included fallow periods, so only a third of the acreage was available for the cereal crop, much of which was lost to molds and insects because of poor storage. Although humus and dung were added, low yields were a direct result of poor soil fertility.

In 1346 Europe was hit by an epidemic of plague that killed an estimated one-third of the population. A further decline in numbers over the subsequent century can be attributed in part to soil exhaustion resulting from population growth in the twelfth century. The consequences of this demographic catastrophe were immense. Labor became scarce, and technology was needed to increase the productivity of those who remained to work the land. The options were limited: more fertilization and better tillage with new tools. In northern Italy, better cultivation of the land stimulated the rise of the cities and with them a population that was not involved in producing food, yet here, too, the balance was precarious. While city-states like Florence and Siena became the crucible of the market economy, their populations placed great pressure on the surrounding land. In the absence of an international food trade, most nourishment had to come from close by, and even before the catastrophic epidemic of plague this led to local famines despite the wealth of the cities.

Food slowly became more varied, at least for those who could afford a relatively interesting diet. In the Middle Ages the Arabs introduced Europeans to produce from China, including lemons, tea, artichokes, eggplants, watermelons, and spinach, most of it arriving through Andalusia. By about 1500, when the Europeans started their great voyages of discovery, farming was by far the most important means of acquiring food in all parts of the world with the exception of Australia, where the growing of crops and the tending of sheep began only in the eighteenth century. Columbus and subsequent explorers triggered a large-scale intercontinental exchange of species, bringing corn, red peppers, tomatoes, sunflowers, and potatoes to Europe, and along with them novel insects, worms, viruses, and other species that inevitably affected local ecosystems.

From 1750 on the growth of the European population accelerated, probably mainly because of the early age of marriage. More cattle were kept, on land that had not previously been productive, providing more manure for the cultivation of cereals. In combination with further urbanization, specialization emerged across the continent; from 1800 on fewer and fewer people worked the land. The Industrial Revolution led to a gradual replacement of labor by mechanization and with it a steady increase in yields, yet these improvements were no guarantee of a secure food supply. Harvests could still fail because of the weather, infestations, and diseases. Poor grain harvests encouraged the growing of potatoes, which yield a higher number of calories per hectare, feeding two or three times as many people as a hectare of grain. The potato became increasingly popular, even after the terrible failed harvests of mid-nineteenth-century Ireland, which led to the famines and large-scale migration still vividly recalled to this day.

Despite those dramatic events, we should not underestimate the importance of the root and tuber crops derived from South America, the most important being potatoes, cassava, and sweet potatoes. Because their usable parts grow below ground, they do not need to invest so much of their energy in a structure of inedible stalks or stems, unlike grains, which must hold their ears in the air. Cassava and sweet potatoes can be propagated from cuttings, so there is no need to reserve part of the harvest for sowing. In a period of rapid population growth, these crops are unsurpassed, as demonstrated by the importance of the sweet potato for both food and feed in China, where it was first introduced in the sixteenth century.

Yet even today most produce is eaten in the region where it is grown. The staple food of Southeast Asia is rice, not because of chance culinary preference but because in a tropical climate rice is the only viable grain crop. Other grains, and indeed tubers such as potatoes and cassava, are unable to tolerate extreme heat and humidity, the exception being the sweet potato. At higher latitudes (in northern India for example) these other crops are available, but only in winter. The importance of corn, which can be grown in the tropics, is increasing in many parts of the world, mainly as cattle feed, although it is not used as a basic ingredient in Chinese cuisine. Rice from China has become popular in Italy and Spain, because the plains of the Po and Ebro rivers resemble tropical regions in summer, although special varieties are needed that can cope with the far greater day length of those latitudes. The original varieties will not flower and set seed when the nights are short.

Agriculture has had to overcome all kinds of ecological difficulties over its 10,000 years: shortages of soil nutrients, diseases and infestations, and droughts and floods. It eventually became the most successful form of land use, but not until the second half of the nineteenth century did the majority of the population in the West cease to live in constant fear of crop failure and famine. It was only then that humans started to gain adequate control of ecological processes and with them the productivity of labor and soil. The great leap forward is attributable to the discovery, in the early twentieth century, of a way of converting atmospheric nitrogen into ammonia and then into nitrate, known as the Haber-Bosch process. It consumes a good deal of energy, but it makes nitrogen available to any farmer, ending dependence on imported guano and saltpeter. It was an evolutionary breakthrough, too, since along with the mining of phosphate it freed humankind from dependence on "fossil" materials that happened to be lying around.

Just how unproductive farming was over all those centuries is illustrated by the ratio of yield to seed for the next crop. In the Roman Empire, on the best volcanic soils of what is now Italy, at least a fifth of the wheat harvest had to be kept as seed for the next crop. In the Middle Ages the ratio for wheat was on average 1:2–4. In other words, a quarter to half of the harvest was sown as seed. In the seventeenth century this ratio was reduced to 1:7–9, and in the eighteenth century a ratio of 1:12 was achieved. Today, only about 2–3 percent of the wheat crop is needed for sowing, and the seed is always bought from specialist seed producers rather than saved from the harvest. These greatly improved figures are a result of better seed hygiene, tillage, and weed management.

It is a similar story with cattle. In the Netherlands livestock farming was an early form of specialization. On their low-lying fields cattle farmers produced cheese, milk, and meat that they exchanged with arable farmers for food they could not produce themselves, because their land was too wet. In the sixteenth century, daily milk production per cow during lactation was about 4–5 liters, increasing to 6–8 liters in the eighteenth century. The best Dutch cows now produce 10,000 liters a year, and a few individuals produce even more. This is possible only if cows receive optimal nutrition and are free of disease. Supplementary feeding, especially in winter when the growth of grass stops, was problematic for many years, since fodder turnips, for example, in use since the Middle Ages, required land as well as labor for sowing. Feed also had to be stored without significant losses. The growing of cattle feed as a separate activity began in a systematic fashion only in the seventeenth century, and everywhere cattle mortality and forced slaughter as a result of malnutrition and disease remained high.

We can see how important feed and livestock have become over the past half-century from one particularly spectacular statistic: a quarter of farmland in the world is now devoted to feed crops, mainly corn and soy, and if grazing on natural and improved pastureland are added, then two-thirds of farmland today is used for livestock. It is an astonishing figure, even if we take into account that it includes extensive natural pastureland and steppe, in central Asia and Argentina for example, which has few other potential uses.

———————

Contemporary farming still exhibits stark contrasts. Dutch and French farmers can produce almost ten tons of wheat per hectare in a good year, sometimes a little more, whereas in Portugal the average yield rarely exceeds two tons per hectare even today and is often closer to one ton, similar to grain yields in many developing countries. So even in Europe, yields can differ by a factor of nine. Although we should not underestimate the impact of climate (especially rainfall), this shows that there is still plenty of room for increased production, given that average wheat yields across the world currently stand at a little more than 2.5 tons per hectare. In India good rice harvests in the irrigated Punjab are 4–5 tons per hectare, but in China, where half of all farmers now plant hybrid rice, the figure is already far higher, at 7–8 tons. Hybrid rice is around 20 percent more productive, but better management is an even more important factor. Without irrigation, rice yields in India are 1.5 tons, as they are in Africa.

———————

From their hesitant beginnings more than 10,000 years ago, barely noticeable ecologically, arable farming, livestock farming, and forestry have become the predominant forms of land use. We consume only a fraction of the earth's edible species, but because of the size of the human population, with its eating patterns based increasingly on animal protein, humankind occupies a unique position. In the course of our short history, farming has allowed us to become the most important user of sunlight, with 30 percent of the surface of the earth in use as farmland or pasture. Our food connects us directly to all the great ecological cycles of our planet. All our food, whether peanut butter, risotto, or veal steak, is produced at the expense of the cycles of other species, but it also makes a contribution, because our agricultural waste ultimately benefits the earth's ecosystem.

Only in those few remote places where agriculture is more or less self-sustaining are the cycles almost closed, simply because so little food is removed from the ecosystem. Household waste from food acquired from woodland, gardens, and fields returns to the ecosystem and to surface water by means of the latrine and the compost heap. Something is always lost, but it is replaced by erosion from elsewhere, as tiny particles of clay are brought in on the rain and wind. For centuries this was the case in many parts of the world, until the rise of cities and the globalization that began with Columbus.

The great difference between undisturbed natural ecosystems and modern society is that much of what we consume does not come from where we live. Even when animals draw on several ecosystems, like antelope and hen harriers, it is they who move, during their annual migrations. People, in contrast, continually transport and concentrate their foodstuffs: Brazilian soybeans feed our chickens or the chickens of China and with them we eat rice from Vietnam, beans from West Africa, or tomatoes grown in Spain or California. Farming in its current globalized form is therefore always an unnatural process, as we cream off parts of the ecosystem for our own consumption and send the food we produce to other regions of the world. Few city dwellers are able to comprehend that food is always acquired at the expense of something else and that it causes the relocation of chemical substances—sometimes across vast distances and in huge volumes, as in the case of cattle feed. Modern shipping has helped facilitate this use of resources from other parts of the globe. Once cows had to graze next to the arable fields; now ships can transport manure and cattle feed over huge distances. The most important supply route in the world is between Brazil and China, carrying soy to feed Chinese cows.

Through trade and the application of scientific knowledge, people have managed to become increasingly independent of ecosystems in the places where they live. Not only can we reshape our immediate environments, we can also add needed resources to them from far away, in the form of energy, food, species, nutrients, even labor. The slave trade between Africa and the New World and later the supply of workers—from the Indian subcontinent to the Caribbean region, for example—amount to the adding of energy to a local ecosystem, however inefficient and cruel from a human point of view. The gradual abolition of the slave trade, beginning in Britain in 1834, helped create the need to replace human labor as far as possible with energy from fossil fuels, especially in the richer countries in the twentieth century. This led to the new techno-logical highpoint represented by modern greenhouse cultivation, which draws much of its energy from the sun, closing the circle that began with the protection of wild plants that required little energy other than direct sunlight. We are now able to create completely closed systems of horti-culture that no longer even need soil, fed by a nutrient-rich fluid flowing through rockwool. Soon we will use solar energy to regulate the climatic conditions and even supplement sunlight with lamps where necessary, as well as stimulating plant growth with extra CO_2 from oil refineries.

In a natural ecosystem a new species can become established only where food is available, which usually means making some other species less prevalent. It will generally arrive only if its seeds or spores happen to land at the right place, having been carried by wind, water, or animal excre-ment. Compare this to ecosystems dominated by humans. We introduce species from other continents, or change the characteristics of existing species so that they fulfil a new function. By importing foodstuffs from far away, even from other continents, we disrupt ecological cycles all over the world. The replacement of human and animal labor by fossil fuels in production, processing, and transportation was decisive in bringing about a situation in which fewer and fewer people were needed to pro-duce food. At the same time, more and more food is available increas-ingly cheaply.

This ability to acquire food from elsewhere has produced great diver-sity and material wealth. Hunter-gatherers required 50–100 hectares of land to feed one person, whereas today 0.25 hectares per person is suffi-cient. The result has been astonishing population growth, especially over the past two centuries and above all since 1960. Two thousand years ago there were no more than 200 million people in the world. This increased to one billion in 1800 and 2.5 billion by 1950. Never before in history has population growth been so great and so rapid in a few generations. Those of us born between 1940 and 1960 recall a world with less than a third of today's human population. No wonder so many people are nostalgic for a golden age of empty beaches and virgin forests.

Unfortunately the evolutionary success of farming has led to an accumulation of nutrients outside their original ecosystems, one example being manure surpluses, whether animal or human. In the Netherlands these surpluses result mainly from nutrients from Brazil and Morocco, arriving respectively in the form of soybeans and phosphate as fertilizer, and supplemented by nitrogen from fertilizer factories that manufacture it from fossil fuels. Along with the United States and Brazil, the European Union (EU) is one of the biggest exporters of farm products, but it is also the biggest importer. Farming has now come to dominate not only the supply of food but also the earth's biogeochemical cycles.

Agriculture as a Matter of Public Interest

The considerable difference between us and our closest relatives, the apes, lies in our greater ability to cooperate and our willingness to invest in cooperation in the long term. We did not evolve to gather food by individual strength and ingenuity. Instead we take care of people outside our circle of close relatives. Partly because of the emergence of language, and well before the development of farming, we started to exchange labor and ideas, for example, when hunting our prey. Over the centuries, unprecedented ecological opportunities have opened up. It is farming above all that has prompted us to take a longer perspective, thinking in terms of seasons and years, and to engage in increasingly specialist tasks. Conversely, agriculture has freed us to do more than simply gather food. Unlike other primates, we have developed a consciousness of the public interest in general. This is not to say that other animals are incapable of sacrificing themselves for the greater good. We only have to think of worker bees or worker ants, or of weak herd animals that go to stand on the edge of the herd when a predator attacks. But the first is a genetically determined specialization and the second can be understood in terms of the principle of the survival of the fittest (weak animals are by definition the least fit to perpetuate the species).

What makes the human experience radically different is the conscious realization that the public interest must be served if human beings are to survive. There are now more than seven billion people on earth and only a few thousand apes. We are not the only successful species, of course. Estimates suggest that the total biomass of termites exceeds that of humans. All the same, surely this is no accident; termites also survive through cooperation.

———

The insight that the food supply is a matter of public interest and demands organized and often specialized cooperation emerged early in human history. Rulers and large landowners, monasteries and city-states were always concerned about what should be constructed and how, whether they were building the temples of Luxor, the estates of Lucca in Tuscany, or the Great Wall of China. The Code of Hammurabi, written 3,800 years ago and one of the earliest known legal texts, distinguishes among different classes of farmers and peasants and indicates the work that is necessary for irrigation and the importance of smithies for ploughs. In the Middle Ages a number of countries introduced laws regulating the production, sale, and pricing of food, one example being England's Corn Laws, introduced in the twelfth century and not repealed until 1846.

Despite this cooperation in the public interest, hunger was common for centuries. Europe could barely feed itself, there were no reserves of food, and a bad harvest meant almost immediate disaster. It is hard to believe that we have only recently emerged from that time. In the early nineteenth century, farming in Europe began to change fundamentally with the application of science, fertilizers, and mechanization. Colonization by the great powers, developments in North America, and international trade led to a stream of new and additional foods, including meats, grains, and sugar. These developments had a major impact on small-scale farming and the landscape it created. The most beautiful paintings of the time, such as "The Glebe Farm" by John Constable of 1830, portray a landscape that was already disappearing. Efforts were made to make parcels of farmland more contiguous; yields increased; wasteland, such as moorland, previously used for the cutting of peat and for grazing, slowly lost their function; marshy land was drained by the digging of wet ditches and the straightening of waterways; transportation routes were added; and forests were planted, partly to provide timber for pit props. Landowners remained obstructive for many years, because their interests meant they opposed both free trade and farmland consolidation.

The combining of small fields and the digging up of hedgerows was a major focus of debate in first half of the twentieth century. In Britain and continental Europe this was not a matter of the nationalization of large estates, as in Latin America, but of supposedly making farming more rational. No matter how sensible and indeed necessary for the securing of the food supply, this trend, which accelerated after the Second World War, altered the landscape forever in many places. The disappearance of characteristic and ecologically functional hedgerows is perhaps the best-known symbol of what many see as a grave violation of nature.

As a result of trade, increased yields, and specialization, fewer and fewer people are directly responsible for their own food supply. Or rather, the world is now divided into areas where a small professional group of farmers is hugely productive—such as northwestern Europe, North America, parts of Brazil, Japan, and Australia—and areas where production is largely in the hands of small farmers, mostly on family farms, where yields remain small and a poor harvest can make the difference between going hungry and going to school. Despite low productivity in many parts of the world, global food production is steadily growing, at a faster rate than the population, achieving more than 2,800 calories on average per person per day. The trend is toward fewer farmers and a continued increase in the productivity of their labor. In the Netherlands the number of farmers has halved over the past fifteen years, while farms have increased in scale. It's hard to imagine that, short of major disaster, many more people will find jobs in farming and food processing in the future than do now.

––––––––

Governmental intervention in farming has a long history. The European Common Agricultural Policy, of which Dutch politician Sicco Mansholt was one of the founders, is in many ways its culmination. European integration has been among its benefits. In many respects it is comparable to current policy in the United States, Japan, and many other countries that traditionally protect their farmers economically to minimize the dependence of national food supply on other countries. The classic instruments of agricultural policy are subsidies and market regulation. Governments decide who is allowed to sell what, how much and at what price, who is guaranteed a minimum price, and who receives income support. From the 1960s on, partly in response to hunger during the Second World War and a sense of vulnerability during the Cold War, Europe used farming policy to increase its self-sufficiency. Slowly the realization dawned that unchecked growth in food production has an ecological downside as well as being extremely expensive. To many people, farming is a water-devouring, tree- and bird-destroying human activity from which we should desist. Support for the Common Agricultural Policy has declined as a result. In non-Western countries, fierce opposition is growing to the protectionist nature of the American and European markets and their systems of subsidies. In response to such feelings, and to worries about the landscape and the environment, much has already changed. Today's farmer has social goals alongside food-production targets. Policy has evolved and continues to evolve beyond price fixing and income support for farmers and now encompasses improvements to the countryside and the protection of landscapes. We have not heard the last word on any of these trends.

So in a surprising way the circle has closed. Moving far away from the laborious efforts of the first farmers to interrupt natural ecological cycles, we now see farmers consciously stimulating those cycles and applying ecological principles, attuning themselves to the culture of the countryside. The latest development is the replacement of opposition to nature with a desire to make use of the ways that nature regulates itself. It is surely appropriate for governments to take responsibility for both the effects of farming and the survival of cultivated landscapes.

As a direct result of continual improvements to agriculture, the human population has passed seven billion. We might regret this fact, but we should surely be in awe of the slow revolution that the discovery of farming set in train. It has made our species by far the most influential on the surface of the earth. Most of us, six out of seven, no longer live in conditions of scarcity. Each case of acute hunger is unacceptable, of course, but that death by starvation is now the fate of a mere 1 percent of the world's population is an unparalleled triumph when seen from a historical perspective. Who could have imagined that at the time when Adam and Eve were thrown out of paradise to fend for themselves in an inhospitable wilderness?

FOUR

Bread: The Most Iconic of Foods

How simple/you are, bread,/and how profound!/.../Now,/whole,/
you are/mankind's energy,/a miracle often admired,/the will to live
itself./.../Then/life itself/will have the shape of bread,/deep and
simple,/immeasurable and pure./Every living thing/will have its share/
of soil and life,/and the bread we eat each morning,/everyone's daily
bread,/will be hallowed/and sacred,/because it will have been won/by the
longest and costliest/of human struggles.   PABLO NERUDA, "Ode to Bread"

The whiter the bread, the sooner you'll be dead!   *American saying, probably
originating with British wholesaler Yates, an advocate of wholegrain bread in the early
twentieth century*

Bread as a Symbol

The smell of freshly baked bread in the oven, the scorched crust crum-
bling crisply under the knife, the tearing of the soft, elastic risen dough,
dry unleavened loaves with their powdery snow of finely sieved flour, old
bread given a new life as toast or bread pudding, a crooked slice on which
to drizzle olive oil, those narrow baguettes known as *flûtes* in the early
morning in a French country town.... Bread, the oldest of staple foods,
appeals to all our senses. Bread tempts us to eat. As a child I secretly ate
the bread that I was supposed to feed to the ducks, and I still enjoy dry
bread. Almost everyone likes bread. You see it in restaurants, where the
bread basket quickly empties while people wait for their meal to arrive.
Bread doesn't just symbolize food, it represents life itself. We speak of our
daily bread, earning a bread-and-butter income, bread and circuses, and
breaking bread. Bread fills and fulfils us.

Bread is a collective noun for all those diverse forms of baked dough,
from baguette to pizza, ciabatta, pita, and chapati, from wheat bread to
dark rye bread, from multigrain to white sliced loaves, from Indian naan
and roti to the bagels and blinis that crossed the Atlantic with Polish
immigrants. In Kazakhstan and Pakistan I've seen bread baked in round
stone ovens like beehives, stuck with water to the inner walls above a fire

lit from one side. Such ovens perfectly fit the descriptions that have come down to us from Mesopotamia 5,000 years ago.

Bread is part of a tradition as old as the domestication of the first cereals. But the apparent immutability of baking techniques and forms of dough masks a continual succession of influences on bread and how it is eaten. Bread is not merely a staple food, it's a snack and a treat, both fast food and slow food, carrying a spread or a salad, eaten on the run, at work, at home, or at celebrations. Bread is not just any old bread. People can be firmly attached to the special qualities of their favorite bread and will drive to a particular bakery, or ask for a loaf baked dark or light. If they don't get what they're after, there's no end to the complaints. Flaubert wrote of the dirt found in bread. A concrete ball with a hole, I once heard someone say of the American donut. There are hundreds, perhaps thousands of variations on the theme of flour and water, with or without salt and yeast, with additives too numerous to mention: salt, raisins, honey, butter, ground chestnuts, white cheese, cumin.... Bread can be classified by criteria including type of dough, shape, consistency and volume, the flexibility or versatility of the final result, and its additional ingredients. In every loaf we can read our history, ancient and modern.

There's a beautiful passage in the Gilgamesh epic, a story written down more than 2,000 years before Christianity. It refers, as do many Old Testament passages, to periods even earlier. Enkidu, who lives in the wilderness among the animals, is presented with bread and wine. He doesn't know what to do with them, because he's used only to the milk and flesh of wild animals. Eventually he relieves his hunger, and by eating bread and drinking wine he leaves behind his "wild" state as a nomadic hunter. That gesture alone qualifies him as a fellow townsman to Gilgamesh. Agriculture and bread, prerequisites of urban civilization, are contrasted here with the primitive food of Palaeolithic hunter-gatherers.

Bread and its related products are not always made exclusively of wheat or a mixture of wheat and rye. Other grains or ground nuts may be mixed with wheat, as in the flat breads of barley and wheat in Scandinavia, or the corn bread of the United States. Bread need not even look like bread as we know it, or be made of grain at all, to fulfil the same role of staple food and tempting snack. English explorer William Bligh, captain of the HMS Bounty, where that famous mutiny broke out in 1789, blamed his crew's revolt on the breadfruit. Tahiti, where the ship was traveling from, had made a great impression on the mutineers. As Bligh writes, they found there "abundance, on one of the most beautiful islands in the world, where they did not need to make any effort." There was never any shortage of food on Tahiti. The generous source of this tempting, ready-to-eat food was a tree with the appropriate name of the breadfruit tree (*Artocarpus altilis*), which produced white spongy fruit that could be eaten ripe or unripe and quickly filled the belly. To Bligh the mutiny was ultimately caused by this particular food; his sailors wanted only to lie on the beach and eat. Contemporaries described the breadfruit as food from before the Fall of Man and the island as paradise.

––––––

Western art includes countless depictions of bread, including seventeenth-century still lifes like those of Pieter Claesz, where a voluptuous, buttock-shaped loaf lies next to the herring. Picasso painted many tables bearing bread, fruit, and a carafe of wine. Bread is at once simplicity and luxury, necessity and pleasure. In the pre-Islamic and Islamic art of the Middle East and Asia, in contrast, bread barely features at all. I can only guess that this is a consequence of the fact that still lifes and domestic scenes were not seen as fit subjects for artworks (and as we know, under Islam images of people and household objects are usually forbidden). Bread is present in Arab and Persian poetry, however, as one of many symbols associated with food, life, and love, as in the famous line by eleventh-century Persian poet Omar Khayyam: "A loaf of bread, a jug of wine, and thou, my Love."

Bread is irresistible to anyone who feels like a bite to eat and especially to anyone truly hungry. It stands not only for love, plenty, and pleasure but also for the opposite, for poverty and hunger, scarcity and want. As a Sicilian saying aptly puts it, *A pani schittu, lu veru cumpanaggiu è lu pitittu* ("With dry bread the true filling is hunger"). This loses something in translation, as in Sicily bread is eaten with everything, not merely with spreads and fillings, such as cheese, meat, or jam. There are countless stories of the proverbial poor thief who steals a loaf for his children. It is a classic theme used by Victor Hugo in *Les Misérables*, where the central character, Jean Valjean, is sentenced to nineteen years' hard labor for stealing a loaf of bread. The novel is based on the true story of a man who stole a loaf to feed his sister's seven children. Here bread is life in a particularly graphic sense; Valjean realizes in jail that for that one loaf, society has taken nineteen years of his life. Indian leader Mahatma Gandhi made a direct connection between bread and poverty when he asked: "But how am I to talk of God to the millions who have to go without two meals a day? To them God can only appear as bread and butter." It is telling that Gandhi, whose focus was on the poor of India, did not speak of rice, or even of the Indian forms of bread, roti or chapati, but instead drew on a universal metaphor. After all, bread and butter, in 1931 at least, were not part of the Indian diet.

Bread can actually taste of poverty. I recall baguettes in Lagos made of expensive imported wheat flour that was illegally mixed with chalk and cassava meal. It was sold at the city's main bus station to hungry, tired travelers and poor immigrants from the countryside. Even though it was bitter and dry and stuck in your throat, people bought it because it filled the stomach.

From southern Italy comes the bread of Matera, food of the poor, unforgettably described and drawn in charcoals by writer and artist Carlo Levi, who was exiled there during the Second World War. In the hard, almost black crust and the golden yellow interior he saw the suffering of the people in their rocky fastness. The bread he depicts in black smudges is a wounded mountain; a lonely human being; the globe in black, white, and gray.

Bread symbolizes food in the broadest sense, the relief of hunger and the sharing of scarce resources. In the three main monotheistic religions, loaves, leavened or unleavened, represent divine benevolence and human hospitality. Bread is hearth and home. Anyone who offers bread is opening the door to strangers, to outsiders, breaking bread with them. Bread is not just the staff of life, it also defines who you are. The way that bread is prepared and eaten, and presented to guests, reflects a society's cosmology, the rules that govern the hierarchy of gods, humans, and nature within it. In the Middle East, bread and salt (along with dates) are a symbol of hospitality to travelers.

Any food that forms the basis of the diet of a civilization will be bound up with religion and spirituality. Uncertainty about the food supply prompts the invocation of a higher power, as does gratitude when sufficient food is available, something inevitably seen as the result of divine intervention. This applies to other important crops too, such as rice in Southeast Asia and potatoes in the Andes, each of which has its own gods.

Bread is mentioned in many religious texts and has a place in ritual festivities. In Egypt—known to the ancient world as the land of the bread-eaters—bread was among the sacrificial offerings to priests and gods. Bread was given to the dead for their journey to the underworld. Many Egyptian temple paintings show wheat, the grinding of flour, and the baking of loaves. The Greek gods received gifts made of the three ritual foods: wheat flour, wine, and olive oil. Bread features in many superstitions. There are still elderly people in Ireland who put a piece of dry bread in their pockets against the evil eye. Babies taken outside after dark must be protected against witchcraft by a piece of bread wrapped in cloth.

In Judaism and Christianity especially—two monotheistic religions closely connected with the emergence of agriculture and the spread of wheat and bread baking—bread is symbolic food. Both religions feature it in a wide variety of forms: the unleavened matzah for the Jewish feast of Passover; the Old Testament manna, bread of heaven; the loaves and fishes that miraculously multiplied to feed the 5,000 in the New Testament; the bread of the Last Supper or of the Lord's Prayer ("Give us this day our daily bread"); and the bread of the Christian Eucharist, which is Christ's body. The name "Bethlehem" actually means "city of bread," and in the Old Testament story of the prophet Elijah (I Kings 17:11–14) a description of the ingredients of bread (flour, oil, and water) is linked to one of the many predictions of an end to famine and the coming of plenty; the flour and oil used to make bread will never be used up or run dry. In the orthodox Jewish tradition, whoever cuts the loaf must first wash their hands and while cutting not say a word, out of respect for the bread. Such respect can also take the form of attributing one's own identity to the bread, as if it were a living being to whom we can speak, as Pablo Neruda does.

Bread is barely mentioned in the Koran, occurring only in the Surat Yusuf, in a dream about bread pecked at by birds. Occasionally mention is made of grain, but not specifically of wheat. We shouldn't be surprised by this, as the Koran is the product of a culture of nomadic herdsmen, who, in contrast to the cultures that produced Judaism and later Christianity, had not made the transition to agriculture and so could not domesticate cereals or bake bread.

In other cultures where bread is historically important, it has a comparable spiritual significance. Examples include central Asia, northern India, Nepal, and Pakistan, where wheat has been grown for thousands of years. In Egypt we find the oldest references to bread in the myth of the goddess Isis, who transformed wheat into bread. Isis is—inevitably—the wife of Osiris, god of agriculture.

Since the European voyages of discovery and the colonizations that followed them, which spread Judeo-Christian ideas and laid the basis for expanding global trade, bread has become common property, and its metaphorical significance along with it. In some languages, including English, "bread" and "dough" also mean "money." In much of the world "bread" is now a generic term meaning food for body and soul. In regions where bread was introduced relatively recently, such as parts of Africa and Southeast Asia, the eating of bread distinguishes the city from the countryside and is therefore a sign of modernity.

Bread as a Staple

Wheat is the most important crop in history. It is eaten in all regions of the world and produced in widely differing climatological and ecological circumstances, from the endless wheat fields of Canada to the narrow terraces of the Ethiopian highlands. No other source of sustenance has fed so many for so long. A fifth of the daily caloric intake of humans today is in the form of wheat. How could a puny grass from western Asia become so successful in what is, in evolutionary terms, a short span of time?

The first wild grasses to be domesticated in that gradual process of protection and cultivation that started 12,000 years ago were all ancestors of or closely related to wheat (*Triticum* spp.). Nevertheless, there is a crucial difference between wheat and other cereal crops and wild grasses. Only wheat (if we take it to include the *Triticum* species einkorn and spelt) contains enough of the elastic proteins called "gluten" to allow dough to rise. Gluten may make up three-quarters or more of the total protein content of wheat flour. Rye has only a little gluten, so rye dough rises hardly at all, and barley, although a close relative of wheat, requires wheat to be mixed with it before it can be used to make bread. Pure barley bread, on proud display at whole food shops, does not actually exist. Its usefulness in dough goes a long way toward explaining the inexorable rise of wheat.

———

Millstones, mortars, and pairs of rollers are about 10,000 years older than agriculture, going back some 20,000 years, but they do not in themselves constitute proof of the invention of bread. Archaeological remains suggest that all kinds of crops were ground or crushed, including hard seeds and tubers from plants of the grass family. Milled and flattened grains were initially used to make pottage. When wheat was first planted as a crop and its grains harvested, all kinds of experiments may have been carried out with heated mixtures of water and coarse flour, but without producing anything that could be described as bread, leavened or otherwise. The domestication of wheat made it possible to separate the chosen grain from wild grass seeds and steadily to increase the proportion of wheat in the harvest. Soon the best land was being used for wheat. Barley, rye, and other cereals remained important crops on dry and poor soil.

Two types of wheat are major ingredients in bread making, and they differ botanically, genetically, and chemically. Durum wheat (*Triticum turgidum* sp. *durum*) grows well in a Mediterranean climate. Its protein content is high, at 15 percent, and it contains plenty of gluten, but its yield is generally low. Durum wheat is used mainly for making pasta (especially hard pasta, such as spaghetti), bulgur, and couscous, but bread is also produced from it, both with and without yeast. Bread wheat or common wheat (*Triticum aestivum*) is found mainly in temperate and cool climates, from North and South America to northern China, and it is well suited to the making of bread and soft pasta, typically noodles. Bread wheat accounts for almost 90 percent of the world's wheat acreage. Pasta made from durum wheat lasts far longer. There are written reports from the Italian peninsula in medieval times of pasta that remained good for many years. Nitrogen fertilizer can increase the protein content of both types of wheat, and both, like barley, have some resistance to drought, no doubt as a result of their origins and domestication in semiarid regions and later in irrigated fields. Durum and bread wheat are sometimes mixed to help the dough double in size.

Bread was invented several thousand years after the start of agriculture. Almost 6,000 years ago, the Sumerians baked unleavened bread, which was probably heavy and crumbly. It is not clear whether sourdough bread is even older. It could have been made with the aid of sour milk. The Sumerians knew about yeast, as they used it to make beer, but it did not occur to them to combine the two processes. With the coming of cities, the need arose to store grain centrally and to keep a check on it, as indicated by the Old Testament story of Joseph in Egypt, in which he collects all the surplus grain grown in Egypt in years of abundance and stores it in the cities (Genesis 41:48). Leavened bread certainly existed 4,500 years ago, and its invention is attributed to the ancient Egyptians. Bakers in the Nile delta gradually developed fifty recipes for bread, biscuits, and cake. In the time of the pharaohs wages were paid in bread and beer, and the oldest depictions of bread date from the same period. The traditional flatbreads of the Middle East that we can now buy so easily in Europe from Turkish and North African bakers are not entirely yeast-free, because spontaneous reactions with yeasts in the air while the dough is rested cause it to rise slightly.

––––––

The Greeks developed bread into a staple food with countless variations. Bakers were highly respected, and they were exempt from military service, since their expertise was regarded as essential. The Greeks also perfected the bread oven, with its typical conical shape. By Roman times, specialist bakeries were producing bread in large quantities, as we know from inscriptions found at Pompeii. In Rome, which had a million residents in the time of Emperor Augustus, there was a famous bakery that produced 150,000 loaves a day at its height. Rome had hundreds of bakeries in those years; the terms "early" and "traditional" certainly do not always mean small scale. Bread was so important in ancient Rome that the killing of a baker was punished three times as severely as the killing of an ordinary citizen. Bread was regarded as more nutritious than other food. Although the people of Rome never demanded "bread and circuses," they certainly demanded bread, which was distributed regularly by the emperors to stave off mass revolt. The later, Spanish variant, *pan y toros* ("bread and bullfighting"), is a common expression to this day. In the fifth century AD, the Jerusalem Talmud addressed the vexed question of whether cooked pasta could be regarded as unleavened bread.

In urban centers in the Middle East, such as medieval Baghdad, there were countless types of *khubz* (bread) as a result of the mixing of different historical influences, including those of the oldest unleavened loaves of the fertile crescent and those of Arab traders who had come on different types of bread on their travels. Where the soil was too poor and the climate too cold, rye was used to make bread mixtures, as in rural Bulgaria under the Ottoman Empire. In Western Europe of the Dark Ages, bread and pottage were made with rye or buckwheat mixed with other cereals. In the Middle Ages bread became increasingly important, partly because of technical improvements, especially in milling techniques, ways of making dough rise, and the quality of yeast. Rye nevertheless remained the main ingredient of bread for the poor, and only the rich ate bread made purely of wheat. Stories abound about employers during and after the Industrial Revolution who had a preference for white bread (once it became affordable) over rye bread, because rye is a laxative and it therefore caused workers to spend more time on toilet breaks.

―――――――――

As bread became more important, feudal overlords and governments interfered increasingly in its production and distribution. In feudal Europe as well as ancient Rome, rulers were simply unable to leave it unregulated. From the eleventh century on, Europeans had to pay taxes on each stage of the production of flour and bread. Most bread, whether made with sourdough or yeast, was a mixture of wheat and rye and therefore had a grayish color. Until the late nineteenth century it was relatively expensive, partly because of taxation, partly because of the price of wheat, which could not be grown everywhere by any means and still had a low yield. Deforestation in Western Europe made fuel for bread ovens more expensive as well. So as urbanization increased the demand for bread, supplies ran short. When international trade took off in the eighteenth century, high tariffs and strict regulation of the export and import of grain made the situation even worse. Farmers were themselves heavily taxed, having to forfeit as much as half their harvest. So regular shortages of bread and wheat occurred, and bread dough was supplemented with roots, beech mast, dried vegetables, and all kinds of other ingredients. When the potato began to spread across Europe in the sixteenth century, it was seen as a logical alternative to expensive wheat. Potato flour became popular for various uses and was added to bread dough.

As urbanization increased in the eighteenth century, and with it the revolutionary potential of urban populations, bread was of growing significance. Government intervention included rationing, and the poor were regularly given bread vouchers. Citizens repeatedly rose in revolt to demand cheaper bread, the two most famous occasions being the protests that led to the storming of the Bastille and with it the French Revolution, and the bread riots of 1917 that heralded the Russian Revolution. In both periods one explicit demand was for white bread, in other words bread made purely with wheat, which had always been unaffordable for any but the elite. (The story that Marie Antoinette said "let them eat cake" rather than bread is apocryphal.) Governmental interference has echoes even today. Many Italian loaves still contain no salt, a relic of popular resistance to paying the salt tax. In other countries, such as the Netherlands, people are used to relatively salty bread with added iodine, which is one of the factors that explain their high consumption of salt.

Over the course of the nineteenth century, the Industrial Revolution brought about a series of significant dietary breakthroughs, and bread was no exception. Thanks in part to Louis Pasteur, who built on the earlier work of Antonie van Leeuwenhoek, the nature of yeast was better understood, and its production became more efficient. Bread was no longer dependent on yeast from alcoholic drinks or sourdough. In many cities more checks were conducted on the quality of bread and attempts made to detect illegal additions of chalk and cheap grains. In most countries the composition of bread flour and the size and weight of loaves is still laid down precisely in law, although taxes on milling and bread flour have been abolished everywhere. Better grain yields as a consequence of the use of artificial fertilizer and better tillage of the soil caused the price of wheat to fall steadily from the late nineteenth century on, and a further contribution was made by the introduction of steamships, which brought cheap American grain to Europe. The advent of mechanized mills led to the introduction of bread factories and further falls in the price of bread. Spreads and fillings became popular in Western Europe, whether in the form of jams and syrups or Italy's chocolate and hazelnut paste (Nutella).

All these developments caused the consumption of bread to rise markedly. In 1918, when the First World War ended and people stood waiting in endless bread lines and protested at the prices asked, bread came to be regarded as a matter of national security in some countries, including the United States and France. Mechanized production took off in the United States during and shortly after the Second World War, when Americans had to maintain long supply lines. The white bread distributed in liberated Western Europe and elsewhere, sometimes dropped from the air, made a great impression. America's Wonder Bread contained added minerals and vitamins, part of an attempt by the U.S. government to prevent deficiency diseases at home and abroad. Only in the final quarter of the twentieth century were price controls on bread abolished practically everywhere.

The bread we eat today is therefore the product of a long history in which technology, economics, and politics dominated by turns. Bread is now a staple food all over the world, not just in Western countries and western Asia, where wheat was first domesticated, but in the temperate regions of Asia; North, South and Central America; and North Africa as well. It is even increasingly important in tropical regions. Bread quickly staunches hunger and is particularly satisfying because of its combination of a crispy crust and an elastic interior. It is easy to store and transport, and it can be combined with practically all other foods. Bread can be served with sweet or savory spreads and fillings; dipped in animal fat, oil, or sauce; made into a pudding; or even function as a fork or spoon for wiping or scooping up other foods. In Latin culture it is perfectly acceptable to clean your plate with bread.

Bread was a "convenience food" long before the term was coined. As tradition would have it, in the mid-eighteenth century the fourth earl of Sandwich asked his butler to put his meat between two slices of bread, so that he could play cards and eat without getting his fingers greasy. The now fashionable finger food for eating at the computer or while making a phone call can be regarded as a direct descendant of this innovation. Bread offers flexibility; you can eat it at any time of day, while on the way somewhere, at work, or even while shopping. It's easier to carry portions of bread than cooked cassava, noodles, or rice, which also decay faster in warm climates. This flexibility makes bread attractive in a part of the world where you would least expect to find it: Africa. It's not unusual these days to see people in tropical Africa standing in line at a bakery, waiting for fresh bread. If you stop to think about it, this is astonishing. Little wheat is grown in Africa, and there is no tradition of it there with the exception of Ethiopia and the highlands of ex-colonial East Africa, where it was introduced by the British. Small amounts of wheat and bread came to Africa from the Mediterranean region from the ninth century on, along trade routes across the Sahara or via the east and west coasts, but they were initially intended for communities of Arab traders. The sixteenth-century European adventurers and missionaries and their successors brought bread with them, and in the nineteenth century freed slaves returning from South America introduced bread as part of their diet. Yet it was only in the 1960s that bread spread right across Africa, largely because of aggressive export policies on the part of the United States and Europe. As a result of falling wheat prices on the world market, Africa was able to buy cheap wheat for many years. For short-sighted governments it presented an easy solution to shortfalls in the production of local grains, especially in urban areas. Artificial exchange rates kept the price of wheat low, while subsidies on bread and wheat encouraged consumption and imports. Food aid to Africa, which included the distribution of bread and wheat, did the rest. As a result bread is now a staple food throughout Africa, while African wheat production is limited to cooler regions or high altitudes, and even there yields remain low. These policies have often proven a reckless course to take: imports in place of local production and the handing out of subsidies for bread (or indeed of free bread) have been common practice, standing in the way of investment in sustainable means of combating poverty.

South and Southeast Asia—China, Korea, Japan, Indonesia, and the tropical parts of India—are an important exception to the worldwide dominance of bread. Soft bread wheat was introduced to China at an early stage, but in contrast to other countries it was used mainly for steamed or boiled pasta products, such as dimsum and spring rolls. Although consumption of wheat there remained undiminished, bread was relatively unimportant until recently. In the early 1980s and as part of the rapprochement between the United States and China, an American bakery opened in Beijing. The loaves it produced fairly flew out the door. Bread confers status. The success of bread led not just to increased wheat imports, as the Americans were probably hoping, but to an ambitious program of Chinese wheat production. In Japan, too, the young urban classes like to eat sandwiches, although with typically Japanese fillings, such as raw fish and seaweed. In most Asian and African countries, people prefer white bread, because white is a sign of status. In Djakarta the temptation of bread is so great that members of the middle class are prepared to spend an average of eight dollars per day per household on muffins and custard buns. Indonesia is Asia's biggest consumer of bread.

———————

At the start of the twenty-first century, bread is not just a generic product. Any decent bakery offers a choice of dozens of loaves and rolls. Having started out as the simplest food a person can make—water, flour, and yeast—it has become the packaging for all kinds of additional ingredients and therefore of additional calories. Bread is still sold by bakers, but supermarkets are steadily encroaching, and small bakeries are declining in number all over the world. Where they remain, a new structure is in evidence, whereby the bakery becomes merely an outlet for the products of the bread factories that supply them with partially or fully baked loaves. This development may be regrettable, but it is understandable in the light of how hard a baker has to work. Even now that the mixing and kneading of the dough is done by machines, hefty sacks of flour have to be moved around and heavy trays lifted in and out of ovens in a hot, damp, and dusty atmosphere with a day-night rhythm that takes a heavy toll on a baker's health. Small bakeries can now survive only by specializing, serving a niche market in urban areas.

Of all Europeans, the British buy the highest proportion of their bread in supermarkets, almost 98 percent. The Dutch come next. Although the term "factory bread" is hardly a recommendation, the diversity of the breads found in supermarkets in northern Europe is remarkable. In this sense Germany comes out on top. At the same time, by means of the packaging chosen and by finishing the baking process in the shop (oh, that irresistible smell of fresh bread!), supermarkets are doing all they can to give us the illusion of eating handmade, traditional bread. More and more often, bread products are sold in canteens, cafeterias, hamburger chains, gas stations, and all those other public places that the eternally restless modern human passes through. Social class still determines choice, with the more educated opting for whole grain and "ethnic" bread and the less educated preferring white.

At the same time we're seeing what I would call a new bread "consciousness." Typical of the renewed attention paid to food by the upper middle classes is their concern for tradition and freshness. Bread must not look as if it came out of a factory even if it did, let alone as if it had been baked yesterday. When I once gave a talk and suggested that we could eat old bread and that there was no need for shops to remove all that day's bread every evening, the response was a storm of criticism. Yet we ought to stop and think about the fact that a third of all bread in Europe is thrown away while still edible. In blind tests, consumers cannot tell the difference between two-day-old bread and six-day-old bread. One of the reasons the consumer throws away so much bread is that the traditional bread box is no longer used. Bread is now often kept in the fridge, where it quickly dries out and takes on the smells of other foods.

The type of bread you choose to eat and what you do with it has become a test of socially responsible behavior. The purchase of whole grain bread is a sign that you give some thought to food and to the environment. Those who eat white bread are different from those who eat sourdough spelt bread, or at least they think they are. Expensive, authentic bread, made from sourdough with mainly organic flour—which its advocates like to call "honest" bread with "real" flavor—is rising in popularity among the well-off middle classes. Here and there we're seeing the return of something that disappeared centuries ago, in cities perhaps as early as the end of Roman times, namely, the regular baking of bread in individual households, which was taken over first by professional bakers and later by bread factories. Amateur cooks distinguish themselves by kneading dough and baking it at home, whether in the oven or in a fully automated bread machine. Of course, purists look down on machinery and do everything by hand. Supermarkets capitalize on the trend by selling prebaked bread in plastic packaging that needs only a few minutes in the oven to create the illusion and smell of home baking. Bakeries advertise with slogans like "baked with passion." The better restaurants serve bread made with special, sometimes even local, grains according to traditional recipes, such as Tuscany's saffron bread. In such loaves we see the craftsmanship of culinary literacy.

In California, during my TED talk about bread, I asked the audience which they preferred, a handmade whole grain loaf from a stone oven or white sliced Wonder Bread. As expected, 99 percent of those present opted for handmade bread. My advocacy of the white loaf was not a defense of the quality of white or commercial bread but a plea for an understanding of how important the large-scale and mechanical production of bread and other foods is in our history, and the extent to which technical progress has made it possible to feed the world. Rarely have I received so many critical reactions as I did to that question and my answer. Of course, I too prefer to eat whole grain bread, and of course whole grain bread is healthier, because it contains the entire grain, but white bread is not the unhealthy calorie bomb some diet gurus take it for (and anyhow, it's fortified with vitamins and minerals). Those who are not fully aware of the source of their whole grain bread or why white bread has been so important geographically, historically, and technologically ought to pipe down a little.

The extraordinary story of the grass that provides bread flour because of its gluten and has changed the world is far from over. More than ever, wheat—and by extension, bread—in all its forms has become a plaything of the world market. The demand for and cost of bread continue to develop. The price of wheat has risen, as part of a general rise in food prices since the start of the twenty-first century. The reasons have to do with occasional bad harvests, unwise government policies, and declining stocks, but mainly with a lack of investment in agriculture. Wheat prices fell over decades, reaching a historical low around 2000. Average wheat yields have since fallen by some 0.5 percent per year. From 2005 on wheat prices began to fluctuate wildly, and they have doubled in relation to their lowest point, yet these developments are barely reflected in the price of bread, which has risen only slightly. The price of wheat on the world market accounts for less than 10 percent of the final price that the consumer in rich economies has to pay for a loaf. In Paris, wheat prices determine a mere 8 percent of the bread price. The average Western European spends only a little more than 1 percent of his or her income on bread, as opposed to 5 percent fifty years ago. Before the Second World War it was not unusual for poor families in Europe to spend half their income on bread. The victims of price fluctuations have up to now been primarily farmers and poorer consumers in wheat-importing countries. In Madagascar the price of wheat on the world market determines half the price paid for bread by the consumer.

Despite the importance of bread in our history and the great diversity of it, the number of calories derived from bread in Western countries is falling. This is especially true of Europe. At the end of the nineteenth century, the French ate on average more than 900 grams of bread per person per day, which gave them 70 percent of the calories they needed. Today Western Europeans eat about 150 to 200 grams, which covers a quarter of their daily caloric requirements (these figures alone show that our bread is now considerably richer in energy). This is a result of the increasing variety in our diets and the growth in their fat content at the expense of carbohydrates. As the twenty-first century progresses, the importance of bread in the rest of the world will probably grow for a time, with increasing demand in places where wheat and bread have not been a major part of the diet before, such as Africa and Asia, where most of today's megacities are to be found.

Carbohydrates

Nowadays the baker sells low-carbohydrate bread. What an irony of evolution! Carbohydrates (collectively known as starch) have been of crucial importance in human history, helping to make us who we are. Having realized we were consuming them in excessive quantities, or simply consuming too much food altogether, we now prefer to avoid them. Agriculture has drastically altered the human diet. Farmers have far more starch at their disposal than hunter-gatherers, in the form of grains that store well. The first domesticated crops all contained starch, and they were mainly grasses or similar species. In the Andes, for example, before the introduction of wheat the native population ate unleavened bread made of the local grain quinoa (*Chenopodium quinoa*, a species of goosefoot), which is related to the vegetables amaranth (which also produces a kind of "grain") and spinach. Where no cereal crops have been domesticated, another botanical species will be a source of starch that can be stored successfully, whether because the roots (cassava, for example) can remain in the ground for a reasonably long time, or because the tubers (potatoes) keep well in dark, cool places, or because the stem (sago palm, *Metroxylon sagu*) can be left standing and harvested at a convenient time. Plantains and ensete (both a kind of banana) decay relatively slowly as well. The breadfruit, which is now quite commonly found in tropical gardens, is an exception, as it gets its name from its white consistency rather than its storage properties. The great advantage of cereals is lost in the humid tropics, where grains sprout too quickly, so rice is the only successful grain crop there, and to a lesser degree, corn. Worldwide just as many calories are derived from rice as from wheat, at 20 percent. In the early twenty-first century, more than half of all the calories we consume still come from grains.

Beans, too, which were domesticated fairly soon after cereals, contain a high proportion of starch. So everywhere in the world, people have always had a preference for foods rich in carbohydrates. For almost a hundred centuries, until well into the twentieth century, carbohydrates were far and away the most important source of energy for humans. The foods that provide it are known as staples. Along with wheat and bread products, the other two grains of worldwide significance are rice and corn. Then come the three tuber crops: potatoes, cassava, and sweet potatoes. Others, such as yam (*Dioscorea* spp.), taro (*Colocasia* spp.), and ensete are important locally, as are quinoa and teff. Far more limited to specific regions are such sources of carbohydrate as sago palm and *Xanthosoma sagittofolium* (known variously as arrowleaf elephant ear, tiquizque, macal, nampi, or malanga).

Cassava, corn, rice, potato, and sweet potato are world travelers like wheat. With the exception of rice, domesticated in Asia, they all come from

South America and have spread across the world in the centuries since the sixteenth-century voyages of discovery. Corn and sweet potatoes are increasingly important as cattle feed. Wonderful stories can be told about all these staple foods. Rice and potatoes are as symbolic in their home cultures as wheat and bread are in the West. They are not merely food for the body but strength-giving in a spiritual sense and are deeply rooted in rituals that are still significant today. In recent decades in Western countries, rice and potatoes have been through the same development as wheat and bread: a shift from mass product to high-status specialty. Nowadays even a relatively run-of-the-mill supermarket in the West sells a wide assortment of both. No one is any longer bemused by basmati or jasmine rice. Traditional varieties of potato are returning to favor, such as the Opperdoezer Ronde and the Malta in the Netherlands, and new varieties are continually being developed for specialist market segments. The potato named after the Dutch crown princess Amalia, for example, is particularly good for making French fries, while the variety named after her sister Alexia is perfect for ready-made potato salad. Potato, and to a lesser extent rice, is fashionable as a snack and as an ingredient in all kinds of foods, but no source of carbohydrates is so flexible, so varied, and so popular as bread.

Bread and Health

As well as being a source of carbohydrates (55 percent) and proteins (7–8 percent), along with a small percentage of fats, wheat bread is an essential source of fiber and of iron, copper, magnesium, and, in tiny quantities, folic acid, iodine (through added salt), B vitamins, selenium, and zinc. Salt not only improves the taste, it makes bread dough easier to knead by improving the elasticity of the proteins. Whatever most people may think, whole grain, spelt, rye, and white bread all contain roughly the same number of calories (about 200 calories per 100 grams of bread). It is a quite different story once additives come into the picture, such as seeds, nuts, raisins, butter and other fats, or milk. Muesli bread has half as many calories again and a croissant twice as many. Luxury breads with additional ingredients are no recent invention, of course. In ancient Rome bread dough was mixed with cheese and eggs to make high-calorie loaves. I always chuckle when I see multigrain bread on sale, often promoted by bakers who blithely claim it contains seven or even twelve types of grain. How could it? There are no more than about seven grains in existence, and to bake bread with all seven would be a major achievement, since many are not readily available and are extremely difficult to bake with because of their low gluten content. It seems likely that these types of bread, for a niche market, contain sunflower seeds, pine nuts, and other high-calorie ingredients that are counted as grains.

The permanent availability of energy-rich wheat-based products is new. They are no longer the festive exception but have become ubiquitous. The additional ingredients may be baking promoters and bread improvers (usually fatty liquids), or sugar, nuts, and oils—to say nothing of fillings and spreads. We increasingly eat sandwiches prepared for us by strangers, as convenience food for when we are out and about. In these and all kinds of similar products for the hurried urban consumer, including filled baguettes, wraps, pizza slices, and hamburgers, bread is merely packaging for the filling or topping. The thicker and more concentrated the layers of bread dough, the more voluminous and substantial the layers in between or on top can be. The trend toward whole grain bread is therefore double edged, satisfying our desire for healthy options while also forming the packaging for even more calories. Put simply, such bread can hold more cheese. Whole grain bread may not be as whole grained as the color suggests, incidentally. It is often made to look darker by the addition of malt flour (made from sprouted wheat, rye, or barley).

A decisive event in the history of bread consumption was the invention in 1873 of a steam engine that could grind wheat in such a way as to produce fine white flour. It put soft white bread in the reach of ordinary people, a product that until then had been costly because of the inefficiency of flour mills. In the decades that followed it became increasingly clear that such refinement had a downside. Epidemiological studies looking at dietary patterns and chronic illnesses such as cardiovascular disease, certain forms of cancer, and diabetes, showed that whole grain bread is healthier. For a long time it was assumed that the decisive factor here was the indigestible fiber known as roughage, but we now know that various ingredients of wheat grains, such as vitamin E, other antioxidants (including polyphenols), and anti-inflammatory agents all have a part to play. Most of these active substances are in the outer part of the grain, which is lost in the making of white flour (unless deliberately added back in by the manufacturer or consumer). International studies are under way that look at various methods of increasing the proportion of antioxidants, vitamins, and minerals in wheat to compensate for this loss.

All kinds of properties have been attributed to whole grain bread. The bread diet, popular of late, advocates eating nothing but whole grain bread on certain days, in the expectation that the average number of calories consumed daily will be reduced because whole grain bread is more filling than other foods.

The reputation of bread, our historical staple, has plummeted. It is now often seen as the cause of obesity. Countless diets—from Montignac, Atkins, and South Beach in the last quarter of the twentieth century to all kinds of "carbohydrate-free" prescriptions of the present day—blame bread for our own undesirable increase in volume. Diet gurus still often want to ban or reduce carbohydrates, despite evidence that diets with very little carbohydrate content are almost impossible to stick to and can have all kinds of negative effects. A false contrast is often suggested between bread and other sources of carbohydrates, such as rice, barley, and spelt, the idea being that the last two are more primitive and therefore less refined and healthier, which is simply untrue. There is also a suggestion that rice makes you slim, as evidenced by the Asian silhouette. In reality the percentage of carbohydrates, fats, and proteins is more or less the same in all grains, so they have a similar caloric content. This has nothing to do with the degree of refinement; in fact for many decades those who refined flour chose cereals with better nutritional qualities. The difference between types of bread lies not in the botanical species but purely in the degree to which the entire grain is used: brown or white bread; brown or white rice. The belief that bread is fattening stems from our use of it as packaging for sugars and fats and just the occasional green leaf. The soft, fat-absorbing bun in which the hamburger is wrapped is the prime example. The fault lies not with the bread but with what lies on or between the slices. (If anything at all is at fault; the occasional hamburger will not ruin your health.) It's been a long time since people were happy to eat "dry bread," in other words, a slice of bread without anything on it, not even butter.

The final step in the development of this ancient staple is functional bread, to which all kinds of things have been added to make it more healthy. This is generally white bread, which many people and especially children prefer. There has always been some opposition to white bread as unhealthy. One of the advocates of good bread at the end of the nineteenth century was a British doctor called Thomas Allinson, and the bread named after him is still popular today. Improvements that began in the twentieth century with the addition of vitamins and minerals have now made it possible to produce white bread with exactly the same nutritional value as whole grain bread, (including the fiber content, partly by means of adding a group of polysaccharides called inulins). The possibilities have by no means been exhausted. Other examples include the addition of phytoestrogens, extra antioxidants, and, for the elderly, calcium and iron. Given current concerns about aging populations, we are likely to see further work on the latter two additives.

———————

The Dutch poet Ida Gerhardt once wrote: "We eat our early bread dunked in sun." It's true. Bread is the best example of captured sunlight, the source of all life transformed into the most iconic of foods. Eating bread gives us a chance to think about the long chain that explains how bread reaches our plates (or our hands, if we've given up bothering with a table), starting with the first Neolithic farmers who selected their *Triticum* grasses, then the first bakers in Mesopotamia and Egypt, the large-scale bakeries of ancient Rome, the laborious production of wheat across the centuries, the invention of artificial fertilizer, the steam power used to mill grain, and the baker or factory worker of today who ensures we can obtain our daily bread as if by a miracle, with no effort at all on our part. Bread binds us to all those who came before us and all those who will come after us, as well as to those who will have no bread today, or too little. It remains an icon of human development, a staple food from the Neolithic era on, the food of rituals and religions, a cheap and healthy source of calories for the poor (as long as not too much unimproved white bread is eaten), a luxury snack that may cause obesity, and a vehicle for that other icon of modern life, the hamburger.

But bread is ultimately the food of simplicity. Nothing beats a slice of fresh bread dipped in olive oil, spread with a modicum of butter or topped with a raw tomato and a little garlic. As the early twentieth-century poet Khalil Gibran wrote: "For if you bake bread with indifference, you bake a bitter bread that feeds but half man's hunger." Eating bread with indifference—that is the ultimate sin.

FIVE

Meat: Necessity and Luxury

As many hairs as the slain beast has, so often indeed will he who killed it without a (lawful) reason suffer a violent death in future births.... Meat can never be obtained without injury to living creatures, and injury to sentient beings is detrimental to (the attainment of) heavenly bliss; let him therefore shun (the use of) meat.   MANU, *Dharmaśāstra* 5.38–48

So saying, he laid hold of a kettle, and dipping it at once into one of the half-jar pots, brought up three pullets, and a couple of geese. "Here," said he, "eat, make a breakfast of this scum, and see if you can stay your stomach with it, till dinner-time."   MIGUEL DE CERVANTES, *Don Quixote* II, 3

Perhaps the most important issue surrounding food, scarcity, and abundance concerns meat, dairy products, and fish, or more generally the consumption of animal proteins and its sustainability and ethical justification. Meat is particularly controversial. After all, meat eaters are increasingly blamed these days for deforestation, animal suffering, climate change, and even aggression in social intercourse, as well as for causing themselves cardiovascular disease. Yet throughout human history an abundance of meat has symbolized unbridled pleasure, lavish hospitality, and pure manliness. A true hero—such as those of ancient Greece—eats no fish, let alone vegetables, but rather meat and preferably red meat. This is still what we expect of a cowboy or anyone wanting to resemble one, of the Australian outback or a barbecue in the back yard. Meat has a supernatural power of attraction that surpasses the effort it requires. It seems to be something the earth produces continually, as Herodotus claimed was true of Egypt, where meat simply grew out of the ground. Meat is a magical force, the most nutritious food we can eat. No other category of food is surrounded by so many commands and prohibitions, myths and customs, and deep feelings of aversion and preference. Fish, in contrast, are cold-blooded creatures, far less like humans than are the warm-blooded animals from which we obtain meat and less visible to us because they live in water. Although in some places fish is an important source of animal protein, it has a less prominent place in human evolution than meat.

Meat, with its animal origin, is the food that most closely resembles human beings themselves, their own flesh. Our complex relationship with meat is made all the more so by the fact that animals are so close to us that meat eating can be seen as a form of cannibalism, against which strict taboos exist for most societies. We have a profound moral aversion to cannibalistic rituals performed by "primitive" peoples and are horrified even by cannibalism in the animal kingdom, at least among the higher animals, even though it might be seen as an evolutionary adaptation, an efficient means of both acquiring food and regulating the population. Cases of cannibalism have been observed even among the mainly vegetarian chimpanzees. Claude Lévi-Strauss argued that all humans are cannibals deep down and called the practice "nutritional incest," a reference to another, no less strict taboo. The most convincing way in which we can identify with another is by eating him, he wrote. Among so-called "primitive" tribes, cannibalism is a spiritual act focused on the dead. It is generally a gesture of respect and even intimacy, or a way of subjugating the enemy by absorbing his powers. Human sacrifice, too, whether by the Aztecs or in the story of Abraham and Isaac, is never taken lightly. Lévi-Strauss was the first to make a connection with organ donation. Is there a difference in principle between eating and receiving an organ? And what about breastfeeding? Or giving blood? Stretching things only a little, you could see these not just as acts of self-sacrifice and love but as a form of cannibalism. If there is nothing either casual or violent about cannibalism, if it is truly a sign of respect, then the eating of an animal could also be seen as an act whereby the power of the animal is transferred to a human. That interpretation of meat eating is at odds with the metaphor of cannibalism that the animal rights movement uses to express a sense that the eating of meat is a violation. Those who eat meat eat their own species, some say, because animals are the equal of humans.

Few of us remain indifferent when thoughts turn to meat. I'm no exception. From the age of eighteen, when I began my studies at Wageningen University, I became more conscious with each passing year of how problematic meat, dairy products, and fish are. In Wageningen a certain level of suspicion concerning meat was and remains in vogue, because the production of meat is bad for the environment. It begins with a vague awareness that meat production is inefficient. Plant products, in contrast, are "good," because the transformation of sunlight into digestible proteins and carbohydrates is beneficial for both humans and the earth as a whole. That was all it took to persuade me to give up eating meat while I was a student. I remained a vegetarian for many years, until finally I discovered that such a stance lacks an adequate basis in science and cannot always be adhered to in practice. I do not want to be one of those vegetarians who regard eating meat as a sin, any more than I want to resemble those Hollywood stars and starlets who parade their new-found vegetarian sensibilities.

My simple view of the world—eat no meat—soon began to show cracks. What about fish? Or cheese, milk, and eggs? Both at home and abroad, problems soon emerged. Are cows that have roamed the African savannah all their lives bad or good? Should we be eating fried beetles? Insect foods are said to be good for the environment, yet they meet with a certain hesitation, or worse. What about the black Iberian pigs that live on the acorns of wild oak woods near the Mediterranean coast? Some of my best friends cook and eat meat with great enthusiasm, yet they have the best of intentions regarding the future of the world. What should I tell my doctor, who sometimes mutters that it's sensible to eat the occasional steak? I make an exception of pork, which I decline on principle, not so much as a protest against the meat industry—as there is no theoretical difference between the production of pork and of chicken—but because of the symbolic importance of pork in the Jewish-Islamic tradition and the way in which pork in particular has been an instrument of discrimination and oppression. The decision to eat no meat brings us up against all kinds of ethical dilemmas. If a friendly peasant on Java insists on slaughtering her last chicken for me, then a haughty refusal based on fine Western principles become impossible. My Italian friends always prepare a stew for Christmas with a lamb brought to them by their neighbor, a shepherd. You surely can't refuse that, can you? His lamb is almost a wild animal, which puts it into a different category. Or does it?

I feel the same degree of ambivalence toward meat that comes from hunting. There is little to be said against game as a necessary supplement in regions where protein is scarce, but even so I cannot be indifferent toward the actual act of killing. I know that animals released into the wild have to be kept under control, given the limited capacity of most nature reserves, in Europe at least, where their size and composition is usually such that the regulation of numbers no longer happens spontaneously.

This ecological argument for hunting remains rather artificial, however, in a modern society where we release animals and then pretend that the "wild" products of the hunt are "natural" food. In any case, hunting does not resolve the ethical issues surrounding the killing of animals.

Over the years my personal rule has developed into: eat little if any meat in restaurants (aside from the occasional medically prescribed steak), and apart from that eat meat only in socially unavoidable situations. I never prepare it in my own kitchen. I opted for fish instead, until recently, that is, when that rule was thrown up in the air again by threats to fish stocks and by dubious fishing methods. Should I stick to vegetarian dishes, with all kinds of soy products? I don't want anything to do with soy disguised as meat, since why would you pretend it's something you are consciously trying to avoid? On all official occasions I ask for the vegetarian menu, but with increasing reluctance, because it's sure to consist of pastry with great slabs of greasy cheese. I eat yogurt daily, which means I'm helping to sustain the dairy industry. These are the everyday compromises I feel forced to make. Refusing meat sometimes feels uncomfortably ostentatious. With each mouthful I'm aware of the inadequacy and inconsistency of my choices.

Many people share my worries about meat, which still has a powerful moral charge in our secularized societies. It has become the touchstone of political correctness and at the same time evidence of refined taste, the showpiece of the top chef. The fundamental question is, should we still be eating meat? Or should we instead collectively convert to artificial meat made of soy, algae or—the ultimate in desperate measures—switch to consuming insects, which can be produced without environmental damage and seem unaware of suffering? Insects already end up in food products more than some would like and most realize, in tomato ketchup, for example. Or is it enough to eat less meat? Is a vegetarian diet good for our health, the forests, and animal welfare? Meanwhile, demand for meat is growing in the non-Western world, where half the population still consumes too little protein, meat is highly regarded, and the sensitivities of the Western middle class are rarely shared.

Meat and dairy products are extremely diverse ecologically, economically, and agriculturally, and even within those categories there are differences that determine how we should regard them. Pork cutlets cannot be lumped together with veal steaks. Milk, cheese, butter, and eggs each belong in a separate category. So it's impossible to generalize about meat, dairy, or animal proteins. Nonetheless, there is a general question that needs to be asked: why do we produce and consume animal proteins at all? It seems to be natural to eat such products, but the reasons are less than obvious. Theoretically you might say that the human species could have evolved as almost exclusively vegetarian, like some of our close relatives among the primates. There are various explanations for our consumption of animal products, and only when we understand those can we talk about whether we should continue to eat meat or drink milk.

The Omnivorous Human

The weightiest argument for the consumption of animal proteins, particularly meat, is that humans have almost always eaten them and that this has conferred on us huge, perhaps decisive evolutionary advantages. The very first hominids, *Australopithecus* and other forerunners of the species *Homo*, probably had the same diet as chimpanzees today: leaves, perhaps a few roots, and just possibly some soft grass seeds. They may also have eaten insects or small rodents, but they were primarily vegetarians. They did not remain so. Humans soon became omnivores. By about 2.5 million years ago the diet of the ancestors of modern humans in the East African savannah changed radically. It was there that *Homo habilis* began to walk upright and to eat meat. It was there that dexterity developed along with the use of tools, mainly fashioned from animal bones, which made it possible to hunt and to cut meat, or at least to tear it. It was a self-reinforcing process. Cutting and eating meat required certain skills, and the manipulation of tools in turn made it possible to hunt more often, to butcher more carcases, and therefore to eat more meat, which in turn rendered up more bones for the making of tools. A relatively meat-rich diet also led to a shorter suckling time for infants and therefore faster reproduction.

That these first people really did eat meat we know with near certainty from the isotopic composition of carbon (the ratio of ^{12}C to ^{13}C) in the ivory of their teeth and from the way the muscles were attached to their jaws. *Homo habilis* ate animals that grazed on tropical grasses, such as the forerunners of the antelope, and perhaps small rodents, but few if any grasses or seeds that were tough to chew. We know this because tropical grasses have a specific isotopic composition, a result of their having a different photosynthetic process (the C4 instead of the C3 cycle) from grasses in temperate regions. By eating grazing animals, people gain access to proteins and minerals in grasses, which they cannot digest.

Our Pleistocene ancestors were omnivores with a strikingly varied diet. They ate not only large grazing animals but also birds, rodents, crocodiles, turtles, and hippos, depending on availability and the effort required to make the catch. We should not imagine meat consumption by hunters in the tropical savannah as the polite consumption of a steak but as the tearing apart or rough cutting of entire animals, including the nutritious inner organs, blood, stomach contents, and bones. The liver is a particularly rich source of vitamins. Cooking was a significant step that increased the nutritional value of meat. In Ethiopia, incidentally, traces of the mass slaughter of animals by humans have been found that are 150,000 years old. The killing of animals for meat on a large scale must therefore have been a feature of human life at an early stage.

Some 50,000 to 60,000 years ago, the forerunners of modern humans left the East African savannah and swarmed out over the rest of the world. During that expansion, humans remained hunters and meat eaters, although vegetable food sources and insects, and where available fish and shellfish, were an important supplement to meat. This predominantly carnivorous pattern changed only 10,000 years ago with the development of farming. From a reduction in the length of the human skeleton and the weight of the bones found at Neolithic sites, we can deduce that this development was initially accompanied by a reduction in the consumption of animal proteins.

We can really only guess why the development of agriculture and especially arable farming as the main source of calories led to a lower consumption of animal proteins. On the one hand it is likely that farming developed where rainfall declined, and as a result, wild animals became more scarce, so that hunting was less productive. On the other hand the domestication of animals for farming, as draft animals and as a source of such products as milk and wool, makes them less attractive as a source of nutrition. Furthermore, farming may have caused a local increase in the human population, which was now sedentary, such that the number of wild animals available per head became too small for the hunt to be relied on for sustenance. In the first millennia after the introduction of farming, the eating of cattle must have been almost unthinkable, because the meat of animals that have worked the fields or produced milk over a long period is far too tough for consumption and young animals are too valuable to be eaten. The distinction between edible animals and working animals is clear: as recently as the era of the Byzantine Empire, the word "meat" was used exclusively in connection with pigs, sheep, and goats— never for cows and oxen, which were regarded as a separate category of working animals. Just how valuable and intimate the relationship with farm animals was is evident from a beautiful Sumerian statuette from the city of Nimrud, on the banks of the Tigris in the north of present-day Iraq. It is made of white ceramic and shows a cow with a suckling calf. In 3,000 years the realistic expression of the cow and her hungry calf has lost none of its eloquence. It is all but indisputable that the artist observed the animals with love.

After agriculture had been practiced for a few hundred or possibly a thousand years, the domestication of poultry began, including chickens, geese, and ducks. This happened in various places independently. Chickens may have been domesticated as early as 8,000 years ago in Vietnam, and in China they were present in large numbers by 7,000 years ago. They were shipped eastward via Polynesia to South America and westward via India to Mesopotamia, Egypt, and Roman Europe. For the ancient Greeks a chicken was still in a sense an exotic bird. The domestication of geese from wild populations of northern parts of Asia and Europe is of a much later date. In Central America, turkeys and certain species of duck were domesticated and then brought to Europe by the conquistadores in the sixteenth century and from there taken to Asia. This complicated early globalization of poultry is reflected in the confusion over names. White Barbary ducks were brought to Europe from Mexico (Barbary suggests "unknown region"), but they were also known as Muscovy ducks. As is clear from countless seventeenth-century European paintings, they were much in demand.

The first few thousand years after the start of farming were therefore accompanied by the development of a predominantly vegetarian diet, but the invention of farming certainly did not mean that hunting and fishing disappeared everywhere. In regions including New Guinea and the Amazon, proteins derived from fish and wild animals are still an important part of the diet, in some cases the most important. Greenland has no sources of vegetarian food at all, aside from a few mosses. The same goes for all regions where arable farming is impossible, or no longer possible, or where it produces little in comparison to hunting and gathering. In some places the land can be used only as pasture. Where hunting still provides sufficient food, there is little reason to switch to the labor-intensive growing of crops, except perhaps as a supplementary activity undertaken by women. For nomadic herders the consumption of meat and milk has of course always been part of the diet, although in moderation. It generally does not include young animals, which are often used in sacrifices and rituals. The popularity of sheep in the Middle East has been attributed to their high productivity, their generous fat content, and their relatively low price. Goats, which are often put out to pasture along with sheep, are held in rather less high esteem, possibly because of the strong flavor of the meat and its lower fat content. Arab peoples have always eaten camel meat, whereas horses and especially donkeys are regarded as barely edible, possibly because they are far more useful as working animals. Horsemeat is still unacceptable in Britain and North America but is regarded as perfectly normal in continental Europe.

Some nomadic peoples, such as the Masai, drink blood directly from the jugular veins of their cattle, sometimes mixed with milk. The eating of blood products is not a custom confined to herders and hunters—you only have to think of the European blood sausage or blood pudding. Those who hunt and those who herd differ greatly in their attitude toward the killing of animals. The latter are extremely reticent about killing their livestock, which after all represent their capital, and eat relatively little meat. In contrast, hunters impose no restrictions on the killing of wild animals, and their consumption of meat is higher. Other population groups might look down on hunters as people with blood on their hands, even though their hauls provide important proteins and fats. Hunting as a leisure activity indulged in by an elite is a fairly recent phenomenon in evolutionary terms, whereas the eating of large wild animals was for centuries the preserve of the aristocracy. In China bear's paws were a delicacy, imported from Cambodia.

Birds and small animals such as rabbits fall outside any restrictions on meat consumption, both among farmers and among herders, and are freely hunted, kept, and eaten. It is rare to find a farming household without chickens or ducks ranging around freely. In ancient Greece not only were hares and rabbits eaten but hedgehogs and foxes as well. With the rise of cities, the meat of small animals became a luxury. In Italy songbirds are still regarded as delicacies, although the hunting season is now strictly limited. Larks were part of *haute cuisine* in France until the early twentieth century, and pigeons are still eaten by almost the entire population in poor countries.

———

Over the course of history, ecological and cultural factors influenced consumption and the value placed on animal products. For most of the past 10,000 years, animal proteins have been a luxury, which only the rich and the wealthy bourgeoisie could indulge in every day. The exercise of the privilege of eating meat has sometimes taken decadent forms. In Byzantium (now Constantinople) there was a tradition of serving a whole roasted sheep with live starlings in its stomach cavity. Elsewhere, meat, because of its scarcity, remained an obsession, a symbol of unimagined abundance. In the famous painting by Pieter Breughel the Elder called "The Land of Cockaigne," a caricature of paradise, we see a pig depicted as a kind of medieval fast food, walking about with a knife in its back.

The best way to regulate scarcity is to impose limits on consumption. In the Middle Ages, during the many fast days, people were sometimes allowed to eat fish but not meat. "Carnival," the binge before the start of the long fast in the run-up to Easter, is a word derived from *"carne vale,"* farewell to the flesh. The terrible magnitude of the Black Death in the fourteenth century paradoxically presented a chance to eat more meat. There were fewer people to feed and therefore more farmland was available per person; at the same time fewer farm laborers were able to work the fields, resulting in a tendency to concentrate on animal husbandry. The net result was a rise in food prices. Several centuries later, increasing urbanization meant that more and more people found themselves without any access to animal protein. They were unable to hunt, and even keeping chickens was problematic. So the consumption of meat began to fall again, and from the start of the Industrial Revolution it fell even further.

Over the past two decades we have seen an unprecedented rise in the consumption of meat, dairy products, and—to a lesser degree—fish, especially in the developing economies. Since 1950 world cattle stocks have quadrupled. The consumption of animal proteins grows as incomes rise. The connection is in the form of an "S," with consumption increasing gradually, then speeding up before flattening out at an annual income of about $10,000 a head. People with low incomes consume little meat, but as soon as they start to earn more, their consumption increases rapidly. Only with very high incomes in OECD countries do we see a slight decline in meat consumption among the middle class, at least as far as the number of calories derived from meat is concerned. In parallel with the growth of meat consumption, a shift toward higher quality meat takes place, with more beefsteak and above all less pork, and higher consumption of meats that are seen as healthier, such as chicken and turkey.

So we eat meat (and fish) because we are the descendants of carnivores and omnivores who developed a meaty diet 2.5 million years ago. Nevertheless, the consumption of meat has varied greatly in both amount and type, depending on availability, price, and preference or taste. Only Hindu societies, especially in India, have deliberately avoided eating meat on a large scale and over a long period, irrespective of availability. India did not start out as a vegetarian society; the oldest Vedic texts frequently mention meat eating. That changed radically over the course of a few centuries, as is clear from the pronounced aversion to violence expressed in the Upanishads. Vegetarianism is a logical consequence of the Hindu conviction that animals and humans are part of the same system, and that one of the ways a person may return after death is in a new life as an animal. Meat eating therefore seems very much like cannibalism. This is confirmed in the Ramayana, where apes appear as surrogate humans with the power of speech. Reincarnation goes hand in hand with *ahimsa*, basic nonviolence, which applies to animals as well as to humans and therefore precludes both animal sacrifice and slaughter. It does not involve any intrinsic concern for animal welfare. The norm of purity among the Brahmins and other groups forbids not only meat and fish but also onions, tomatoes, and other products, quite apart from further restrictions during fasting.

In the philosophy of reincarnation, the cow is the symbol of peace and selfless generosity, since it is the only animal that by giving milk can feed a person without dying. There may be another, material, reason for the taboo on eating beef. Oxen, buffalo, and other draft animals are essential in irrigated agriculture, which requires the ploughing of extremely heavy soils. Furthermore, their efforts make them inedible. This is confirmed in the Indian constitution, which not only forbids the slaughter of cows, calves, and other milk-giving animals but of draft animals too. Yet despite what many Westerners think, far from all Indians are vegetarians. No more than 25–40 percent decline to eat beef, and other meats are allowed. Vegetarianism is therefore more than anything an ideal, most strictly adhered to by the highest castes and especially by the Jain.

Essential Nutrients

The second explanation for human consumption of meat and dairy products is that from a physiological point of view, we need animal proteins, and without the concentrated nutrients derived from animals we might not have become what we are. Proteins are made from amino acids, and essential amino acids are those that our bodies cannot make for themselves but need to derive from food. Without proteins and amino acids there is no life at all.

Animal products contain different proteins from foods derived from plants, and they have a higher protein content than the latter. Yet for the world as a whole, plants are still the most important source of proteins, especially three grains: wheat, rice, and corn. Even in Europe, grains still meet a quarter of the protein requirement, while in low-income countries the proportion is far higher. Humans need about 0.8 grams of protein per kilogram of body weight daily. Those who eat no meat but derive protein from dairy products need not worry about the effects on their health and welfare in the long term. Vegans, who take their proteins purely from plant sources, have to eat both more varied food and more of it if they are to consume all the amino acids they need.

However important proteins may be, there are other things humans require. One reason almost all cultures have developed a liking for meat is that other essential nutrients, such as minerals and vitamins, are present in meat and dairy products in a form that is concentrated and easy to absorb. Useful minerals such as iron, as well as vitamins A and D, for example, are available elsewhere, but meat is almost indispensable as a source of iron that can be taken up readily by the human body. A carefully balanced and varied vegetarian diet can in theory achieve comparable levels, although for the nonexpert achieving this is not always easy. As we know from Popeye, we can become strong as oxen by eating spinach. But with an ageing population, the importance of a source of minerals and proteins that is concentrated, easily absorbed, and readily consumed is increasing, and in that sense dairy products are superior to both meat and fish.

Almost everywhere, with the exception of strictly vegetarian Indian population groups, there is a belief that meat is particularly strength-giving because of its composition. Many myths surround these special properties. As tradition among the Ashkenazi Jews would have it, chicken soup is the only substance capable of combating the influenza virus, while in Jewish households on the Iberian peninsula the traditional taboo on pork may occasionally be broken to help sick people recuperate, ideally in the form of the refined pata negra ham.

The only nutrient found almost exclusively in animal products is vitamin B12, mainly in the form of cyanocobalamin. Small amounts can be found in some yeasts and a few algae and seaweeds, so strict vegans can obtain it from Marmite, or from Vegemite to which vitamin B12 is added, although they will have to eat a fair quantity every day. Certain types of polyunsaturated fatty acids, omega-3 and omega-6 (alpha-linoleic acid and linoleic acid, respectively), cannot be made by the human body; they are derived from fatty fish and to a lesser extent the meat of grazing animals. Neither source actually manufactures these substances, incidentally, but must derive them in turn from, respectively, algae and grass.

Dairy products contain extremely diverse quantities of nutrients, from the very fatty protein-rich reindeer milk to low-fat buttermilk and cheese made from semi-skimmed cow's milk. The distribution of dairy products varies, depending on the availability of milk-producing animals and the related ability to digest milk. Goat's milk contains less lactose than cow's milk. Storage life is another factor relevant to availability. It explains the centuries-old preference for cheese, which is after all nothing other than milk in a different form. Cheese may have been discovered by accident, when milk was transported in the stomachs of slaughtered animals that still contained rennet, a key component of which is the enzyme chymosin. Archaeological remains of sieves suggest that cheese may have been made in the Alps more than 5,000 years ago.

In short, the quantity, quality, and absorbability of a number of essential nutrients—including proteins, iron, and fatty acids—are greater in animal products than in foods derived from plants. It is owing to our almost continual partiality for meat and fish that as humans we have become bigger and bigger, with long bones and a broad skeleton, with enhanced resistance to disease, greater physical strength, and a higher survival rate among newborns. In that sense the consumption of animal products has undoubtedly been a successful human strategy.

But we know that results attained in the past do not guarantee positive outcomes in the future. In Europe we currently consume an average of 100 grams of protein per person per day, which is more than we need. Animal sources account for 60 percent of this protein. High protein consumption, especially high consumption of red meat combined with saturated fats, is associated with chronic ailments, such as cardiovascular disease, as well as certain types of cancer. Incidentally, in Europe the consumption of red meat is still lower than in the United States and parts of South America.

Meat as an Unavoidable By-Product

As well as the evolutionary and the physiological there is a third and at least equally important reason people eat animal products, particularly meat: we are able to produce it and sometimes have to. In some situations we have no choice: we cannot preclude the production of meat or we cannot avoid engaging in the production of meat and dairy products. In the former case meat is the by-product of the keeping of animals for other purposes; in the latter case there is no other way of using the land except as pasture.

The very earliest domestications of animals, 8,000 to 10,000 years ago, were focused on goats and sheep. Wool, for clothes and household goods, was the main reason, but it soon became clear that whoever wants wool will get meat as a derivative. Milk production was a second goal of domestication, and if we are to obtain milk, lambs or kids must be born. So at first unintentionally and later deliberately, meat became part of the diet. The liking for meat increased as it became clear that sheep's meat is nutritious and high in calories. Keeping sheep for their mutton became a new activity.

A second situation in which meat and dairy foods are by-products arose with the domestication of cattle several millennia later. In the evolution of agriculture, cows, more even than sheep and goats, were essential, both as providers of manure and as draft animals. Without animal manure the same piece of land can hardly ever be farmed for years on end, even with the low yields of those days. The need for manure was the main reason for keeping animals. Similarly, buffalo meat was a by-product of the traditional draft animals of the Indian subcontinent and Southeast Asia. In the dairy industry these reasons remain relevant today: without calves, and therefore veal, there will be no milk. It's no different with mixed farms, where arable farming and livestock keeping are combined. In the Netherlands, such farms produce 90 percent of the milk and 70 percent of the country's mutton, lamb, and goat's meat. Even for specialized herdsmen, meat is not the primary focus, because livestock are their walking capital. Historically meat is less often the product about which everything revolves than a spin-off of other ways in which animals are used.

By the same token, much of our meat is the residue of the production of high-quality meats such as steak. The processing of waste from meat production increases the efficiency of the use of grasslands, feed, and animals, so it ought to be encouraged rather than banned. It is in this light that we should see the rise of the hamburger, not as a goal in itself but as a cleverly devised use for an unavoidable by-product of farming, namely, meat that cannot be sold in any other form. It may seem counterintuitive, but restrictions on the hamburger and other ways of using "residual meat" (some forms of sausage; manufactured pizzas and soups) might lead to more scarcity rather than less, because both land and animals would be less efficiently used. The hamburger is the ideal recycler. In addition, today people are increasingly reluctant to eat offal, although it is the richest source of nutrients. Destroying or recycling it, in cat food, for example, means that nutrients are removed from the human food chain.

––––––––––

Meat is therefore sometimes either a by-product or a necessity. Large areas of the world are mainly suitable as pasture. About 30 percent of the surface of the earth, with the exception of Antarctica, is connected in one way or another with the farming of livestock, whether directly, for grazing, or indirectly (a third of it) as land used to produce feed. In areas with erratic, seasonal rainfall, whether or not in combination with infertile soils (such as the pampas in Argentina and much of Australia), or with long periods of cold (the Alps, Mongolia), or large differences between day and night temperature (as in the Andes), or a high water table (such as the wet peat soils of the Dutch province of Friesland) as well as much of the Middle East, the most productive and often the only way to grow food is by grazing herds of ruminants, be they cattle, sheep, goats, or such locally important animals as dromedaries or llamas. In these situations, meat is the unavoidable outcome of land usage, because grazing is the only means by which the proteins from the natural vegetation can be made available to humans. If they are properly managed, grazing animals cause less harm to biodiversity and the soil than the growing of crops.

Over the course of history, humankind has domesticated two types of animal. On the one hand we have cows, goats, and sheep, which have more than one stomach. Known as ruminants, they predigest plants and therefore do not compete with humans. On the other hand there are such creatures as ducks, pigs, and chickens, which are monogastric (meaning they have one stomach) and therefore do compete with us. They eat what we eat—grains and proteins—and they require more water than do ruminants. Grazing animals need space, all the more if the grassland is of low quality. Supplementary feeding with feed grown elsewhere, sometimes even on another continent, makes it possible to keep the animals in their stalls and to intensify production. Even chickens, ducks, and pigs, which naturally forage for food, have been increasingly kept indoors worldwide over the past few decades, so that they convert their food into meat more efficiently. Everywhere the growth of cities and changing diets in the second half of the twentieth century have led to a huge expansion of the livestock industry, and the proportion of monogastric livestock is still increasing. The outcome of the intensification of production is today's bio-industry, with its worldwide tentacles and its trade in cattle feed from South America to Southeast Asia and especially China. Half the pigs on earth live in China, Thailand, and Vietnam.

Animal Proteins Have a Place in Almost All Cultures

The final reason we eat meat is habit and custom. Over the centuries meat and dairy products have gradually become part of any number of cultural traditions with their own norms and values, which regulate and reinforce their consumption. This is especially true of meat, which is part of the human diet all over the world, and of eggs, which are eaten frequently in most places; but it is rather less relevant to milk products, as they are by no means in use everywhere. Cultural values anchor the biological value of meat and dairy.

It was in Australia that I first became aware of how important meat is for humans. I was minding a house and thought I'd be doing the owners, who were about to leave for a trip to the outback, a favor by preparing breakfast for them. As far as I was concerned it was a delicious and well-balanced meal, with a soft-boiled egg, croissants, and muesli. My hosts consumed it all with relish, then departed with the words: "Fortunately we'll still have time for a steak in the village, to keep us going on the journey." Breakfast without meat is no breakfast. It's no different in rural Ireland. In all the pubs there, breakfast is a mixed grill: large quantities of fried sausage, bacon, and other meat. Until a decade or so ago, most people in rich Western countries believed that a warm meal should always include meat.

As a biological species people limit themselves to a mere fraction of the available sources of animal protein. Which particular meat and dairy products are consumed is genetically, ecologically, but above all culturally determined. It is genetically determined in the sense that many species cannot be kept as herd animals, such as antelope. We can eat their flesh, but they have not been domesticated. The ecological limitations are simple: in the Netherlands there have never been any dromedaries or kangaroos, so the Dutch do not eat them. No ostriches are found in the wild there either, but because of the country's historic ties with South Africa, they have been on the menu at the more adventurous restaurants for a decade or more. We eat whatever is going: animals that have been domesticated and, to a lesser extent, meat acquired by hunting and then imported.

Contacts between cultures through migration and trade—first regional, later global—removed the original ecological boundaries. In theory this brought new proteins within reach. One of the earliest examples is the spread of the domesticated pig from the Middle East. It reached northern France 6,000 years ago. What arrived was not merely the animal but the idea that domestication was possible. Soon local wild swine had been domesticated as well, and they replaced the "foreign" sort.

The first great voyages of discovery and sixteenth-century international trade brought two previously unknown animal species to Europe, the turkey and the Muscovy duck. By similar means, cows, goats, chickens, and sheep were taken to North and South America. The old and new ecological worlds, separated until then, were bound together for good from that moment on.

The strong growth of world trade toward the end of the twentieth century perpetuated this trend. The main effect of trade is to increase the volume of goods available; it rarely brings new animal species to our plates. These days our diets are no longer determined by what is available locally. Now that products can be brought to the supermarket by plane and truck within two days, we can choose anything that is on the market. The Dutch have an old saying: what the farmer doesn't know, he won't eat. That may once have been true of farmers, but it certainly does not apply to the twenty-first-century consumer. People in developed countries now eat beef from Argentina and prawns from Thailand. Aside from a little ostrich or crocodile, however, there has been no significant growth in the number of new animals introduced to diets in Europe and rich countries elsewhere. Kangaroos and antelope, from Australia and Africa, respectively, are rarely found on restaurant menus outside their own ecological areas. They probably have too great a cuddliness quotient to become popular as meat in Europe and America. This Bambi effect also applies to fallow deer, which are kept in European parks. All the same, there is no historical reason to assume that in the long term the current culturally determined preference for certain animal species and sources of animal protein will never shift.

So although trade has largely done away with ecological limitations, cultural differences remain relatively strong. Cultural traditions and aversions are in fact particularly stubborn when it comes to animal products, in contrast to items derived from plants. It's easier to get consumers to switch to kiwis and avocados than to fried grasshoppers or crocodile liver. As a result we see huge differences in consumption, even between northern and southern Europe, and they can be traced back directly to centuries-old feeding patterns. The Irish get less than two grams of protein per day from eggs, the French more than double that, Italians eat the most offal, and the Dutch are by far the biggest milk drinkers in the world.

These ancient patterns of animal consumption do not mean that diverse beliefs and feelings about meat remain constant through time. In the past few decades our choices have reflected changing cultural values, secularization (less fasting, fewer dietary rules), and concern about food safety and animal welfare. Quail and small songbirds were eaten all over Europe in the past. The practice is still common in France and Italy, but not in northwestern Europe. In former centuries the elites of Asia and Europe ate swans, which we would now find shocking. The reverse, a new openness, has arrived as well. In the Netherlands your local café may well serve snails these days, which would have disgusted most people half a century ago. In today's top restaurants, offal is cautiously being consumed again, including tripe, brains, and kidneys, items that horrify many people and in many cases were once seen as the food of the poor.

The boundaries between acceptable and unacceptable nevertheless remain firm. Marinated dogs and cats are absolutely taboo in the Western world, partly because pets live close to people and are sometimes experienced as full members of the family. The same applies, for other reasons, to fried moles, horse milk, and snake's eggs, foods that are enjoyed in Asia. Raw lapwing eggs are a good example of food gathered from the wild. Until quite recently, the finding of the first egg of the season was publicly celebrated in the Netherlands, but most Dutch people no longer touch them. Python prompts disgust, although from my own experience I can tell you that python in tomato sauce, which was once prepared for me from one that my gardener had caught, tastes like a cross between chicken and freshwater fish. I wouldn't go out of my way for it again, but it was certainly edible. We can discuss matters of taste, but they are an expression of culture. Despite small changes—offal, ostrich—most of our old preferences seem unalterable, in the short term at least. During an outbreak of swine fever in the Netherlands in the 1990s, consumption of pork among the Dutch fell only briefly, soon returning to its old level. Consternation at the slaughter of goats as a consequence of the Q fever that broke out in the Netherlands at the start of this century (a disease transmissible to humans) did not lead to avoidance of goat's cheese by the Dutch consumer. Similarly, mad cow disease has not led to a substantial reduction in demand for beef in Britain.

The culturally determined liking for meat is less pronounced in women than in men. Historically, in times of scarcity, the most nourishing food went to men and boys, and still today women express less of a preference for meat than do men. This difference reflects the fact that modern women are more conscious than men of the relationship between food and health (and appearance). If I go out to eat at a restaurant with a woman, I can be almost certain that she will choose fish or a vegetarian dish. If women do choose meat, they generally want smaller portions, partly because they need fewer calories. Women also consume less milk and fewer eggs than do men.

The general assumption is that men associate meat more directly with strength and heroism than women do. Nevertheless, it is hard to attribute specific psychological characteristics to meat eaters. The idea that they are less respectful toward others, more aggressive and more egotistical, or even have a liking for discipline and order, turns out to be a myth. It's possible that fervent meat lovers classify edible animals as low on the scale of things to be valued and experience less empathy for them. The stereotypical association of male courage and virility with large quantities of red meat certainly exists. The introduction of the Quarter Pounder as a larger-sized hamburger was a carefully considered step aimed at freeing the hamburger from its image as a family meal and turning it into food for tough young men. Who knows, perhaps the fact that more and more women are choosing to work in cattle farming and as vets will soon start to affect public perception of meat and animals.

More than any other foodstuffs, meat and fish—in other words, animal proteins—are linked to religious and moral codes and taboos. There is probably no religion on earth without rules governing the consumption of meat and fish. This reflects their costliness and importance, but also our ambivalence about the killing of animals, especially warm-blooded animals. Many religions have detailed classifications of meat, fish, and dairy products, whether wild or domesticated, and rules about how animals are to be slaughtered, which parts are to be eaten, and by whom. These classifications are based on complex worldviews with their own internal logic concerning the place of humans in the world, moral and religious purity, and good and evil. Sometimes we can trace some of that logic back to scientific principles, but far from always. In any case, the emergence and persistence of taboos confirms the role of the group and the identity of the individual. Such prescriptions and prohibitions resist simple, one-dimensional explanations involving, for example, hygiene. The perception of pork as "unclean" in the Judeo-Islamic tradition cannot be put down to the risk of parasitic infection with the larva of the round-worm (usually the nematode *Trichinella spiralis*) from raw or undercooked meat, because the parasite occurs in other meats that are not forbidden.

Taboos surrounding animal products gain an extra dimension in the light of the prehistory of humankind as a carnivore and the paradise story. In the first book of the Bible we read that as soon as Adam and Eve were created, God told them what they could eat. God said: "I give you every seed-bearing plant on the face of the whole earth and every tree that has fruit with seed in it. They will be yours for food." (Genesis 1: 29). So despite the abundance of wild and tame animals in paradise, and despite the long evolution of humans as hunters, they are not allowed to eat the animals. In other words, the first religiously prescribed diet was vegetarian, not because of any shortage but by deliberate choice. For some groups this is still reason enough to claim that eating meat is wrong. There is even a movement among American preachers that has developed a raw food diet based on Genesis.

In the Bible, however, the vegetarian diet is superseded. According to tradition, two millennia later—after the flood—God decides on a change in food policy and speaks to Noah: "Everything that lives and moves about will be food for you. Just as I gave you the green plants, I now give you everything." (Genesis 9:3). Of course Jewish commentators have looked for a sound agricultural explanation for this radical change of course, writing that God knows that after the flood it will be a long time before the earth dries out sufficiently for cereal crops to be grown again. So humankind must switch to eating everything that moves. With one exception: God says nothing about the option of a diet of aquatic plants and fish, although you would think it might be the obvious solution after a flood. Instead he gives permission to regard everything that moves as meat. Only two restrictions are placed on such food in the Bible: meat that still contains blood may not be eaten, and neither may fat derived from animals. Later many other rules followed, which collectively make up the dietary laws, laying down which foods are suitable, or allowed (known respectively as kosher and halal). These laws are made yet more detailed by the classification of animals according to the shape of their hooves or whether they are ruminants.

That we still have comparable classifications today is clear from the expression "neither fish nor fowl." It says something about the fact that organisms that fail to fit into a category, such as slugs and jellyfish, are unattractive to us. Metaphorically, the saying "neither fish nor fowl" implies an ambiguity, ambivalence, or a lack of clarity.

Meat is simultaneously the most desirable type of food and the type most bounded by taboos, rules, and a sense of disgust. Within the rules, meat means to most people mainly status and enjoyment. A rich person eats meat; an even richer person eats the best, most uncommon meat. In Western Europe "best" means beefsteak or big game, such as venison and wild boar. Restaurant menus demonstrate the growing appreciation of meat as a superluxury product with a stated origin, by analogy with wine: Texel lamb, poulet de Bresse, Parma ham, or better still pata negra from wild Iberian pigs. The liking for meat as a luxury product exists everywhere, with the obvious exception of India, where the higher classes are demonstratively "pure" and eat no meat. It is a feature of human culture that almost everyone has a preference for meat, except for a growing but still small group of vegetarians. Meat, or the refusal of it, and the nature of the meat eaten still confirm the identity of the diner. In classical Greece, members of the Pythagorean sect were vegetarians, thereby indicating that they did not accept the rules of the city-state. The relationship between meat and identity is far weaker with dairy products, which are less sensitive to status and rarely bound by proscriptions, with the exception of eggs.

So most of humanity eats meat and dairy products regularly, often daily, because we are omnivores, because they chime with our evolutionary and cultural preferences, and because we can produce meat and in some cases have to. Human history is closely bound up with meat and in some regions, including northwestern Europe, with dairy produce. We also consume animal proteins because the worldwide bio-industry has made them cheap and available to all.

Unease and Change

Several years ago, designer Christien Meindertsma set up a project about an individual pig, PIG 05049, and the 184 products in which the remains of that one slaughtered pig were incorporated or for which pig products (especially gelatin) were needed during the manufacturing process—from liquorice to toothpaste, photographic paper to heart valves. In a series of photographs she made visible, by artistic means, something that remains hidden from almost all of us: the astonishingly complex interconnectedness between our lives today and animal products. Animals give us not only milk, butter, cheese, wool, leather, and meat (including all that residual meat that ends up in hamburgers and other meat products) but all kinds of other things too. As ever, little is wasted, but the uses have become far more diverse.

A movement is coming into being that radically rejects the keeping of animals that live purely to meet our needs, including those that produce products it's hard to imagine modern life without, such as leather for shoes, furniture, and bags, or the ubiquitous gelatin from skin, bones, and other parts, which is used in sweets, medicines, and cosmetics. Opponents of those who object to the slaughter of animals like to point to what they call "hypocrisy": moral indignation about the eating of meat in those who nevertheless benefit from the by-products of meat production.

We might indeed wonder what future archaeologists will think if they ever dig up the physical and virtual remains of cities in which they find citizens who are pathologically obese; battery cages; vast abattoirs; and factories that transform animal remains into all kinds of things, including unrecognizable, pink-dyed, plastic-wrapped food items. What will they think of the felled forests, the eroded pastures, the increasing emissions of greenhouse gases by livestock and the growing of feed crops? They will wonder what drove us, what kind of culture produced all this, in short what induced people to behave as they did at the start of the twenty-first century.

It is the scale, the transportation over long distances of feed and animals, the conditions in which animals live, and the effects on the environment that give us—in the rich countries at least—more and more reason to stop and think about the consequences of our liking for meat. Food and power are closely connected, and the relationship between people and the providers of animal proteins, the animals themselves, is one of power. We alone determine how and how long the animals live, and if we put them in battery cages or closed stalls, we can control their environment totally. In our dominance over other species, which began with the domestication of crops, lies the evolutionary success of the human species. But where the complete dominion over plants and their environment in greenhouses barely prompts a moral reaction at all (although it is becoming clear that plants can experience stress), control over animals meets resistance because of its scale and its inhumanity. The efficiency with which, biologically speaking, we control not just the living conditions of animals but their genetics, makes us increasingly uneasy, as does the scale on which livestock businesses operate. However logical as the next step toward greater efficiency, the move toward ever larger dairy facilities and feeding lots does not have the support of the public. The cost of our evolutionary success seems far too high—in theory, that is; the price tag in the supermarket usually remains the deciding factor when it comes to what meat to buy.

There are countless ethical and moral objections to the keeping of animals in inhumane conditions and to the killing of animals purely to satisfy our hunger for animal products. Many of these objections have been expressed frequently down the years, by famous vegetarians, including Voltaire. But the form taken by current objections is new. Abstract philosophical principles are less central now that more people identify with the individual animal, for example, in reportage that follows the short life and death of one or two chickens or lambs. Then there are those who oppose the artificial insemination of cows, believing that a cow has a right to pleasure, or at the very least to "real" insemination by a bull (forgetting that the weight of today's prize bull might well crush the poor cow). Our relationship with our pets is increasingly normative. For generations they have been included in family portraits. In some households they sit at the table to eat like members of the family, and their deaths can lead to more grief, or at least more expressible grief, than the death of a partner. From far-off cities, the same norms of cuddliness are projected onto domesticated farm animals as are applied to pets.

Everywhere there is a growing distance between the consumer and the animal, first as a living creature, then dead and as food, processed or otherwise. That distance from the reality of production creates room for the consumer to see the animal as an individual, with emotions comparable to our own. So we convince ourselves that cows are "happy" in meadows, while the chicken surrounded by others in battery cages has come to symbolize the loneliness of the individual in a mass society, the futility of human aspirations. The typically Western conviction that an animal is "innocent" and therefore can look "soulful"—as if it too had a soul—proves just how much we have come to see them as human.

The anthropomorphic and ethical approach to animals also prompts us to go in search of those responsible for the unhappiness and exploitation of animals. We do not need to look far; it is surely the modern bio-industry. The tone of resistance to intensive cattle farming and slaughter has become harsher and in some cases more radical. We are growing used to such slogans as "Meat is murder" and "Are clothes to kill for?"

In the Netherlands a political party has been established that aspires primarily or even exclusively to represent the interests of animals. It seems to me no accident that the Partij voor de Dieren ("Party for the Animals") has emerged in the Netherlands, that densely populated, highly successful country where people cannot escape the reality of intensive meat production and where increases in scale are so visible (and until recently so smellable) in the landscape. A divide is opening up such that on the one hand cattle farming is becoming increasingly professional and animals are seen primarily as the means of production, and on the other hand the general public has a growing tendency to regard animals as more or less human. After all, were the animals not created along with us? Do they not come from the same paradise? Do they not feel almost the same things as we do? They're just like us, and we're not cannibals—are we?

The idea that animals have rights or even, as some claim, should be liberated, by analogy with women and slaves, is entirely in keeping with this development, certainly in Europe, North America, and some other OECD countries. Although the legal basis for animal rights has not yet fully crystallized, more and more people agree with the assertion that an animal is not an instrument for our use or simply a production factor. The theory of evolution tells us that animals and humans share many characteristics, not just physical features but—certainly in the case of warm-blooded animals—such emotions as altruism that we formerly thought of as exclusively human. The recognition of the need to protect animals has already led to extensive legislation. Animal welfare is seen as primarily a Western achievement, but we should not allow ourselves to forget that its history has a dark side. The most advanced laws for the benefit of animals originated in the Germany of the 1930s.

The relationship between humankind and livestock is seen as less problematic as long as there is little distance between farm and fork, in a geographical and technical sense. In earlier centuries that was the case; in fact it remained so until about fifty years ago. Carcasses were hung in butcher's shops in plain sight, and butchers served their customers wearing blood-smeared aprons. Many still lifes show a table on which the animal is presented in a recognizable form. In a painting by Frans Snijders from the mid-seventeenth century, one of many of its type, we see a dead deer, gutted but otherwise intact, next to the head of a wild boar and a whole lobster, all on an amply laden table. We certainly do not want to see our meat like that any longer. The time when rabbits were hung by their furry paws in the window of the poulterer's (another forgotten trade) is long past in much of Western Europe and North America. We have systematically removed butchery entirely from the view of the consumer, to the point that meat is packed in plastic on neutral pink pads or, even more often, processed into sauces and ready meals (ready-made meals), so that nothing is left to remind us of the animal.

In rich countries protests against the agro-industry go hand in hand with the glorification of tradition, of the farmer who knows all the cows in the herd and slaughters them on the farm, using every part of the animal. In France and southern Europe there is little hostility to meat as such, which has always been associated with authenticity—*localité* and *terroir*—in other words, local produce and traditional recipes. Instead opposition to meat consumption is opposition to large-scale farming and globalization. We like to ignore the fact that mass slaughter has happened before, not only of East African game but of the North American bison. Inhumane practices in abattoirs were denounced in the late nineteenth century, especially in Chicago. What is new is that protest is now accompanied by more scientific suggestions for ways of preventing animal suffering, along with greater openness in the media and a lack of knowledge among much of the population about methods of production and slaughter.

We want to avoid seeing meat as the consequence of the recognizable death of animals, just as we want to avoid the thought that frolicking lambs will inevitably be transformed into lamb chops. Ideally we would like to consume meat but no longer as meat. Typical is the latest culinary fashion aimed at making food completely unrecognizable through molecular cuisine: bite-sized pieces that no longer resemble what they are and no longer have any structure. They enable us to banish the thought that we are descended from meat-eating hominids with powerful jaw muscles.

In a stubborn form of cognitive dissonance, many people are concerned and express their outrage at the production methods of meat and dairy products, but at the same time they close their minds to the causes and take advantage of the low prices that result from those production methods. The willed blindness of consumers in rich countries makes it possible for the majority of the population to profit from the abundance of cheap animal products while not knowing the unpleasant details. We end up with a difficult balancing act, cherishing the romantic image of the small famer looking after farm animals as if they were beloved pets, as opposed to the horrors of the battery cages and abattoirs used by that very same farmer. Both images are a distortion. The old-fashioned farmer did not treat farm animals as if they were children, and conditions in large-scale meat-production facilities, abattoirs included, have improved considerably in recent years. We also need to recognize that protest against industrial farming is very much tied to place, class, and time. It barely exists at all in countries where protein consumption is low and pets may end up in a casserole when need becomes acute.

Traditional and Ritual Slaughter

Many societies have rituals in which animals are asked for forgiveness before being slaughtered. But such customs do not automatically go together with more tender-heartedness at the moment of killing or the avoidance of animal suffering. In poor countries, crowds gather at places where slaughter takes place, where living and dead animals are evaluated and offered for sale. There are no grounds at all for praising traditional methods of slaughter, given the countless tales of screeching piglets and blood-drenched scenes in the courtyards of the past.

In recent years the Netherlands has seen a wide-ranging debate about ritual slaughter, and a similar controversy has raged in France. The Dutch Partij voor de Dieren introduced a bill to forbid ritual slaughter without stunning, or rather to end the exception made for Islamic and Jewish slaughterers. They enjoy an exceptional position in this sense in Britain as well, with slaughter without stunning banned by law except in the case of those two groups. Numerically, ritual slaughter is an insignificant issue, accounting for a total of less than 1 percent of animals slaughtered in the Netherlands (the number slaughtered in conformity with Jewish rites accounts for less than 0.1 percent). The argument was that freedom of religion should not lead to "additional and unnecessary animal suffering." Representatives of the Jewish and Islamic communities claimed that eating kosher and halal meat was an indispensable part of their identities.

The debate turned on the question of which method of slaughter caused the least pain. According to Jewish and Islamic slaughterers, the animal dies almost immediately after the severing of the carotid artery and the windpipe. There is also criticism of the conventional methods of stunning animals in abattoirs by electric shock, a blow to the head, or a bolt driven into the brain, which are no more animal-friendly. Alternatives are more expensive or little better. Administering a mixture of CO_2 and carbon monoxide, possibly with a little oxygen as well, causes a slower and still not entirely pain-free death.

According to Jewish ritual, in fact, animal welfare is central. The animal is taken aside a day before slaughter and put in a quiet place. The knife must not be sharpened within sight of the animal, which must also not be allowed to witness the slaughter of another animal. This shows that the concept of animal welfare, far from being a twentieth-century invention, goes back to ancient times. The appeal to tradition as an argument for ritual slaughter is less convincing, because even though tradition is essential for identity, it is not set in stone. Those who propose banning ritual slaughter have another argument at their disposal: anyone who believes meat from animals stunned before slaughter is haram or *treif* (not kosher) should simply become a vegetarian.

In Judaism and Islam the ritual slaughterer will ideally be trained to treat the animal with respect and avoid suffering prior to the moment of death. In the Jewish tradition this is strictly supervised, in theory, but there is often a gap between the rule and its application. Little objective comparative research has been done on what the animal actually experiences, nor has there been research on whether a difference exists in practice between Islamic and Jewish slaughter. Then there is the question of whether an animal experiences more stress prior to slaughter in the legally permitted system than in the ritual form. An animal that is calm and approached calmly will surely feel less distress than one carried into the abattoir on a conveyor belt. In the end what matters is not just slaughter without stunning but the way in which an animal is treated throughout its life.

––––––––––

The example of slaughter without stunning raises a far broader question. Were it to be banned in one country, the result might be an increase in meat imports from abroad. After all, the practice is allowed almost everywhere, with the exception of a few countries, such as Finland and New Zealand (which do not have significant Muslim or Jewish minorities). It is conceivable that conditions for animals in stalls and abattoirs in countries where ritual slaughter is not banned might be worse. Animal welfare is currently not an acceptable reason for blocking the import of meat, according to the rules of the World Trade Organization. Unilateral measures might lead to people in one country salving their consciences by forbidding unpleasant practices at home while benefiting from the fact that they are allowed elsewhere.

Dangers of Livestock Farming

Animal welfare, slaughter, and animal rights are the things that most concern the urban consumer in the West, but attention is turning to other problems in livestock farming. Partly because of shocking statistics of the type "a steak is as bad for the environment as flying twelve kilometers," the impression has taken hold that meat and dairy products are inherently problematic.

The question that frequently arises is: have we reached the limits of livestock production and should a limit be set on the number of animals kept for this purpose? Some even say that livestock farming should be made independent of exports and imports, with each country becoming self-sufficient. That would be impossible, because many countries are utterly dependent on imported cattle feed. In fact there are plenty of arguments against, say, limiting Dutch exports of meat and dairy products, quite apart from the loss of income and employment. The efficiency of production in the Netherlands and similar countries means that the costs to the environment are less than elsewhere. Methane emissions per liter of milk are far lower in the Netherlands than in Ethiopia, for example, and from a global perspective there are convincing reasons for trying to ensure that as far as possible the production of food happens where it is most efficient.

So do we want large-scale industrial production of meat? What rules should be imposed? It is after all the intensity and scale of livestock farming that is causing concern. In the Netherlands the number of agricultural enterprises has halved over the past fifteen years, but the number of chickens and cows has increased. The trend toward an increase in scale can be seen among goat breeders as well, with a doubling of the number of large enterprises over the past fifteen years and almost a tripling of the number of animals each of them owns. Again we see the same dilemma: livestock farming is more efficient in the Netherlands but this brings with it exports and possible risks to public health. Male kids are an inevitable by-product of farming for goat's milk, and until recently there was no market for them at all in the Netherlands. People in southern Europe and tropical countries are happy to eat goat's meat, so they buy Dutch exports. Worldwide, 80 percent of goats are kept in poor conditions with very low yields and considerable damage to vegetation and soil.

The greatest problems of intensive livestock farming in Europe are the manure surplus, which leads to unacceptable concentrations of ammonia in the soil and in surface water; emissions of greenhouse gases; and risks to public health. Energetic attempts are under way to combat the first two. New types of cattle shed, developed in cooperation with environmental organizations, have led to a considerable reduction in emissions of ammonia and greenhouse gases. Yet here our anthropomorphic view of animals clashes with atmospheric chemistry and veterinary science: animals seem "happier" on straw than on concrete, but the use of straw can lead to fermentation and therefore to more emissions and the faster growth of bacteria.

The health risks are now seen by consumers as increasingly serious, as the general public learns about zoonotic diseases, which can be passed from animals to humans. Examples include foot and mouth disease, bovine spongiform encephalopathy (BSE, or "mad cow disease"), Q fever in goats, and possibly the recently discovered Schmallenberg virus. Each of these diseases, which seem to arise with increasing frequency, has a different cause and demands a different set of measures. Migratory birds probably spread the H5N1 strain of bird 'flu from Southeast Asia to other parts of the world, via the Black Sea to the Mediterranean and then along the Atlantic coast into Europe. The transportation of animals transmits infection too. Many people feel their governments have given them insufficient information and intervened too late to tackle the sources of infection. The sense of risk is reinforced by growing concerns about the use of antibiotics and the resulting threat of resistance to them developing in bacteria that affect human health. The animal sector is seen as too close to the pharmaceutical industry, as routinely putting profit above public health, and as having been too complacent for too long before attempting to reduce the use of antibiotics. A succession of crises in the production of animal-based food products (such as infection with dioxins or salmonella) not only in Europe but also in areas of intensive production in Asia has shown that the entire food chain and its relationship with the environment are at stake. Most importantly, better cooperation among veterinary services, doctors, and producers is required.

––––––––

The connection between livestock farming, water shortages, and the loss of biodiversity is complicated. Deforestation to create meadowland, fertilization of pastures, erosion by overgrazing, and the production of manure can each have a detrimental effect on the diversity of species. For example, the number of uncommon species is often enhanced on infertile grassland. It has also been clear for some years that livestock farming makes a considerable contribution to greenhouse gas emissions. Such ruminants as cows and sheep produce methane, one of the most potent of greenhouse gases, three-quarters of which is produced by their breath, the rest by their dung. Laughing gas is also released by manure (as well as by arable farming). The total contribution of livestock farming to greenhouse gases, including CO_2, has been estimated at 18 percent of worldwide emissions. That is more than from motorized traffic, at least if deforestation is, biologically speaking, taken fully into account (and whether it should be is quite controversial; some estimates arrive at half the figure, 9 percent). Deforestation leads to a considerable release of CO_2, but the calculations are complex, because not all deforestation is connected with livestock farming. In the tropics there may be various motivations for deforestation: to assert land rights; to lay roads or build cities; to provide grazing land; or to grow oil palms, eucalyptus, or such feed crops as soy and corn. Moreover, forests grow back. The contribution to greenhouse gases by nonruminants (such as pigs and chickens) is far lower than by cows, where it mostly comes indirectly from CO_2 in the feed. Europe, especially the Netherlands, is a large importer of soybeans and corn as cattle feed.

New Proteins, New Ideas

Worldwide demand for animal products continues to grow, as there are 3.5 billion people on earth who are currently ingesting insufficient proteins and other nutrients. Poor countries will take decades yet to catch up. It has been estimated that to feed 9 billion people in 2050, 75 percent more animal proteins will be needed. In Africa and Southeast Asia the figure is as high as 150 percent. This is considerably more than the projected increase in grain production. There are many reasons to investigate whether this necessary increase in animal proteins could be met by new methods and new products. At the moment what are called "new proteins" are generating a great deal of interest as replacements for animal proteins. These are mainly, though not exclusively, plant proteins that can replace meat, such as those found in soybeans, lupines, and algae, as well as milk proteins. Up to 30 percent of the animal proteins in such processed foods as sausages and cold meats could be replaced with proteins from other sources without the consumer noticing.

Soy is a prime candidate. It is the only plant that approaches meat in its protein composition. The problem is that raw or incompletely processed soy contains substances that inhibit the uptake of proteins. An enzyme known as a trypsin inhibitor makes it impossible or extremely difficult to absorb proteins from soy. Fermentation, common in Southeast Asia (as we see with products, such as tofu, tempé, and soy sauce) solves the problem, although phytase remains, another inhibitor, which can hinder the uptake of calcium and iron. Other sources of protein, such as yeasts and bacteria, may be good alternatives as supplements to a plant-based diet.

Mushrooms are sometimes proposed as an alternative to meat, but their nutritional value is often overestimated, perhaps because a fat mushroom like *Boletus edulis* has a texture rather like that of steak. Meat contains about eight times as much protein as mushrooms, whose proteins are also of a relatively low quality, with few essential amino acids, and are harder to digest. Mushrooms also have low levels of other nutrients and sometimes contain heavy metals. There is little convincing evidence of their health-giving properties for humans. Protein can be garnered from mushrooms for further processing as a meat substitute, and something similar applies to the proteins found in milk, which are already being extracted for all kinds of pharmaceutical applications. They too are used in meat substitutes, in combination with fibers from algae or soybeans. Nuts are another candidate, but they are too expensive and too high in fat to serve as a substitute as yet.

A very different alternative is in vitro meat, but growing meat in the laboratory from muscle cells or stem cells is still impossibly expensive; a 1-kilogram steak would cost about $200,000. Of course, animals cells are needed to start the cultivation of tissue, so this method does not enable us to completely avoid the need to kill or wound animals. In vitro meat will not help us change or increase meat consumption in the short term.

But in theory, it enables us to achieve what no other substitute can, be it soybeans, algae, or insects—namely, the production of a steak. Yet in reality early experiments have produced meat that merely resembles mince and is therefore not superior to vegetable substitutes that can be used in a similar way. There may be a place for in vitro meat with special medicinal properties, for example, as protein-rich food for cancer patients.

Insects are another option. In many cultures they are already regarded as a delicacy. I still vividly recall my first palm weevil larvae, fried as meatballs on a palm oil plantation in Burundi almost thirty years ago. The eating of insects demands a mental step that most Europeans and Americans will not be quick to take, despite the rightly enthusiastic stories told by entomologists. Anyone who does take that step will discover that insects are not just nutritionally valuable, they also can taste very good. An estimated 1,800 species of insect are edible, mostly beetles, ants, caterpillars, grubs (including pupae), grasshoppers, and crickets. In Southeast Asia crickets are already caught for consumption. Insects offer countless advantages. With the exception of termites they emit far fewer greenhouse gases than cows or pigs. Being coldblooded, like frogs and snakes, they convert food more efficiently than warm-blooded animals can. Keeping insects on a large scale poses fewer risks of disease that can be transmitted from animal to human, unless the insects are vectors for pathogens from elsewhere.

Paleontological finds indicate that insects were part of the diet of early hominids. It is interesting that they are also part of Judeo-Christian and Islamic culture. In the Bible grasshoppers are recommended in Leviticus yet forbidden in Deuteronomy. A ban on the eating of insects suggests the existence of a tradition. Such food taboos carry mainly symbolic weight. That is certainly true of the aversion to insects in today's Western culture. We think of them as scary. This is odd, because we eat sea creatures that closely resemble them, such as prawns, lobsters, and glass eels, although we like to call them "seafood" or "fruits de mer" to disguise their animal origins. Incidentally, the Arabic word for "grasshopper" means something like "prawn of the sky."

Insects might make a major contribution in the form of "processed meat" for inclusion in sausages, soups, sauces, or pizzas. This would take them far beyond their niche as a delicacy to replace a proportion of the meat used in those products today. They would work best in combination with plant-based proteins. The meat content of a sausage might be replaced by a combination of 30 percent meat, 35 percent vegetable protein, and 35 percent insect protein. Everywhere in the world, partly as a result of urbanization, people are increasingly eating ready meals (ready-made meals), especially meat dishes, so this substitution might make a tremendous difference.

The importance of insects is not confined to their being an alternative source of protein. Anyone who eats insects develops a new perspective on his or her diet and the degree to which it is normal or natural. Food is not merely a matter of biology or history but of negotiation and choice. Eating insects opens the way to the eating of many other species that are lower down on the food chain, such as snails and algae, which would also help increase world food supplies. The great thing about eating insects is that it makes us conscious of our own place in the food chain and of ancient traditions, of what we take for granted, and of new possibilities.

Warm-blooded animals should not be excluded completely when we consider future supplies of meat. In Australia the consumption of kangaroo meat seems a natural step. Kangaroos produce relatively little methane, and many people appreciate the quality of their meat, partly because of its low fat content. These animals could perhaps be introduced in regions with a comparably dry and warm climate. That remains something for the future, although the prospect of kangaroos hopping across Africa is a cheering one. Horsemeat, although not permitted in Judaism and Islam and abhorrent to the British and others, might yet return to favor.

Initiatives aimed at reducing the distance between producer and consumer are popular. Most people would be able to start a vegetable plot, although that is often not nearly as simple as its advocates seem to believe. Animal husbandry is harder. Most people would have trouble keeping a cow or a goat, let alone milking or slaughtering it, and even keeping chickens is problematic in a city. One recent method of bridging this gulf is by paying to "adopt" an animal, usually a pig or a chicken, whose picture can be found on a website. I fear that not all the adoptive parents realize that at some point their animal must be eaten, even if they have adopted it for the wool. A similar trend is toward attention in the media on individual farmers, which makes the story of food production more personal and accessible, the idea being that if we hear more from farmers, their relationship with consumers will improve. It is a unique selling point to be able to say that dairy products are made on the farm itself rather than in a factory, or that sheep graze outside and can be visited.

———————

Even in livestock farming as it exists now, new ideas are being developed to moderate the effects of the means of production on animal welfare, public health, and the environment. Small-scale farming, however much it may be professed as an ideal, has little chance worldwide. Already 75 percent of poultry live in large-scale production centers. There is no way back, if only because it's impossible to prove that increases in scale equate to increases in stress in animals. The consensus among experts is that the solution lies not with less intensive, smaller-scale farming but with sustainability and careful management. There are countless ways to achieve this, for example, through sustainably produced feed and new ways of processing manure. Introducing certain bacteria into the bowels and guts of ruminants can influence their digestion in such a way that they emit far less methane. Manure surpluses can be effectively controlled by means of better feed and low-emission stalls, and by injecting dung into the ground instead of spreading it on fields. Currently 50–90 percent of the nitrogen and phosphates given to cattle end up in manure. The use of the enzyme phytase in pig feed causes the animal to absorb nutrients far more effectively, leading to savings and to a reduction in environmental damage. The addition of polyphenols to feed has a comparable effect and improves the soil as well.

———————

Another useful initiative is the imposition of a phosphate tax on artificial fertilizer and phosphate emissions, which encourages the development of better techniques. All such attempts come down to better use of water, energy, and other resources. With regard to animal diseases, it is probably not the scale itself that needs to be addressed, but rather hygiene and the possibility of isolating animals in smaller units. Strict guidelines about the use of antibiotics might help prevent an increase in resistance among bacteria harmful to humans, although the livestock industry will probably be in trouble in the long term if no new pharmaceuticals are developed. Feeding animals well can reduce the need for antibiotics. As for damage to landscapes, large feeding lots could be placed in industrial areas rather than in picturesque countryside.

We are also seeing new ideas about how to improve the quality of meat or milk, whether by genetic modification or by other means. These ideas include increased amounts of omega fats, which are found not just in oily fish but also in Iberian pigs and ducks, and increased levels of the vitamins and minerals that are important for the elderly. Science knows no bounds.

———

The search for alternatives and improvements raises questions about science itself. What do we learn from data suggesting that the most efficient production methods are generally those that best meet norms of animal welfare, or that chickens in battery cages have lower levels of stress hormones in their blood and convert food more efficiently than free-range chickens? Who could be left unmoved by the fact that a farmed sow gains 110 kilograms in 120 days and produces twenty-eight young? To some this is sufficient reason to reject science with its own invented norms once and for all. Yet we have to wonder where on the road that began with the first domestication of animals the limits of science and ethics lie. To be even more provocative: should we, again with or without genetic modification, breed animals that manufacture so many endorphins in their brains that their well-being in factory farms can be guaranteed forever? Might that be the future of the debate about animal welfare? Most people will respond with horror, but it wouldn't surprise me if thinking along those lines emerges somewhere in the world fairly soon.

Meat Avoiders, Meat Reducers, and Flexitarians

The high consumption of animal products in rich countries and by the middle class in developing economies reflects a time of plenty. Almost all Europeans eat meat on most days of the week, people in South and North America eat it on average once a day and often several times daily. In rich countries meat is available in large quantities almost everywhere, at a price that continues to fall. In the rest of the world eating meat daily is an ideal, although not achievable for a large proportion of the population. There is no brake on our consumption, and the consequences of that for the environment, animal welfare, and public health are at best unpleasant. We consume the abundance that has been more or less tossed into our laps for several generations now. Our appreciation of animal products, especially meat, or indeed our fierce longing for them, is the consequence of thousands of years if not hundreds of thousands of years of scarcity. We continue to eat something that apparently demands no effort and no sacrifice (material or otherwise), while in truth we need meat only in very modest amounts.

––––––––

Can we adjust this behavior, determined as it is by evolution and culture? Part of the solution lies of course in the means of production. Fortunately there are more and more sustainable options when it comes to reducing pressure on the environment and raising standards of animal welfare. But that is not enough. We know from the automotive industry that technological solutions do not lead to changes in behavior. Our cars are many times more efficient than they were thirty years ago, but we correspondingly drive many more kilometers, so that the positive impact on the environment is zero or less than zero. Adjustments to our systems of producing animal feed are a necessary but not sufficient condition of an improvement in eating patterns. The consumer needs to be central, especially the consumer in wealthier countries, who already consumes enough protein.

In the Netherlands no more than 4.5 percent of people are vegetarians, in Germany perhaps 9 percent, and in Italy 10 percent. In other rich and developing economies, with the exception of India, the figure is far lower. Yet 50 percent of people in Europe say they think more consciously about meat than they used to and are prepared to reduce their consumption of it. Red meat seems to be the target at the moment, while chicken and fish are exempt. The rise of vegetarian butchers who sell meat substitutes and butchers who present meat as a delicacy is undoubtedly helping.

Developments in the rich world do not have a great deal of influence on the growth of demand worldwide, but we can afford to look at possible ways of reducing the consumption of animal products. The options are clear: scrap meat and dairy products from the menu, or reduce consumption of animal proteins, perhaps by replacing them with vegetable products that resemble meat.

Banning the consumption of meat and fish completely would be impossible, and to demonize them would be undesirable. Demonization fails to do justice to the place of meat over thousands of years, and its continued importance for children and others who need additional nutrients. To demonize meat consumption from a single dimension, perhaps from the point of view of the environment, public health, or animal welfare, would be to ignore the desire for meat that exists in almost all cultures. We set meat before guests and give it a special place in feasts and festivities. A ban on meat would also lead to the development of a black market that might feature some truly horrific conditions for both animals and those who work with them.

The question is whether something can shift in the cultural attachment to meat and its iconic significance, at least in regions and groups where too much of it is consumed from the point of view of public health. If eating meat were no longer held in such high esteem, if people on the street or in restaurants were stared at if they consumed vast quantities of meat, such behavior might be reduced. Little by little, such a shift is already being brought about by a health-conscious and environmentally aware elite in rich countries. The number of "flexitarians" and people who prefer to avoid meat is growing. Flexitarians are people who enjoy vegetarian meals and deliberately opt for them but have not given up meat altogether. They often avoid meat or are keen to reduce their consumption of it; they seek alternatives, and when they do eat meat they prefer animal-friendly local produce.

The reduction of meat consumption to, say, 80 grams three times a week is therefore a more realistic option than forgoing it altogether in the medium term. Yet the initiative cannot lie with the consumer alone. Governments must take responsibility too. At the very least, public and semipublic establishments should set a good example by regularly offering exclusively vegetarian meals or cocktail party snacks. If the vegetarian option is presented as the normal option, meat becomes a "special dietary preference" that you need to request explicitly. A serious first step might be a differentiation in rates of sales tax, so that the most ecologically damaging forms of meat production are taxed most heavily and vegetarian foods fall into a category for which tax rates are lowest.

Information about meat and dairy produce that makes clear their effects on and importance for human health might help. Labeling along the lines of "Meat endangers the environment and your health," as some activists have advocated, cannot be justified by science, if only because there are so many sorts of meat production and some countries have no other option but to produce meat and export it. Sometimes activists call for an extra tax on meat. That would be unwise, unless it was a matter of the sales tax rate, since such a tax would disproportionately affect low-income groups, which would then be at greater risk of an unbalanced diet and a lack of essential proteins. Unbalanced diets need to be addressed as a whole.

Anyone who wishes to avoid meat because of concerns about climate change, the environment, health, and animal welfare should also avoid dairy products. Cheese, including sheep's and goat's cheese, is no alternative, because meat is a by-product of the production of milk from which cheese is made. Nor are eggs a vegetarian option, since for eggs you need hens and that inevitably means killing male chicks. Most people do not stop to think that a purely vegetarian diet based on grains also leads to the deaths of countless animals during ploughing and harvesting, and in pest control during storage. Vegetarians have on their hands, inadvertently, the blood of countless mice and birds.

Our attitude toward animal products must ultimately be inspired by what we know, from science but also from history. We are primates and throughout our past, meat and dairy products were scarce and at the same time essential to our survival and our evolution. Animal proteins have made us what we are. This fact is expressed in our cultural and religious convictions. Now, however, a new situation has arisen because of the effects of the scale on which we consume animal meat. We can no longer ignore the impact on the environment, our own health, and the animals themselves. Everywhere a consciousness is growing that the damaging effects of intensive livestock farming on the environment and public health must not be subordinated to economic interests. The way forward will consist of a combination of improvements to classic livestock farming, a reduction in consumption, and the search for alternative sources of protein. This may sound like a case of "neither fish nor fowl," but in my view we do need to curb the casual way we currently deal with the abundance of animal products.

We do not think about meat and the killing of warm-blooded creatures with complete indifference. This was probably the case from the moment humans started to hunt. Dutch artist Berend Strik has created an intriguing work on the subject. He took a photograph of a bloody carcass in a butcher's shop and used deep-red velvet to give it an abstract, three-dimensional depth from which you return to reality with a sense of shock. He makes visible what we do not want to see: the fleshiness of meat and at the same time our inability to resist it. Meat is the ultimate temptation.

SIX

Liquid Paradise: Food from Water

Perhaps it was a sin to kill the fish.... You did not kill a fish only to keep alive
and to sell the fish for food, he thought. You killed him for pride and because
you are a fisherman. You loved him when he was alive and you loved him
after. If you love him, it is not a sin to kill him. Or it is rather more.
ERNEST HEMINGWAY, *The Old Man and the Sea*

Darting Fish and Dark Monsters

In the history of our food, fish, shellfish, and other water creatures occupy
a special place. They're more mysterious than land animals, literally and
figuratively harder to grasp. More often than not they're invisible. Their
way of life, the long distances some of them cover to breed, and the stages
of growth they go through were mysterious for centuries and gave rise
to any number of myths. We've all heard of crosses between people and
fish, like the little mermaid, symbol of the unfulfilled longings of those
who belong neither to the land and humanity nor to the water. Many such
creatures are regarded as dangerous, because they're a departure from the
established order, like the Greek-Roman semidivine Nereids, who can
cause ships to sink purely by their presence. In this context of chaos and
danger there are many sea monsters, starting with Leviathan, the terrible
sea serpent whose prey only God could protect. According to Jewish tradition, the flesh of Leviathan will be served to the righteous at the end of
time. In the Christian Middle Ages this monster represented the devil and
even the mouth of hell. Homer's Odysseus, incidentally, had his hands full
with what was possibly a distant relative, Scylla, a former nymph who had
changed into a terrible sea monster. Creatures of the water, in other words,
are closely associated with evil and therefore evoke mixed feelings. Until
well into the Renaissance, sea monsters were depicted on nautical maps.

Fish has also had a negative reputation since early times because of the
bones, the strong smell, and its short storage life, even if dried, salted, or
smoked. In the Egypt of the pharaohs, for example, fish were eaten by
poor peasants along the banks of the Nile, but they were not used in ritual sacrifice. They are missing from lists of food given to the dead to take
with them to the afterlife.

Yet not everything that comes from the depths is evil. Countless mythical figures are associated with the sea in a positive sense: beautiful Aphrodite was born out of sea foam, and in Buddhism and Hinduism we find kings who fish. The Inuit of Greenland believed that humanity was created by being combed out of the locks of an underwater goddess. Last but not least, early Christianity used an anagram of the Greek word for fish (*ichtus*) to make a spiritual association between fish and being saved by Christ, describing believers as a shoal of fish. In China the rearing of red or gold fish was for many years the preserve of the imperial court. This had more to do with the fish as a symbol of happiness and well-being than with cultivation of it as a food source. There is a beautiful multicolored vase from the Ming dynasty showing red carp swimming among aquatic plants, including lotuses, ferns, and lianas, along with sea creatures resembling crayfish.

The contrast between living and dead fish is striking, even more so than is the case with domestic or wild animals. A living fish, radiant in its silver, or in all the colors of the rainbow and always moving, almost impossible to hold, is in death no more than a lusterless, cold creature with dull scales. The modern city dweller hardly ever sees whole dead mammals at the butcher's, let alone at the supermarket, but with fish it is different. We seem to be less disturbed by a confrontation with dead fish that are recognizable as such than with dead cattle or poultry. Many people would be horrified by the carcass of a cow with its eyes open, whereas they have no trouble at all looking into the staring eyes of a dead fish on a market stall or inspecting a dead lobster to see how fresh it is. Fish and arthropods simply don't arouse such emotions in us as warm-blooded animals do.

In modern times fishing has been reduced to a sport, usually known in English as angling. The performance it requires—throwing out a hook with live bait—meets with less resistance from the general public than the paraphernalia of hunting as a leisure activity. Shooting a deer seems to most people very different from catching a whiting or even a tuna. That revulsion at the killing of warm-blooded animals doesn't necessarily have any connection with the association of hunting with the rich, with the lifestyle of a wealthy leisured class, therefore seeming to belong to the past. Although fishing as a sport was traditionally an activity of the Western working class, some varieties of angling are strictly a luxury for the rich, such as taking a helicopter to a remote Scottish river to catch salmon. For almost every non-hunter, hunting is higher up the hierarchy of social distaste than fishing. I have to admit, however, that the soundless suffering of a wriggling fish on a hook, as I remember it from village harbors along the coast of the Mediterranean, seemed to me as a child worse than the fate of other animals.

———

Their cold-bloodedness makes fish seem very distant from us, even though humans originate from the long evolutionary line that, for more than 500 million years, developed from fish, amphibians, and reptiles to give rise to mammals and primates. We feel less affection for fish and crustaceans than for mammals, but if you are sensitive to it, you'll have to admit that something majestic resides in their silence and their inability to communicate with us. To anyone aware of that majesty, as Hemingway was, a speechless fish is a symbol not of stupidity but of silent pride and defiance.

Even the waters in which fish, shellfish, and other animals live evoke mixed feelings. According to the myth related by the Maori, the native peoples of New Zealand (which the Maori call "Aotearoa"), the oceans were created by the tears of the God of the Sky, shed when he was separated from the Goddess of the Earth. Whatever its origin, the sea has for millennia been a source of fear, because where sea and sky meet was the end of the world. The sea is empty and dark, as is the water of great rivers and lakes and even pools. It is treacherous, because you cannot judge its depth or its fickle currents; the water is sometimes opaque with floating sediment, sometimes so clear that you seem to gain brief access to an impalpable mirror world that is then dimmed again by a single gust of wind. Fish and aquatic animals live in an environment in which humans cannot survive for long, usually only briefly. Water rarely allows us in, because we don't belong there; our environment is on land. As a result the important place of fish and other water creatures in the functioning of wet ecosystems, their relationship with terrestrial ecosystems, and the complexity of the aquatic food pyramid were hidden from human observation until quite recently.

———

Fish, crustaceans, and shellfish—indeed all creatures we take from the water—are therefore surrounded by a complex ambivalence, but it is precisely the ungraspable, fluid nature of the waters and their inhabitants that give the impression of an endless supply of food. In the watery environment limitations remain invisible, and populations of fish and other species seem inexhaustible. In the darkness and depths there must always be more to be found. A poor catch may mean only that the currents have shifted, an unfavorable wind has got up, or the water gods are in a bad mood. From land we cannot survey all the water that covers three-quarters of our planet. As long as fish are constantly brought ashore, the image of an inexhaustible paradise, where you have only to throw out your net to catch something, will continue to be reinforced. The waters, and especially the depths of the seas and big lakes, are still largely out of our reach. In places we cannot visit or even see with our own eyes, myths live on. Only when Jacques-Yves Cousteau, with his ship *Calypso*, started filming the silent undersea world in the 1950s did the vulnerability of ocean ecosystems start to dawn on us.

It is telling that fish, lakes, and seas are a metaphor for inexhaustible plenty that can be drawn up from unfathomable depths "naturally" and without great effort. Legends and folk tales abound concerning rivers and lakes full of fish. The miraculous catch is a familiar image in many cultures, not least in the Christian New Testament, which tells a tale not just about spiritual sustenance but also about actual and self-evident plenty. That is how humans experience the waters, as a miraculous and infinite supply of food. In a painting by Raphael, for example, we see the apostles hanging over the side of a boat on Jesus' instructions to haul in a huge catch from the Sea of Galilee, while several cormorants watch (the painter knows his food pyramid). The reality of the fishing life is one of hardship, poverty, and danger, but in mythology the fisherman has only to throw out a net to harvest all that God has set swimming for him. The ocean becomes a liquid paradise, an ecosystem just as impossible as the earthly paradise in which everything serves as food for humankind.

The elusive, ungraspable character of fish and other marine creatures made is clear by their absence in the paradise served up to us by the main monotheistic religions and traditions. Although water is often depicted or described, it takes the form of streams that bring moisture and fertility to the landscape. It is seldom mentioned as a source of food. This reflects the ecology of the Middle East with its rivers and oases. Genesis/Bereshit begins, as do the Sumerian creation myths, with a god separating earth and water. On the third day of creation he names the water "ocean." Then, on the fifth day, living beings are created in the oceans, including specific, named sea monsters, which come even before land animals. Humankind is charged with ruling over these marine creatures, but they are not mentioned as food, unlike plants on dry land (animals are designated as food only after the flood). Genesis 1:28 does make reference to fish when Adam and Eve are banished from paradise. God's ultimate blessing of them includes an injunction to rule over the fish, the birds, and every other living creature on earth, although the reader does have the feeling that this is mainly about creatures that "move along the ground."

Human and Fish

The consumption of fish and crustaceans by humans does not go back as far as that of meat, because in the East African savannah where our species first emerged, fish is not readily available. Nevertheless, the eating of fish may have been of crucial importance to the development of *Homo sapiens*. To the south and west of the savannah, where our predecessors once hunted, are the lakes of the Great Rift Valley. They have existed for 15 million years, although they only gradually acquired their current form and ecology. It is not yet clear to what extent these lakes served as a systematic food source for the earliest of our ancestors, the various *Australopithecus* species (which go back some 4.5 million years) and later *Homo habilis* (2.5 million years), but there are indications that the availability of fish was important for humans and their ancestors as long as 2.5 million years ago. The qualitative improvement in nutrition that occurred around that time seems to have been brought about partly by fish. Two aspects are important here: proteins and fatty acids. By analyzing the carbon and nitrogen content of human bones, we can determine the relative contributions of various sources of protein: plants, land animals, fish, and shellfish. It's possible to deduce that beginning about 2.5 million years ago, consumption of fish may have increased. Even more fascinating is the finding that the long, multiple unsaturated fatty acids that are found in particularly high concentrations in tropical fish and aquatic animals may have been essential in the development of the human brain. Around 60 percent of our brains consist of fatty acids, and unsaturated fatty acids promote the growth of the central nervous system without any accompanying increase in the total weight of the skeleton. A larger supply of fatty acids through the diet may have triggered the development of a hominid with a bigger cortex. In other words, a qualitative improvement in the human diet, with proteins and fatty acids derived from fish, may have allowed the intellectual powers of human beings to increase.

Traces have recently been found that suggest the consumption of freshwater fish may go back 380,000 years. This would mean that the rise of the modern human, *Homo sapiens,* which began 200,000 years ago, is partly attributable to the fish-rich waters of East Africa. The development of fishing techniques and tools may have further aided the development of the human brain, just as hunting implements did. Although much is uncertain, we are justified in cautiously speculating that if our ancestors had not lived close to tropical waters teeming with fish, evolution might have taken a very different course.

The catfish, an important source of unsaturated omega-3 fats, was one of the fish species most often consumed, at least until 40,000 years ago. Ancient catfish bones have been found with traces of tool cuts. Beginning 160,000 years ago, sites near the coasts of seas and lakes show increasing evidence that fish and aquatic animals were part of the human diet. It is fairly easy to distinguish between the shells of salt- and freshwater creatures, incidentally, because they have a different isotopic composition. In what is now France, traces of shellfish consumption 300,000 years ago have been discovered, and rather less-ancient finds have been made in a wide diversity of regions from South Africa to Vietnam and New Guinea. Archaeological remains show that early humans in China were eating fish 40,000 years ago. These finds take the form of the remains of shells and fish bones, fish hooks fashioned from animal bones, and tools and ornaments made from shells. Nonetheless, it's extremely rare to find prehistoric depictions of fish on cave walls like those of mammals in the caves of Lascaux or Altamira. Fish were probably important in human history, but they don't generally seem to have had the same universal status as wild land animals or livestock.

It has been speculated that one of the factors involved in the disappearance of the Neanderthals was that they did less fishing and therefore ate less fish than did *Homo sapiens.* Relevant here are not just the proteins and fatty acids fish provide but also the increased variety of food sources, which raises the chances of survival in periods of scarcity. Paleontological remains show, incidentally, that Neanderthals wrapped shellfish in algae to help preserve their moisture and quality, as fishermen in northern Spain still do. At the Strait of Gibraltar, where the fish-rich waters of the Atlantic Ocean and the Mediterranean mix, recent archaeological finds suggest that the Neanderthals held out longer there than in most other places.

After the last ice age, 10,000 years ago, worldwide consumption of shell-fish increased significantly.

––––––––

In contrast to fishing in fresh water, the systematic exploitation of the sea as a source of food is a relatively recent development in human history, probably dating back some 40,000 years. In North America, fishing did not begin until the Holocene, or 10,000 years ago. In terms of efficiency measured as production per unit of effort, hunting for large mammals comes out best, better than hunting for small animals and much better than gathering wild plants. As far as sea creatures are concerned, gathering shellfish is far more productive than fishing out at sea, but shellfish contain few calories, unlike marine mammals, with their high fat content, which supply at least as much energy as land mammals. Sea creatures in the tropics are more diverse, but they have a lower fat content. The general rule is: the colder the water, the fattier the flesh will be. Salmon is a good example. Another general rule: the higher the latitude (so in the case of the northern hemisphere the farther north), the more humans make use of fish and other sea creatures. Protein content varies too. Shellfish contain relatively little protein (about 20 percent), but it is easily digested, even if they are eaten raw. Interestingly, shark's fins, that famous and controversial Asian delicacy, have extremely beneficial ratios of amino acids. Seaweed, the most important vegetable food source in the sea, contains as much protein as the best grain crops (13 percent of dry weight). The sea is an important supplementary source in coastal areas at times when the amount of protein available from plant sources declines in the spring, when the next harvest is not yet ripe. This co-incides neatly with the fact that spring is the time when many sea organisms reach their highest fat content. The sea therefore provides a chance to reduce the risks of food scarcity on land. Food from the sea is rarely the dominant source of nutrition, except in regions that are too cold for agriculture or animal husbandry and the hunt provides too little, as on the coasts of Canada.

Humans quickly discovered that animals could be domesticated. Farm animals and pets reproduced successfully in circumstances dictated by humans. Hardly any edible fish species are suitable for this kind of husbandry. Moreover, farm animals provide more than just food: pulling power for ploughing and transportation, guard duties (geese and dogs), bones for tool-making, hides, and manure for the all-important fertilization of fields. But fish and sea creatures provide us with virtually nothing besides edible flesh. Their by-products are few, and with the exception of blubber and oil from whales and cod-liver oil they are never the main purpose of the catch. The use of whalebone for corsets or umbrellas was always a secondary concern. Fish skin is occasionally used for making high-end shoes or handbags, but that is nowadays just about all. Fish and other aquatic creatures are therefore mainly a source of food, for humans and increasingly for animals. The importance of fishmeal as feed for cattle and fish has increased markedly in recent decades. Aside from shells for decoration, music, rituals, and as a form of currency, and shellfish as a source of dyes (especially purple dye), few aquatic species have more than one direct function for us.

Like hunting, fishing is a matter of technique, but fishing is more complicated, because it requires a way of moving in and across water and of keeping one's bearings without landmarks. Fish in seas or rivers are even harder to find and catch than prey on land. It therefore seems likely that the first food from the water took the form of shellfish, which move little if at all. Tidal pools and rivers and ponds that dry out in certain seasons are ideal, because fish, shellfish, and animals such as turtles can simply be lifted out of the water, without any need for tools.

Everywhere that fish and sea creatures are visible and can be reached, people have developed fishing techniques, from the South Pacific to Arctic waters, from the Nile to the Amazon, the Caspian Sea to Lake Victoria. River species probably supplemented the diets of the first farmers. In some areas the exploitation of creatures from the sea and large rivers and lakes was so successful that extensive trading networks developed. This was the case until the mid-twentieth century in the Trobriand Islands near New Guinea, where shells for armbands and necklaces were a currency that facilitated a complex exchange of goods and brides. But far earlier, in Roman times, the city of Carthage on the mainland opposite Sicily derived its wealth not just from the grain trade and mining but also from the trade in salted fish. Even before that, some 3,000 years ago, the Phoenicians developed a de facto monopoly on salt pans and fish processing, especially along the coasts of what are now Portugal and Spain, with their rich fish stocks.

Fish has always been an important part of the daily diet on and near the Mediterranean coast, as is clear from the wonderful Roman mosaics of darting fish and prawns. A floor mosaic from Sousse in present-day Tunisia reads like a modern poster of fish species of the kind found on the walls of some fish restaurants: flat fish, anguilliformes (types of eel), and tuna caught with either nets or spears; lobsters, sea urchins, and squid as big as gondolas trapped in earthenware pots; sponges and shrimps. Such accurate mosaics are evidence not just of the existence of extensive fishing but also of an early awareness of the ecosystem and of the pleasure and usefulness to be derived from the diversity of life in the sea. Other mosaics from the same period show fishermen in action, pushing boats laden with baskets and three-pointed spears, and a vat filled to overflowing with fish and octopus.

Whereas hunter-gatherers move with the wild animals and become sedentary only if they come upon rich hunting grounds or begin to farm the land, the economy of the community of fishing folk is very different. Fishermen cannot move with the shoals. Traditional fishing communities are made up of small groups of sometimes no more than twenty people, who settle permanently on the coast near good waters rich in fish. This seems to apply to all climatic regions: to the original coastal inhabitants of Sarawak and Fiji in the tropics, to those of that part of the west coast of South America affected by the Humboldt Current, and to the native tribes of the cold west and east coasts of Canada. Of the latter groups we know that fish was a supplement to a diet mainly made up of the meat of elk, reindeer, and beaver rather than the principal constituent, but exactly what they ate depended on the seasons and the alternatives available. Climate was decisive in that sense.

In the evolution of human civilization in the tropics, the fish catch was of secondary importance almost everywhere, with the exception of the coral and atoll islands of the South Pacific, where little vegetation can grow. In general the contribution of fish as a direct source of calories increases with the latitude and reaches its high point in subarctic areas, where again the vegetation is insufficient to sustain human life. In the very coldest places, such as the regions inhabited by the Inuit, sea ice limits the catch of fish and marine animals for much of the year, so the importance of the hunt (for polar bears and seals) increases again.

This ancient pattern, set by local conditions and ecology, has been turned on its head by the large-scale intercontinental trade in fish and other products of the sea. While the trade in dried fish in the Mediterranean basin dates back to the time of the Phoenicians, the Vikings were the first to trade in fish on a large scale, especially dried cod from Lofoten, a group of islands off northern Norway. These trading networks are at least 1,000 years old. All major cities near the sea have centuries-old fish markets; that of Rome is said to date back 2,500 years.

Fishing does not take place everywhere and where it does, not everyone fishes. There are fishing communities in which some members specialize; communities in which most people fish from time to time; and communities in which no one fishes, and all the fish come from elsewhere. All major cities fall into this last category, even those that have fish markets, but so do semiarid regions where fish is scarce. This division of labor is not static. In Hawaii, for example, the land on the islands was traditionally divided up in such a way that every village had a wedge of land that ran from the center of the island to the coast. As the population increased, the land was further divided, so that some villages no longer had any land on the coast and could not fish, while inhabitants of other villages were forced to concentrate exclusively on fishing and to barter fish with farmers farther inland.

Almost without exception, those who fish are men, although women are involved in mending nets and processing the catch, and in some cultures they set traps for aquatic creatures that can be fished by hand. Women also trade in fish. In traditional communities in the South Pacific, women are kept out of the boats. Once, in New Britain (part of Papua New Guinea), I said I might like to go by boat to a nearby bay and was severely reprimanded. Women bring fishermen bad luck (even worse, the close proximity of a menstruating woman can make a boat permanently defective and scare away the fish for good). Like the oldest of farming communities, fishing communities are closed and usually poor. In situations of great uncertainty, rituals and behavioral rules provide a way to deal with chronic scarcity and temporary abundance.

Hunting for wild animals and fishing were originally each other's ecological equivalents, but there is a great difference between the exploitation of aquatic creatures and that of the animals and plants found on land. The oceans, seas, and other bodies of water are far more extensive than land, and they have escaped human influence to a much greater degree. With their limited means, fishermen had relatively little effect on fish populations even after the invention of the steamboat, the notorious exception being the whaling industry. Locally some seas or lakes were fished out, but fish stocks were often replenished naturally, or other species moved into the vacated niches. Until the twentieth century, fishing techniques remained largely unchanged. Spear and harpoon, nets and—in rivers— poison, often derived from plants, are the classic instruments of the fisherman. Nets have changed most in size and shape, and especially in the way they are pulled along. Dynamite and poisons like cyanide supplemented this arsenal for many years, but in most countries these methods are no longer permitted.

Until the nineteenth century the influence of fisheries on most wild populations was minimal, in contrast to hunting on land where, after the invention of gunpowder and above all in the nineteenth century, wild animals were killed with gay abandon. On land agriculture expanded for centuries, leaving fewer and fewer undisturbed areas of vegetation where wild animals could hide and reproduce. So the pressure on terrestrial resources led far more quickly to the need to intensify food production. As part of that development, hunting as a source of food became less important. It was replaced by animal husbandry, while gathering gave way to the growing of crops, including trees.

This change has taken place in fishing here and there, but only in Southeast Asia has small-scale fish farming developed as a significant replacement for traditional fishing, mostly in combination with wet rice and the raising of lobsters, oysters, and mussels. Those traditional forms of aquaculture have changed out of all recognition over the past decade: such fish as pangasius grown for export is now said to make up 10 percent of the Vietnamese fish trade.

If there has been a partial transition in some places from fishing in the wild to the farming of domesticated fish, then it took place many millennia later than the development of farming on land. The earliest known aquaculture started about 4,000 years ago in China, more than 6,000 years after the farming of crops. The oldest known written culinary recipe, dating from shortly after the Chinese script came into being, originates from South China. It is 3,000 years old and describes how to prepare a spicy marinated carp salad, a dish that would not be out of place on a menu today.

However important for human evolution, the contribution of fish to the total worldwide human diet is and remains limited. Around 16 percent of animal protein consumed by humans globally comes from fish. This does not mean that fish is of little significance: as well as being a source of proteins and essential fatty acids, it makes an important contribution to our intake of vitamin D and iodine. In populations that live far from the sea, such as those of the African interior, a relatively high percentage of people suffer from a shortage of iodine, which in its more extreme form results in goiter, a swelling of the thyroid gland, and can lead to a serious and sometimes incapacitating mental and physical developmental disorder called "cretinism." The condition is easy to prevent by adding iodine to the diet, as is done routinely in many countries by means of a standard addition to table salt. Unfortunately iodine deficiency still occurs in isolated villages; I recall women in the Central African Republic with swellings in their throats the size of a grapefruit.

Historically the consumption of fish was concentrated on the coasts and the banks of large bodies of water. Still today, almost 90 percent of fish that are caught come from the seas and oceans. In coastal areas most of the fish consumed is local, although delicacies—in the case of Europe the porpoise, for example—were soon being shipped in for the governing classes. Given that the transportation of fish is difficult and costly because of its short storage life, the ability to serve fish conferred extra status, especially where the elite lived far from rivers, lakes, or the coast. Recipes of the Chinese and Mongolian courts include many ways of preparing fish and marine animals: steamed, marinated, in brine, or grilled. In Europe fish consumption increased in the Middle Ages, partly because of the Christian rules on fasting. On certain days meat was forbidden, but in some cases fish was allowed. Many cultures have rules and taboos about fish. According to Jewish dietary laws, fish without gills and scales (such as eel, catfish, and shark) are not to be eaten at all, while in Africa and the Amazon basin fish is generally taboo for pregnant women.

From Fish 'n' Chips to Sashimi

From a culinary point of view little can beat a fresh sardine on the beach (of the Atlantic Ocean that is, as in the Mediterranean they are endangered), straight from the nets, grilled over a charcoal fire with just half a lemon and some salt to season it. This partiality applies not just to me or most Europeans but to many generations before us. Only the lemon is a recent addition, brought from China to the Mediterranean region by the armies of Alexander the Great before moving on from there with Columbus to reach America. The grilling of fish and seafood in this way is tens of thousands of years old, so it dates from long before the start of agriculture.

Unlike the plants and farm animals we eat in the twenty-first century, it's quite possible that today's fish tastes more or less as it did then. Apples, tomatoes, and lettuce have been selected and improved over thousands of generations to make them taste less bitter or sour. Vegetables and fruit are noticeably less fibrous today and therefore more tender, and they are infinitely sweeter than a century ago, let alone thousands of years ago when they were first domesticated. Pigs, chickens, and cows are less fatty and tough, and have a far less pronounced taste. But fish and shellfish have not been subjected to a centuries-long process of breeding or to means of production—especially feed—that affect their flavor (the exception being fish from modern fish farming, which is a very recent development). So the difference in taste between wild salmon and salmon from fish-rearing ponds strikes us immediately. Of course the composition of the water, vegetation, and sediment may have changed as a result of erosion from land and the flushing of pollution and nutrients from farming into the sea and into lakes near the coast, which may have affected the aquatic food chain. But I would venture to say that the enormous capacity of the oceans as a buffer and the fact that pollution in them is not usually concentrated in one place mean the flavor of seafood caught in the wild has remained virtually unchanged. Ways of preparing fish are generally identical to those of earlier centuries too: we bake, grill, boil, steam, marinade, and ferment to this day. That last technique, which enables us to keep fish longer, is a method the Phoenicians had mastered. In Vietnam the famous *nuoc mam* sauce, derived from fermented fish, has existed for centuries, with variations in neighboring countries. If we ignore for a moment the effect on flavor of large-scale freezing and stick to the freshly caught sardine on the beach, then it is exciting to think that we are tasting roughly what our ancestors tasted, not just 10,000 years ago but perhaps 200,000.

There is another way in which fish differs from plants and animals: the immense diversity of supply. This is mainly the result of great local variation in the species caught. At a random fish market on a random day, anywhere in the world, you can easily find dozens of species. Some occur only locally; others—such as bluefin tuna—are found in virtually all the seas of the world and are traded globally. The market in products from salt water and fresh water, including fish, prawns, lobster, and other shellfish, is so diverse that in the United States alone more than 700 species are traded. The average Dutch supermarket sells dozens of processed products derived from fishing and fish farming, and perhaps twice as many are available at the local fishmonger's. Alongside prawns, mussels, cod, and tuna, new acquisitions from the tropics, such as tiger prawns, pangasius, and tilapia, are becoming commonplace. Yet the range of fish available in northern Europe is still far smaller than in southern Europe.

Of necessity fish was originally mostly eaten close to the coasts, and although trade in dried and salted fish has existed around the Mediterranean since ancient times, fresh fish was a luxury product for centuries. Only since the Industrial Revolution has it been available to all. The increase in fish consumption by urban populations runs in parallel with industrialization and the move to the cities. The building of harbors, railroads, and factories in the nineteenth century meant fish could be transported inland in significant quantities and quickly processed, making it a product more and more people could afford.

Nothing makes this clearer than the fact that for much of the twentieth century the English working class lived on fish 'n' chips. Although this was cheap food designed to stave off hunger, never a rival to meat, it was a successful combination. Starting out as food for the poor, it developed the status of a convenience food before the term was invented, especially in cities, where the middle classes were happy to call in at a chip shop. It is amusing to think that the dish would never have existed if the potato, that efficient source of calories from which the "chips" (French fries) are made, had not recovered from the terrible crop failures of the nineteenth century. The potato indirectly stimulated the demand for fish. Fish 'n' chips remains such an attractive formula that it can be found in all regions of the world, having arrived there in large part because of the British Empire. Plaice, whiting, cod, haddock—all kinds of whitefish can serve as the basic ingredient, depending on availability. As a quick and easy snack, fish 'n' chips and fried fillets were controversial from the start. Sanitation, waste, and the quality of the oil used for frying often left much to be desired, especially in densely populated urban areas.

Over the past twenty years, demand for fish and seafood has grown, slowly but surely, the world over; consumption now stands at a little over sixteen kilograms per year per person, but variations are large, with the highest consumption in Asia and the countries around the Mediterranean. The European catch, even supplemented by fish farming, will probably not be able to keep pace with growing demand, which means that over the coming decades more fish will have to be imported from other parts of the world. The growth in demand can be put down to better supplies of fresh fish and to the idea that fish and seafood are a healthy alternative to meat.

It's not simply that we are eating more fish. Fish and seafood are increasingly popular among different strata of the population and at the same time have a higher status than they once did. Fish is not just for Catholics on Fridays, for a herring stall, or for the inevitable fried plaice option in restaurants; it has become a delicacy proudly shown off by the domestic cook or the renowned chef, a far cry from the grilled fish stick. In most rich countries, huge shifts have taken place in the frequency of consumption, the quality, and the type of fish consumed.

Take salmon. Until twenty years ago it was an exclusive product, but now farmed salmon can be found in the sandwiches in any canteen. Aquaculture has made it a cheap snack; wild salmon, in contrast, is an expensive luxury. All Atlantic salmon now comes from fish farms. How things change. A century ago salmon was nothing special, at least not for those who lived near the rivers up which the salmon swam to spawn before returning to salt water.

Another new group of fish products comes from Japanese cuisine. At the forefront are sushi and sashimi, which have also broken free of their exclusive reputation and are now available in every supermarket as ready-made snacks. They are popular among busy and health-conscious young professionals. The main ingredient of sushi is rice, usually prepared with vinegar, on top of which is draped a scrap of raw or cooked fish, a prawn, or sometimes a piece of vegetable. Sushi dates from a time when rice cultivation was dominant, about 2,000 to 1,500 years ago. Sashimi is primarily finely sliced very fresh fish, intended as a delicacy. Sashimi and sushi are the perfect answer to the complicated desires of the modern Western consumer: health and convenience, and less and less confrontation with the origins of the product. They both present a neutrally colored morsel of fish flesh that in no way reminds us of the great proud bluefin tuna and its bloody death. For the fashionable city dweller this makes such Japanese methods of preparation, psychologically at least, the modern successor to fish 'n' chips and the fish stick, that strip of fish fried in batter that spared the housewife and the diner the unpleasant work of filleting fish and could be placed in front of the family, because nothing about it made anyone think of an actual fish. With the popularity of Japanese cuisine, interest is growing in other products of the sea, such as seaweed and the sea cucumber (which is not a plant but an animal).

The same goes for fish as for all our other food. Western countries and the rich middle classes in developing economies are eating more and more prepared products, and fish is no exception. New, healthier options are replacing fish sticks. Regional, historically determined differences remain—fresh octopus is not highly valued in Eastern Europe; salted herring is not greatly appreciated in China—but everywhere regional choices are coming under pressure from the development of products for which demand is global. It's not so much that we'll eat different species over the coming decades, but clearly the preparation and nature of fish products is changing fast. The move toward ready meals featuring fish and other seafood is partly due to the growing range of products available in supermarkets and increasing consumption outside the home, in canteens, restaurants, and fast food chains. In countries such as Britain, France, and Germany, almost three-quarters of fish products are sold through supermarkets. It's worth noting, however, that supermarkets in southern Europe usually have proper fish shops in them, where every day a selection of wonderful fresh fish and seafood is on sale, laid on shards of ice, that bears no resemblance to the items in plastic packaging found in northern Europe.

The supermarket meets the needs of the hurried modern consumer who wants fish that looks as little like fish as possible and, as with meat, bears hardly any resemblance to a living creature. So fish must be odorless, boneless, skinned, with no trace of blood or internal organs, and preferably sold or served in the form of fillets. The same applies to prawns and other crustaceans: preferably sold peeled and frozen, so that they can go straight from the freezer into the pan. This is the writing on the wall. Most people have no idea what kind of fish their food contains.

Given that knowledge about how to cook fish is also declining rapidly, it needs to be processed as far as possible before sale. Increasingly we see precooked fish on offer, with instructions for boiling or frying, and herbs and sauce to go with it. Or merely as an ingredient in a product: a cod burger, crab salad, marinated salmon for sandwiches, or steamed mussels. As far as I'm concerned the epitome of all this is the "fruits de mer salad," of which the origin and even the ingredients are vague. Various fish and shellfish species are combined in factories into a global mix, so we can buy tubs with labels that, in barely legible script, inform us that the ingredients are from the Indian Ocean, the South Pacific, and the North Sea. Only true enthusiasts still go to the fishmonger to buy whole fish, using the bones to make soup. The modern urban elite can now gain status by preparing fresh fish and thereby showing off culinary skills.

––––––––––

Alongside the growth in lazy eating, however, a consciousness is emerging, among some consumers at least, that fish can be a problematic product just like meat. With the remarkable equivocacy that characterizes so much of our attitude to food, it's possible to eat cheap fish and at the same time to be concerned about intensive fish farming and overfishing. As with meat, dairy products, and vegetables, some consumers thus are willing to pay more for an ecologically sound product, such as fish labeled "sustainable seafood." Yet in many ways fish remains a little-known product, especially when you think of the importance attached to meat and the information on offer about it. Few people eat fish more than once a week. It's a remarkable paradox that flexitarians, in trying to limit their consumption of meat, generally opt for fish (avoiding that standard alternative, cheese). There are even people who call themselves vegetarians yet do eat fish, because it's an efficient source of nutrients. In their view fish is unproblematic, and fish and crustaceans seem a healthy choice, more friendly to both the environment and the creatures concerned. This is true only to a limited extent.

Seas of Plenty

Foam flies up between the large bodies, the sea turns red, men labor away at the flesh with hooks and harpoons, the by-catch of thousands of little fish is thrown back dead or damaged—the reality of fishing is as unbearable as the slaughter of domestic animals in the most uncontrolled, brutal conditions. This applies both to the modern, industrial catch and to traditional fishing, which we should not idealize. Particularly notorious is the catching of bluefin tuna, or almadraba, at Cadiz in southern

Spain, or off Sicily and Tunisia, where passing shoals are caught with nets that end in a kind of narrow chamber. Nobody who has seen it or read about it will have any illusions about the mortal fear of those creatures when they are caught in these nets.

That traditional fishermen catch as little as possible out of respect for the sea is a myth. They too kill more fish than can be consumed locally. The only difference between them and large-scale commercial trawlers is that the traditional catch is concentrated in the spawning season and its scale is limited to what local fishermen can haul in with relatively limited exertion. Fishing is all the more horrifying to watch because so many creatures are killed that don't belong to the species sought. That animal rights activists do not find this at least as controversial as the killing of farm animals emphasizes once again the difference in status and importance between meat and fish.

The use of modern fishing methods, including dynamite (which is now declining, fortunately) and motorized shipping—first steam, then diesel with refrigeration on board—has made it possible to exploit all the earth's seas on a vast scale for a century now. In recent decades new techniques have further intensified our efforts: geographic information systems to trace fish shoals, synthetic fibers for larger and larger nets, powerful motors for trawling, and rapid freezing systems. Trawlers using modern fishing techniques can have disastrous consequences for the marine ecosystem, for the sea grass that protects young fish, for example. The industrialization of fishing took place mainly in the first half of the twentieth century, but in the tropics it is not yet complete. Only there is a fishing life still extremely dangerous, whereas in the rest of the world it has increasingly become an industrial occupation. There we still hear echoes of the words of Kniertje, the despairing fishwife in the famous Dutch play *Op hoop van zegen* ("The Good Hope") by Herman Heijermans, who tries to dissuade her son from going to sea like his father.

Populations of fish and aquatic animals are threatened not only by fishing but also indirectly by other forms of human intervention, such as the introduction of new species that bring greater profits. The technique is not new. The Phoenicians and Romans introduced fish from the Black Sea and the Sea of Marmara into the western Mediterranean. The most notorious case concerns Lake Victoria in Africa, where humans have severely disrupted the extremely diverse ecosystem of inedible types of cichlid by introducing the dominant Nile perch as a food resource. Yet human intervention does not always have a negative impact. One of the most extraordinary introductions of exotics—fish outside their original habitat—resulted from the opening of the Suez Canal in 1869. Shortly afterward, dozens of fish species from the warmer, saltier Red Sea became established in the Mediterranean. They are now an important part of the fish catch there. This invasion does not seem to have been at the expense of the original species of the eastern Mediterranean. Similarly, oystermen have profited from the introduction of the Japanese oyster, which has spread successfully in Dutch waters and is even moving on to the mussel banks of the Wadden Sea.

No matter how vast the seas and waterways, human influence extends almost everywhere, directly through fishing and indirectly through countless human activities that gradually influence the biological and chemical characteristics of the water close to the coasts. The nutrient composition of coastal waters is now powerfully affected by phosphate, as a consequence of inefficient farming practices and industry, and this represents a considerable threat to fish stocks. From the Yangtze in China to the Nile in Egypt, the building of dams and pollution by industry close to rivers has resulted in dramatic episodes of countless dead or dying fish.

Agriculture can sometimes be a competitor to fisheries. Its direct effects include the removal of water for irrigation, as seen with particularly poignancy in the drying up of the Aral Sea. Indirect effects include the flushing out of chemical pesticides and herbicides, animal manure, and artificial fertilizer into surface waters, which can have devastating consequences. Extremely harmful substances that are hard to break down, such as mercury and dioxins, can be stored in fish fat, which has consequences for human health, although their effects are slight in the case of fish that are low on the food chain and do not live long, such as herring. Irrigation can sometimes have positive effects locally, in that the storage of water in shallow fish ponds creates a new environment for fish that live on the sea bed, such as tilapia. These ponds are quite common in regions with small-scale rice cultivation. After a while an oxygen-poor zone develops in such reservoirs, however, which depletes fish stocks. Irrigation also causes the transportation of soil particles in suspension, making the water less clear, especially if currents are slow. In the tropics high fish production is achieved in clear irrigation water when there is plenty of sunlight, but sometimes algal blooms can occur. Salty and brackish coastal morasses, generally an essential link as an incubator for marine species, are threatened by erosion as a result of agriculture and urban development, or by drilling for oil as in the Niger Delta. And indeed, these incubators are also threatened by dikes built to protect human habitats against high water levels, as on the Mekong Delta or the Lower Rhine, in addition to the deliberate draining of marshland, often for farming purposes.

––––––––––

Throughout human history we have unthinkingly treated rivers, lakes, seas, and oceans as a liquid paradise, where we can draw without limit on an abundance of valuable food rich in minerals, oils, and proteins. Fish (taken broadly to include shellfish and other aquatic creatures) forms a distinct category of food in the sense that it can still be harvested from the wild on a large scale, without cultivation, as nothing else can. Estimates suggest that between 25 and 30 percent of all fish populations are currently threatened or are being overfished. More than half are fully utilized, meaning that the catch cannot grow any further, and only 16 percent are underexploited. Almost 80 percent of the catch from the wild is intended for human consumption; the remaining 20 percent is used to make fishmeal or fish oil to feed cattle and farmed fish.

Fish from the sea is the great anomaly of our food supply: it is the only category for which we have not until very recently taken the step to intensification and cultivation. We have done so for freshwater fish, although not until thousands of years after the start of agriculture, and mainly in the tropics, generally in combination with the growing of rice.

Fishing is a prime example of what is known as the tragedy of the commons: if something is common property, then no one feels responsible for it and there's no reason for any individual to treat it less exploitatively, because there's no guarantee that others will moderate their behavior as well. It's actually quite striking how easily humans have been able to exhaust fish stocks when you compare them with animal populations on land, which occur in greater density and are far more visible. In the vast expanse of the seas and oceans you'd think that most fish would be able to escape humans quite easily. But that's an illusion: fish are not evenly spread across the oceans, and some species, such as the bluefin tuna, always return to the same place to spawn. In rich fishing grounds they are easy to catch, and now, with sonar and the Global Positioning System, fishermen are much better able to locate fish stocks.

As with land animals, predators at the top of the food chain, such as the lion and the tuna, are especially vulnerable because of their small numbers.

That we've continued to fish from the wild for so long has to do with the fact that the sea has no real boundaries and little in the way of property rights, and until recently it seemed to have inexhaustible stocks. Generally speaking there's far more space in the seas and in large lakes and rivers that is not claimed exclusively and permanently by specific owners. If wild animals, pasture, or agricultural land are exhausted, people leave, following the animals, or they move their herds or improve their yields. In any case there is a limit; land is scarce and rarely unused. Anyone who leaves to follow wild animals or their own herds will soon come into conflict with other land users and hunters. The scarcity of wild creatures combined with increasing rainfall, which makes grasses produce more grain, was one of the decisive factors in the replacement of nomadic hunting and gathering by permanent agriculture. Scarcity of land in turn led to technological improvements, such as the fertilization of fields and pasture, irrigation, and the supplementary feeding of livestock. These are self-reinforcing effects; the success of the first farmers led to population growth, so more land was needed, which prompted technological advances. Improvements in technology made possible the growth of cities and better lifestyles, which created a demand for further improvements. None of this applies to the seas.

The realization of just how abundant life is in the seas and lakes—and how vulnerable—has slowly got through to the general public, partly because of steadily improving techniques of underwater photography and voyages of discovery in the wake of Cousteau. The unique ecosystems of the oceans deserve our attention for the value they have in their own right, as our collective biological heritage, and they change continually even without human intervention. Justification for the protection of the sea can lie only to a very limited extent in its value as a source of food for human beings. With marine creatures, as with animal species on land, there is no relationship, or possibly an inverse relationship, between species diversity and food production. The coral reefs, which are home to almost a quarter of all marine species, are impressive in their diversity and therefore of great value as biological heritage, but they have no place at all in the world food supply chain.

Taming Fish: Aquaculture

Anyone arriving by plane at Ho Chi Minh City, Bangkok, or Manila will see it from the air: flat land along the shore with a mosaic of ponds and rice paddies framed by narrow earthen dikes. Increasingly it's not rice being grown here but the far more lucrative fish. In Asia a close relationship between fish and rice cultivation has existed for thousands of years. Fish, ducks, and rice use the same water, made fertile by the excrement of humans and animals, and sometimes surrounded by leguminous bushes and trees (which fix nitrogen from the air by symbiosis). The mud from the ponds, rich in undigested nutrients, is used on the fields. Such traditional small-scale systems have higher productivity (in terms of the total biomass of plant and animal species) and can be extremely stable. Along European and American coasts as well, more and more aquatic animals are being farmed, from mussels and oysters to salmon.

Fish farming is not a purely Chinese or even Asian invention, although the lion's share of it takes place in the east. Hundreds of years before the present era, the Etruscans farmed fish on the coast of Tuscany, and along the Danube the farming of carp goes back to the Middle Ages. Asia still dominates the production of farmed fish. Traditional methods are often used, but production for export is increasingly intensive. Two-thirds of farmed fish worldwide comes from China, and roughly two-thirds of it is carp. Shellfish farming is increasing by 8 percent per year, primarily in China but also, for example, in Chile. A little less than half the fish eaten by humans is farmed, and that number is certain to grow. Fish farming is showing the strongest growth in the protein production sector, and it is the fastest growing food sector in the world, output having doubled over the past ten years.

Modern fish farming is the wet counterpart to agriculture. It too is aimed at protecting the desired species, eliminating other species, and optimizing the environment for the desired species so that yields are as high as possible. It would actually be more accurate to say that fish farming is the wet counterpart to livestock farming, because in both cases the species concerned cannot themselves engage in photosynthesis. As with livestock farming, there are two forms, an open form that uses existing ecosystems (such as coastal morasses where cages or nets are placed) and a closed form consisting of systems of ponds lined with concrete or plastic: pasture as opposed to cowsheds, so to speak. Most fish farming takes place in fresh water. Farming in cages in open sea, fjords, or bays is a more recent development. Toward the end of the twentieth century fish farming developed into a large-scale commercial practice, comparable to the earlier rise of the bio-industry. Neither has a good reputation, partly because of the use of hormones and antibiotics, as well as the resultant water pollution and damage to coastal areas, such as the mangrove swamps of Vietnam. No one who has seen the density of salmon in huge floating cages, for example, will be able to resist the comparison with cattle in vast feeding lots.

These problems can be resolved to some extent. In the short term we can reuse the nutrients from the water of fish farms, in horticulture, for example. Aquaculture therefore looks like a logical alternative to fishing in the wild. But this transition is by no means straightforward. Most fish are not easy to farm because of their susceptibility to disease in captivity and low yields. In evolutionary terms this is logical, because for most species we have only just started farming, so we have little experience with breeding and feeding. Arable farming has a head start of at least 9,000 years on the farming of a species like tuna, which has only just begun.

Even the best fish farms use 1.2 kilograms of fishmeal to produce 1 kilogram of valuable fish, such as salmon (the ratio is 1:1 for anchovies). The less efficient farms use more than 4 kilograms (and a good deal more than this, if we base the calculation only on the edible part of the fish produced). For carnivorous fish, feed means, or has meant until recently, fishmeal and fish oil from other fish. So the problem is simply shifted elsewhere. Improvements to fish farming would therefore involve not merely converting feed into fish more efficiently but substituting fish oil and fishmeal with feed from vegetable sources or from creatures lower in the food chain, such as worms or insects. A shift to herbivorous fish species, such as tilapia, might be a solution, as then the feed can consist of vegetable matter, possibly waste, for which only a little extra land is needed. The use of more vegetable feed seems to lead to changes in the composition of fatty acids, however, with the result that the proportion of polyunsaturated fatty acids is reduced. The color of farmed fish is grayer, so a (harmless) dye has to be added to the feed to compensate at least visually for the antioxidants that wild fish obtain naturally and that are lacking in farmed fish because of the different composition of their feed.

––––––––––

Sustainability and ethical treatment are also a challenge at every step in the fish-farm chain, from the use of energy, genetic contamination of wild fish stocks, water pollution by disease-control substances, waste management, and the minimizing of suffering among the fish all the way to farm sanitation and working conditions. Susceptibility to disease in intensive fish farming means that infection can quickly spread, endangering wild populations if cages or nets in open water are used. Cases have been known of mass escapes by farmed fish through holes in the nets. Antibiotics can lead to resistance, with the possibility of serious consequences for humans and other species. Closed ponds have the advantage that—at least in theory—no pollutants, harmful microorganisms, or fish can escape. Upstream of such ponds, however, there may be ecological effects, because water needs to be diverted. Almost without exception, fish farming requires a great deal of space and can lead to serious pollution or damage to coasts and coastal marshes.

The most popular species, such as tuna and salmon, turn out to be the most problematic to farm. They are carnivorous and prone to disease, and a lot of time has to pass before they are ready for slaughter. This is clear from the farming of species of the *Salmonidae* family, usually referred to as salmon, although they include, for example, sea trout. They represent one of the most important branches of aquaculture. Salmon are kept in ponds on land or in cages in bays and fjords, especially in Norway, Canada, and Chile. They need to be grown for three years on a diet of fishmeal, fish oil, soy, and vegetable oil.

––––––––––

Improvements by means of genetic modification would appear to be the next step, but as yet this has always met with fierce objections from consumers, especially in Europe. There is a fear of bloated salmon by analogy with the big, bloated tomatoes of a few decades ago and more recently cheap and bloated supermarket chickens—even though those tomatoes were not produced by genetic modification, of course, any more than today's salmon are. More importantly, critical consumers have ensured that quality is now a priority for those hoping to improve species. The clearest justification for genetically modified fish and crustaceans concerns disease resistance (as it is with genetic modification of food crops, incidentally). When it comes to species that cannot be kept in captivity, or only with great difficulty (such as the sturgeon, or the bluefin tuna so popular in Japan), biotechnology may be able to help.

Despite all this, aquaculture is the way forward. It is a logical and inevitable step toward sustainable intensification of the use of the earth's resources. Farmed fish has a lower CO_2 footprint per kilogram than any other source of animal protein. Substitution of a proportion of the feed with vegetable sources or species lower in the food chain is crucial. Fish farming has a great deal of catching up to do compared to arable and livestock farming, but the road ahead is clear. Some whitefish species are already more efficient than chickens at turning feed into protein. The expectation is that by 2050 the farming of fish and other aquatic species will be as important as that of poultry. In China, fish farming is already as big as chicken farming.

From Plenty to an Awareness of Scarcity

For all food products, whether potatoes, bananas, or pork, production shows an increase that corresponds with the sum of population growth and income growth (and is therefore greater than population growth alone). This is not the case with fishing, however, although it does hold true for fish farming.

Over the past century, the catch has declined in specific parts of the ocean, like the cod catch around Newfoundland, and in rivers, as with salmon, which once swam in great quantities in the Rhine and its tributaries. In the Volga the wild sturgeon (the source of black caviar) has declined by 99 percent, mainly because of illegal fishing. The failure of the catch to grow at the same rate as that of the productivity of other food sources and the exhaustion of stocks are direct consequences of the absence of intensification in fishing. In other words, while yields on land are not static but grow per unit of land area because of investment in artificial fertilizer, pesticides, herbicides, and better tillage methods, what happens at sea is precisely what was feared on land several centuries ago. The seas, rivers, and lakes are not becoming any more productive (and are suffering from pollution and drought), but we are extracting more and more from them.

The exhaustion of fish stocks does not mean, incidentally, that the fish have disappeared altogether, merely that populations at certain places are so small that it is no longer worth the trouble of finding and catching them. Large predator fish are relatively easy to catch, and their absence has a disastrous effect on the rest of the food chain. Initially, exhaustion leads to the increased exploitation of fishing grounds elsewhere and to deeper fishing, then to the catching of younger fish and of other species lower in the food chain. In the North Sea more fish are being caught now than in the past, but the total weight is lower; fish seem to stay smaller and spawn earlier as a survival strategy. The extreme pressure on some fish stocks means that different species are caught in succession: first the large, then the middle-sized, and finally the small. Overfishing does not actually reduce marine biodiversity, in fact it can have the opposite effect. Some of the more somber estimates suggest that by the middle of this century all species now caught will reach a point at which the replacement rate falls, so that populations steadily deplete and there is a risk that they will be wiped out.

The solution lies not in banning the use of fish or parts of fish, as has been suggested for sturgeon and shark (because of the demand for shark's fins); the risk of a growing illegal trade leading to exhaustion is too great. The illegal trade in caviar from the Caspian Sea is now five times as great as the legal trade. We would do far better to consider a shift from fishing to the farming of aquatic species, but fishing for wild fish must be reformed as well. This is happening already to some extent, and there are good opportunities for further reform based on a combination of better technology and international agreements.

But like the meat trade, fishing is a sector of great contrasts, from primitive fishing from canoes in the South Pacific to the most modern refrigeration and satellite technologies that allow fish to be caught and processed thousands of tons at a time. Ironically, increases in scale actually produce more responsible behavior. It's impossible to make agreements with tens of thousands of small fishermen about moderating the catch, let alone to carry out checks on them, but it can be done with a small number of large ship owners. This explains why cod and herring stocks, with just a few major businesses sharing the catch, have returned to their former levels. In the North Sea a temporary ban on catching herring during the two decades from 1980 worked well and has helped make herring fisheries more sustainable. It seems that because of a temporary ban, the cod near Nova Scotia and Norway are recovering from overfishing. After years of monitoring we can conclude that fish species that form shoals can be managed well by a quota system. Without such a system, it is unlikely that these populations will increase.

Binding agreements are therefore necessary, and it seems they can be made. The countries with the largest fish catches are China, Peru, the United States, Indonesia, and Japan, but countries like India—already in the top ten—are increasingly active. Ninety percent of fish stocks currently being fished are within 200-mile coastal zones, in other words, within national jurisdictions, so nation-states can make agreements domestically and with their neighboring states about fishing limits and government policy. What matters is sustainable exploitation, so it is essential to know how many fish can be caught without depleting wild populations. All the countries named here have quota systems at least in theory.

Few consumers realize that fisheries, just like many other sectors in agriculture and food production, are subsidized to the tune of tens of billions of dollars a year and are regulated by fishing quotas. Those quotas actually stimulate the size of the catch, because everyone wants to fill their quotas. For a long time now, researchers and environmental organizations have been advocating a reduction of fishing quotas. An alternative might be regulation by means of a maximum number of days that fishermen are allowed to operate at sea. Fishing for species subject to a quota naturally leads to by-catch, at a ratio of 1:1.3, or 1.3 kilograms of by-catch for every 1 kilogram of the target fish. Those other fish species are not counted in the quota, but they are removed from the marine ecosystem. So damage is often far greater than the quota suggests, and damage is also done to the seabed by the heavy nets used by trawlers. Still, there are few indications that the exhaustion of species at the top of the aquatic food chain leads to the collapse of the entire ecosystem.

It will also be necessary to create marine reserves to combat overfishing. A mere 1 percent of the sea is now protected in some way. This is all but insignificant, and reserves are not like parks that you can protect with a fence to keep welcome species inside and unwelcome species out. Only the protection of very large areas will guarantee that ecosystems remain intact. The most urgent protection is needed, on ecological grounds at least, in the case of coral reefs, which in some regions are still fished with dynamite and threatened by pollution, rising water temperatures, and the decreasing alkalinity (that is, the slightly increasing acidity) of the oceans ever since the Industrial Revolution.

Fishing is similar to hunting in that it can be curbed only if we stop assuming that the oceans and seas are a kind of paradise where abundance comes free of charge. Fishing rights, known as concessions, are one solution. These concessions could be auctioned in an international market, with the additional advantage that poor countries that govern some of the fishing grounds, such as Ecuador and Mauritania, could earn extra income from the sale of these concessions.

There are many more questions to be asked about working conditions for fishermen and workers in the fish and shellfish industries. There too we see that the fishing sector is lagging behind compared to labor legislation in agriculture and elsewhere in the food industry. Much of the work has barely been automated if at all, such as the peeling of prawns, which are moved back and forth between northern Europe and Morocco, so that processors can take advantage of lower labor costs.

The fishing sector has taken the initiative over recent years by introducing labels marked with quality guarantees, as well as setting up roundtables to bring together all those involved in the fish farming chain, including supermarkets and, not least, nongovernmental organizations. Under the flag of the United Nations, international commissions have been set up to control fish stocks in the Atlantic and the Indian Ocean. In that sense the fisheries are more progressive than the meat sector, where production is still regulated by nation-states, even though feed may be imported and the final product exported. An active search is under way for more responsible alternatives and for ways of improving the quality and flavor of ready-to-eat fish products while still ensuring they meet the current demands of ease and convenience.

Some quality labels and guidelines exist, including those of the Marine Stewardship Council (MSC) and the Aquaculture Stewardship Council. The latter is not yet highly developed and is open to criticism. Even the MSC stamp of approval cannot guarantee that no more than a sustainable catch is landed, but it does aim to indicate that the wild fish concerned has been sustainably caught without damage to the environment. Such stamps of approval offer a more usable guide to consumers than red lists of threatened species or national fish guides. Nevertheless, they are still a source of confusion, and adherence to their guidelines does not provide any guarantee that fish populations will increase. The fact that the guidelines are related to spawning seasons makes them complicated, so they are often difficult for consumers to use. This kind of certification alone will not regulate fishing; it needs to be part of a wide range of measures to limit the catch from the wild. The industry as a whole has for some time had a Code of Responsible Fisheries, a general list of agreements among countries about fishing methods. It has no sanctions and no checks, however. There is no such thing as CO_2-neutral fish, incidentally, unless you go off in a rowing boat to fish for it yourself with a line made of wild fiber, and eat your catch immediately, raw.

Fish welfare, by analogy with the welfare of domestic animals on land, receives little attention from the public at large. Again this reflects the time lag between fisheries and fish farming on the one hand and agriculture and livestock farming on the other; in other words, it reflects the "primitive" character of this aspect of our food supply. The circumstances in which an animal is kept or caught to provide food for us characterize the relationship between humans and other species. Only if this realization penetrates public consciousness will there be a chance of a responsible relationship. Fish and aquatic animals are still taken for granted, and the conditions in which they live are still largely invisible. Moreover, there is still a great deal of controversy about how fish can best be kept. Some supermarket chains have stopped selling eel, whereas producers are trying to encourage people to buy sustainable eel that is allowed to pass through an entire life cycle.

Aquaculture is a necessary development, but we should not assume that it's a solution to the depletion of fish stocks in the oceans. Fish farming changes our relationship with the sea, unless we move all aquaculture onto land. Should we place restrictions on fish consumption as a whole, because of its damaging effects on the seas, marine biodiversity, and the environment? I think that would be the wrong route to take, if only because almost half a billion people, especially in Asia, are employed in fishing and fish farming. Better production methods, protection of species and spawning grounds, and above all a reduction—within a clear international framework—of the use of fishmeal and fish oil as fish feed would probably be a more successful approach. Governments and fishing organizations will be essential in achieving these goals.

We can and must take another fundamental step in our evolution, which will bring about a structural change to our relationship with the seas. From the point of view of health and the environment, we must start eating other marine species instead of fish, such as seaweed and algae. We might look at it this way: fishing is analogous to hunting, fish farming to livestock farming, and algae cultivation to arable farming. If we take the step of consuming vegetable organisms from water, it will be as important an evolutionary transition as starting to grow crops. It will mean a fundamental change in our use of water, by harvesting the lowest species in the food chain, which like land plants fix energy by means of photosynthesis. Seaweed—which is now grown only on a small scale, mainly in Japan, and is elsewhere harvested from the wild only to a limited extent—contains in its dried form a high proportion of protein and other nutrients and is easy to transport and store. One additional aspect is that algae and seaweed can absorb phosphates held in solution in seawater, which come partly from the fertilization of farmland. We need marine farms with floating islands of seaweed instead of fish. An intermediary step would be to combine fish farming with sea vegetable farming, a system known as aquaponics. In a closed system from which no nutrients are lost, vegetables benefit from the nutrients in waste water from fishponds, and the filtered water that results is used to replenish the ponds, resulting in extremely high crop yields (the ratio of vegetables to fish is 50:1).

If fast food chains were to put seaweed or marsh samphire sandwiches on the menu, it would be a sign of our new relationship with the seas and oceans. That will only happen when everyone comes to realize that the time of the liquid paradise where everything was possible and plentiful is over for good—and when the intestinal flora of the whole of humanity are as adapted to the digestion of seaweed as are those of the Japanese.

SEVEN

Hairy Apples: The Challenge of Biotechnology

I read and re-read her letter and some softened feelings stole into my heart
and dared to whisper paradisiacal dreams of love and joy; but the apple was
already eaten, and the angel's arm bared to drive me from all hope.
MARY SHELLEY, *Frankenstein*

> The world's wealth would be won by the man who,
> out of the Rhine-gold, fashioned the ring
> which measureless might would bestow.
> WAGNER, *Das Rheingold*

On Chaos, Monsters, and Paradise

At first sight it looks like an ordinary apple that's been in the fruit bowl
too long. You see it from one side: yellow underneath, the skin a little
dried out. Toward the top it has turned a reddish brown, as if the flesh
is already beginning to rot. Only then do you notice that the apple has
short, downy hair on top, so that it suddenly seems as if you're looking
at a baby's head or the pate of an elderly man, or perhaps the hide of an
unknown animal. The delay to the shock doesn't make it any less intense:
this is an unnatural object, a being that smashes right through the harmonious relationship between humans and nature.

The hairy apple is not the only example of its kind. On the Internet you'll
find pictures of apples with zebra stripes, pears with frog's eyes, a sheep
with the body of a cauliflower, and more delights along the same lines—
all unappetizing crosses between animal and plant. Occasionally you'll
find hybrids of humans and plants, such as apples with human teeth that
bite back. They are all fantasy images, of course, not things that actually
exist. They're intended purely to arouse disgust.

Even though we know these are manipulated images, they disturb us
nevertheless, and not without reason. We have a deep aversion to everything that crosses the barriers between human, plant, and animal. The
advertisement showing the hairy apple comes from a Spanish campaign
demanding that warnings be printed on the labels of all genetically

171

modified products similar to those on cigarette packaging: Danger! Mutated apple! Can kill! Will damage your health! The campaign was discussed in the French art magazine *Beaux Arts* under the title "Forbidden Fruit"—an interesting illustration of how art is involved in criticism of technology and society. The article opens with the question: "What if one day fruits became horrific, hairy creatures? The work of arrogant researchers and greedy capitalists, the Frankensteins of the orchards, these fruits will bear the mark of guilt and sin." It goes on to suggest that we'll soon find winged bananas and one-eyed apricots in our supermarket trolleys.

Fear of crossing species boundaries is a fear of the unknown, the indefinable, the unnatural, a fear of chaos. Fear takes particular forms in each culture, but the opposite of this fear is identical almost everywhere; at the other end of the spectrum from chaos is the divine order of paradise, that comprehensible world of distinct species living side by side without conflict, each with a place of its own. In paradise every species has a natural role, so they all know their boundaries. The same is true, especially so, for human beings. Adam and Eve are forbidden to eat from the tree of knowledge; seed-bearing plants alone may serve as food (a command revised only outside paradise, after the flood). Paradise represents a natural order, set in stone for eternity, where everything is in its place and nothing may be tinkered with, genetically or otherwise. This natural order is of course fictional, because ecosystems and societies are neither stable nor orderly, and species and their genetic characteristics are continually evolving. But that biological fact does not alter the human desire to eliminate chaos.

The desire for harmony explains the universally felt aversion to hybrids of animal and plant, human and animal, plant and human—to hairy apples and frog-pears. Almost all cultures have stories about creatures that are half-human, half-animal. They go back a very long way, beginning with the fire-breathing Chimera—part lion, part goat, part snake—which features in Homer, and they persist today in countless role-playing games and in the Harry Potter stories. They are possible only by means of sorcery (as with Harry Potter), divine intervention, or the work of alchemists and dangerous researchers. The tradition is certainly not confined to the western hemisphere. We find hybrid figures elsewhere, such as the Hindu Narasingha, half-lion and half-man, and the Japanese Tengu, a cross between a man and a bird that also appears in mangas. Then there is the Greek Minotaur, half-man, half-bull. The were-jaguar of the ancient Olmecs combines the power and aggression of the jaguar with the intelligence and spirituality of the human.

There are countless fables featuring near-human creatures that look like animals or even plants. Almost without exception they are the helpers of the gods, or gods themselves that adopt a variety of forms. Generally speaking they have evil intentions and may bring diseases or natural disasters. Sometimes they are neutral and only very occasionally do they show themselves to be benevolent toward humankind, like the elephant god Ganesha in India. All such examples of crossing species boundaries are the result of divine intervention. They are never initiated by humans. It is not human beings that manipulate species but the gods. Humans are in fact warned time and again to keep their distance. Monsters that combine human, animal, and plant are the stuff of nightmares or dark fairytales, not of human dealings. At their best they challenge the heroes among humankind to demonstrate their extraordinary human characteristics of determination and courage; at their worst they sow death and destruction. All these monsters are supernatural. They can do more than humans, animals, and plants put together, because they are immune to the natural laws of space and time.

In a few cases the belief in the existence of mythical hybrids seems to arise from a misunderstanding. There is a wonderful story from Central Asia about the discovery of a cross between a lamb and a plant. It can be traced back to an unusually hairy variety of cotton—we suddenly seem to have found an ancestor of that hairy apple. All these mythological examples suggest that under the right circumstances hybrids possess a supernatural strength, but it is almost always associated with a threat to human beings.

Hybrids are different from transformations from one state to another, which can be rather less threatening. Ovid tells how the nymph Daphne took the form of a tree to escape the advances of Apollo. Bernini's wonderful statue of them shows her fingers and locks of hair turning into leaves. Crosses between human and animal can get out of hand and turn against humanity without hesitation. Such creatures are the domain of the gods; they alone can keep the forces released by such hybridization under control. This idea is echoed in the words of Britain's Prince Charles, who believes that genetic modification is in conflict with nature and takes us into "realms that belong to God and God alone."

Yet we ought to be thoroughly familiar with hybrids of all kinds, if only in an evolutionary sense. We share an important part of our genome with other species, going back to the very first simple, one-celled prokaryotes. Without crossing—or, more generally, without the mixing of genetic material from different individuals and populations—there would have been no photosynthesis, nor any oxygen, so mammals, including humans, could not have come into existence. We are increasingly discovering that nature scatters DNA around with apparent carelessness, both among and within species. That we are so troubled by genetic exchange and recombination, and that genetic modification is equated in some circles with playing god and creating foul monsters, has nothing to do with biology but rather with old fears of chaos and our longing for a paradisiacal harmony among species. Religions tell us that nature is governed by the gods, and humans must not intervene. But if we look at our past, especially since the beginning of farming, it is clear that we have intervened continually.

Genetic Intervention as Part of Our History

In paradise, that impossible, inexhaustible ecosystem, the apple trees and the grain fields live forever. There are no seasons and, if we are to believe tradition, fruits and vegetables are harvested only little by little. If plants grow ceaselessly without setting seed and animals have no need to reproduce, then the obverse of this continual stream of food is the absence of genetics and evolution. Genetic selection, the survival of those individuals most fitted to survive, works only if there are offspring that react to the environment in different ways, responding differently to heat or cold, rain or drought, disease and threat. In the ecosystem of paradise there are no fluctuations in the weather, any more than there are crop-eating insects, viruses, or predators. Humans in paradise do not engage in genetic selection. Eve takes the apple that's offered to her, she doesn't seek the nicest apple so that she can plant its seeds and breed more apple trees from it. The apple tree worthy of paradise already exists, in paradise, and all its fruits are equally beautiful and perfect. In paradise selection is senseless. In fact it's impossible.

PLATE 1 The connection in paradise among diversity, plenty, and well-being is beautifully depicted in the variety of open and dense vegetation in a landscape with a great range of colorful animals and plants. Adam and Eve are on the point of committing the original sin, but the painters suggest they are enjoying this diversity and abundance for one moment longer. Partly because of such depictions, which are associated with the paradise myth, diversity has acquired a positive moral charge (Chapter 9). "Earthly Paradise with the Fall of Adam and Eve"; Peter Paul Rubens and Jan Breughel the Elder, 1615–1617; Mauritshuis, The Hague / The Bridgemen Art Library.

PLATE 2 Painters rarely if ever aim to offer a photographic or realistic picture of the landscape, let alone of agriculture, but they give us pointers toward the continual presence of the agrarian: the grazed fields, the felled trees, the grain in the distance, the cow at the water's edge. Here too nostalgia lurks, because in fact by 1830 this small-scale landscape was already disappearing (Chapter 3). "The Glebe Farm"; John Constable, c. 1830; Tate Gallery, London.

PLATE 3 The ecology of paradise is miraculous, as befits a divine creation. Painting elaborates on these ecological miracles. Whereas Genesis speaks merely of fruit-bearing trees and seed-bearing plants, Hieronymus Bosch turns paradise into a climatological potpourri: a hilly landscape of temperate trees with an elephant, a unicorn, deer, and an overwhelming number of birds and cacti (Chapter 1). "The Garden of Earthly Delights," detail; Hieronymus Bosch, 1480–1505; ©Museo Nacional del Prado, Madrid / Getty Images.

PLATE 4 The theme of paradise is not confined to the West. This book of miniatures from thirteenth-century Baghdad about the characteristics and uses of animals, called *Manafi al-Hayawan*, includes a picture of Adam and Eve surrounded by a decor of flowering shrubs and grasses. We can identify pomegranate bushes by their red flowers, with two multi-colored birds perched in them (Chapter 1). "Adam and Eve"; Anonymous, late thirteenth century; miniature from *Manafi al-Hayawan*; Pictures from History / Bridgeman Images

PLATE 5 This horrifying picture of the expulsion from paradise does not show paradise at all, but instead the desolate world outside it, a bleak moonscape, a colorless place devoid of plants and animals. Its negative view depicts the lush plenty of paradise all the more sharply (Chapters 1 and 3). "Expulsion from the Garden of Eden"; Masaccio (real name Tommaso di Giovanni Cassai), c. 1427; fresco in the Brancacci Chapel, Church of Santa Maria del Carmine, Florence; akg-images / De Agostini Picture Lib. / A. Dagli Orti.

PLATE 6 Even in cultures that do not have a paradise story, such as that of the ancient Romans, the garden is the archetype of civilization and therefore of the idealized harmony between humankind and nature. This fresco showing the garden of Empress Livia depicts untroubled security and fertility in the form of water and laden fruit trees. To this day the garden perpetuates the illusion of paradise (Chapter 1). "Garden"; Anonymous, c. 30–20 BC; fresco at the Villa of Livia, Primaporta; Museo Nazionale Romano, Rome, Italy / Bridgeman Images.

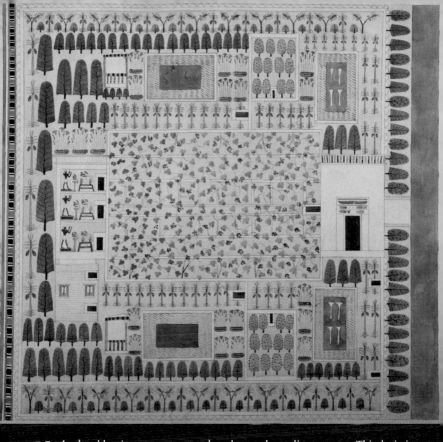

PLATE 7 In the oldest images, ornamental gardens and paradise converge. This depiction of the walled garden of Sennefer, a senior civil servant under Amenhotep III (also known as Amenophis III), was found in a grave in Thebes, Egypt. An avenue of trees runs along the periphery and other avenues divide the garden into eight planted areas surrounding a vineyard. There are two rectangular lakes with lotuses and ducks. This geometric division perfectly matches what we read in Genesis. The river that waters paradise splits into four arms, a pattern seen elsewhere in the Middle East and in the Islamic gardens of Andalucía (Chapter 1). "The Garden of the High Official of Amenhotep (Amenophis) III," also known as "Sennefer's Garden"; Anonymous, c. 1417–1379 BC; Kingston Lacy, Dorset, UK, The Bankes Collection / National Trust Photographic Library / Derrick E. Witty / Bridgeman Images.

PLATE 8 This fragment of white ceramic from the city of Nimrud, on the bank of the Tigris in what is now northern Iraq, shows a cow with a suckling calf. It's 5,000 years old, but the lifelike expressions on the faces of the cow and her hungry offspring are utterly contemporary. The artist must surely have observed the creatures with love, thereby demonstrating how highly valued domestic animals were even in that era (Chapter 5). Plaque fragment with a cow and suckling calf; Anonymous, 3,000 BC; Metropolitan Museum of Art, New York; akg-images / De Agostini Picture Lib. / G. Dagli Orti.

PLATE 9 This 150-kilogram steel hamburger represents the Chinese dream of the West. When the father of one of Liao Yibai's classmates went to the United States on an official trip, the class begged him to bring back a sample of the mysterious hamburger. On his return the father showed them a thick envelope bearing the words "Top Secret." Inside was a hamburger, an almost otherworldly brownish-green thing giving off such a foul stench that the schoolchildren were immediately convinced of the perversity of capitalism. Only much later did Liao Yibai realize that what he had experienced was not the smell of the American system (Chapter 2). "Top Secret Hamburger"; Liao Yibai, 2009; courtesy of Mike Weiss Gallery, New York.

PLATE 10 The Land of Cockaigne is paradise in overdrive, where absolutely everything consists of food ready to eat, up to and including the buildings with roofs made of pancakes and the landscape of rice-pudding hills. The food makes its own way to the eaters, sometimes by means of animals that offer themselves for consumption, such as the pig on the right, walking around with a knife in its back. The weird exaggeration surely shows relief from toil, from chronic food shortages, and from a monotonous diet (Chapter 1). "The Land of Cockaigne"; Pieter Breughel the Elder, 1567; Alte Pinakothek, Munich / Bildagentur für Kunst, Kultur und Geschichte, Berlin; P. Brueghel t. E. / Cockaigne.

PLATE 11 This loaf of the poor, from southern Italy, is by writer and artist Carlo Levi, who was exiled there during the Second World War. In the hard, almost black crust and the golden-yellow interior he recognized the suffering of the people in the inaccessible landscape. His loaf, drawn in streaks of charcoal, is a wounded mountain, a lonely human, the globe of the earth (Chapter 4). "Il Pane"; Carlo Levi, 1971; charcoal drawing; Fondazione Carlo Levi, Rome.

PLATE 12   The relationship between human beings and farm animals is experienced as less problematic when the distance between them is small. Until fifty years ago, animal carcasses were hung up in plain sight in butcher's shops. On dining tables, and in many still lifes, the animal was presented in a recognizable form. Here we see the dead stag, gutted but otherwise intact, next to the head of a wild boar and a whole lobster on a lavishly overburdened table. This is not how we wish to see our meat these days (Chapter 5). "Still Life with a Dead Stag"; Studio of Frans Snijders, 1630–1650; Mauritshuis, The Hague; © Rijksmuseum, Amsterdam.

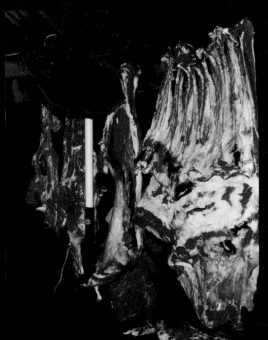

PLATE 13   That meat and the killing of warm-blooded animals no longer leaves us unmoved is demonstrated by Berend Strik in his adaptation of a photograph of bloody carcasses, for which he used dark-red velvet. It gives the image an abstract, three-dimensional depth from which you return to reality with a shock. Strik makes visible what we do not wish to see, the fleshiness and at the same time the irresistible nature of meat. Meat is the ultimate temptation (Chapter 5). "Suspended Blurr"; Berend Strik, photography by Gert Jan van Rooij, 2011; Fons Welters Gallery, Amsterdam.

The challenge to human ingenuity begins only at the point when we free ourselves from the drip-feed of this artificial, mythical abundance of food. Only after the expulsion from paradise do we begin the learning process that enables us to use other species to feed ourselves. So a straight line runs from paradise and the Fall of Man to genetics and biotechnology in modern farming. Agriculture always involves genetic intervention, even if hardly any modern consumers are aware of the fact. Even as hunter-gatherers, humans developed a preference for certain species and certain individuals, but only as herdsmen and farmers did they start to make choices that influenced the genetics of all the species around them, both useful and unuseful: yes to wheat and to the wheat with the fullest ears, no to the fungi that cause stem rust on wheat; yes to the tamest horses, no to those that refuse the harness. Human selectivity with regard to what is sustained, protected, and selected goes far further than evolution's natural selection.

Whatever our staple diet may be—steak 'n' chips, vegetarian lasagne, rice with chicken and soy sauce—almost all our food (with the exception of flesh from wild populations like tuna) is derived from organisms that have been not merely caught or harvested but also cultivated and domesticated. By definition, farming entails domestication. Domestication means intervention in genetics by selecting from a population only those individuals that have the characteristics that suit us. We choose the biggest, reddest apples, not the most unsightly and maggot-ridden, and plant their pips. It's a process that repeats itself over many generations of apple trees, sheep, or wheat plants. Through domestication, and therefore by means of individual selection, a shift slowly takes place in the genetic composition of populations of those apples, sheep, or wheat. This doesn't happen purely as a result of the deliberate human selection of individual plants or animals the farmer wants to reproduce, it also happens indirectly, because some individuals react better to environments that are controlled by humans. Some individual vegetables will grow better with the extra water and nutrients that accumulate in gardens close to human dwellings, for example. Plants that quickly bolt in response to the extra nitrogen available in vegetable plots and therefore produce little seed or fruit will not be well represented in the next crop. A genetic shift will naturally take place toward plants that do not bolt too soon.

Human influence on the genetic composition of nature is not limited to domestication. As farmers we don't just intervene, consciously or unconsciously, to promote useful species, we also intervene in entire ecosystems. Farmers are always eager to limit the population of other, unwanted species: weeds, insects, ticks, predators, and any other species that threaten the selected plants and animals. It starts with burning off vegetation to hunt or to make room for crops. In forests we want to maintain coppices and oak trees for building, but not too many squirrels that will consume the acorns our pigs would otherwise eat. Nettles, woolly aphids, leaf curl viruses: we try to wipe out all these unwanted species by systematic and purposeful means that do not exist elsewhere in nature. This too is a form of genetic intervention. Then there are the indirect but immense effects of humankind on other species in the surrounding area or in arable fields and meadows—creatures that are not directly damaging or even unwanted, such as ground-nesting birds, badgers or bats, frogs and algae, whose environment is damaged by us. Over time, entire ecosystems have disappeared as a result, such as primal forests in temperate regions, while others have been radically changed by cultivation; the introduction of new species; the change from open fields to hedge-bounded enclosures and back again; fertilization; or the alteration of water courses by irrigation, drainage, and dams.

Domestication has its limits, because we can choose only among individuals that have spontaneously reproduced or hybridized. In other words, domestication makes use only of the relatively limited variation that already exists in a population. Very occasionally a population will include an individual that has crossed with a related weed or undergone a spontaneous mutation. Another still relatively unknown source of variation is epigenetic, meaning that although the genes have not changed, their activity has—that is, their state of being switched on or off.

The arsenal of genetic features cannot be expanded by combining species that, by definition, do not interbreed (rice and apples, for instance, or even apples and pears, even though they are closely related). Domestication can create very little variation in plants that reproduce vegetatively, such as cassava and bananas, because they will be genetically identical to the mother plant unless a spontaneous mutation takes place. Vegetative reproduction is in fact the same as cloning, so breeders seek the best mutants among clones with virtually identical genes.

Much more dramatic than the genetic effects of domestication and land use is the introduction of locally novel species by travel and trade. They may be useful species, such as cassava and corn in Africa, or those many unwanted exotics that became major plagues, as rabbits did in Australia, and the countless pathogens that traveled along with our livestock. The powerful dominance of these introduced species, which have no natural enemies, has had a huge impact on native species. Conversely, the arrival of exotics has created unprecedented risks. This is tragically illustrated by the potato, which originated in Peru and came to dominate farming in mid-nineteenth-century Ireland in particular. A local soil fungus, *Phytophthora* sp., to which the potato plant had no resistance, completely destroyed the crop within just a few years, including the seed potatoes.

Agriculture, therefore, put the relationship between humans and nature on a new footing. It meant a break with everything that had gone before in evolution, because human intervention is systematic, cumulative, large in scale, and mostly irreversible. No other species can match us in this respect. In the hundreds of thousands of years before farming began, humans as hunters and as gatherers of wild fruits, leaves, and roots were of hardly any ecological significance. The extremely sparse human population of that long period—far less than one person per square kilometer— shows that "exploitation," the use of the ecosystem by humans, was not particularly successful, because otherwise the capacity of that ecosystem (that is, its productivity) and the number of humans would have been higher. Conversely, that relative lack of success shows that human influence on the ecosystem was very limited, otherwise the human population would have been able to grow more quickly.

The effect of the Neolithic hunter was no different from that of meat-eating predators at the top of the food chain, such as lions, coyotes, and wolves. Hunting implements like axes, traps, or bows and arrows would have had an influence on local populations of prey, such as gazelles, but early humans did not interfere directly with the genetics of their populations. The loss of the weakest animals to predators is after all part of natural selection. The dramatic eradication of bison or elephants took place far later, when humans had modern weapons at their disposal. The control of fire, with which animals were flushed out and food cooked and dried so that it would keep longer, represents a breakthrough, but it did not usually affect the ecosystem any more permanently than spontaneous sources of fire, such as lighting and volcanic eruptions, the consequences of which are insignificant on a time scale of decades, let alone centuries.

Since time immemorial, genetic selection has been a subjective process: the farmer's eye determines the choice. Somewhere in those first centuries after the start of agriculture, people became aware that they could purposefully influence inheritance. It is sometimes said, jokingly, that the first plant breeder was a Neolithic woman, because she was the first deliberately to choose ears of grain to keep as seed for planting the next year. The first farmers must have realized that strong parents bring forth strong offspring, even if only because that was their experience with human children.

It has been only just over a century since we first used statistics—rather than looking at just one or two characteristics—to resume selection by chance in a population to increase genetic variation in that population. The greater the variation, the more potential there is to choose interesting offspring. Perhaps selection has had unintended effects. In the case of many vegetables, over the centuries specimens have been chosen to delay their seed germination until after harvest, because gemination before affects the vegetable's flavor and results in lost seed. Thus in the case of most modern vegetable varieties, the seed no longer germinates spontaneously at all; it has to be treated in some way first. So without human intervention, these vegetables will die out. That is the ultimate consequence of domestication: most agricultural species will not survive without us.

The most radical and permanent effect of humans on plant genetics is that through farming we have created entirely new species out of wild plants, species that do not occur in nature and bear almost no resemblance to their ancestors. Once, some 7,000 years ago, selection began in the case of a plant called teosinte (*Zea mays*, sp. *parviglumis*), from which modern corn is derived. But this ancestor bears hardly any resemblance to the modern crop. Teosinte is a low plant, not unlike grass, and instead of corn cobs it bears many featherlike ears holding triangular seeds. It can still be crossed with corn, if with some difficulty, so it has to be regarded as a subspecies. Over time, domestication causes shifts away from the original population that lead to distinct changes to the phenotype or outward appearance of a plant. Such changes happen gradually, until a time arrives when the original populations can no longer cross with the domesticated species. That is the point at which a new species has come into being, one that differs from its ancestors both genetically and phenotypically.

Just how complicated the effects of domestication can be, whether intentional or not, can be seen from the genome of the apple, which has more than twice as many genes as a human being. At some point in the selection process, the number of genes doubled. This means that the apple has far more chromosomes—seventeen, to be precise—than its closest relatives in its species, *Malus*, or its family, the Rosacaea, which have nine or fewer. This genetic plasticity perhaps explains why the apple has adapted so well to so many different regions of the world. The apple, the first cultivated fruit tree, is unusual among farm crops in that the varieties now grown do not belong to a different species but to that of the original populations in the mountains between China and Kazakhstan.

––––––––––

We have engaged in genetic modification throughout the history of farming to a far greater extent than most people realize. It first came about because farmers always used the best individuals among their plants and animals for breeding purposes, and for the past century or so breeders have engaged in systematic and scientifically calculated hybridization using the most promising stock as parents. Agricultural crops and animals are truly new species or subspecies, created by humankind.

Genetic Modification as Continuity and Discontinuity

Domestication did not stop after the Neolithic era or somewhere in the Middle Ages. It's a process that continues to this day and will continue for as long as humans engage in farming. The most recent forms of domestication are now taking place in horticulture as a response to growing demand for vegetables and fruit. We have recently started growing arugula, or "garden" rocket (*Eruca sativa*), which is less bitter and more productive than its wild relative. Perhaps the greatest success of recent domestication is the kiwi, known the world over, of which the next step in evolution has just reached our supermarkets in the form of the Zespri varieties, developed from the most golden and sweet kiwi fruits. Another well-known recent product of domestication is the nectarine, which is not (as many think) a cross between a peach and a plum but a chance hairless mutation of a Chinese peach that would have little chance of survival in nature because of its vulnerability to insect damage.

Modern plant breeding of the twentieth and twenty-first centuries, including biotechnology or genetic technology, is an extension of 10,000 years of domestication. What began with a search for individuals that happened by chance to be unusual or particularly desirable has become a systematic approach to breeding plants and animals based on scientific research. This step was made possible by an increased knowledge of genetics and the rediscovery in the late nineteenth century of Mendel's laws of inheritance. Mendel showed that the characteristics of the parents are "discrete," in other words they are passed down to the next generation intact and not mixed: a pink flower and a yellow flower do not produce a plant with orange flowers, instead they produce pink- and yellow-flowering plants in predictable ratios. You can select the plants with pink flowers and continue to cross them until the gene for yellow almost completely disappears. From the 1950s on, as the molecular basis for inheritance, DNA, was becoming increasingly well understood, the breeding of farm species grew to become an important field of science and an industry worth billions. Genetic improvement went hand in hand with the application in agriculture of other scientific advances, such as the use of artificial fertilizer, drip irrigation, and mechanization. Combined with genetic improvements, these technologies have accelerated the increase in both yields and the quality of food production in a way that is truly staggering.

The changes that flow from all this are so extensive that we are increasingly worried about the effects of our intervention. It seems as if agriculture and food production have become independent forces, outside of ourselves, and we are in a permanent state of unease about them. Can we keep a grip on the consequences of our own existence? We are the only species on this planet to have become, over the past two decades at least, increasingly aware of our responsibility for the earth and for nature. Our uncertainty and sense of responsibility are most evident in relation to biotechnology, especially the genetic modification of organisms. More even than erosion or the felling of forests, this technology seems to cross a line, perhaps precisely because the line is invisible.

To what extent does biotechnology truly mark a new course? Its advocates say it is nothing of the kind but at most an acceleration of what we have been doing for many years, only by far more efficient means and more focused methods. For at least 10,000 years we've had such an effect on the genetics of plants and other animals that species have emerged that would not have evolved and could not survive without us. If biotechnology fits seamlessly into a continuity of human intervention, then the fear that it will create monsters is nothing more than the ancient fear of chaos in a new guise. At most it is amplified by the uncertainties brought about by secularization, modernization, and globalization.

But it's not so easy to push aside the often fierce emotions that accompany opposition to biotechnology. Opponents are not simply hostile to modern technology; they claim a completely new situation has arisen in which humans have taken control of nature and gone beyond natural limitations. It's no accident that their fear is often expressed in eschatological and religious terms: genetic modification is a violation of the sanctity of life. In the eyes of activists this justifies the use of violence in the destruction of trial plots of genetically modified plants.

The deadlock between those who see a discontinuity and those who see continuity is made all the harder to resolve because most people have little understanding of genetics. We are witnessing a triumph of Babel-like confusion and biased language. There is often a failure to distinguish among modern breeding, biotechnology, and genetically modified or transgenic crops. DNA, that ribbon-like carrier of inherited characteristics in every cell, on which genes are grouped, remains a mystery to many. Genes themselves are nothing more than instructions for the making of proteins in a cell, and they determine the function and appearance of cells and the substances within and around them.

Breeding, the search for plants or animals with better genomes and the perpetuation of them, takes place via three routes. Classic breeding, or a continuation of domestication, involves repeatedly crossing individuals to find the best combination of features. Unwanted characteristics result as well, and these must be eliminated by further crossing (rapid growth, for example, may be accompanied by low sugar content and therefore less flavor). The mid-twentieth century saw the beginnings of mutagenesis, in which radioactivity or chemicals were used to produce mutations. This turned out to be a process governed by chance, impossible to steer. The third way was that of biotechnology, also known as "genetic modification," a general term for a broad range of techniques that allow us to profile and use precise genetic information. It provides us with a toolkit that includes such techniques as tissue culture, DNA fingerprinting (identification based on short pieces of DNA), marking specific genes, mapping genetic sequences, cloning, embryo transfer, using restriction enzymes (molecular scissors, so to speak, that can cut DNA at specific places), and the methods of recombinant DNA, which use all these techniques to introduce a new gene into a genome.

The improved profiling of the genetic composition of crops, farm animals, trees, and fish is in itself a fundamental improvement on searching for a needle in a DNA haystack in order to track down favorable features of a plant or animal. After all, these emerge only after the offspring have grown, and in the case of trees, for example, it may take years for the desired qualities, such as larger fruit, to become evident. As for resistance to diseases or infestations, you might have to wait for many generations to be certain that susceptibility has really been reduced. Means of categorizing certain features can in themselves help accelerate classic methods of breeding and lead to new insights about how genes are interrelated, without having as an end result any modification of animals or plants. With animals that reproduce only with difficulty and in small numbers, such as older breeds of cattle, or fish used in fish farming, the use of techniques involving embryos is of immense value.

Genetically modified organisms (GMOs), sometimes called "transgenic organisms," represent just one specific application of biotechnology, although they are the outcome that has attracted the most attention by far among the public at large. Modification involves the artificial introduction of a desired characteristic. Special techniques are used to create a parent plant or animal that has cells in which one or more genes are present that do not occur in the original species. This parent is then used to create new varieties, cultivars, or breeds. The modification may be transgenic, in other words, genes derived from a species with which it would not be possible to cross the plant or animal concerned, as with the introduction of a gene from a bacterium into a cotton plant. Then there is intragenic modification, which involves a plant or animal that could be used for breeding, except that the genes concerned would not naturally combine in the desired way. Cisgenic crops, currently mostly apples or potatoes, belong in a category of their own as well; they involve the introduction of a gene from a closely related species, often a wild ancestor. In the case of potatoes this technique is increasingly being deployed in attempts to introduce resistance to fungal disease. Cisgenesis is seen by some opponents as the "least bad" form of biotechnology, since no "frightening" crosses can occur; everything stays in the family, and the same combination could in theory occur spontaneously. It serves mostly as a way of developing resistance to diseases and infestations, because the likelihood of finding truly new features in related species, families, and varieties is small by definition. Unfortunately, neither politicians nor the general public have learned to distinguish among these different forms of genetic modification.

In nature, too, "foreign genes" can sometimes be introduced spontaneously. This generally results in nothing unusual, but occasionally it produces extremely advantageous adaptations. Crosses between unrelated species are therefore not entirely the preserve of human intervention; in fact, exchanges of DNA between species are quite common. The difference between this and genetic modification by humans lies of course in its speed and scale. With spontaneous transgenic offspring, hundreds or thousands of years may pass before the new variety or breed is present in large numbers in nature, and there is a good chance that it will not survive the pressure of natural selection, however advantageous the specific new adaptation may be. We know that bacteria and viruses can quite easily penetrate the cell membrane of other species and introduce their genetic material into the host, thereby producing transgenic cells spontaneously. This capacity is used in breeding to send a package of genes, as it were, into a cell.

It is correct to speak of genetically modified food if a GMO is directly eaten (a transgenic tomato, for example) or if GMOs are used in the production of a dish, whether as the main ingredient (for example, starch or oil from genetically modified corn, soy, or rape) or as an additive or flavoring (such as sugar syrup from modified corn). Substances used in processing, such as rennet or yeast, do not count.

––––––

Although biotechnology as a whole is controversial, the genetic modification of organisms raises questions about our most profound relationships with other species. Are we lord and master of this planet, or should the purposeful manipulation of other species be reserved for God, or for nature and natural processes? Many religions share the idea that all knowledge is of divine origin and the use of it by humankind must be punished if it leads to conceit, arrogance, greed, and high-handedness. Strictly orthodox religious groups are opposed to technological innovation, because it brings with it a modernization of norms and values, introducing individualism and personal choices that detract from the dominance of religious leaders. The temptations of curiosity, the feeling out of boundaries, and experimentation started in a sense with Eve and the eating of the fruit of the tree of knowledge, with all that followed from it.

Despite secularization, the idea that people should not simply apply "divine" knowledge, and a sense that knowledge is inherently dangerous, is widespread in the Western world, especially among new ideological groups, as well as consumer, ecological, and nature-loving movements. Science and technology are seen as opposed to what is thought of as local or traditional knowledge, and the secrecy of closed laboratories is contrasted with the proud farming families that welcome visitors with stories about the traditions of their farm. Modern science "tampers" with nature, so lovingly cared for by those who resist modernization. This is a caricature, of course. That technological knowledge and love of nature and tradition are not necessarily opposites but can go well together is demonstrated by Dutch dairy farmers who experiment with the most modern cowsheds, with the welfare of both animals and the environment in mind, and at the same time regard all their cows as individuals. Conversely, the treatment of animals in so-called traditional societies leaves a lot to be desired, as demonstrated by the fate of donkeys in Marrakesh so movingly described by Elias Canetti. History is full of examples of ignorance disguised as traditional knowledge that should not be idealized, from the letting of blood to the incorrect pruning of fruit trees.

Biotechnology is an emotionally charged subject for another, related reason. Modern farming is increasingly synonymous with increases in scale, globalization, and the worldwide feed and food supply chain. Even if modern techniques like irrigation or the application of artificial fertilizer are bound to a specific place and deployed only locally, the products of farming and the food industry touch all of us: mass chicken farming in Asia is dependent on genetically modified soy from Brazil, and Indian consumers buy soft drinks sweetened with American corn syrup. Seed from genetically modified plants is spreading all over the world, driving out traditional varieties. From that perspective genetic modification seems essentially to be a conspiracy against the traditions of the countryside and old ways of eating, setting small-scale enterprise, collective activity, and local values against large-scale business, trade, and material gain. Traditional, honest farmers know their plants and animals almost as individuals, because they selected them personally, whereas modern managers in their combines are at a great distance from the genetically modified rapeseed they grow and do not know what happens to their product, except that it is shipped all over the world. This is the stereotypical picture of two opposing worlds.

To me the knowledge of genetics and its application to the improvement of farm breeds of animals and plants, and ultimately of useful insects and other creatures, is an extension of what humans undertook long ago, using methods increasingly based on science. It is therefore as much about continuity as it is about a qualitative break with the past resulting from the scale and speed with which knowledge is deployed. Nevertheless, there are potential consequences for humans and the natural world. Biotechnology is not merely a perpetuation of earlier human dealings and existing biological knowledge. It is a fundamentally new step in the sense that it enables far more goal-oriented work and a search for characteristics that have always been impossible to introduce or perhaps did not even exist.

One clear example is the "silk potato," with a gene taken from a silk-weaving spider that enables the potato to produce an extremely strong silklike fiber that has countless industrial applications, with yields far higher than those of the spider. The same process has been applied to goats, which produce silk fibers along with their milk. These are fundamentally new steps, because new materials are manufactured that were unavailable using conventional techniques. The creation of animals or plants with the aim of making them serve our needs is experienced by most people as a step that puts us on the level of divine creator. Yet this too is a continuation of an old development: for centuries we have made use of silk from living organisms, silkworms. Everything that humans grow or breed, from orchids to chickens, serves us and us alone.

We could engage in a long philosophical debate about the boundaries of the role of humans, and we would probably never reach a consensus. My own pragmatic approach is rooted in the idea that this is all about how we will deploy the knowledge we have or are developing to ensure better food supplies for everyone. Genetic modification, like any technology, can be used for good or ill. It's impossible to generalize about good and evil. After all, the significance and the possible risks lie in the details: for what purpose do we deploy which techniques, and who will control them?

The End and the Means

The hairy apple and the pear with frog's eyes are symbolic of a fear that people will use their knowledge to play god in nature. In that vision, not just knowledge itself is evil, the goals for which it is deployed are no less the object of condemnation. Spurious aims and above all ends that are in themselves considered morally wrong, such as resistance to herbicides, are targeted in particular.

In retrospect, this last application, developed by Monsanto (a well-known multinational based in the United States) and one of the most commonly implemented genetic modifications, has been a catalyst for opposition to biotechnology. I regard this situation as a collective historical error by business, government, and science, stemming from a complete lack of insight into how citizens would react to a technology that brings two "evils" together: chemicals in the form of herbicides and interference with the genome. I think the history of acceptance or rejection of modern farming and breeding would have been different if the first commercially available modified varieties had included genes intended to produce substances that protect against cancer or blindness, or had served some other socially uncontroversial end.

That the first applications were aimed at herbicide resistance in large-scale crops, such as corn and soy, which are used mainly as cattle feed or ingredients in industrially produced foods, has compounded the distrust of critics. Biotechnology seems to be an instrument in the hands of big business, which aims to dominate the market and subdue nature. To environmentalists the destruction of the rainforests is a direct result of genetic technology. Its application more or less coincides with the start of globalization, so everything seems to be connected: China's demand for feed is increasingly met by countries like Brazil and Argentina that grow genetically modified soy on huge stretches of land. That this land is mainly in the Cerrado (savannah), far from the vulnerable forests of the Amazon, is a detail that usually escapes the attention of critics.

As a result we lose sight of the fact that, despite the extremely unfortunate decision to pursue herbicide resistance in combination with crops grown on an industrial scale, there really is continuity and logic in the technological development itself. Herbicides, which are increasingly biodegradable, are an important part of a combination of new growing techniques aimed at minimal tillage, such that seeds are sown directly on the soil. By avoiding the need to plough, erosion and energy costs are considerably reduced, the level of organic matter in the soil is better maintained, and water use is more efficient. Direct sowing without ploughing does mean, however, that farmers will have far more trouble with weeds that inevitably compete with the young plants. They have to be destroyed, which is not easy since the most persistent weeds often look much like the crop. Given the large scale and the jumble of plants, this can be done only by using chemicals that will not harm the young soy or corn. The crop therefore has to be made resistant to the chemicals used to kill the weeds, hence the need for herbicide-resistant soy. Not only will the herbicide kill the weeds and not the crop, in doing so it will create a thick layer of dead organic matter that helps protect the soil against high temperatures and heavy rain, both of which are disastrous for the organic content of the soil and therefore its fertility. One risk, which is not in itself inherent to herbicide-resistant transgenic crops, is that in the long run the weeds will be harder to kill as they become more resistant to herbicides.

There are many positive ecological aspects to minimal tillage, even though it is primarily suitable for mechanized farming. Herbicide resistance makes sense, and indeed varieties with this characteristic are being used on an increasing scale in countries including the United States, Brazil, and Argentina. Moreover, they are part of a larger package of measures, such as introducing a fungicidal coating on the seed and various other treatments designed to make the plants come up more quickly. In the end companies like Monsanto are not concerned just with the sale of herbicide-resistant seed but also with a range of related products, including the herbicide itself. No one could seriously be opposed to attempts to optimize the growing conditions of the crop, but criticism of the lack of information about the substances used and the downplaying of the side effects, which has been going on for too long, is justified.

Negative reactions to herbicide resistance mean that the second and now most common application of genetic technology has also been placed in a bad light. The introduction of genes from the soil bacterium *Bacillus thuringiensis,* Bt for short, is intended to afford broad resistance against such species as moths, flies, wasps, and beetles. The bacterium forms crystals that are toxic to these insects and to some soil organisms. In solution, Bt has been in use in farming for almost a century, organic farming included, and as far as we know it has had no negative effects on other organisms. Genetic modification with a number of genes from these bacteria is now being applied in countless crops, including cotton, soy, corn, tobacco, potato, eggplant, and papaya, to combat a very wide range of damaging organisms.

Two-thirds of the cotton grown in India is now Bt cotton. Giving plants an ability to resist insects makes insecticides almost completely unnecessary. This saves farmers money, reduces the number of accidents with chemicals, and means the end product contains fewer chemical residues. In contrast to herbicide resistance, therefore, this technology is about eliminating the need to use chemicals by ensuring that harmful organisms do not feed on the crop. Another spectacular application is found in Hawaii, where papaya farmers have been hit by papaya ringspot virus. As a result of mass replanting with papaya trees made resistant by a gene derived from the virus itself, papaya growing has been saved from ruin.

In the case of animals, biotechnology is aimed both at increasing meat and milk production and at producing useful substances. It began in 1990 with Herman, the first genetically modified bull in the world. His DNA includes a gene from human DNA that codes for the making of lactoferrin, used to treat diseases including rheumatism, which is now produced by Herman's female offspring in their milk. The use of animals and plants in the production of medicines is sometimes called "pharming," but it is not part of food production.

The gene for high milk production has been identified, as have various genes that determine the fat content of pigs, so improvements to food production using transgenic animals are only a matter of time. Some countries are said to be selling milk from cloned cows already. Many people are not aware that almost all cheese, traditionally produced or not, is made with rennet that includes chymosin taken from genetically modified microorganisms, rather than, as it once was, from calves' stomachs.

Despite successes in application and attempts to introduce a more nuanced discussion, a standoff between critics and proponents of these technologies has developed, especially in Europe, such that constructive dialogue on this subject seems impossible. Its advocates promise huge benefits for our health and world food supplies; opponents see the danger of dependency on specific businesses, poisoning of the environment, and other developments that threaten humankind. The consumer responds with concern without always knowing exactly why. Authoritative scientific institutions, such as Britain's Royal Society, have published assessments time and again that show the risks to be minimal or negligible. Governments hesitate nonetheless, not wanting to side with the majority of researchers against their uncertain and distrustful voters. When proponents and opponents feed the debate with terrifying images and demagogic statements, the paralysis is complete. This deadlock is typically European, although there are differences in attitude among European countries. Positions are less clearly staked out in North America, and in developing countries and emerging economies, aside from a few Western-inspired campaign groups, biotechnology is seen as a positive development and there is incomprehension regarding the European attitude and a lack of clarity as to what is or is not permitted on the European market. One side effect is that a great deal of breeding research is moving out of Europe.

Biotechnology, Hunger, and Poverty (1): The Case of Cassava

Despite the bogged-down debate in Europe, it's impossible any longer to imagine farming without genetic technology. Since the commercial introduction of genetically modified crops in 1996, they have been planted on more than a billion hectares of land in over thirty countries. Those countries represent some four billion people, more than half the world's population. Two-thirds of these countries have developing and low-income economies. Between 1996 and 2010 growth in the adoptions of this technology increased by a factor of 87, making this without doubt the fastest growth of a new technology in the history of agriculture. Of the more than 15 million farmers who grow genetically modified crops, an estimated 90 percent are small farmers, like the growers of Bt cotton in India. So it is certainly not the case that these technologies are suitable only for rich countries and rich farmers. Nor are we any longer talking only about crops of which a single characteristic is genetically engineered. The number of crops with more than one altered feature is increasing rapidly.

Nonetheless, the majority of transgenic crops have been developed to reduce the costs of labor and chemicals, and far less with the aim of addressing problems of poverty, hunger, and environmental degradation. Even today, little is being invested in the most important food crops in the tropics, such as cassava, sorghum, pearl millet, chickpeas, pigeon peas (*Cajanus cajan*), and peanuts. Work is under way on modifications to rice, the most important food crop in the world, both to increase its nutritional value and to improve its resistance to insects and disease.

For agriculturalists, a first crop is a first love, and they will always feel a bond with it. In my case that crop is cassava, an unsightly root, originally domesticated in northeastern Brazil, that is the most important food in large parts of Africa. Although it is also used as cattle feed and as a biofuel (ethanol in China and Brazil), cassava is primarily the food of the poor, a plant that produces at least something in even the most unfavorable circumstances, although it has very little nutritional value. More than 800 million people are dependent on cassava for their immediate food needs. When conditions are good, the plants grow two meters tall and have bright or dark green, edible, palmate leaves that are a source of iron and vitamins. Their potential yield in optimal growing conditions in Brazil is high, at 70 or more tons of fresh weight per hectare.

Unfortunately, when you come upon cassava plants on fields tended by poor farmers, they look like crooked, insect-eaten bushes with crumpled pale-green leaves. This is the result of countless viral and bacterial diseases and insect infestations, combined with generally poor soils and a lack of fertilizer. Despite its miserable state, cassava is essential for the poor, because nothing else will grow on such infertile land. Cassava is reasonably resistant to heat and drought, as it can stop growing temporarily in adverse conditions. It is reproduced from cuttings, which farmers take from old plants, so no seeds are needed, but diseases are transmitted along with the cuttings. The harvest may take place gradually over a number of months, with the soil serving as a storage place for unharvested roots.

The roots of cassava, and to a lesser degree the leaves, contain a glucoside (a kind of sugar) that liberates hydrogen cyanide as it decomposes. This chemical can cause severe poisoning, even death, so before it can be consumed cassava has to go through a complex fermentation process to drive off the cyanide. The widespread growing of cassava as a crop shows that its advantages outweigh the problems of hydrogen cyanide and low protein content. Cassava was introduced from South America into various places in Africa over the course of the nineteenth and twentieth centuries and became essential for poor African farmers who can grow little in the way of cereal crops.

There is yet another complication. Cassava turned out to be vulnerable to diseases and infestations already present in Africa, to which it had not built up resistance (a situation rather similar to the sensitivity of the potato to *Phytophthora* in nineteenth-century Ireland). Moreover, the natural enemies of similar plagues that occur in South America were not brought with it to Africa. So cassava falls prey to woolly aphid, red spider mite, and insects that spread viruses and bacteria. Despite them, the plant will still produce a few roots and leaves and offer some sustenance to people who have nothing else to eat and little energy to farm the land, such as HIV-positive people in southern and East Africa.

In the face of this almost hopelessly complicated reality, we need to ask whether biotechnology has anything to offer cassava compared to conventional methods of plant breeding. We can dream of all the things that might be improved about the plant: a reduction in its glucoside content, better resistance to disease and infestation, a higher protein and vitamin content, and better yields. Each of these aims raises countless fresh scientific questions. The degree to which it is toxic, for example, has to do with how the hydrogen cyanide escapes the cell, which enzymes liberate it, at what temperatures and level of acidity, and so on. But then there are the circumstances in which the plant is grown, and the genetic variation between individual plants and within a variety. There are also indications that the glucoside or cyanide content may offer some protection against insects and, conversely, a lower protein content may offer an evolutionary advantage by making the plant less attractive to other species, such as small rodents.

In cases like this, classic breeding methods concentrate on looking for differences among individual plants. This involves reproducing them sexually, from seeds, which is difficult in this case, because cassava flowers rarely if ever and may not produce viable seed even when it does. That's why farmers reproduce it vegetatively. But breeding from seed is only the first step, because then you need to carry out experiments on many generations of plants to discover which genes are associated with, for example, amino acid content (which determines the protein composition), the enzymes that regulate its cyanide content, and features that protect against infestation (plants with hairy leaves, for example, are less susceptible).

Because classic breeding is so difficult, it seems obvious that biotechnology should be deployed, as it requires no seed. Relevant genes can be tracked down more quickly and if necessary taken from other sources. We should not assume this task will be easy, incidentally, because at some point reproduction is needed, so techniques must be developed that allow the growth of tissue in nutrient solutions and enable embryos to survive. Moreover, several different genes are responsible for the cyanide content, and "introducing a gene" is a good deal less simple than it sounds.

Work is already under way to produce transgenic cassava, but it is primarily aimed at improving the starch content. That would be advantageous for cassava used as feed and biofuel but irrelevant for poor farmers. Two genes have been identified that inhibit the first step in the formation of the glucoside that leads to the production of cyanide, making it possible to grow roots with only a fraction of the usual cyanide content, but they are unable to survive on unfertilized fields with a heavy burden of disease and infestation. Researchers are also looking at genes that increase deposits of proteins, or amino acids, but the altered plants do not yet have an improved protein content in the leaves. The entire genome of the cassava plant has now been sequenced, which gives us a basis for new applications.

The example of cassava shows the extent to which biotechnology could offer solutions, but it is a complicated, time-consuming, and therefore expensive business. This is the most important reason little has been invested in crops that are not commercially interesting or in which seed is not traded. When investment does take place, new technology is deployed initially for purposes other than combating poverty. In the case of cassava there can nevertheless be no doubt that improvements are possible that cannot be achieved by classic means, even if improved yields and a reduction in toxins are a long way from reaching poor farmers. I believe that in this case the end—better nutrition, less poverty—does justify the means, transgenesis. A possible further step would involve improving the composition of cassava by introducing extra vitamins (such as vitamin D) and micronutrients (such as zinc), and this is now being worked on as well.

But there is another sequel to the story of cassava. For several years, a mutation in a geminivirus has been causing an epidemic in African cassava of the devastating brown streak disease. The virus is transmitted by a type of whitefly and it also affects the stalks, so farmers are left without healthy cuttings to plant for the next harvest. Genetically, cassava has no resistance at all to this disease, but a resistant substance has been found in tobacco that works against both subtypes of the virus. Here there can be no doubt: genetic modification—the introduction of tobacco genes into cassava—is the only possible way to save from famine the 250 million Africans who are completely dependent on cassava. This example alone causes African researchers to say: Africa missed out on the Green Revolution but it must not miss out on the genetic revolution. Who are the Europeans to keep this technology from us?

Combating poverty and ensuring food supplies in the future calls for unorthodox methods. For many people the fact that in the coming decades another 2 billion people will need to be fed with products grown mainly on the same land area justifies the use of biotechnology. Yet this quantitative argument is inadequate. With current knowledge of classic breeding methods, the systematic use of fertilizers and irrigation, and the availability of existing varieties of food crops, far higher yields could be achieved even without biotechnology. The yield of cassava roots achieved by a poor farmer in Central Africa is only 15 percent of that achieved by a modern farmer in Brazil with comparable soil. There is thus a great deal of room for improvement using existing techniques, even if a woman in Africa will never produce as much per square meter as the average Brazilian farmer. Improving yields is therefore not a decisive reason for genetic modification. On the contrary, improving the potential yield is pointless unless other production factors are improved as well: if no water and no fertilizer are available, if there are diseases and infestations, then no plant can grow optimally, however much it may have been improved.

The tragedy of low yields in poor countries has at least as many technological as socioeconomic causes. Yet the recent example of brown streak disease and the problem of low nutritional quality in cassava show that other applications of genetic modification may prove essential, as long as improvements are also made in market and production conditions. All the same, even if a great deal of money is spent on advanced technology for poor people's food like cassava, and on characteristics that are directly relevant to feeding the poor, it remains to be seen whether the technology is effective and reaches the people it is intended to help. Illustrative of this is the example of golden rice.

Biotechnology, Hunger, and Poverty (2): Golden Rice

Malnutrition takes many forms. Depending on the year and the estimates used, between 800 million and a billion people still have an absolute lack of calories, for at least part of the year, in seasons when the land cannot be farmed or just before a new harvest, when food is scarce and expensive. They and another billion, so 2 billion in total, suffer from a shortage of micronutrients, minerals, and other essential dietary components. Not all of them live in low-income countries, incidentally. In rich countries too we see people deficient in specific nutrients who are severely overweight or obese. A balanced diet contains enough micronutrients, so the way to solve a deficiency is to ensure that everyone has enough food with a balanced composition. But not everyone is in a position to eat sufficient vegetables, fruit, and protein. For a long time, therefore, supplements have been used, such as vitamin pills or cod-liver oil, to avoid shortages of particular elements, as has fortification or enrichment of the composition of specific foods. Fortification is done in such a way that there are no extra costs to the consumer, and almost half the daily requirement may be covered by supplements. In Ivory Coast 80 percent of bread is enriched with folic acid and iron; in China and Vietnam iron is added to soy sauce; and in many countries, including the Netherlands, vitamin A is added to oils and fats, and iodine is added to table salt.

Since the early 1990s it has been believed that the micronutrient content of food could be raised using biotechnology. What makes this belief so novel is the idea that biotechnology can be deployed not just to increase the quantity of nutrients already present but also to introduce entirely new micronutrients, something that conventional breeding cannot do by definition. This is not just a matter of introducing a single gene; it means creating a whole new route of biochemical synthesis. The most famous project along these lines is responsible for something known as "golden rice." The word "golden" refers to the yellow-orange color of beta-carotene (a precursor to provitamin A, which is itself a precursor to vitamin A). Golden rice is said to be capable of preventing poor sight and blindness as a result of vitamin A deficiency in 500,000 children per year. To ensure that each rice grain contains beta-carotene, four enzymes have to be made by it that do not normally occur in rice. To this end two genes are used, one from a soil bacterium and one from the daffodil. For something as apparently simple as the introduction of these two genes into rice, around seventy separate biochemical steps are required. All in all the approach has turned out to be successful in theory, so follow-up studies are now going on that concentrate on crossing golden rice with local varieties in Asian countries where rice is a dietary staple.

Golden rice is the result of extensive international cooperation between public and private parties. The DNA sequence of rice is now publicly available to all researchers. Nevertheless, golden rice has been the subject of fierce criticism from the beginning. Some say the beta-carotene content is negligible, others that it is too high and therefore presents a risk to health. From some areas there have been reports that consumers are distrustful of rice that's not white. It also turns out that anyone eating golden rice needs to consume enough fat, otherwise absorption of pro-vitamin A is insufficient. Work is going on to raise the beta-carotene content further and improve its digestibility by humans.

There is continual concern about the ecological impact. After twenty years of experimentation, no negative effects have yet been found. The rice plant itself seems unaffected by the new synthesis. Rice is self-pollinating, and so are weeds related to rice, so genes do not simply "escape" to other plants, a prospect that causes great disquiet among environmental groups in the case of corn, which cross-pollinates. Regulations have been established for the many patented steps in genetic modification, for which those who produce or use the resulting seed in theory need to pay. It has been agreed internationally that farmers with an income of less than $10,000 a year will not be expected to contribute to the extra costs for the patents attached to golden rice.

Golden rice is the first transgenic crop to be produced with an indisputably positive goal in mind, although of course it is possible to criticize fortification in the sense that supplementation (put simply: handing out vitamin pills) is comparatively cheap and easy. The commercial partners have negotiated from the beginning to enable the giving out of humanitarian licences for procedures to which they have a specific title.

So is golden rice widely available to poor farmers and to consumers in developing countries? No, that is still not the case. What works in the lab is not yet growing in the fields, let alone being eaten by those who need it. To achieve that, not only must the time-consuming process of producing large amounts of seed take place, but also a whole series of unavoidable steps that fall under the heading of "regulation." They include national procedures for the admission of genetically modified products, based on risk assessment, before either field trials or commercial growing can take place, which means that each country needs to introduce rules and the accompanying legislation. Regulation can begin only once the results of research are clear and consistent. In response to public concerns, more and more safety requirements have been placed on new varieties by politicians, which entail longer and more extensive field trials. These make the costs higher and higher. Regulation is a political process, which means that all kinds of objections can be made, and it sometimes takes longer to address these objections than to conduct the original research. The road to real change in the nutritional condition of the poor by means of genetic modification will be a long one.

Golden rice is fortunately not the only step along that road. The most important humanitarian and geopolitical decision of recent years in agriculture is one that hardly anyone in the West will have noticed. In November 2009 the Chinese government decided to allow the growing of genetically modified varieties of rice and corn. This happened after extensive biosafety tests, followed by standard field trials and only then commercial growing. Rice has been made resistant to certain kinds of infestations by the introduction of the Bt gene, derived from the bacterium *Bacillus thuringiensis,* as mentioned earlier. As we know from other Bt crops, this leads to a considerable reduction in the use of chemicals and therefore positive effects on the environment and public health, partly because the risks of incorrect use of agricultural poisons are lessened. In China alone, rice is grown by more than 110 million farmers on 30 million hectares of land.

At the same time, China has allowed the production of corn with an added enzyme (phytase) that improves the take-up of the amino acid phytin by animals, especially pigs and poultry. As a result they display faster and healthier growth, and phosphate pollution through their dung and droppings is reduced. The use of transgenic corn that expresses phytase means that farmers need to buy and add few if any feed supplements containing phosphorous. Corn, the most important cattle feed crop in the world, is grown on 30 million hectares in China, by almost as many farmers as those who grow rice. The country has an estimated 500 million pigs, almost half the pigs in the world, and 13 billion chickens and ducks.

The Chinese decision to allow genetically modified crops for human and animal consumption, having earlier given the green light to Bt cotton, is significant for the rest of the world. China hopes this will first of all be a way of increasing its self-sufficiency in food and animal feed, but at the same time it is signaling a firm faith in modern biotechnology. It is worth noting that research and development were carried out by the Chinese Academy of Sciences and a national company, so not, as many assume, by a Western multinational. This decision will undoubtedly influence other countries, such as India, that still have their doubts about genetically modified food crops.

Risks and Continuing Controversies

A great many of the arguments against biotechnology and genetic modification concern not the techniques used but the whole concept of genetically modified plants, the way in which they come into being and are made available, especially in developing countries, as well as intellectual property rights, risks, and regulation. The objections fall into three main categories: risks to the health of humans and farm animals, effects on the ecosystem, and the impact on economic and political power structures.

As far as human health is concerned, in the more than twenty-five years since the first products of GMOs came on the market, no indications have been found on a significant scale that the risks of toxicity or allergy are higher or essentially different from those of products produced in a conventional manner. Estimates suggest that more than 10 percent of the world's population now fairly regularly eats food products that contain ingredients derived from genetically modified crops. Worries about unforeseen allergic reactions seem so far to be without foundation. Fragments of the bacteria used to insert foreign genes into DNA turn out to exist in nature, and they have not up to now increased the likelihood of allergies. The most famous case of allergic reaction concerned a gene derived from the Brazil nut, so it was not an unknown allergy and it was immediately identified in tests.

Still, the absence of proof is not proof of the opposite. The possibility cannot be excluded that when more and more products with multiple changes to their genes are consumed, the likelihood of interaction among those products will increase, perhaps leading to allergies or illness. The only solution is to keep a finger on the pulse, as we should with all technologies, and to carry on looking for possible unforeseen side-effects. Farm animals that eat genetically modified corn and soy have not so far been harmed. Not so far. We should be clear about one thing: milk and meat from animals fed with genetically modified crops are not themselves transgenic products.

<hr/>

When it comes to the environment, a great deal of evidence has accumulated over the past two decades to show that there seems to be no cause for concern. No genes "escape." Even to put it like that is nonsense. We do need to ask whether, if GMOs are planted in the fields, resistant weeds or related plants might come into being by cross-pollination. This can happen here and there, as with a transgenic zucchini that was found to have crossed with a wild zucchini found in the southern United States. From time to time we hear reports of resistance among harmful insects or damage to other insects. Up to now, however, these have not turned out to be systematic effects of biotechnology. What are known as "superweeds" emerge in conventional farming too. Organic farmers close to fields of genetically modified crops are particularly concerned about possible contamination. In a few rare situations of "coexistence," as it is called, a small number of plants have indeed been found that originated from neighboring land with genetically modified crops. This can be dealt with by introducing a sufficiently large buffer zone to prevent insects and wind from transferring pollen.

Nor does there seem to be any evidence of an increasing disturbance of soil organisms, or any other effects on organisms lower in the food chain, such as leaf-eating worms, for example. This could theoretically be a problem with the breaking down of leaves of Bt-resistant crops, because they contain antibodies that might damage organisms found in the soil. In general the potential effects on the surrounding ecosystem are far harder to trace than those on humans or farm animals, because hundreds—and if we include the soil perhaps tens of thousands—of organisms are involved. Less is known about the tropical soils that need to serve as a standard against which future changes can be measured. The risks to soil organisms therefore seem the greatest and the least understood, and more attention should be paid to them. Mass mortality in the monarch butterfly in the United States, the focus of widespread dismay a few years ago, turned out not to have been caused by genetically modified plants.

But there remains a whole range of socioeconomic complications and objections. Despite what is often claimed, genetically modified crops are not the preserve of the big and the rich. Small farmers can also profit from them, as we see from cotton production and can hope to see soon with golden rice and modified vegetables. Genetic modification is not necessarily related to the scale of the farming enterprise. If new characteristics are present in the seed, it will make no difference to the farmer how they came about. Only when new varieties require extensive and complex techniques does the small farmer encounter barriers, as with herbicide-resistant soy, which is used in conjunction with heavy machinery. Many of the objections concerning scale do not apply only to biotechnology but to all agricultural innovation and unequal opportunities in the market.

Another cluster of objections focuses on the supposed dependence on large multinationals, which are said to be forcing farmers to their knees with their monopolies. Are seed companies becoming dominant, as some fear? Are traditional varieties being lost? No more so than with other seeds, because again this is not a problem unique to biotechnology. As with classic hybridization, new seed usually has to be bought every season, but in almost all cases the cost of the seed is a small fraction of the total production costs. Hybrid corn has been present for decades in Africa, and it is grown by small farmers. In China and other Asian countries, those developing new technologies tend to be state companies rather than multinationals. There is certainly a dominance of scale in the market for soy and corn. Small and medium-sized seed companies can rarely afford the expensive technology, partly because of extremely costly admission procedures and licenses. There is no doubt therefore that both farmers and consumers benefit from a business sector that is as diverse as possible.

A related objection is that biotechnology undermines local traditions. This too is not a specific consequence of genetic modification; it applies to all innovation. After all, agriculture is not an open-air museum but is constantly evolving. Which tradition should be saved, that of ten years ago or a hundred years ago? We need to decide what we want to preserve when it comes to the diversity of landscapes, traditional varieties, and other desirable species, such as ground-nesting birds. We would hate to lose beautiful landscapes like those of the Frisian forests, the rice terraces of Bali, or the hills of Umbria, which without intervention will be destroyed by the increased scale of farming or by neglect. These are issues entirely independent of biotechnology.

––––––––

The reduction in the number of varieties, modified or not, is a result of the modernization of agriculture. Genetic narrowing is not an automatic result of modernization: even though the number of varieties at any given moment in any given region may not be particularly great, they are replaced time and again over the years. Precisely because pathogens can become resistant, plant breeding is in a constant race to produce new cultivars. So it is unlikely that a virus or bacterium will suddenly emerge that will damage the most important food crops worldwide. The need for continual development of new varieties is one reason to advocate broad cooperation between business and governments.

––––––––

Where sustainability is concerned there is again no reason to assume that different factors are in play with genetically altered crops than with other agricultural innovations. Convincing evidence shows that Bt-gene crops have helped limit pesticide use and that the average yield and income of farmers has increased. Other characteristics might also have favorable outcomes for sustainability, such as the more efficient absorption of artificial fertilizer and water. One negative effect might be an increase in the amount of land used for agriculture as more genetically modified crops are grown. It might, for example, become possible to grow rice on salty or brackish land; mangrove swamps might then be stripped of their vegetation, and a fragile ecosystem would be lost. This is no reason to forbid salt-tolerant cultivars of rice, however, whether obtained by genetic modification or otherwise. It is a reason to protect the mangrove swamps.

––––––––

To me the objection that outweighs all these is that so few of the results of genetic modification have so far truly been part of an effort to improve the diets of the poor or the productivity of small farmers, or to solve environmental problems. Experience with cassava and golden rice shows how difficult this effort is.

Another good example is resistance to drought, the showpiece of plant breeding. It turns out to be far more complicated than an outsider would think. By means of molecular marking, genes have been identified in a wild plant (*Arabidopsis thaliana* or thale cress, a model organism in the plant sciences whose DNA has been sequenced) that have an effect on the stoma (pores) through which a plant loses water. The way in which photosynthesis takes place also suggests points of departure for researchers. Some tropical plants, such as grasses (sugarcane, for example), have a photosynthesis route known as C4 that uses water far more efficiently than that of other plants. The same is true in even greater measure for succulents, but we have a long way to go before those genes can be built in to rice or wheat.

Other possibilities include the development of plants with a good root system that are better at taking up water, growing rapidly, and adapting to water stress. Biotechnologists are increasingly looking at the potential to stack several useful characteristics in new plant varieties, with or without improved nutritional values. Corn has been created in the lab that has high levels of beta-carotene, vitamin C, and folic acid.

A different approach entirely is the use of modified microorganisms to clean up water for farming. Yet in attempting to combat the loss of harvests to drought, genetics is only one of many relevant factors, along with the frequency of rain, the characteristics of the soil, and the use of fertilizers. Ultimately the most important ways to address poverty and hunger are bringing peace to war zones and providing job opportunities.

Promises about the contribution of genetic modification in the short term to reducing greenhouse gases and climate change are as yet no more than that. But there are possibilities here too, especially when it comes to the reduction of methane emissions from wet rice cultivation and the stomachs of cows, and the reduction of laughing gas emissions from dung. In both cases attempts are being made to modify the bacteria that live in symbiosis with, respectively, rice and cows, and lower organisms are undoubtedly simpler to genetically modify. This may in fact be where the future lies, because the modification of lower life forms is less controversial. Other applications that look achievable over the next few years include the conversion of cellulose, lignin, and other fibers by means of genetically modified molds and their like, making it possible to use vegetable waste as biofuel.

I actually expect that in the long run there will be a major role for genetic modification in organic farming, because resistance will mean that herbicides and pesticides can be avoided and plants will become better able to take up organic fertilizer. The selective acceptance of biotechnology by organic farmers might perhaps be the real key to its normalization. It's likely that even in Europe there will be increasing acceptance of applications that do not have to do with food, such as biodegradable fibers and plastics, or modified cotton and jute. Another successful line of research is looking at ways of causing such plants as soybeans to make important fatty acids like omega-3 for use in soups and sauces, so that these do not always have to come from fish and we no longer have to rely entirely on the inefficient conversion from algae to fish.

Biotechnology and genetic modification are not the panaceas their advocates so eagerly claim them to be. They don't offer a solution to the shortcomings of markets, lack of buying power, or an absence of infrastructure and artificial fertilizer. But on specific points there is a place for biotechnology and GMOs, namely, where conventional scientific solutions fail and the need is clearly formulated and urgent. There must be a context in which the monitoring of unpredicted consequences is guaranteed, so it's impossible to come to a general judgment about biotechnology. It all depends on the goal, the characteristic to be manipulated, the gene or genes to be introduced, the crop or animal, and the region in which it takes place.

Even though the likelihood of spontaneous cross-fertilization is minimal, I would be extremely cautious about transgenic crops in centers of genetic diversity where many wild ancestors are found, for example, in the regions where wheat and other cereals emerged in the Middle East, or the Andes in the case of the potato. Because biotechnology and transgenesis are so multifaceted, the only sensible approach is to test each product, as we do with new medicines.

In light of all the theoretical risks, doubts, and objections, testing and regulation are crucial. More and more often the question arises of how they can be organized internationally. In Europe both individual countries and the European Union (EU) can choose whether to allow GMOs, which inevitably leads to confusion. There is a great deal of disagreement, so it is not the EU that puts forward proposals for the introduction of genetically altered crops; that is a decision it prefers to leave to individual countries. The EU has only one type of argument at the moment for refusing GMOs, namely, the risk to humans, animals, and the environment. If no risk has been demonstrated, then the current rules of the World Trade Organization do not allow any crop or product to be kept off the European market. Some argue that socioeconomic aspects should be considered, one example being the question of whether a technology or a particular variety would have a negative impact on small farmers. There is little if any evidence for such arguments, however, and such a change would mean that all kinds of accords and existing negotiations, such as the Doha Developmental Round (a stalled attempt to lower trade barriers), would have to be interrupted or revised. These developments are looked at with suspicion in developing economies, where the West is suspected of using such arguments to throw up new trade barriers.

Low-income countries often lack the regulatory framework necessary for the introduction of GMOs, particularly when the end product needs extra safety tests or where competing claims could arise. The problem could be solved if testing were done by an independent international organization, or if existing testing procedures were recognized worldwide.

Last but not least are worries about the independence of farmers and consumers in the face of large companies that hold patents on genetic sequences and techniques and keep them out of the public domain. The case of golden rice makes clear that public-private cooperation is possible, but examples abound of cases in which genetic material has been patented by companies, or attempts have been made to do so, one being an Indian tree called "neem" (*Azadirachta indica*), which has insect-deterring properties, and another the fragrant basmati rice. Such cases are regarded by campaign groups and by the countries concerned as downright bio-piracy. There is increasing moral pressure on companies not to keep any genes outside the public domain, but commercial interests are huge. Counterpressure, along with current practice in the pharmaceutical industry (where patents play a prominent role), is overwhelming. The seed sector has an annual turnover of 30 billion dollars. The challenge is to keep genetic variation accessible to plant breeders all over the world while respecting the huge investments made by private companies, and not to allow businesses to protect their work with patents to such an extent that the free exchange of genes and genetic techniques is threatened.

In farming, and especially in the Netherlands, there is a long tradition of accessibility as a result of the recognition of breeder's rights, which are not overruled by the practices of other sectors, such as the pharmaceutical industry. This is the biggest economic issue surrounding biotechnology, and it points to a need for the far-reaching reform of older and (until now) reasonably well-functioning agreements on intellectual property rights.

Genetic Resources Aplenty

God is not a breeder, let alone a biotechnologist. The abundance of paradise excludes all genetic modification and domestication, because biotechnology exists by virtue of variety among and within species. In the garden ruled by God, biological diversity and genetic stagnation are a given. In this mythical context there are no genetic resources, because the genetic composition of all living things is fixed for eternity.

In earthly evolution, outside of paradise, genes do continually combine, and new species emerge. In nature these combinations have no value besides that of their own survival. Only when humankind comes on the scene and intervenes in nature by means of farming does genetic material become a resource with an economic value, just like oil or gravel, with which new things can be achieved. Once genetic material becomes a resource, the way is open for the development of entirely new species or products. Anyone who can discover a wild organism with genes that prevent colon cancer and introduce them into wheat for bread-making will become immensely rich, as will anyone who can develop a gene that prevents plants being affected by frost or chickens by bird 'flu.

But who are the owners of the original genetic information and the genes that are present in useful plants and animals? And who are the owners of the improvements that are introduced by breeding new varieties from existing plants, by crossing them with other existing agricultural varieties, wild relatives, or different organisms altogether? The current farmers or their ancestors, who once selected suitable plants, the companies that carry out breeding work, the scientific researchers who laid the basis for breeding programs, or the governments who pay them and in whose countries the original plants and animals are found? What about organisms from the deep sea or the Antarctic? Clearly all these parties have a more or less reasonable claim. Without the original varieties and selection by farmers there would be no cultivars for agricultural use. Without the efforts of scientists there would be no innovation, and much of that work is time-consuming, expensive, and risky, because success is not guaranteed. Companies and universities are prepared to undertake innovative research only if they are rewarded for their creative efforts.

Ownership rights in genetic resources are necessary as a mechanism for rewarding earlier investment and to finance the creation of new cultivars in the future. You cannot simply copy a building designed by an architect, or a book you've bought, and you cannot simply make use of genetic resources or seed for commercial ends. But you are allowed, indeed encouraged, to be inspired by them.

International breeder's rights have been in place for about a century, as a way of recognizing the efforts of breeders. This gives them the opportunity to keep working on characteristics or on cultivars developed by others without having to pay. As a result the route to innovation remains open for all; only when seed or sperm come on the market does remuneration fall due. The law governing breeder's rights is democratic, small scale, and accessible.

But because modern breeding is concentrated in the hands of a few multinational conglomerates, which have often bought up smaller companies, significant power blocs arise on the world market. The big players in breeding—especially plant breeders, who concentrate on a limited number of commercially interesting crops, such as corn and soy—claim that patents are unavoidable, because patents represent the only way for their investments to yield a return. Patent law, whose origins lie in industry, regards a new variety or a new characteristic as a new human invention, like a new kind of vacuum cleaner. A patent establishes rights to that invention, owned by a legal entity.

––––––––

At first sight this seems impossible to apply to genetic information, which after all existed long before human beings and was not invented by them. But in several parts of the world, including the United States and Europe, it has been possible since the 1990s to claim rights in a particular sequence of base pairs in a genome as long as it exists outside the cell, since then it is said to be an arrangement of "components," just like other inventions that use existing components. A complete DNA sequence cannot be patented, nor can selection or crossing with marker technology. Patents are not allowed exclusively for GMOs, incidentally; crops improved by means of biotechnology but not genetically modified can be patented too.

The pressure to patent is immense. Since 2004 more than 150 patents on vegetables have been applied for in Europe alone, and many have been granted. The European legal framework for biotechnology asserts that a patent on a product is valid for all the material incorporated into the product that has a function. In a recent judgment the European Court declared that patents are not valid for situations in which the genetic product has no function. Flour made from transgenic herbicide-resistant soy may contain introduced DNA sequences, but these sequences do not fall under the patent, because they have no function in flour. Where a patent exists, other users must pay or they may be refused access to the material. Because a patent is not immediately public and is often not granted for several years, other breeders sometimes find themselves in a blind alley, since with hindsight they realize they are dealing with an existing patent. The Netherlands, with its long plant-breeding tradition, was the last country in the EU to recognize this patent law, and it insisted on a partial exemption for plant breeders.

Rice illustrates how complicated patenting is. The rice genome is the smallest found in any grain crop, and in 2000 it became the first of them to be mapped, after worldwide efforts, all the way from Japan to Brazil and the United States, with public and private programs working in parallel, including dozens of institutes and large companies. Much of the information is available from public sources, but the companies involved have applied for patents to many of the sequences, even though these have been published on the Internet. In practice, when it comes to scientific applications without any commercial objective, the patent holder will not be quick to take court action.

Applying for patents is expensive and legally complicated, so it is rarely a realistic option for small businesses or small countries. The use of material patented by others involves paying the company that supplies it for expensive licenses. It is clear from the successful modernization of agriculture in the past, based partly on new cultivars and breeds of plants and animals, that patenting is not a precondition for improvements. We are now seeing a shift, however. The power of the large breeding conglomerates is such that patent law has the upper hand, and classic breeder's rights are losing out increasingly often. When conflicts arise, court judgments are decisive, and we may wonder which will weigh more heavily: a patent or an earlier agreement under breeder's rights.

Although this battle is by no means over, a solution is starting to emerge. More and more of the complex breeding work now going on requires a combination of public and private institutions, because all the existing techniques need to be applied, such as the use of bacteria as a way of introducing new genes. Various groups who own rights in these techniques waive them for use for scientific purposes, but a limitation of such cooperation based on an exchange of patents without detailed publication is that outsiders are no longer informed. The absence of critical evaluation goes to the very heart of science and may restrict innovation in the agriculture and food sectors.

By analogy with the world of computer software, geneticists have therefore proposed that all genetic resources and improvements on them, certainly where biotechnology is used for food crops, should be regarded as open source. That would make them part of a democratic process whereby anyone can contribute material and improvements and everything remains available. In the development of software this is all about making source code available; transposed to agricultural biotechnology, it would mean making public genetic sequences and methodologies. It would be possible, because the genomes of some twenty important food crops are now known, and the data are accessible to all. They include the potato, rice, wheat, and the tomato. So there is a shared communal space, a "commons" (a word derived from the old village "common," where all residents could graze their animals). The analogy with programming software holds true only up to a point, however, as biotechnology is not an activity that can be carried out by motivated young people in attic rooms; instead such research always requires substantial investment, access to complex technology in advanced laboratories, and persistence over a long period.

The questions remain as to how these intellectual property rights in genes should be expressed in financial terms, and how businesses or countries can claim that a variety or a combination of genes is their property. There is a market for seed and sperm, but it bears no relation to the value of all the genetic material stored away in the tropical rainforests, for example, possibly containing new characteristics that may be useful in the development of new plant cultivars. We have absolutely no idea of the value of bacteria and viruses. How much do you pay for potential, and to whom? These are difficult questions, and they have been the subject of long negotiations in the United Nations, through the Convention on Biological Diversity and the International Treaty on Plant Genetic Resources, in which the rights of farmers are laid down. It is possible that a voluntary code of behavior might help. Comparable codes, in the fields of sustainability, tropical hardwoods, child labor, and pesticides have produced some reasonably positive outcomes.

Biotechnology and GMOs seem likely to continue to come up against resistance and revulsion for some time to come. The deadlock in the debate and therefore in regulation will not be resolved quickly, although I do see a growing openness among individuals in their twenties, who readily embrace most new technologies. One of the surprising developments is the emergence of biohackers, young people experimenting on their own initiative with DNA sequences. This can't do too much harm, and it breaks down the barriers to genetic technology, just as the original hackers did for computer coding. I also suspect that research into ways of applying biotechnology to improve the health of consumers by means of food will lead to greater acceptance. Even though there are so far no indications of increased risk, we have no reason to play down the objections. Far more than other technologies, biotechnology raises questions about consumer choice. A sharp distinction exists between biotechnology and, for example, nanotechnology and information technology, which are not associated in the public mind with age-old images of mythical monsters—or at least not yet.

An important parallel can be seen between biotechnology and robotics. As soon as robots start to show human characteristics, they frighten us just as much as images of strange hybrids. This brings us back to the apple with animal or human hair. There is still a powerful taboo against crossing the barrier between types, especially that between human and animal, human and plant, and human and machine. Even though there will never be any question of monsters like hairy apples or pears with frog's eyes—because the end product will never look like a literal hybrid of phenotypes with a mix of external characteristics—the fear of biotechnology can be traced back to a fear of dehumanization as a result of our own hubris.

On the one hand this comes about because of stories that lead a mythical life of their own, such as the tale of strawberries with a protein for frost resistance taken from fish that live in the Antarctic. On the other hand it arises because biotechnology uses methods that are themselves thought of as "unnatural" and therefore seem inhuman, because intervening in the genome to change characteristics is seen as radically different from other human activities, although this is largely untrue. That in the United States since 1980, and in Europe since not long after that, it has been possible to apply for a patent for a living organism or material (whether a bacterium or Herman the bull) means to many critics that a firm boundary has been crossed. They believe this represents a failure to do justice to the unique biological nature and significance for humanity of farm animals and other organisms, such as the yeast used in food processing.

At its most fundamental, the controversy surrounding biotechnology is about the issue of where the boundaries of humankind lie and what the true source of knowledge is—science alone, or also faith, or emotion, or intuition? It's no accident that this controversy has arisen at a time in which, in Europe at least, many people no longer believe in institutionalized religion but instead in "something" that shapes our lives despite all our progress and affluence. Biotechnology, an invention of the West and especially of the dominant United States, stands for Western hubris, for our arrogant opposition to the natural order of things. Ironically this feeling resonates particularly in the secularized countries of the West. Outside the West and Western culture (and therefore even more in Asia than in Latin America) this feeling does not lead to opposition to modern science in most of the middle class, and certainly not among the better educated, but instead to the desire to acquire the technology, to improve it, and to use it to their own advantage. In Argentina or Vietnam there is no sign of the doubt and caution we see in the Netherlands, Germany, Italy, and Austria. On the contrary, in the late 1980s, when I was in China to take stock of previously unreported research on the sweet potato, I was struck by the great enthusiasm about gene banks and the use of genetic material and techniques—in those days mainly for genetic characterization and for tissue culture. In the years that followed, China, along with Argentina, became a leading player in transgenic research. This is not simply a consequence of the lack of active nongovernmental organizations, as they nowadays have a strong presence in most emerging economies.

Frankenstein nightmares are not linked simply to monotheism but to the "old" Europe. We see this in the ready acceptance of genetic technology in the predominantly Catholic Latin America and its broad acceptance in North America. The relationship between biotechnology and religion is not straightforward, incidentally. Whether products made with transgenic crops are kosher remains a matter of debate in Judaism. The

Vatican has not as yet adopted a definitive position. A recent decision by the religious authorities of the global Muslim community determined that genetically modified food is halal, or accepted, as long as it is made with products that are acquired by means that meet halal criteria and have been through all the normal tests regarding health and the environment. So as far as Islam is concerned genetically modified food need not be rejected on religious principle.

This is quite remarkable, because there is much hesitation within orthodox segments of both Judaism and Christianity. In other religions too, such as Hinduism, the gist seems to be that because the technology is not inherently dangerous, its application cannot be rejected outright. Nonetheless part of the high-profile middle class in India is ill disposed toward biotechnology, and in 2010 the Indian government announced a moratorium on the first genetically modified, insect-resistant food crop, Bt eggplant, despite a positive assessment by scientists.

The best guarantee for the future introduction of transgenic crops and products lies in a society in which transparency in scientific research and regulation makes it possible for everyone to gain insight into the risks and uncertainties of new technologies. That few people can assess the technical details on their own merits and many remain dependent for information and opinion on government, scientific organizations, science journalists, campaign groups, and representatives of specific interests constitute a barrier, one found with regard to all modern technology and complicated issues, such as climate change, health, and energy policy. The acceptance of diverse voices, emotions, and prejudices offers a better guarantee of sensible policy, even if at the moment we find ourselves more or less stuck in a dialogue of the deaf. Biotechnology benefits from a free press and transparency, but also from a recognition that we will see progress only if the different parties listen to one another with respect for others' arguments and for the facts, and if untrue assumptions are corrected. Unfortunately this is by no means always the case, so the debate often runs aground after irrational reactions have been flung back and forth: utopian promises about all the things biotechnology can do as opposed to fears of the dark forces it will unleash. If only biotechnology could flourish in a democratic society in which well-considered decisions are made about necessary changes, rather than only in situations where too little debate takes place and decisions are made out of sight of ordinary citizens.

Its application in nondemocratic societies should actually worry us most, because public control and debate are sometimes entirely lacking. In most Western countries, where the concept of individual freedom is deeply rooted in parliamentary democracy, the introduction of biotechnology means that consumers will demand the option to avoid buying transgenic products, which will have to be labeled or coded in some way. Labeling is easier to propose than to implement, as keeping supply chains separate is extremely costly and complicated, although not impossible. Just as in many countries we have the freedom to avoid vaccination (no matter how strongly advocated by medical science), we must also have the option to avoid consuming transgenic products. The formulation of criteria and the checking of compliance must happen internationally and be carried out by independent organizations—but we are a long way from that as yet.

Gloom and fear with regard to biotechnology are a luxury we can ill afford. Progress comes from the courage to apply new knowledge in the right way and to learn from it. This is a continual process. The course taken by biotechnology and genetic modification will probably resemble that taken by the development of the automobile. The first cars were death traps, without brakes or lights, with laborious and dangerous ignition systems such that anyone cranking up an engine might well be forced to run for his life. But gradually cars became immeasurably safer, and people were taught how to drive; roads were widened and fitted with traffic lights, markings, and curbs; pedestrians were persuaded to obey rules; and laws were formulated. Every significant new technology demands far-reaching change.

But however it may go with biotechnology, fast or slow, people have lost forever the innocence of paradise. The history of farming is a story of increasing control over the environments and genomes of other species. Biotechnology continues that process, but in a more fundamental way. From now on we no longer live in a world where we passively wait to see what natural evolution has to offer. Since the beginning of agriculture, and to a rapidly increasing extent since the start of genetic modification several decades ago, humans now hold the cards. Few yet understand just how revolutionary this is. In the longer term, biotechnology is as dramatic a step as the development of agriculture itself. Just as space travel and knowledge of the universe make it possible to go beyond the boundaries of our planet, so biotechnology allows humans to go beyond natural selection, which has shaped life on this planet for roughly 4 billion years. This ultimate consequence is not inherently more dangerous than space travel, but the optimism with which the advantages are celebrated passes over the deep emotions it evokes in many. The accompanying responsibility toward other species and new species is morally comparable to the care with which we need to deal with the effects of the Industrial Revolution on the atmosphere and on the earthly cycles of water and resources. No longer are the divine order of paradise or the slow processes of evolution normative, but instead we are ourselves, as human beings.

EIGHT

Homesick for Paradise: "Organic" and "Natural"

The ultimate goal of farming is not the growing of crops, but the cultivation and perfection of human beings.   MASANOBU FUKUOKA, *The One Straw Revolution*

"I would like to know what life was like ten thousand years ago," Pepe was saying. "I think of it often. Nature would have been the same. The same trees, the same earth, the same clouds, the same snow falling in the same way on the grass and thawing in the spring. People exaggerate the changes in nature so as to make nature lighter.... Nature resists change. If something changes nature waits to see whether the change can continue, and, if it can't, it crushes it with all its weight! Ten thousand years ago the trout in the stream would have been exactly the same as today."

"The pigs wouldn't have been!"

"That is why I would like to go back! To see how things we know today were first learnt."   JOHN BERGER, *Pig Earth*

"Organic" and "Natural" as a Moral Choice

The biblical myth of paradise offers not just a story of creation and sin but also a perspective on the relationship between humankind and nature. In the three main monotheistic religions, paradise has for centuries been an image of what nature ought to look like, in all its benevolence. The garden is a moral guide: nature without human intervention is good, an idyll. Few people are insensitive to this image of a manageable environment in which we are cared for, where nature and the elements generously contribute to us their abundance, and no complicated decisions are demanded of us. Just as you can sometimes look up at a starry sky and experience yourself as part of a great cosmic whole, so you can feel part of the harmony of a mild, human-friendly nature. Almost all of us will have had such moments of more or less spiritual intensity at some point. You can experience it in many landscapes: in the water meadows of the Lower Rhine, the hills of the Auvergne, the Fergana Valley in Kyrgyzstan, or amid the proverbially emerald-green rice paddies of Bali. It seems as if nature will always exist to share its immeasurable fruitfulness with us, as long as we respect her and know our place.

Plainly we feel most at ease where a human presence is noticeable, in land-scapes that look like gardens. We generally experience the greatest harmony in our existence not in the harsh nature of the deserts or in impenetrable forests but in a half-open, parklike landscape with fields here and there and some livestock. That harmony is different from what we experience when looking at the Milky Way. In cultivated landscapes, as they are known, it's not awe and insignificance that attracts us but a sense of security. In count-less depictions we recognize the charming landscape where garden and nature coincide, sometimes even in the form of an actual pastoral, as with paintings by the fifteenth-century artist Giorgione of High Renaissance Venice, in which the light is always soft. We see the same orderliness in the geometrical, almost abstract but perfectly balanced fields of Paul Klee in his "Ebene Landschaft" or his "Blick ins Fruchtland."

The tamed, static ecosystem on a human scale has for a very long time been the accepted model of the relationship between humans and nature. In that view of the world, human intervention is barely necessary. On the contrary, according to the paradise story, it's human beings who disturb the balance. At the point when humans do something—taste the forbid-den fruit—the spell is broken. The stress on harmony as valuable in itself is above all a modern European or Western development, starting with Romanticism, which has everything to do with the fact that increasingly we control nature. The irony is that control of nature makes us nostal-gic for a pseudonature, for the idyllic. It's no accident that from the end of the eighteenth century, when urbanization and rising incomes were placing greater demands on nature as farmland, ideas about nature as an inspiration for moral action arose. According to that vision, nature itself encompasses the source of truth, beauty, and honesty, and people should take their cue from it.

In the romanticizing of nature, then, a longing for purity is accompa-nied by sadness about what has been lost. We experience the advantages of human dominion over nature (which allows us to acquire more food) but at the same time we are troubled by it. Every depiction of landscape is in fact a reflection of the struggle between nature and culture. Nature affords security, as long as people know their place and are corrected where necessary. This is expressed perhaps most beautifully of all in the nineteenth-century American Hudson River school, which includes paintings by Albert Bierstadt, who depicts nature as sublime, majestically illuminated by the sun. For some romantics, nature is a primal force to which humans must submit by accepting nature in themselves, in the form of their urges and passions.

The notion that nature is well disposed toward us and shares with us its paradisiacal plenty—even if we take account of the reservations expressed by Bierstadt and painters like him—is not a self-evident assumption everywhere. In most contemporary non-Western cultures, the relationship between nature, landscape, and humans is precarious, and the gods of nature (in the form of earth, plants, water, fire, insects, and seeds) have to be placated continually. Nature is untamed and unpredictable, too much a source of uncertainty and fear to be the subject of romantic feelings. Anyone who lives in the primal forest, on coasts subject to hurricanes, or in swamps with a tendency to flood, lives in a world of spirits that by their capriciousness—in the form of rains; tidal waves; and diseases of humans, plants, or animals—make the difference between death, famine, and life. Only when modern technology allows humans to begin to dominate food production can such an individual idealize nature and declare her harmless.

Throughout history people have tried to ward off the hostility of nature by attempting to live in harmony with her, to make up for the violence that inevitably accompanies food chains. Humans intervene as farmers, they plough and burn and harvest, but nature hits back with drought, rocky soils, and disease. Eating and being eaten are the everyday reality of life. Unfortunately, real nature is not a benign mother or father figure but a neutral, ruthless, and apparently "cruel" force, with evolution as its engine. That side of nature used to be assuaged by sacrifices and now, after secularization, it's a reality we prefer to forget. The modern urban middle classes are all too ready to ignore the fact that we now leave it to farmers to keep nature in check. Nature as found in paradise is in reality only a moral guide, not a practical one.

That our desire for harmony also—in fact above all—extends to food and agriculture is obvious. Farming, including forestry, is the most visible form of disturbance to the ecosystem. No other human activity has such large-scale effects on the earth's surface, not even mining, which is always concentrated, although extremely disruptive where it takes place. In food, humans meet nature: we consume nature and by doing so become part of nature, every day anew. In paradise a connection is already in place between nature (the garden), food, and morality. The apple is food and warning in one. What you eat is a moral choice. Food is our most intimate way of interacting with nature; with every sandwich, every strawberry, every plaice fillet, we digest part of the ecosystem. Entirely in accordance with Genesis/Bereshit, it remains true today that food can be dangerous, but it can also uplift us. We feel that opting for natural, good food makes us better people, and vice versa. So what's good for the ecosystem is also good for humankind.

As a reward, it tastes good too. One Dutch manufacturer exclaims of its dairy products: "100% delicious, 100% pure nature!" In the mythical nature of the post-Romantic city dweller, apples and tomatoes are always delicious, because they are caressed by beams of sunlight and bathed in gentle raindrops, having been pollinated by languid, lumbering bumble bees. Everything works together for the good. In this version of nature the ears of grain wave heavily laden between the cornflowers, the cows and goats lovingly donate their milk, and the piglets grunt blissfully in the clean mud. Animals are addressed by name and stroked daily. The garden paradise, on the boundary between nature and culture, wild and tamed, has been since time immemorial the domain of a god or the gods, with whom we like to compare ourselves or in whose protection we love to nestle. There, nature is benevolent not just to the apples and piglets but above all to us.

This nonexistent but oh so tempting idyll is in stark contrast to the reality of the modern world. In the West there are no women singing songs as they pluck the apples from the trees one by one but robots with metal grabbers. Where children help to harvest crops by hand, in poor countries, their working conditions are hardly romantic. The desire to follow nature is almost always a longing for the past, for a time when everything was good, or at least looked good compared to the present. The tragedy is that we are not innocent today but know all too well that nature in its archaic manifestation is disappearing in many places, and where it is not disappearing it's the victim of exploitation by advertising and tourism. We, modern people, are to blame. That realization makes our longing for the past all the greater. The past must be protected, because that is the only way to protect ourselves and our happiness. It's the only way to safeguard our moral purity.

For well-to-do citizens of postcapitalist societies, food is the ultimate symbol of the past. The past has a taste and a smell (sensations that penetrate directly to us through the brain stem): the sensation of grandmother's apple tart made with those russet cooking apples that are so hard to find these days, long summer evenings with pancakes spread with elderberry jam, or at least the imaginary taste of the memory of the food of the past, which was simply delicious and unproblematic. Far more than cars or houses, which inevitably have to conform to modern demands (no one wants to go without safety belts or central heating), food offers the illusion that we really can return to the harmony of the past. Not only that. At least as attractive is the conviction that with our nostalgia for the nature and food of the past we are fulfilling a moral duty.

In many social movements that seek "real" and natural food, the starting point is the connection between humankind and the ecosystem. Those who choose to eat pure, organic food do so to ensure the health both of themselves and of nature. From that perspective it seems logical to regard the inspiration of nature as the one and only guide to farming. If harmony and nature represent goodness, this makes clear demands concerning what should be produced and how. In its most extreme form the idyllic image of nature implies that intervention is not allowed at all, or at any rate should be kept to a minimum. If we stick to that, is the implicit promise, then there will be no rot or insect damage, failed harvests, or poverty. Everything will come right, just like in paradise. It's an attitude that regards nature as the opposite of technology, the opposite of human hubris that tries to turn nature to its will and therefore steps onto morality's slippery slope.

Farming naturally, a movement originating in Japan that is more far-reaching than organic farming, is based on the philosophy that humans themselves cause the greatest disturbance and that doing nothing at all is the best farming technique. So no artificial fertilizer is allowed (instead only naturally fertile soil is used), no tillage, no machines, as little weeding as possible, and only straw serves as mulch and compost. This approach goes even further than respect for tradition. At its purest, natural farming, also called "do-nothing farming," is a form of mediation, agriculture without any human intervention in which people at most sow seed and wait to see what the earth provides. It's a direct extrapolation from gathering. If wild animals or fungi destroy the crop, then that's simply an unavoidable aspect of life. Such natural farming, which makes humans subordinate to nature, is practiced hardly anywhere. Instead it's a rare experiment, contradicting the nature of farming itself, in which humans keep control as far as possible. Its philosophical way of being is beautifully portrayed in the documentary *Taimagura Grandma* by Yoshihiko Sumikawa.

In the modern world, where we're merely an insignificant cog, where our food comes from all points of the compass, and where no god any longer accompanies us as individuals, we express our moral choices through our patterns of consumption. Tell me what you buy, and I'll tell you who you are. What you buy doesn't just have to perform an obvious function (such as garments to keep you warm) or raise your status (designer clothing), above all it must bring intellectual, cultural, and even spiritual fulfilment (for example, clothes labeled socially responsible). For anyone taking nature as a guide, that translates as the conviction that by buying organic and related products you are opting for a better planet, without deforestation, with fewer chemicals and cleaner water. For some this goes even further and choosing organic is an explicit political act. Don't vote once every four years in an election—vote every day with your shopping basket. Doing the shopping gives you the chance time and again to do "good" and to feel morally principled. Change your buying behavior and you'll change the world. Resist economic growth and consumerism, oppose poison and polluted water. Buy organic! If only it were that simple.

———————

The image of harmonious nature also leads to an idealization of farming life. We demand that the farmers, with their uncomplicated existence, close to the seasons, compensate us for our lost paradise. Rural simplicity, working close to nature with everyday things, has become a metaphor for the happiness that has escaped us, because our existence is shaped by stress, anonymity, and sophisticated equipment. True luxury is now clad in hand-knitted sweaters that sell for good money in specialist shops. In the predilection for romance and innocence that is so powerfully present in today's rich middle classes lies a coercive demand for privilege: the privilege not to have to deal with the disagreeable details of tractors, chemicals, and abattoirs, nor to become immersed in the tough economic reality of struggling subsistence farmers and agricultural laborers who every day stoop to pick the most delicious raspberries. In their more extreme forms, in some TV shows, sensational restaurants, and the fanatical search by weekend cooks for unique ingredients and perfect kitchens, farming and food are beginning to verge on entertainment. If the viewers want to see anything about the production process at all, then it has to amount to an enjoyable or at least pleasant distraction. Sausage-making again becomes a leisure activity at which you can excel, as does a hiking trip with an organic shepherd. Perhaps this is the ultimate form of amusement in a society of abundance:

being able to return briefly to the supposed delights of the farming and food supply of the past, without any adverse effects for yourself or anything else, without the burdens or the life-threatening poverty.

Related Ideas

The longing for an unspoiled garden and an idyllic farming life is part of a far broader revival of attention to nature, the natural, tradition, and the countryside, and of resistance to mass production and industry. The words "biological," "local," "traditional," "small scale," "handmade," and "sustainable" are often used in one breath, but they are not identical. They arise from two tendencies that are partially connected: a growing consciousness of nature and the environment, and opposition to urbanization, industrialization, and globalization. Much of the confusion among consumers comes about because the motives behind various movements for reform are comparable, while their effects are different. The call for local, whether organic or not, for example, is an attempt to provide an alternative to the long and complex food supply chains that reach their ultimate absurdity in the now-famous transportation of piglets from the Netherlands to Parma and back in the form of the district's famous ham. The latest development in this trend toward local, however, has a cosmopolitan streak: local cuisine with ingredients from all over the world.

There is another mainstay of interest in "organic" and "pure nature": the fear of unsafe food, a legacy of widespread panic over diseases caused by food, such as Q fever in goats, bird 'flu, or the mad cow disease of previous decades. The positive counterpart to this is attention to the relationship between dietary patterns and health problems, especially obesity, diabetes, cancer, and cardiovascular disease. For the first time a broad agreement has emerged that human health and the state of the planet are inseparable. Local and traditional seem healthier for both the planet and humans than distant and modern.

Around these thoughts we find a group of unconnected ideas that shore up organic and traditional farming. Over recent decades a belief has arisen—in fact a truth long recognized by anthropologists and historians— that food, or more precisely specific dishes and culinary traditions, are part of the human heritage. Not long ago, UNESCO, the United Nations cultural organization, canonized Mediterranean, Mexican, and French cuisine as part of world heritage. This is merely the start. German bakers have started a campaign to have the huge range of German bread recognized and placed on the same World Heritage list. The diversity of German bread is unique; nowhere else in the world have so many different kinds of grain been made into bread in so many different ways over such a long period. Wheat, rye, barley, spelt, buckwheat (not actually a grain), with the addition of sunflower seeds, pumpkin seeds, other seeds, herbs and spices, coarse and less coarsely ground flour, sourdough or yeast, risen or twice risen—the list seems endless, partly because of the slight regional variations added to it. We are certainly not talking only about bread baked with organic grain (even sourdough bread is not necessarily organic). It's no accident that the call for recognition for German bread comes just as Germans, like other Europeans, are starting to eat less bread, the number of bakers is falling, and the competition from other breads (often French, Turkish, or Italian) is growing. Importantly too, Germany is now increasingly importing grain from abroad.

The campaign for the preservation of bread and culinary traditions by, for example, putting them on the UN World Heritage list is based on a misunderstanding. Just as industrial or architectural heritage changes over time, what we eat is a reflection of many influences, and our eating patterns change rapidly. Two generations ago the Dutch ate mainly potatoes, meat, and greens. Now pasta and rice—easier to prepare and to store—have partly driven out potatoes, our vegetables have become incomparably more varied, and we have moved away from meat in its old standard forms (stuffed beef rolls, braising steak, sausages) to all kinds of cuts, plus fish and shellfish. Vegetarian alternatives have penetrated almost every household in northwestern Europe, even if eaten only occasionally. Modernization is not a reason to abandon tradition, but a question needs to be asked here: what is original Dutch, Swedish, or German cuisine? Just as with the preservation of landscapes or plant species, there is always something arbitrary in any decision about how far back to go and what should be labeled "original." What is the original recipe? The one used thirty years ago or a hundred years ago? On top of that, anyone wanting to keep a tradition going will need to perform all the labor by hand. Few are prepared to do this nowadays, and those who are tend to be poorly educated immigrants. When Indian workers from the Punjab have to be brought to the Po Valley to make classic Italian cheeses like *grana padano*, because young Italians no longer want to do this kind of work, we might well ask where the boundaries of tradition lie.

Following naturally from the idea of heritage is the desire to restore to favor old varieties and forgotten ingredients. This is mainly a matter of vegetables and fruit. Traditional varieties are dug out of national collections or gardens, and seed is gathered from heirloom vegetables. Apple breeding, for example, is now focusing on optimal combinations of modern characteristics of storability and disease resistance with traditional taste and appearance. Parsnips, purslane, Jerusalem artichokes, turnips, black salsify, Swiss chard, and pumpkins, once available only in specialist shops, now enrich many a farmer's market and can be found in the supermarket, We have also seen the return of beans (borlotti beans, broad beans, chickpeas), small cucumbers, and a wide variety of tomatoes, cabbage, and lettuce. Color, flavor, and size are receiving more attention, with a new preference for the small. There is even a search for edible flowers, which have little if any place in existing eating patterns. Increasingly popular too are microvegetables, in other words all kinds of seedlings that are used as garnish and appetizers, such as alfalfa or mustard sprouts. Not all these varieties are organically grown; the production of bean sprouts is often a large-scale enterprise. Older grains and grain-like crops—including buckwheat, barley, bulgur, and quinoa—are also becoming popular, partly under the influence of whole food shops and diet gurus. Older breeds of animals are receiving more attention, especially chickens (for example, the snow-white poulet de Bresse), pigs, and cows (such as the fawn-colored blonde d'Aquitaine). There is great variation, with breeds imported from specific parts of Europe. Rediscovered foods include curds, stewing pears, liver, and whiting, preferably slow-cooked on a paraffin stove or in its modern equivalent, the steam oven.

Behind our desire for the organic, traditional, and local or regional lies another issue, one less often mentioned—namely, the loss of old-fashioned skills and creativity. What used to be bitter necessity, doing it yourself, from the vegetable garden to the preserving jar, is now the height of culinary, status-raising experience. Anyone who really wants to make an impression will show off homemade strawberry jam made with strawberries from the garden. A diffuse movement of groups is trying to revive traditional skills in the broadest sense, including food production and preparation. It has become the new luxury, because handmade products in natural materials command far higher prices than industrially produced products. It's depressing to think how much has disappeared, even among culinary traditions alone, that current generations cannot even imagine, skills every housewife used to possess, from bottling, pickling, or making pâté and pasta to cheese-making or the baking of bread and biscuits, not to mention slaughtering and processing all parts of a pig, smoking fish, or making stock from leftovers.

There's a good reason, however, why the traditional and handmade are disappearing. Women no longer have either the time or the inclination to knead everything by hand, and it's been a long time since home slaughter was permitted, with considerations of hygiene in mind. I fully share the sorrow at the loss of craftspersons who could make something unique and all those common or garden skills, but unless we completely reorganize our economy and our education system to pass on such knowledge, the reality is that in rich countries handmade food, like handmade shoes, is the preserve of a small, wealthy group. It's possible to schedule bread making from time to time into our busy lives, in fact it's even "cool." But there's no way we can bake bread every day. Food and food preparation are ingredients of the way you distinguish yourself from others. This is important in modern societies in which traditional bonds, such as class and religion, have fallen away.

Some take all these trends even further than seeking out old breeds, recipes, and skills. They want to go right back to basics, to the ultimate biological experience: gathering and perhaps even hunting and fishing. The collecting of edible wild plants, from dandelions to seaweed, from horse radish to wild mussels and algae, from mushrooms to moss, is making a modest comeback among true devotees—often men. By fetching your own food from the wild, you are confirming your masculine toughness (there is a misunderstanding here, because even though men did the hunting and fishing, it was mainly women who did the gathering, but never mind). In the most prestigious and award-winning restaurants you'll now find wild foods on the menu, especially moss and mushrooms. These are not organic in the strict sense, as they are not cultivated, but the philosophy of submitting to what nature offers sits easily alongside the organic approach—with the proviso that if this kind of gathering was adopted on a large scale, there would soon be no edible food left in the wild.

Opting for organic, pure, and/or natural food doesn't necessarily entail a vegetarian or vegan diet. These movements do not coincide completely, but they do overlap. Vegetarians and vegans are more conscious of what they are eating and so have a greater tendency to choose organic produce. Conversely, quite a few professional chefs, home cooks, and eaters of organic meat now consciously reject vegetarianism and want to go back to buying meat direct from the farmer, preferably slaughtered by them on the farm.

Although our food is increasingly safe, partly because of more meticulous and advanced checks, concern about safety has increased significantly. Organic food, mainly because of the absence of such chemicals as synthetic pesticides and artificial fertilizer, has reinforced the association between natural and healthy. Pure means natural, and that means without additives, whether they be preservatives, flavorings, or colorings. To some who strive to eat "honest" food, what comes out of the factory or is made with fabricated ingredients is suspect or contaminated and is assumed to be harmful to humans and the ecosystem. Those who prefer natural and organic food are automatically opposed to biotechnology and genetic modification. Sometimes other modern techniques are rejected too, such as hybridization. So all kinds of ideological, social, and socially critical movements come together around organic food. In the image of the harmonious human-made landscape in which the traditional farmer is part of nature lies resistance to the large-scale and to industrial intervention in agriculture. The desire for the organic and traditional is the greatest change in modern farming of recent decades. The importance of food as a mark of status presents an opportunity to make yourself distinctive that is not offered in the same way by houses and cars.

What Exactly Is "Organic"?

Natural, organic, pure, traditional, authentic, old-fashioned, and ecological, or local, ecologically aware, ethical, egalitarian, and honest: the number of concepts associated with food has multiplied at a great pace. Everyone can project their own meaning onto these words. As in many fields where powerful convictions and desires have a large role to play, there is considerable confusion. "Pure," "honest," "ecological," and "natural" are labels strewn about at will, first of all in advertising, but in fact they have no other meaning than that they are attractive to the conscious (meaning well-educated and Western) consumer. "Traditional" and "old-fashioned" are no less arbitrary, to say nothing of "egalitarian" and "authentic." Often the type of packaging is enough to suggest something attractive: grains in brown paper bags with a see-through window, pots of jam with a checkered cloth over the lid or lentils wrapped in linen. The packaging links tradition with a sense of honesty.

———————

The only one of these terms that has a formal definition is "organic." On the one hand organic farming refers to a way of running a business and on the other to a system of labeling and checks that is laid down by law in most Western countries. It does not make any claims about the quality of the product, only about the production process. This is logical, because the sugar molecules in an organic apple are the same as those in an ordinary apple. "Organic" guarantees that no artificial fertilizers; radiation; or chemical pesticides, fungicides, or herbicides have been used during production and that no residues of them can be detected in or on the product. None of these chemicals will be found on organic apples, therefore, but this sounds more significant than it actually is. In almost all high-income countries, no such residues are allowed on apples at the point of sale, according to law.

Organic farming is therefore a precisely described, legal, and quantifiable concept, unlike ill-defined and mostly vaguer terms like "ecological," "integrated," "local," or "sustainable" farming and products, or, even less clear, "low external input agriculture." There are also "biodynamic" farmers, although they are in a tiny minority. They have to comply with the specific demands of biodynamic agriculture, which regards a farm as an organism. "Dynamic" points to the anthroposophical approach, which assumes a connection between plant, animal, soil, and cosmos, so there are guidelines concerning, for example, the phases of the moon at which sowing can take place. The range of ideas not laid down in law— everything that is not formally organic but is promoted as natural, ecological, local, and so on—contains many comparable elements, such as an emphasis on closed ecological cycles, energy saving, the shortening of supply chains, and a personal relationship between producer and consumer.

The term "organic" says a great deal, because it so clearly refers to nature as an ideal that humans fit in with. Let organisms do their work, and all the abundance of nature will come to us of its own accord, is the suggestion. Organic thinking thereby aligns itself with the mythical paradise. After all, if we take the term literally, then every form of farming is organic. In this respect there is nothing fundamental that distinguishes organic farming from ordinary farming, so it becomes a rather empty definition. Photosynthesis remains photosynthesis, with the same molecules, no matter how the organism, in this case a plant, is treated. Farming is always about protecting, reproducing, and harvesting the desired species at the expense of other species, and the same chemical conversions take place. Yet we instinctively know what is meant by "organic." The difference lies in the degree to which agricultural species are protected and selected and the effects this has on the environment. Therein lies the crux and the attractiveness of organic farming.

"Organic" is also used outside agriculture to indicate biological control of pests or weeds, using natural enemies, such as parasitic wasps or substances derived from plants. The use of biological pest control in tomato growing, for example, is not enough to make a farm organic in the legal sense, so its products cannot be labeled organic. Although conventional pesticides and herbicides are banned, this does not mean that organic products are grown entirely without "chemicals." All kinds of nonorganic ingredients may be used as pesticides, fungicides, or herbicides, such as copper compounds, chlorine, or ammonia. This makes sense, given that organic products have to be protected from organisms that would otherwise feed on them.

The official guidelines with which organic farming has to comply include matters such as obligatory crop rotation (not growing the same crop on the same land every year, so as to avoid diseases and soil exhaustion), the use of organic fertilizer and natural additives, a ban on chemical and synthetic pesticides and herbicides, animal welfare through spacious living conditions, the minimizing of antibiotics in cattle farming and of concentrates in feed, and a ban on genetic modification and its products. These guidelines have been translated into concrete production and processing rules in the EU and in national legislation. In each country, a recognized, independent organization will check compliance at least every two years and decide which farms will be able to label their products organic. For fish the process is still in its infancy. Consumers are not yet sufficiently aware that much of the fish in supermarkets is produced by fish farming in its various forms, and therefore complies with highly variable standards. Only a small fraction could be called "organic," so generally accepted norms and checks still do not exist.

The introduction of organic farming is limited not just by its lower yields (a result of the ban on artificial fertilizer and the greater likelihood of disease) but also by the cost of certification and a difficult, often lengthy switch from conventional farming. Farmers who want to convert to organic farming will sometimes have to wait several years before their soil is more or less free of artificial fertilizer; they also have to ensure that a large enough buffer zone exists between their fields and those of their neighbors to prevent unwanted cross-fertilization with GMOs. Sometimes the benefits—the higher prices commanded by organic produce—do not outweigh the higher costs. Organic farming is certainly no way to make a fortune. Most enterprises are small and not particularly productive; farmers do not include their own labor in their accounts, and far from all are insured against crop failure. They can just about get by, if they have plenty of land, perhaps inherited. In Italy I've seen farmers working for far less than the minimum wage producing meat and cheese on 80 hectares of land.

The strictly legal definition of organic farming means that most farms in poor countries, where few if any chemicals are used for lack of capital, are not labeled organic. Two-thirds of agriculture in Asia and perhaps 90 percent in Africa could be called "organic perforce," because small farmers cannot buy the chemicals that would increase production. But such farming is far from environmentally friendly, because farmers are repeatedly forced to fell trees to open up fertile land, which causes erosion, and because if chemical fertilizers or pesticides do become available, they are used indiscriminately.

Increasing interest in the organic and the authentic, and the demand in rich countries that arises from it, means that the professional market for organic products from poor tropical regions is growing, especially for vegetables and fruits, such as bananas, mangos, tea, coffee, cocoa, and rice and increasingly for specialist products, including spices. Countries like Argentina, Brazil, Chile, India, and Kenya have recognized the potential of this organic export market. In those countries the organic movement has therefore departed from its more socially critical roots to become a commercial activity like any other. These emerging economies have set up an extensive certification system to comply with international rules. The sticking point is now with the farmers, who often have little education, whose yields are low, and who need help to make the transition to organic farming. This almost always means they need governmental support and will have to organize to sell their products cooperatively. The availability of biological pesticides and organic fertilizers needs to increase as well. In poor and developing countries the labor is available that makes the switch to organic production so difficult in richer parts of the world.

Organic farming presents opportunities to poor farmers, but that certainly does not mean that organic products imported into the West are CO_2 neutral. The EU (especially Germany, France, and Britain) and Japan are the biggest importers of organic produce. In the United States many organic products are sold, but fewer are imported. Worldwide only a few percent of the products bought and sold are organic, with a few exceptions, such as coffee and cocoa.

According to official statistics, about 2 percent of the farmland in Europe complies with the norms of organic farming, although some organizations representing the organic movement put the estimate at 8 percent. The statistics concerning organic acreage include land that is being converted from normal farming and is not yet productive in that sense. The figures are extremely variable. Austria has the highest score (at almost a fifth of farmland), followed by Switzerland, Norway, and Sweden. The figure for the Netherlands is about 3 percent. The percentage of organic farmland is increasing only very slowly; in 2005 it was 1.5 percent across Europe. The most important areas of growth are hothouse production and grassland. Initially the aim of the Dutch government was to have 10 percent of farmland organic by 2010. Clearly they have fallen well short. In North America the percentages are comparable to Europe. These average figures say little, however, about the share of organic farming in various categories. In the Netherlands it is growing fastest in dairy production and especially egg production, and that growth does not express itself in expanded acreage, because the chicken feed is imported. Feed for hens producing organic eggs is not by definition organic, and given its limited availability it rarely is—another illustration of how complex the concept is, even with all its legal frameworks.

Is Organic Better?

Aside from the motives and moral convictions of consumers of organic produce, the most crucial question is whether organic products and means of production are better for humans, animals, and the planet. Unfortunately it's impossible to give a straightforward answer. It depends on many factors. For a start: to what are we comparing organic farmers? To the average farmer and horticulturalist, to farmers in Europe or across the globe, or to farmers in the same climatic zones and similar market circumstances? Or should we compare them to the best of farmers, those in the vanguard who have already introduced all kinds of improvements, whose production methods are the most environmentally friendly and take account of animal welfare? And what exactly does "better" mean? Are we talking about the long or the short term?

The comparison is far from simple. As with everything surrounding food and sustainability, here too we need to look at all sorts of dimensions that are hard to compare, and there the dilemmas start. What is good for the planet? Is it the same as what's good for humanity? Our knowledge of food and soil has gaps in it, too, so we have no final answer as to what is "better"—we are still learning, bit by bit. Because we're trying to compare apples with oranges, it's impossible to reach a final judgment. It's always a matter of details, of the product, of the production process, and the specific comparison. One thing is clear: when comparing organic and conventional farming we need to go further than "there's no harm in trying."

Anyone who buys a product grown without artificial fertilizer is opting for a lower yield per hectare. After all, farming means that with every harvest the nutrients taken up from the soil into the plant or animal are transferred to humans. Although for a while this will do no harm, eventually the loss of soil fertility has to be corrected, which is not easy. Estimates of yields diverge markedly. Almost all studies show that yields from organic farming are lower than those of farms using conventional production methods. They may be lower by a quarter or by three-quarters, depending on the research and the product. In organic farming, such plant nutrients as nitrogen, potassium, and phosphate are almost always the limiting factor. Proportionately more land is needed to achieve the same amount of produce compared to conventional farming.

If we buy organic produce, we're opting for the use of more land for farming, irrespective of the need to compensate for lower yields. After all, ways of keeping up the level of nutrients in the soil without artificial fertilizer include letting the land lie fallow for a year or more; crop rotation with green manure (using such plants as clover or beans that fix nitrogen); or the addition of animal manure, mud, or humus from forest or heathland. Each of these solutions requires extra land. Even minimal crop rotation, with wheat harvests interspersed by one year of lying fallow or of leguminous plants as green manure, means that 25 percent more land will be needed. Animal manure presumes that the animals graze elsewhere and are given supplementary food in winter, such as silage. Plaggen manuring requires the stripping of heaths, while other humus has to be taken from forests. Only in rare cases of extremely fertile soils, such as on the slopes of volcanoes or on terraced riverbanks, can one avoid having to fertilize the soil for a long time (and even then not forever).

Putting more land into production doesn't seem too much of a problem, as there's always a bit of unused land somewhere, but this is an illusion. Far more is needed than is available either locally or on a global scale. There is something else too: using more land means using more fuel for tillage and transportation (and therefore creating more emissions of greenhouse gases). Putting land into production also presumes land clearance, which entails further emissions of CO_2 and other greenhouse gases.

The scarcity of land is not all that should trouble us; there is also the issue of the most efficient use of resources. This is complicated but essential to analyze for a proper understanding of the future of food and the earth. For a long time people thought that in farming, as elsewhere, the laws of diminishing returns applied, that as levels of production rose, the effects of contributing extra units of, say, nitrogen or water would be reduced. Diminishing returns arise, for example, in a situation in which you've already eaten a good many hamburgers (or apple pies or whatever). The pleasure (or nutritional value) of each subsequent mouthful declines, whereas if you're hungry, the pleasure in each bite of the hamburger (the marginal return) is enormous. It turns out, however, that with the growth of plants, additional nitrogen or water at any level of production—the highest and the lowest and at all levels in between—is used equally efficiently. So there are no diminishing returns; returns are constant. This is only possible if all other resources are available at optimal levels as well.

If a great deal of nitrogen is supplied but little potassium, then the amount of potassium—the element that is available in the lowest quantities in relation to what is required—will determine the yield, not the higher level of nitrogen. The effect of a resource is limited, therefore, by the amount of other resources available. The minimum is decisive. To put it yet another way, economically and ecologically it's extremely important to look for a means of deploying all resources simultaneously as efficiently as possible, because they'll be wasted if they are not all available in optimal quantities at the same time. This is precisely what's so difficult with organic farming: the use of animal manure or leguminous plants as green manure results in a wide variation in the nutrients available, and they are not deployed optimally but always at a level that is slightly too low. This explains why yields in organic farming are consistently depressed.

Because no artificial herbicides are used, weeds can be a persistent problem, leading to considerable losses. Weeds compete directly with crops for nutrients and water. Weeding by hand is expensive, and mechanical weeding leads to more CO_2 emissions. The zero-tillage method, which leaves the ground undisturbed and simply sprays all weeds with herbicide once, a technique that has proven successful in large-scale conventional farming, obviously cannot be applied in organic farming. So ultimately "organic" means agriculture with lower yields than would be possible given the same conditions. That may not be too much of a problem on an allotment or a vegetable plot, but it certainly is a problem if we're talking about world food supplies. From that perspective, organic farming is not an innocent option but an implicit decision to use land and resources inefficiently.

In the eyes of those who sell organic produce, organic methods are a solution to all the evils of modern farming. Yet the scope of organic farming, as defined in law, is limited. It's striking that such methods are not aimed at reducing effects on the climate, at efficient use of energy, or at the reclaiming and reuse of such nutrients as phosphate. Nor are there any rules about recycling water. Organic farming, aside from deploying biological controls rather than pesticides, concentrates mainly on ways of using leguminous plants to compensate for the absence of artificial fertilizer. This does indeed create savings, because the production of artificial fertilizer requires a great deal of energy in the form of natural gas and such substances as phosphorus and sulphur. That advantage, however, is largely negated by the larger land area needed, which leads to additional energy costs for cultivation, tillage, and transportation.

Organic livestock farming also presents a mixed picture. Not all animal-friendly produce is organic, but organic farming always demands certain standards of animal welfare. Animals have to have a minimal amount of room to move around, and indoor facilities must not exceed a certain maximum size. This is in sharp contrast to the image most people have of conventional livestock farming: the modern sow or chicken with barely enough room to move, fed by computer-controlled machines, with the farmer as a manager at a distance. Although in the conventional cattle farm in the EU and several other developed countries, the housing of animals has recently been improved in response to new legislation, all cowsheds in intensive livestock farming are the result of the development in the direction of better control of living conditions, resulting in lower costs per product. Organic livestock farming therefore seems to have the edge when it comes to animal welfare.

Yet this claim cannot be completely substantiated by science. The latest developments in intensive livestock rearing, such as the Roundel housing system for chickens or the most modern cattle feeding lots and pigsties, do not emerge in research as systematically more detrimental to animal welfare than smaller accommodations. Animals that do not need to compete with one another for food and have enough space to show varied, natural behavior generally have lower levels of stress hormones in their blood. The organic label imposes restrictions, too. Animals cannot be kept on concrete floors but have to be able to walk outside in the mud. Some pig farmers who would like to go organic object to this, since in places with high summer temperatures or with long sunny days pigs can get sunburn, and in the mud they may pick up infections. There is no room for flexibility in current legislation. The attractiveness of the organic livestock model is most striking when compared to the horrifying past of intensive industrial farming, the great blemish of the 1970s that is gradually disappearing. Beyond that it's largely a matter of projection and perception, of animals that look "unhappy" to us because they can't wander about freely.

In organic livestock farming antibiotics are banned. This ban is useful, because their preventive use in conventional farming creates a risk of the development of resistance in bacteria, which could have serious consequences for human health. Preventive use of antibiotics is most frequent in large-scale enterprises. Although infections do not spread any faster there than on small farms (despite what many people think), the consequences are greater. Consumers associate the transmission of diseases from animal to human, be it Q fever or mad cow disease, with large barns and feeding lots, but it can happen at any scale. Moreover, a farm may be large but made up of relatively small cowsheds, so any infection can be confined to specific units.

In general, organic farming has advantages over conventional farming in this respect, although the EU has recently adopted new guidelines aimed at limiting the use of antibiotics in farming as a whole. One disadvantage of organic farming is that animals that range freely have a greater chance of picking up infections from the soil or the air, from wild birds for example, than they do indoors. The term "organic" says nothing about the fact that the stomachs of organic cows produce greenhouses gases just like conventional cows. This makes the difference between organic and ordinary cheese and dairy products fairly slight when it comes to the consequences for the climate.

As for biodiversity, that issue is equally complex. Less artificial fertilizer often means a greater diversity of plant life on organic fields and pastures. A fallow period, if it lasts long enough (which means several years) can work well for the preservation of species. The absence of pesticides has favorable effects on insects, especially bees, whose populations are dropping dramatically for still unknown reasons, as well as on birds and small mammals. But these effects are not large, and they are variable. Organic farming is not always insect-friendly, either. Sometimes so many predator insects are left alive that other insects are eliminated.

We should not overestimate the positive effects. Even on organic fields the number of species is very limited compared to undisturbed nature reserves. Because organic farming requires a larger land area for the same level of production, there are indirect negative effects on biodiversity, because more land must be stripped of its natural vegetation. Some studies have actually found more birds on conventional farms. But even if organic farming is beneficial for birds, butterflies, and other insects, we still have to weigh up the negative effects on those same species of bringing more land under cultivation. Still, the message is clear: the less chemicals are used (especially if they are slow to break down), the more species there will be, including useful species, such as bees that pollinate certain crops. Too much fertilizer is often applied in conventional farming, with negative consequences for surface water and biodiversity. The solution to this, however, is not necessarily a switch to organic farming but rather to limit fertilizer use by means of strict regulation, dissemination of information, and taxation on the principle that "the polluter pays."

Organic pest control—the deployment of predator organisms to combat damage and infection by insects—was not invented by organic farming. It is a technique copied from nature, and it now has countless applications, in both conventional and organic farming, in the open soil and in greenhouse cultivation. The most advanced applications are found in closed greenhouses. The predator organisms can be insects, molds, nematodes, parasitic wasps, mites, viruses, or bacteria. Substances derived from plants, such as pyrethrum, are also used to combat damaging insects. In this sense organic farming is not so very different from the best practices in conventional farming, and it is not the case that no insecticides are used in organic farming, it's just that they're called "natural" rather than "chemical" or "synthetic." "Natural" does not mean innocuous. Some of the substances used contain copper, sulphur, soap, and oil.

So what about public health and the safety of organic produce? The use of animal manure instead of artificial fertilizer increases the risk of the spread of bacterial infections originating in the intestinal flora of animals. This can be overcome by sterilizing the dung or radiating the food, but neither is an option in organic farming. Some of these bacteria can be life threatening for the elderly or sick, such as specific forms of the bacterium *Escherichia coli* (enterohemorrhagic *E. coli*, for example); others may be resistant to conventional antibiotics and therefore difficult to treat (such as extended spectrum beta-lactamase–forming bacteria). Cases of typhus, cholera, and amoebic dysentery have resulted from eating organic produce. Sometimes the source of such infections in humans can be traced back to vegetables grown on organic farms that were eaten raw or were inadequately cooked. Animal manure is a bigger problem in vegetable cultivation than in fruit farming, because fruit is generally more acidic and therefore better protected against bacteria. However, fruit that has not been treated with fungicides is more susceptible to molds. Extended spectrum beta-lactamase–forming bacteria are most often found in chickens, incidentally, as a result of high antibiotic use in conventional poultry farming. In that respect the organic approach has a significant advantage.

That organic produce has no residues of synthetic pesticides, herbicides, or fungicides is obvious, given that they are forbidden in organic farming. Whether that makes any difference to public health is unclear, because the amounts of such substances allowed on or in nonorganic produce are extremely low and are well below the level at which they could represent a danger to consumers. It's a different story in poor countries, where too many chemicals are often used in high doses and are mixed by hand, with dangerous methods of application (such as rucksack nebulizers). Every year people die of poisoning, partly because of poor storage of these agents. Reducing their use is a worldwide priority. Ironically, it's not organic farming but the introduction of genetically modified crops, such as insect-resistant cotton (known as Bt cotton; see Chapter 7), that is now making the biggest contribution to the reduction of insecticide use in developing countries.

Various conflicts are currently going on between organic farmers and companies producing genetically modified crops, for example, between bee-keepers and farmers on neighboring land who are growing genetically modified corn, because a tiny percentage of the honey will be made from corn pollen. According to the norms of organic farming, this honey must be removed from sale as "contaminated."

———

Signs of the health benefits of organic produce are far from unambiguous. In general there is no evidence that the consumption of organically grown food is healthier than that of conventionally grown products. This is mainly because "organic" is not a guarantee of the composition of the end product, as the label refers only to the production process. Organic farmers sometimes use alternate varieties or breeds to those used in conventional farming, so you're not actually comparing production methods but the combination of methods and types of plant or animal (which may differ slightly in their chemical composition). The association between healthy and organic is more likely to point to a relationship in the opposite direction: people who eat organic food are more healthy because they have a more conscious attitude to food and health. That people say they feel better if they eat organic apples, bread, and so forth is probably mainly attributable to the placebo effect.

Here and there we find a few indications of possible differences between organic and conventional foods. Organic milk is said to contain more omega-3 fatty acids. Higher levels of antioxidants have been measured in organic vegetables and fruit. Sometimes more vitamin C is found in organic vegetables, along with more iron and zinc. Different studies come up with very different results, however, and even these effects are not always found. Up to now most of these differences are barely significant, if at all. Moreover, it is very hard to make proper comparisons, because almost all the research has looked at crops from existing fields, so no claims can be made about strict experimental conditions, and all kinds of environmental factors could be involved, such as small differences in soil composition or local microclimates. In theory a higher antioxidant content in organic produce is explicable. Organically grown plants are more likely to be affected by insects and molds, because no pesticides or fungicides are used. This causes a defensive reaction in the plant, and the production of antioxidants is part of that reaction.

Organic vegetables usually contain less nitrate (which comes from artificial fertilizer in conventional farming). But whether nitrate content, at least in the amounts found in Europe and other OECD countries, makes any difference to health has not been satisfactorily determined and seems increasingly unlikely. As far as the health effects of organic produce are concerned, all we are left with is that they may contain higher levels of healthy substances, or to be precise, substances that may have a positive effect on health, such as antioxidants. But the presence of these slightly higher levels of antioxidants or omega fatty acids is not in itself proof of a positive impact on human health. It's quite possible that these substances don't survive human digestion or have no effect in low concentrations. What is healthy is determined by the diet as a whole, all the products consumed, not by tiny variations, if they are measurable at all, in specific substances. The rich West has no lack of vitamins, minerals, proteins, and other nutrients, so it probably doesn't matter whether a product is organic. None of this excludes the possibility that in the future significant differences will be found, with beneficial effects.

So does organic produce at least taste better? Although its consumers think so, there's little evidence from blind tastings. Where there is a qualitative difference that cannot be traced back to the use of different varieties or breeds, it may be attributable to shorter supply chains. Anyone allowed to pick their own produce or who buys vegetables and fruit that have reached the market quickly, perhaps at a farmer's market, will find that well-ripened produce has a better flavor than unripe produce transported over a long distance or kept in a cold store. That advantage is not inherent to biological produce, but it is rightly made a selling point by organic growers.

For meat there is usually a difference in taste. Because animals on organic farms usually live longer and weigh more, their meat is firmer and the flavor a little more pronounced, but the same applies to older animals in conventional livestock farming that are given more room to move around.

Perhaps this too is the wrong comparison. Just as a specific dish or a specific wine tastes better on holiday, or because you've paid rather more for it, or are drinking it in the company of loved ones, organic food may taste better because you know it's organic and feel good about that. Organic is above all a moral and social choice.

————

As far as the sustainability of production is concerned, the ultimate balance between organic and conventional farming doesn't favor organic, because of the far greater acreage needed to achieve the same level of production and lower efficiency in the means of production. If we take into account lower yields, fallow land, crop rotation, and animal manure, we would theoretically need five or six times as much land for organic farming as is in use for conventional farming now. It's therefore not an appropriate answer to the world food problem. But even in the case of mushroom farming, for example, organic is less sustainable, because the fermenting of organic compost leads to more emissions of ammonia and yields are again lower. Organic farming makes no contribution per unit of production to reducing greenhouse gases or to saving water.

In poor countries it's always a matter of weighing up a reduction in the use of pesticides and herbicides against lower yields. In that situation we need to ask whether the absence of chemicals is worth the larger acreages that are needed and the lower yields achieved. Concerning meat production, the balance is more favorable, mainly because of the ban on antibiotics, but even here it is not decisive. Effects on biodiversity, which are difficult to measure and mainly attributable to the ban on the use of chemicals, are partly negated by the larger acreage. It has yet to be proven that organic production is any more healthy for humans than conventional.

The Weight of Good Intentions

Food is a matter of both consciousness and conscience. If you think you know that you're eating something good and by doing so are making a contribution to the planet and that it's good for your health as well, then it will taste better. Organic therefore becomes a self-endorsing label, a quality mark for the soul. One indication of the degree to which such concepts have lodged themselves in our thinking is that "organic" is now used as a noun rather than merely as an adjective. We say "I eat/buy organic" rather than "I eat/buy organic food." Shopping organic becomes part of your identity, comparable to the way in which a car or a fashion label can be. It indicates that you identify with a specific group of people and thereby distinguish yourself from others. Organic is a mark of quality, literally and figuratively. Literally because countless companies use the word "organic" to recommend their products. Figuratively because "organic" is a metaphor for opposition to the modernization and increases in scale that the middle classes in Western countries so dislike. The same goes for other terms, like "natural" and "honest." They too have become labels, ways of setting yourself apart as a business or as a consumer.

———

True to my profession, I have for many years not been shy of asking people in the Netherlands, Europe, and beyond why they buy organic food. I wouldn't say there are as many answers as there are buyers of natural and organic produce, but certainly I have heard a wide diversity of responses. Some people prefer the shops that sell organic food because they're more spacious and less crowded; others have health benefits in mind, or say it's better, without any further specification. Many people buy only certain organic products, because they prefer the taste, such as organic yogurt and bread. Others buy organic food for special occasions, such as parties, or as gifts. Or they may simply want to try it out, if organic and conventional products are displayed next to each other on the shelves. In some areas organic vegetable subscriptions are available; a box or bag of seasonal produce is delivered to you every week. Those who take out a subscription build a direct personal relationship with the producers. That satisfaction alone can be a reason to buy organic. One variation on this is the right to harvest vegetables from an organic field every week. "Know what you're eating" becomes "know who's producing your food."

A small percentage of the total supply of food in the Netherlands is organic. In Europe as a whole the figure is slightly higher. The market share of organic produce has risen sharply in recent years in relative terms, but it remains very limited as a proportion of the total, at around 1 percent worldwide. This is disappointing, given the decades of effort by its advocates. Such growth as there is can be explained by more and more consumers opting for a few carefully selected organic products. It's not that those who buy organic are buying more. It seems organic food is an alternative for only a few categories of food, not for the diet as a whole. Even based on a conservative estimate of 20 percent as the number of consumers with above-average to ample incomes, organic products are underconsumed. Many more people could afford organic products, and many more people say they are interested in organic food without actually buying it. The potential market is therefore far bigger, and the shortfall in consumption is actually even worse, given that young people with low incomes, such as students, quite often buy organic products, however selectively.

It seems there are deeper reasons that—despite good intentions, despite all those positive verbal responses, and despite the disquiet expressed by many consumers—organic food has not really penetrated daily life. On the one hand it's a question of price, even though the price of many products is not much higher and in an absolute sense it can't make a great deal of difference, like the extra €0.15 on a liter of milk costing on average less than a euro. Even for people on low incomes this is a small if not insignificant sum, as even if they drink a liter of milk a day it will cost only an extra €55 a year. For meat, cheese, and some vegetables the difference can be greater than 30 percent, which is certainly a limiting factor.

The recent growth can be largely explained by big supermarket chains offering an increasingly broad assortment of organic products. This lowers the barrier—almost half of all sales of organic produce now take place through supermarkets. Several new luxury organic supermarkets have appeared in big cities, offering a combination of status, awareness, and gastronomy. These shops strive to shorten production chains by buying locally. Those shopping in them present themselves as critical, progressive, and environmentally sensitive. The slightly depressing side effect is that with the clientele for organic produce no longer restricted to small, specialist shops, these shops are disappearing, because they cannot compete with ordinary supermarkets offering organic products. The increasing professionalization of organic food chains has also led to takeovers of small suppliers, such as butcher's shops and bakeries.

The limited commercial success of foods with an organic label suggests that faith in organic food has more adherents than buyers. There is certainly a growing trend toward a desire for the natural and traditional and for a more conscious approach to food, but it by no means always leads to changed behavior. The long-awaited breakthrough of organic produce has not arrived, which reflects a lack of conviction: we prefer to desire it than to act. Consumers continue to ask themselves, in their hearts at least, whether organic really makes a difference. They are not wrong: the scales do not ultimately tip toward organic. The question is how much this matters.

I think the consciousness boosted by organic producers, chefs, and consumers forms an adequate basis for change in the long term to farming and food supplies. From that perspective there is no need to stimulate organic production as a separate branch of the food business, other than as a niche market with a focus on enjoyment and an above-average lifestyle—rather than the natural sobriety and other ideals that were present at the start of the organic movement. I believe we should strive for the integration of the best organic and biological with the best conventional techniques, so that the two become increasingly alike. This is already happening on pastureland, because on more and more meadows, few if any artificial fertilizers or other chemicals are used.

The great merit of the organic movement and related schools of thought is that food, in rich countries at least, has again become a full part of our existence and is recognized as being of cultural value. Although this awareness certainly cannot be attributed exclusively to the organic movement and related groups, such as the slow food movement—because it is also the work of various progressive chefs, gardeners, and farmers— the organic movement has restored the link between the means of production and the consumer. That the movement has taken off precisely where consciousness of production methods was disappearing—among the urban middle classes who no longer had any contact with farming and clung to a romantic view of nature—therefore makes sense. Their image of nature and farming is entirely different, however, from that of most farmers. All the farmers I've met are keen to work in ways that are environmentally friendly and good for animal welfare, but they want to use the most advanced and labor-saving methods available. None are contemplating a return to a romantic alternative of manual labor and small-scale production from which neither they nor their children can hope to earn a living.

Everyone agrees that organic farming has shifted the emphasis from productivity and increased output to the desire to make farming more benign for humans, animals, and nature. Organic increasingly stands for quality and flavor, even though little sound evidence supports this connection. The basis and motivation come from nature. Nature leads the way.

The weakness of the organic approach, however, is that taking nature as a guiding principle can be interpreted as a longing for the past and for tradition. Nostalgia for a world in which the relationship between humans and nature was still perfect is not a reliable guideline at all. The garden of paradise never existed. Most of the techniques and assumptions of organic farming do not lead to objectively better results, and they can have negative effects, especially when it comes to the use of land and other resources. So in contrast to what people often think, "organic" and "sustainable" are not one and the same concept. Even agriculture ministries in various European countries and the European Commission have a tendency to assume that organic is a necessary part of sustainable food provision. This assumption is incorrect, given organic farming's greater land requirements and its suboptimal use of nutrients. The organic label does not mean anything regarding emissions of greenhouse gases, water use, transportation, effects on land use, fair trade, and many other factors that determine sustainability. Organic farming cannot offer a solution to the challenge of feeding the world. It can merely fill a niche market in rich countries and among higher income groups elsewhere, with its own specialist producers and distributors. By doing so, organic farming helps increase consciousness of natural cycles and of nature as a whole.

———

Taking nature as a starting point is not in itself a guarantee of better production methods. Organic is not necessarily better for nature, humans, or animals. Nonetheless, the latest insights in the field of ecological processes can help clarify and reformulate the assumptions of organic farming. A great deal can be said for keeping ecological cycles closed as far as possible. Thinking ecologically does not automatically coincide with traditional and low-tech, however. On the contrary, some of the most sustainable systems have emerged in experiments with closed greenhouses that involve neither soil nor direct sunlight. "Sustainable" is not by definition "natural" in the naive sense of resembling nature as far as possible. Ecology presents all kinds of opportunities for a modern technology that is far more precise; that looks far more carefully at how substances can be reclaimed from natural cycles; and that studies how the genetics of plants, insects, and animals change and how those developments can be steered. Other innovations lie in the field of organic pesticides and fungicides in combination with biotechnology to increase disease resistance, the exploitation of energy cycles, and the recycling of nutrients and water. We can progress only with the help of organic techniques validated by research. The terms "organic" and "ecological" (in the scientific rather than ideological sense) can be very close in meaning. It is counterproductive, however, to reject artificial fertilizer and genetic modification a priori, and it muddies the debate about the real contribution environmentalism can make to the modernization of farming and the food supply. Unfortunately, organic farming remains too conservative.

That is a shame, and it confronts me with a personal dilemma. Adherents of the organic movement are genuinely committed, and many of their aims are worth striving for. But dissatisfaction with a Western bourgeois way of life sometimes borders on the naive, on a view of nature as paradise, nature as a guide that must be listened to. Natural and organic are by no means always better for the environment, no matter how much we intuitively want them to be. Organic farming as a whole is a mishmash of valuable goals and ideas that have either been insufficiently tested or are completely misguided. The result is polarization between organic and conventional farming, which means no progress is made.

Food always reflects the identities of individuals and groups. What makes our own era extraordinary is our huge freedom of choice when it comes to food. We no longer eat whatever is available but reject standardized food to opt for individual freedom of expression. Buying organic produce is above all a confirmation of who you are, of your intentions and lifestyle, rather than a well-considered political choice, let alone one based on sound science. Just as consumers selectively combine expensive designer labels with cheap products when buying clothing or furniture, so they may go by car to the organic bakery and then drive on to the supermarket for other items produced by conventional farming. The irony is that organic consumption is possible only in a worldwide postcapitalist society, in which you can opt for variety instead of uniformity, small scale rather than large scale, personal in place of anonymous, regional rather than universal. What strictly organic thinking rejects—globalization and modern technology—is precisely what makes that option possible. It's only because we no longer have to worry about consuming sufficient calories tomorrow that we have scope for new and in many ways less efficient approaches.

Those who buy organic are making a choice, even if it's not one that will save the planet. "Organic" and "natural" are ultimately about ideology, about food as lifestyle, advocated with honest intentions. The strength of the organic movement and all movements like it is that in the end they offer a story, a story about harmony and provenance, about love of nature, about a romantic landscape on a human scale, about devotion to traditional skills, about a longing for an uncomplicated world in which we are safe. These are all things that seem to be lacking in today's global society. Organic products also tell a personal story, in which the producer—the farmer, the grower, the fisherman—has a face and sometimes even appears in advertisements or in discussions with consumers on the Internet. The consumer too likes to appear in these stories. It is perhaps this new intimacy that we find most satisfying of all.

That story, far more than the objective characteristics of organic food, is what attracts so many people. The story of a paradisiacal environment in which nature and the elements generously provide us with their abundance and where we have no worries—where we can even be happy amid all that plenty—is made visible in the most modern of organic supermarkets. As true organic paradises, they tempt us to consume— who knows, perhaps also to overconsume—with their shelves stuffed with fresh produce in attractive packaging. There are shops in which the vegetables are regularly sprayed with water, to the accompaniment of the sound of thunder, to give consumers the feeling they are standing right out amid the natural world. The organic story is not merely used to attract the food consumer. It can be seen, for example, in architecture and fashion. The story lifts us out of anonymity and gives meaning to our existence, especially when it offers a sense of purpose as we engage in those unavoidable daily activities that consumption involves.

Which is why all too often I buy organic products, such as bread, vegetables, and yogurt, sometimes even against my better scientific judgment. I'm not immune to the desire for a story about a better world, as reflected in the archetypal garden of paradise.

NINE

Biodiversity: From Landscape to Gene

Landscape [is] ... a text on which generations write their recurring obsessions.
SIMON SCHAMA, *Landscape and Memory*

> in a field of rapeseed
> they enjoy the blossoms—
> these sparrows
> MATSUO BASHO

Ask people what they find attractive, or with what they feel the greatest affinity, and it will rarely be anything boring, uniform, monotonous, or large in scale. People dressed in precisely the same way, especially large crowds of them, or cities with endless lines of identical tower blocks make us feel ill at ease. The same goes for landscapes and food. Vast fields of corn or soybeans, or immense barns full of battery-farmed chickens are experienced as repugnant compared to a varied landscape of woods and hills. Variety or diversity means small, at least on the scale of human observation, which makes events understandable and manageable. The idea that diversity is not just attractive and a delight to the senses but morally good for us is therefore deeply rooted.

Diversity has gained a new meaning in recent years, namely, the acceptance of those who are different from the local norm. Translated into policy it means everyone must be given equal opportunities. This stands alongside the biological meaning of biodiversity. The positive value given to social diversity is recent. For a long time those who were different were not welcome. The emancipation of minorities has forced us to adopt a diversity policy, and it now contributes to the feeling that diversity is always good. Biological diversity is increasingly appreciated as well.

Evolution began with biological diversity, which therefore precedes social diversity. The image of plenty in paradise that is so dominant in the main monotheistic religions, and exists in other cultures too, presents a partial explanation. The abundance of food in the paradise of Judaism, Christianity, and Islam is after all a direct consequence of the diversity of biological species. All depictions and descriptions of paradise make explicit this connection among a wealth of species, food, smallness of scale, and human well-being. Biological diversity, or biodiversity, has traditionally been seen as positive, because God given. Social diversity is now established by law in many countries, so biological diversity is also becoming a goal in its own right. All diversity is worth pursuing, is the idea, even though biological diversity is the outcome of climate, soil, the range of species, and other circumstances and has no moral significance in itself.

In paradise abundance arose by itself in conditions of—to put it rather disrespectfully—divine landscape management and species control, according to a biblical biodiversity policy. The image of this naturally charming garden, which needs the help of a divine hand only occasionally if at all, is contrasted with the wilderness outside paradise. There Adam and Eve encounter a monotonous, interminable landscape without any variety in its flora and fauna. In the untamed natural world of scarcity and deprivation, they are vulnerable and insignificant. In other religions the picture is no different: the land is desolate and empty and can be cultivated only with divine help. It is the gods and goddesses associated with farming, from the Greek and Roman Demeter and Ceres to the Chinese Mang Shen, who create order out of chaos and make the desert manageable, in other words, usable for humans, a place where they can grow their own food. In a Laotian creation myth, for example, the god of gods sends his son, Khun Borom, who plants a rice paddy, and from that point civilization begins. An ordered landscape, neatly arranged biodiversity, and food belong together.

In Europe the connection among paradisiacal diversity, abundance, and well-being has become rooted in the culture through tradition and art. This can be seen from a painting of 1615–1617 titled "Earthly Paradise with the Fall of Adam and Eve," painted jointly by Jan Breughel the Elder and Peter Paul Rubens, with its variety of open and thick vegetation and its great array of colorful animals and plants. The viewer keeps discovering more species. Adam and Eve are about to commit the original sin, but the painters suggest that they can still enjoy all this diversity and plenty for a moment longer. It may be partly because of such images, associated as they are with the paradise myth, that diversity has gained such a positive moral charge.

For most people biological diversity is equivalent to a multiplicity of species. The Bible provides a foundation for that idea too, in the story of Noah, who is charged with saving not nature (or the ecosystem) but its expression, the species. Scientifically speaking, biodiversity relates to the different but connected forms of "miscellany" or "disparity," on a variety of scales from landscape to species and genes. Diversity at the level of species means, simply put, that the more species there are in a given surface area the more diversity there is. Within species it means: the more variation in the form of varieties and breeds and differences among individuals, the more diversity of genes there is. We increasingly look beyond species to the functions they fulfil in an ecosystem and how different species fulfil the same functions, and vice versa—for example, which species can serve as hosts for useful insects. Measuring biodiversity, or its loss, in terms of the number of species is no longer so relevant.

Landscape, the visible expression of an ecosystem on the land, is a combination of biological species in a given physical setting—soil, climate, topography, hydrology—and human disruption through agriculture and building. At one end of the spectrum are completely untouched ecosystems in which only evolution provides variety. Here it's usually the case that the older the landscape, the longer evolution has been at work and so the more variety there is. The Amazon rainforest is one of the oldest landscapes, and much of it remained undisturbed by the last ice age, with the result that it has the greatest biodiversity per square kilometer of any area on earth.

As soon as farming begins, or human intervention of any sort, all kinds of disturbance takes place. Cultivated forest with spontaneous new arrivals, patches of nettles, and messy little fields were for many years excluded from what we thought of as nature, but appreciation for them is now growing. One of the most interesting scientific discoveries of recent years is that even in disturbed forests and in urban areas, examples of truly rich biodiversity can be found.

Disturbance as a result of small-scale farming has created new landscapes. These human-made or cultivated landscapes arose in areas with a variety of altitudes, soils, and water-retention properties, with agriculture stretching back for centuries: poppies among the rocks, olive groves and almond trees on steep slopes, or birds nesting beside wet ditches. The diversity in fields and meadows, the variety of cereals and apple trees and of local sheep but also of weeds and insects—all these things are a consequence of farming.

Biodiversity is certainly not merely a technical concept. For many it relates to an ideal of what the landscape, the countryside, and farming should be like. The word "landscape," derived from "the condition of the land," already contains a suggestion that the land has been shaped by gods or humankind and has not simply evolved. It is associated with human or divine intervention intended to make something that pleases the eye with its harmonious variety. Now that cities with impersonal suburbs and high-rise dwellings are expanding everywhere, and with them motorways and industrial zones, now that farms are bigger than ever and the countryside is scattered with ugly structures, we are overcome by a sense of loss. Unless we try to protect it, the landscape will have to give way to our collective drive to expand. For a decade or so, the middle classes have associated biodiversity with everything that is vulnerable and defenseless. Biodiversity is the victim, and humans and above all farming are the culprits.

It's not that simple, because farming also creates biodiversity in cultivated landscapes, and it does so in all kinds of unexpected ways. That is what makes the subject so difficult. Anyone wanting to understand what biodiversity means must look not only at biological aspects but also at the small scale of agriculture in the past and its traditions. It then becomes clear that the management of biodiversity has everything to do with lifestyle and traditional values, and with restoring them. Nothing makes this clearer than recent changes in how we value the landscape.

The Renaissance of the Countryside

The people in the photographs all look short and thin. Their skin is dark and wrinkled. Most are not wearing shoes, or only worn-out boots without laces. The women wear headscarves that cover their foreheads and shoulders; they are picking up leftover ears of grain from the freshly harvested fields. The men stand next to a cart that has no wheels, levering it through the mud with their hayforks like a kind of sledge, aided by white oxen with twisted horns that are led by a rope through their nostrils. A beggar with a stick and a bundle of clothes brings news in exchange for somewhere to sleep. There is a well covered with stone slabs that freezes in winter and dries up in summer. A woman lifts a jug onto her head with a gracefully curved arm. In a kitchen—no more than a scorched hole in the wall—two children with sunken eyes stand next to a rudimentary chair.

The yard is bare, aside from a few woven baskets. You imagine this must be the Middle Ages, North Africa, or Central Asia, but these photographs were taken in the first quarter of the twentieth century in Umbria, Italy, by Swiss ethnographer and linguist Paul Scheuermeier, who recorded countless apparently insignificant details of daily life in the countryside.

――――――

Ninety years later I, like so many people, love visiting Umbria with its alternating valleys and thick forests (from which it probably gets its name, a reference to the darkness). In the hills south of Lake Trasimeno, where I often walk, there is almost nothing reminiscent of the past that was captured by Scheuermeier. The messy fields, pools of mud, and coppiced woods have been transformed into a landscape that is pleasant to wander in, where associations with fear, hard work, and poverty seem to have been eliminated for good. Three generations later the region is at the cutting edge of a new lifestyle. The tumbledown farmhouses have been perfectly restored, retaining the original materials yet now with the latest devices for heating and security. Farmhouses and workers' cottages have become second homes, with luxuriantly blossoming oleanders and lavender around courtyards with white umbrellas. Surrounded by olive trees and manicured lawns, bright-blue swimming pools glitter. Antiques shops sell the simple furniture of the past for dizzying multiples of the original price; coarse hand-embroidered linen sheets (the traditional dowry) are worth hundreds of euros each. In the picturesque villages the only shop, which sold everything from bread to carpentry saws, has gone, making room for delicatessens and galleries. The poor man's food of old, *la cucina povera*, with dried tomatoes, pancetta from your own pig, and wild artichokes, is celebrated in culinary guides.

Foreigners are all too fond of staying in former cowsheds that have been transformed into holiday residences for the benefit of *agriturismi*, where they can enjoy the landscape, culture, and culinary pleasures in discreet luxury. What an irony. Their own ancestors were probably from countryside that looked very much like the old Umbria. The same development took place earlier in Tuscany and on some Greek islands, and several decades before that in large parts of France and Spain. Unless extended economic crises follow one on the other, there is every reason to think that comparable developments will take place in all regions where the landscape is attractive, the climate less than extreme, and traces of the old cultural and culinary traditions have been preserved. First may come the relatively undiscovered countryside of Hungary, Romania, and the Balkans, but this kind of tourism might just as easily take off in North Africa and Turkey, in Central America, Sri Lanka, or Bali. Agritourism is not an exclusively European phenomenon, and it in no way resembles the mass tourism of the coasts. It's a more conscious return by rich city dwellers to the countryside as a symbol of authenticity, the beauties of landscape, and pleasure.

Economic growth after the Second World War brought work opportunities to the countryside, especially in southern Europe (but also elsewhere in the world), first of all in farming, then in food processing and other industries. In Umbria everyone became richer. Tourism, restored village centers, luxury shops, new roads, and second homes are some of the ways in which this wealth expresses itself. Small-scale farming, which years ago ceased being able to compete with efficient agriculture elsewhere, has survived only because of EU subsidies. Most farms are now switching to the production of vegetables, goat's cheese, and olives, whether organic or not. This means the landscape is preserved: gray-green olive groves alternating with cereal crops and coppiced woodland, unpaved roads and overgrown streams. Except that the oxen with their wooden carts have been replaced by noisy tractors. In the fields manual labor is now done by the elderly, with the help of Bulgarians and Romanians and the occasional North African. The latter also collect garbage and do the washing up in restaurants. They are today's poor, although their working conditions are better than those of the 1920s. Often these new laborers come from rural areas that are little different from Italy just after the First World War. They have done just what Umbrians did a generation or two before them: left in the hope of a better life somewhere else. In their countries too, whether in Eastern Europe or North Africa, innovation is hesitantly beginning, at least where investment is available for the modernization of farming and there is a new middle class that can send money home to its childhood villages.

So the countryside has been through a real renaissance in the past few decades all over Western Europe and little by little elsewhere. As a child, in the mid-1960s, I saw villages in France's Massif Central with open sewers and collapsed houses surrounded by rising scrub. What made the greatest impression on me then were the stooped old women who let out a cry of alarm at the sight of strangers. Where entire villages were abandoned, more than half a century later tradition and culture are flourishing, or at least a selective version of them, along with the semblance of old values, in the form of "genuine luxury" and "the natural life" for the spoiled urbanite.

It's a reversal of all values. The countryside, so recently synonymous with poverty, backwardness, and hard physical labor, has been transformed into a desirable place where the cosmopolitan urban middle class loves to linger. Country life has come to symbolize an ideal, a return to the values of a mythologized past, a paradise. This, thinks the city dweller, is how real life ought to be, so simple and unhurried, with good food from the garden or the region every day, prepared and grown with care by farmers who work the land with respect. This is the quiet natural counterweight to the frantic life of the city, where we degenerate at our computers and in our cars into consuming robots, surviving on fast food and stress.

The trek to the idealized countryside embodies for us the desire for the past, for nutritious food that is simply set before us, for idyllic sunsets and singing birds. In the rich parts of the world where fewer and fewer people work in agriculture, where food is cheap and free time plentiful, we have seen the countryside this way ever since the Renaissance. There, laboring on the land, working with your hands, seems like an attractive form of gardening and the countryside a paradise of freedom from care, without agricultural poisons or tractors, farmers crippled by back pain, gruesomely slaughtered pigs, and vicious guard dogs.

———

This reborn idyll contrasts markedly with many parts of the former Soviet Union, Africa, Asia, the Middle East, and South America, where many people in rural areas would drop everything tomorrow if they had a chance to leave for the city. Seventy percent of the very poorest (with a daily income of less than $1.25) live in rural areas, and in southern Asia the figure is as high as 80 percent. Isolation, low labor productivity in agriculture and other sectors, lack of education, insufficient availability of credit and agricultural products (such as artificial fertilizer and tools), lack of transportation and roads, too few schools and clinics—there are countless reasons for the link between poverty and the countryside. Those left in rural areas are increasingly the poor, the elderly, and the weak.

Mahatma Gandhi apparently said that anyone wanting to get to know India must study its villages. In his day he was right, and now it's true in a different sense. The countryside reflects the world. It's there, in the poor countries and in the rising economies like India and China, that great changes will take place in the coming decades, following patterns we have already seen in Europe and the United States.

It starts with the emptying of the countryside, where there is no money to be earned. Those who leave for the city usually send money back to relatives in their villages, for modest investments, not only in better accommodation but also in new means of production, such as artificial fertilizer, seed, and livestock. At the same time demand for food in the cities grows, in volume but also in diversity, so in the fortunate areas—the most fertile and accessible—farms increase in size, business operations are rationalized, and entrepreneurs are attracted. Small farmers and growers give up; parcels of land and herds are combined. Higher labor costs near cities and new export opportunities encourage further modernization and labor-saving investment.

So the countryside grows apart. On the one hand economically viable regions emerge where the old way of life, and with it poverty and hard labor, quickly disappear, even if the farming life remains relatively tough and underpaid compared to work in industry and the service sector. This is the countryside that feeds the cities and fills export orders. On the other hand the less favorable areas are further marginalized by depopulation and governmental neglect. Until suddenly this poor, unmodernized, and almost abandoned countryside, where the old buildings, small fields, hedgerows, and terraces still remain, is discovered by the urban middle classes. With their money and their interest in authentic food and a down-to-earth lifestyle, they become the instigators of the renaissance of the countryside, with the willing cooperation of the original inhabitants. Fields become golf courses—why not? Entire villages are rebuilt by travel companies, which renovate them as "authentic" villages with luxury apartments. In Umbria and Tuscany the olive growers have become gardeners, who uproot their old olive trees and plant them among the lavender and swimming pools in the gardens of those second homes, and then plant new olive groves on their own empty fields to qualify for European subsidies.

With the growth of the world population and greater mobility, many regions are seeing a reduction in the sharp contrasts between city and countryside. City dwellers return to the countryside for recreation or to live the outdoor life when their working lives come to an end. The image of the idyllic countryside is so powerful that it has become the inspiration for newly developed city districts. The Garden City movement that emerged in the late nineteenth century has acquired new zest in the past twenty years. In suburban areas the attractive aspects of the countryside are replicated: green courtyards, wide verges, orchards and vegetable plots, even ponds that naturally filter water.

So what about the original rural inhabitants? They leave for the city to seek their fortune, study, and earn money, but they often keep in touch with one another in the districts where they end up. In old age they like to return to their native villages. In a continual, slow migration, city and countryside residents circle around each other. If you look carefully, the village is not what it was, with its satellite dishes, city skyscrapers on the horizon, with the arrival of modern transportation, new customs, and new residents who want to eat sweets and truffles and to take up paragliding. But the village does exist again, because the countryside has been reborn.

With the disappearance of the old life of the village, however, something immaterial has been lost, and it is precisely that for which the city dweller longs. What is it? We always need to be careful about idealizing the community spirit of old, because no one wants to return to that relentless social control and the hopelessness of shared poverty. That which really has disappeared is the indomitability, the sense of pride and knowledge of the landscape, the ways of the clouds and the paths of the wild boar—that specific identity of place and time that has not found any substitute in the new globalizing world, except in the nostalgia of the urban middle class.

From Countryside to Cultivated Landscape

The moment humans laid out their first fields and pastures, the countryside came into existence. Perhaps we would do better to call them "rural areas," from the Latin *rus* ("open land"), derived from the Greek for ploughing and cultivation. In any case I am referring to the area outside settlements and towns or cities, where fields, herds, and humans meet the wilderness. Such areas—a succession of fields, meadows, and coppiced woodland, the sum of human effort—constitute a new diverse landscape, shaped by humankind.

The renaissance of the countryside is not just a recent phenomenon, the consequence of increased spending power and the desire of better-off urbanites for an idyllic counterpoint, or a contrast to the modernization of farming elsewhere. Long before the twentieth-century renaissance of the countryside, we gradually came to see rural areas as landscape. You might say that the countryside is the human side of agriculture, whereas landscape is the physical and spatial structure where biodiversity can develop. Wherever we find it, landscape can be read like a history book: the position of the trees and woods, how big the fields are, whether the farms are far apart, whether there are animals or once were. All this can be interpreted if you take the time and already know something of the history of the area. Countryside and landscape are our memory.

Even though we are usually unaware of it, most of the landscapes we love are a product of farming, which has created and sustained their various forms of diversity. As with those pictures used in psychology tests in which you see either a vase or the faces of two women, depending on how you look at them, we see the areas outside the city as countryside or as landscape, as places of work or as green space. At the start of the twenty-first century, when city dwellers want to know as little as possible about the realities of farming and when the real work of food production has moved to large-scale enterprises and thereby has been removed from sight, landscape and the countryside coincide again. The idealized countryside becomes a desirable landscape, onto which an idyllic way of life is projected, an ode to diversity. Only recently have we started to see that you can also quite literally create a collection of landscapes, as has been done in the Netherlands, for example, with everything from medieval peat polders to reclaimed moorland. This gives the diversity of cultivated landscapes a value in itself, just like a collection of paintings. Landscape has become art.

This is no accident. It was art, especially European painting and to a lesser extent literature and music (think of the nineteenth-century "landscape composers," like Smetana or Beethoven) that taught us to see the countryside as an artificial landscape and not merely as a place of rural labor. What we admire most of all, in Italy, France, or the Netherlands, is a safe parklike decor in which people experience not their insignificance but their connection with the diversity of nature around them. Painting shows us how attractive and human the diversity of agrarian or human-made landscape is, in contrast to virgin nature with its breathtaking cliffs, desolate plains, raging rivers, or impenetrable conifer forests. In the countless cultivated landscapes immortalized by painters, we feel at home. This is true not just of the many wheat fields with crows that Vincent van Gogh painted in Provence, such as "La Moisson" ("The Harvest") of 1888, but also of the views by John Constable, in which he so often depicts meadows and farmland close to towns and villages, as in his "Salisbury Cathedral from the Meadows." Of course it's rarely if ever a painter's intention to offer a photographic or even realistic depiction of landscape, let alone of agriculture, but nonetheless these paintings do unintentionally point to the continual presence of the agrarian.

From the Middle Ages on the landscape of Europe was stripped of its divine orderliness to become a subject in its own right, first as a background in the form of a view, the *veduta*. Paintings from the Renaissance often show an idealized agrarian landscape in the background, like the fifteenth-century "Adoration of the Shepherds" by Andrea Mantegna, with its olive groves on terraced slopes, barely distinguishable from those found there today. The landscape was for a long time a popular subject, because the hand of God could be seen in it, creating order. The Romantic period ended with attention focused on the dramatic and the wild, but painters like Jacob Philipp Hackert, a contemporary of Caspar David Friedrich, repeatedly depicted farmed landscapes, as in his "Villa of Maecenas and the Waterfalls at Tivoli," in which we see sheep peacefully grazing in the foreground accompanied by resting shepherds and shepherdesses, and in the background meadows denuded of trees. In reaction to nineteenth-century urbanization, which brought change on an unprecedented scale, idyllic rural landscapes were painted remarkably frequently: the wilderness tamed by agriculture.

In no country in the world are landscape and farming so interwoven as in the Netherlands, and nowhere else have they shaped our image of beauty and nature to the same extent. Despite the dramatic skies over the flat land, the human scale dominates, as in Jan van Goyen's "View of Haarlem and the Haarlem Lake," in which the low horizon and the vast space of the flat landscape make people look small but in no sense insignificant. The two resting farm laborers are entirely in proportion to the polder they look out across. Other paintings, such as Paul Gabriël's "Watermill in Polder 'de Leidsche Dam' near The Hague" interrupt the vast sky with unmistakable signs of human activity: the cows and especially the mill that towers high above the land. Without exception, Dutch paintings exude calm and self-confidence. This is a safe landscape, where the trees often stand motionless and the sunlight falls in parallel beams, creating intimate vistas, as in "The Farmstead" by Andreas Schelfhout. This is a countryside in which people can move around care free. The mainly green fields and the plentiful trees reflect the fertile soil. The skies are vast but not overwhelming, with clouds that predict mild rain rather than storms. Landscape and town are closely interwoven. In "Little Rope Walk" by Joris Herst we see cows in the meadow just beyond the fence. In views of towns the agrarian is always close by.

This version of the Netherlands is inhabited by people who know that they rarely need be afraid of nature, because the landscape itself is largely made by human hands. The farmer with barns and animals is never far away. We see farms and farmhouses, dikes and ditches, horses, cows and sheep, planted trees, and neat grassland. The fields form a variegated patchwork of green. This is a land of water and sky, but the water is above all functional, in drainage ditches, canals, and rivers that are used for transportation. Even if humans appear to be absent, as in a painting of the wild forest titled "The Origin (Wooded View at Ooster-beek)" by Matthijs Maris, there is no mistaking the human influence: the tree roots have been washed bare, the fertile layer of humus has been partially dug away, trees have been felled, and any fallen wood has been removed.

Wouter Johannes van Troostwijk's "A Barn on the Bank of a Stream in Gelderland" is a wonderful example of how painters can give the natural-ness of the agrarian landscape a beauty of its own. By doing so they pre-pared the way for a new consciousness of the landscape as something that must be preserved. Because of them, because of the frame they put around nature, we learned to look at landscape as valuable in its own right and therefore as something that must be preserved.

It is perhaps not by chance that toward the end of two centuries of pro-ductive landscape painters, the first efforts were made to protect the nat-ural world in Europe and the United States simultaneously. In the early twentieth century in the Netherlands, Jac. P. Thijsse and Eli Heimans set up both the Vereniging tot Behoud van Natuurmonumenten and the Nederlandse Natuurhistorische Vereniging. In the United States a book of paintings of birds by John James Audubon inspired the founding of the Audubon Society. Campaigns by the pioneers of nature conservation were inspired by a desire to protect the environments of breeding birds. Later their efforts were extended to all landscapes.

It soon became clear to them that not only wild and apparently unused nature should be protected but also all those diverse areas of transition between farm and raw nature, between forest and meadow, moorland and valley, dry and wet, slope and riverbed, fertile and infertile, rocky land and deep soil, wind and lee, and sun and shade. It is often the case that the steeper the gradient (in other words, the degree of transition), the greater the diversity will be of biotopes and therefore of species. Farmers have made use of this variation in landscape for centuries. The richer and better watered the soil, the bigger the fields can be and therefore the more uniform the agriculture practiced there, giving non-farmed species less chance of survival.

Sometimes we trip ourselves up. We have such a clearly defined image of what beauty is—a mixture of trees, bushes, and tall grass—that we no longer find acceptable the burning off of vegetation that happens regularly in nature and in traditional farming and hunting. Cultivated landscape and "natural" or "organic" are two sides of the same coin. The first, the landscape, is the bearer of diversity; the second is a guide to how to use the land as naturally as possible. They are different but fundamentally similar images of the landscape as a garden that has wrenched itself free of the wilderness, and they have become part of our culture. By means of the detour that is farming, humans return to the paradise of a landscape on a human scale that radiates peace and self-confidence, the divine garden where we know we are safe because nature, well-disposed toward us, presents us with its diversity.

Farming and Biological Diversity

Our appreciation of the beauty of agricultural landscapes and the countryside goes deeper than painterly aesthetics or our longing for simplicity and pleasure. It makes sense that we feel most at home in a diverse, open landscape with parklike areas, fertile fields, and meadows. In the Dutch version there is heathland as well, in the humid tropics here and there a little woodland still. All such landscapes feature a great wealth of flora and fauna. Our spontaneous appreciation of variety is historically determined.

Diversity—the existence of variation or differences—is both a precondition for the start of farming and a historical consequence of it. The first farmers made use of variety to select the best plants and animals and breed from them. In areas where variety was greatest, because of differences in the gradient of the hills, the angle of the sun, rockiness, and moisture, farmers began their efforts to plant wild grasses. Diversity, and particularly biodiversity, is a vital necessity. Without biological variation there would be no domestication of species, no plant breeding, and no biotechnology.

But outside of undisturbed ecosystems, biodiversity is also a product of agricultural intervention by humans. Without farming there would be no hedges or open fields, no ploughed soil or grazed pasture. Farming, and more generally the use of land and water (for example, for peat cutting and watermills), has created various new biotopes—environments for plants and animals—where new species establish themselves and develop, and old species are at home. The swallow that once spent the night in a fringe of reeds has found a new habitat in those fields of corn that humans so often hate. The biological diversity of the cultivated landscape is an unintended by-product of farming.

But the results of farming are by no means always so arcadian. Humans not only create biodiversity, they destroy it as well. Almost everywhere with sufficient rainfall, where the climate is not too cold and the soil not too rocky, the original wilderness was primeval forest. Only in the sparsely populated humid tropics (the Amazon and Congo basins and parts of Southeast Asia) does the forest still remain. Everywhere else, farming has gradually destroyed the forest. This started to some degree even before farming, because people have always used the natural world around them, not just for hunting and gathering but also as a source of firewood and structural timber, fiber, and other useful products. With the coming of agriculture, however, the destruction of the original vegetation became more extensive and more thorough.

From pollen analysis, especially of the kind that studies the relationship between the seeds of grasses and trees, we know that in most parts of Europe the original forest began slowly disappearing 5,000 years ago. Humans cut down the trees to create pasture and fields. Sometimes farmers had to withdraw for a time, and the livestock disappeared from the meadows, allowing the forest to return spontaneously. In wetter areas too (sometimes now seen as "natural" pasture) there were almost always trees. Over time, precisely because of livestock keeping—the grazing and trampling of young seedlings; the effects of nitrogen-rich dung—the forest lost its ability to grow back.

These effects turn nature into countryside and then into an agricultural landscape, and the effects of human influence are more or less irreversible. From the Middle Ages on, the use of land in Europe became more and more intensive, based on a combination of crops, timber, fruit trees, and livestock. This first created a parklike landscape, with the remnants of forest here and there. As the use of land became even more intensive, it was degraded into grassland and moorland, especially on wet or sandy soils (with the risk of sand drift that created landscapes we now also regard as natural). In temperate climates this intensification meant not just grazing, the felling of trees, and cutting of reeds but also the use of the fertile upper layer of soil from woods and moorland to enrich farmland elsewhere, or as a fuel, leaving the high-altitude strips of the open field system so typical of northwestern Europe.

From the Industrial Revolution on, the countryside became the arena of commercial production for the cities, while at the same time a countermovement arose that valued the arcadian or pastoral scene. Agriculture had an impact not just on humans themselves, their diet, population growth, and the freedom to undertake other activities, but also on all the species around them, which were given preferential treatment if useful or eliminated as soon as they became damaging or inconvenient. Hedges were laid to separate fields and to shelter them from the wind, soils were ploughed, stones removed, rivers diverted, and weeds and pests killed. Even where humans did not intervene directly, they left traces of their presence downstream and in the air, by damming water courses, through salinization and erosion, and eventually by using chemicals to fertilize and protect crops. Only slash-and-burn agriculture—the least intensive form of farming with very low yields—which takes place on small areas of burned-down forest that quickly grows up again, has no irreversible effects, as long as the land lies fallow for long enough (which generally means for decades). Such agriculture barely exists anywhere any longer, even in the most remote tropical regions.

The astonishing growth of the human population in the twentieth century meant that agriculture had a particularly damaging impact on the natural environment. Natural ecosystems, and indeed many of the older cultivated landscapes, disappeared as a result of increases in scale, intensification, and the rationalization of farmland and farming practices. The striking and tragic paradox is that the very same agriculture that created the landscapes we love became the destroyer of them as a result of the growing demand for food and other agricultural products. Such demand became the engine behind the expansion of farming and the unprecedented destruction of ecosystems. The application of artificial fertilizer and chemical herbicides and pesticides leaves chemical residues and unfortunately kills helpful insects along with the rest, as well as birds. Forests and fragile river deltas are stripped of trees, drained, and turned into wide plains planted with uniform crops. The indirect effects also can be disastrous. The extension of farmland means that wild areas are fragmented and wild species no longer have sufficient space. Add drought as a result of drainage and the removal of groundwater, and further species, such as amphibians, become seriously threatened as well.

It's impossible to say how great the combined influence of humans has been through agriculture, agrarian industry, and distribution systems. Some say it's destroying the world, others that farming was merely the start of all the disasters humans have called down on themselves. The most illuminating way to see that influence in its proper proportions is to view the role of humans as being of the same order as that of other forces of nature, such as volcanism and continental drift. This human impact is so great not just because of the amount of land we use but above all because of the far-reaching effects of land use and the speed at which we are cultivating more land in more and more places.

Yet farming has not destroyed all natural diversity. In contrast to the impression most people in densely populated areas have, worldwide less than 12 percent, or 1.5 billion hectares, of all the land on earth (not counting the Antarctic) is in use for arable farming. That is a little more than a third of the land theoretically suitable for the production of crops without the use of irrigation. This may not seem like much, but it is 12 percent more than forty years ago, an average increase of 4 million hectares a year. Most of this growth (58 percent) has taken place in Africa and South America, the least populous continents. Only in Europe and North America has the area under cultivation shrunk a little in the past fifty years.

We do not farm all the land, because not all of it is suitable. Most of the earth's surface that is not covered in water is too cold, too wet, too dry, too stony, or too steep to farm. There we find more or less untouched areas, and we have come to believe that they must be protected as nature reserves and as human heritage. Although controls are not yet sufficient, no country on earth has a government that claims nature reserves should be cultivated as farmland, although some do want to drill them for oil and gas.

The concern expressed by many environmentalist organizations that tropical forests in poor countries, especially around the Amazon, are being sacrificed to make hamburgers for wealthy consumers—by turning forest in to grassland for meat production—reflects a long history of exploitation in which felling did indeed take place without a second thought. With a few exceptions, however, this is no longer going on, if only because deforestation can now be detected by means of satellite images. If we want to slow down the future increase in farmland or even limit it to protect natural ecosystems then, paradoxically, farming must become more intensive and modern and therefore less diverse. The higher the yields are on farmland, the better biodiversity outside agricultural areas can be protected.

———

Sometimes changes to the landscape caused by farming are so dramatic that few are able to see anything positive in them, such as the endless cornfields of America's Midwest or even the geometric Dutch polders. Characteristic of farming is the dominance of one or at most a few species that are actively favored: grass and cows, barley and olive trees, rice and carp. The more efficiently the land is farmed, the less diversity there is, both in the landscape and in the fields. We now have vast areas devoted to a single species, perhaps potatoes or corn. A field or pasture is never uniform in the strict sense, even if it may appear so, because many of the lower species associated with the agrarian ecosystem are diverse but unseen, such as molds. A rice paddy cannot survive without the presence of insects like predatory wasps that make short work of caterpillars and other pests, nor without useful soil bacteria, and it will always suffer from invisible underground infestations of such species as nematodes.

There is much resistance to what is often called the "monoculture" of modern farming. Strictly speaking, monoculture means that the same crop is grown year after year, but the word is often used to express repugnance at the lack of diversity and the sense of monotony such farming evokes. Although many people regard it as such, monoculture is not inherently irresponsible, as long as fertilization, soil protection, and the combating of infestations is appropriate.

Monoculture is not new, either—just think of the rice terraces where nothing but rice has been grown for centuries (sometimes with a short vegetable crop between two rice crops). Or look at the growing of olives in Andalusia, where a single variety (*picual*) has been planted in the same orchards for more than 200 years. Still, in modern monoculture there is almost always some form of crop rotation, for example, the growing of cereals after one or two years of potatoes to prevent any build-up of pathogens. This rotation is not possible with irrigated sugarcane or rice. They make special demands of the soil, which must be wet and is therefore unsuitable for other plants of the grass family. With almost all field crops (grains, potatoes, and so on), modernization leads to increases in scale.

Small-scale farming means intensive cultivation. It may take the form of "polyculture," which involves growing many different species. We find small-scale cultivation mostly in horticulture, in areas with plenty of labor available (as in many poor countries), and in mountainous areas where large fields are not possible. Farming has the greatest impact on the landscape in fertile and flat river valleys, where agricultural yields are highest. Modern greenhouses and extensive complexes built for indoor animal husbandry also contribute to a loss of diversity, and they are a conspicuous presence in the landscape.

If farming techniques created the cultivated landscape and made a renaissance of the countryside possible, then the same processes can be deployed to preserve it. The landscape and its diversity, once an unintended consequence of traditional farming, can become the main product, at least where modernization and rationalization are impossible or undesirable. But by definition, the deliberate preservation of cultivated landscapes means they are barely viable economically, if at all. If you ask farmers to look after the landscape and promote its wealth of species, then you are asking them for more than the normal way of running a business can produce. Indeed areas where the landscape itself is becoming the main product are very often areas where farmers are leaving the land. Were we to abandon the Dutch river deltas or the Tuscan valleys to their fate, impenetrable and uninteresting vegetation would soon take over.

Abandoning farmland does not mean that biodiversity will return. On the contrary, because of disturbance by ploughing and fertilization, or because of the selective coppicing of woods, it can take decades before a natural landscape emerges. The preservation of landscape elements in cultivated landscapes is therefore a job for farmers. If we want to retain the diversity and appearance of the landscape, then society must reward farmers for performing such unprofitable ecological services.

It all requires extra effort by farmers, perhaps in the form of delaying mowing or not mowing buffer strips to protect birds and wild plants at the expense of agricultural production. The smaller the bits of natural or cultivated landscape, the more labor-intensive it is to preserve them. This is the reason European subsidies, once intended to secure food production, are increasingly being used to protect nature, landscape, and the quality of life in the countryside. Collectively we find landscape and diversity more important than food production, so we pay farmers to maintain cultivated landscapes.

Our prizing small-scale cultivated landscapes so highly and idealizing them has to do with their intrinsic diversity. Because humans are unable to control everything in this kind of low-productivity farming, there is naturally space for species we like to see, such as cornflowers and larks, badgers and bilberries. On small, relatively unproductive fields the largest trees are left standing, because they provide shade and useful products like fruit or leaves for cattle. There are some wonderful examples of this in Spain's Extremadura, with its parklike landscapes of oak and cork oak (*encina* and *alcornoque*), beneath which grain is traditionally grown, with sheep that graze on the stubble and the famous *pata-negra* pigs that eat the acorns.

The open, gently undulating landscape with ancient trees is nothing less than a park or a garden. That is where our relationship with the landscape is heading, toward the mythical image with which our relationship with nature began. Gardens, not for many years any longer the preserve of the rich, are more popular now than ever. Garden centers are flourishing, even though fewer and fewer of us have any expertise on the subjects of plants, animals, or insects. What was once common knowledge— methods of weeding, sowing, and fertilization, making flowerbeds, grafting, and training new growth—are now skills for which we need courses, how-to newspaper columns, and TV programs, In fact garden plants have become throwaway items that you buy and toss out when they've finished flowering. In our gardens we create a brief illusion of paradise, or at least a substitute for it: the diversity of the small scale.

Diversity and Food Security

Biodiversity is often spoken about in terms of stewardship. The word implies that only the interest may be enjoyed while the capital must be left untouched. The most urgent question then becomes whether the loss of capital, or the "stock" of biodiversity, is such that the world's food security is at risk.

At first sight the situation looks alarming, but biodiversity creates its own rhetoric. In 1990 activists wrote with some feeling for drama that general genetic erosion (the loss of species) meant we were on our way to a rendezvous with extinction. Indeed, despite many international agreements about pushing back the loss of biological species, including the United Nations International Convention on Biological Diversity, little progress has been made. In the past forty years total biodiversity in the tropics is said to have declined by 60 percent, largely as a result of urbanization, farming, and forestry. According to the United Nations, in the twentieth century three-quarters of the varieties of essential food crops in the world were lost. Of local breeds of domesticated farm animals, 20 percent—hundreds in absolute numbers—are on the point of extinction. The world's food supplies are now said to depend mainly on an agricultural biodiversity of just a few species. We see time and again that biodiversity is the backbone of economic development and of measures to combat poverty.

A quarter of a century has passed since that warning about a rendezvous with extinction, and there is little sign of a tipping point, to use a fashionable term, where the balance will shift irrevocably toward food scarcity. The world's population has grown by at least 1.5 billion since then, and partly because of the liberalization of world trade the quantity and quality of the diversity of food supplies have increased almost everywhere. In many parts of the world we eat a more varied diet than our grandparents did. We live longer and healthier lives, consuming both local foods that we had almost forgotten about, such as black salsify, and foods from foreign parts that we've only recently encountered, such as passionfruit. The degree of deforestation in the tropics as a result of agriculture has been reduced in recent years.

Not all developments are equally rosy. New threats like steadily increasing meat consumption and subsidies for biofuel lead to greater land use.

There are also growing worries about food prices, public health, and intellectual property rights of genetic material. Population growth is slowing and will eventually stabilize before dropping sharply in the twenty-second and twenty-third centuries, as better fed and educated women have fewer children and delay childbirth, which gives reason for hope. In the short term the effects these trends are negated by changing consumption patterns, especially the trend toward more animal protein.

The questions remain whether biodiversity is declining and whether it threatens food supplies, or the reverse: Do we need to sacrifice biodiversity and the diversity of landscape to food production? Can food security and biodiversity go together? To put it another way, can the demand for food security for 9 billion people and their food needs be met in 2050 without further damage to natural ecosystems, let alone their loss?

The answers depend on how much land is taken into production at the cost of natural ecosystems. In Africa, Latin America, the former Soviet Union, and to a lesser degree parts of East Asia there is certainly room for the expansion of farmland (in theory more than 4 billion hectares). Some expansion seems inevitable, but we should try to cultivate as little additional land as possible. After all, what is now unused has mostly been left for good reasons, perhaps because it has been designated as a nature reserve but usually because both the infrastructure and the production potential are lacking.

Sustainable intensification is the only answer to the threat to biodiversity from the increasing demand for food: more production per unit of scarce resources—that is, per unit of land and water and chemicals (and of labor, but that is a different story)—while also reducing damage to the environment. This will certainly not be easy, but it is in the realm of possibility, and we are getting steadily better at it. How much we can spare by raising yields can be seen from estimates that the Green Revolution, especially the new cultivars of rice, corn, and wheat, have saved an area as large as the Unites States since 1960, land that would otherwise have been needed to cope with a doubling of the world's population and an even greater increase in the demand for food. Intensification in northwestern Europe has led on average to a quadrupling of yields and saved a huge amount of land that is now available for other uses.

In fishing we find a special version of the issue of intensification. The decline in both fish species and fish stocks as a result of overfishing (partly stimulated by subsidies) is best addressed by the establishment of marine reserves. These are protected areas that can serve as breeding grounds for new populations of fish. The special characteristic of fish—their mobility—means that it is not intensification of the catch that protects nature reserves, as on land, but precisely the opposite.

Intensification has to take place where the circumstances are most favorable: on the most fertile land, in the most accessible places where soils are rich and yields are highest. It is precisely there, however, that farming is threatened by urbanization and diminishing water quality, especially in developing countries. Intensification does not need to coincide with increases in scale, as can be seen from the intensive rice paddies in Southeast Asia, but it does require optimal control of water, nutrients, and infestations.

What happens to biodiversity on the field itself where farming is intensified? Uncontrolled intensification and increases of scale in farming lead to impoverishment in terms of the variety and quality of the landscape. Everywhere in developed countries, the number of farms has decreased, along with the number of farm laborers (in the United Kingdom, for example, three-quarters of jobs in agriculture have disappeared). These workers have been replaced by machines that are more efficient but require larger and more uniform fields, so that trees, hedges, and verges disappear and with them bird habitats. Autumn tillage and autumn sowing also mean that fewer crop remains are left as shelter for insects and small animals out on the fields in winter. The number of chemical treatments on the fields has increased markedly since the 1960s, even if the amounts of chemicals used per ton of harvest are much reduced and chemicals are now more easily biodegraded.

All these changes have a price. No matter how carefully we measure out doses of artificial fertilizer and minimize the use of herbicides and pesticides, sustainable investment always leads to disturbances of the environment of wild species on farmland itself. And in many places investment in modernization takes place, but the farming that results is not sustainable. The use of artificial fertilizer has more than doubled the amount of nitrogen and phosphate in the global system and has caused widespread water pollution. No one denies that useful nonagricultural species, such as pollinating insects and soil organisms that ensure biological activity in the soil (so that nutrients are better taken up by plants), are under pressure from modern farming.

Food security is not only a matter of yields, it also concerns genetic diversity and a possible loss of genes. We hear alarming reports about this as well, but genetic variation *within* identical or closely related species, the potato for example, can be enormous. There are seven species of cultivated potato, including the most commonly grown *Solanum tuberosum*, which itself has seven subspecies, and another 199 wild relatives of the potato that also produce tubers. The same goes for farm animals, for example the variation between red-and-white and black-and-white cattle, both of which are *Bos (primigenius) taurus*.

The question is how much of the variation in breeds, species, and varieties of plants and animals will disappear because of human activity. This genetic erosion could be a threat to food security, although it is not easy to work out exactly what is being lost or where, for what reasons, how serious it is, and how irreversible. The great fear is that because of a lack of variety, the risk of diseases and infestations will increase. Many blame the loss of breeds and varieties on modern capitalism and globalization, but that is not always the case. Even in 1970, long before its period of economic growth began, it was discovered that in China only fifty of the 8,000 landraces of rice in existence before the Maoist revolution of 1949 remained. In the United States more than 80 percent of named apple varieties disappeared over the course of the nineteenth century.

All the different forms of genetic diversity came into being through a long process of selection of the more desirable characteristics, or those that happened to accompany them, and over the past century through modern breeding methods. Improvements to crops and farm animals were possible only because of diversity among individuals within a species or between related species. Particularly important are landraces, local varieties and breeds that have come about through traditional selective breeding. It is possible that the conscious use by farmers of traditional diversity, in the cultivation or husbandry of more breeds and varieties, is a form of insurance. If one variety suffers from drought, another may cope better, so there will always be a harvest somewhere. This is especially pertinent for low yields. In modern farming it is not diversity in the field that provides the best insurance but the level and reliability of yields.

Modernization all over the world, both in temperate regions and in the tropics, has led to the large-scale introduction of modern varieties of grain crop, which have replaced landraces almost everywhere. The most important reason for this replacement is that the new varieties react far better to artificial fertilizers and water; are often more resistant to diseases, infestations, and storms; and therefore produce higher yields. This is partly because they are shorter (and therefore often called "dwarf varieties"), so that they have a more favorable ratio between grain and stem. Thus more grain is produced per plant, and the crop does not fall over in response to a greater availability of water and nitrogen. The latest varieties also absorb more sunlight. Landraces are at a disadvantage when modern means of production are used. They are almost always best adapted to less fertile conditions, even if they are grown on relatively good soils. Some do better than modern varieties if no artificial fertilizer is used, but often even in the absence of artificial fertilizers the older varieties are less successful. Almost without exception, as soon as artificial fertilizer is introduced and farming therefore becomes more intensive, modern varieties have to be grown and traditional varieties are lost. It has been claimed that traditional crops or landraces are more resistant to drought, but under dry circumstances all plants do very badly.

———————

Breeds and varieties, traditional or modern, evolve slowly over time, with slight changes in each generation. This process is called genetic drift, and it results from growing conditions combined with selection by the farmer. The great difference between old and modern varieties is that the latter have been developed by much quicker and more purposeful breeding. In modern plant breeding continual efforts are made to develop new cultivars that are better able to resist new diseases or to respond to new requirements, such as enhanced nutritional value. In other words, agricultural biodiversity in space (many landraces and traditional varieties in the fields) is being replaced by agricultural biodiversity in time (successive generations of modern breeds crossed with traditional breeds and wild relatives to produce specific characteristics). The idea that modern breeds narrow the genetic basis of farming and are therefore a threat to food security is not generally true. Variety remains, but it is different.

Intensification doesn't only cause the disappearance of landraces and old varieties, however, it also contributes to the loss of entire species, such as traditional grains and leafy vegetables. In traditional agricultural systems, different crops are usually grown next to one another or in rotation in what are known as polycultures (the opposite of monocultures). Unfortunately, these broad mixtures of plants do not bring in enough money and are too labor intensive to be sustained when farming modernizes. So the breeds and varieties that are not particularly suitable for a modern system disappear.

There are few indications that modernization and loss of diversity amount to a threat to world food security. Much of the evidence for the loss of breeds and species, especially in developing countries, is anecdotal. We do not know how things stood two generations ago, let alone two centuries. For several decades now, systematic efforts have been made to store landraces and traditional varieties in gene banks or genetic collections. These are buildings housing huge refrigerators with drawers containing sealed packets of seed, each with its own code. Collections in national and international gene banks tell us something about the variety that exists, but not much. There are more than 20,000 registered types ("accessions") of rice in Asian gene banks, for example, but the documentation is often so inadequate that no one knows how many different varieties or species they represent. On Spitsbergen island, Norway, the first international gene bank for food crops is now slowly being filled. Its establishment is one outcome of the International Treaty on Plant Genetic Resources for Food and Agriculture of 2001. But storing away seeds does not amount to evidence of the importance of diversity in food production. Even if all these accessions have different local names and, were they planted out, possibly a slightly different appearance, this is still not proof of real genetic diversity. The same variety can be known in different regions under more than one name, and a plant with a slightly different appearance does not necessarily have completely different genetic characteristics, and vice versa. The rice genome was sequenced some years ago, but even so we cannot determine whether all the various types are truly genetically different. Just how problematic the numbers are became clear during a recent inventory carried out at a data bank of tropical plants: there were twice as many names as there are existing species. Naming mistakes and typing errors led experts to conclude that perhaps a third of the accessions are erroneously labeled—and even that figure is by no means certain.

The consequences for food security of the disappearance of traditional varieties of rice and their wild relatives can be assessed only by weighing up the undoubted rise in yields produced by modern varieties against the potential risk of genetic narrowing and therefore the likelihood of widespread disease, along with the need to use varieties from wild relatives and landraces to develop new forms of resistance. The real doomsday scenario would be a disease or infestation that wiped out at a single blow one of the essential sources of carbohydrate (rice, corn, and wheat, which between them provide 60 percent of our calories). It's hard to imagine how this could happen, however, with plants that grow in different seasons around the world, because they could not all be affected at once. The spread of plant diseases, unlike bird 'flu, for example, is slow and takes several years. The existence of far better international communication than in the past concerning possible diseases and infestations also helps guarantee that widespread outbreaks can be prevented.

As far as genetic doomsday scenarios are concerned, there are no real indications they will come about. Many people see genetic uniformity as a risk directly connected with hunger, but this is largely based on the tragedy of the Irish famine (1845–1857). It was caused by the infection of the potato by the mold *Phytophthora infestans* (strictly speaking a funguslike microorganism called an "oomycete"), and the end result was the emigration of between 1 and 2 million people and the death by starvation of another 1 million or more. But it was an extremely unusual situation, one that is not representative and will not be repeated. The cause of the Irish tragedy lay in the large-scale introduction of a crop foreign to Ireland, of which individual plants were genetically almost identical (because they were vegetatively reproduced using tubers) and still without natural defenses to combat local infections and infestations, combined with the compulsory export of grain to the colonial rulers, the British. The resulting loss of the harvest to potato blight, reinforced by an inhumane policy on the part of the British government, led to a terrible famine that left many with no choice but to emigrate. The Irish Famine was above all political, not genetic, disaster.

Nowadays hunger is the result of a lack of buying power, natural disaster, and civil war, not genetic uniformity. In the fifty years since the start of the Green Revolution, when modern breeds were first introduced, not a single widespread epidemic in modern food crops has occurred. All breeding research is focused on preventing the breakdown of resistance to disease, and famine as a result of genetic erosion is very unlikely. The notion that genetic modification will lead to narrowing or genetic erosion is incorrect. Better profiling of the characteristics of different breeds and varieties—ancient or modern—helps evaluate and preserve them. The genetic narrowing that we do see (in space, not in time) is the result of the planting of large areas with modern varieties, independently of the issue of whether they have been created by genetic modification.

Because of their higher yields, modern varieties have certainly displaced traditional food crops, in the Andes, for example, where the cultivation of such tubers as ullucus (*Ullucus tuberorsus*) and such grains as quinoa (*Chenopodium quinoa*) has declined markedly. Although these can be important locally, it is unclear how much they contribute quantitatively to the food supply in terms of yield and consumption.

In recent years, attention to "lost" varieties and breeds has fortunately increased, partly under the influence of organic farming and culinary movements. Large-scale migration from the tropics to the north has caused some products to gain hugely in popularity, such as cassava and amaranth (a leafy vegetable), which can now be found at most street markets in Europe. Breeders are also increasingly looking at interesting old varieties or landraces, not just from the point of view of food security but also as part of a search for such qualities as flavor and coloring, in pear and apple breeding, for instance. An incidental advantage of older fruit trees is that they are attractive as a feature of the landscape, because they are grown as standard trees. One interesting question concerns the availability of insects that could supplement protein consumption locally. Here too, the picture is unclear. Some insects are threatened by agriculture, others boosted by it, like the popular palm weevil, found in palm plantations, that is relished by local people.

Do old breeds and varieties have greater nutritional value? The evidence is mainly anecdotal. There are a few indications that, for example, guava and papaya can have a favorable effect on cholesterol. Quinoa and other grains are said to have a higher protein content than wheat (11–14 percent as opposed to a little more than 8 percent), as well as greater quantities of amino acids, such as lysin and methionin. The fruit mass of the baobab tree is rich in vitamin C. Traditional vegetables are sometimes advocated for their vitamin A content, but evaluations often fail to distinguish between vitamin A and beta-carotene, and the biological availability of beta-carotene is far more limited (quite apart from the method of preparation; cooking in oil rather than water makes it more readily available). Figures from small sample surveys are difficult to interpret without knowing the circumstances of production and preparation and the variation between varieties and between individual plants. In a normal, varied diet the differences are insignificant, but it is possible that they might be decisive for people who have little opportunity to eat a wide range of foods.

No one knows the economic value of the species that could be lost if they are driven out by modern breeds or by the expansion of farmland or changes to the countryside. In Africa, 900–1,000 species could in theory be used as vegetables, and nearly all of these are not now grown as crops. Estimates suggest that in Asia there are 3,000 species of tropical fruits and nuts, with a comparable number in South America. Most are rarely if ever farmed; they simply grow spontaneously in fields or in verges or woods. If they are eaten at all, most are gathered from the wild in small quantities, so they cannot really be said to contribute to world food supplies.

New species do have potential, however, certainly given that trade in tropical fruits has increased significantly with the liberalization of international markets and better international agreements about pesticide residues. All the same we should not expect a sudden revolution. Before these new species have been bred to be able to withstand transportation over long distances, and are of a sufficient quality with high enough yields, years if not decades will have passed. The success of the kiwi and the nectarine are the exceptions that prove the rule.

Biodiversity is seen as having countless positive aspects, aside from food security. It is said to be the key to our health. This too is not as simple as it sounds. Areas with the greatest biodiversity are certainly not the most rich and healthy. In fact there seems to be an inverse relationship: some of the poorest regions of the world, such as the Amazon and Central Africa, are the most diverse. This anticorrelation can be explained by the lack of development and cultivation, which might have reduced diversity. All the same, diversity in the diet does make a contribution to health.

PLATE 14 Western art includes countless images of bread, as in this seventeenth-century still life, where a voluptuous, buttocks-shaped loaf lies next to the herring. The image is both simplicity and luxury, relief and pleasure, and perhaps also a warning against temptation and excess (Chapter 4). "Still Life with Herring, Wine and Bread"; Pieter Claesz, 1647; Los Angeles County Museum of Art.

PLATE 15 Émile Zola called the immense complex known as Les Halles Centrales "the belly of Paris." In a series of cathedral-like spaces with much glass and iron, surrounded by courtyards and squares, everything the population was consuming in ever greater quantities could be delivered during the night. Here we see one of the open-air markets where vegetables were sold (Chapter 11). "Le Carreau des Halles"; Victor-Gabriel Gilbert, 1880; Musée des Beaux Arts, Le Havre; akg-images / Erich Lessing.

PLATE 16 In China the imperial court had a monopoly for many years on the farming of red and gold fish. These were not merely fish for consumption but fish as a symbol of good fortune and well-being. Here large red carp swim among lotuses, ferns, lianas, and crustaceans (Chapter 6). Goldfish Vase; Reign of the Jiajing Emperor, Ming dynasty, 1521–1567; Musée Guimet, Paris / Réunion des musées nationaux, Grand Palais; Photo © RMN-Grand Palais (Musée Guimet, Paris) / Thierry Ollivier.

PLATE 17 Fish has always been an important component of the daily diet around the Mediterranean. This floor mosaic reads like a modern poster of types of fish, of the kind found on the walls of the better fish restaurants. It shows flatfish, eels, and tuna, caught with nets and spears, and lobsters, sea urchins, and squid as big as gondolas, which were trapped in earthenware pots. Such accurate mosaics are evidence not just of the existence of extensive fisheries but also of early knowledge of the ecosystem, and of the pleasure and practical benefits derived by humankind from the diversity of life in the sea (Chapter 6). Necropolis of Hermes, floor mosaic; second century; Musée Archéologique de Sousse, Tunisia; akg-images / Gilles Mermet.

PLATE 18 Countless mythological examples exist of crosses between humans and animals or between humans and plants, such as the Greek Minotaur, half man, half bull. They do not bode well, and today they fuel the fear of genetic modification. Sometimes it's not a matter of an actual hybrid but of a change in the human shape, which serves to reduce or eliminate danger. Ovid tells how the nymph Daphne assumed the shape of a tree to escape an importunate Apollo. Bernini's statue shows her fingers and hair turning into leaves (Chapter 7). "Apollo and Daphne"; Gian Lorenzo Bernini, 1622–1625; Galleria Borghese, Rome; akg-images / Nimatallah.

PLATE 19 This bleaching field in the Dutch province of Gelderland shows how painters have given a beauty all its own to the apparent naturalness of the agrarian landscape. By doing so they prepared the way for a new consciousness of the landscape as something that must be preserved. Through them we learn to look at landscapes as valuable in their own right and therefore worthy of protection (Chapter 9). "A Barn on the Bank of a Stream in Gelderland", Wouter Johannes van Troostwijk, 1805–1810. © Rijksmuseum, Amsterdam.

PLATE 20 "Dinner's ready!" The cry that marks the start of a meal always relates to a place. It may not be a table, but there is always a location where the meal will be served: a picnic in the grass, on a spread tablecloth, on the open hatchback of a car beside the high-way, or on a rickety folding table on the balcony. Even in the famous painting by Manet with an undressed lady sitting on the grass, something that looks like a crumpled table-cloth lies next to the fruit—or is it her dress, serving as such? (Chapter 10). "Le Déjeuner sur l'herbe": Edouard Manet, 1863; Musée d'Orsay, Paris; akg-images/Laurent Lecat

PLATE 21   The topography of the table sets the mood. Those who eat facing each other will pass the pots or dishes between them and are virtually forced to look into each other's eyes. Is the taste of the food influenced by the company and the seating arrangements? Those dimensions are illustrated by this painting in which two women sit across from each other at an almost empty table in a simple Chinese restaurant in New York. The table is the center of a universe (Chapter 10). "Chop Suey"; Edward Hopper, 1929; Collection of Mr. and Mrs. Barney A. Ebsworth / Bridgeman Images.

PLATE 22   In such political cartoons as this we often see monstrously fat capitalists and workers who are nothing but skin and bone. Anyone who had little if any need to work, and was therefore rich, was overweight. Being corpulent remains an ideal and a mark of beauty in societies where an abundance of food is the exception to the rule (Chapter 15). "Le Banquier"; Honoré Daumier, 1835; Bibliothèque nationale de France, Paris; Robert D. Farber University Archives and Special Collections Department, Brandeis University.

PLATE 23 Allotments for the poor were established in many cities in the nineteenth century. During the Second World War they were of great importance, supplementing a meager diet. Vegetable plots always re-emerge in times of crisis. In the gardens of Montmartre in Paris, which Van Gogh painted several times, people grew their own grapes (Chapter 11). "Montmartre, behind the Moulin de la Galette"; Vincent van Gogh, 1887; Van Gogh Museum, Amsterdam (Vincent Van Gogh Foundation).

PLATE 24 In this idyllic landscape, all attention is concentrated on a traditional plough drawn by a blue ox and a red ox, and atop it a computer on a wooden pallet. With his left hand the farmer taps at the keyboard, with his right he holds ropes to steer the oxen. The screen shows the Cuban flag—in mirror image. The plough with its computer refers to the new, computer-guided cultivation of the soil (developed, incidentally, for genetically modified, herbicide-resistant soy) (Chapter 16). "El tiempo Moderno"; Julio Breff Guilarte, 2009; artist's collection; by permission of the artist.

The question is then to what extent the loss of biodiversity, however intangible, has negative effects on the feeding of the population, especially of the poorest. In today's global economy, a varied and healthy diet is mainly a question of buying power rather than local diversity. This conclusion is of course not a license to neglect biodiversity. Poor urban populations eat too much fat and have too monotonous a diet. The most vulnerable groups live in urban agglomerations in poor countries and in places like the former Soviet Union where food distribution is poor, choice is limited, and the alternatives (such as harvesting plants or insects yourself from the wild) are barely viable any longer, with the exception of mushroom picking. Many people simply do not have the money to buy a wide range of food. In the case of poor rural populations that can still go out and find food in the natural world, the diversity of the landscape does perhaps help supplement diets.

The range of species and breeds or varieties is connected to food availability mainly in an indirect sense. It's not so much the declining availability of landraces or the disappearance of traditional foodstuffs that amounts to a danger but the loss of the genetic diversity they represent, which could be used in modern breeding. The source of variation is important for the future development of new breeds or, as I called it earlier, biodiversity through time.

How dangerous, then, is the fact that most of the calories for the world's population come from twelve species of plant and fourteen species of animal? At first sight this seems very few, especially if we compare it to the hundreds of species of plant and animal eaten by, for example, the !Kung people of southern Africa or the indigenous tribes of the Amazon. Consumption of hundreds of species, however, means only that most of those species are eaten perhaps twice a year. It says little about food security. Moreover, these tribes are not farmers but hunter-gatherers. As soon as agriculture develops, the number of species eaten falls rapidly. This does not tell us anything about the risk to food supplies, because dependence on far fewer species has not stood in the way of a continual growth of the world population. It seems that dependence on a few dominant species is not so very risky, because each species and each variety is constantly being improved.

All these developments require one essential condition, namely, that we protect the sources of diversity for future use (until the theoretical moment when we can ourselves construct plants, as radical biotechnologists say we one day will). Diversity has to be protected in situ, in the regions of genetic differentiation where our vital food crops originally grew, such as the Middle East, Central America, China, and the Andes, as well as ex situ in international or national gene banks, which are increasingly working together. One of the political hot potatoes at the moment, as discussed in Chapter 7, is whether payments should be made for the use of genetic material, and if so to what value. Countries with the most valuable genetic resources to offer agriculture in the form of animals and plants are of the opinion that they deserve remuneration, perhaps even retrospectively. This seems impossible, given that it is not at all clear exactly where a specific crop, wheat for example, with its complex evolution, actually comes from (Turkey, Syria, Jordan, or Israel?) and who should be paid: governments or the descendants of the original breeders, the Neolithic farmers?

As long as we cannot construct artificial genes, genetic resources, of both agricultural and other species, will remain important. Only by introducing new varieties can we develop new crops or breeds that are resistant to continually evolving pathogens, are adapted to new limitations, such as the higher nocturnal temperatures in the tropics that may result from climate change, and have new characteristics that are important for our diet and health. The use of foreign genes (in other words, genes from outside the species concerned or even its family) is increasing and with it social resistance. Yet for plant breeders this is often a route to avoiding old diseases: resistance to mildew in grapes is a characteristic that currently comes not just from the genome of wild grapes but from barley and even from silkworms. It has prompted critics to talk of "Frankenwine."

We need not be too pessimistic about biodiversity and its benefits for the food supply. Some species and varieties have been lost, perhaps many, and this process will continue, but the diversity of species and food security are not one and the same. There is a trade-off between variety and yield that we sometimes prefer not to acknowledge. Monocultures are a better guarantee of world food supplies than the low yields derived from mixed cultivation or polyculture. This is not to say that mixed systems, including mixtures of livestock and crops, do not have other important functions, if only for the landscape. Such systems may also create variation in local diets, but the urban masses cannot rely on them.

Fortunately a large proportion of the variety of genetic material is still available to us, from wild plants and from gene banks. Moreover, the value of tradition and traditional varieties is increasingly being recognized. Organic farming and movements such as slow food have played a useful role here, even though they may sometimes have overestimated the importance of landraces and local species. There seems to be little evidence for the alarming reports that say it is the poor who suffer most from the decline in biodiversity. The poor, those without land at least, are in fact the first to profit from higher yields, as a result of intensification and the reduction in food prices that goes with it.

All the same, intuitively almost everyone feels that biodiversity is good for us. Or, as a former Dutch agriculture minister wrote: "Biodiversity works for nature, for humans, forever." The United Nations says that the loss of biodiversity touches us culturally and spiritually. One reason is that we think of biodiversity in terms of species, preferably cuddly species of the kind Noah took into his ark. We also associate biodiversity with smallness of scale. Diversity conjures up an image of the small and varied, of landscape on a human scale, something we can manage and understand. Our first mythical encounter with nature was after all a garden, a paradise, with a vast wealth of species. Scaling up may in many ways guarantee food security, but the immense fields of corn in the American Midwest or the Brazilian *cerrados* magnify our sense of insignificance, of dependence on forces outside ourselves. In farming we are still dependent on nature.

Biodiversity rouses deep emotions, because it is an aspect of ancient images we have passed on from generation to generation. Biodiversity is partly an ideal and an ideology, partly science, and the two do not always sit well together. Much is counterintuitive to those who like to think in simple terms of good and bad. "The more diverse the better" simply does not hold true. Farming sometimes leads to more biodiversity (for example, through the extensive grazing of meadows that gives orchids a chance), sometimes to less, such as when grazing causes rare butterflies to disappear. The absence of farming sometimes means the landscape is more monotonous, covered in thick forest without clearings and without transitional areas that attract biodiversity.

Biodiversity can be an inspiration for agriculture in addressing biological pest control or ways of implementing organic principles. The presence of more species sometimes means better ground cover and less erosion—at least on small plots, because on larger fields such techniques as the monocultures used in conservation agriculture (no ploughing, direct seeding, often without the removal of weeds) work better. Less biodiversity is not always a danger, and sometimes it can be a blessing if it means more food is produced. In other words, the wealth of species so often celebrated seems to be primarily made up of species that occur infrequently and make little contribution to world food security, even though they may be important locally.

Much of the concern about biodiversity is in fact about something else: the loss of traditional ways of life, cultivated landscapes, well-being, and knowledge. We should not downplay these things, but their relationship to food supplies is unclear. In almost all traditional societies, eating habits are such that women and children may become chronically underfed, so tradition is no guarantee of food security.

Appreciation of biodiversity arises in part from a longing for a reborn countryside, for an ideal agricultural landscape, an idyllic environment in which nature, because of its abundance of species, guarantees an abundance of food and well-being. As an idea, biodiversity appeals to a feeling of harmony, of being close to nature, a counterweight to the urban and modern. Biodiversity remains important for the future in all its forms, in the landscape, in the fields, and genetically, but we will have to keep weighing up when and how biodiversity, and exactly which biodiversity, should be retained, and at what cost.

TEN

Roast Wolf and Deconstructed Olive:
Cooking and Eating as a Worldview

Since Eve ate apples, much depends on dinner.   Byron, *Don Juan* (13.99.8)

Indian food made me more English. Like most Englishmen of my generation
I now think of ... Indian food as a native dish imported centuries before....
    My grandmother, who had made her way from Pilvistok to London via
Antwerp, knew nothing of salad and she had never met a green vegetable she
could not torture to death in a saucepan.   Tony Judt, *The Memory Chalet*

Cooking and Eating in the Food Chain

A great deal has to happen before we can eat. It demands the physical
and mental work of animal husbandry, planting and harvesting, hunting, fishing and gathering, or at least doing the shopping, followed by
preparation, presentation, and consumption itself. In modern societies it's
extremely rare for all those steps to be undertaken by one and the same
person, but ultimately everyone has to do something to be able to eat,
even if it's only to choose a ready meal, pay for it, and consume it. The
final step prior to eating is the preparation and presentation. Eating and
cooking seem like two sides of the same coin, even if the cook is by no
means always among the diners. Anyone who cooks or prepares food,
even in a factory, does it for someone to eat, however unknown and far
away that person may be. And whoever eats knows that there is someone
somewhere who prepared the food—or are we forgetting even that? Food
is always more than passively waiting for roasted doves to fly into your
mouth as they do in dreams of Cockaigne.

    The notion, first mooted in science fiction films of the 1950s, that one
day a simple pill would replace our meals and we'd be able to dispense
with the complexities of food preparation and with time-consuming
meals (there are no dining tables in spaceships) has not been borne
out. The science fiction food pill reflects a bygone era of simplistic faith
in technological knowledge and functionality that seems almost unimaginable today. Such a pill, we now know, would be impossible,
because healthy eating is not a matter of compressing a few micrograms

of nutrients into a pill. We need more ingredients than that, not least fiber.

A pill is the very opposite of all the things food can be, both as an expression of individuality and as a sign of an individual's place in society. Although the idea that food is also a medicine is certainly still with us, modern diets have not developed in the direction of a magic pill. On the contrary, increasing affluence in large parts of the world has caused two apparently contradictory developments, which if anything make eating more complicated than it used to be.

On the one hand, in the West, and in middle class districts elsewhere in the world, in cities and even in villages, much and sometimes all of the effort involved in preparing food at home has been taken out of our hands by the food industry and the supermarkets: we no longer store apples and potatoes over winter, or can green beans, let alone slaughter our own livestock, make sausages, or dry fish. We no longer even slice all our own fruit and vegetables but often buy them ready washed and cut, in plastic bags, after which we keep them for days in the fridge without fearing they'll wilt or go moldy. We buy vacuum-packed fish that stays "fresh" for weeks and—by some miracle—tastes that way too.

Anyone for whom this is not enough can choose from a whole range of ready meals, each presented on a throwaway plastic tray that has only to be heated up in the microwave and put on the table, or more likely the lap. Americans devote only thirty minutes a day on average to meal preparation, including clearing away and washing up. This is shockingly little, even when we consider that reheatable food in throwaway packaging is a blessing for overworked single mothers (if consumed in moderation, in versions without too much salt and fat). Even the filled rolls, sandwiches, and wraps available all over the place are put together in factories, and their fillings are not simply cheese but all kinds of appetizing combinations of hummus and eggplant, goat's cheese with arugula, and so on.

Even in megacities and developing countries we see this trend toward a separation of cooking from eating, linked to the rise of ready meals, although this may not be a result of people being unable to find time to cook. In the West we no longer see people cooking in the street, with the exception of hotdogs, spring rolls, and other oily snacks, and roasted chestnuts in southern Europe, but it is still a prominent feature of Shanghai or Delhi. Their creations are stacked up by ingenious means and carried to offices and homes.

More and more people take advantage of the affordable and effort-free abundance of the food industry, but its very convenience creates uncertainty. Many experience it as a loss of control and worry about the health effects of modern food. There is a fear that the industry itself, with its impenetrable factories full of gleaming, mysterious tanks and pipes, is a threat to our health. After all, who adds all those E numbers, and where does the contamination come from that is a threat to our food security? Objectively speaking our food is safer than ever before, but this reassurance is negated by the invisibility of the preparation process. There's a striking ambivalence here, because most people are critical but don't want to know too much about how our food is produced; they'd rather not see how gelatin from animal bones is used in making sweets and puddings, or how "fresh spaghetti sauce" is made with freeze-dried vegetables (allowing it to make its claim to freshness).

But as a counterweight to the professional processing of our food and the uncertainty or even distrust it evokes, food and cooking have acquired a new meaning. For the middle classes in the West at least, and for an increasing proportion of the rich in developing economies, eating is becoming less about absorbing sufficient nutrients and more about pleasure, status, and self-expression, even recreation. People who have time because they are not occupied all day with survival will inevitably seek out experience and significance. Becoming once more an active part of the food supply chain, rather than just a passive consumer, is the new challenge.

Preparing and eating food are the final two steps in the long food supply chain. Cooking and eating have become the determining factors for what happens earlier in the chain, in production and especially the many steps involved in processing. Farming and food, production and preparation, and then eating itself are ultimately closely connected. This is so obvious that it is astonishing that the disciplines at the root of it all, agricultural sciences and food sciences, have until now existed in almost completely separate realms.

It took me a very long time to start thinking in terms of the entire food supply chain. During university studies and for years afterward I focused mainly on the first part, production, and never paid much attention to the final steps of cooking and eating, or at least only in that slightly ridiculous way that students act out their burgeoning scientific obsessions. I still recall long discussions about the foam on the dried beans when they were boiled. (Was it caused by denatured proteins or not? And if so, could you reuse them?) Or about the optimal quantity and timing for the addition of salt to peeled and unpeeled potatoes.

In my years in the tropics I more than once saw real food shortages and I was brilliant at thinking up new ways of preparing peanuts, rice, and plantains, the only foods available in Central Africa. But that was merely scientifically inspired amateurism. Only gradually did I become aware of the importance of cooking as the penultimate but crucial link in the chain, the identity issues bound up with it, and the countless complex changes that occur in human diets. Slowly the significance of cooking dawned on me—especially in the years when I lived in Italy, a country where talking about recipes and ingredients has raised cuisine to the status of a high art, and you simply cannot avoid thinking about food and cooking. Everyone has advice for you, about the preparation of fish, about the mushroom season, about the best bread (which since the Middle Ages has come from Lariano in Lazio).

Reasoning from the point of view of production is logical in a world where scarcity prevails. There everything depends on the farmer, the land, the crops and animals, and the weather: What is grown where? How suitable is the soil or the climate? And what is limiting the yield? Only when scarcity slowly makes way for variety and surplus does the question arise of what people want to eat.

After all, you can't eat farming, nor even most of what comes from a farm. People don't eat calories or kilograms per hectare, they eat ingredients combined into dishes, which are then combined into diets. Farmers and fishermen don't produce either dishes or ingredients, only the raw materials for them. The expression "to grow food" is actually misleading. Bread doesn't grow in the fields, only wheat, and many steps are needed before wheat becomes bread and bread becomes a sandwich on your plate. Olives are edible only after fermentation, or if oil is pressed from them. There are exceptions, such as the produce from a vegetable plot or orchard, things that we buy at so-called farmer's markets (where most of the produce doesn't actually come straight from the farmer and has often been processed on the farm in some way), or farm cheese perhaps, or the fresh sea urchins you can buy from fishermen in Greece and slurp straight down. Most of what we eat has a long trail behind it of transportation, processing, and packaging.

A person can eat alone, but not in isolation. Food forms one of our most intimate connections with nature; you partake of the world. Our bodies consist of atoms derived from other organisms, which they in turn derived from other organisms, from organic and mineral substances, in the endlessly complicated cycles of the food chain, around and around from the soil to the stomach. They once arose from a tiny quantity of stardust. The cycle is complete because nutrients return to the ecosystem through rubbish dumps and sewers and after our deaths in the form of our corpses or ash. "Soil" should be understood broadly here, because some elements, such as nitrogen and sulfur, go through gaseous phases, and many end up in groundwater or surface water, ultimately flowing into the oceans. Even packaging materials (made of leaves) and utensils (wood) used to be part of the chain, and by means of a long detour the same goes for modern packaging made of paper and biodegradable plastic. Food is ultimately about life, waste products, and death.

In that fundamental sense, food is part of a sustainable cycle that will endure for eternity, or at any rate as long as life on the earth exists. Everyone who prepares food and everyone who eats is linked to those cycles of nutrients in the world, to other species and other people—past, present, and future, here and elsewhere. Every mouthful we eat connects us with those who long ago started to domesticate plants and animals, with the migrants and traders who spread them across the world, with the researchers who bred them and developed techniques for making agriculture and food potentially safer and more productive, with the farmers who are proud of their land and their work, and with the laborers who pick beans and mangos and pack them and in some cases endure appalling working conditions. It connects us with the bakers who knead dough in the early hours even now (if usually by machine), with the butchers and fishermen who have the most difficult and often the most degrading work in the whole human food supply chain, and ultimately with those who will use the land and the genetic material after us and to whom the world must be passed on in as good a condition as possible.

<hr>

Cooking determines how we experience food, but cooking and the rituals surrounding food always arise out of a worldview. Those who fry a hamburger or steak will be eating a symbol, and they want to show that they share a world with others. Those who cook organic parsnips are doing exactly that too. A hamburger stands for the world of urban youth with a Western, materialistic lifestyle. Sashimi is simply another variant of that, with health and foreign travel as additional associations.

I fall short almost at once, because despite my experience in many different countries and climates, my repertoire as a cook is simple, verging on the sober. I'm not usually the sort to prepare fennel mousse with lavender, or sheep's cheese with truffles, let alone foam from the fat of an Iberian pig. Vegetable soup, grilled mixed vegetables, with coarse bread, olive oil, a glass of red wine, and hard cheese with cherries (in summer only, of course)—for me that's pretty much as good as it gets. According to many criteria I'm a failed cook, but it's not because of fear or lack of knowledge, it's because I'm satisfied with simplicity.

Cooking is a matter of copying and combining, more association and memory than science. The years I spent in countries of food scarcity still influence me, even though I've returned to the lands of plenty. It remains routine for me to first think what's available and what could replace something else. No cheese? Then strain some yogurt and add salt. No sugar or honey for a cake? Then caramelize a few mashed bananas. When there is little to be had, you learn that almost everything can be combined, and it's a sport to make something work rather than dash to the shops. Cooking is a matter of reacting to what happens to be nearby. Sometimes "nearby" is a shop, sometimes a market, and occasionally it is a place where you can pick your own green asparagus and mushrooms, or an apple orchard. Sometimes "nearby" is simply your own cupboard, where you happen to have a bag of lentils from last summer. My friends for all seasons are tomatoes, fresh or canned, because something surprising always emerges when you use them: thick sauce or thin, sweet or sour, the scent of spring in the mountains, or combined with sea lavender from Walcheren, so that the tomato suddenly seems to belong on the North Sea coast, where it certainly doesn't come from and rarely grows.

<hr>

Eating, because of its immediate importance for human survival, is probably one of the most ritualized of human activities, along with sex and childbirth. There is no greater diversity to be found than in rules about food, about what can be eaten and how, where, when, and with whom. The meal is a thing of immense variety. Many of the rituals, rules, and customs surrounding food are ultimately about regulating scarcity. This is not to say that all meals are frugal as a result, as the regulation of surpluses (usually temporary) is of great importance if scarcity is the norm. Men and adolescent boys have a right to the most protein and mineral-rich parts of the animal in almost all traditional societies, often the inner organs, such as entrails and liver. Women and girls eat later, with more carbohydrates and fewer calories. Almost everywhere, including Europe, there are strict ideas about what women should eat, or not eat, during pregnancy. Many such physiologically understandable preferences, which stem from the era of male hunters and female gatherers with their different energy requirements, are still part of today's dietary rituals. When you dine out with others, you can test this for yourself.

Ultimately, doing the shopping and cooking are only the preparatory stages of what food is all about: satisfying mental and physical hunger, taking time to sit at the table with friends, celebrating, listening to one another and determining our place in the world. Food means sharing and hospitality, but also exclusion and distinction. Those who eat pigs, grasshoppers, snails, raw fish, or dogs seem initially to be fundamentally different kinds of people from those who regard such things as inedible. At the same time, food can bring us together, because without even noticing we slowly adopt one another's habits and ingredients over time. Indian dishes in the United Kingdom, Polish-Jewish recipes in the United States, and elements of Chinese cuisine in the Netherlands now belong to those national cultures. As American as apple pie suggests authenticity—but apple pie has been eaten in America only for the past century and a half or so.

Raw, Cooked, and Pure

The story about the bite Eve took out of the apple may not be the first but it is the best-known story in which food has a symbolic meaning. Food and eating are the basis for our survival and, I suspect, they were always woven into stories and myths, in the Middle East and elsewhere.

Yet the Bible has far less to say about eating and cooking than about farming and making sacrifices in the temple. It doesn't contain many detailed recipes, although several specific dishes are mentioned; from the story of Esau's red lentil dish it's clear that people cooked. An important and well-known reference to cooking is the complaint by the Israelites to Moses that in Egypt the pots of meat are full while in the desert they don't even have bread (at which point manna comes down from heaven). From time to time actual directions are given, as in this recipe for concentrated meat stock: "So heap on the wood and kindle the fire. Cook the meat well, mixing in the spices; and let the bones be charred" (Ezekiel 24:10).

In other religions, agricultural and culinary instructions can sometimes be more closely connected. In Aztec mythology there is a striking parallel with Eve in the figure of Xochiquetzal, who eats a forbidden fruit, falls for the sexual advances of a deity, and is chased out of paradise as a result. Outside paradise she becomes the goddess of plants and corn and at the same time, in another incarnation, she is Tonacacihuatl, the goddess of food supplies. She thereby combines farming and food, a reflection of the fact that at the start of the development of agriculture, farmers and cooks were close together, not separated by a long food supply chain as they are now.

Cooking does not occur, of course, in the perfect ecosystem that is the mythical paradise. Seeds and fruits are available for immediate consumption, according to divine instructions. No other references to eating are made at all, as if Adam and Eve, in a kind of superhuman symbiosis, automatically absorbed enough proteins, minerals, and vitamins. In later depictions and descriptions of paradise there are no knives, plates, pots, or pans. The suggestion is clear: amid such self-evident plenty even the notion of elaborate preparation is unnecessary. In fact the story of paradise anticipates in that sense our current ready-to-eat fast food paradise: there is enough; you only need to open your mouth and the calories will pour in (and the money pour out). Images of Cockaigne, where prepared and directly edible food is everywhere, fit in this sequence, which runs from the symbiotic plenty of the Garden of Eden to today's fast food paradise.

Adam and Eve ate neither stewed apple nor dried apple slices, only raw apple. They didn't need to cook, because food in paradise was immediately digestible and healthy, and above all available in unlimited quantities and suitable for storing. This notion is so powerful that there are still people for whom the fictional uncooked food of Adam and Eve is a guide to how to eat, such as the American preacher who launched the "Hallelujah Diet," which is limited to raw fruit and vegetables, seeds, and nuts. In exceptional circumstances, he says, a maximum of 15 percent of the vegetables can be cooked, although it is unclear on which Bible text that precise percentage is based. The conviction that nature was perfect in paradise has given rise to the still-widespread misconception that raw food is healthier than cooked food.

The Fall of Man marks the end not just of divine plenty but also of the automatic guarantee that food is of high quality and is digestible. Most of the fruits that Eve and her descendants will have to pick and gather outside paradise in no way resemble the sweet, gleaming jewels of the Tree of Knowledge but are bitter, fibrous balls with a hard peel, barely edible raw. Apples, funnily enough, are an exception, as the earliest apples were in many ways like those we eat today.

But precisely because it is so hard to find digestible food, the Fall was a blessing for humankind. Not the high-value plenty in paradise but universal food scarcity makes demands of human creativity and our ability to innovate. With banishment from paradise the search begins not just for edible plants and animals and ways to breed from them but also for techniques of processing raw food direct from nature into edible dishes. It's a search that ultimately led to far more than edibility and digestibility. It produced the greatest culinary refinement and the most incomprehensible taboos, imperial banquets and hamburgers, star chefs and food as an expression of highly individual identity, and even food porn, as TV programs and photo series in culinary magazines are ironically called when they present food in all its exuberant sensuality. Women used to paint or make pottery; now, along with more and more men, they express their creativity by taking cookery courses. Food preparation has gained status.

What is said in the paradise story in the main monotheistic religions—that all plants are food—refers to a primal state, before the discovery of cooking, that is far older than agriculture and urbanization. Before the use of fire, human evolution involved the eating of raw and unprocessed food, at best soaked and dried in the sun. Exactly when the first humans became able to command fire at will to cook food is a matter of scientific controversy. Some control of fire is likely to have arisen 1.6 million years ago, but it could have begun even earlier, with the first *Homo erectus*. Cooking—in the broadest sense of heating food by some means—is the most essential human adjustment to banishment from the mythical paradise, an adaptation that arises from scarcity and makes that scarcity manageable. Processing food with a heat source first of all makes it easier to store, but it also becomes easier to digest. Protein-rich meat can then be dried and smoked, so prey that is caught decays less quickly. Grass seeds, tubers, and fruits can be kept longer after they've been dried, and heating also makes vitamins and minerals easier to absorb. Heating and processing almost always make food more digestible.

In a physical and chemical sense, cooking simply entails the transformation of the tissues of plants and animals by slicing, peeling, soaking, and heating, so that something edible emerges that we can more easily digest and is therefore more nutritious. We also find a combination of cooked food tastier than the separate raw ingredients. At its simplest cooking means the addition of water and heat, or even heat alone in roasting or grilling. At its most complicated cooking means embellishing, combining, coloring, and deconstructing according to the techniques of molecular cuisine until we can recognize nothing of the original food and see only its pretentious deployment.

Long before the invention of farming, people managed to overcome at least in part the inherent limits to the quantity of food to be found in nature. There is increasing evidence that cooking made us who we are, *Homo sapiens*. The use of fire to prepare food distinguishes us from the animals, especially in combination with other complex ways of processing, preparing, and sharing food—to say nothing of all the religious, moral, and cultural meanings we attach to food preparation. Chopping, mashing, grinding, soaking, fermenting, but above all roasting, baking, boiling, drying, or in some way heating food with hot water or steam, hot stones, or hot air—these things have changed us fundamentally.

That is not the case only in a sociological sense but physiologically too. It made our brains bigger. The preparation of food by heating was essential, as is clear from the fact that the direct ancestor of *Homo sapiens*, *Homo erectus*, despite having small jaws and molars, unsuitable for tearing off raw meat, was so evolutionarily successful.

The only explanation for this success is that through a self-reinforcing evolutionary process, more protein was consumed, because meat was heated, which made for a greater concentration of nutrients that were also more easily absorbed, and at the same time the requisite organization and tools were developed that went along with cooking. The use of the precursors of utensils and eating sticks increased human dexterity. We have recently learned that Neanderthals not only controlled fire but also actually cooked. Traces of roasted meat have been found, even barley grains and vegetables that have evidently been boiled in water. The heating of food leads to the partial relief of quantitative and qualitative scarcity, partly because of storability, and therefore to the availability of more nutrients and calories. Moreover, people eat more if dietary fibers are broken down by heating, and time is saved too, because the food does not have to be chewed for so long.

The outcome of this evolution is that in all human societies, cooking almost always takes place daily. The only exception are the Inuit, who survive largely on raw fish, birds, and meat; their only fuel is whale oil. Aside from that rare situation, a meal is ultimately always a cooked meal, wherever in the world it may be, or at least it involves food that has been prepared in some way. Even someone who idly takes an apple from a bowl is eating the result of processing, in the sense of packaging, refrigeration, transportation, and treatment to protect against insects. In Japan and the United States the apple will probably have a protective layer of wax. Even the typical Dutch lunch of filled rolls is in reality cooked: the wheat flour was ground and baked, the ham or sausage was boiled or at least sterilized and dried, the cheese is made of warmed milk, and so on. The slice of tomato on the bread may be raw, but it is the product of a long process of breeding and selection to make it taste better and be more digestible, so it is never "natural."

Depictions of paradise suggest that humans and nature are at one: what nature supplies feeds us. That image can be used in all sorts of ways to reinforce advertisements. The slogan that returns in countless variations is "the natural goodness of" (fruit, yogurt, vegetable soup, and so forth). The implication is plain: what comes from nature is directly and inherently good. There is not even any need to use the word "nature" to have the desired effect: "grass-fed butter" sounds better than simply "butter." Just as nature cannot simply be a guide to the way we produce food as organic farming assumes it is, the idea of "naturally pure" food is based on a misconception. Consumers who opt for "natural" in preference to "processed" fail to realize that hardly any of our food comes straight from nature. Almost without exception, our food is the product of many centuries of genetic selection by humans. It is protected by chemical or mechanical means against being damaged by insects or bacteria during production and transportation, and it's almost always processed in some way in factories and kitchens. Even raw fish caught in the wild are not eaten unprocessed but cleaned and usually vacuum-packed.

––––––––

The idea that "nature" offers better, healthier food than anything processed by the food industry is one of the most stubborn myths of our time. It can be explained only as a consequence of the distance that now exists between the consumer and food production and processing. City dwellers in particular, who have no experience at all with the production and processing of food, long for an ideal of untouched food that has the purity of the pre-industrial era or even an era far longer ago. Resistance to ready meals is at its most pronounced in the desire for wild food collected directly from the natural world by the cook. The "Palaeolithic" or "Neanderthal" diet, based on meat from animals killed by the cook along with raw plants, has a growing number of adherents. The male as hunter-cook is on the rise again, as can be seen from all kinds of recent instruction books about the spearing of fish and shooting and cleaning of game. Hunting or gathering from the wild guarantees true purity. Excursions in search of wild plants, under such headings as "urban foraging," can count on growing enthusiasm: the nettle and the dandelion—the food of the poor—are being restored to favor by connoisseurs. A derivative of this is the increasing use of extremely expensive bean sprouts and sprouted seeds, and edible flowers as a delicate garnish that you can pluck yourself from a plastic box. They include sprouted mustard seed or chives, colored variations on watercress and increasingly Asian varieties as well, such as edible mini-orchids.

In light of this it's striking that one of the most prestigious restaurants in the world, Noma in Copenhagen, works with wild berries, moss, and nuts. That hunting and gathering are a luxury solution for a small elite is all too eagerly forgotten. In a surprising historical twist we see the ultimate stage of this revival of pre-Neolithic gathering of food in the so-called dumpster divers, who search for unsold and rejected food at the exits to supermarkets at the end of the shopping day. Of course these gatherers are protesting against the excesses of the consumer society, but they are also idealizing a pseudo-autarchic way of life. The raw food diet, or its modern variant, the Paleolithic diet, therefore represents a huge step backward in evolution. Just like the Hallelujah Diet, it's a sign of our times, in which people increasingly have little idea of the long distances their food has traveled before ending up as a meal on their plates, and of how much that meal has changed in the course of history.

––––––

"Pure" doesn't mean what it used to mean. I have a well-thumbed copy of a classic cookery book from the Amsterdam domestic science school. It's undated, but I would say it must be from the early twentieth century. It includes an advertisement for vegetable oil from Delft, praised for being "completely pure" and "extremely nutritious." In those days, indeed until after the Second World War, the primary concern of every housewife was that food must be nutritious and pure. The word "pure" meant untainted and unadulterated. For centuries people ate food with additives that made it impure: water in the wine, beer, or milk; chalk in bread flour (a practice that goes back to Roman times); sugar in the honey; and cheap vegetable oils and water in the butter. A lack of purity was not simply fraud—the addition of cheap ingredients—it could be deadly dangerous: red pepper was often mixed with an extremely poisonous substance containing mercury to improve its color; mushroom sauce was made with an extract of rotting horse liver. Such adulteration took place on such a large scale that in 1820 a German chemist wrote about "death in the cooking pot."

Purity is the opposite of adulteration. Describing a product as pure means promising that it contains no undeclared ingredients and, at least as importantly, no bacterial infection and no rat droppings or traces of strange chemical substances. It's hard for us to imagine just how common those things were. Reports of the stench in Amsterdam and London in the eighteenth and nineteenth centuries are evidence of just how much the quality of hygiene and garbage collection left to be desired.

Pure in the sense of untainted is still relevant, of course. Infection by bacteria and other pathogens happens everywhere, especially in the case of salmonella and *E. coli*, which find their way into the food chain via the intestines of people and animals. This can mean that a Dutch vegetarian is made sick by a salmonella infection in chickens that has spread to other products, such as bread or salad, via equipment or unwashed hands. Diarrhea is to blame for 20 percent of child mortality worldwide, mainly as a result of contaminated food and water. In rich countries the greatest danger lies in the notorious dish cloth and cutting board in the consumer's home.

Despite all these risks, our food is safer than ever. The scale of the modern food supply chain makes a systematic approach to inspection possible. Where once tens of thousands of small dairymen had to be visited for random sampling to trace, for example, tuberculosis in the milk, now every milk delivery from every farm is automatically sampled on collection. Of course global networks present risks of their own. A European can be made ill by a pathogen that was originally introduced in another country or even on another continent. The infection of German bean sprouts with enterohemorrhagic *E. coli* bacteria in 2011 had its origins in an organic farm in Egypt that used animal manure. Stringent international agreements are in place regarding the maximum permitted residues of antibiotics, cleaning products, or heavy metals, but the use of antibiotics has nevertheless led to the development of resistant bacteria in livestock farms (for example, in chicken), which are a serious danger to public health. The purity of food will always remain a concern.

Pure, however, means far more than hygienic, uncontaminated, and unadulterated. Almost all cultures exhibit a concept of "pure" in the sense of spiritual purity and balance. Those who eat a macrobiotic diet avoid foods that are too yin (such as fruit) or yang (meat), sticking to foods in between, such as grains. As an ideal, in Hinduism for example, eating is a carefully considered act of self-control that allows the mind to concentrate on the divine. A great many foods are forbidden either because they are holy (like the holy cow of Hinduism) or because they are unclean (several fish types along the Amazon). Whether you do or do not eat a certain food isn't a question of avoiding physical discomfort, such as diarrhea— no, it guarantees the purity of the soul. If you don't stick to the rules, you'll be breaking religious laws. Although the goal of those laws is sometimes associated (often wrongly) with hygiene, as the ban on pork in Judaism and Islam has been, the ultimate aim is not to avoid infection but to preserve the unity of the group and the social order. A modern, extreme variant of this avoidance of forbidden foods is known as orthorexia nervosa, an obsessive desire for purity in the diet.

The broad, modern interpretation of the concept "pure" is far less old and is not simply inspired by religion. Pure food fits with a modern lifestyle that pays attention to health and nature. Living healthily is not just a matter of exercise or walking but also of eating food that's labeled "naturally pure" and is produced according to natural methods (whatever they may be) and contains no unnatural additives. This conviction arises from opposition to the modern food industry that may have given up using dangerous substances like mercury but now uses countless flavorings, E numbers, structure improvers, and so on, which to some consumers are just as bad. Ironically, many of these are useful and "natural," such as vitamin C (which has several E numbers for its different chemical forms), but that does nothing to reduce the psychological resistance. Chemical and processed are now equated with tasteless and risky, even if that is generally not true.

The issue is even more complicated, in fact. The food industry can produce synthetic flavors that are several times stronger and more effective than natural extracts. Some are indistinguishable from the "real" thing. However bizarre this seems, from the point of view of sustainability and nature conservation, there is a great deal to be said for an artificial strawberry taste for which no strawberries need to be grown. After all, strawberries require a great deal of water, pesticides, fungicides, and herbicides and are difficult to transport.

Yet artificial strawberry extract is a long way from what most people would describe as natural. "Natural purity" is ultimately an ethical concept, with a partially concealed meaning. Nature is not as innocent as it may seem. Fresh milk, straight from the cow, can be a source of brucellosis. Even plants cannot be trusted. In rhubarb we find oxalic acid; in salad, nitrates; and in almonds, hydrogen cyanide. Yet the attractiveness of "pure" food is overwhelming, even in the absence of any scientific basis. Many Dutch people drink mineral water because it's "purer," even though Dutch tap water is the purest in the world if we are talking about levels of bacteria, contaminants, and substances in solution. They do so because for them it's all about an image of a crystal clear stream of water dripping down from the rocks under a rainbow, the sun glancing off it. "Pure" is becoming a hedonistic view of life.

This vision of natural food can flourish only in conjunction with the comforts of an urban life that features no physical effort, hunger, or poverty, among those who have profited most from human progress and yet feel deeply uneasy about that progress. The price of progress seems too high, so people want to fall back on the simplicity of the past, on the purity of the farming life at a time when the fields were still full of cornflowers and poppies, and the farmer's wife made her own cheese and bread. They have a feeling they've lost something essential if industry determines what we eat. Food is always connected with a worldview, and most people in rich countries cannot accommodate in their worldview the idea that industry and purity go very well together.

The value of the debate about purity, "the poison-free kitchen," and natural food is that food has returned to the collective consciousness. Our tastes and preferences have evolved from pure, uncontaminated, and unadulterated several generations ago (although with strange, unknown substances added) to authentic, natural, and honest today. The very concept of "pure" is changing. Its meaning is a product of our knowledge and desires—and sometimes our prejudices. Who knows, perhaps in fifty years from now we will, after all, think of "pure" as a handful of pills that contain precisely the right nutrients to keep every individual healthy.

Food as a Mirror of a Changing World

It was not until the twentieth century, or even the past few decades, that quantitative scarcity was relieved for large segments of the world's population, but the diversity of the human diet began to increase far longer ago. In the first millennia after agriculture began, there was very little variety: unleavened bread and a gruel made of cooked grains or lentils combined with leafy vegetables and olives from gardens or the wild; honey; and, with the rise of dairying, milk and a very limited amount of meat. What people ate was determined first of all by what the land produced, both from farming and from gathering and, although less and less, from the hunt. Over the centuries, trade became more important, so food became regional rather than local. Migration and trade routes allowed plants, animals, and methods of preparation to spread. The introduction of new crops brought major dietary changes, starting with wheat and other cereals in northwestern Europe, followed by the potato. Long before the current wave of globalization, and without anyone really noticing, cuisine became international.

We usually forget within a few generations the foreign origin of food-stuffs that have quickly become part of our own tradition and identity. One good example is cassava, now universally thought of as a traditional African food, although it originally came from northeastern Brazil. The striking thing is that cassava was introduced to Africa at various different places and times by freed slaves, Portuguese traders, and missionaries, which meant there were extremely diverse methods of preparing it. Because cassava contains a glucoside that can liberate hydrogen cyanide as it decomposes, it has to be processed so that an enzyme is released that breaks down the glucoside. It's precisely those differences in processing—grating, soaking, heating, fermenting, roasting, and mashing—that tell us where and by whom cassava roots were imported, mainly in the nineteenth century. Yet consumers of each of these different products all insist that their own is the truly original African one. Comparable variation in preparation and consumption can be seen in the case of wheat, with all those different forms of bread, and of course meat products. Not just individual foods but entire dishes are regarded as part of a tradition, like the Dutch rice table or the British curry.

For a long time the history of our diet was characterized by a combination of local foods, which were readily available, and foods from far away, which were exotic and therefore scarce and desirable. But now that the world is growing smaller—now that products from everywhere are brought to us and few seasonal limitations exist any longer—the exotic is losing its value, and the desire for local and even anachronistic foods is growing. Not pineapples and bananas, let alone oranges, excite the consumer, but self-picked wild strawberries, sea lavender, and elder blossom. If the cook still uses pineapple, then it must be prepared in a special way: a mousse or a marinade.

However important the desire for local ingredients may be among those who can afford them, the dominant trend in the history of food is toward the globalization of ingredients and eating patterns. Cooking and eating are always an expression of international relations. One good example of early global cuisine is a curious handbook from 1330 titled *Yin-shan cheng-yao* ("Proper Essentials of Drink and Food"). It was written in Chinese by one Hu Szu-hui and as well as travel stories, it contains about 200 recipes for the imperial court, many of them illustrated, including quite a few that seem wildly exotic to us now, such as *shulen* ("banqueting soup"), which is made of swan and roast wolf, the organs of the snow leopard, sun-dried sheep's stomach, fermented mare's milk, and sorbet of rose petals. The basis of the classification is the distinction between "soup," food that gives strength, and the lighter, liquid dishes and drinks. Some of the ingredients in the handbook are typically Mongolian, such as sour apples, roasted grains, mutton, and fermented milk. Others come from the Turkish and Islamic traditions: chickpeas, steamed and baked loaves, and preserved fruits, syrups, and jam. The author obtains the wolf's meat from the Russian steppe, larded with olives from the coasts of the Black Sea. The recipe for curry with fennel bread, in contrast, is from Kashmir. From Persian cuisine come spices, such as cinnamon, saffron, rosewater, black pepper, and fenugreek. Typically Chinese components include cabbage, onion, carp, fermented soybeans, soy sauce, and of course sticky white rice.

The author, Hu Szu-hui, is the personification of this early globalization, a fourteenth-century Uighur who spoke Turkish and Chinese and served as personal physician to various Mongol emperors. The handbook therefore includes extensive rules for health, based on the premise that "food is medicine and medicines are food." As a member of a minority group—neither Mongolian nor Chinese—Hu Szu-hui was a master of culinary politics. He understood only too well that he would have to combine ingredients from different parts of the Mongol Empire in his kitchen to serve meals acceptable to his masters. He operated as a culinary entrepreneur who instructed the imperial cooks, sent envoys to all part of the world to collect seeds and recipes, and set gardeners to work to acclimate the new plants and to breed and crossbreed them. The kitchens, gardens, and extensive storerooms were a central feature of the imperial establishment—the result of careful political calculation, gastronomy, and health policy. As with the banquets held by the Romans or the French kings, excess was possible only because of an extensive and well-functioning trading network that could supply fresh food quickly and intact, along with cheap labor to process and prepare it.

Hu's recipes reflect the first truly international cuisine, a kind of "fusion cooking," long before the term was coined, which emerged along the Silk Roads almost three centuries before the Columbian globalization began with the European discovery of America in 1492. Just how revolutionary Hu was is clear from comments in later sources, which complain of the unfortunate incursion on refined Chinese cuisine by primitive Mongol customs. Hu's "soup for the emperor" was soup for an empire.

The West has the Silk Roads to thank for all kinds of food that is now commonplace. Eve's apple arrived in Europe via the Middle East from the forested mountains of Tian Shan on the border between Kazakhstan and China, along the various Silk Roads, as did several related fruit trees, including cherries, walnuts, and peaches. The most important source of carbohydrates to come from the East is rice. As ever, what arrived was not just the crop but also ways of preparing it. With rice, brought by the Arabs via Spain, noodles also arrived, as well as curry and risotto.

A multiplicity of stories has grown up around all these dishes to explain their origin and supposed characteristics. The success of rice growing in the region of Valencia and in the Po Valley from the fifteenth century on is a direct consequence of the increase in the urban population and the need to cultivate flat river valleys. The wet and regularly flooded soils are not suitable for wheat, and they had never been farmed successfully until rice found a niche there. So rice quickly became a staple food, despite the danger of malaria. The Italians replaced the original Arab recipes for sweet rice cooked in almond milk, honey, or fig juice with versions that suited their tastes better, such as risotto with saffron (*Crocus sativus*, from Turkey). The story goes that the idea of combining saffron with rice to make the famous golden grains was the brainchild of a Flemish pupil of the creator of Milan Cathedral's renowned stained-glass window, as a way of qualifying the pupil to ask the artist for his daughter's hand in marriage.

From the time of the European voyages of discovery in the sixteenth century, the number of new crops and dishes that spread from one part of the world to another increased rapidly. This is true not only of Europe but also of China, for instance. Intensive cultivation of irrigated rice dominated Chinese farming, along with the planting of horticultural crops on the dikes around rice paddies. As early as the sixteenth century, corn and sweet potatoes arrived from America. They didn't have to be grown in damp river valleys but produced good yields on slopes and in the cooler mountain regions. The result was spectacular population growth and a revolution in Chinese agriculture—as well as serious erosion as a result of the migration of peasants to the mountains and the creation of fields on slopes. A comparable success story, though without the erosion, was the introduction of the potato to Europe. Within a century the European population doubled. With the new crops came new recipes, such as the Dutch stamppot, made with mashed potatoes. Beans from Central America (*Phaseolus* species and a few *Vigna*) were quickly adopted too. Wheat arrived in Central America and the south of what is now the United States along with the Spanish conquistadores. In Africa, too, diets based on millet and plants collected from the wild were changed radically by the arrival of rice, brought by the Arabs in the Middle Ages, and by corn, cassava, wheat, and American beans. The trading and spread of new species involved not just food crops but also crops that produced other raw materials, such as cotton, rubber, and palm oil, as well as spices and drinks, including coffee. Sugarcane is a special case, because it is a food crop but also an essential item of trade with temperate regions, where workers benefited from cheap calories until trade barriers and the development of the sugar beet put an end to cane sugar imports. The creation of plantations for various trade crops had a knock-on effect on the amount of land left for food, including food for agricultural workers, and often it was disruptive. As plants and animals spread across the world, such spices and herbs as nutmeg, pepper, and cinnamon became extremely important, as a way not just of introducing new tastes but of masking decay.

It was the wave of globalization after 1990, however, that truly turned the world on its head. What people eat now is no longer determined by supply—mainly from local agriculture and fisheries and local trade—but by demand, that enormous intangible conglomerate of large groups of anonymous consumers, bound together by supermarkets, that control farming worldwide. Want a strawberry in winter? At your service: they come from Chile. Fresh vanilla pods from Madagascar for self-indulgent yuppies? Of course, the local vegetable boutique will have them—at least for anyone who lives in the best districts of the city. In poor suburbs of American cities the scarce supermarkets sell only packaged, high-calorie fast food and soft drinks, and half of all Americans goes to a hamburger chain at least once a week.

Taste is a function of time, place, and income. Diets are therefore never static. They change continually and rapidly. It's not yet thirty years since Dutch people ate a meal of meat, potatoes, and an overcooked green vegetable almost every day. That is unthinkable now. Pasta, pizza, and rice have partly driven out the potato, vegetables have become infinitely more varied, and from meat in its standard forms (braising steak, sausage, and meatballs) the Dutch have switched to a wide range of meat, fish, and seafood, not forgetting meat substitutes and vegetarian products. Even the sandwich, still the basis of lunch, is gradually being replaced by wraps and filled rolls. Mediterranean cuisine, so highly praised for its healthy ingredients—lots of vegetables, plenty of fish, olive oil, carbohydrates, and little meat or saturated fat—is in decline even in the Mediterranean region itself. Purists who idealize it don't realize it also includes recipes for finely sliced boiled udders in tomato sauce. The Mediterranean diet was born of necessity, from a lifestyle of hard work, frugality, and community spirit. In their food choices and their tendency to be overweight, adolescents in those countries already seem very much like their northern contemporaries. The next phase will likely favor the Scandinavian diet: rye, fish, seaweed, milk products, cabbage, and a lot of berries, with rapeseed oil instead of olive oil.

———————

All these changes make nonsense of the concept of local cuisine. There is hardly a single original local cuisine whose traditions are fixed. Except in the case of the most isolated tribes—in the Arctic, the Amazon, or New Guinea—there are always outside influences. Those influences are considerable, and the adoption of new foods happens far more quickly than we think. In reality this was always the case. Attempts to recover the past, perhaps through the slow food movement and UNESCO (which has labeled certain dishes as "world heritage"), are well meaning, but they fail to recognize something essential about our culinary history: even original recipes are constantly evolving.

There are good reasons for the changeability of food. Supply and techniques of preparation evolve, while alternatives emerge and are adapted. One good example is the wrap, a pancake of thin dough with a filling. Originally an Indian tradition of wrapping food in certain kinds of bread, such as *naam*, it combines the exotic with the modern need for convenience food. It's easier than a sandwich for busy Western office workers at their computers to eat with their hands, because the filling cannot fall out, and there's no temptation to make it yourself every morning. In that sense it's very much like the hamburger, made to be eaten without utensils, usually on the way somewhere. The wrap, vegetarian or otherwise, is the hamburger for the hurried professional class—which makes many people think it's something new.

That traditional handmade food has largely disappeared in rich countries, especially in the West, is easy to understand. Avoiding work like kneading, sieving, and stirring is an important motivation for women in particular. Considerations of hygiene also deter us from, for example, slaughtering animals at home or making sausages. Instead we stick to the more controllable techniques that are now allowed in abattoirs. Although modern slaughtering methods are facing criticism, they were and are an enormous improvement on past practices. Rigid approaches to culinary heritage, insisting that things have to be cooked in this particular way and not that or they will not be authentic, demonstrate a refusal to acknowledge the continual change that is part of human dietary experience.

Cooking as Construct and Philosophy

Not only at the Mongolian court but everywhere and always, what we cook and eat is a reflection of a worldview and of changes to the world. Our worldview has moral significance; it reflects what is good or bad for us to eat, for body and mind, and why. To comply with such rules requires careful decisionmaking and a complex organization of food supplies. This is true even in situations of absolute scarcity and isolation. Even native tribes in the Amazon or poor farmers and landless peasants in rural India have extremely precise, well-reasoned classifications of what is edible and what is not, why, and in which combinations. This limits what they consume from their surroundings, despite scarcity: a certain plant or bird is dangerous, another beneficial; one may be eaten only in the rainy season, another only by men and never by pregnant women.

Even in the very earliest civilizations, values were attributed to food that go far further than its contribution in the form of proteins and calories. Food offers a framework for ordering the world around us. For Westerners at the start of the twenty-first century, whose choices are barely limited (if at all) by availability or cost, food is a statement, a series of implicit and explicit assertions about what we regard as good, healthy, and status-raising. Through our diets we declare openly who we are, who we want to be, and what we believe the world is like.

Cooking brings about a biochemical transformation, but it has a philosophical dimension as well. Preparing food is a civilized act. For a long time, a diner was considered more civilized the more preparation had gone into the food and the more ingredients it contained. Now we see a movement in the opposite direction to some extent: toward the raw, the simple, the pure, and the unique rather than a combination of flavors. At the same time the search for refinement goes on. The more work and ingredients go into the food, the more expensive and valuable the result. The growing status and pretentions of restaurants and chefs, coupled with the increasing number of people who can afford to eat out (and therefore do not need to cook), are reflected in all kinds of artificial, artistic, and frenetic creations. Where once live birds were baked into pies, or human-sized ice sculptures were presented to diners, now the challenge lies in applying chemistry and physics in the kitchen. The chef becomes a scientist, or at any rate a star, to judge by the endless stream of TV shows—and even dedicated TV channels—in which food is philosophized over, and sometimes even cooked, as well as by foodie films and those expensive, hefty cookbooks that present themselves as bibles of good taste.

Ferran Adrià is head chef at the most famous restaurant in the world, elBullí in northern Spain, which claims to receive 2 million applications every year for a maximum of 8,000 places. He has documented his creative methods in a photo book of more than 500 pages, intended as art, that records every minute of the daily work of the restaurant, from sunrise over the sea to the extinguishing of the last lamp, including the washing of tablecloths and napkins and the extensive administration involved with the dishes and ingredients. Various philosophical concepts are applied to the ingredients and the food served, such as association, minimalism, symbiosis, spherification, reconstruction, and deconstruction. Adrià is one of the chefs in the forefront of molecular gastronomy, the application to cooking of scientific insights and techniques, especially from chemistry and physics. In his case this is mainly about the design of a gastronomic style and experience, a way of experiencing food as never before. Some scientists have gone before him, such as French chemist Hervé This, who investigated exactly what happens when proteins solidify and foam is beaten firm. In the molecular kitchen, instant freeze boxes that use liquid nitrogen, vacuum cookers, and CO_2 injectors are part of the standard equipment. The application of ultrasound to form tiny cavities makes for an extra tasty crust. Chemistry, which so often frightens consumers, is suddenly in fashion.

In the molecular approach of Adrià and his colleagues, pure sensation is central. Typical is the fluorescent orange ball of foam that dissolves in a flash in the mouth, leaving nothing but the texture-free taste and scent of carrots. In cases like this, the end product has barely any recognizable visual relationship to the original ingredients or the dish from which it was derived. There is also a class of produce that deliberately puts the diner on the wrong track, such as mousses and creams in diverse colors. Yellow tomato mousse looks like orange Bavarois but tastes of sour tomatoes. And the reverse: tomato juice turns out to have been made from oranges, and pannacotta from stockfish. This is incidentally one way of making the hamburger attain new high point. After dipping it in liquid nitrogen, the frozen exterior can be fried crisp while the interior remains tender because of its lower cooking temperature.

The technological pinnacle of this approach is undoubtedly represented by products that are apparently identical to the original but came about in a totally different manner and are in fact a deconstructed form of it. Emblematic of them in Adrià's recreation of the olive in the form of a little ball of freshly pressed olive oil that is given its olive shape in a bath of sodium alginate (a polymer derived from brown algae) and that "explodes" on the tongue. It looks like an olive and is made of olive, but it's a concentrate, a human fabrication. Using the same technique Adrià has made caviar from apple juice, and one of his colleagues has deconstructed moussaka. The most brilliant creations are those featuring new combinations of ingredients, such as lobster foam with white chocolate mousse.

Although molecular chefs are usually interested in local foods and *terroirs* (areas with specific ecological and cultural characteristics resulting in original and unique products), their worldview is diametrically opposed to that of slow food, organic farming, or those who look for "honesty" in nature. Molecular cuisine is based not on the past but on the future. Local products are at best a stimulus to create something new, not a goal in themselves. In a great leap forward, the molecular chef wrests him- or herself as a designer from the straitjacket of natural evolution and the slow process of the domestication of species. The molecular designer no longer sees ingredients as a given with which dishes are compiled; instead tastes and sensations are built up from the first molecule to achieve the effect of complete ingredients and products. The deployment of advanced chemical and physical technologies means food can be made "larger than nature." Not nature itself but modern technology takes the lead. The revolution of modernism has reached the kitchen. With food as design, molecular or not, humans have definitively broken with nature. The brain of the diner has to be led up the garden path; food and the environment must be manipulated so that new associations arise. Not all chefs go this far, but the increase in the number of creations made with molds or based on microscopic structures confirms the trend. Chefs are the new emperors, exercising ultimate and virtuoso control over newly created nature. It makes them both cooks and artists, and they join the ranks of artists and designers whose goal is to recreate food and food experiences: meals as works of art, bright color combinations or monochrome dishes, dining in the dark or while looking at photographs of ingredients—situations in which tables, plates, and food flow into one another. The restaurant has become a branch of (expensive) entertainment.

Slow Food and Whole Food

The molecular movement and slow food may be opposite poles philosophically, but together they are at the forefront of innovative cooking and eating. Slow food arose as a reaction to the opening in 1986 of a branch of the hamburger chain McDonald's right next to the Spanish Steps on the Piazza di Spagna in Rome. A hamburger restaurant, complete with plastic tables and soft drinks in giant paper cups! Next to one of the icons of the incomparable beauty of Rome! For the Italians this was nothing less than an imperialist provocation by the American superpower, which by imposing its abject eating habits was attempting to corrupt the ancient and rich Italian culture.

The indignation was indescribable, and the reaction as inevitable as it was typically Italian. It was typical too of all differences of opinion about food. Only one response was possible: demonstratively emphasize the uniqueness of the Italian culinary identity. The slow food movement was set up with the goal of providing a counterweight to American fast food culture and restoring the honor of uniquely Italian cuisine. In Italy the movement quickly took off, and the rest of the world eagerly followed. Who isn't opposed to the hamburger as a symbol of Western excess and of eating without thinking? Apart, that is, from a whole generation of young Italians and other Europeans, who pay little attention to all the commotion, and a few molecular chefs.

—————

As its declaration of principle states, slow food "promotes the right to enjoyment, at the table and elsewhere by studying, protecting, and making known agricultural and gastronomic traditions from all parts of the world, in order to pass on today's pleasures to future generations." This is not a plea for a return to nature, but it does extol a past in which farmer, gardener, and cook coincided or at least were geographically connected with one another. Slow food contrasts itself with an era that took the machine as a model for life and enslaved us to speed. "Fast life" has penetrated our living rooms and forced us to eat fast food. Slow food is the only real advance that combines knowledge and enjoyment: know what you're eating and enjoy both what you know and what you eat.

Slow food insists that small-scale, preferably traditional farming is necessary for us to achieve this, along with a close bond between consumer and producer. Over time, slow food has built up an impressive national and international network of chefs, farmers, and others interested in gastronomy. The slow food movement organizes an annual Salone del Gusto, a trade fair devoted to flavor, and is working on an Ark of Taste, an encyclopedia of local production methods and products. The use of the symbol of the ark is of course a reference to Genesis and indirectly to the paradise story and the Fall of Man. A typical example of research work carried out by the slow food movement is the documentation of more than 200 Italian cheeses, all irresistibly described. It has helped to gain each of them their own *appellation còntrôlée* or a comparable stamp of originality of origin or production method. Slow food also organizes annual meetings of "food communities" and traditions, called "Terra Madre."

—————

Ancient traditions, breeds and flavors are key words in this new culinary approach by restaurants and delicatessens. Growing your own veggies, keeping animals, and gathering ingredients from the wild are ways of reducing the distance between producer and consumer. Fortunately we don't have to start doing such things ourselves; it's enough if the cook does them for us. In its search for purity, slow food is combined with elements from exotic cuisine: unsprayed muesli has given way to wild rice with chicken in chocolate sauce and wild asparagus.

Slow food is the chic scion grafted onto the food counterculture that started more than a century ago with the biodynamic and whole food movements. It advocates organic food only if not grown on too big a scale and it regards non-certified local produce, as long as it's sustainable (something it does not define in detail), as an equally valid option. Slow food builds on the achievements of earlier campaigners who wanted to restore respect for the small scale and for local knowledge—the small-is-beautiful attitude of the 1970s—and on the growing interest in communities that are still "connected with the soil," including hill farmers and nomadic herdsmen. Slow food is the movement best known in Europe, but it's certainly not the only one. In almost all urban centers related initiatives have developed over recent years, with farmer's markets and local produce and shops selling "natural," "green," "honest," and "organic" food. New types of farmer's market have collectively rescued environmental awareness from its association with scratchy woollen socks and mouse-dropping-strewn whole food shops. With attractive designs and trendy shopping spaces, they have made traditional and local food acceptable to the growing number of double-salaried, middle-class professional, urban households. These new chains are supplied by a network of food-processing companies, such as soup factories, that share their aims. A decade or so earlier, shops run by immigrants from Morocco or Turkey, with their flat loaves, lamb, zucchinis, almonds, hummus, and a wide range of tomatoes, originally intended for clients from their own ethnic group, became popular with people who had discovered those countries as tourists. The positive contribution made by the slow food movement lies not only in its discussion of traditions and the origins of our food but also in its ways of restoring the link between producer and consumer, between farmer and cook.

In the United States a similar tradition arose even earlier in the sixties counterculture of California, with its bread baking, its vegetable plots on campus, and food as a symbol of protest against capitalism. The *Whole Earth Catalog* (1968–1972) boosted the autarchy of the hippies: you can be truly independent of mind only if you provide your own food. In practice a rather miserable picture of such autarchy emerges: the vegetable plots became overgrown and full of aphids, and not many people knitted jumpers with home-spun wool for long. In about 1980 a new phase dawned. From protest the philosophy shifted toward pleasure, toward food that could claim authenticity—ideas very close to those of the slow food movement. Professionalization and commercialization took shape as a result of the setting up of The Whole Food Markets in Texas by a group of business people who were looking for an economically success-ful approach to the alternative circuit.

Advertisers in the West are more than happy to play on nostalgia for the real food of the past. Marmalade is sold in old-style angular canning jars, and bottles of pear juice are given an extra paper lid tied with a string to suggest that grandma herself stood at the kitchen table making mar-malade and boiling down fruit. Farmers, to the disaffected city dweller once synonymous with a deeply conservative class of songbird-killers, poison-sprayers, and veal calf slayers, are on the up-and-up to an un-precedented degree. The epitome of this trend in the Netherlands is an immensely popular reality TV program called "Farmer Seeks Wife." It's impossible to imagine a series called "Builder Seeks Wife."

Behind slow food, whole food, and the modern organic supermarket is a worldview that links the authentic and elitist with a sincere desire to do something good, sustainable, and honest, as part of a new, if selec-tive, interest in the countryside. The original approach of the slow food movement—eat and enjoy according to local tradition—is the preserve of those who can afford a trip to that one special truffle restaurant high in the hills of Piedmont, where the prices match their spending power.

"Local" does not necessarily equate with quality or diversity. Taken to extremes, after all, the stress on local food would mean that northern Europeans could eat no citrus fruit, and Morocco and Israel would have to give up growing oranges for export. The arbitrary nature of the concept "local" is demonstrated by the wide range of interpretations. Sometimes it's regarded as covering anything within 700 kilometers, sometimes just a few dozen. All the same, a great deal can be said for collecting forgotten varieties of vegetables and fruits, documenting old recipes, and stimulat-ing the production of handmade sausages, bread rolls, cheeses, and jams. The desire to reduce the food supply chain to a local or regional scale is understandable, even though the diversity we so enjoy is attributable pre-cisely to the fact that so much of what we eat is not local.

Anyone who simply wants to go back to the handmade, local, and small-scale—radical regionalism—is ignoring not only the continual nature of evolution but also that such an approach cannot feed the world and would make food prices impossibly high. Ultimately it's all about avoiding excesses and responding to justifiable doubts about large-scale food transportation, especially of cattle feed, all over the world, even though it's essential for the production of meat proteins in Asia.

The slow food and whole food movements are a response to the desire by the urban consumer to belong to the small-scale, the genuine, the way things used to be. They bridge the huge gap between urbanized globalization and the village by looking back to a past of tradition and solidarity. But anyone wanting to return to the past should understand that tradition can be preserved only if it's paid for, and only a small percentage of consumers seem prepared to do that.

The ideas behind whole food have also been given a powerful boost, even undergone a reincarnation, among the urban professional classes in Europe, South and North America and Australia, as a result of increasing concern about climate change and the concept of sustainability. While the supermarkets specializing in slow food and whole food and related produce have to be careful not to become a paradise for snobs, the standard supermarket chains and food manufacturers are rapidly catching up. The selection of foods with green, sustainable, organic, and fair trade labels in the average supermarket has expanded massively. Although products stamped "organic" still only represent a small fraction of the market, "sustainable" and "green" labels are becoming mainstream in the larger supermarkets. The resultant confusion has not been helped by the increasing number of products that have labels telling the consumer what is sensible and responsible. All the same, the message is clear: make the right choice and you'll be caring for yourself and the environment, and it's affordable to do so. Pleasure and the authentic are thereby made to seem achievable, every day, in a malleable, manageable existence. The new maxim is: tell me where you shop and what you buy, and I'll tell you who you are.

Dinner's Ready!

Between us and our ancestors, who tore apart their half-raw, half-burnt meat with their teeth, or the women of Mesopotamia who ground flour to bake bread, food traditions have piled up and up. Food is no longer a matter of survival, nor purely power; it confers the status and identity with which we distinguish ourselves from others and at the same time gives us the sense of community we seek. Those who eat as we do have a connection with us; they are as we are.

"Dinner's ready!" is the traditional cry with which Western mothers used to call their playing children indoors and grab the attention of their newspaper-reading husbands. "Dinner's ready!" We're about to eat, so drop what you're doing. The call represented the most important moment of the day, a confirmation of family life, of the caring role of the mother and the authority of the father. So it went on for many generations, in many countries.

The table is a place of memory where we, whether because of the Proustian madeleine or not, become aware of who we are and with whom we are. Around the table, all previous meals come together in every meal, in an endless succession of memories and associations. The table is the place where the family gathers, the symbol of solidarity, or indeed the backdrop to family rows and childhood tragedies. At the table the eater is tamed. At the table we relive our youth through the recipes of the past, our hatred of endive or liver, teenage love through that first failed canard à l'orange, the sadness of the unarticulated apology, the tears of loneliness that mixed with the burnt cauliflower, the sensuality of fingers dipped in an airy sauce mousseline.

Eating around a table means both eating and talking, if only to say a few words of praise for what is presented to us. At the table we talk about what we've eaten before and what we're going to eat and everything in between. If we say nothing at the table, then there is always the refusal of food as the final word. With that same sensitive organ, the mouth, we taste and consume, speak and kiss.

How food is experienced has everything to do with the decor, with the rituals surrounding the meal, with the company, and with the experience. Everyone knows the trap of the Vinho Verde: that famous Portuguese wine tastes so much better when drunk in a sun-drenched restaurant garden than at home with central heating and a view of a rainy street. Simple wooden tables and farmyard cutlery appeal to our emotions, just like damask tablecloths and crystal wine glasses. Food is drama, the table the stage, and the cook is the tamer and hero. People eat more if the food is presented festively even if the taste is no different—important to remember if you are trying to encourage an elderly person to eat.

"Dinner's ready!" calls people to a specific place. The dining table may be round or long, of wood or plastic, covered with a luxuriant cloth and monogrammed table napkins or with reed placemats that have seen better days. Sometimes the table is bare and shows traces of previous meals. On the top of my French farmhouse table, 200 years old, are diagonal scratches from the breadknife of an unknown cook. "Dinner's ready!" is always a call to a specific place where the meal is being served, whether or not it includes a table: the picnic in the grass on a blanket, or on the open hatchback of a car beside the highway, or the rickety folding table on the balcony. Even in "Le Déjeuner sur l'herbe," that famous painting by Manet with a nude woman sitting on the grass, something that looks like a scrunched tablecloth lies next to the fruit. (Or could it be her dress, being used for the purpose?)

The words "Dinner's ready!" denote a state of mind determined by the topography of the table. People sitting opposite each other inevitably pass dishes or pans, and are almost forced to look each other in the eye and to converse. People sitting next to each other look at a third person, or out of the window, or at a wall. Does that looking, or indeed not looking, make the exchange of confidences easier? Is the taste of the food influenced by the company and the seating arrangements? These dimensions are beautifully illustrated in Edward Hopper's painting "Chop Suey," in which two women sit opposite each other at an almost empty table in a Chinese restaurant in New York. The table is the center of a universe in which we seek our place, revolving like planets around the sun, drawn by the gravity of the regularity of eating and the longing for company.

At the table it's all about receiving food, or at least the ritual of serving and eating. Every meal arises from a series of specified acts, even if only an improvised picnic or a chocolate cake consumed alone. Something is revealed, from a dish, box, or picnic basket, steaming plates are brought in, pan lids are lifted, and vinegar and oil poured, there is stirring and slicing. Even where a lonely diner picks sweets out of a bag with bare fingers, a rudimentary ritual exists, a moment of pleasure, no matter how ambiguous or guilty. This symbolism of the meal applies to politics as well. The table is functional; formal dinners confirm the state of negotiations and at the same time demonstrate the power and opulence of those attending. Every meal, however simple, has a beginning and an end, marked by the unfolding of napkins and the deployment of cutlery, or by a prayer, a speech, or a toast, or a satisfied leaning back in the grass as the last glasses are emptied.

The human is the only animal species that surrounds its food with rituals and takes account of hunger among others who are not direct relatives. The table makes us human. Cooking is the basis for relationships. We distinguish ourselves from the animals not by our use of tools—the stick other primates use to extract honey from a honeycomb could with a bit of a stretch be called a "fork" or "spoon." No, we distinguish ourselves by the fact that we eat at a table, or at least a specific place intended for a meal, such as a mat on the ground. We don't eat as soon as we get our hands on food, to stifle hunger; we usually eat together, if less than we used to and at more flexible times. We generally wait—although again less than we used to—until everyone has food on his or her plate, and we don't regard the meal as over until everyone has eaten enough. In urban families where older children remain at home and everyone goes their own way, people increasingly eat alone, or at any rate no longer with the whole family gathered at a specific time. The rhythm and communality of meals is declining in single-parent families too.

The call "Dinner's ready!" was until recently a sign that a particular time had been reached, a specific part of the day, in harmony with the rhythm of the seasons, determined by cultural preferences: is the midday meal most important or the evening meal? The sandwich at a quarter past twelve or the Spanish *el amuerzo* (lunch) at three in the afternoon? The call to the table marks the moment in the day at which everything else must give way to communality: toy bears are abandoned, school textbooks closed, computers put on standby, and work stopped, at least for a while. In Western Europe there used to be three meals every day, but elsewhere too the meals determine the hour, even where breakfast consists of nothing more than the cold leftovers from the previous evening and lunch is carried out to workers in the fields, even where little remains to serve as an evening meal.

How far back does the dining table go? For much of the hundreds of thousands of years of human evolution we did not sit at tables at all. The Roman emperors lay on beds beside low tables, the poor of the Middle Ages had little more than wooden troughs for their food, and in Africa and India people eat crouching down or in the lotus position on the ground. Estimates suggest that a quarter of the world's population doesn't eat at a table but around a mat, or standing in the mud of a market with a narrow plank for support. In poor countries, where mothers and children often eat separately from men, usually in or near the kitchen, the cry is not "Dinner's ready!" but "Come and eat!"—just as the usual greeting in many countries is "Have you eaten yet?" Why should we assume that dining at a table marks a high point in our evolution? Humans are not simply what they eat but how and where they eat. And with whom; in eighteenth-century Dutch a good friend was called a "table friend."

The dining table is disappearing. Fewer are being sold now in rich economies, apparently. This says a lot about the times we live in. The table is less and less the center of family life. We eat at the computer, standing in the kitchen, lounging on the sofa in front of the television, in the car, or walking along the street. Best of all we like to graze all day. If we do still eat at the table then it's no longer a dining table but one where eating shares space with other things, such as a computer, a television, or newspapers. Sales of plates are declining too, and even more so serving dishes and cutlery designed for serving from them. More and more of the food we buy is ready to eat, in throwaway tubs or trays, or designed as finger food to be eaten with one hand and no cutlery. What's the point of a table if we can devour a microwaved ready meal on our laps? We say we have no time to cook, although on average we watch hours of television every day.

With the disappearance of the table as the center of existence, a new emotion is coming to the fore. The table exerted a certain discipline; now we feel conscience stricken because we eat too much, while neglecting to cook and forgetting how. Is the table not becoming the place of sin, of guilt about our desire to eat, now that we no longer dare to enjoy food uninhibitedly? Increasingly we eat alone, and what solitary diner bothers to lay the table?

Something comparable is happening to the kitchen. Avant garde kitchens are becoming living spaces with a built-in library and bar, the ultimate thus far being Berloni's Not For Food kitchen in which a desk, sofa, and kitchen are fused into a single whole. Nostalgic farm kitchen or high-tech laboratory: the irony is that the more a kitchen is visible as a symbol of status and identity, the less it is used. The dining table and the old-fashioned kitchen are becoming anachronisms.

Eating and Cooking as a Dilemma

In an urbanizing society in which hardly anything reminds us of soil, grass, and grain, the dining table and kitchen are the theater of alienation and confusion about what we eat and what the other is eating.

Nothing is any longer self-explanatory; the taboos have worn away, and new, contradictory rules are shooting up like mushrooms. All the food of the world is available to us, so we eat things that were impossible and unimaginable until recently: Chinese turtle soup, papayas from Ivory Coast, raspberries from Chile—or is it Israel or Italy? We no longer notice or care about the origin. The decline of the table also stands for eating without knowing, without wanting to know how the chicken (battery farmed or free range?) was transformed into that white slab on our plates. The modern diner, unless schooled in the meat-eating tradition of slow food and the organic butcher, is disgusted at the thought of calf's tongue and head cheese, of the bloody details of animal carcasses and sharp knives. With the decline of the old taboos come new taboos and coercive rules: meat is bad and a moral hazard; salad, peanut butter, and eggs threaten our health (or do they?); oolong tea is the new champagne.

If you're poor, food is an obsession; if you're rich, it becomes one again. The inhabitants of Europe and other rich economies, and the rich classes in the rest of the world, now eat safer and more varied foods than ever before. Diets have changed rapidly all around the world over the past three decades, primarily as the result of economic growth and increased production, which has meant that spending on food has fallen on average. We should not be complacent, however: a billion or more people still spend most of their incomes on food. They have the most to gain by falling food prices. The situation for the poorest classes in poor countries is very unlike our own, because corruption, inadequate legislation, and a lack of oversight often lead to shortages and unequal shares, infected products, or terrible food-poisoning tragedies.

For the extensive middle class that is looking for something different, the rules of the World Trade Organization designed to promote open markets and quality control have made the export of tropical products possible on a vast scale. Tourism and immigration have stimulated interest in the exotic and rural. For city dwellers who for years bought their food at the supermarket without giving it any thought, a new form of self-expression is emerging. Through food we demonstrate our aspirations: sun-dried tomatoes express the carefree feel of a Mediterranean summer, hot curry the exoticism of Asia, ostrich the wild expanses of Africa. Domestic cooks now want to serve Thai and Tuscan (not merely

Italian) dishes. Cooking and eating, whether of ready meals or food prepared by hand, at home or in restaurants, have become the driving forces behind the new stories and rituals surrounding food.

Even though the rich countries make such huge profits from globalization and from specialization in the food supply chain, or perhaps precisely because of that, everything that has to do with cooking and eating has become troubling to the citizens of these countries. I would explain this as a result of the way that the preparation of food is increasingly being taken out of our hands at the same time as it has come to determine our identity so powerfully. Many people feel alienated and confused about what good food is. As a result we eat too easily, too much, too quickly, too thoughtlessly, too guiltily, because we are aware we know better. While some 15 percent of people in rich countries seek culinary refinement, a majority wolf down ready meals more and more often, sometimes at the computer or with a phone or remote control in one hand. While busy yuppies both male and female indulge in fancy cooking on weekends, unafraid of making their own ravioli with truffles, more than 20 percent of our meals come from gas stations, train and bus stations, and other places that until recently sold no food other than a few chocolate bars. Oddly enough, these are to some degree the same people: special ingredients and luxury utensils for the Saturday extravagances in the kitchen; on weekdays a quick snack on the road with lack of time as an excuse. We have become so uncertain about how to prepare food that every year there's a world market for 24,000 books about cooking and food preparation.

The irony is that the rich are now searching for what served the poor as food for centuries: *la cucina povera,* beloved of the slow food movement. Much is paid for very little, served in a luxurious, authentic setting. The rehabilitation of the food of the poor is accompanied by culinary snobbery and strict rules about what belongs to it and what does not. This while the cuisine of the poor consists largely of local produce, because little else is available. Interest in the poor is selective: what the poor in Africa eat has a quite different status from the food of the Mediterranean poor. Northerners have a strong tendency to associate good food with relaxing in the sun, failing to realize that the *dolce far niente* was in fact more a consequence of joblessness and a harsh climate than a conscious preference for stress-free leisure time.

Alienation from the industrialized food supply chain has evoked its own response, the countermovement among the richer classes, who want to return to the earliest stages of food preparation and processing and to hunt out original recipes—at least on days when they choose to spend time on all that at home. Whether it's a matter of exclusive restaurants, sustainable local produce, or fast food at the gas pump, of designer kitchens or simply shopping for the evening meal, cooking and eating will never again be simple and self-explanatory.

ELEVEN

Paradise on Every Street Corner: Food in the City

Iam quidem hortorum nomine in ipsa urbe delicias agros villasque possident. [Now Epicureans have the comforts of the country in the town and they name it gardens.] PLINY THE ELDER, *Historia Naturalis*

If you haven't been in Paris in a long time, you probably don't know the new markets. It's only been at most five years since they were built. Over there, you see, the pavilion next to us, that's for fruit and flowers. Further down is the fish market and poultry, then butter and cheese. There are six pavilions on this side and over on the opposite side, another four: the meat market, tripe and organs. ÉMILE ZOLA, *The Belly of Paris*

Onions beside the Highways

In Taiwan I once rented a bicycle to explore the suburbs of Kaohsiung, a large container port in the south of the country. You don't need to go far from town there to see how quickly the asphalt roads turn into unpaved tracks. Some are barely wide enough for a bicycle or a motorized cart. Yet you don't find yourself cycling among farmers but instead in a no man's land that has no identity as yet. The transition from countryside to built-up area is far from abrupt; the city creeps out between the farmhouses and fields. It shows itself first as light industry, next come homes, and only then do you reach the paved roads. Next to a large chicken run is a small factory making cattle feed. A little farther on you get to an enormous gray barn, where plastic granules are molded into buckets and bowls. Electricity pylons with a tangle of cables stride across the fields and ditches. You pass a rice paddy, the hanging ears radiant yellow, almost ready to harvest, and find right next to it the skeleton of a block of apartments just going up. The concrete mixers stand among the stubble of what was until recently another rice paddy. In the long evolution of this farming system, crop rotation ends for good after the final rice crop with a factory or an apartment building. There will never be a rice paddy here again.

In Niamey, the capital of Niger in West Africa, I've admired the bananas, squashes, cabbages, and tomatoes grown by residents along the banks of the Niger River, just beyond the last of the houses. The soil is clay, and in good years it holds enough moisture for horticulture even in the dry season—*la contre-saison*—when water levels in the river fall. These city gardens bring in a great deal of money, especially in the hungry months when no vegetables are left from the previous growing season and grain stocks in the circular storage huts have reached their lowest levels. There is always a rich family prepared to pay for scarce vegetables. But the land along the river doesn't belong to those who tend the gardens, and every year they have to wait to see whether their work will be tolerated by the owners, who are often speculators waiting for land prices to rise even higher. A square meter of building land brings in more money than the city gardeners will earn in a lifetime.

A different place, a different development, but comparable all the same: in the mountains above Marbella, in southern Spain, dusty almond trees, barley fields, and dry meadows where sheep grazed have given way to the most lucrative form of land use in southern Europe. Where once in hot summers clumps of grass struggled to survive here and there between the thistles, and the animals squeezed into the shade of a solitary holm oak, bright green fields stretch out, generously irrigated. They are golf courses, which have expunged the last remnants of traditional farming. Here it's not the city itself that's expanding, with houses or factories, but the city dweller, in search of high-value entertainment, a city dweller who may not even come from this area but from far away, sometimes a different part of the world altogether. That's how far the city's tentacles reach. In contrast to Taiwan, here in Andalusia it's not a matter of loss of productivity, because this marginal land never produced very much. The loss lies in encroachment on the old landscape, the disappearance of rural ways of life, the use of scarce water, and the effects of that on horticulture downstream in the river basins. The profits lie in the incomes of the landowners and, to a limited extent, of the former farmers who have found work in the tourist industry.

The development of the relationship between food and farming affects not only rural areas but also cities. Mumbai (formerly Bombay) is a city of more than 12 million inhabitants and an average of more than 35,000 people per square kilometer. At least 10 million of its residents live in slums, in concentrations of more or less improvised houses. Such places have only footpaths, so they're barely accessible by public transit or car.

Every square centimeter is in use, and opportunities for food production are extremely limited. In the dry season water is scarce and almost always heavily polluted; in the rainy season the sewers overflow, and any crops will be washed away. But the need for food and income is so great that attempts are repeatedly made to use land in all kinds of ingenious ways. Rice, lentils, or other sources of carbohydrate cannot be grown on such a small scale, but the residents do manage to produce spinach, onions, and eggplants, and sometimes a little fruit. Here and there a papaya tree is nurtured, crammed between two houses. Young cabbages are planted on the edge of a scrap of land where a house has collapsed, next to a garbage tip. In Dharavi, the largest slum, I've seen eggplant and onion fields no bigger than a bath towel, on either side of the railroad tracks. Every time a train comes past, the women doing the weeding have to jump aside. This kind of horticulture does not produce much, but this is an economy in which every calorie and every rupee counts. In Nairobi's Kibera, the largest slum in Africa, corn grows on the slopes of the waste heaps. In Hong Kong, with 55,000 residents for every square kilometer of rocky terrain, the only chance to grow greens is in a window box.

The Dutch have a long tradition of allotments in and around their cities, scraps of ground made available by local government for "ornamental and secondary crops" or "for pleasure and for supplementary nourishment." Just how much farming and the city touched on each other is clear from the many paintings of Dutch cityscapes in the seventeenth and eighteenth centuries, in which the houses border directly on pastureland. In London countless names recall how the countryside was woven into the city, such as St. Martin-in-the-Fields or Covent Garden, where there were orchards and meadows from the thirteenth century on. During industrialization in the nineteenth century, land was made available to workers and their families in most northern European countries, including Britain, Sweden, and Germany, so they could supplement the food they were able to buy with their wages. I've come upon them in photos in all kind of places in the literature, dating from the late nineteenth and early twentieth century: small strips of ground between blocks of housing, mainly filled with cabbages, with here and there a pecking chicken. The distinction between rural and urban farming—or to be more precise, horticulture—has always been a matter of degree. Even the better-off residents experimented with vegetable plots and orchards in the cities or just outside them.

In Amsterdam the allotments or "people's gardens" (*volkstuinen*) have their origins in an initiative by the Maatschappij tot Nut van het Algemeen ("Society for the Benefit of All"), which dates back to 1784. Land was rented out to workers for a minimal fee, so they could grow their own potatoes. In the twentieth century, clubs of allotment holders appeared all over the place, sometimes reserved for specific target groups, such as dockworkers. In 1917, as food supplies diminished because of the First World War, the Bond van Volkstuinders ("Union of Allotment Holders") was set up. During the Second World War these gardens were again important in supplementing food supplies. Vegetable plots always come back in times of crisis. In the Paris district of Montmartre, vines grew in allotments—Van Gogh painted them. In Russian cities, where the residents always tried to keep a vegetable plot, ideally at their dacha outside the city, such gardens have become popular again in recent decades as incomes fall relentlessly. After 1945, however, the emphasis in the West came increasingly to be on recreational gardening. If beans and tomatoes are still grown it is mainly for the pleasure they give. But here and there real vegetable plots are still found, even in the Netherlands. When out cycling I happened upon one near Amsterdam, at Durgerdam, with neatly tied beans, eggplants, tomatoes, and apple trees. Because of urban expansion, sports fields, new nature reserves, industry, and infrastructure, European allotments are threatened with elimination or are being forced to move, just as they are in India, Niger, or Taiwan.

An abundance of food has made the city possible, and vice versa: because of its buying power, the city prompted the production of abundance. Cities are a direct result of agriculture being so successful that it frees workers to move to urban areas, where they can spend their time on things other than food production. That is the case historically, and it's still the case today. Without food production outside the city boundaries, city dwellers wouldn't survive. Rural areas are not just grain stores but reservoirs of workers, or indeed redundancy pools when the city has an excess of labor.

From the very start of farming, the development of urban communities took place in stages. In the first 3,000–4,000 years the transition was made to sedentary farming. At first the villages were improvised; they then slowly grew and stayed in the same place for longer. Beginning about 7,000 years ago, farmers became able to sustain themselves by systematically harvesting seed for planting the next year and keeping herds of selected animals. Architecture adapted: huts became houses of sun-dried bricks, food stores were built, and fields were irrigated.

The second step, another 2,000 years later, was the result of a combination of "dry" rain-dependent fields and irrigation with water from the Tigris and the Euphrates. Beginning about 5,500 years ago, villages grew into more or less permanent towns. A self-sufficient rural economy gave way to a market economy. Only then was sufficient food grown to sustain an urban, nonagrarian population and to enable the arts, religion, and science to flourish. The development of writing was essential. The spectacular thing about cities, in terms of human evolution, is the exchange of food for other services by unrelated strangers. Whereas in a farming society everyone, or at least every family group, possesses more or less the same skills and produces the same things, urban living alters human relationships radically. Cities are the product of specialization, and they lead to an even greater division of labor, sometimes over huge distances. Such specialization demands trust and a universally accepted means of exchange, so that food can be delivered to city dwellers who are neither farmers nor relatives but unknown craftspersons or soldiers: wheat in exchange for furniture and woven cotton, or for money to buy tools.

In the end, in Mesopotamia, the farming that laid the foundation for cities was destroyed by declining yields. Food shortages arose. Large-scale deforestation led to erosion, and salinization resulted from inexpert irrigation. All this and the wars that followed meant no trace was left of those famous first cities save a few dusty hills scattered with the remains of building rubble and ash. The pattern repeated itself in many places, sometimes made worse by fluctuations in the climate, sometimes by civil strife, sometimes by invasions and infectious disease—but everywhere a decline in food supplies was ultimately decisive.

Because dependence on long supply lines made cities vulnerable, food often needed to be grown in and close to the city rather than only outside it or far away. You could rewrite the history of urbanization as a continual battle between bricks and concrete and edible plants (as well as ornamental plantings). In the course of history the importance of horticulture and farming in or close to the city varied enormously. This is still the case in poor countries, and even in Western economies, whether in the twentieth century or today. The general trend is that urbanization and trade will always quickly introduce food supplies that are less dependent on the city, and vice versa:

trade blockades or the decline of cities usually cause a return of farming and horticulture to the city. This happened during both world wars and not only in Europe. Even the United States saw the return of growing one's own food. In 1944–1945, 40 percent of American vegetables came from specially laid out Victory Gardens. This sounds rather more spectacular than it was, because the range of vegetables grown, mainly carrots and cabbage, was far smaller than it is today.

In spatial terms the city is the visible outcome of a thousand-year process of separation between production and consumption, even though the splitting apart of town and countryside happened in fits and starts, and they remained interwoven to some extent, especially in the megacities in poor countries that have expanded only recently. Toward the end of the Roman Empire, Rome fell to its ruin partly because supplies of grain from North Africa were interrupted. In the Middle Ages, Rome was so depopulated that goats grazed on the Forum. Conversely, the famous food markets on the Campo de' Fiori in Rome today are on what used to be meadows, as the name suggests.

So we shouldn't imagine urban growth as a continual process. In about 1700 a third of the Dutch population lived in towns, but as the eighteenth century went on the urban population declined to such an extent that houses were demolished to make way for vegetable plots and pasture. In the late eighteenth century, Middelburg lost a quarter of its inhabitants within a generation. Residents of the city were woken by cocks crowing. This was followed by a period of ruralization of the economy, and farmland became a source of wealth again. Perhaps in areas of demographic shrinkage, today's residential areas will eventually become not just parks but also vegetable plots.

City and country, farming and food are opposites, and they complement each other. The city is home to people who need food but don't grow it, people who provide labor but don't deploy it in farming. The city is the source of demand, with buying power, money paid for food that can be invested partly in agriculture. So there's a flow of material and financial resources between city and countryside. The material flow consists of food on its way to the city and with it nutrients. Along with food, soil nutrients enter the city, such as nitrogen and phosphate, so the land is gradually depleted. At the same time the density of the urban population produces a concentration of waste and manure, in other words, soil nutrients. In the period prior to the invention of artificial fertilizer in the mid-nineteenth century, it was of crucial importance to return that manure and other waste to rural areas. If manure were not returned, the countryside would suffer a net loss and the city a surplus, with unpleasant consequences for both. This imbalance is still a problem in poor countries. Until recently "night soil" (feces) was collected in China, for example, as a thing of value.

In the densely populated west of the Netherlands, manure and urban waste have been a problem ever since the Middle Ages. Between there and the higher, sandy land in the middle of the country, manure boats plied back and forth along the inland waterways. It was not a matter of human manure alone; horses, for centuries the most important means of transportation, produced millions of kilograms of manure every day in large cities, such as New York and London. In 1894 *The Times* predicted that by 1950 the streets of London would have disappeared under three meters of horse dung. A disaster of unprecedented proportions was in prospect. At that point no one could imagine that an entirely new solution was at hand: the replacement of the horse by the car.

Food waste is an increasing problem in urban areas. Rich cities produce more garbage, but as so often with relationships between wealth and environmental pressure, the amount of waste falls again at a certain level of income. The megacities that will produce the highest percentage of food waste in 2025 are all in poor countries: Mumbai, Delhi, Karachi, Dhaka, Calcutta, and Lagos. More than 45 percent of the food that enters those cities remains uneaten. Kinshasa comes in first at 70 percent. The cause is mainly inadequate storage and distribution.

———

Peri-urban developments almost always occur in fertile areas, with good access by road and river, where the soils are fertile and there's enough moisture in the form of rain or river water. This makes sense, because these places can best feed a concentrated population. The expansion of cities therefore generally happens at the expense of farmland, as can be seen most clearly in large cities, including Manila, Shanghai, Bangkok, Lagos, and Mexico City, where the city's infrastructure is overwhelming land previously used to grow food. Between the concrete pillars of hastily constructed ring roads lie vegetable plots, rice paddies, and small orchards. In Bangkok and Dhaka, fishermen stand patiently on the riverbanks, while traffic thunders by on the viaducts above their heads.

Agriculture is threatened not only by the disappearance of fields and waterways but also indirectly by the destruction of mangrove swamps and lagoons. In Ho Chi Minh City or Abidjan, such swamps are home to many bird species that feed on the insects and slugs that threaten the harvest. Drainage of the swamps for building purposes damages both nature and the food supply.

Most conflicts between city and country are a result of the enormous speed with which cities, especially in poor countries, are developing, the lack of planning and supervision of that growth, as well as indifference and disdain toward farmers, who are regarded as less civilized than city people. It's true that we shouldn't exaggerate the amount of space cities take up, as they cover no more than 1 or 2 percent of the total surface of the earth, but that small proportion of land will soon be home to two-thirds of humanity, which must be fed by just a handful of farmers who are responsible for a considerable proportion of the remaining 98 percent (which of course includes wilderness, unusable land, open pit mines, and forestry plantations). The empty areas are usually empty because they are infertile or inaccessible, and we want to leave them untouched as far as possible.

You might say that over the course of history, towns and cities have always had the character of farms, markets, and eating places, in varying proportions. The city as a farm has been pushed into the background over the past few centuries, but in the West attention is turning to it again. This is undoubtedly a reaction to the high degree of urbanization and the sense city dwellers have of being a long way from the countryside. Whereas untainted food and clean water were scarce commodities in the city in previous centuries (as they still are in the megacities of poorer countries), in the twenty-first century healthy, varied, and sustainably produced and distributed food is central. For a long time the countryside suffered at the hands of powerful cities: farmers were at best neglected, more often exploited, to feed the city. Every dictatorship—including the most atrocious in recent times, such as those of Stalin, Pol Pot, and Mao—has tried to squeeze the countryside dry to maximize food supplies for workers in the cities. Since the liberalization of world trade, beginning in the 1990s, the world's abundance has piled up in the modern city. By 2050 more than 6 billion people will live in cities. In Europe as much as 90 percent of the population will be urban. The city's functions, as farm, market, and eating place, will change to a breath-taking degree once again.

The Belly of the City

Émile Zola called it "the belly of Paris": Les Halles Centrales, that immense complex in the oldest part of the city that at its height covered 10 hectares. The first market halls date back to the twelfth century, and for 800 years all kinds of buildings were in continual use there for the trading of food. The culmination was reached in the mid-nineteenth century with the building of the new Halles, a series of cathedral-shaped halls in glass and iron with courtyards and squares, where everything was delivered during the night: butter from Normandy, mussels from Brittany, coal, live cows, and round golden cheeses—everything that Paris was consuming in ever greater quantities. From the beginning to their recent demolition, the Halles were a perpetual building project, subjected to increasingly strict regulations, especially regarding hygienic slaughter and the disposal of waste water. When in the 1970s it was recognized that the rapidly expanding city could no longer be supplied from its center, fierce debates ensued before the Halles were finally demolished and re-located to the edge of town.

City dwellers are by definition unable to supply their own food directly, or at least not enough of it. If there is any room to grow food, then it's a matter of a garden, a few small domesticated animals (such as chickens), and occasionally a spot of fishing. At best this can supplement the diet, and even this level of production is achieved only by a small minority. Almost all calories and animal proteins for growing cities come from out-side their boundaries. The cultivation of carbohydrates, with such crops as wheat or rice, and the production of animal proteins simply require too much space. It usually cannot take place even close to the city.

Cities therefore require food supply lines. Some can be very short, but often they are long, and many connect different continents. Just how dependent the present-day city is on other places is illustrated by the vast transportations of Brazilian soy to Chinese megacities as chicken feed. This dependence is nothing new, incidentally. Rome depended on grain from the rest of the Mediterranean region, while medieval Amsterdam was reliant on the Baltic trade.

Food is delivered to the urban consumer from dealers rather than directly from producers. The intermediate step may be the street seller, the grocer, the market, or its modern reincarnation the supermarket. They all buy food from processing companies, hardly ever straight from the farmer. Most of these complex links in the chain are invisible to the people of the city. Trading in food takes place day and night, as sales and distribution are not limited to the hours of daylight; in fact shops and markets need to be supplied at night when the streets are less busy. In Asia the liveliest markets start trading when darkness falls. In Islamic countries the evening market is the central focus of the city during Ramadan.

The sale of food on the street is as old as the city itself. What's new is that because of longer and longer supermarket opening hours, there is hardly a pause in food trading. In some cities, not only in the United States but also in Asia, food can be bought twenty-four hours a day. The introduction of Sunday shopping and the growing number of outlets have made impulse purchases increasingly easy in Europe as well. In many cities across the world, the larger shops are open sixteen hours a day, seven days a week, far longer than a generation ago.

The food trade itself is extremely diverse and always has been. In the Middle Ages markets and stalls were in covered porches (*portici*) on the ground floor in front of the houses, as seen today in Bern and Bologna. All our cities still have local markets, covered or not, some with permanent stalls or counters, others set up from scratch every time. Street stalls were originally intended to sell food to migrants, travelers, or workers who were far from home in daytime, and they still function in this way today, which is why they are often close to stations and traffic intersections. In many European inner cities in the late nineteenth century, open air markets were replaced with covered market halls, for reasons of sanitation and to channel the influx of people and vehicles. In Spain and Portugal these *mercadillos* were often tiled, sometimes with attractive designs and depictions. The interiors and exteriors of market buildings reflected their importance as meeting places. Until the mid-twentieth century Western European food shops usually specialized, selling either bread, dry grains, spices and beans, meat and poultry, fish, or dairy products. In smaller population centers milk was delivered to homes until very recently.

Unfortunately many local markets and independent shops disappeared from city centers in the 1970s and 1980s as a result of the expansion of offices and commercial districts. The number of independent grocers, greengrocers, butchers, and bakers is declining everywhere. A concentration of well-off consumers and hence the presence of a potential market does not mean therefore that food supplies in the city will develop satisfactorily of their own accord. The supermarket is not a paradise everywhere. Food supplies are precarious in fast-growing suburbs, not just in slums. Shops may be few, and the range of goods limited.

The United States has notorious food deserts, neighborhoods that lack shops providing affordable fresh and healthy produce. There you find only large grocery chains selling convenience food like pizza, cakes, ice cream, and chips. Such food is high in calories because of its fat and sugar content, and it has little nutritional value, but it sells rapidly to overworked mothers and to young people who have never learned to cook. As a result there is no demand for fresh vegetables; people have neither the time nor the knowledge to prepare a proper meal. The poorer a city district in the United States is, the greater the likelihood that its diners and supermarkets sell mostly fast food. In the south of Los Angeles three-quarters of the restaurants sell fast food (and even in richer districts the proportion is an astonishing 40 percent). This overabundance of fast food is leading to so many health problems that the city has decided not to allow any more hamburger, taco, or pizza restaurants in areas where a high proportion of the population is overweight. The reactions to that decision have not been entirely positive; the government should concentrate on the real problems, people say, and not ban the food that's especially valued by poorer ethnic groups. Research also shows that eating habits are little influenced by the proximity of fresh, healthy food. Availability, even on the street corner, is not sufficient to change behavior.

The lack of fresh food is not an American problem alone. In Australian, Canadian, and European cities too, there's a risk that healthy alternatives will become hard to find because there are too few supermarkets, while the small shops sell mainly prepackaged convenience food or are extremely expensive. The only small shops that can survive the battle with the supermarkets are delicatessens selling vegetables, cheese, bread, and pastries.

Despite relentless modernization, there is still room for street sellers and open-air markets. In busy urban areas like New York's Manhattan, street vendors, often recent immigrants from South America, stand on every street corner selling wares that vary according to the time of day. Even in the Netherlands, with its many supermarkets, fish stalls can be found here and there, and the ice cream seller comes by on a bicycle. In every Asian city you can find a wide range of hot noodle dishes to eat outdoors until late at night. The vegetables are sliced on the street and cooked in a wok on a cart, which is also equipped for washing up. The customer stands, or sits on a plastic stool.

In European cities sales in the open air are declining. I saw that very clearly in Rome, where the small food shops, the *alimentari,* and the little markets of three or four stalls in the inner city were slowly being pushed out by the supermarkets. Everyone regretted this, but when I questioned them, all my neighbors said it was an inevitable development. The little shops had insufficient turnover, there were bad patches on the tomatoes, the salad was wilted, the bread not fresh, and the ricotta had a crust of orange mold that wasn't supposed to be there. The children of grocers and street traders don't want to take on the hard life of their parents. No, they were happy to shop at the supermarkets with their range of fresh vegetables, bread, and fish and their fixed working hours for the staff, who were at least paid, even if not very much. The same is happening with mom and pop stores in the United States. My local greengrocer in Amsterdam will be retiring soon and has no one to take over the shop.

It looks like an unavoidable development: the transition from family businesses and street traders to larger shops run by staff who have no connection either with the customer or with the food they're selling. But along with better quality and availability comes a loss, an unraveling of the social fabric of the city. We are also losing the sensations that enrich city life. Who can forget the smell of roasted chestnuts wafting toward them in Paris in winter? Food at markets and in roadside stalls appeals to all our senses, if mostly to our sense of smell. That too has changed. The aromas we now encounter in the average shopping street are those of fried chicken and pizza, if not the used oil of a shop selling French fries. Still, the stench of the waste from the markets and abattoirs of the past must have been considerable. That direct confrontation with food at markets and stalls or in open market halls did bring us far closer to what food actually is than the supermarket does, where almost everything is prepackaged and odorless. It's typical of them that supermarket chains have started putting out the smell of fresh bread to mimic that direct sensation and increasingly display their vegetables on open shelves rather than in plastic bags. The chance to touch or even just to see food appeals to our deepest desires, to our longing for unlimited variety, for plenty, for an abundance that seems to emerge right in front of us. No one is left unmoved by the sight of beautifully stacked colorful wares, such as you see in many places at markets in tropical countries: deep-pink papayas, purple potatoes, red onions next to white garlic, artful little mountains of turmeric and ground red pepper—just as no one remains indifferent when faced with the tempting abundance of cheeses and sauces in the average French supermarket. In a Dutch supermarket I recently counted almost thirty different kinds of tomato sauce.

The diversity of food available in cities has increased partly because of immigration, both in cities in rich countries in temperate climates and in cities in formerly developing countries. It's a phenomenon seen in all eras; migration changes eating patterns. You only have to think of American cuisine, a combination of Eastern European, Italian, Irish, and French elements with one crucial Native American ingredient: corn. Yet what is happening now is something special, of a quite different scale and speed. Traditional urban food markets have undergone major change as a result of the arrival of migrants with their own food preferences. At the Albert Cuyp Market in Amsterdam you can buy cassava, yardlong beans, and sweet potatoes as well as coriander and mint. All of it fresh. Chinese, Turkish, and Moroccan shops are flourishing, not just because of their ethnic clientele but also because the indigenous inhabitants of the large European cities are eating more and more dishes from other parts of the world. Owners of Moroccan and Turkish shops do not have too many problems handing businesses on to their children, and they often have their own family capital, which ensures their independence. In Brussels, close to the Gare du Midi, a real souk has emerged, a covered North-African market.

The arrival of shopkeepers from North Africa has had an unforeseen effect on the wholesale market by increasing demand for such vegetables as tomatoes, eggplants and onions. The growth of tourism has also changed European diets in ways no one could have expected. People who eat couscous or pilaf on holiday want to try it at home as well, encouraged by restaurants and cookery columns. Conversely, in tropical countries food from temperate climates is becoming dominant, especially cheap carbohydrates, such as potatoes, pasta, and bread, but also apples and even the ingredients for imported dietary components, such as breakfast cereals. Although such Western food is mainly for those who have traveled or studied abroad, the effect on the rest of the population should not be underestimated. Sugary buns can be found in almost all poor urban districts, even in countries where no wheat is grown.

The metaphor of the market as the belly of the city is still applicable today. It's not just a matter of the machinery, the city's digestion, including waste. Émile Zola used the term partly to depict a world where everything revolves around food and gluttony, abundance and fullness, and their opposites, hunger and poverty. Now that hunger is unknown to more and more people, or only as a memory, intemperance and greed are gaining the upper hand in the unrelenting effervescence of the urban economy. Far more than the countryside, the city is the place of food plenty, and at the same time the place where the contrasts between rich and poor are at their most distressing: mansions right above slums, as in Rio de Janeiro; filthy street children begging at the exits to luxury supermarkets; and illegal immigrants searching the dumpsters outside supermarkets in the middle of the night.

Daily Temptation: The Supermarket

It seems New York has a supermarket called Garden of Eden, a paradise where the consumer is encouraged to spend by the most tempting produce, romantic music, and smiling staff. There could be no better image of the supermarket as paradise on the street corner: temptation and abundance in one. Never before have so many people had access to so many diverse food items from all parts of the world, all the year round and for such low prices. Every year, an estimated 17,000 new products are added to the stock of supermarkets. The supermarket phenomenon is rapidly penetrating even the poorest countries. There are said to be some 20 million supermarkets in the world. Although everyone knows the names of the biggest companies, such as Ahold, Carrefour, Tesco, and Walmart, they represent only 10 percent of the world market; the rest are regionally and locally important chains. In the Netherlands around three-quarters of food is bought in supermarkets, and ten supermarket chains have three-quarters of the market. They regularly become caught up in price wars, despite high commodity prices.

"Ethically responsible" and organic supermarkets are increasingly successful as well.

Although supermarkets are slowly expanding their range of nonfood items, that particular piece of jargon only serves to confirm that they are primarily places for food shopping. Super-market: the food market that goes beyond the boundaries of ordinary life. In the supermarket the food is there for the taking, no longer behind a barrier in the form of a shopkeeper who serves you, or a counter with goods stacked up behind it. First you're encouraged to take all kinds of things from the shelves, with the most expensive products at eye level, and only later do you see a sum that you can trace back to the individual food items by studying the cash register receipt. The separation of desire from price is almost complete. There is no longer any indication of the costs involved in the production of each of those foods. Even the vegetables from the fields have no trace of mud on them. The farmer who got up at five to milk the cows is at best reduced to a romantic picture on the carton.

In the view of critical consumers, supermarkets are often the powerful villains that push unhealthy and expensive food on us and exploit farmers. The role of supermarket chains is indeed crucial; they occupy a position between farmers who produce commodities, the processing industry that produces the food, and the consumer. As the largest and often the only buyers, they determine not only the price farmers will receive but also the strict specifications with which products must comply. The globalization of the past twenty years and the takeovers of companies that have flowed from it have led to the emergence of larger and larger conglomerates of wholesalers that span more than whole continents. Rising commodity prices put these large concerns under pressure, given that power now seems to be shifting to the suppliers. Sometimes these are farm cooperatives, but more often buyers come between the two, who themselves squeeze the farmers. On the other side of the supermarkets are consumers who, especially in times of economic crisis, balk at price rises and show barely any loyalty to brands or to shops.

In this complex economic game some international wholesalers have gone through a huge about-face in the past decade or so. Aware of their crucial role, they have put several principles into practice in the areas of healthy eating, food safety, animal welfare, sustainability, fair trade (including working conditions in the food processing industry), climate change, and relationships with local communities. Sometimes they have done this in cooperation with other wholesale chains and with their suppliers, sometimes as the single dominant player. Repeated attempts have been made to render these good intentions concrete and measurable, perhaps by publicly stating the reduction of CO_2 emissions per square meter of shop space or the percentage of healthy and certified products being offered. One good example is the fitting of refrigerated shelves with doors or see-through plastic strips to keep the cold in, and another is the introduction of LED lighting. The reason for this turnaround is not altruistic; instead it comes from more long-term thinking and a determination to combine sustainability and cost reduction. Ultimately, supermarkets gain nothing by having unhealthy customers who buy too many unhealthy products. Which is why many large supermarkets, in cooperation with governments, are now associating themselves with programs aimed at preventing childhood obesity.

Most supermarkets also encourage their staff to adopt a healthy and responsible lifestyle. It turns out that companies that have socially responsible aims and act in socially responsible ways—and make this obvious in their annual reports and other publicity—attract more motivated and better qualified personnel. This does not apply to shelf stockers in temporary jobs. Between them and the permanent staff there is still a wide gap, and they have little contact with the notion of responsible enterprise.

One of the most engaging things I do with my students from time to time is to go on a supermarket safari. As on a real safari, the aim is to observe without prejudice, to look straight through the "undergrowth" (the shelves and the packaging) without disturbing the ecosystem (the customers and staff). The quarry—food and its supply chain—allows itself to be caught only by those who have plenty of patience and good powers of observation. Those who know what to look for will find their eyes popping out of their heads. A multitude of questions: how much diversity is there in a product group, such as apples, milk, or bread? (In Amsterdam we counted more than sixty kinds of bread or related items such as French toast.) How many different vegetables are sold? Does a choice between forty kinds of jam serve any purpose, and in whose interest is that degree of diversity? Do diversity and temptation coincide?

It is remarkable how vast and varied the range of products in an average Western supermarket is, and how quickly it changes to reflect new trends. Not only are organic and fair trade products freely available, there are many products that were not present in such quantities until recently: dozens of kinds of dry and fresh pasta and pasta sauces, and all sorts of nuts and tropical fruit. Certain things are disappearing, too, such as glacé cherries and canned pineapple. What are the most expensive and the cheapest products? How many truly unprocessed products are there? Where do the products come from, and is there any relationship between price and distance? There turn out to be three types of food on sale: ingredients for home cooking (such as spaghetti, bread, and cheese), ready meals (like salads, or spaghetti with sauce that only needs warming up) and food for eating on the go that can be consumed immediately, sometimes even before you reach the checkout register (including snack bars and yogurt drinks).

Again and again the question arises of what the right amount of information is for the customer, what people should know or want to know. This information goes beyond simple facts like the caloric value and fat content, or relatively vague concepts, such as "ecological," "organic," or "local," which most people would have difficultly defining. At a minimum you should know what the origin is, and the composition, the nutritional value and shelf life. It would be good to know about the packaging and production methods. Consumers often have few answers to simple questions, such as: what is harvested at this time of year? Why is it strange to find apples in a European or American supermarket in May?

Developments in the sale of food can be summed up as more diversity, more information, more demands, and more goals. The times when large food retailers only needed to keep their shareholders happy has gone for good. Customers expect ethical considerations, even if most of them choose products based purely on price. They like to buy things in "good" shops. As a result, supermarkets have to cooperate more than before with governments and nongovernmental organizations, and not least with consumers. A supermarket that wants to sell animal-friendly meat needs the support of the government and of animal welfare organizations, which between them have set the norms (for example, the amount of space per pig and the ban on castration) and monitor compliance. In response to the wish of some consumers to buy "honest and fair" products, most supermarkets now have such categories as "free range" or "fair trade." Suppliers, such as dairies and farmers, need to adjust to this new reality. For pork it may mean that the animals not only get more space but also are fed only locally produced food, or at least no genetically modified soy.

Most supermarkets sell three types of products: the famous top brands, their own home brand, and a cheap brand (usually displayed on the bottom shelf). The producers of the top brands set their own norms, so the supermarket simply has to decide whether to buy them, but these brands are only a small part of the turnover. Home brands are crucial. Therein lie the big differences, although we may wonder how much attention buyers pay to the norms selected. The economic crisis has led to a shift toward cheaper versions of products that generally do not meet the new goals concerning the environment or animal welfare, or meet them only in part.

Because of the great volumes they represent and the number and frequency of customer visits, supermarkets hold the key to food consumption. They offer abundance on every street corner, to such a degree that supermarket stress is a real phenomenon: the tension produced by an overwhelming range of choice. Buying is an emotional business, especially in the case of food.

At the same time, supermarkets also have it in their power to make consumers aware of the instinctive behavior that surrounds food buying. One telling example is that if consumers are asked whether they want a receipt rather than automatically having one printed for them, they have to think about what is really a small decision. The consequences cannot be dismissed lightly. In the Netherlands alone, not printing receipts saves 50,000 kilometers of paper strip annually.

Something similar applies to the seemingly trivial issue of plastic carrier bags, the supermarkets' bestselling product. Because the price is so tiny, shoppers repeatedly ask for new bags. In Spain the government has forced supermarkets to stop giving them away almost for free but to charge a reasonable price, which has led to a decline in their use. That is a better approach than switching to paper bags. Most studies show that even if they are made of paper certified as being from sustainable forests, paper bags are little different in their environmental impact from plastic bags. Best, as ever, is to encourage the shopper to recycle, whether paper bags or plastic, by setting up collection points in the shops for excess used bags. More expensive bags made of plant fibers such as jute or cotton with an environmentally friendly appearance do indeed last longer, but even the production of these fibers damages the environment, if only because fields of cotton or jute are not being used for food, and quite a lot of water is needed for their cultivation. Then the bags have to be transported long distances, to say nothing of the chemicals used in the cultivation and production of cotton.

Not just in their choice of products, packaging, and bags, but in other ways too supermarkets affect the behavior and consciousness of consumers. Because of strict rules of sanitation, food that no longer complies with shelf-life rules (food past its sell-by date) cannot be given to the homeless, as it is in some countries, or used as cattle feed. As far as possible it is converted into green energy by fermentation, or simply burned, while the packaging is recycled. Consumers are rarely able to distinguish between situations in which consumption after the sell-by date is not hazardous (as with dry pasta) and those in which the product really should be thrown out (like moldy bread). This is a dilemma: young people dispose of things sooner than necessary, while older people keep food too long, to avoid wasting anything.

Anyone who has ever seen a documentary about how much food is disposed of in rich societies will surely have been astonished by the negligence of modern humans. In rich countries, 100–150 kilograms of food per person per year is thrown away. In Africa the figure is 6 kilograms, at the level of the consumer at least. There losses take place before sale to the consumer—after harvest, during transportation, and in storage. Bread is the category in which the most waste takes place, because modern consumers cannot imagine buying or even eating yesterday's bread. This is very much a dilemma of modern times. A great deal is thrown away because we want to reduce the risk of tainted food to almost nil. Sour milk—common until recently—is now rare because of better handling at the dairy and during transportation. We still throw out so much milk simply because the huge diversity of the food available makes planning difficult. However good its consumer research may be and no matter how effectively it steers demand by means of special offers and advertising, the supermarket cannot know for sure how many people are going to eat pizza, cauliflower, or steak on a given evening. The consumer shuts his or her eyes to waste as firmly as to the way lambs are transformed into chops. We don't want to throw away food individually or collectively, but we do demand perfectly safe and fresh food and as much choice as possible. These aims are simply irreconcilable, a fact that most supermarket shoppers prefer to forget.

––––––––

Supermarkets reflect essential changes in the food chain over recent decades, in a positive and a negative sense. For consumers it remains hard to say what the best options are. Buying food always serves different aims, and consumers have their own priorities. One wants to shop quickly and looks for food that's cheap and quick to prepare; another hesitates and wonders whether organic is better or whether soy would be better than meat. Animal proteins are the trickiest category for many reasons. So much is involved, from animal welfare to world trade, from health and shelf life to associations with "real" food. One and the same consumer reacts differently on weekends than during the week.

A good example of a dilemma on a small scale is salad greens. As conscious consumers should we buy prepackaged, washed salad or unwrapped lettuces? Prewashed leaves sealed in plastic look like a bad choice, but it's not that simple. They don't last quite as long as a whole lettuce, but washing in the factory uses far less water than washing in an individual kitchen, and most consumers will throw a considerable portion of a lettuce away. Another often-heard objection, that a head of lettuce from the supermarket has no flavor compared to one from the farmer's market, has been disproven by blind testing with tasting panels. So is it the lack of diversity that critics deplore? No, not any longer. The modern supermarket is characterized by diversity, more than the traditional greengrocer's, where turnover is less and the risk of decay greater. In the average supermarket in most of Western and southern Europe, you can buy oak leaf lettuce, iceberg lettuce, wild and cultivated arugula, red lettuce, lamb's lettuce, and plenty more besides. Shopping is a tricky business.

The City as a Public Eating Place

It's not the supermarket alone that looks like paradise, with its effortless abundance. In more and more cities in Europe, North America, Australia, and South America, and in shopping malls for the rich in emerging economies in Asia, leisure zones have developed where eating, relaxing on a café terrace, and shopping are closely connected. Entire shopping streets and squares have been made pedestrian friendly, starting with those iconic Halles in Paris, where you can now wander around the Forum des Halles, and the pavement cafés are crammed from the first day of spring sunshine. From Seattle to Berlin and Istanbul, from Bogota to Prague and Bangkok, from Tokyo to Taipei, the middle classes gather under the umbrellas, and whenever necessary the outdoor heating is ready and waiting. These zones, playgrounds for the upper and middle classes and young people, are the closest thing to a paradise, in which every imaginable kind of food is waiting to be eaten and can be had almost for a song.

The Mediterranean culture of pavement cafés is flourishing in city centers where a generation earlier it would never have occurred to anyone to sit outside, let alone to eat there. In some town centers practically all you can do is eat, with one outlet after another, fast food restaurants alternating with snack bars, sandwich shops, and bars for coffee and fruit juice. In cities like Montreal where it's too cold in winter to walk outside, let alone to sit or eat, underground food halls and food courts have been set up with multiple eating places. Those who refuse to allow themselves to sit down will find countless places in almost every city where they can buy food to be consumed on the move or while driving.

––––––––––

Food has become a pastime. The middle classes of the world have a boundless desire for entertainment and distraction. One of the most astonishing aspects of modern city living is therefore that eating and drinking go on continually, all over the place. The temptation to eat urges itself on us as a result of the long opening times of shops and restaurants and the increasing number of choices available. Snack bars and convenience food outlets match the trend by diversifying, selling shawarma and falafel. The hamburger joint now draws the whole family, even the vegetarians among them, with its specially adapted range of offerings, its toys, and its cheerful decor, but later the same place becomes the terrain of young people who feel like a greasy snack after a night out. Food is play, play is food, and everything is decor. Convenience is decisive. More than a third of the total amount Dutch people spend on food goes on ready meals and eating out. Open kitchens in restaurants and take-aways show their wares as never before. Bakeries and butcher's shops become catering outlets with hot displays and steaming pans of soup. Doors and windows are rebuilt into glass serving hatches wide open to the street, so that there's no longer any barrier between consumer and product. Come and see and smell and taste. And above all: buy!

With the growth of wealthy modern town centers, even in developing countries, eating as a social phenomenon is gaining new dimensions. We're far removed from the hungry factory workers of the nineteenth century in their dilapidated housing, and from their modern equivalents in equally wretched concrete blocks. We're even further removed from peasants barely able to survive to the next harvest, and from beggars, or children who live on rubbish dumps. In the urban domain of the global middle class we eat in public—to look at passers-by and be seen by them, to display our wealth, our latest fashions, our most attractive purchases, and the company we keep while acquiring it all. Public space has become a public eating place. Those who don't talk, chew, and those who do talk chew too. Where there are no pavement cafés and restaurant terraces, or where they are too expensive, young people sit on curbs and steps or in parks. In rich countries the city has become a snacking paradise. This very often results in filthy streets, overflowing garbage bins, and plagues of rats, although not in Tokyo or Vienna.

Life in the city changes what we eat and how we eat it. Without urbanization and suburbs there would be no hamburgers or hot dogs, no snacks such as grilled chicken legs, not even fries. Without a class of students and young professionals there would be no fast food or ready meals. Convenience food is intended for people in a hurry, on the way somewhere, and that's what we all are, those who work and commute, but also families with their double careers, countless after-school activities for the children and ambitions for personal development. Fast food is often associated with the low-income classes in the city, although it's eaten far more widely than that. There could be no better symbol of the Dutch urban food culture than the famous Rotterdam-Turkish "barbershop," a horrifying mix of meat, chips, cheese, sauces, and salad. But even fast food is no longer homogeneous—even though most of it is still a variation on greasy and calorie-rich themes—despite the symbolic slice of tomato or onion. Fast food has acquired new dimensions under the influence of the choosy rich and the health devotees. With its vegetarian and low-calorie options it's coming back into favor among ambitious urban professionals. The rise of the soy burger with low-fat fries (which absorb less fat during frying) is imminent.

The great majority of convenience food remains unhealthy, however. That quick bite means consuming a large number of calories in a very short time, despite attempts to reduce the salt and fat content. The liquid calories in soft drinks and fruit juices, which are usually high in sugar, play their part. This is a pattern of consumption that has become a way of life, especially among younger generations, and it will not be quick to disappear. Those alone in the city want to be like others and not feel lonely. Fast food is proof that you've become a city dweller. It helps overcome the heterogeneity of a city's residents, offering the uniformity they cherish. Those who feel undervalued for whatever reason and try to emulate the richness of the shopping streets don't necessarily want to spend what little money they have on sensible food. Those who are relatively poor may seek comfort and identification with others. Large amounts of cheap calories from fries, tubs of dessert, and ready-made pasta dishes are a solution, sometimes against the consumers' better judgment. Changing this will require more than information or a supply of healthy or even subsidized food in every neighborhood.

The city brings out the best and the worst in *Homo sapiens* the eater. The onward march of convenience food culture does not alter the fact that without the city there would be no Michelin-starred restaurants or culinary tours de force. After all, the court culture that once encouraged haute cuisine has all but disappeared. The number of restaurants and cafés has grown considerably in all countries, although we have no precise figures. Along with the famous chains, which without exception have been attempting to double the number of outlets they own, the number of top restaurants is growing. A cautious estimate suggests that in the rich economies there is almost one restaurant, bar, or café for every 220 residents (if you count every place where you can sit down to eat and drink) and one for every 600-plus residents in low-income countries.

Catering is an important landing stage for migrants, because it offers both work for the uneducated or barely educated and opportunities for young entrepreneurs. This is one of the reasons local cuisine has become so varied everywhere over recent decades. An additional reason is that new migrants are often from tropical or subtropical regions, and they have brought a very different cuisine with them than the European migrants took to the United States. After the end of the Vietnam war, refugees referred to as "boat people" arrived in France and not long afterward the rest of Europe and America. They started restaurants, not unlike the Italians in Little Italy, Manhattan, in the late nineteenth century or the Mexicans now. The Chinese in the Netherlands started out cooking for their compatriots, but after Indonesian independence Dutch colonials returned, and the number of "Indonesian" restaurants grew rapidly. Today's skilled migrants often choose to maintain their own traditions and seem unwilling to adjust to the Western diet. Whereas Norwegian, Irish, and Polish migrants in nineteenth-century New York tried to adapt as much as possible, the Hispanics, Asians, or Africans in Europe and North America have no need to do so. Because of much improved transportation, they can easily buy all those exotic products familiar to them in markets all over the city. The indigenous population takes full advantage of this. There is no better example than the replacement in Europe of canned pineapple by fresh, or, even better, slices of pineapple prepared the same morning in West Africa.

So it comes about that for anyone who pays attention (and can ignore the aroma of fast food), the streets of Europe no longer smell of sauerkraut and sausage but of coriander and garlic. The almost unnoticed changes in our diets represent the permanent success of the multicultural society of the twentieth century, here and everywhere in the world where cities have absorbed immigrants. Nothing remains of the smell of boiled cabbage. In the Netherlands all this started with Chinese food, followed by French and Italian cuisine, then Greek, Spanish, and Indian, and now there is nothing too outlandish to be found there: South African, Mongolian, Peruvian, Filipino, or Ethiopian. What applies to the Netherlands is even more true of countries elsewhere in Europe that once had a whole portfolio of colonies, such as the United Kingdom and France, or that received many immigrants, such as Spain and Italy. The globalization of our tastes seems complete.

Meanwhile a remarkable paradox is emerging. While the attitude of many people toward immigrants sometimes resembles barely concealed hostility, there nevertheless seems to be increasing adventurousness in the culinary field. The question is whether this is a matter of broad cultural curiosity (or rather a touristic adventure and a desire for novelty) or simply the temptation of an increasingly diverse range of options. Plus universal laziness, as much of that international cuisine has been transformed into its urban fast food version: falafel, tacos, wraps, or sushi.

Despite various countermovements, such as slow food, whole food, and the import of many exotic ingredients and dishes, the paradox is that the globalization of taste leads to uniformity. Even though the diversity of foods available seems to be growing and all kinds of items are on the market, city dwellers increasingly choose to satisfy their daily needs with a limited range of convenience foods. International studies show that pizza, pasta, and chicken are the favorite or at least the most appealing foods of almost everyone on earth, with an important place reserved for comparable categories, such as lasagne, spaghetti, and hamburgers. This is not to deny that many people like eating red meat if they can afford it, especially in Russia and South America. The attraction of Western food in poor countries is undoubtedly a matter of status or, if you like, a regrettable outcome of colonialism, or the result of clever marketing by hamburger chains, or more likely a combination of all these things and price. Pizza, sushi, pasta, chicken drumsticks, and tortillas fit perfectly with youth culture: ready to eat, of international appeal, and relatively cheap. Variety is provided not by the dish itself but by the sauces and spices that enable us to eat more or less the same thing every day. The global market for snacks is still growing and will continue to do so as long as urban populations are increasing, even though I do expect to see an irreversible shift toward more healthy or at least low-calorie snacks.

Food and Green Places as Urban Counterculture

Despite this global trend, resistance to urban food culture—with its unbridled consumption and laziness—is growing: resistance to the artificial gulf between city resident and farmer, the stench of oily snacks, the straitjacket of the supermarkets, and what is seen as standard fare from the food factories. For some, especially the rich middle classes, the globalization of our cuisine is kept in balance by a countermovement favoring "the past" and "local," black salsify and Texel lamb. This is the clientele of the specialized restaurants, the farmer's markets, and gourmet shops, mainly focused on individual pleasure and barely if at all on social action.

But there is also more radical resistance that harks back to the counterculture of the 1970s, with its mild or less mild anticapitalist slant. The way in which our food gets to us, by means of supermarkets and long supply chains, is to this movement proof of the perversity of Western consumer society. This resistance takes all kinds of forms. It comes, for example, from those who steal along the streets at night and fire darts holding flower and vegetable seeds over walls. Guerrilla gardening, they are proud to call it. They clear away rubble and lay fresh soil on waste ground or in unused containers; they weed and they water. With true disregard for danger, they hoe busy roundabouts, or the land under bridges and along railroad tracks. No flat surface is safe from them. They plant everywhere, using buckets and cans if there is no soil. Gardeners pop up as revolutionaries in the city, in New York and Vancouver but also in Melbourne, Munich, and the cities of the United Kingdom. The very fact that what they are doing is illegal (because the land is not their property) makes the work attractive to activists. In their illegality they seem remarkably like the women of Mumbai or Niamey who garden on just as precarious a basis, without any rights to the soil, although for the latter it really is a matter of survival.

————————

The radical counterculture doesn't limit itself to production but extends its reach—how could it be otherwise?—to the market and the market mechanism. Here and there subversive markets have arisen, at secret places, where alternative farmers and gardeners sell their wares outside all the usual channels and checks. Above all they barter, as a form of resistance to "corrupting" money. Dumpsters are raided, even if only for use as compost in the gardens, because waste is a sick perversion of capitalism. The movement allies itself with radical cuisine: the hunting and gathering of local wild food. Although its methods may be questionable, especially concerning food safety, the message is clear: food must be returned to the city, and local initiatives must be decisive, not the big companies: away with the lawn; long live the vegetable plot outside the door.

Farmer's markets were originally part of this radical philosophy. They started in California in the mid-1970s with the aim of repairing the rift between town and countryside. Those early, subversive farmer's markets represented opposition to the market economy as such. Farmer's markets now seem to be commonplace in many Western cities, and they tend to specialize in organic and local produce, but often what is called a "farmer's market" is nothing more than a marketing mechanism for small to medium-sized businesses (a good thing in itself, but hardly radical). They attract mainly the higher income groups, while households with lower incomes use the cheaper supermarkets. Farmers have discovered the Internet, too, and they shorten supply chains by skipping the distributors and delivering straight to the customer.

Following on naturally from the original farmer's market and new initiatives aimed at developing local neighborhoods are the school gardens and community gardens in which children in urban areas are given a chance to discover how tomatoes or beans grow. In the most idealistic vision, this caring for green spaces and vegetables by children from disadvantaged backgrounds will create better people. Many of these ideas have a charitable component, in that some of the profits are given away. For a long time in Toronto there has been a movement that provides poor families with healthy, fresh food, not through food banks but by handing out boxes of vegetables grown in the city. We see something similar in poor countries. In Manila, where vegetables and fruit can be harvested all year round, school gardens have been created as part of a collaborative effort by the government, seed companies, and schools. This project is innovative but not revolutionary, unlike the promotion of community gardens. In the original counterculture, sharing and bartering were central concepts. Working in someone else's garden gave you the right to some of the produce. Something similar exists in the Netherlands, where for a season you take a share in a garden. Some groups in the United States also cultivate other people's allotments, at which point the market mechanism comes into play again.

From the start of these countercultural movements, artists saw the radical potential of the confrontation among humans, food, and nature. Food is war to some, war against the establishment that regards self-sufficiency as illegal. Artists have also become involved with the green city by creating art that confronts people with the destruction and waste of the conventional food chain and by praising the authenticity of home-grown food. A field of corn in the city becomes an installation.

Outside radical circles too, change is continuing. Just as the counterculture of squatting in the Netherlands eventually led to better and more affordable housing (and more diversity in the way city centers are built and lived in), and just as the radical women's movement led to more freedom of choice for the majority of women, so some of the alternative ideas about greening the city are slowly filtering through into mainstream thought. Famous chefs confess that they pick their herbs at secret places in the city. Catching fish and collecting crustaceans from urban rivers or the seashore is for some enthusiasts the ultimate statement. Urban green space and food are becoming radical chic. The day that wild herbs from city parks are sold in supermarkets cannot be far off.

City Farming: The New Interweaving
of the City and Food Production

So radical ideas about food in the city offer inspiration for innovation in urban life. After all, now that the majority of people on earth live in urban areas, and that majority will continue to grow, governments and ordinary city dwellers are feeling a need for a renewed link with food production. Even among the middle classes in developing countries such a need is arising, which leads to the hypocrisy that sings the praises of horticulture while gardeners in the slums have to fight for water and space. This is not completely new. A century ago in Britain, as a response to the expansion of cities, the garden city was invented. What until recently was harsh necessity—and in many poor countries still is—has been transformed into a new ideology with unprecedented success. In theory at least.

If we are to believe the countless websites and glossy publications, urban farming is the miracle cure for the future. A related idea is found in metropolitan agriculture, a broader concept that concerns food supplies in a sometimes quite large area around a city, not just within its municipal boundaries. In the past decade initiatives have emerged everywhere aimed at engaging in urban agriculture in a new form. All kinds of local authorities in Europe have launched plans for green roofs and walls. Some have no hesitation in taking up suggestions about turning parks into vegetable plots. On the roofs of apartment blocks and garages, in verges, in combination with solar panels, on walls that become vertical sources of food, or as decoration on famous buildings—everything is conceivable if not actually tried. This movement is not always about food; sometimes it's merely a matter of green prestige projects, such as plans for vertical forests on balconies and apartment buildings in Milan (BioMilano), but growing food is popular among politicians. As part of a worldwide program to create sustainable cities, the mayor of London decided in 2012 that the number of such gardens must be doubled. Michelle Obama stirred up a fuss with her vegetable plot on the White House lawn. In the Netherlands there are plans for an entirely new scheme for green spaces in Almere, for example, and a network of green landscapes between The Hague, Delft, and Rotterdam, as well as new ideas for a regional food strategy for the metropolitan region of Amsterdam.

The new allotments and urban farming are part of a broader set of ideas about sustainable "green" cities that are intended to address some environmental problems. The ambition of urban farming is far more than to produce food. In a sweeping gesture, the whole city is to be turned on its head, creating nothing less than a new urban ecosystem, especially in public areas, for which no one feels responsible. The potential effects are breathtaking. The range of vegetation in gardens, which is often far greater than in nature reserves, can form a new habitat for useful insects and small animals as well as regulating the flow of air between buildings. This so-called natural or wild gardening, which is not purely aimed at food production, is a way of creating gardens that are as natural as possible and absorb excess rainfall. Waste timber and even chunks of concrete or shipping containers are used to create such gardens.

Urban farming is also intended to contribute to the generation of sustainable energy, the storage of CO_2, to reduce heat storage in the concrete of the built environment (which causes the city to cool down more slowly than the surrounding countryside), and to benefit biodiversity. Gardens help combat air pollution and waste, regulate traffic, strengthen social cohesion in neighborhoods, and provide caring environments for children and young people. They are even said to reduce criminality and to increase security through social control. What could be better than a group of weeding and hoeing adults and children to keep an eye on young people hanging about in the streets? Each neighborhood could grow its own specialties, make apple pie and cherry jam from its own crops, and swap them with nearby neighborhoods. City gardens could even be fitted into programs designed to combat obesity and promote healthy living, for example, by linking the gardens with information centers about healthy eating and sustainable production and by encouraging children to help tend them. "Through urban gardening you change the world" is the alluring slogan.

The concrete ideas behind urban farming are fairly diverse: from green zones around the city where care for the elderly, recreation, and energy generation with small windmills is combined with agriculture to compulsory roof gardens and new collective allotments. There are many designs for green roofs that reduce the speed of rainwater runoff so that water is used for the growth of plants while sewers are relieved. Countless varieties of the Earth Box are doing the rounds, a minigarden that needs no land. It consists of a box the size of a suitcase containing seeds, fertilizer, and soil that only needs a scrap of space. Then there is microgardening, in containers of less than a cubic meter specially developed for balconies on blocks of apartments in poor countries. It can get smaller still, in the form of narrow window boxes or bags to fit on the front wall, for growing herbs, strawberries, tomatoes, and leafy vegetables.

As with all wide-ranging ideas, there's a gap between intention and reality, if only because the amount of space available in cities is so limited. City farming was not thought up by agricultural experts but by city planners and architects, environmentalist groups, community centers, and artists. Proposals therefore quite often suffer from unrealistic expectations and a lack of realism about what is technically possible when it comes to food production. It's simply not true that most weeds are edible, let alone form the basis for a delicious pesto sauce. (Yes, the young tops of the dreaded ground elder can be eaten, but unfortunately they don't taste very nice.) Fruit trees in shallow containers on balconies catch the wind and are sensitive to drought and frost. Urban beekeepers may encounter difficulties with inquisitive children. A good many square meters of unused land may be found in cities, but much of it has been polluted with heavy metals over a long industrial history, or has too little water available or is shaded by tall buildings. Not everyone is prepared to sacrifice garden space to community cows (which then need feeding in winter). The effects on vegetables of vehicle emissions and nearby factories should not be underestimated. It's also almost impossible to grow vegetables without any artificial fertilizers and pesticides at all, but the aim of urban farming is always implicitly or explicitly to grow food using organic and environmentally friendly methods.

I have done an extensive search for reliable information about yields from urban farming. Sadly, there are still no well-documented quantitative assessments of its contribution to food supplies. We need to be realistic. The value of urban farming for the city itself will never be more than minimal, and it will mainly be a matter of vegetables and fruit suitable for the climatic zone in which the city garden finds itself. It can never replace arable farming and livestock keeping with their international distribution networks. Carbohydrates and proteins take a lot of space and are therefore not suitable for urban farming (the occasional potato field and a few goats do not alter that fact). The most useful aspect of city farming seems to be its ability to connect urban consumers with producers. Food does not need to be the main goal of the edible garden. Cabbages, zucchinis, beans, and rhubarb, for example, are decorative too. Nurturing an understanding of how our food is produced is as least as important as growing green beans to meet the demand for them.

There is no shortage of good intentions and romantic ideals. The pretentions are great, the slogans attractive. Unfortunately, the actual application of many plans for urban farming—or rather, urban gardening—is still beyond reach. Not only are the costs often higher than expected, for the cleaning of land, for example, but also labor is scarce and far from free. Sadly that is the element lacking in almost all enthusiastic stories about urban farming: labor in cities is expensive, even in poor countries. Young people rarely want to work the earth with their hands, volunteers are not always reliable, and the number of farmers has been declining for decades.

Urban farming demands continual and expert attention. Nonetheless, twenty years ago the idea of returning food production to the city was unthinkable. Now we are starting to see cities as ecosystems in which sustainable food supplies are an essential component. This type of thinking is an advance. Something as simple as the growing demand for edible plants in garden centers proves that gardening for food, on a modest scale at least, has penetrated all classes in the West.

The High-Tech Green Metropolis

Imagine: artificial trees that filter the air and at the same time serve as solar panels; light-producing vegetation; reservoirs with fish that purify waste water; buildings with green walls that look like lush slopes; vertical, angled, or terraced gardens with trees, planted in a lightweight substrates with closed watering systems containing fertilizers in solution; horizontal gardens one above the other; orchards and vegetable plots alternating with windmills; multistory farms with pigsties on the roof; methane from animal husbandry used for biofermentation; algae and fish farming in underground tanks in parking lots; micrologistical horticulture, where computer-controlled production takes place in closed ecosystems.

Along with the romantic desire for the new-style vegetable plot, an entirely different school of thought has emerged. Rather than small-scale farming by hand in local neighborhoods, it is high-tech: the smart city, with a closed, circular economy. Realizing this vision in the center of the city will be difficult, because each square meter simply costs too much to be used to grow food, and the investment needed would be far too high. Integration into newly built neighborhoods seems more achievable or, even better, focusing on industrial areas just outside the city. High-tech agriculture and horticulture are a mixture of existing techniques and futuristic elements. Much can be automated, according to the model of the most advanced greenhouse cultivation, such as the control of temperature, feed, and sunlight. The integration of high-tech urban farming in neighborhoods yet to be built will generally demand an architectonic tour de force. Thus a significant gap yawns between this dream and that of the motivated city dweller, who longs for cornflowers, pick-your-own strawberries, and a chance to bake elderberry tart along with the man or woman next door.

Other innovations in high-tech urban farming are emerging in the fields of water purification and energy. The high concentrations of people and therefore the need for soil nutrients from elsewhere (especially potassium and phosphate) mean that the city of the future must make efforts to recover as many nutrients as possible from sewage purification. Waste can be converted into substrate. In addition, the use of specially adapted lamps and light regimes with suitable plant varieties can raise yields significantly, but at this point it's too expensive. In this vision it seems natural that robots will be needed, and infrared scanners to judge the degree of ripeness.

Whatever the future of urban farming, it will often mean that we need to think again about spatial planning in the city and outside it. For a long time zoning schemes have been all about separating agricultural land from building land. This picture has been transformed into one whose motto is "every citizen has a right to green areas, preferably producing edible produce." Several studies show that green vegetation does indeed have a positive effect on people, especially their peace of mind. In all highly populated countries, areas of transition between city and countryside are continually under pressure. The infiltration of buildings, industrial zones, and homes in former agricultural areas means local authorities must adapt their rules and make space for food production, whatever form it may take. A great deal more needs to be said on the subject in the bureaucratic Netherlands and in other developed countries.

From the point of view of food production, the sustainability of cities is determined by the size of the areas on which they depend and the distance between cities and the places that supply them, otherwise known as "food miles." In the current global economy there is no city of more than a million on earth that is not connected in dozens or hundreds of ways with other continents. We import lamb from New Zealand, rice from Southeast Asia, and bananas from Central America, which we wrap in paper from Indonesia and treat with chemicals from Europe and the United States. These products will not ever be produced in European cities, or at least not in sufficient quantities. "Local" will therefore always be a relative concept, used rather loosely even by devotees of urban farming. The value of the "food miles" concept is that it makes the interconnection visible and provides a basis for decisions about whether to do things differently if possible. It would be a nice idea for supermarkets and restaurants to estimate food miles and indicate the result for each product they sell.

The city is the place where plenty and scarcity come together, where temptation lurks on every street corner, along with poverty and hunger, both physical and mental. Sustainable food supplies in the city mean that residents have enough healthy and diverse food at reasonable prices; their food can be transported and stored properly, and where necessary refrigerated. It also means that city residents have sufficient knowledge to consume food sensibly. Feeding our cities in the twenty-first century is undoubtedly one of the greatest challenges for agriculture. The other challenge, related to it, is to increase productivity and promote dignified working conditions in farming. The sticking points for urban farming remain that, by definition, there will always be far too little space in the city for growing crops, even in the most high-tech scenario, and that the buying power of a large majority of city dwellers is low. No big city, let alone the metropolis of the future, can feed itself from its own vicinity. Anyone wanting a radical return to local food supplies will have to abolish the city.

The desire to watch your meal grow around you and the distrust of large-scale and industrial production—and of fast food culture—force us to think about how the city and farming have always been interlinked. The benefit to be gained from the urban farming movement and the green city does not lie in their contribution to urban food supplies or in the replacement of global food supply chains but in an understanding of how much food affects the culture and life of the city dweller, from hamburger to wild nettle. It also forces us to think about what land in the city is used for and by whom. The green city with its vegetable plots and edible parks may yet be able to present a vision of paradise, not because of its unbridled abundance but as a result of its citizens' involvement and attention to what grows there.

TWELVE

An Embarrassment of Riches: The Food Chain

Carbon is again among us, in a glass of milk. It is inserted in a very complex, long chain.   PRIMO LEVI, "Carbon," in *The Periodic Table*

Mother's cooking was with rare exceptions poor, that good old unpasteurized milk touched only by flies and bits of manure crawled with bacteria, the healthy old-time life was riddled with aches, sudden death from unknown causes.   JOHN STEINBECK, *Travels with Charley*

The Long Road from Farm to Fork

A Sunday morning—at last there's time for a proper breakfast. First a cup of fragrant tea, perhaps Darjeeling. Then yogurt with muesli, kiwi, or banana; perhaps a soft boiled egg or even an omelette, a brown roll with sunflower seeds, filled with mozzarella and tomato; a glass of fresh orange juice; and a cappuccino to finish.

There are as many breakfasts as there are breakfasters: from bread and peanut butter or French toast with sheep's cheese to rye bread with bacon or salmon. In France many people still dip croissants into their *café au lait*. The Italians do something similar with a *cornetto* (croissant) or biscuit, as do city dwellers in Latin America. In the countryside of southern Spain the traditional breakfast consists of old dry bread with olive oil and grated tomato. In North America various cakes and pastries are eaten, such as bagels with cream cheese or sweet muffins, but they are accompanied by yogurt and the increasingly popular fruit juices and soy drinks. Or perhaps it'll be a full English breakfast, with eggs, bacon, sausages, sometimes blood pudding and baked beans, or even fried fish. In parts of East Asia steamed or fried snacks dominate, and vegetables or noodle soup. In Africa there's sometimes bread with margarine, a ball of *fufu* (pounded boiled cassava), or cold rice with a little palm-oil sauce.

One of the most striking developments of recent decades is that this great range of food arrives on our plates as if by its own accord. Not just at breakfast but for every meal, every single day. In the Netherlands alone, with more than 16 million people—each of whom has specific eating habits and consumes three meals a day—this happens tens of millions of times. Every meal is a miracle of organization and hardly anyone stops to think about the complexity of all those supply lines. Fresh food, frozen food, processed food, with ingredients from all over the world—it's almost impossible to grasp how much has to happen before we find ourselves looking at a bowl of muesli or a cheese sandwich.

The multiplicity of ingredients alone is dizzying. The average bowl of muesli contains fruit from all over the world: raisins from southern Europe; dried apple that may come from Poland; hazelnuts and almonds from California, Turkey, or Spain; coconut or banana from the tropics. Each of these ingredients is harvested, cleaned, and traded fresh or dried. Muesli also contains such cereals as wheat, oats, and spelt, rolled into flakes, and most will be from abroad. Even if they're grown nearby they require artificial fertilizer that is usually made of raw materials from Morocco or Canada. The soft-boiled egg exists by the grace of chickens nourished on feed partly imported from Brazil and on vitamins from the pharmaceutical industry. That great addiction of so many in Europe, North and South America, and increasingly China, the cup of coffee, is from the tropics, where the beans are picked by hand, roasted, and fermented. It can be even more complicated if you're after particular coffee beans, such as pure Arabica or a special Robusta. If you don't want just any old tea but Assam or Darjeeling, then you'll be drinking the result of a yet more detailed process of selecting the leaves from tea plants of a special variety in a clearly defined region.

The production and transportation of all those different items with their history of domestication and distribution across the world—tomatoes and sunflower seeds from America, cow's milk from Central Asia—are a miracle, but so is the processing. Take something as simple as semi-skimmed yogurt. It starts with milk of the correct protein and fat content, which has to be brought from the cow to the factory as fresh as possible and therefore with speed. To make semi-skimmed yogurt, the fat content of the milk first has to be reduced to 2 percent, and then the milk must be reinforced with extra milk protein, milk powder, and other ingredients, including whey and sometimes gelatin or another binding agent. Then two to four types of bacteria are needed that have to grow in the correct balance. Sanitation and temperature have to be controlled constantly. A few degrees too hot, or slightly too few of one of the bacteria, and the end product will be too acidic or watery or not creamy enough. Then fruit or flavorings may be added, introducing another story about ingredients brought from elsewhere and processed: vanilla, mostly from Madagascar, has to be fermented to produce an extract, unless artificial vanilla flavoring is used, which comes from another factory; the fruit to be added must be chosen, washed, blanched, pureed, and mixed with sugar. Whole libraries of documentation exist about the production and history of sugar from sugar cane or sugar beet. Then the yogurt has to be packed, in cartons or plastic tubs, in individual portions or larger, with or without a lid but in any case with color printing. If the packaging is partly made of paper, then it may be recyclable, or not, or made of wood waste from the Netherlands or Scandinavia or India. Next comes the trip in refrigerated trucks to the distribution point for the local shop or supermarket and from there to the breakfasting consumer's fridge. But the story does not end there. The life of a pot of yogurt is not always a happy story, as we regularly throw some of it away, sometimes a great deal. The packaging, often a hard-to-process combination of plastic and paper, goes into the trash bin and is mostly burned, perhaps to generate electricity, perhaps not.

This is to say nothing of the many steps that precede the arrival of the milk in the factory, the selection of cows and ways of keeping them healthy, the feeding, and the daily milking. Then there is the story of the industry behind dairying and the transportation of milk: the stalls with their complex delivery and cleansing systems for air and dung and feed, the milking robots with their sensors that can recognize a cow and immediately determine the health of her udders, the steel milk tanks—all of these are areas on which demands are made every year, for the sake of sanitation and animal welfare, but about which difficult decisions continually have to be made concerning profitability: Should the cows be let out to pasture or not? Should the stalls be open or closed? How often should the animals be milked, and when should they calve?

The technological achievements of our day make us forget that earlier generations too were involved in long food supply chains, and we should not underestimate their complexity. The Romans ate grain from North Africa, grapes and raisins from Greece and Asia Minor, and fish from the Strait of Gibraltar. The imperial kitchens of medieval Mongolia used ingredients from Turkey, Russia, and China. Food has always been an important aspect of trade flows. The history of the Dutch East

India Company and later the Dutch West India Company can be seen as successful attempts to expand and reinforce the European food supply chains. The Dutch brought pepper, mace, nutmeg, and other spices to Europe from Southeast Asia, which served not only to improve flavor but also to make food last longer. At the same time the ships of the East India Company stocked up on rice and sugar cane in Asia as a regional medium of exchange, so that they could buy other products for the European market. Almost all colonial empires were after not just such commodities as cotton, copper, or silver, but a diversification and expansion of food supplies. In the eighteenth century Britain's relationship with China was focused on tea, mainly because it might serve as a way to reduce dependence on the national drink, beer.

More and more food is processed and brought from elsewhere. This applies not just to Europe and the West but increasingly to people in poor countries. In the slums of Kinshasa, for example, people now eat bread and margarine, both imported from other parts of the world, and rice from Thailand rather than Africa, because Asian rice is cheaper. It's therefore not the case that poverty means eating local produce only. In fact the price of imports often forces more expensive local products off the market. Local production in poor countries unfortunately often means lower quality and far less variety, especially when it comes to vegetables, fruit, and fish, because of diminished control in the supply chain, leading to poor storage practices. Yet importing food into such countries often leads to exploitation by middlemen and a reduction in quality because of inefficient distribution. The poor certainly do not escape the worldwide food supply chains.

I find it disconcerting every time I see canned pineapple and instant coffee served for breakfast in an African city. These are products produced locally, but the raw ingredients are then exported, processed in Europe, and imported back by their countries of origin. This may make economic sense, but everyone feels it's an undesirable state of affairs. Such illogical detours in the food supply chain are the consequence of a lack of processing capacity, trained personnel, and quality control in the countries from which tropical products are sourced. Coffee-growing countries like Ethiopia and Uganda therefore have no opportunity to make a serious profit on the valuable coffee beans they produce, so they cannot invest in improvements to the processing industry. An African coffee farmer receives on average less than 10 percent of what the consumer ultimately pays. Roasters, middlemen, and coffee retailers earn most, although the situation is slowly improving.

So every cup of coffee, every bowl of muesli or rice, every bite links us with the past and with countries and regions elsewhere in the world. A tangle of chains, miraculous, with a long history, precedes every meal. As a consumer you see less than the tip of the iceberg, merely the end result, that one tub of yogurt surrounded by abundance in the shops and your own fridge. This kind of abundance means that supermarkets have all their products on their shelves all year round, which necessitates continual supply from all over the world, and perfect storage. Hardly any of us have any idea what this involves; we become aware of the chain only when something goes wrong.

Safe, but Not Risk Free

During the holiday season and New Year's celebrations in 1992–1993, on the west coast of the United States, 700 people became seriously ill, many of them young children. It was one of the most extensive cases of food poisoning in history. They suffered from diarrhea followed by kidney trouble. Several died, others had to undergo painful operations. Eventually the cause was traced: a dangerous strain of the intestinal bacterium *E. coli* on a hamburger. A hamburger?! The epitome of American food, a symbol, at that time at least, of a nation of contented parents and smiling children in the suburbs, of sensible food for the whole family. The shock was even greater than the shock caused by the widespread food poisoning itself.

A comparable situation with a potentially deadly variety of this bacterium (enterohemorrhagic *E. coli*) occurred in 2011, with thousands of infections and an estimated 50 deaths in northern Germany. To blame this time were not hamburgers but sprouted fenugreek seeds. Examples abound of food poisoning. As well as dangerous or lethal forms of *E. coli*, salmonella, listeria, and other microorganisms are often found on food, as are the pathogens that cause hepatitis. Watermelons, chicken, milk, peanuts, canned fish, onions—anything can be a vector for disease.

Other types of disturbances to the food supply chain can occur. In China and Bangladesh, melamine, used to make artificial resins, was found in milk powder. More than 50,000 babies became seriously ill, and several died. Because Chinese dairy products can be found in countless food items that are exported all over the world, the incident caused widespread disquiet. Cases have been documented of pesticide and coloring residues, even nails, sawdust, cockroaches, and many other contaminants, or the use of tainted ingredients.

This is generally the result of a lack of hygiene or extreme carelessness, but it can also result from incorrect measurements and other understandable mistakes. Sometimes gross negligence is discovered, or even deliberate acts, such as the irrigation of horticultural crops with water from a sewer or the addition of cheap material to increase product weight. The melamine in China was used to mask the addition of water to the milk. Animal droppings used as fertilizer in the cultivation of vegetables and soft fruit, such as strawberries, are a recognized hazard. In each of these cases, the entire supply chain has to be traced and every possible connection checked to identify where things went wrong. Infections often spread to other products via equipment and unwashed hands. Human feces are another potential source of infection. Where supply chains connect countries or continents, it can be extremely difficult to trace the cause.

———————

Foul-ups in the supply chain are nothing new, incidentally; in fact they're as old as humanity. Only in paradise were there presumably no problems with dangerous organisms, contamination, or food poisoning. Although … the apple is a well-known risk factor. Tragic cases of E. coli infection have resulted from apples falling to the ground and then being used in unpasteurized apple juice, or simply being eaten unwashed. The biblical choice of an apple (or related species, such as cherry or apricot) as the tree that bears forbidden fruit may not be entirely accidental.

For centuries reports have emerged of flour being mixed with chalk and beer diluted with water. Standards of sanitation, waste disposal, and abattoir practices must have been terrible in earlier centuries. Think of all those reports of the stench in cities like Amsterdam and London. It was a long time before people realized that damaging organisms transmitted from animals or plants to humans were a particular danger. They might be viruses, bacteria, or fungi, or the substances they produce.

In the past Europe was regularly hit by deaths attributable to rotten meat or moldy grain. One of the more notorious cases involves ergot, or *Claviceps purpurea*, a fungus that grown on ears of wheat and produces hallucinogenic alkaloids related to LSD. Whole villages were sometimes wiped out. The last known case of mass death occurred as recently as the 1950s in France.

In about 1800, Frenchman Nicolas Appert proved that he could make food keep for years by heating it in glass jars and then closing them with an airtight lid—an invention of which Napoleon's army made grateful use. It was only after the work of Louis Pasteur three-quarters of a century later that it became clear why this treatment works. Pasteur showed that every form of decay in food (the souring of milk and wine; the rancidity of butter and meat) was caused by a specific microorganism. Heating, now called pasteurization, was almost always sufficient to kill the microorganisms. It soon became clear that microorganisms also have a positive role to play in the food supply chain. They are used to make cheese, yogurt, bread, and alcoholic drinks. The ability to produce yeasts and chemicals on an industrial scale gave a huge boost to the food sector.

Almost all problems of contamination can be avoided in principle by applying strict hygiene measures to plants, animals, and humans, and by defining and applying legal norms concerning the percentage of additives and contaminants. Scandals generally lead to improvements, as was the case with melamine. After that scandal the Chinese government not only punished those responsible severely but also specified the maximum amount of melamine allowed. Heating, freezing, and to some extent cooling reduce many of the risks presented by pathogens, but they do nothing to ensure the absence of toxins and contaminants. The large-scale application of techniques for curbing or killing microorganisms, such as salting, roasting, drying, bottling, pickling, pasteurizing, and more recently canning and radiation have made food supplies incomparably safer over past centuries.

The rules imposed on factories are increasingly strict, and a hamburger or a piece of chicken on display at the famous outlets must be sold within thirty minutes, not a second longer. Anything unsold at that point is destroyed. This reflects the increasing sensitivity to matters of food safety and food quality, not just in the West but also in Asia. Given the enormous number of meals and the number of activities involved in getting them to customers, the conclusion should not be that our food is dangerous but that problems are the exception, however serious. Almost always, in the vast majority of those billions of daily meals, everything works out fine.

The demand for local produce—in other words, for shorter food supply chains—is becoming more and more fashionable among an advanced guard in the West. It arises in part from the idea that anything coming from close by and directly from nature must be safer than something that reaches us via all the detours of the supply chain. Unfortunately, local and "wild" food is not necessarily safe. Wild berries may contain the tapeworm *Echinococcus multilocularis*, which causes serious intestinal problems. Game, European or otherwise, may be infested with the roundworm *Trichinella* sp. (yes, the same roundworm sometimes used to explain the ban on eating pork and horsemeat in Judaism and Islam).

I believe people only really became aware of our heavy dependence on the existence of extremely long and complex production chains as a result of what became known as mad cow disease (bovine spongiform encephalopathy) and its consequences for humans. In 1996 the world was shocked by the deaths of young people as a result of a variant of Creutzfeldt-Jakob disease, until then an extremely rare disease that caused elderly brains to degenerate. In the United Kingdom alone, the death toll has been put at more than 170 by 2012, with an average age of twenty-eight, after an average incubation period of sixteen years. The disease turned out to be the consequence of an infection in cows, and it probably originated from freely grazing sheep, in which the pathogen is endemic. The reuse of potentially dangerous parts of the cow carcass in feed for cows kept for meat production allowed the disease, with its long incubation period, to spread.

Mad cow disease is not the only dangerous epidemic in animals, and it increased public sensitivity to other infections in the years that followed, each of which led to the slaughter of tens of thousands—sometimes hundreds of thousands—of animals. Although most animal diseases have been known about for centuries, the frequency of outbreaks—foot and mouth disease in cattle, swine fever, bird 'flu, and Q fever in goats—has been one reason to look critically at the animal food supply chain. It seems that cost considerations drive us to adopt practices that can lead to unacceptable risks. Nonetheless, since the 1990s the number of checks on food safety has increased markedly.

"Food safety" is the general technical term for a guarantee that food will not harm the consumer as long as it is prepared and eaten as indicated (so the fact that raw kidney beans can make you ill is not an issue of food safety). Factors that make food unsafe may be chemical, biological, or physical. There are also all kinds of adulterants to be avoided, in other words, the undesirable and unintentional introduction of contaminants or infections. Safety is a necessary but not sufficient condition, because food must also be "suitable" (acceptable) for human consumption. Dog biscuits aren't dangerous to humans, but they are not acceptable as human food. Food safety requires national and international legislation, the cooperation of businesses in giving out information and adjusting processing methods, and responsible behavior by the consumer. When did you last check the temperature of your fridge?

There is no such thing as a risk-free food supply. Its complexity is an unavoidable by-product of a society in which 97 percent or more of people have been liberated from the need to take care of the production of their daily bread. There is only one way forward, however, and that is not to allow ourselves to be panicked or to feel insecure. Politicians must have the courage to show leadership and not immediately point the finger if there is insufficient evidence (remember how the cucumber was unjustly blamed for the German enterohemorrhagic *E. coli* infection in 2011). Legislation and checks must be adjusted and optimized. With an eye to cases of unexpected infection or contamination of the food chain, we must improve our readiness and, where necessary, national and international coordination. Only transparency about the true scale of the risks— what we know and do not know and what serious scientific research can provide—will help us move forward. The saying "the fear of suffering is worse than the suffering itself" applies to food safety.

Yet there is a tendency, certainly in the media, to be extremely suspicious of farming and the food industry. A caricature emerges, in which the farmer ruthlessly mows to death the young field mice and the cornflowers, the vet torments the animals with antibiotics all the way to the abattoir, and the industry pumps our food full of forbidden chemicals. This image is not merely unjustified when applied to the food industry as a whole, as abuses are rare, it creates another serious problem. The more society distrusts the farming sector and demands more controls, the fewer young people will want to become farmers, horticulturalists, or fishermen. These are already jobs that often earn less than the minimum wage. Because of the high investments needed in these sectors, family businesses often have to go deeply into debt and thereby take on huge economic risks. These businesses are already strictly controlled by national and European laws. Discouraging young people from working in the farming and food industries inevitably means we will become dependent on other countries, where food may be produced with less concern for the environment, public health, and animal welfare. Howling with the wolves about the dangers of the food supply chain is an extremely dangerous and short-sighted tactic.

Chained by Chains

The animal production chain, with its ethical dimension, is perhaps the most visible and the most controversial food supply chain, but our dependence on global chains and their vulnerability is a feature of vegetable food production as well. The greatest source of disquiet today, in Europe at least, is the issue of whether to allow the use of genetically modified soy from the United States and South America in pasta and other foods. According to modern science, genetic modification does not represent contamination, nor is it pathogenic. Formally and empirically speaking, food safety is not at risk, because no evidence suggests that health problems can be caused by genetically modified products. Many in Europe, however, are intuitively opposed to the genetic modification of plants and would like to eliminate the resulting products from the food supply chain.

Aside from this issue, it is true that a balance must always be found between safety and efficiency. Farmers and growers are struggling to survive in an environment in which competition is increasingly fierce. A rumor about a bacterium, an emotional reaction among consumers, an importing country that closes its borders—any incident of that sort can mean huge damage to thousands of farming families. The food supply chain is as much emotional as it is economic, and fear and a lack of information can be infectious among consumers.

The contemporary farmer is competing not against neighbors but against tens of thousands of unknown fellow producers, many miles away. Farmers no longer deliver to local villages or a nearby town but to anonymous food processing companies and big supermarkets. This is true not only in rich countries but also increasingly in developing countries, where food exports may be the most important source of income.

In the most competitive sectors, such as horticulture, it's not sufficient to be the best in the region or the country. A producer needs to try to be the best in the world, best at producing the highest consistent quality at the lowest cost. This is possible only through specialization and continual technological innovation, with a keen eye for how the needs and tastes of customers are developing. After criticism of Dutch tomatoes for being "water bombs" (a criticism not backed up in blind panel tests, incidentally), horticulturalists looked for alternatives that not only had a better flavor but were smaller, so they would be easier to eat as a snack. The dark-red vine tomato, with its visible stalks as if only recently plucked, is in tune with the desire for authenticity and Mediterranean tradition. Partly because of rapid innovation like this, and the application of extremely precise irrigation and feeding systems, Dutch growers are among the most successful in the world.

I expect the health properties of vegetables and fruit to be the next arena of competition. People will want tomatoes that are not just juicy and aromatic (another dimension that's increasingly valued) but that also contain more beta-carotene, iron, antioxidants, and eventually other substances that protect us against the diseases of old age.

What exactly is this "food supply chain" that determines and connects so much? The term is not unambiguous, and it is used rather loosely. In an evolutionary sense we are all part of the totality of biological food chains and cycles of our planet, that immeasurable recycling of atoms and molecules that regroup, bind, and react, only to become inert again for millions of years. We share that position with the tigers, elephants, oak trees, cockroaches, and bacteria. There is no living organism on earth that is not a link in one of the many food chains. All living beings consist of atoms of the same interstellar origin: weighed on the scales of the universe we are all merely a handful of stardust.

In an abstract sense that one all-embracing cycle exists, but in practice there is not a single food chain or ecological cycle but many: the leaves of the trees that die and rot in the soil; the peregrine falcons that eat mice; the viruses that make wheat stalks wilt. Most of these biological chains are fairly short, with just a few links, and they are above all bound to a specific place, at least in the short term. The peregrine falcon catches mice in its own environment. Swallows migrate, but they eat insects on the way and excrete them in their droppings as they fly, so that the quantity of nutrients they move around is minimal. The minerals from the fallen leaves of a beech tree in a forest will at some time wash out of the soil into a river, which will then deposit them along with its sediment on new riverside terraces, which will gradually evolve into soils and provide nutrients for other, new forests and soil organisms—but these are processes on a time scale that stretches far beyond that of a single human being.

Human food supplies are unique in their geographical freedom and extent, and in the huge numbers of people connected with them in some way. Globalization has expanded our food chains, but ever since trading began many people have been dependent to some extent on food from areas other than where they live. This makes us fundamentally different from other species, which after all do not engage in trade and have to find food in their own environments if they are to survive. Actually the word "chain" is the wrong one for what we see today; we are actually part of a worldwide network with multiple branches in the form of supply lines and discharge routes, a spider's web of food-based relationships.

Sometimes I try to look around me at sportsmen and sportswomen or dancing crowds with the eyes of an extraterrestrial or an ant, to appreciate how only one species on earth can permit itself to waste so much energy systematically on efforts that have nothing to do with physical survival. In contrast to the rest of the planet, our food supply chain is not there to minimize energy expenditure but to optimize the various values we derive from food. Relaxation through sport and dance is a value practically everyone will recognize as such, so a proportion of our food serves to subsidize that extra effort. It's not only the quantity of food that is decisive. Food also has to be attractive, not just functional, and this is reflected in the food supply chain. We grow not just the most productive variety of tomatoes but the one that bears the reddest, most aromatic fruit, and preferably more than one, for variety's sake.

We are unique in yet another way, as the only species that does not continue to grow and expand once the supply of food is sufficient to the point that it's unlimited. An oak gets bigger and taller and produces more acorns if more sunlight, water, and nutrients are available. If an animal's food is unlimited, the number of descendants increases. Antelope in a profuse savannah continue to reproduce, although that population growth is soon regulated by lions and other predators. If the food supply remains plentiful, both species continue to increase in number. We grow as individuals, becoming heavier and taller than earlier generations, although that growth in height is now slowing. But the growth in the total number of people is declining. It will eventually stabilize and, according to the latest estimates, decline markedly in future centuries, even though food will not become any more scarce. Current studies predict a gradual drop in the human population after 2050, although that could all change if China, after decades of a one-child policy, suddenly starts to encourage people to have more children.

The way in which most of the global food supply is organized is a result of the small proportion of the population involved in food production in rich countries. In the rich northwest of Europe the figure is no more than a few percent; in very poor regions far from cities and industry, such as Central Africa, it is 60 percent or more, but all over the world the percentage is falling fast. This is the driving force behind the search for greater efficiency: more production per worker, so that more people are freed to concern themselves with other things. Of course there is a limit to this trend, but when I look at the most modern greenhouses in the Westland in the Netherlands, where almost everything is automated, or the Cerrado in Brazil, with its army of giant seed-planting and harvesting machines, then I realize that at least in these places the minimum has almost been reached: one lonely farmer in the middle of a huge area of land that produces a mountain of food sufficient to feed thousands of people. This efficient specialization is one explanation for the unique character of human food supplies, but at the same time it is also the basis of the sense of alienation and anxiety caused by dependence on distant strangers.

The food supply chains that feed us can be imagined in a simple form as consisting of six great links, each of which has countless links of its own, which are manifested on various scales: global, national, and local. The first link consists of suppliers of the means of production, such as artificial fertilizer, seed, irrigation equipment, tools, tractors, herbicides, and pesticides—all those things that are needed before production can even start. These suppliers are increasingly extremely large businesses, each of which forms a complex chain. For the production of artificial fertilizer, for example, raw materials are needed, such as potassium and phosphate, that are to some extent mined and to some extent result from chemical processes. For that, too, equipment is needed, and factories and railroad tracks have to be built. The same goes for seed, which is increasingly produced and marketed by specialist companies. Seed is itself the product of years of laboratory research. Even in poor countries that produce hardly any tools or seed, there is still a blacksmith to make machetes and ploughs, and seed is bartered or bought from elsewhere.

The second great link in the food chain is that of the primary producers—the farmers, herders, horticulturalists, fishermen, and fish farmers in all their diversity. They range from smallholders with less than a quarter of a hectare, farmers who make their own cheese, and part-time farmers who run therapeutic farms to those who operate on a massive scale with thousands of cattle or greenhouses covering dozens of hectares, from the most advanced fishermen who sail the world's seas to atoll fishermen on the Pacific Ocean with narrow canoes made of hollowed out tree trunks.

Third in the chain are the traders, who buy up the raw products from producers: the wheat, the peanuts, the cattle, the fish. Often another specialized step takes place between producer and trader. Sugar, for example, is extracted from sugar beet or sugar cane before it comes on the market. Some products have to be processed quickly to avoid decay, such as milk, or grapes for wine, and this often happens on the farm. So by no means all products are marketed as such, let along marketed globally. The majority of such staple grains as rice, wheat, and corn are traded in the country or region where they are produced. For some products farmers have a direct relationship with the factory, as with milk. The Netherlands is famous for its cooperatives that collectively buy the means of production and then collectively deliver the product to the factory that processes it (which is also often owned by a cooperative).

Next in the chain come the food processing industries, where wheat, sugar, and fats are transformed into bread, pasta, biscuits, and so on. Processing companies are diverse too, with their own chains, from small bakeries to large firms with all kinds of factories turning out intermediate products. The small bakery, for instance, buys fats and pre-milled and mixed flour from a factory. Here too are countless supply industries. Just take packaging and pallets. They require chains of producers of paper, wood, plastic, and aluminium, to say nothing of the designers and producers of labels.

As the fifth link in this rough classification of the food supply chain comes the distributers or retailers, first of all the supermarkets and smaller food shops, but also businesses that deliver food or half-prepared food to the final distributer, such as the partially baked loaves delivered to restaurants, the tomato sauce and pizza bases, or the anchovy paste and presliced eggplants for the topping.

———

Only then, right at the end, do we come to the final link in the food supply chain, the billions of consumers, whose desires and ways of acquiring food differ so markedly. Their behavior changes all the time. In cities people not only eat different things, consuming more animal protein, they eat differently, using more ready-made products. This is true of both rich and poor countries. On weekends and during holidays we eat differently than we do during the week, and in winter differently than in summer. Much of the work that was one done by the consumer has now been taken over by the food chains. The following holds true for most people in high-income countries: we no longer bake our own bread, make our own jam, roast our own coffee, harvest our own leeks (or even wash and cut them), and we don't go out fishing. Yet sometimes we do. What for poor people is a necessity has become a pleasurable option for those with both money and time. We may attend a course to learn how to make sausages, or pick apples at a farm to brew our own cider.

This is the food supply chain in the narrowest sense. Around it are many other connections, including the financial sector that invests in and insures food production, processing, and retailing; the researchers in public and private institutes who devise new techniques and study our behavior and our health; the lawyers who concern themselves with legislation and patents; the advertisers and those behind public health announcements; schools and universities that train the people involved in supplying our food; and so it goes on. The food supply chain forms the fabric that binds us all together, including our politicians.

It is simply dizzying to imagine all this complexity, all the more so once you realize that in this food network with all its different branches, so many links affect one another. A change in one place always leads to change somewhere else: falling food prices, as in 2009, which were themselves a reaction to earlier price rises, lead to lower demand for artificial fertilizer, less investment in the fertilizer industry, lower production and delays to innovation, lower incomes for farmers and growers, and smaller margins for the various links in the chain, less bank credit, and so on. Unfortunately, falling prices on the world market rarely lead to a comparable fall in the final price paid by the consumer, whereas rising prices are often reflected in full, so that the consumer notices immediately, especially in poor countries.

The decisive difference between poor and rich areas is a difference in disposable income, which translates into the complexity of food supply chains. In the least developed, poorest situations the producers, the farmers and fishermen, play the main role. They determine what is available to eat. Only in situations where the market barely functions—because people are completely isolated, and there is no transportation or money—do production and consumption coincide. Processing is done by farmers or households; there the rice grains are separated from their husks, millet ground, and beer brewed. Such complete self-sufficiency at the level of a household or village with a completely local food chain was normal for years in rural areas, but it is extremely rare today. Always, even in the most remote parts of the Amazon basin, Sarawak, or Central Africa, ingredients from elsewhere are used. In the rich countries and urban areas, each of these steps is much more specialized and geographically spread. The distributers and consumers are both in the driving seat: in a spiral of reactions, supply and demand push each other ever upward.

Demand should not be seen as a series of explicit desires among consumers ("We want chocolate muffins with roasted walnuts!") but rather as the strategy of the supermarkets, which anticipate future and usually vague consumer preferences that are then translated into the demands made of buyers and primary producers: more food items, or snacks, with nuts and darker chocolate because of the presumed effects of both on health as a result of the antioxidants they contain. The tomatoes must be smaller, sweeter, and more environmentally friendly. The bread must have more fiber. Hamburgers must contain less fat and be "greener."

Meanwhile, all over the world, as a reaction to the search for efficiency and cost reduction, we see a trend toward further integration of steps in the food supply chain. Traders make long-term contracts with the providers of the means of production; supermarkets sign contracts directly with farmers to cut out the middlemen; the processing industry buys companies that supply seed and artificial fertilizer. Entire countries take part in this game of concentration and integration, such as China, which seeks out potassium mines and other raw materials for its own agriculture and rents or buys land in Africa to increase production. Such vertical integration can make those at the ends of the chain—farmers and consumers—vulnerable unless they are well organized.

The Dilemmas of Human Food Supplies

If you think about what you eat at every meal, to say nothing of snacks, then you cannot fail to be impressed by the dizzying abundance that falls into our laps. It seems that more than a fifth of humanity, citizens of the OECD countries along with the rich middle class elsewhere, are now living in a paradise, where safe and diverse food is available every day without any limits and without requiring any particular effort.

Of course our food is not free, but its physical and economic price bears no comparison to its value for our survival. In terms of our universal medium of exchange, money, food is not expensive, at least in comparison to other items of expenditure, such as clothing and holidays. In most rich countries we spend between 10 and 14 percent of our family budgets on food, including eating out. A little over half a century ago that fraction was 50 percent. Even in China, where memories of scarcity and deprivation are so recent, people now spend an average of only 30 percent of the family income on food. Only in poor countries can the percentage be as high as 60.

Our food is cheap in terms of energy too. This again points to how unusual the current situation is for the human species. Only a small fraction of the calories provided by our food each day are required for the physical effort of shopping and food preparation, and even those efforts are quickly being reduced by the growth of ready meals and delivery services. A larger and larger number of people make hardly any physical effort any longer to get food, either directly or indirectly through the work that provides the income to pay for it. All other species on earth adjust their efforts to match their caloric requirements, so that they eat what they need to survive and reproduce, before becoming food themselves for other species.

People are different. Not just because of the ingenious manner in which we have liberated ourselves from much of the physical work required but through the way in which we look at food. Whereas in the nonhuman food chain everything is focused on survival, and therefore on energy and getting hold of the necessary nutrients, human food supply chains are about far more. We are the only animal that does not eat purely because of a shortage of energy, purely to absorb calories and nutrients, but for pleasure, out of loneliness, to reinforce the community spirit, or for reasons or luxury and status.

———————

In the main monotheistic religions, the first image of the food chain was paradise, that remarkably static ecosystem. Paradise is the antithesis of a food chain, a static system from which nothing disappears and where nothing arrives, where the trees always bear fruit without fertilization or pruning, and water flows without interruption. Here there is no growth, no change, nothing is lost, and nothing is transformed: no rotting leaves, no human feces, and no dung beetles. It is also a system of very low productivity, because Adam and Eve do not really eat, and they have no house, furniture, or clothing and need no firewood. All they ever harvest is that one apple, and as far as we know it was not processed into sauce or cider, nor was it sold. To put it irreverently: it's not hard to evoke abundance in a comfortably lush landscape with only two naked people and a handful of grazing animals. The food supply chain could not be shorter and simpler than it is in paradise.

This powerful image of an unchanging balance and effortless plenty, where food causes no harm and is within reach of Adam and Eve, still plays tricks on us when we try to understand how our food reaches us. The paradise model echoes implicitly in the call for shorter, less artificial, more small-scale and therefore more sustainable food supply chains. As urbanization gathers pace, we are increasingly under the impression that it's unnecessary and undesirable for food to travel long distances, or to be produced by industrial methods, and for modern agriculture to cause so much permanent ecological damage compared to the farming of the past.

Often the word "uniform" is heard in this context: products from the food supply chain are the same everywhere; identity has been lost. Many in the West want to retake command of their own food supplies as an emotional counterweight to the immense international complexity of the current system and their vulnerability to failed controls. Pessimism dominates, the sense that everything is getting worse, from the climate to the flavor of food, from the welfare of cows to the dangers of mistakes. Things that are invisible, like viruses and bacteria, or difficult to interpret, such as climate change, make us feel insecure. Diminishing trust among consumers in the quality of food and in the role played by large food producing conglomerates are evidence of this disquiet.

In this sense too, zoonotic diseases, which can be passed from animals to humans (like mad cow disease), have altered public opinion. People have started to believe that our food supply chain is slowly changing from a blessing into a nightmare. The shock of mad cow disease has led people to think of it and Creutzfeldt-Jakob disease as a punishment for misbehavior. We are guilty, because we have acted against the natural order of things, turning cows into cannibals by making them eat the remains of members of their own species. That was the result of our greed, our immoderate search for cheap abundance. The modern reincarnation of the snake, the food industry, has tempted us to eat the gleaming apple of capitalism. The contemporary Fall of Man is our insatiable hunger for an abundance of cheap products that makes us play fast and loose with the natural character and lives of other species.

These somber guilty feelings are the breeding ground for fierce reactions to disruptions to the food supply. In times of uncertainty as to where the world is going and what is happening to our land, our neighborhood, or the economy, we must at least be able to depend on our food. If it turns out that we can't, even for the duration of a one-off incident (let alone because of structural defects), then emotions flare up, and trust drops to zero. Such disasters as infection with variants of E. coli demonstrate to many people that their distrust of the quality of food and the role played by large conglomerates, a distrust nourished by political movements and activist groups, is well founded. In the face of such strong emotions, scientists (supported by the occasional politician) do not make themselves any more popular by appealing to reason.

One good illustration of the dilemmas consumers face is the radiation of food to improve food safety. The use of gamma rays or high-energy electrons makes it possible to penetrate solid food uniformly and destroy microorganisms deep inside. Despite its inherent safety (it involves energy, not radioactivity, just like light or the microwaves in a cooker), consumers have the feeling that radiation is dangerous. Many do not want their food irradiated, although it greatly improves shelf life with hardly any loss of quality. Radiation is rarely mentioned on the packaging, any more than we see the word "gassed" to indicate that the CO_2 content inside the sealed plastic has been increased, at the expense of oxygen, to stop vegetables decaying so quickly, or that the contents have been treated with nitrogen.

Even aside from anxiety about food safety, the food supply chain is a focus for vague feelings of unease about globalization and our powerlessness in the face of all the rapid change that is coming our way. In light of this the desire for an existence we can comprehend, including simple food, is understandable. This alternative seems almost impossible to resist: organic landscape-friendly "natural" farming, preferably vegetarian, without genetic modification, producing food processed in the shortest possible food supply chain without intervention by outsiders. There would be just farmers and their consumers, who if possible know each other because they live in the same neighborhood or region. Or perhaps the most extreme alternative of all: growing or gathering your own food. Not everyone wants to go that far, even in theory, because it is clear intuitively that only a few people would be able to feed themselves by their own efforts alone, but it does sound attractive to shorten and simplify the food supply chain. Local food seems less polluting, because it doesn't need to be transported so far, and it is less risky, as there are fewer steps between producer and consumer and no large-scale industrial production. Clearly, however, a shorter distance is no guarantee of food safety.

This is the kind of reasoning that uses terms like "food miles" and "ecological footprint" (or even the derivative "foodprint"). Food miles are calculated based on the total distance covered by the food before it reaches our plates. It can be a revelation, in the case of coffee, for example, when we discover that it returns to Africa as instant coffee.

The concept of an ecological footprint involves such issues as the origin of the ingredients (whether local or from far away), the degree of processing involved, and whether the product is fresh or frozen. The frequency of the consumption of meat and fish is also of relevance. The result is expressed in terms of the number of hectares needed to sustain a person for a year. Methods vary a good deal, and they do not allow for a precise calculation. Anyone trying to work out their own ecological footprint quickly encounters insurmountable problems, because the concept leaves no room for nuance.

The calculation is based on what you normally eat, but no distinction is made, for example, between fresh tomatoes from a greenhouse and those grown in the garden, or the amount and type of meat rather than the frequency of meat consumption. If we calculate footprints for large population groups rather than for individuals, the differences are immense. For example: 8 hectares to feed a European as opposed to 1.5

for an African. The United Arab Emirates comes out at the top, at 9.5 hectares, a little more than the United States. On average, humans now need 2.7 hectares each, whereas 1.7–1.8 hectares per person would be the measure of a sustainable life that does no damage. Conversion to surface area, however, says nothing about sustainable intensification. A hectare of wheat in northern France can feed many hundreds of people, whereas a hectare of millet in West Africa will not even feed a family. The same kind of confusion is created by calculations concerning "how many earths we are using." We would do well to see that image not as a quantitative measure but as a vivid illustration of the fact that humanity is using an increasing proportion of the biological capacity of the earth, so much so that its regeneration is at risk.

A special form of footprint is the water footprint, or the total amount of water necessary to get a product to our plates. This is sometimes called "virtual water," because it is water you cannot see and is not reflected in the water content of the end product. The figures can diverge markedly, especially concerning animal products, as they include all the water used to produce cattle feed as well as the water the animals drink and that is needed to keep cowsheds and abattoirs sanitary. According to such calculations, a hamburger made of pure beef and the famous soft bun with a little salad requires almost 2,500 liters of water, a chicken drumstick perhaps about 600, and a bowl of rice more than either of them. These figures are only rough indications, because everything depends on the specific production process, what yields are like, and whether or not the water is recycled.

Although it is useful to realize how far our food travels, there is—quite apart from questions about methods used and apparent exactitude—a fundamental problem with these concepts. The suggestion is that a shorter food supply chain and a smaller footprint would be the best solutions for feeding the world. For many reasons, this ideal is an illusion. First of all, in almost all countries apart from the very largest, such as the United States and Brazil, it is impossible to derive all food from local production. Even in Europe as a whole it could not be done. A strict shortening of the supply chain would result in monotonous diets. In Europe we would eat hardly any meat or dairy products; these products would be very expensive (because of the need to import animal feed); and no oranges, bananas, pasta, rice, coffee, or tea would be available. There would be no chocolate and no chocolate ice cream. Even for the fans of slow food, this would be going too far. It's unlikely that many people would accept such drastic limitations. This is not to discount the pleasure local produce can bring, such as sheep's cheese from that nice farmer on the edge of the city. But more fundamentally, sticking to a strict norm for food miles would be biologically unwise. It would mean not intensifying where it is appropriate and also sustaining inefficient and costly production (to take an extreme example: growing wheat in Saudi Arabia). Where the soil and climate produce the highest yields, we collectively place the least stress on the environment.

Something else is wrong with being attracted by short supply chains. In the experience of most critics, they go along with concepts such as "simple," "low-tech," "close to the land," "small-scale," and "human." They are rarely associated with a computer-controlled greenhouse just outside the city, where plants no longer grow in soil, or huge feed lots for cattle in industrial areas a few miles away. Yet short supply chains and high-tech intensive production certainly can be a sustainable combination, especially in horticulture, minimizing energy use for production and transportation. Gamma radiation suits them very well, another thing few people associate with a local food chain. Technology will increasingly be an essential ally, such as lasers that can detect the ripeness and quality of products under the peel, and plant breeding that produces vegetables and fruit whose ripening can be steered. Transportation is the first thing critics of long chains think of, but that is only one of many aspects of sustainability. The length of the chain does not necessarily determine either the degree to which technology is used or sustainability.

Nor can short food supply chains prevent problems surrounding food safety. That idea is understandable but unsubstantiated. Short chains certainly do not guarantee that infection will not take place: cow dung at the organic farm around the corner can be a source of harmful bacteria; free-range goats can transmit Q fever. Moreover, no business can function without products from elsewhere. Substances to prevent diseases in plants and animals—including those allowed in organic farming—are not made by the businesses that use them. Seeds and seed potatoes almost always come from elsewhere and may be infected. Tools, even the simplest (such as a spade), may transmit pests, and even a trip on a tractor along a country road can create problems. So again there is no automatic relationship between shortening supply chains, banning imported food, and guaranteeing food safety. Regionalizing supply may be a solution if we keep an eye on efficiency and sustainability, but for many products, such as fruit and vegetables, it's impossible because of the climate. The advantage of a more regional approach is that any problems that do arise with food safety do not immediately take on global proportions and disrupt world trade.

We must not downplay problems in the food supply chain, but we should not exaggerate them either. Every day, billions of acts and decisions concerning food go well. Rationality and proportionality are essential. In all sectors mistakes and neglect take place occasionally, but just as we don't appoint an inspector for every car that rolls off the production line, we cannot install a food safety lab for every farmer or every fishing vessel. Many people find it strange that the farming sector is not responsible for checking food quality, but there are legal frameworks that have to be complied with, for example, concerning levels of pesticide residues. Food safety inspectors carry out spot checks. The automobile industry guarantees the quality of its cars within agreed norms, just as the medical profession places itself under the supervision of health inspectorates and medical boards. There is no intrinsic reason to assume that more dirty tricks go on in the food sector than elsewhere.

However, economic pressure on the food sector in the past has led to abuses. Dependence on rapidly fluctuating prices can lead to dubious or even criminal practices in the pursuit of profit. In the past the reputation of the livestock sector in northwestern Europe was damaged by scandals involving illegal growth hormones—practices that have probably not been eliminated elsewhere in the world, incidentally. The use of cow carcasses in feed for cattle was the consequence of severe economic pressure, and it seemed rational, because they are a good source of nutrients for use in concentrated feed. The spread of mad cow disease is the result of a mistake that should never have been made, scientifically speaking, but it should not be used to condemn the use of concentrates as such.

The consumer wants two incompatible things: food that is 100 percent safe but not too expensive. We have the last word, all the same. We decide what to buy and at what price. Unfortunately, there seems to be a sharp contradiction between the principles we voice and our cash-conscious behavior. Still, because the consumer can respond instantly by not buying a product as soon as there is even a suspicion of a safety problem, the food sector cannot permit itself many moments of carelessness—in contrast to the medical sector, for example, where abuses can remain hidden for a long time in the guise of differences of opinion among specialists.

The desire for a short, manageable food supply chain is ultimately an expression of an identity crisis among the middle classes in urban, post-industrial societies. They seek refuge in proximity, wanting to distance themselves from the large-scale, the threatening outside world, and the rapidity of change. I too am far from immune to the desire for an understandable world in which we sit together around long tables after a long day at work to eat what the land offers us, as if in paradise. But local, low-tech, short food supply chains offer only a partial and very limited solution that doesn't bring us any closer to fulfilling the essential demand that our future food supplies must be more sustainable and must take into account many more people in the world who require a sensible and varied diet.

Reading Food: Logos, Certificates, and Labels

Much of the unease about our food supply chain is expressed in a call for more information about how our food is produced. This is a justifiable demand, especially in a time of more openness and more responsibility on the part of citizens themselves. There is no quality stamp for food safety, of course, because unsafe food is banned, and all the food in the supermarket must be taken to be safe—in countries where the market functions properly, that is. Poor countries have no such certificates either, obviously, no matter how great the need for them.

What consumers want goes well beyond food safety. Some want information about environmental impacts, sustainability, and animal welfare. With imported products, people are interested in working conditions, agricultural training, the environment, and fair trade. We are used to seeing fair trade coffee. Other branches of the food industry too have shown themselves to be progressive, taking the initiative by entering into agreements with producers and nongovernmental organizations in an effort to make supply chains more sustainable. There are currently international guidelines and framework agreements, or agreements in preparation, concerning soy, palm oil, fish, biofuels (important because of possible competition with food crops for land use), and wood (important for packaging). Quite a few criteria are intertwined, so such agreements can be complicated and therefore hard for the consumer to assess. At this point the supply of certified sustainable products limits the application of the agreements: the product streams are simply too small.

The sustainability of a specific product is not a simple thing to ascertain. Comparing different products is even harder. What is sustainable butter? Butter from cows in a meadow? From cows not fed concentrated feed, or only a little? From cows that keep their calves with them for a long time? From cows from your own country, or a neighboring country, or a different continent? How do you know for certain that one pack of butter is more sustainable than another? What about coffee? Does sustainability mean bushes grown on small areas of land on the margins of the rainforest? Or in large plantations where water usage, pesticides, herbicides, and erosion are strictly controlled? And what about artificial fertilizer?

Unless you're an expert and have all relevant information available as well, you don't know where to start. You simply have to trust the producer. But consumers doubt the objectivity of producers across the board, especially when it comes to elusive concepts like sustainability. There are also too many quality certificates, invented by individual small producers, with the best of intentions, and they are not systematically verified by third parties. There is no quality certificate that applies to all meat. Of course advertising only adds to the confusion, as no producer will ever say its product is not sustainable. Every producer these days presents an environmentally friendly image.

Consumer consciousness of interlinked food supply chains has grown over the past decade in another way, thanks to environmental awareness. More and more attention is being paid to the life cycle of machinery; to the possibilities of recycling it or at least of converting waste into energy; and to the development of degradable materials, not least those that end up as landfill, such as biodegradable plastics or packaging made of straw or corn leaves. By regarding all waste, including energy, as future "food"—in other words, as an ingredient for other production processes—we can close our production cycles.

On our planet, that vast but finite ecosystem, waste does not disappear. It will always be somewhere and is always either reused or very slowly degraded. New designs are helping us to reuse things in the best ways possible. Take furniture with a wooden frame, cushion covers, and stuffing that can all be reused, or greenhouses that store the sun's heat underground. That idea of reuse or multiple use can also be applied to food for human consumption: waste becomes compost, while leaves and stems (biomass) become an ingredient for packaging or for generating energy (biofuel). This development too is more than anything a matter of awareness, and it is not essentially new, because poverty has always stimulated recycling. In the Philippines, for example, rice straw is used for growing mushrooms; as stuffing for mattresses; for heating; and, when mixed with mud, as a building material.

Most consumers feel misled by the product information they read on packaging—the small percentage of shoppers who read it at all, that is, who tend to be people who think about what they are eating. The average consumer wants to do the right thing but does not know how and will probably not look up each product on the Internet or use the apps now being developed to make information available right there in the shop by means of a phone or tablet. Does "ecological" mean "sustainable"? Or "fair trade"? Or does it signify both? What is the relationship between local and sustainable? What about labels saying "Rainforest Alliance," or "EU organic"? There does not seem to be a single objective source of information about what arrives in our shops. No wonder we are inconsistent in our shopping: we buy fair trade coffee, or an expensive Italian brand without the fair trade logo, but at the same time we buy cheap pairs of jeans that were almost certainly made using child labor.

There are three things here that can easily become mixed up. First are the various certificates that guarantee certain qualities of the product, such as fair trade or organic farming without artificial fertilizer and chemical pesticides, fungicides, and herbicides. These certificates are recognizable by their logos. Then, more broadly, labels offer information about the origin and composition of the product, sometimes comparable with the guarantees given by the stamp. Third is the important issue of who ensures the quality assessment has been carried out correctly. This is called "certification" and ideally it ought to be in the hands of an independent organization that is not involved in either producing or selling the product. Certification is an additional instrument for overseeing the food sector itself and any international agreements it makes about improvements.

Because of this mass of certificates, logos, and information, almost all consumers are confused. On top of that, on several occasions the reality of production has turned out to be not as suggested. Far from all marks of approval can be trusted. Small farmers do not always receive a fair price, and the use of chemicals is not always cautious, especially outside Europe. The pretentions are high-minded but also rather vague. "Ecological" can be a variant on "organic," meaning no artificial fertilizer, but that says nothing about the effect of cultivation on the landscape and the soil and therefore about ultimate sustainability, whereas the label suggests that the environment will not be harmed in any way. Certificates and logos are used by countless producers, producers' organizations, and supermarkets. Currently everyone is free to invent one, and the result is a flood of information with no clarity about independent verification unless it is specifically mentioned. One example of truly independent certification is the stamp "UTZ certified" (which in the case of coffee, tea, and cocoa guarantees both sustainability of production and a fair income for producers), but there are few supervising institutions, so a monopoly could conceivably emerge in the sense that a single organization could corner the market in verification. At the moment the majority of world food products by far, perhaps well over 90 percent, are not certified.

The various actors in the food supply chain, from producers to supermarkets, are in discussion nationally and internationally with the aim of bringing clarity to all this. But as long as there are no independent international institutions checking claims, comparing different quality assessment processes in different countries will remain difficult. Nonetheless, the quality of certification schemes is improving, and the number of different logos is likely to be reduced.

The consumer wants to know not only whether the supply chain is sustainable and safe but also what exactly is in the product. Given the growing share of processed products and increasing anxiety about allergies, this is extremely important. Is apple juice made only with juice from apples? What is in fruit juice? Does it include gluten, or added sugar? A "gluten-free" logo now exists, and added sugars have to be mentioned on the label. Consumers have become more critical about claims concerning the effects of foods on the environment and on their risk of causing cardiovascular disease.

One of the most important sources of uncertainty and confusion are E numbers, which arise from a European system for the coding and classification of additives. Additives are extremely diverse. They include colorings, thickeners, and emulsifiers, but also antioxidants and antibiotics, and chemicals that influence flavor and acidity. Products with E numbers are regarded by many consumers as unnatural, synthetic, and even dangerous, so a market has emerged for "E-number-free products." Yet E numbers are also allocated to innumerable natural substances, such as vitamins. Their absence merely means that nothing has been added. An E number is given only after the substance has been approved based on extensive scientific research. Most rich countries outside Europe have a comparable system.

Almost everything stated on the label and almost every decision about the composition of food is the result of international negotiations and agreements. These are partly laid down at a European level, under the supervision of the European Food Safety Agency, and in the United States by the U.S. Food and Drug Administration. Then there is the Codex Alimentarius, which is the responsibility of specialist agencies of the United Nations, a system of standards of food composition that are of great importance for food safety. This codex determines not just what can be called "frozen peas" or "apple juice" or "pure chocolate" but also what the acceptable quantities of pesticide residues are.

A serious point of contention in recent years has concerned the labeling of foods that contain ingredients derived from genetically modified organisms. This applies especially to soy and corn (in cookies, for example). Labeling would involve extra costs, because product streams would have to be kept separate. The United States, and almost all other countries growing genetically modified crops, think this would be pointless, because there is no difference in risk between these and other products. Europe, however, insists that the consumer has the right to know what is in a product, above a critical threshold of 1 percent.

Information by means of a quality stamp, logo, or label gives no guarantee of sustainable shopping, but it is a necessary condition for the encouragement of more sustainable behavior. At first sight a label seems a good thing, and the more information the better, yet there are complications to giving detailed information, quite apart from the confusion it can cause.

So every mouthful remains an act of conscience and consciousness. Those who eat link themselves to thousands of others who work in the food supply chain, not just farmers, growers, and fishermen but also truck drivers and breeders, checkout clerks and traders at the Chicago Commodities Exchange, and politicians in Brussels or Moscow who make decisions about subsidies and import tariffs. There is a great deal of room for improvement with regard to food safety, working conditions, and fair prices for producers and workers. Even if in the long term the food network becomes more regionally oriented, complex global interconnectedness is here to stay. Not everything can be produced everywhere, and food security is best guaranteed by producing things where they are best produced, where the soils are most fertile, water most easily available, the climate most suitable, and trained workers available. At those places on the earth—and fortunately there are many of them—the best food can be produced at the lowest cost and with the least damage to those other food chains, the natural cycles that bind all life together. There may be countless other reasons to promote or maintain regional food chains—from sheep's cheese to olive oil and "wild" strawberries as a niche market—to improve life in the countryside and maintain landscapes, for example. But even then we are bound by what we eat to all others in the chain who make possible the abundance we take for granted.

THIRTEEN

A Shrinking Paradise: Back to Scarcity?

It frequently happens that in spots where forests have been felled, springs of water make their appearance, the supply of which was previously expended in the nutriment of the trees.   PLINY THE ELDER, *The Natural History* (XXXI: 30)

The only true paradise is paradise lost.
MARCEL PROUST, *Remembrance of Things Past: Finding Time Again*

Paradise in Crisis

"I had a farm in Africa, at the foot of the Ngong Hills," runs the famous first sentence of *Out of Africa* by Danish writer Karen Blixen, published in 1937. Anyone reading the book or watching the romantic film based on it will be unable to escape a feeling of intense nostalgia for the time when antelope and lions still roamed freely across the savannah, proud as the nomadic Masai, and coffee plantations blossomed "like a cloud of chalk." Karen Blixen first came to East Africa in 1913. When she left again twenty years later, the hills were no longer virgin territory, partly because of the influx of British colonizers and their capital.

I first visited Ngong in the 1980s, seventy years after the writer. Much had changed. Along what was once the quiet country road to the Ngong Hills stood rows of huts with traditional reed roofs, interrupted here and there by gray concrete structures. In the shadow of rubber trees women sold beans and corn laid out in heaps on mats.

Today, a century after Karen Blixen's arrival, the suburbs of Nairobi stretch as far as Blixen's Ngong Hills. The roads are asphalted; droning trucks and buses drive back and forth. Of the forests in the valleys only occasional clumps of bushes remain. Nowhere will you find the wilderness out of which the leopard appeared that ate Blixen's beloved dog close to her home. Over the city hangs a permanent stench of gasoline and rotting detritus.

All these changes have one fundamental cause: the growth of Nairobi. When Karen Blixen and her husband arrived, fewer than 25,000 people lived in the city. That number had doubled by the time she left. Now its population is more than 3 million, and it is one of the most dangerous cities in Africa, with the continent's largest slum. The land, with its fertile volcanic soil, the best in Africa, produces an average of a mere 1.5 tons of corn per hectare, no more than in Blixen's day. The modest nature reserves close to Nairobi bear no resemblance to the paradisiacal landscapes that Karen and her lover admired from their single-engine plane. The wild animals have become a tourist attraction. Most distressing of all to my mind is the sight of ten parked Land Rovers with filming and flashing tourists surrounding an old elephant that has nowhere left to hide.

Faced with this image and all those other images of clear-felled forests and dried-up riverbeds, the thought is unavoidable: how can it be that in less than a century humans have completely destroyed this African paradise and all the other paradises? How could we have got it into our heads to rob the earth of its harmony in the name of progress and food? With so little success, too, given the persistent poverty and hunger. Of course these are not rational questions, because all kinds of logical explanations can be given for the growth of the human population and the disappearance of wild animals, such as better healthcare and damage to nature by roads and cultivation. Medical care, especially the reduction in child mortality, has not been matched by increased crop yields or trade, so everywhere more land is in use at the expense of nature.

This explanation does nothing to assuage the feeling of sadness at what has been lost. With that feeling comes a need to apportion blame, for many people at any rate. Is all this the fault of colonialism and capitalism, or of individual greed and exploitation, with or without the collaboration of local elites, or is it a more subtle, more unmanageable process that human beings cannot control? The most worrying questions are whether we'll survive it and whether the earth will survive us. Are we heading for a breakdown of society, partly brought about by economic crises, in which it will be every man for himself? In other words, does the triumph of agriculture and the globalization of the food supply have a dark side?

We are daily bombarded by talk of loss and calamity. It's impossible to turn on the television, look at the Internet, or open a newspaper without coming upon iconic images of the desperate state of the planet: crowded cities with children begging at the traffic lights, families living in cardboard boxes or under a sheet of plastic, ramshackle factories belching black smoke, and mountains of waste where disheveled people fight for the last scraps of food. Only one conclusion can be drawn from all those dried-up lakes, polluted rivers, women at deep wells with greenish foamy water, rusted taps that have run dry, and cracked earth where emaciated animals lie dying: the world is going to rack and ruin.

Or take those devastating floods caused by rivers overflowing their banks, swollen by uninterrupted monsoon rains and washing away people, houses, and livestock. Water seems to have become our enemy, and at the same time we are the enemy of water. When it comes to wasting water, no greater example of cynical disregard can be found than the creation in deserts of golf courses, which need sprayers going all the time. Everywhere we see signs of destruction. Oceans are becoming acidic, fish stocks are disappearing, and coral is being bleached. Such natural disasters as hurricanes, floods, forest fires, even earthquakes and tsunamis all seem to be warning signals, symptoms of a sick, overexploited planet.

Our concern about the planet, our guilt, and the surrounding controversies converge in the issue of climate change. It's our greenhouse gas emissions, a consequence of our use of fossil fuels, that are affecting planetary processes so profoundly. Never before in all those hundreds of thousands of years of evolution has humankind manifested itself on such a scale. Earlier consequences of human intervention were always local: erosion, silted up rivers, deforestation, or drainage of marshes. Now everything is different, and we are like sorcerer's apprentices, powerless and astonished at what we have done. The effects of climate change on food production seem irreversible and unavoidable. Farmers can no longer depend on the seasonal rains; it rains more or perhaps less often, in different seasons, but generally harder than before. The cultivation of crops that require plentiful water, like rice and vegetables, is becoming more difficult. Diseases and infestations are increasing as a result of moisture and high temperatures, causing yields from crops and livestock to plummet.

———

Humanity is not threatened by natural phenomena alone; the market too, that epitome of human invention, has escaped our control. Prices fluctuate more and more unpredictably and can rise at a terrifying rate. Governments react in blind panic with measures that are counterproductive, such as market-disrupting subsidies or the closure of borders to exports, so that prices are driven up even further. Experts warn that the era of cheap and readily available food is over for good. Poor countries are at risk of widespread hunger; refugees crowd at the gates of Europe and the

United States. In big cities food riots are becoming more common, and they are violently put down. Even in the rich West, food is so expensive for some that food banks have become essential. The prices of food and oil fluctuate simultaneously, more dramatically than ever before.

Energy and food are, after all, inextricably linked. High oil prices make artificial fertilizer expensive and raise the cost of tractors and transportation, refrigeration and processing. This puts yet more pressure both on farmers, forced to produce food for the lowest possible price, and on consumers, for whom food becomes almost unaffordable. Part of this scenario is the production of biofuels, which have turned out to be a spurious solution to the problem of sustainable energy production. They are helping neither to reduce energy prices nor to stabilize the output of greenhouse gases. Worse, where biofuels are grown there is no room for food crops. Farming for purposes other than food production, to produce fuel or plastics, comes at a direct cost to the poor. In an unrelenting vicious circle, this leads to inflation, unrest, and financial speculation. How can we have sunk so low that we allow unscrupulous traders to speculate with futures contracts for food and biofuel? To say nothing of the governments that subsidize it all.

There is more: population pressure, toxins, and climate change lead to the loss of species diversity on earth. Soon, it seems, only nettles and grass will grow outside our cities. The sources of genetic variation are drying up and with them the potential for finding life-saving genetic characteristics that could increase yields. Genetically modified seeds are said to be intruding on nature, threatening biodiversity and even human health.

Poor farmers are the ultimate victims in this doomsday scenario; their land produces so little that they don't even have enough seed for the next crop. So they are tied hand and foot to traders who sell them seed at extortionate prices. The despair is so great that they give up farming and sometimes see no other way out than to kill themselves with agricultural poisons, as the tragic statistics from India demonstrate, where more than 200,000 farmers are said to have taken their own lives. Anyone who is still producing food watches it rot at the roadside. Drought and overpopulation drive environmental refugees into cities and to rich countries in their millions. Diseases and infestations are said to be increasing, while at the same time such useful insects as bees are dying en masse because of the use of all-destroying chemicals.

Even in rich countries farmers seem to have no choice, caught up in the maelstrom of modernization, the exhaustion of ecosystems, and ever-narrowing profit margins. All over the world the countryside is left impoverished, populated by elderly people who lack the strength to feed themselves or to run a business. Where farming still goes on, massive machinery ruins the landscape. Chickens are stuffed into cages in their tens or even hundreds of thousands; cows never see the light of day. Without noticing, we have all fallen into the hands of big businesses allied to the food industry, which decide how we live.

Tied up with this narrative is a sense that our decadence and decline are nowhere so clear as in what and how we eat. Food is becoming an industrial product, high in fat and calories, a throwaway item. Old skills are being lost forever. Farmers are seen as merciless exploiters of animals and sprayers of poison who have no choice but to think only about economic gain. The more animals in a barn the better; the more they are pumped full of hormones and antibiotics the faster the meat-on-legs can be got to the abattoir to be processed into packets that are then sold in the supermarkets for rock-bottom prices, or further processed into unspeakable ready-made snacks that end up at gas stations, where they are gulped down by hurried travelers.

Then it's only a small step to the conclusion that the violation of human rights is closely linked to the stripping of the planet. Two billion people are said to be in a downward spiral of malnutrition and despair, and if they try to make their voices heard, they are silenced. Even food aid is not a solution, if only because the most generous contributor, the United States, uses its food surpluses as a tool for political coercion. In addition, 40 percent of the food we produce never reaches our plates. No less disturbingly: how can it be that just when the number of overweight people exceeds the number who are hungry, the incidence of eating disorders such as bulimia and anorexia is increasing?

All these arguments lead to just one conclusion: something has gone irreversibly wrong in our relationship with food and farming. The food crisis is said to have become linked with a broader economic and financial crisis, causing a general feeling of gloom and powerlessness. We watch as the world order undermines itself, while the United Nations and international forums are incapable of turning the tide, and politicians, blinded by a lust for power in the short term, fail to make choices and leave consumers to make them for themselves. The whole earth seems to be in an existential crisis, with the risk that peace and security will be lost forever.

––––––––

If you set all these images down together, the result is a caricature. Yet I haven't made any of this up. This narrative is what most of the media like to serve up to us, and what many people in Europe and the rich world fear. This is the world of what I call the "shadow thinkers," a neo-Malthusian vision painted by despondency and powerlessness, reproducing the conclusion of English cleric Thomas Malthus that we will soon all be destroyed by overpopulation and the exhaustion of the earth.

At the same time something remarkable is going on, because that despondency has little real influence on daily life. Most people carry on shopping, traveling, and living without adjusting their behavior very much at all. Without exception, all studies show that the majority of the population in most countries feels reasonably happy. Of course, people are always ready to say that everything was better in the past, but that translates into at most a vague feeling of unrest and uncertainty. A somber, indeed tragic, vision of the world is difficult to reconcile with the other side of the story: the growing prosperity of so many, with more diverse food and less hunger. I don't mean by this to downplay concern over the state of the planet. The questions are, however: what precisely has gone wrong, why, and how irreparable is it?

Nature and Guilt

The idea that people cause the earth irreversible damage by their food needs and their insatiable desire for more is far from recent. Four thousand years ago the success of the Sumerians' irrigated food production went to their heads. Ever larger areas of land were brought under cultivation and increasingly too much water was used—to supply food for trade with the rest of the Middle East. This expansion could not go on for long. Increasing soil salinity and the drying out of riverside farmland were the result of what we would now call unsustainable practices. In a few dozen years the capacity of the grain fields fell to almost zero. So began the fall of the great Sumerian Empire.

Two millennia later, something comparable happened to the ancient Romans. The growing demand for timber, farmland, and pasture led to large-scale deforestation in what is now central Italy and elsewhere. On the slopes of the Apennines great mudslides occurred that were described with horror by chroniclers of the time, such as Pliny the Elder. The mass slaughter of bison herds in North America (carried out partly to deprive the Native Americans of food) remains a symbol of the capitalist expansion of the nineteenth century.

In our own time many people, especially in the rich West, are convinced that most if not all of what people do is bad for nature, whereas nature ought to be our guide. Farming is one of the biggest culprits, because more than any other sector it damages the planet's land surfaces and depletes freshwater reserves. For most of humankind, however, the ability to subdue nature has always been a sign of power and of reassurance that humans can escape their fate and need not be victims of merciless nature. Abundance as a result of farming—or, put another way, the maximization of produce from the ecosystem—has almost always and everywhere been interpreted as a sign of divine blessing.

In the main monotheistic religions the harvest proves each year anew that original sin (the eating of the apple) and the expulsion from paradise that followed have been forgiven. All religions assume that we cannot take the divine benevolence of nature for granted. It must be secured afresh time and again through the respect shown for the god who governs all and through recognition of the humble place of humankind. Farming and food are by their nature always dependent on natural processes, such as rain, sun, and disease, which humans cannot influence and which can be controlled only by a divine power. If people start to tell themselves they are the masters of nature, instead of being led by divine nature, they will be punished for their arrogance.

This was the thinking in the ancient world, when Prometheus, of divine origin but well-disposed toward humans, stole fire from the gods to help mortals, thereby challenging the divine order. Zeus's fury was terrible, of course. Nevertheless, the story created the image of a human who thinks he can be cleverer than the gods, and over the course of history the word "promethean" came to be synonymous with human hubris and guilt. With the decline in importance of a god for whose mercy we must pray and the rise of science, humans moved to the foreground. No rain? Instead of praying to a god for rain, we install irrigation systems. Caterpillars eating the crops? Then we spray them with pesticides, preferably in a scientifically sound way.

The recklessness with which we have subjugated nature to satisfy our desires is now turning against us. In these secularized times we can no longer blame the capricious gods of weather and water for failed harvests and setbacks; we are ourselves responsible. This sums up the attitude of the shadow thinkers, who see only the dark side of the human presence on earth and believe that from now on things can only get worse. It's a revived form of magical thinking. Not the weather gods determine the climate but humanity itself, through emissions of greenhouse gases and by influencing water cycles. Those greenhouse gases have become the symbols and consequences of our greed. Whereas the weather gods could once be appeased by sacrifice, the image of humankind held by the shadow thinkers offers no hope at all. Our destructive and greedy nature means that we humans are ourselves guilty for what is happening to ecosystem earth. This is the new original sin. Once we were sinful because we were driven out of paradise; now we are sinful because we are born in paradise.

There is only one form of redemption from that sin. We can mitigate it a little by having a new respect, even a new reverence, for nature. For most people today in prosperous, temperate regions, nature is no longer a force to be conquered and used for purposes of self-interest but a value in itself that must be respected, if not venerated. Farmland must make room for nature where necessary. In the Netherlands, polders with fertile land are being given back to the sea or to rivers. Civilization is now measured by the prudence with which a culture treats nature. We make continual attempts to give nature space. We no longer see nature as something to be bent to our will but instead try to empathize with it, as it were, as well as creating space for it.

Nature therefore becomes our guide and at the same time a reflection of our morality. The natural is good, the natural must be emulated, the natural is our only certainty. In a high-tech society in particular, in which so much of existence is experienced as artificial, nature becomes an ideal, a counterbalance to coldness and to a sense of being lost in the crowd. Over the past few centuries we have quietly begun to associate nature with mildness and the small-scale, with benevolence toward humanity, and with health. Farming and food must be "natural," because then all things will be well. For agriculture this line of thought means that by using natural processes—for example, by deploying natural biological enemies of pathogens in plants—we hope to create sustainability. There is a great deal to be said for this approach, even if the pointers given by nature are rarely clear. In nature there is no harmony, however much advertisers and environmentalists try to make us believe there is, only a life-and-death struggle.

To inspire us, reference is often made to the traditional practices of farmers and hunters, who are said to have respected nature far more than we do now. The respect for nature found in traditional farming societies is fundamentally different, however, from the idealization of nature in modern urban societies. Traditional farmers had no choice but to adjust to the whims of nature. They learned from hard experience that poor land had to be left to lie fallow, that you cannot grow the same crop in the same soil year after year or graze too many animals in one meadow. Nature leaves us no choice. To ensure this adapted behavior and to prevent individuals from violating the rules at the expense of the group, strict, often religious laws are essential. One famous example is the agricultural sabbatical, the command to let the land lie fallow in the seventh year.

For the traditional farmer, nature's abundance is something that must be extracted by appeasing and "feeding" nature, perhaps with sacrifices or rituals. This respect is born of need, of a fear of failed harvests and of gods who turn against humans. It has nothing to do with a deeper wisdom, a desire for harmony, or idealism, which is all too clear from the terrible damage that can be done by those same farmers if the old rules fall away or can no longer be enforced. The destruction of the Kenyan savannah around Blixen's Ngong Hills is one distressing example.

There is huge gap between traditional communities with their fear of nature and modern society which embraces nature, makes space for it, and spends large amounts of money on it. Because yields in rich countries are so high and they have enough money to import food and animal feed from elsewhere, citizens of the developed world can permit themselves not only to avoid exploiting nature but also to leave it untouched. The "giving back" of fertile land to nature, as if nature were a being with requirements and rights, has become a moral duty. It is compensation for the destruction of nature carried out in pursuit of riches.

Growing concerns for animal rights and their welfare are part of this worldview. Having served us as meat or to carry loads and pull vehicles, animals are now symbols of free nature, especially those ancestors of the animals in our meadows, the aurochs and the wild horses. Nature and animal protection in our own countries or elsewhere are a way of recompensing for things we do elsewhere to meet our needs. Animals are regarded as having intrinsic value and as deserving respect for their needs and environment, even if they are in the end a commodity, serving our own purposes.

We are complex and contradictory creatures, inspired by religion and by mythical ideas about nature but at the same time by the promethean idea that humankind, mindful of the Old Testament, is made in God's image and must subjugate nature. We are caring steward and ruler in one. At first sight it seems a paradox, but from the idea that we must let nature take its course it's only a small step to going beyond nature. We ask, proudly, why we must take the difficult route of acquiring milk by breeding animals who make it from sun and grass when we can create the same amino acids in bioreactors. Or why, if we do use cows as milk producers, we shouldn't have them manufacture useful by-products as well, such as insulin and lactoferrin. This brings us to the crossing of boundaries between humans and nature, which we see reflected in the debate about genetic modification and food with pharmaceutical properties.

We not only dominate nature until it is exhausted, we can where necessary manipulate it to make it produce what we need, with molecular precision. We use bacteria to move DNA from one cell to another for us or insert the light-emitting molecules from jellyfish in plants to make the latter glow in the dark. Our influence stretches from molecules to the entire planet. Because of us, the ice caps and permafrost are melting; because of us, it's raining more, or perhaps less; we've caused the rivers to change their course. In this vision we've had the audacity to step right into the domain of God or the gods. It is a step in human evolution that goes far further than the domestication of species for food production.

More than any other modern medium, video in the form of documentaries and feature films shows the extent to which people are destroying the earth. There is no more gratifying sensation to be had than by looking at disasters for which we collectively bear the blame yet which we can enjoy in luxury cinemas and our own well-heated homes, ideally with the symbols of our guilt—popcorn, hamburgers, pizza, and soft drinks—in our laps. I do not mean films that play on the classic fear of uncontrollable nature, such as *Jaws*, *The Birds*, or *King Kong* (where the monster does have some human characteristics), but films that take as their subject human mismanagement. In many films it turns out that if nature is polluted (*The Day after Tomorrow*) or commercially exploited (*Jurassic Park*), it turns against us—as if nature has its own coordinated will.

Anyone who lines up all those images of the deterioration of the planet will be forced to conclude that the audacity of modern humans has brought about a disastrous situation. But has there not always been human hubris when faced with the limits of nature? Pride and arrogance have always been the motive for all the improvements we have reached collectively. Those who never experiment will never discover the limits of their potential or test new solutions by trial and error. If Neolithic farmers had not discovered that they had to burn forests to create fertile, weed-free fields for crops, and that they could divert streams, and if twentieth-century chemists had not discovered that artificial fertilizer could be made in factories using synthetic ammonia, all of us would still be engaged throughout our lives in the struggle for food. The essential difference is that there are far more of us now, with far more ambitious hopes for our well-being, and that the means available now have far more large-scale, lasting, and drastic effects.

Pride is not in itself a negative force, but its scale and the things we make the target of our exuberance, from fossil fuels to genetic modification, from nuclear power to artificial intelligence, should give us pause. Our creative curiosity is one side of the coin, our destructive recklessness the other. The question we face is how to find a balance, just like the balance between defeatist doom-mongering and short-sighted optimism. How can we channel our curiosity in such a way that we truly learn from our mistakes? That humans never learn, as some shadow thinkers insist, is pure fiction. Wallowing in guilt and personal impotence is too easy as well. It gets in the way of the learning process and fails to do justice to the vision of the majority of the world's population. In Asia, in Africa, and in South America, people are striving for progress. There, far more explicitly than in developed countries, they want to free themselves from the limitations of nature. So huge dams are built, lakes drained, insecticides sprayed, and so on. These actions sometimes lead to disaster, and they certainly aren't all sensible, but most mistakes are eventually rectified, especially now that knowledge and technology no longer have political boundaries and the most sustainable techniques can be brought in from elsewhere.

So a different story can be told, one of hope and gradual improvement, a story rarely featured by the media, because hope is modest and accounts of it are generally far from spectacular. In contrast to shocking pictures of famine and ravaged soil, we know that rice yields have doubled in China as a result of the planting of hybrid rice, the debilitating cattle disease rinderpest has been eliminated in Africa, algae is used instead of fishmeal in fish farming, and nature is protected or even replenished even as it is also farmed to provide food (such as in fish farming in the Doñana Nature Reserve in Spain, at the mouth of the Guadalquivir River). The history of human intervention is not simply about example after example of destruction but includes a positive sequence of events as well: increasing recognition of the planet's ecological limits, technological curiosity, and the elimination of hunger and of conditions unfit for humans and animals.

How Scarcity Disappeared

Anyone who truly wishes to understand the negative effects of food production must first gain insight into the history of human intervention on earth. Expulsion from paradise marks the mythical moment when the first two people were thrown back on their own resources in a world of scarcity. No longer did everything serve as food for them, no longer did roasted doves fly into their mouths; they had to survive by their own strength, in their own sweat. We should take this literally. Farming and food demand manual labor—a lot of it—and result in low yields and frequent failed harvests. Throughout most of history a field of wheat or barley yielded not much more than a hundred kilograms per hectare, which could be increased only by irrigation.

It took another 4,000 years before animals were tamed to become draft animals and working the land grew a little easier. During the thousands of years that followed, people increasingly learned to bend the ecosystem to their will to make it produce what they needed. With every step, human control of natural processes increased and with it the precision and purposiveness of their work. The invention of the planting stick and later the plough, the selection of the most productive plants and animals, the use of water for irrigation, the adding of nutrients to the soil—each of these technological innovations led to higher yields and therefore greater extraction from the ecosystem. Scarcity and hunger were part of the picture throughout those years, however. A majority of the population had access to only minimal calories and ate a monotonous diet with few animal proteins.

Then came a thunderclap on the evolutionary stage. In the second half of the nineteenth century these gradual developments gained momentum as a result of the Industrial Revolution. A radical change came about through the sweeping away of the inherent limitations that had applied everywhere until then. Human and animal work were replaced by energy from fossil fuels, so that far more land could be put into production and more food moved around the world more quickly. The development of means of preservation and cooling meant food could be made available for longer and transported in good condition. Artificial fertilizers multiplied the productivity of the land. When in the course of the twentieth century other chemicals followed to combat loss to insects and weeds, yields grew again. The combined consequences of the expansion of acreages by mechanical cultivation, storage and preservation methods, and increased yields per hectare and per hour of labor brought about an unprecedented revolution. From the land of scarcity we found ourselves—potentially at least and far from everywhere—in the land of plenty. The inherent fertility of the land, diseases or infestations, and the seasons now determined how much food could be produced in a given place, rather than the amount of human energy deployed. The whole world with all its ecosystems was suddenly at the disposal of humans, wherever they lived.

As soon as food becomes available in abundance and the number of calories per head of population gradually starts to rise, the predictable happens. As with other species, expansion of food supplies is accompanied by demographic growth. Improved hygiene and medical care reinforce this effect. In a little more than two centuries the human population increased sevenfold, and life expectancy more than doubled. At the same time the number of people engaged in agriculture and food production fell spectacularly. Per hour of human work, productivity shot up and with it, well-being. Then another change in the trend occurred. All the studies concur: the constant availability of food and medical care eventually leads to a fall in the number of offspring and to longer, healthier lives with more individual freedom to spend time on things other than taking care of the basic necessities of life.

So in the course of the second half of the twentieth century we arrive at a new earth system, created by humans, in which there is no longer any visible relationship between human effort and the ecological consequences of food production. Because other activities are making human influence felt as well, from industry to urbanization, transportation and tourism, it is right to speak of a new geological period that began with the Industrial Revolution: the Anthropocene. The term, drawn from the natural sciences, does not fully reflect the fact that this era is also a new cultural and mental phase. Since it began, technology has been the greatest of cultural forces. Collectively we in the rich countries have forgotten the labor and sweat of those thousands of years of history. Life is starting to look increasingly like the mythical paradise, with food available in unlimited quantities at almost no cost. Cheap calories are now taken for granted. We are no longer confronted daily by the seasons and by limits to the capacity of the land. In our cities and supermarkets it is always summer, always harvest time, in a continual feast of plenty. No wonder our wastefulness and desire to consume are boundless. Consumption is turning from a necessity into a fashion. We drink imported mineral water that comes in a bottle, rather than water from the tap, even though in most developed countries tap water is as good (or better) bacteriologically and often contains less salt. If you take account of the entire production chain of bottled water and its transportation, then tap water is 150 times cheaper, but such considerations no longer count.

At the same time a feeling is growing among large segments of the population that something is fundamentally wrong. Since the end of the Second World War living standards and the quantity and quality of our food have risen steadily, but we no longer take these improvements for granted. It begins with worries about chemicals. The image arises of a world without forests and bees, without birds, where the rivers are polluted. This is the prelude to a broader anxiety about human pressure on the environment and fossil fuels, as expressed in the report of the Club of Rome in the 1970s. Yet in the decades that followed, gloomy reports about overpopulation and the destruction of the earth turned out time and again to have overstated the case. The population bomb is not a bomb; the image of the earth as a burning candle or a lifeboat is an exaggeration; new reserves of fossil fuels are constantly being exploited, resulting in increased supplies; and more people are better fed, healthier, and employed than thirty years ago. In almost all fields, from water purity to air quality, the figures show that the situation has not worsened in proportion to population growth; in fact in many cases it has improved despite this growth. Our wealth makes it possible to protect land and its diversity of species, to filter water, and to make stringent demands regarding industrial emissions. This is true not only in the rich West but also increasingly in poor and emerging economies.

But these hard facts, which should make us relatively optimistic, do not ease Western concerns at all. The malaise is caused more by a change in perception than by the facts themselves. Many people in developed countries have lost faith in science. Anyone who reacts based on a sense of guilt and lack of knowledge will distrust the facts and suspect a conspiracy among scientists. Because researchers in the fields of agricultural and nutritional sciences, as well as economists, sometimes find themselves in direct opposition to nongovernmental organizations and action groups (which carry out their own research), the consumer is left confused. An unbridgeable gap yawns between the general gloom of the Western shadow thinkers and the technological optimism of such countries as Brazil and China. Precisely because there is no consensus, unease persists, and with it a need to blame a specific bogeyman.

Trouble in Paradise: Real Scarcity and Shrinkage

We should not downplay damage to the ecosystem, but neither should we make a caricature out of it. There is no reason for widespread alarm or apocalyptic scenarios. Pessimism can all too easily become a self-fulfilling prophesy that leads to apathy, defeatism, and reactionary dogmatism. That we have been so successful so far despite all the challenges is no guarantee for the future, however. The notion that everything can be shaped to suit us, the blind optimism that insists all problems are solvable quite rightly has many critics. Some types of food production may be in danger, probably not worldwide but locally and regionally, unless we apply new production methods and introduce policies to secure them. We also know that a ruthless pursuit of increased production without any scientific foundation leads to horrific tragedies, as the history of China, Russia, and Cambodia demonstrate.

So is paradise really shrinking, in the sense that fewer resources will be available in the future? The superficial answer is: "Yes, but...." Here too, it's the details that count. The human population is after all still growing at a rate unprecedented in our evolution. Between now and 2050 another two billion people will be added. Thus we will have less of everything per head of population: farmland, water, artificial fertilizer, fossil energy, and so on. This is one reason shadow thinkers always insist that population growth must stop. But the assumption that it means everything automatically becomes more scarce is based on a fallacy.

The relationship between population and economic growth is multifaceted. Even if a billion people are suffering from hunger now, this is not a matter of absolute shortages but of the distribution of purchasing power. It's not food that's the scarce resource, now or in the future, but economic growth and incomes. Halting population growth would in any case be impossible, as only the most draconian measures stop people having children. More importantly, we don't need to intervene, because growth will soon flatten out. Now 1.2 percent per year, growth will fall to 0.9 percent and after 2030 to 0.6 percent. For the sake of comparison, in the decade between 1960 and 1970 the world population grew by an average of 2.2 percent per year. Consistently negative population growth is predicted for the twenty-second and twenty-third centuries, when the number of people will fall rapidly. Some estimates suggest that by 2200 Italy will have fewer than a million inhabitants. Sufficient food, hygiene for children, and the education of women that leads to a higher age at marriage and improved knowledge about reproduction naturally lead to a reduction in the average number of children people have. This is the case everywhere, although in Africa the reduction has been very gradual as yet.

Population growth is an engine of economic growth and higher labor productivity. Without it there will be no care or pensions for those who are not working. We would therefore do better to worry about the prediction that from the end of this century the world's population will shrink. The real problem of population growth is after all not the absolute number reached but the speed at which it happens. This is particularly worrying in Africa and parts of Asia, in situations where scarce resources are not always available or are poorly managed.

A point that we tend to notice rather less concerns the growth, or indeed lack of growth, of rural populations. The ratio of those who produce food to those who don't is becoming increasingly detrimental all over the world. Fewer people are left to farm the land, with the result that production per worker will have to increase faster than productivity in the population as a whole. More than 2.2 billion people live in economies where agriculture is one of the dominant sectors, but nonetheless, most young people even in those regions do not see agriculture as their future. Young people, especially young men, do not want to work the land and prefer to leave for the city. An estimated 70 percent of arable farming in China is carried out by women. This problem can be solved only by investment in farming and appropriate types of labor-saving mechanization. These investments would allow incomes to rise and working conditions to improve, making farming attractive again as an occupation. Such changes will not happen quickly, so we should be concerned about the fall in the number of people available to work in food production and food processing.

In the end it's all about the combination of population growth and diets. In the coming decades the growth of the middle class will drive major change. The middle class in many Latin American and Asian countries is increasing by more than 10 percent a year and with it demand for animal products and luxury items. The greatest challenge will therefore be to supply sufficient animal protein. Were we dependent on livestock alone as a source of protein, the scarcity of animal proteins and animal feed would be a major worry. But the way forward will probably be to replace meat and fish to some extent with vegetable proteins and with creatures lower down the food chain, such as insects and algae. Substitution offers a way out, so there is no reason in principle to assume fundamental scarcity or shrinkage.

So will we have enough land in the future if the amount of it per head shrinks as a result of population growth and it comes under increasing pressure from the requirements of livestock farming, and the need for animal feed, and biofuels? Yes, we have enough, although fertile, well-watered land is not evenly distributed across the earth. A decade ago we still thought that the amount of land suitable for crops and grazing was running out, but it now appears that with the right techniques, previously unused land can be cultivated, such as the Cerrado in Brazil. As well as the total of 1.5 billion hectares of farmland now in use, in sparsely populated regions of the world (with fewer than twenty-five people per square kilometer) there are still almost 500 million hectares of potentially suitable but unused land, 200 million of which are in Africa south of the Sahara, more than 100 million in Latin America, and 50 million in Eastern Europe and central Asia. This land does not include valuable natural landscapes.

There is something else that eases concerns about the amount of land available. Yields per hectare can be increased relatively easily. The outputs of most fields where crops are grown are now well below their potential; on average, current yields are in the order of 30 percent of what could be achieved.

Is there a maximum number of people the world can feed? Yes, but the estimated theoretical biological maximum (around 50 billion, if we use all the available surface area, including the tropical forests, and if everyone is strictly vegetarian) is so far in excess of the expected 9 billion that we have little reason to worry. Local shortages of land may well occur, however, if population growth outpaces the increase in food production, and if pollution and poor irrigation techniques make land unusable in the short term. This is already the case in highly populated areas and close to cities, as in the Nile delta.

Land is not scarce on a world scale, but locally it is, as well as for countries that want to secure their own food production. This explains the tenfold increase in foreign demand for land, sometimes called "land hunger" or "land grabbing." Before 2008 only 4 million hectares in the world were in the hands of foreign investors. Just a few years later the figure had risen to almost 50 million hectares. China is the biggest investor in this sense. Three-quarters of land held by investors is in Africa, in countries including Ethiopia, Mozambique, and Sudan. The fear is that this will lead to scarcity for the local population. It is striking that only in a small minority of cases do the investors actually use the land to produce food. It seems it is mainly being acquired as a kind of insurance. There seem as yet to be no detectable gains or losses for the local population, but the transfer of land may well cause scarcity, especially if it is used for biofuel, as some plans suggest it will be.

The positive side of land transfer (which often takes the form of long-term rental contracts rather than purchase) is that it facilitates investment in improving yields, which are currently far too low. In addition, in several sparsely populated countries in Africa, including Zambia and Sudan, less than 1 hectare per person is farmed. The reasons for this underuse are not lack of fertility or water but other factors, such as market dysfunction and low investment. Large-scale production by investors could therefore in theory contribute to a rise in food production, as long as a number of conditions are met. Responsible investment by foreigners in land involves paying attention to the environment and social conditions, contributing to local food security, and allowing those affected to have a say.

This is not about surface area alone, however. The usability of land can be severely affected by a deterioration in its chemical, biological, and physical properties. The fertile layer of humus may be washed away, and land can become too salty or too acidic if it is used badly. Acidification can result if what are known as acid sulfate soils or cat-clays—types of sea clay that form in oxygen-poor conditions—are drained inexpertly. Over-fertilization can have countless damaging consequences too. According to some estimates, in certain vulnerable areas 5 tons of fertile topsoil is lost per person per year. This kind of damage cannot be repaired in the short term. If erosion happens more quickly than the formation of a new layer of topsoil, then the land is not being used sustainably, and irreparable damage is being done on a human timescale. In the humid tropics it can take 100 to 1,000 years for a new layer of soil to form. On a fifth of the arable land and a tenth of pastureland some form of degradation has taken place, but on the same percentage of ground we see improvement, especially in irrigated areas.

The cultivation of more land and the intensification of production on current farmland have consequences for natural and quasinatural ecosystems. To judge by random checks, almost two-thirds of the ecosystems on earth have already suffered damage. A concern common to all those involved in nature conservation is that biodiversity—in other words, the variety of species and habitats—declines as a result of food production. This stance puts farmers and conservationists in direct opposition to each other. The short answer is that encroachment on the ecosystem for purposes of agriculture always leads to a loss of diversity, even if biodiversity on arable fields is deliberately fostered. Biodiversity increases the longer the ecosystem remains undisturbed, and in general it is higher in tropical regions and on poorer soils with transitions from wet to dry or shady to light conditions. As far as biodiversity and the landscape are concerned, it is indeed true that the more people there are, the greater the pressure on the land, which leads to a real reduction. The untouched ecological paradise is becoming smaller. But at the same time, high productivity in agriculture without excessive use of chemicals leads to less pressure on the land and higher incomes that can be used to protect nature in other areas.

The total quantity of available food is not now declining and will not decline, unless an unforeseen disaster occurs on a planetary scale. In contrast to what many people think, on average more is produced now than we need—by around a quarter—and if we add up everything we now waste or use as biofuel, we are producing twice as much food as we need based on calories alone. In rich countries we throw away 100–150 kilograms of food per person per year.

But that is not the full story. If prices rise further, people whose incomes do not allow them to buy enough food will experience shortages. To ensure food supplies for the poorest people, more must be produced than is strictly necessary, so that prices stay low and stocks are sufficient to even out price fluctuations. To feed 2 billion additional people plus the 1 billion who now eat too little and the billion who do not consume sufficient minerals and vitamins, about 70 percent more food will be needed by 2050. That is a huge amount, but less than half the growth in food production achieved over the past fifty years.

Are yields shrinking or stagnating? Worldwide average grain yields are still rising. In the second half of the twentieth century the *increase* in yields grew from 2 kilograms per hectare per year to 50 kilograms per hectare per year. In developing countries yields grew by 3 percent annually in the first decades of the Green Revolution (from 1965 on). Now the figure has fallen to 1 percent, but that is still an increase, not a drop or stagnation. The decline in growth is mainly the result of inadequate investment in farming, poor farming techniques, uncertain markets, and environmental norms that lead to suboptimal application of artificial fertilizers. For many crops, yields could yet grow spectacularly almost everywhere.

Nonetheless, the growth of yields is also slowing under the best of circumstances, such as at testing stations. So we need to look for fresh breakthroughs, such as plants that capture sunlight more efficiently, make better use of water and nutrients, and are less susceptible to pathogens. Nowhere does it seem as if we have reached the biological limits of what can be produced, even if we may be close to it in some places, such as in the Midwest of the United States, the Dutch polders, or the Île-de-France (an area around Paris).

The raw materials for artificial fertilizer are not as scarce as the doom-mongers claim, certainly not as far as this century is concerned. Nitrogen is not a problem at all, because it is derived from the air, and considerable stocks of potassium and phosphate still exist: enough phosphate probably for hundreds of years, enough potassium certainly. Although at this point no alternative has been found to artificial fertilizer, it is already possible to reclaim nutrients, even if it is not yet economical. Who knows? Perhaps in a hundred years we will find alternatives to potassium and phosphate, or discover new stocks or ways of synthesizing them from other molecules.

Will we have enough insects left to pollinate crops, or will the disappearance of bees present a serious danger to production on arable farms? Here we have reason to be worried. The chronic exposure of insects even to low doses of neonicotinoid insecticides (an alternative to even more harmful substances) is comparable with exposure to carcinogens. Many biocides are soluble in water, with serious consequences in wet regions. But again, the ultimate balance is not as negative as the shadow thinkers imagine it to be. Other insects can fulfil the role of pollinator. More importantly, many arable crops are self-pollinating, rice for example, or reproduce vegetatively like the potato, so they have no need of bees to help them produce seed. The problem may affect fruit trees and several other horticultural crops that depend on pollination. If not performed by insects, it must be done by hand. But fruit, however useful and tasty, is not the most crucial of crops when it comes to feeding the world.

Is there enough water for our food? Yes and no. The total amount of water on earth doesn't shrink. Unlike other resources, water is not scarce on a world scale, and it doesn't vanish. What evaporates and washes away, or becomes polluted or salinized, still remains part of the hydrological cycle. Even water that ends up in the sea evaporates again and returns to us as rain. Water problems are therefore regional or local in nature. Shortages may exist in some places, as well as problems with quality and quantity. A great deal can be done through better management. In the long term some areas will prove unsuitable for the cultivation of crops, but they may be usable for extensive livestock farming—the Sahel, for example. Increasing drought will lead to the relocation of agriculture here and there, as has been the case throughout history. The Sumerians left their lands, and the Toltecs in the twelfth century migrated as a result of persistent drought in Central America. In some parts of the world we are currently using more water than is available from durable sources, so water levels in the soil are falling, and fossil water reserves are being drawn on.

Globally, farming is the largest user of water: about 70 percent of all the water from durable sources is used for agriculture. The required increase in food production of 70 percent does not mean, however, that 70 percent more water will be needed. The growth in water use can be held at considerably less than that of food production. The key lies in producing more food per unit of water, in other words, in using water more efficiently. The expectation is that a growth of 45 percent in the amount of water available will be sufficient for a growth of 70 percent in food supplies.

That is still a lot, but it's not unthinkable, especially if climate change alters rain patterns in some parts of the world. The amount of water on earth is limited, but water is present in huge quantities, even if we ignore the salty and frozen water that accounts for 97 percent of the total. Every day the rivers bring a vast volume of unused fresh water to the sea. The Amazon alone pours more than 200,000 cubic meters of it per second into the Atlantic Ocean.

Water scarcity is a separate issue from climate change, but it may be made worse as a result of that change. Countless proven techniques exist for using water more sensibly and efficiently, such as irrigating less but at the right moments, improving water infiltration and the water-retentive properties of soils, limiting the outflow of water, and capturing dew. We could also grow less water-hungry crops (jute in place of cotton, for instance), and a great deal of surface water in lakes and rivers could be used for irrigation. Think of Lake Malawi or the Congo River in Africa. Only 4 percent of the land south of the Sahara is irrigated. Worldwide 20 percent is irrigated, and that land is responsible for 40 percent of food production. Sensible irrigation really does pay off.

The amount of water is important, but so is its quality. The eutrophication of surface water and groundwater, arising from an oversupply of nutrients in the form of artificial fertilizer and animal dung, is leading to local shortages of clean water in rich countries. Eutrophication is primarily a problem for ecosystems rather than for agriculture, with the exception of organic farms. For the Netherlands, with its great density of animals and of people, all of them needing green areas, this is a reason to consider reducing the number of livestock.

Animal production is the direct or indirect cause of an unprecedented expansion of cultivation, tree felling, and swamp drainage. Much of this kind of cultivation is intended to bring land into use, rather than to produce food. This is clear from the extremely low density of animals in the largest areas of felling; in the Amazon basin less than one cow is grazed per hectare. Nonetheless, most of the problems of sustainable land use are in the livestock sector and there the fear of—or indeed, the call for—a shrinkage in the numbers is greatest. Animal production, including fisheries, will be the touchstone of how we deal with land sustainability and food. Already 13 percent of cereal production in the world is used for animal feed, and that percentage will rise. Deforestation for feed crops or pasture has increased in the past century, but it has always existed. Iceland was a green island 1,100 years ago, but overgrazing and logging destroyed the forests, and because of the unfavorable climate, woodland vegetation has not returned.

The greatest risk to public health from animal production is presented by animal diseases—namely, zoonoses (diseases that can be passed from animals to humans). They represent a source of potential infection in highly populated areas in particular. The use of antibiotics in animal husbandry and especially poultry farming might lead to the emergence and spread of potentially life-threatening antibiotic resistance in bacteria that infect humans. This problem is not a result of shrinking resources, however, but of incorrect dosage and irresponsible practices, which must be tackled by legislation.

I don't believe anyone has calculated whether a biological limit exists to the number of farm animals (cattle, poultry, and pigs) the earth can sustain. In theory the limitation lies in the amount of feed and therefore of feed crops we can produce, which will be far more than it is now. In huge new, animal-friendly indoor feeding lots and dairy facilities, we could keep far more animals if we wished to, and in a much more efficient and safe way. The current limit to animal production lies in the inefficiency of small-scale systems. In recent decades yields of meat and dairy products have risen spectacularly: by five to ten times in the case of chicken (Brazil) and dairy (China). Productivity could certainly increase further, with better feed, genetic selection, and disease control. Here again there is no physical shrinkage in prospect, although there may be social reasons for not increasing the numbers of livestock.

Changes in rainfall patterns and possible climate change may limit production, because land may become drier or wetter and seasons shift, and storms or frost may damage crops. No matter how serious the effects for farmers, however, these events will not be a decisive factor that endangers food production. Certainly, higher night-time temperatures and humidity, for example, can lead to a reduction in yields, but those effects will be dwarfed by the huge gap that still exists between average yields and the best possible. Since the start of agriculture, farmers have had to adapt to variations in the weather in the short and long term. Crops have been abandoned because of cold—think of the grapevines in southern Scotland in the Middle Ages. Desertification is not merely a contemporary phenomenon; it ravaged China for periods that sometimes lasted thousands of years. The expansion and contraction of deserts in Africa goes back millions of years and may be related to the expansion of ice caps at the poles. Conversely, civilizations have profited from periods of higher rainfall, as the Roman Empire did in what are now North Africa, southern Italy, and Spain. The climate has rarely been stable, even across human generations, let alone centuries.

Adjustment is possible by means of better, more water-saving agricultural techniques and, for example, crop insurance. Some areas will benefit from more rain and warmth, others will suffer. The effect of higher CO_2 levels, which stimulate photosynthesis and with it the growth of plants, is still unknown. The net effect of climate change is far from clear, but it is not purely negative, and its challenge invites new, creative solutions.

Improvements to yields and increased work opportunities and incomes are ultimately the best protection against climate change for vulnerable groups. Ways of reducing emissions of greenhouse gases in farming and the food supply are still in their infancy, but they are certainly possible, even in livestock farming. Agriculture and forestry can contribute to the effects of climate change or mitigate against them by storing more carbon in the soil and by recycling plants and crops back into the soil. This does make less land available for growing food, and such measures require extra labor.

The shadow thinkers who worry about a scarcity of resources point above all to Africa. In no other part of the world are the disasters that threaten our planet and the effects of exploitation more visible, they say. The continent does indeed have the largest population growth, at 2.3 percent per year. There will soon be a billion African mouths to feed. Climate change and fluctuations in the climate may have more negative effects there than elsewhere. But look at the statistics: Africa accounts for 11 percent of the world's agricultural potential and only 15 percent of its land is currently used productively. In Europe we have an average of one tractor for every 26 hectares of farmland, in Asia one for every 72, whereas in Africa there is one tractor for every 307 hectares. That is to say nothing of the many tractors standing rusting for lack of parts or fuel. A full 90 percent of energy use in African agriculture consists of work by humans or animals, and 20 percent of African soils are eroded. Irrigation is negligible. Africa uses only 10 kilograms of artificial fertilizer per hectare, and only 5 percent of seed is improved (hybrid), whereas the figure for Brazil is 90 percent. Those billion mouths to feed can also be seen as a billion pairs of hands to take care of food production, especially because in contrast to other continents, most Africans live in the countryside. Rather than proof that our planet is doomed, Africa is the continent of potential.

———

So what about the Netherlands? It's the most densely populated country in the world, a major exporter of agricultural products and other goods, with a great deal of livestock, energy-intensive industry, and a high volume of commercial traffic, partly because it's a transit country. Horticulture in Dutch greenhouses emits a greater net quantity of CO_2 than the same sector elsewhere, even if transportation is included. The Netherlands has the largest phosphate surplus in all of Europe, and it also produces a great deal of ammonia and nitrogen dioxide. The country exports animals and animal products as well as horticultural products, but the manure stays put. As a result the Netherlands experiences a high degree of environmental pressure per head of population compared to other OECD countries. At the same time, this pressure stimulates the search for solutions, including the reduction of greenhouse gas emissions from cowsheds, nature conservation, and the reclamation of nutrients from animal and human waste. These are great challenges, but they do not imply that resources or food production are systematically shrinking.

Paradise Won and Lost

According to tradition, one of the possible locations of paradise lies where the Tigris and the Euphrates flow together to become one river, the Shatt-al-Arab, in the lowlands of Mesopotamia not far from the sea, near Basra in present-day Iraq. Little is left of that paradisiacal river. Large parts of the delta where the Marsh Arabs once lived have been drained to provide farmland and living space. The delta has been disputed territory since time immemorial. A generation ago Iran and Iraq fought over it, and it was one of the battlegrounds of the Iraq War. As a result of neglect and dams and irrigation works upstream, as well as reduced rainfall, the volume of the river and its tributaries has shrunk, and salt water has penetrated increasingly far into the delta. Fish are killed by the salt, and on the banks the salt is making its way under the fields and into the irrigation water. Crop yields are falling, animals lack fresh water to drink, and even the date palms have been affected. The canals of Basra, once called the Venice of the East, are blocked with filth and brackish silt.

I'm not immune to those images. When I look at the earth from an airplane window at night, for example, at roads, cities, and fields, I see endless traces of humans. There are hardly any dark places left on the earth, only parts of Siberia, South America, and Central Africa. Or from another perspective: from my hotel window on the thirty-seventh floor in an Asian city, the sun comes up through a brown haze. Between the skyscrapers lie the slums, tiny and innocuous looking from so high up. Or when on an ordinary working day I see the overflowing waste bins and the garbage in shopping streets with the remains of pizza and soft drinks. Then I wonder yet again how we can restore what we have lost and at the same time supply all those millions of anonymous people with sufficient food.

The loss of that paradise of empty green earth is easy to blame on greed, exploitation, capitalism, colonialism, neocolonialism, and globalization. Whoever wishes to can see tragedies everywhere: in the loss of the countryside; infringements on the landscape; the encroachment of highways and industrial zones; the pollution and poverty in today's slums; or the disappearance of the wilderness, in the Ngong Hills for example, once a paradise to the Western colonial man (and the occasional rich woman). Using words like "globalization" and "exploitation" as pejorative labels will get us no further toward solving the problems, however. These labels are too simplistic and at the same time too negative. Humans destroy and humans build. It has been so since the beginning.

The question that remains after this survey of possible shrinkage and scarcity concerns the combination and sum of all the problems. Perhaps water and biodiversity will sort themselves out, but what if everything changes simultaneously? Will something happen then that makes reconstruction and correction no longer possible? In essence this is a question about the existence and proximity of what are known as critical thresholds in the earth's ecosystem. Is it possible that we will suddenly reach a tipping point, where an entire ecosystem or even all the earth's life-sustaining functions will be lost?

There's little point arguing over the answer. We have only one earth and nothing to compare with it, so we can only speculate. But if we look at the earth's complex processes with their buffers and feedback mechanisms, we realize that extrapolation from ecosystems such as lakes or ant colonies does not offer the basis for an answer. Ants may succumb, the chemistry of lakes can suddenly change, but humans with their intergenerational learning ability are independent of such systems.

Based on what we know now, food is not the weak link in the existence of the earth's ecosystem but it is one that needs to be looked at realistically. The food crisis is not a crisis of absolute and increasing scarcity, nor of an absolute shortage of land, but one of low yields and inefficient agriculture that takes a great deal of space and is careless in its management of chemicals, biodiversity, landscape, and soil fertility. Those are the limiting and vulnerable aspects of our planet. Volatile food prices reflect a combination of unwise policy and agricultural negligence.

We are not in a shrinking paradise. People can acquire more and healthier food without exhausting the planet. That is the case today, and there is no reason to doubt that it will be the case in the coming decades, unless disaster or war erupt on a vast scale. As long as we have an open world economy with adequate control of quality and working conditions, as well as sufficient spending power, local and regional shortages can be overcome.

———

Yet many people are experiencing a food crisis, first of all those who cannot buy or cultivate sufficient food. They need economic growth and work opportunities. Encouraging words about how there need be no scarcity on scientific grounds are of little use to them, but they are even less well served by shadow thinkers who predict the destruction of the planet.

The rich parts of the world, especially modern cities, find themselves in an identity crisis that is unrelated to real food scarcity. That crisis is all about the disappearance of an image of the world as paradise, as a result of the anonymity and scale of production. The distance between farm and fork, soil and dining table, mean consumers have no say about how and where their food originates. Ignorance and uncertainty increase our sensitivity to gloomy depictions of our world. The true food crisis of our times transcends a romantic view of the past; it relates to the failure to value food, the loss of respect for those who produce it, and the loss of dignity both of those who do not have enough to eat and of those who bolt it down without a second thought.

Science does not have an adequate answer. The crisis lies within us, and it is to a great degree a crisis of the West, which has profited so hugely from progress. The loss of self-confidence in rich Western countries is manifesting itself in other fields too, with uncertainty about the political order and the economy. Autarchy and nationalism are not solutions.

Fortunately, the gloom of doomsday scenarios and shadow thinkers has evolutionary advantages. We are shocked and learn from it. So for the first time in decades food has the attention of politicians, scientists, businesses, and citizens. The limits to growth are not the problem but rather the limits to confidence in our solutions.

FOURTEEN

A Paradise within Reach: Sustainable Food Production

Everything else can wait, but not agriculture.
JAHARWALAL NEHRU, 1948

The future is a convenient place for dreams.
ANATOLE FRANCE, *The Opinions of Jerome Coignard*

The Future Is Now

Years ago, in Central Africa, I once stood still with my Land Rover on the edge of a high plateau in what is now Congo. A steppe of tall bleached grass stretched out before me. Here and there the plain rippled, and along the edges ran the jagged lines of landslips. Deep valleys formed by fast-running rivers of black water and edged with the remains of rainforest crisscrossed the plain. Here and there in the depths were a few oil-palm plantations from colonial times. The soil is made up of a thick layer of grayish-white highly leached sand, once blown in from the Kalahari Desert, on top of an old red clay layer that stretches all the way to South Africa. It's a fragile ecosystem, degraded by annual burning and by overgrazing. Where there are no longer any trees or bushes, the topsoil, already poor, disappears altogether, and farmers struggle to harvest a few cassava roots or a little millet from their fields. All the children, without exception, were undernourished, the women prematurely aged, the men absent, having left to seek their fortune in the city. This was underdevelopment—disheartening, desolate.

But hopeless? No. If you leave the plain alone and stop burning it, the vegetation recovers, and a new microclimate develops. This attracts animals again, including birds that bring seed from elsewhere. Organic matter accumulates in the soil. An agricultural scientist knows that this is possible in theory, but not everyone has had the privilege of seeing it happen in practice. Right there in that drab landscape, in the 1980s, the years of the great African famines, something began of which few dared to dream. In the village of Feshi, not far from the Angolan border, a local businessman patiently experimented for years with seeds and methods of cultivation that would allow people to plant trees and improve meadows. It turns out that even without planting, the bushes grow back, followed by the forest, as soon as you protect the land from fire and grazing. The forest remains at risk, because firewood is scarce.

Imagine what this part of Africa could look like fifty years from now: forested along the contour lines to prevent erosion, with fruit trees, and in between them improved pastureland. There could be rice paddies and vegetable plots along the river valleys; here and there fish ponds; strips of woodland; and plantations of coffee, mangos, vanilla and other profitable products. Imagine small tractors, grain silos, properly graded roads, clean abattoirs and markets, and buildings for farmers' organizations.

This is no absurd vision. Despite the gloom of the shadow thinkers, there is much to be hopeful about in today's world. The economic growth figures for some African countries, such as Ghana, are many times those of European countries. In Asia and Latin America, hundreds of millions have been earning incomes above the poverty level for the past decade. In the emerging economies the middle class is growing far faster than expected. In the rich West an awareness is growing that food is the responsibility of us all. Our evolution from peasant to city dweller to sustainable producer and consumer is a learning process that rarely occurs without complications. Development happens in fits and starts, by trial and error—major errors sometimes. Governments are often slow and bureaucratic, farmers can be conservative and risk averse, the business world is too focused on the short term, and consumers are insufficiently aware that their purchasing behavior can be a vote for a change in relationships. There is no single answer. The key lies in the details, the nuances. Each solution invites the next problem, and with it a new solution, sometimes a radical one.

Take poultry farming. Less than fifty years ago chickens were almost always a peripheral part of any farm. Practically all farmers kept chickens, some more than others, but hardly anyone specialized. Chickens provided eggs and meat, and in many countries this is still the case. Over the past decade improved sanitation, optimized feed, economies of scale, and rapidly expanding specialist breeds for either meat or eggs have led to huge improvements in productivity and in the number of birds. Northwestern Europe, the Netherlands in particular, has taken the lead, followed in recent years by East Asia. The shock of worldwide bird 'flu in 2003 led to the preventive slaughter of many birds, but it also brought greater control of production, so that chickens were no longer allowed outside in case they were infected by wild birds. With increasing exports, the final product has changed too: it's not the whole chicken that counts these days but parts of it: wings, breasts, drumsticks. The consequence of all these changes is that farmers are producing chicken for slaughter more and more rapidly. A chicken is now raised to weigh between 2.1 and 2.5 kilograms in just five or six weeks.

There has been increasing social disquiet in recent years about these "bloated chickens," spurred by many groups of animal welfare activists, leading to new EU legislation on chicken welfare to reduce overcrowding. Some supermarkets and large food wholesalers in Europe have decided not to buy these quick-growing chickens at all but to opt for birds that gain weight more slowly and have more space to move.

This is not a complete answer. Slower growth of chickens means the environmental balance ends up being less favorable, because greenhouse gas emissions are greater stemming from both the longer growing time and the less efficient processing and transportation. It is by no means certain that chickens grown quickly really are worse off than those that have more space but are forced to compete for food. And doubts remain about the health risks for chickens that are allowed outside. Furthermore, Dutch poultry farms, for example, are failing to meet the increasing demand for slow-grown chickens, so the supermarkets are buying from abroad, which results in extra transportation and possibly also extra battery farms and environmental damage elsewhere.

Cut-price chicken is a symbol of increases in scale that most people no longer favor, even though the speed of growth of each bird and their numbers—the scale of the operation—are not necessarily connected. Furthermore, the scale of a chicken house or battery-cage facility and the scale of the business are two different things. In the Netherlands a chicken farm is allowed to have maximum of 240,000 chickens, but no rules govern how many can be housed together in a single unit. In total an average of more than 100 million chickens grown for meat are alive in the Netherlands at any one time, of which half are for export. Environmental and animal welfare organizations advocate a drastic reduction in numbers, but anyone who agrees with them should realize that the problem would only be shifted to other countries and not necessarily solved. Setting aside all arguments about the Dutch export position and jobs, it might make more sense to look for other means of production that are better for chickens, farmers, and the environment and promote them both at home and abroad. This does have consequences for the price, so it requires the cooperation of the consumer. No solution will meet all sensitivities of society, all economic interests, and all environmental goals. Simply transposing the problem to another country is as short-sighted as pretending it doesn't exist. In other words: the story of the chicken is far from over.

_____

Or take the issue of fish consumption. There are countless reasons for taking great care of the threatened fish stocks in the oceans and turning to fish farming to fill an important proportion of human demand for fish. Grounds for hope exist here too. What was impossible until recently now seems conceivable: the reproduction of the most popular tuna species. This means that tuna could finally be farmed, so it would no longer have to be taken from the wild, violently and with unavoidable damage to other species. The expectation is that in the long term, cages at sea, with all the problems of pollution and disease risk that they bring with them, will not be necessary. The development of what are known as tritrophic systems looks promising. Fish are held in ponds that have shellfish in or next to them, which filter the waste from the fish and absorb it. The water then flows into ponds containing algae that use the inorganic substances. The result of such a system is three types of products, little or no water pollution, and a more efficient use of sunlight and nutrients.

_____

Finally, look at that other hot potato, transgenic soy from South America. Most people associate it with terrible damage to the environment, but because of the latest transgenic insect-resistant soy, far less insect damage takes place, so far less spraying with pesticides is needed. That is positive for the ecosystem. Land that previously produced little is now profitable and can provide an income and, to a limited degree, work for the rural population. The high yields also mean that no new areas need to be taken into cultivation. The negative perception is caused in part by the confusion between monoculture and environmental damage. Yes, there are fields full of nothing but soybeans stretching to the horizon, but it's not necessarily the case that this ruins the soil. On the contrary, as a nitrogen-binding plant and good soil cover, soy leads to far less soil degradation than, for example, corn. Nonetheless, monocultures can cause the disappearance of useful insects. Thus other ways of using the soil should be sought, perhaps the introduction of broad planted verges around the soybean fields, or inserting strips of other crops, or rotation with every season. The EU has recently introduced an obligation to devote 7 percent of agricultural land to nature. Yes, soy is exported. Without it there would be no cattle feed and therefore no protein for the population of Asia—at least not in the current set-up.

But in this respect too, new prospects are opening up. A proportion of the meat can be replaced by plant proteins, such as lupines, but also algae, or proteins from insects. Or simply proteins taken from parts of plants that we don't currently use, such as the chaff of cereal crops. In the very long term we may possibly need neither animals nor land to create proteins with the precise composition of amino acids that humans need, producing it instead in factories from single-celled organisms. Or we may be able to breed cultivars of cassava and potatoes with a far better protein content. Much is possible, and some of these technological advances are not even too far off. Of course, animals are still desirable for other reasons, to keep the landscape open, for example.

———

Technical improvements are good not just for increases in scale and efficiency but also for authentic, small-scale, traditional farming. More is being done to reintroduce heirloom varieties of fruit and vegetables, from yellow beetroot and Jerusalem artichokes to completely forgotten types of turnip and quince. Genetic technology and grafting techniques make it possible to create crosses that are as robust as the modern disease-resistant varieties and have the taste and smell of the traditional crops, yet can be harvested mechanically if necessary. Infrared detection of damaged plants, advanced chemical treatments, and improved transportation will make it possible to reduce loss considerably. Greenhouses that store solar energy in ground water and burn biomass to provide heating for homes have already been built. Just as CO_2 fertilizer is now used in greenhouses, both increasing production and preventing CO_2 from being added to the atmosphere, so we may eventually be able to use CO_2 in systems that are not closed, such as arable fields. The reclamation of nutrients from waste is already taking place on an experimental scale, and the recycling of struvite (a phosphate mineral) from urban sewers as well as from food not fit for human consumption is only a matter of time. The remainder will be used as biofuel.

In short we now have a great deal of knowledge and technology that could lead, now or in the near future, to more sustainable food supplies. That we need not be concerned about shrinking resources in the absolute and global sense and that there are all kinds of technical possibilities is not to say all the new potential will automatically be used. Some solutions have undesirable side-effects, others are too expensive, and yet others come up against political objections. We are continually on our way to the future, sometimes stumbling, sometimes sprinting, in a perpetual learning process.

Lessons of the Green Revolution

The history of scientific creativity in agriculture and the food supply chain includes innumerable inventors and researchers, with a few famous heroes among them. One is Justus von Liebig, who performed the first experiments with such fertilizers as nitrogen and phosphate in the nineteenth century (and in passing invented the bouillon cube). Or Nicolai Vavilov, the Russian geneticist who in the twentieth century investigated where the original ancestors of our food crops had come from and how they could be preserved for future breeding purposes. Or the Israeli inventors of drip irrigation, the researchers who invented pesticides and later discovered how to use predators against pests. Of course history would not be complete without the mendacious and malign antiheroes, first among them Soviet biologist Trofim Lysenko, who refused to acknowledge scientific genetics and breeding and claimed that plants could "learn" better characteristics. And not forgetting Mao, Pol Pot, and Stalin, who, by insisting on a return to traditional methods and by forcing collectivization, caused unprecedented famines and food-supply disruptions.

The past half-century was marked by the breakthrough known as the Green Revolution, which is linked primarily to the name of one man, Norman Borlaug, who in 1970 became the first and only agriculturalist before or since to win a Nobel Prize. Borlaug and the Green Revolution are icons of the perspective offered by science in the face of hunger and scarcity.

It was in the late nineteenth century that the foundations for the Green Revolution were laid, when in North America, Australia, and Europe, scientific insights were applied to farming and food for the first time. This process might be referred to as the "Western Green Revolution," before the term was invented. At first it was slow. Despite increasing knowledge of fertilization and improvements to methods of cultivation, yields more or less stagnated in the years after 1900. In Britain, for example, the wheat harvest in 1930 was little better than those in the mid-nineteenth century. Trade barriers and a lack of credit were part of the problem, but the biggest obstacle was a lack of nitrogen. Up to and during the First World War, it was available only from guano or animal manure, or by means of crop rotation, using clover, for example. After the Second World War, annual yields grew systematically as a result of the synthesis in factories of artificial binders of nitrogen like ammonia in combination with phosphate.

In developing countries the breakthrough did not come until the late 1960s. In those days famine, as in Biafra and Bihar, still seemed unavoidable. Humanitarian considerations and above all geopolitical concerns, mainly in the form of the Cold War, encouraged the U.S. government and such institutions as the Ford Foundation and the Rockefeller Foundation to invest as never before in the scientific basics of food supply, especially plant breeding. The result was the Green Revolution, a spectacular increase in yields of wheat, corn, and rice in Asia and South America. The new varieties were soon being grown by farmers in countless regions from Mexico to China. Since 1960, production in developing countries has more than doubled, along with the world population, as has production in rich countries. So each year total production increased, and calories became a little cheaper. Households were able to spend progressively less on food and could eat a quarter to a third more than in the 1960s, despite the population increase. This was typified by India, where food shortages had always been common: the country became self-sufficient and then subsequently was able to export its surplus of rice.

Technological progress seemed fairly simple during 1965–1985. Just take the numbers of the most successful rice varieties, IR5 and IR8 (the low number indicates that they were among the first ten crosses of the thousands that were made). The basis for higher yields had become obvious: more nitrogen and other nutrients; sufficient water; shorter plants that don't fall over, have a favorable ratio of grain to straw, and above all are better able to absorb sunlight; control of diseases and infestations; and improved mechanical and phytosanitary treatment of crops after harvest. All this was combined with a shorter period of growth and mechanical ploughing, which meant that crops could be harvested two or three times a year, so that the amount of land available was in effect doubled or tripled. At testing stations—in other words, under the most favorable conditions—yields increased fourfold. It therefore seemed a simple matter to dismiss the demographic doom-mongering of Malthus and company. Hunger is not at all the unavoidable consequence of population growth.

But after a few years all kinds of problems emerged. The social costs of the Green Revolution became obvious when tenant farmers were driven from their land because their labor was no longer needed. The excessive use of chemicals caused illness and death among people, cattle, and insects and led to pollution of the soil and water. The falling price of food limited the investment opportunities for small farmers.

So from about 1980, after the initial euphoria about the Green Revolution, disappointment and even cynicism set in. It seemed as if we could go no further than improvements in a few crops, in a few favorable areas where the soil was fertile, irrigation could be provided, and the local farmers worked hard, were given credit, and could sell their produce. This is probably a law of all economic development: it first benefits those whose circumstances are relatively good and only gradually (if ever) helps the very poorest. Because poverty means difficulties of access and a lack of social networks and markets. The questions always remain: to what extent can new agricultural technologies help the poorest groups, and is there a trickle-down effect of progress to the poorest of all?

The Green Revolution gives us some insight into these questions. In most cases the poorest people do benefit if average production in a village goes up. But it is complicated. Higher yields often mean lower prices, good for those with little or no land, such as poor city dwellers and landless peasants, but bad for poor farmers or tenant farmers who earn less as a consequence. So not all poor people are helped to the same degree. Wealth will trickle down only if facilities everyone uses improve (such as irrigation channels, wells, or markets) and above all if demand for labor increases. Most useful of all, as it turned out, was to develop varieties that produce better yields, perhaps because of better resistance to diseases or weeds, on every kind of farm, irrespective of size and soil type. However desirable, such scale neutrality is limited, because few varieties perform well on all types of soil and under all circumstances. Furthermore, a person who runs a small business has little flexibility when it comes to deploying labor, will prefer to play it safe, and will not be quick to try out new technologies.

These problems, however serious, do not detract from the success of the Green Revolution. It's been estimated that the new techniques have helped feed more than an additional billion people a year. The lesson is not that the scientific basis was wrong or that innovations were adopted incorrectly. The downsides of the success of the Green Revolution helped show us the way forward. It soon became clear that there could be no progress without tackling the ecological effects of the new technologies on farmland and beyond, in the broader ecosystem. We had to learn to stop polluting water by applying too much nitrogen to the soil. It turned out that erosion and the breakdown of organic material could be prevented by ploughing less deeply and keeping the soil surface covered. The amount of pesticide applied can be reduced considerably by using it more carefully and sparingly.

It has also become clear that plant breeders should concentrate not only on resistance to disease and infestation and on increasing yields but also on all the conditions farmers have to cope with, such as unfavorable soils, caused perhaps by too much salt, acidity, or regular floods. Farming needs to be seen as part of a farm ecosystem, in which every change has an effect everywhere on the farm and on everything that lives there. Crossing plants with traditional varieties that are adapted to these stresses has significantly improved the characteristics of modern cultivars. The Green Revolution did prove to have its lacunas, however. Too much emphasis was placed on wheat, corn, and rice, while legumes, root crops, vegetables, and fruit were neglected. The breeding of these crops, livestock—such as draft animals for ploughing, transportation, and milk—and poultry is far more complicated, especially in tropical conditions, than the breeding of grains. The Green Revolution has barely reached Africa at all, because wheat, rice, and corn are less important there, the climate is characterized by more extreme fluctuations, livestock is more important, the population is less concentrated, and less is invested in agriculture there than is the case in Asia.

Insights like these have enabled us to convert our concern about the Green Revolution in developing countries into an essentially new way of looking at farming and agricultural sciences there and here. Technological improvements are not a source of external change that is forced on farmers from outside but the result of the precise adaptation of ecological and technical processes to an existing cultural and social environment.

So it is no longer about developing an insecticide that will target specific insects, but about a combination of genetic changes to a particular variety of tomatoes, or about encouraging predator insects that will keep aphid numbers within bounds, and adjusting sowing schedules so that vulnerable periods of tomato growth do not coincide with aphid cycles and the wettest periods of the rainy season. If pesticides are still needed, then we determine on each occasion how much will have to be applied, rather than giving a standard treatment. Something similar applies to artificial fertilizer. Don't fertilize the soil with the risk of encouraging organisms in surface water (such as blue algae), just fertilize the root zone, and only at times when the plant is in need of nutrients.

The same goes for animals. No blind use of antibiotics to stimulate growth, let alone hormones, but a selective application if necessary, based on monitoring animal welfare and reducing greenhouse gas emissions. Along with this approach comes the use of the biomass that is a by-product of animal husbandry, such as slaughterhouse waste, sawdust, and bedding straw.

Central to the new approach is to take account of what happens outside the farm or cowshed. The agricultural sciences are evolving into the sciences of farming, ecosystems, and the environment. The goal is no longer to promote blindly anything that raises yields but to close the cycles of nutrients, chemicals, and water, so that the effects on the environment are minimized and yet yields are optimized at the same time. This ensures that no more land will have to be put into production than is strictly necessary. Scientists are now concentrating on developing agro-ecosystems that respond flexibly to fluctuating weather conditions and new diseases and infestations, and that use nutrients and energy efficiently.

Comparable changes are under way in the food sciences. The classic idea that calories, proteins, and vitamins or iron are limiting factors for a person's nutritional state has given way to a better understanding of the physiological, psychological, and economic reactions of individuals to the scarcity or abundance of food, and to research into other food elements, such as plant sterols. We have learned that diets are not static but change rapidly, even in one generation, and that price is the deciding factor. Even a modest growth in income leads to a significant and immediate shift toward the consumption of more animal proteins, sugar, and fats. But we also see that with very high incomes that preference declines. Food is decisive for the health of every individual. Most of the ten top causes of death in populations, such as cardiovascular diseases and possibly certain forms of cancer, are directly related to diets and therefore to farming. We are now in a position to make broad connections between health, food, and agricultural production. It is the latest lesson we are learning.

Worldwide changes in climate and ecosystems, of which we were unaware until a generation ago, present additional challenges. Many of them can be experienced locally as a change to the weather, to vegetation, or to watercourses. In temperate climates the changes may be a matter of several dry summers in a row, low river levels, and the drying out of reed beds. These can be serious, but they are not in themselves anything new, because historically there have been countless periods of drought or indeed of flooding. What is new is the combination of many local changes to form global weather patterns, the speed with which they are taking place, and the large number of people affected.

It's impossible as yet to determine whether the ultimate combined effects of changes to the weather and the climate will have a positive or negative impact on total world food production. Fluctuations in weather patterns will probably increase in frequency, especially extreme rainfall and extreme heat. They will cause fluctuations in food production, which in turn will create more uncertainty about supply and price, and with it increased instability. Weather and the climate affect the growth of plants through day and night temperatures, water availability, wind speeds, and the build-up of pathogens, infestations, and favorable insect populations. Higher night temperatures and humidity may cause problems with molds, which might explain why the growth in yields of such grains as wheat and rice is no longer increasing. During 1960–1990 the average yield of wheat, for example, grew by 3 percent a year; now the figure is less than 1 percent. In conditions of such uncertainty, farmers are less inclined to invest in new techniques.

Climate change will not lead to different weather patterns alone. It may also cause sea levels to rise, which in turn may bring higher or indeed lower groundwater levels and incursions of salt water. For relatively rich countries and countries with sparse populations, such changes need not be problematic, because they will happen over many decades or even centuries. Perhaps in the long term climate zones will shift, so that wheat can be grown farther north, or the acreage of cotton in China will expand into cooler regions. Then in the northern hemisphere as a whole, production, at least in theory, may have a stronger tendency to rise than to fall. In the most important regions that will suffer from drought, such as the Sahel, Australia, the Mediterranean region, parts of the United States and Central America, Central Asia, and western China, the productivity of both arable and livestock farming may decline, unless efficient irrigation is possible. This too is something that humanity has experienced before: farming regions have been abandoned many times, or have shifted, starting with ancient Mesopotamia.

Their speed and the number of people affected make these developments fundamentally different today. We cannot simply extrapolate from the successes of the past, even if we can learn from our mistakes and have confidence, based on history, that our collective creativity and willpower will enable us to tackle future challenges. Probably the most important lesson from the past is not that technological solutions exist but that society, and therefore the market and politics, need to make their development and implementation possible.

The Price of Food

Price: see under market and disaster. Because the way in which world food issues have reached us over recent years is through alarming reports about food prices. What we see most of all are rapidly changing prices that seem to lead to social unrest. After decades of stable and slowly falling prices, we find ourselves in a period of massive price fluctuations. In 2007–2008 prices reached record highs, only to fall quickly before rising again to a high level in 2012. In various places in the world food riots broke out. What has happened? Are high prices a sign of scarcity after all? If we are to believe some politicians and commentators, we're on the verge of a calamitous period in which food becomes unaffordable and world peace is threatened as a result.

What we are seeing is actually not evidence of food shortages but of a long period of political neglect, marked by a lack of investment in research and falling real prices followed by a number of destabilizing factors. Precisely because yields kept on increasing until 2000, many people were lulled by the notion that the world food problem had been solved. What was forgotten was that food prices had been steadily declining since the Second World War. The problem, although the average consumer does not realize it, is that food has become too cheap. The rich countries have become so overconfident that they have taken perfectly good farmland out of production through all kinds of subsidies for voluntary set-asides. Until recently Europe was still implementing the McSharry reforms in its Common Agricultural Policy, which meant farmers were paid for not producing food.

The current higher prices are therefore to some extent a correction to extremely low price levels at the start of the twenty-first century. Food riots, such as took place in Haiti in 2009 and Tunisia in 2011, were prompted by food prices, but the deeper causes were almost always social unrest, economic uncertainty, and the frustration of democratic desires among the people. This is not to deny that higher prices have a disastrous effect on the poorest people in the cities, who sometimes spend two-thirds of their incomes on food.

Food riots in unstable countries are not, however, evidence that the world is teetering on the edge of an abyss. Food is not oil. It's a renewable resource that will never run out. It renews itself in every growing season through photosynthesis. The means of production needed for food (sunlight, water, nitrogen, phosphate, and potassium) are not scarce on a world scale, not for the coming century at least, despite all the doomsday scenarios, even if local shortages can occur. Food is grown by almost a billion farmers large and small, who do not in any sense act as a cartel or have transnational power like the oil companies.

Nevertheless, food does resemble oil in the sense that it is an object of speculation. Food production is relatively inelastic, meaning that the supply of food cannot quickly adjust to changing prices. It takes at least a year to switch from one annual crop to another and for trees, greenhouse agriculture, and meat or dairy products far longer. The sudden rapid growth of demand for grain, cattle feed, meat, fish, and beer in China and Southeast Asia, and indeed elsewhere, as a result of huge economic growth, led to a reduction in supplies in the first decade of this century. This growth affects some 1.5 billion people, who have begun to consume more, more quickly than anyone had thought possible. The price fluctuations are first of all a consequence of the reduction in food stocks. Because food deteriorates, supplies cannot be kept for long. Moreover, until well into this century European and American policy was to reduce stocks, as confidence in price stability had increased, whereas now there is nervousness about possible future shortages.

Declining food stocks have created a market that is sensitive to fluctuations in supply and demand. Demand is fluctuating because, as a result of the economic crisis in North America and Europe, money has been freed up that cannot be invested in financial institutions or real estate, so it finds its way into what are known as "soft commodities," especially grains for food and cattle feed, and seeds intended for oil production. Psychological effects such as the perception of shortage, rather than absolute scarcity, have driven prices up further. The increasing and fluctuating price of energy (for the transportation and processing of agricultural produce) reinforces this volatility, as do exchange rates. Fluctuations in supply arise as a result of all kinds of climatological and political causes, such as disappointing harvests as a result of drought in the most important production areas, floods in others, forest fires, and so on. Farming, with the exception of completely closed greenhouse horticulture, will always remain dependent on unpredictable weather factors that humans cannot control. Natural ups and downs are made worse, however, by decisions by governments to close a country's borders, as Thailand, the world's biggest rice exporter, did in 2008 to protect supplies to its home market.

An additional complicating factor is the use of subsidies to divert food, or rather feed, into fuel production, especially corn in the United States. Legislation concerning the compulsory addition of biofuels to fossil fuels has created constant upward pressure on prices. These mechanisms, which reinforce each other, and the complacent attitude of the biggest traders in the market, mean there is every reason to assume we will continue to see higher price levels and more fluctuations in the future. This result is not entirely negative. Higher prices are a precondition for investment in improvements to agricultural techniques. Low prices give farmers and the food processing industry the signal that it is not worthwhile investing in food, and such prices encourage waste by both industry and consumers.

But if the world market is so sensitive to fluctuations, would it not be more intelligent, environmentally friendly, and honest to stand aside as far as possible from its perversities? Shouldn't we grow food close to where it is consumed, as far as possible, rather than hauling it around over long distances? This is happening to some extent. Basic foods such as wheat, rice, cassava, potatoes, and millet are generally consumed regionally. Less than 15 percent of all rice grown comes onto the world market. The trade in bulk products concerns mainly crops for cattle feed, such as corn and soy; tropical fruits, such as bananas; meat and dairy products; fish; and high-value items like coffee, tea, cocoa, and sugar. For many of these products, no local alternative is available. Moreover, we ultimately make the best use of the scarce and vulnerable land on the earth by growing food where it is most suited to grow. Where the land yields most for the lowest cost, the least land is needed. Because land of good quality with a favorable climate is not evenly spread around the world, food must be imported by those in less favorable regions. Trade is a necessity if we are to combat hunger, because it is the only way to resolve local shortages.

We have moved on from the situation of a century or two ago when we occupied other countries as the only way in which to secure food supplies. Thanks to two new factors, the rise in yields per unit of land and the free market (which is to say a market that is regulated but without trade barriers), trade has become the peaceful solution. Our supply of food is greater than ever. Liberalization of the world market has not only brought more goods to more people but has also increased intellectual and cultural exchanges. As a result, not every country nor every farming community has to reinvent the wheel time and again. Knowledge and experience can be shared and the best techniques spread across the globe.

There is nothing straightforward about food. This realization is growing among consumers and governments as a result of higher prices. Still, if farmers get a chance to react to market prices and poor consumers retain access to affordable food, we do not need to worry about price development. There are big differences between the price on the world market, the price the farmer receives, and the price the consumer pays— indeed sometimes there is hardly any relationship between them at all. Price equilibrium and well-functioning markets are a precondition for every step in the food supply chain and are essential for investment in sustainable production. Above all, they are in the interests of the poor.

Sustainability as Political Consensus

The demand made by society, with ever-increasing emphasis, is that food must be produced sustainably, now and in the future. It is an understandable desire, reminiscent of the static abundance of paradise, with its lack of natural cycles, where humans do no harm and the ecosystem remains the same forever. But what does "sustainable" mean exactly? Every citizen may have some idea of what it's about, but abuses are rife, and no one has a quantitative definition to hand. The term "sustainability" may be reaching its sell-by date. Only if we can agree on exactly what we mean by it will the concept of sustainability, or its successor, be able to retain its value.

Unfortunately, sustainability has started to mean just about anything: it's the projection screen onto which everyone can project the societal ambitions of his or her choice. The concept, which originally came from forestry and referred to the amount of timber that could be felled without damaging the forest, became a household term thanks to a UN commission led by Norwegian Prime Minister Gro Harlem Brundtland in the mid-1980s. From Tyneside to Timbuktu, Beirut to Bengbu, everyone has heard of it now. Sustainability has become a playing field for all those who wish the world well, something that relies on enthusiasm rather than coherent policy. Such a broad concept is eagerly seized on and misused.

In the strictest sense every natural process on the planet is sustainable as long as our solar system lasts; on the scale of planetary time and space there is never any loss of resources. Raw materials will eventually form again, eroded soils recover, ecosystems adjust if climates change, species will disappear and others emerge—it's been going on that way for thousands of millions of years. On a human timescale that realization inspires only modesty and awe, not action. Nevertheless an extremely long-term perspective is necessary if we are to understand why we should be concerned about sustainability.

"Sustainability" is a word for the scientific fact that human influence on the earth is now of the same order of magnitude as other processes that shape the planet, such as natural erosion. From that follows the desire to limit our influence in such a way that natural processes on earth are disturbed as little as possible by humans. Sustainable development means that we shape the growing needs of our own and future generations such that they will have as few negative ecological and social effects as possible while still doing justice to human beings' legitimate desire for a better life. We are also responsible for the generations after our own, which must have consequences for our behavior.

The Brundtland report marked a radical break with the earlier generation of doom-sayers. Population growth does not have to be a bomb, nor is the earth an overpopulated lifeboat in which we are at one another's throats. Our effect on the planet is a product of the number of people multiplied by their patterns of consumption. Resources can be exhausted, but we can do something about it if we act in collaboration. The concept of the mutual dependence of all those on earth is reflected in the title of the report: "Our Common Future." During the 1990s a feeling of optimistic consensus took hold of the global community. Many international accords were reached on ways to improve the state of the planet, starting with the declaration by the Earth Summit in Rio de Janeiro in 1992. For the first time, attention was paid to the influence of human activities on a wide range of things, including the climate, chemicals, biodiversity, and water. In the conferences that followed, attempts were made to flesh out these ideas, with varying degrees of success.

Now, in the twenty-first century, it all seems rather less simple. One by one the pillars of sustainability—such as policies concerning the climate, energy, water, and biodiversity—have started to look shaky under the growing weight of demands for more coordination, improved standards, better monitoring, and more workable definitions. Conclusions concerning climate change are also subject to serious and sometimes stubborn criticism by sceptics who represent the entire political spectrum from right to left, in science and in business. An additional problem is that everyone wants sustainability now: countries, companies, action groups, cities, provinces, ministries—all jostling to formulate the best green objectives ever. And consumers? They shuffle along behind, partially motivated, poorly informed, and indeed confused. Because it's difficult. Should they do the dishes by hand or in the dishwasher? Should they buy tomatoes from greenhouses in their own country or from Morocco? Before long you decide that nothing bad will happen in your own lifetime or that you can't make a difference anyhow. The rich like to shift the blame by having production take place elsewhere and by buying carbon credits. The poor can't afford low-energy light bulbs, and if they do save water it's because they have to. Yet in the long term we will all be better off with a planet where the impact of humanity does as little damage as possible.

One serious complication is that again and again it turns out that the positive effects of technological improvements, such as energy-saving cars or lights, are negated by our consuming more rather than less. It seems technology doesn't straightforwardly stimulate improved behavior but instead gives us a license to use more. If we try to consume responsibly, then an odd psychological twist occurs: we buy coffee with an environmentally friendly label, but that's really because it makes us better people— or makes us feel better—rather than because it makes for a better world. There is always self-interest and selectivity in sustainable consumption. Eating less meat may be a reasonably acceptable option among the rich Western middle classes, but so is a great amount of driving and flying. Technology that encourages a change in behavior, such as intelligent metering for energy and water, is still in its infancy.

That the concept of sustainability keeps on expanding its reach is logical, because the more we understand about the earth's cycles, the more involved they turn out to be. The Brundtland commission paid hardly any attention to the greenhouse effect, for example, whereas now we never talk about sustainability without referring to CO_2. We've arrived at a point where nothing any longer falls outside the realm of sustainability: cars, buildings, vegetable growing, Lake Erie, and the Ruhr industrial district, not forgetting poverty in Africa, town planning, the ocean depths, slums, and tropical forests. It has made the concept of sustainability unusable in practice, because by bringing everything into its remit, we've increasingly realized that each aspect can be improved only at the expense of another. Sustainability is always about choices. If we want to stimulate economic development in poor countries, we should eat green beans and mangos from Africa, but because they're flown in to the OECD countries, they're bad from the point of view of CO_2 emissions and food miles. So what do we do?

It seems obvious that a term as broad as "sustainability" cannot be the basis for a manageable approach to weighing up all those different dimensions. As always happens in an international context, when we get stuck, we think up new jargon.

So the concept of sustainable development has been supplemented by three apparently more straightforward criteria: people, planet, and profit—a triple measure against which companies, for example, can test their results. This choice has useful effects, because it makes clear that economic growth is merely one of several dimensions. We also talk about natural capital (climate, energy, biodiversity, and air), social capital (participation), human capital (work, education, and health), and economic capital (investments and knowledge). Recently these have been joined by another threesome: economy, ecology, and equity. But this shift doesn't fundamentally solve anything, because everything still belongs within sustainability. It's clear that for all our good intentions, this kind of potpourri will not lead to a concerted approach to sustainable development. A shopping list of ideas means no one dares to prioritize. Policymakers and consumers would ideally like a simple instruction leaflet to tell them what is sustainable and what isn't, like a guide for a DIY project that only requires a few numbers to be filled in, an $E = mc^2$ for sustainability.

———

Meanwhile there is no shortage of good intentions, nor of clever ideas, from electric cars to biodegradable plastic, from biological photovoltaic cells to the recovery of nutrients from waste water. Slowly a remarkable situation has arisen in which there is no other principle about which we are so united in theory as sustainability and no subject for which so much practical effort is made, in both the public sector and the private sector, while the results are so unconvincing. The sense of stagnation is global, as was confirmed again at the Rio+20 summit in 2012, twenty years after the euphoria of the first summit for a sustainable planet. Apparently we're simply incapable of reaching firm agreements about climate targets or about quotas for renewable energy.

The most important reason for stagnation is a lack of political decisiveness. Internationally this is caused by conflicting national interests. Developing countries, especially the emerging economies, demand the right to be free of restrictions in their development and consumption patterns. They also want financial support from the West to make their economies more sustainable. In contrast, the rich nations believe that rapidly growing countries, such as China, India, Brazil, and Russia, must take responsibility for themselves. National decisionmaking is muddled by the large number of institutions that feel responsible for sustainability.

Sustainability is always a matter of weighing up aims that are very different, and its definition is always a snapshot in time, a reflection of insights that are marching on. Thus it engenders both vagueness and an obsession with details, so that political parties and countries like to get on their hobby horses and engage with a grab bag of ideas big and small, from illegal felling to road pricing, from organic farming to clean water, from windmills to generic innovation subsidies.

Market Failures

The rise of the concept "sustainable development" runs more or less in parallel with the expansion of world trade after the fall of the Berlin Wall in 1989. In those years investment in developing countries with their low wages shot up. Economic growth came within reach of far more areas of the world. However, neoliberal market thinking offers no protection to the weak and defenseless (such as the poor, the disabled, or minorities) or to things that have little if any monetary value, such as nature and culture. Only legislation drawn up for the purpose can help them.

That lack of protection is a form of market failure. If water quality had a price tag, then no chemical waste would be dumped in rivers. If the exploitation of children were taken into account, hand-woven carpets would be unaffordable. Critics fear that the free market is a dangerous aberration that produces modern slave labor, disfigured landscapes, and cheerless high-rise buildings. The end of capitalism is in sight, they say.

Do capitalism and the free market really stand in the way of sustainable development? You might think so. From the great grasping for huge bonuses in much of the business world and the run on stock markets by investors big and small, to the fight for bargains in sales and the dizzying growth of consumer credit, greed and its little brother envy seem to be the guiding principles of humanity. But a glance at history teaches us that such evils have always existed, since long before the Industrial Revolution.

Offhand comments about the end of capitalism reflect the unease of those who have too much rather than too little, an elite that can allow itself to stop buying and to grow more slowly. Ask poor farmers in Rajasthan, Cappadocia, or Mali. All they want is a chance to earn money, so that life for the next generation will be materially better. Ask the first generation of city dwellers in Rio de Janeiro. They all want a house, a television, and meat every day. The triumph of capitalism is that the fulfilment of desires of this sort has become possible for more people than ever. For all its shortcomings, no other system offers a better guarantee of widespread economic growth. However much greedy capitalism and its excrescences may fill us with disgust, the aspirations of the more than 5 billion people who have not reached Western levels of consumption are incontrovertible and can be met only by continuing growth—consumption to be moderated, we hope, just like that of the rich. There is no legitimate basis on which to forbid others to reach a higher level of consumption. All the rich countries can do is, with appropriate modesty, pose questions about the relationship between consumption, social distribution, and the environment. We can philosophize endlessly about why it would be better for all of us on this planet to consume less, but the most urgent question is whether growth can be achieved in better ways, with fewer negative effects on humans and the environment.

The opportunity to correct the market is woven into a democratic system in which abuses can be addressed by elected politicians and the free press. This is what makes the combination of capitalism and democracy so strong, and it also indicates what makes unbridled, uncorrected capitalism in authoritarian systems so dangerous. Where criticism cannot be voiced, or where outlets for it are few, excesses remain unaddressed for far longer. But everywhere correction is gradually taking place, under international pressure, not least from nongovernmental organizations, because no country (with the possible exceptions of North Korea and Burma) still produces goods in isolation. Democracy is a necessary but not sufficient condition, because rich voters have their own interests in mind. Democratic control remains the best guarantee that capitalism will not get out of hand. Enlightened technocracy, as in China, seems also to be capable of producing innovation and legislation, to the surprise of many in the West.

The recent financial and economic crisis has confirmed beyond doubt that more is needed for economic and social stability than the profit motive. Sustainability demands public responsibility for public goods, including correction of the market, by both governments and businesses. Growth without greed: a sustainable world is all about the greatest good for the greatest number. The correction of the failing market demands legislation: factories must comply with environmental norms (the polluter pays); people without work or with a disability must be given financial support and training; children should not be at work until they are sixteen, and if they are already working they must be given time off to go to school; and so on. Factories that put too many fats of the wrong kind into their food or pollute the food chain must be pointed in the right direction by laws and fines. This is perhaps only to treat the symptoms, and to some extent we are playing catch-up, but it works. In Western European and other OECD countries the soil, air, and water are far cleaner and working conditions incomparably better than in earlier centuries, or even fifty years ago.

That success was achieved because a growing number of businesses took upon themselves a social role and embraced the promotion of sustainability. Ethically or socially responsible business practices, once something for softies, have become an integral part of business life. We shouldn't idealize this, because of course some companies are merely paying lip service, and not everything put forward convincingly by top management is always adhered to at all levels. But large international companies especially, which are obliged to present an annual report detailing their social impact, have become increasingly transparent. Without exception nowadays all of them have departments that look at aspects of socially responsible business. The prospect of instant notoriety on the Internet means no company can indulge in irresponsible behavior. Sports shoes manufactured by children, paint factories that dump waste in fragile swamp habitats, all that kind of thing has become harder to do without being detected. One film on social media is enough to damage a brand for years. There's far more reason now to be worried about small, regional, and national companies that neither publish in English nor feel the hot breath of Western consumer and environmental organizations on their necks. Large multinationals realize that they bear partial responsibility for their suppliers, so principles of socially responsible business are gradually spreading.

The goal is therefore shifting from making a profit to contributing to a stable society where buying power increases and can continue to increase because the ecological foundations are not being undermined. Almost all companies in the food sector in rich countries have launched ambitious plans for socially responsible business practices. There are now international agreements about how to monitor progress. The subject is on the agenda of almost every meeting of senior managers. Ambitions extend from sustainable cultivation (including the training of farmers and the establishment of cooperatives) to environmentally friendly processing, a reduction in packaging, low-energy transportation, information provision for clients, and general involvement in social projects. One side effect turns out to be that staff feel motivated by plans of this kind and like to work for a company that's leading the way. Because of all these activities, and because governments have become stuck in fragmented policy, Western companies are playing a large, sometimes decisive, role in the move toward sustainable food production.

Correction of the failures of the free market, step by step, is essential but not sufficient to foster sustainability. The time horizon of capitalism is almost always limited to the short to medium term, whereas to find sustainable solutions we need to be conscious of a more distant future. Changes in the fields of energy and technology demand long-term stability to ensure that investments are not merely responses to short-term fluctuations and subsidies. Currently we set to work on wind or solar energy only if the oil price is high enough, and when it falls again we're left wondering whether we've invested enough to make those alternatives profitable.

Ultimately, sustainable food production is the responsibility of the state. This does not necessarily mean that state intervention is required. The state must create the conditions for sustainable food supply chains to work, through a combination of legal, fiscal, and policy measures. Markets and companies must operate in this framework, and only where markets fail should the state intervene, perhaps when an unforeseen disaster occurs, or when goals other than the production of consumer goods are regarded as important, as with the protection of the landscape.

There are many steps we can take to bring sustainable food production within reach, although our concept of sustainable solutions is sure to evolve further in the future. This sustainability in an immediate if narrower sense can be achieved only if it is economically possible and realistic. Without doubt we need a combination of fiscal measures, stimulation with short-term subsidies (especially for research), government investment, and the workings of a market that makes the polluter pay and creates a level playing field for competition. A new fiscal regime, in Europe's case preferably at the EU level, seems unavoidable to me, so that inefficient production is taxed more heavily than sustainable production, and work is taxed less than raw materials. We should also consider tax breaks for loans used for investments that promote sustainability, in green digesters to process organic waste, for example, or low-emission livestock facilities.

It's essential to specify several criteria for sustainable production and to have them regularly checked by an independent body. For tropical hardwood, palm oil, soy, and fish there are already international agreements on clearly defined rules, such as that no virgin rainforest is to be felled. Fishing methods and the migration of shoals have been looked at as well, but the rules are not sufficiently focused on the entire life cycle of the end product. Many such sustainability criteria are still too vague, but it's a start, as long as product checks are by independent bodies and the rules are gradually tightened.

Small Farms: The Key to Sustainable Food?

Sustainability needs to be translated into ways of making production processes more efficient, replacing nonrenewable resources, reusing raw materials, and redesigning production chains. For large farms, for the producers of the means of production (such as seeds or tractors), for the food-processing industry, and for supermarkets, that transition is manageable, because they are able to bear the risks. But what about small farmers who are barely able to keep their heads above water? Do they hold the key to a sustainable future?

―――――――

You might wish it was so. Who doesn't dream of a nice little farmyard with chickens pecking about, of a vegetable plot with tomato plants and fruit trees and behind it a field of golden wheat surrounded by a flowering hedge full of nesting birds? Or of a farmer leaning over the gate of the cowshed, stroking the twenty cows and seeing that all is well? Or of a Javanese village with bright green rice terraces and a garden full of fruit trees? It is tempting to idealize the existence of small farmers and to see them as a way of producing food replete with local traditions and close to nature. There is only a certain amount of truth in this image.

Few ways of farming are so destructive as the small-scale cultivation of annual crops in the humid tropics. The disappearance of the original vegetation, the influence of sun and rain, the disturbance of the ground, and the harvest all cause erosion and the loss of organic matter in the soil. Having seen the conditions in which small farmers work, I would never have the audacity to sing the praises of such a way of life, no matter how much tradition is to be respected in other ways. Anyone who has spent half a day trying to work the soil with a pick, or to clear scrub with a machete, will know what I mean. I could dig no deeper than a few centimeters into the hard red clay. I have also weeded a rice paddy by hand, bent double and up to my ankles in water. Which is nothing compared to harvesting potatoes in a stony field high in the Peruvian Andes, and then carrying them further uphill. Or slaughtering cows at an open air market, or bringing in the catch in a storm on a rickety little boat. No one should idealize such hard work. Small farmers are also vulnerable to corruption, unscrupulous traders, and criminal or paramilitary gangs that drive them from their land to seize it for purposes of speculation, as used to happen in Columbia. For small farmers, as for everyone else, the only way forward is to improve working conditions and make markets more transparent.

In most countries the position of small agricultural companies will change dramatically in the decades to come, if only because of ageing populations and a lack of successors. Most sons and daughters of farmers take jobs elsewhere, seeing farming as a backward sector. "Small" is of course relative, and it needs to be measured against other businesses in the same area and other economic opportunities. Being a small farmer is more a way of life than an economic enterprise, one that is disappearing as a result of globalization and higher education. Only if young farmers also become entrepreneurs and can therefore invest will they succeed in earning a decent income. Then the farm will no longer be the place to find those left behind, or people with few opportunities, and farmers will be able to take more pride in their efforts. The hope is that they'll have a chance to specialize at least to some degree, while production for their own households falls markedly. It's therefore very important that small farmers have access to credit and don't remain dependent on middlemen to sell their produce. Collaboration (through cooperatives, for example), can improve their lives considerably, as happened in the Netherlands a century ago, as long as the cooperatives don't become an instrument for politicians.

Globalization is leading to concentration. The number of businesses is declining through horizontal integration (of comparable businesses) and vertical integration (in the food supply chain). Such integration can weaken the position of small farmers by making them dependent on a relatively limited number of companies that provide them with the means of production (such as seeds, artificial fertilizer, and tools) and because of the dominance of a small number of buyers. Such "errors" or distortions of the market must become a subject of international concern. Sustainable development means in the long term that in developing countries, as earlier in Europe, a large number of small farmers will have no future where the land is too unproductive for farming to be professionalized and mechanized. It does not mean there will be no more small farms, but they'll become businesses and not just a means of survival. A special role is reserved for small farmers close to cities in poor countries. They are the city's back garden and granary, often supplying the first food to reach the market. There the farm remains a safety net for the city dweller. In Ho Chi Minh City, for example, much of the population has its origins in the countryside. Links with family outside the city remain strong. When there's not enough work in the city, people return to work in rice cultivation for a time. We see this pattern all over Asia.

The limited means available to most small farmers today makes them them unable to feed the world tomorrow, but there are other reasons to invest in them. With the social and ecological role of agriculture in mind, farmers can contribute to the management of landscape and nature, to keeping the countryside an attractive place to live, to agritourism, and to providing a place where the mentally ill, the disabled, and other vulnerable people can find temporary respite from the stresses of modern life. Such considerations have already led to a type of agriculture where production is secondary to the maintenance of a diverse, open landscape, as in Tuscany, where olive production is a by-product of farming, and in the future in the rice terraces of Ifagao in the Philippines. These additional services—for which only a very limited market, if any, exists—are possible as long as there is financial support from outside agriculture for them. This is an element that should be part of any future agricultural policy.

Sustainable Green Revolutions

Opportunities to create sustainable food supplies are within reach. Unfortunately a huge amount still goes wrong, as a result of human error, ignorance, corruption, imbalanced markets, short-sighted government policy, and unscrupulous profit seeking. Thinking in terms of sustainability will not solve any of these problems, but it can help to clamp down on waste. In the past there have been calls for a new or dual Green Revolution that gives a central place to both productivity and the environment. Nothing much has come of these calls, because the idea was too vague and at the same time too all-embracing. The moment has come to free "sustainability" of unrealistic expectations, political fashion, and apparent conflicts of interest. Sustainability is not an absolute concept but an evolution, a learning process. There certainly cannot be a standard model for making the food supply chain sustainable. Many Green Revolutions are conceivable, depending on place and time, and many more will follow them.

Sustainability can be translated into a number of concrete goals. First, we can make production processes more efficient by using less raw material per unit of production or producing more per unit of raw material. Second, we can find alternatives to nonrenewable resources, such as fossil fuels. And third, we can reuse raw materials, perhaps in closed cycles, sometimes called "cradle to cradle" design. Then all products of one process become inputs for a subsequent process in the food supply chain. Waste from crops becomes animal feed, which becomes manure that is partly used as a source of energy or as a source of nitrogen and other nutrients. Sometimes entirely new possibilities are created in this way. The inedible leaves of the pineapple contain a fiber that has the same properties as high-quality linen and has found a use in haute couture.

Through these limited but practical principles of sustainability, forms of sustainable intensification emerge, ways of optimizing production to a level close to the maximum that is biologically possible. Yields must be measured differently, not just per unit of land but also per unit of labor, water, fertilizer, and other limited resources. Optimization does not mean maximizing production, incidentally, because the best, most efficient use of raw materials almost always lies just under the level of maximum productivity. One good example of sustainable intensification is how much can be gained through better fertilization. Most of the nutrients we now use in food production are wasted, in the case of nitrogen half on the farm and another 30 percent during processing and consumption. If we were to optimize the application of nitrogen (precisely the right amount at just the right time) and replace some of the artificial fertilizer currently used with means of natural fixing of nitrogen by a symbiosis between bacteria and plants, the savings would be considerable. Which is good for the economy, people, and the environment.

In the short term the consequence of the increasing demand for food will be an overall rise in the use of artificial fertilizer, pesticides, fungicides, and herbicides, and with them their negative effects on the environment. We already have countless techniques for overcoming those effects in part by reusing water and recovering nutrients, for example. Pulp from the oil palm or from sugar can serve as animal feed or as fuel, but it can also serve as a raw material for the building industry. The use of pesticides can be reduced markedly by better techniques, ranging from biological alternatives to more efficient application. The same goes for irrigation. Anyone who has a garden or even plants on a balcony knows how tempting it is to water too much. The trick is to give less than the maximum, something known as "deficit irrigation," preferably using a drip system. The speed at which such optimization can be implemented depends on the market. We will not make much progress as long as the price of chemicals and water stays low and there is neither a market mechanism nor legislation to take account of pollution or the wasting of water.

A sustainable production system will replace heavy labor and improve working conditions. This seems illogical, because in poor countries work on the land is a way of earning money, and in rich countries more value is placed on craftsmanship nowadays. But as a consequence of urbanization, labor is becoming more expensive everywhere, and fewer young people are prepared to work with their hands. Mechanization is unavoidable, which does not mean economies of scale or vast combines but smart equipment that makes life easier. We already have machines for sowing, weeding, and harvesting no bigger than a vacuum cleaner that are powered by a moped engine. These machines prevent farmers from having to bend and stoop a thousand times. And there are moped-type vehicles for the transportation of produce and fertilizer. The same goes for the processing of harvested crops, the separation of wheat and chaff, drying, grinding, pulping, and so on—the mechanization of which makes life easier, especially for women.

Sustainability means always looking at the entire production chain rather than just parts of it. This calls for clever solutions. To some degree they already exist, but there is room for improvement, as with the use of by-products of agriculture (such as hay and straw) as an energy source for further processing, or for a different purpose (such as cattle feed or the shading of seedbeds). Whether in stalls, greenhouses, or factories, we must strictly control the use of energy, water, and raw materials, with new approaches to waste, packaging, and transportation. Yogurt, for example, should be packaged such that the cartons fit next to one another, so that less "empty air" is transported in boxes. Of course cartons, labels and boxes must be completely biodegradable and preferably made of recycled materials.

A sustainable Green Revolution also requires measures to reduce the vulnerability of food supplies, especially when disasters occur. This means stocks must be kept in reserve, locally but also according to international agreements, to dampen price fluctuations and as insurance for farmers against animal diseases, drought, or untimely frosts. We need not just improved techniques to reduce risks but also ways of managing shortages should they arise, as well as warning systems; safe areas for humans, livestock, and seeds in case of emergency; and infrastructure that can withstand floods, fires, and earthquakes. The best protection against vulnerability remains increased production and the avoidance of loss, resulting in less fluctuation in prices and fewer risks for poor consumers.

The vulnerability of food production is not exclusively a problem for poor countries, but the poorest population groups are most at risk, because they have no reserves, either in the form of food stocks or as money and alternative sources of income. In poorer countries, farmers can barely compete on the world market in the short term, because they're unable to produce food of the right quality or in sufficient quantities, but it's precisely in these poorer countries that agriculture is one of the most important economic sectors. We should consider temporarily protecting the farming sector in some places to allow it to grow and to specialize, even though that would represent a departure from agreements about the liberalization of world trade. This topic will remain one of the most controversial in international politics, I fear.

With the sensible application of current knowledge and a long-term vision, we can go a long way toward ensuring that in 2050 the world's population has sufficient high-quality food and the countryside remains an attractive and viable place to live. But that's not the whole story. Other factors make the future uncertain, among them developments in computing, medical science, and the field of energy resources. All these are outside the domain of food supply but may have a major influence on it. Anticipating the unknown by imagining the future is what has set the human species apart ever since, ejected from paradise, we began farming the land by trial and error.

How can we imagine the rest of this century, or even this millennium, to say nothing of the next 10,000 years, based on what we know now? It's tempting, but probably a sign of an overestimation of our own powers, to regard our own era as a pivotal point between the beginning of farming and the ecological perfecting of it in an era that will last just as long. So let's limit ourselves to the coming century or so.

Food production will remain the most important form of land use on earth and therefore will require the most space. Most food crops are annual plants, which grow for one season, less than a year. They are sown annually, so the soil must be tilled, which requires energy and disturbs the ground. One intriguing question is whether we will succeed in making those dominant annuals into perennials, so that they regenerate after the winter or in the dry season from the stubble left by an earlier harvest. Associated problems would probably emerge eventually, such as a build-up of diseases and infestations, but thought experiments of this kind—rice and wheat as crops that shoot up again like grass—are precisely what we need if we are to look at innovation in agriculture in entirely new ways.

The majority of our calories will continue to come from the land, but we will explore new species, including those in the seas and in fresh water. The continental shelves may thus become a second source of food. The farming of fish, shellfish, and algae could take place there, or on the land, even in or near cities, in large tanks, with new sources of fish food, such as lower organisms and processed industrial waste. Providing affordable, environmentally friendly proteins for all, acquired with proper respect for animal welfare, represents the greatest challenge. Animal proteins must be replaced in part by proteins from plants or from species lower on the food chain, such as algae and insects. The importance of by-products will grow, as we are already seeing with sheep, which are now often kept for both meat and milk.

Food production and the pharmaceutical and chemical industries are beginning to overlap. We will measure production not just in tons per hectare, or calories, carbohydrates, proteins, or fats, but also in terms of other important chemical substances, such as hormones (insulin from cow's milk, for example), or vaccines produced by animals or plants, perhaps against rabies or foot-and-mouth disease. Products derived from milk will be important as easily absorbed raw materials and as carrier substances for medicines and dietary supplements.

Biotechnology is crucial—and not just in the form of genetic modification. Opposition to it will probably ebb away over the coming decade as concern about the risks declines and its advantages become evident. The use of cellulose and related compounds in biofuels will increase, but not at the expense of land for food or of food production itself. This may also lead to production systems in which processing after the harvest will be fueled largely by energy derived from the plants and animals to be processed, as already happens with sugarcane. Such developments will make market-distorting subsidies for biofuels superfluous overnight.

We will not be able to supply the world with food sustainably using only small-scale local produce, organic or not. But we should not be dismissive of interest in it, if only because of the growing environmental consciousness among the middle class. We have opportunities to shorten supply chains by producing food closer to where it is consumed, at least in the case of vegetables, some fruit, and certain kinds of meat, although not for tropical fruit in temperate regions and hardly anywhere for fish, starchy crops (such as rice, wheat, corn and potatoes), or beef.

In such a new Green Revolution, what is the balance between exports and imports of food, or between producing locally, regionally, and far away? I imagine the options as a combination of scale (on a vertical axis) from small to large, as against geographical distance and reach of production chains, from local to global (on the horizontal axis). These dimensions do not coincide. Although we tend to equate them, large-scale is not the same as global, and small-scale is not the same as local. Close to cities of a million or more people, local production may very well be in the hands of extremely large businesses. Conversely, highly specialized companies can produce on a small scale for a world market, as we see with producers of new herbs and dwarf vegetables.

On a third axis we can mark the extent of precision in the production process and control over production factors. The development of agriculture, which began with the haphazard protection and tending of individual plants and animals, coincides with the development of control over conditions of production and over the genomes of species that are useful to humans. The more precisely we control them, the higher the yield becomes. Traditional or primitive farming means nothing less than being at the mercy of the chance availability of nutrients in the soil. With the growing understanding, gained by trial and error, of where plants thrive—on land regularly flooded, on manure heaps, in cowsheds, on the slopes of volcanoes—and as the result of systematic research, people learned that nutrients needed to be added, in the form of humus or animal excrement, later artificial fertilizer, and ultimately in the form of individual nutrients in solution. This latest approach, now found in the most advanced greenhouses and some irrigation systems, involves providing just enough feed at just the right moment, so that the great problem of the second half of the twentieth century—excessive use of superfluous nutrients and water—can be avoided. Figure 1 shows some of these possibilities, with examples.

If we set these three dimensions—scale, distance, and control—alongside one another, we arrive at a number of models for food supply chains. As yet the trend is very much toward large-scale, global chains and as much control as possible over the factors that determine productivity, such as

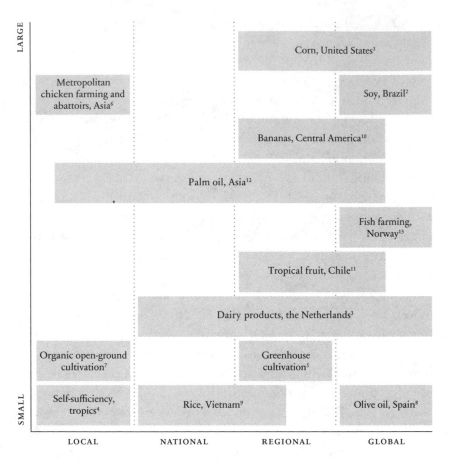

FIGURE 1. **Scale and length of food supply chains.** The third axis, the degree of precision in the production process and control over production factors, has been omitted here for the sake of readability. That dimension is to a great degree dependent on the other two dimensions. The position of the examples is merely indicative and is subject to change. Furthermore, the boxes have been shown as horizontal, whereas some (palm oil, for example) have both small- and large-scale variants and therefore have more height along the vertical axis. The scale is not an absolute measurement but is dependent on the type of production and the agro-economic conditions (for example, climate, soil).

1 Corn, United States: Large-scale production as cattle feed mainly for export, as biofuel and sweetener for domestic consumption; great control and precision in production.
2 Soy, Brazil: Large-scale, genetically modified, mainly for export to China as cattle feed; great precision and control.
3 Dairy products, the Netherlands: Small- to large-scale, cooperative, both national production and global export.
4 Self-sufficiency, tropics: Self-sufficient slash-and-burn agriculture in humid tropics (e.g., Central Africa, Amazon); very low degree of participation in the market.
5 Greenhouse cultivation: High-intensity greenhouse cultivation (e.g., tomatoes); high degree of control over the production process, computer-controlled, biological pest control, export-oriented, especially out of season.

6 Metropolitan chicken farming and abattoirs, Asia: Large-scale battery farming of chickens around large Asian cities, destined for the local market.

7 Organic open-ground cultivation: Small-scale, mainly focused on national market (e.g., beans).

8 Olive oil, Spain: Relatively small orchards, increasingly mechanized but still local; increasing control over production, intended for European export and via Italy the global market.

9 Rice, Vietnam: Small-scale, highly intensive rice cultivation, sometimes in combination with fish, mainly focused on national self-sufficiency, with some export in the Southeast Asian region.

10 Bananas, Central America: Banana plantations, large-scale but worked by hand, control over production variable, focused on regional American and global market.

11 Tropical fruit, Chile: Medium-scale, often irrigated; good control of production process, mainly focused on export to northern hemisphere out of season and to South America.

12 Palm oil, Asia: Plantations of variable and increasing size, focused on production of raw materials for food products exclusively for global processing and export.

13 Fish farming, Norway: Medium-scale, intensive cultivation; increasing degree of control, focused on the international market.

---

water and manure. South American farmers, who with their transgenic, zero-tillage crops leave nothing to chance, deliver to China and the rest of Southeast Asia, where chickens and pigs are being kept on a larger and larger scale. Those same soy farmers also deliver to Europe and Africa, where the feed is used for chickens. And then those parts of the chickens that are not in regional demand, such as the wings, are then traded with Asia. In Europe, such products as eggs and pork are distributed widely.

Alongside this trend is another toward specialized and global chains with tight controls. This applies to tropical vegetables and fruit for export and to such high-value products as olive oil, wine, or foods made from fish. The large-scale, concentrated production of grains, oil seeds, soy, and sugar (for food, energy, and animal feed) will continue to be globally oriented, especially in South and North America and in Europe. Possibly some of these global trading currents will become regional, but livestock production in Asia cannot be sustained by grains from the region. Who knows? Perhaps eventually it won't be the soy that goes to China but the day-old chicks or fertilized eggs that go to Brazil, to avoid shipping huge amounts of feed such a long distance.

Organic food production is by its very nature locally oriented, but as the market grows, exports will increase, both regional and intercontinental. Small-scale production, whether or not linked to local or regional markets—such as rice farming in the Punjab or yam production close to Lagos—will continue to exist where labor is plentiful and investment is sporadic. Or indeed where specialized production takes place for a lucrative market, as for sea lavender and other products of the briny soil of Zeeland in the Netherlands, or the Camargue in France. Self-supporting small farms that are poorly connected to the market will gradually disappear, however. Food is best produced where production occurs most efficiently, but that biological principle is tempered by many other considerations, from animal welfare to landscape and subsidies. I suspect that in the future, as now, Europe and America will have a little of everything: orchards close to cities and multistory pigsties (known as "pig flats") in built-up areas, cereals in the fields, and greenhouses near the ports, as well as far more fish farming along the coast, combined with the protection of farmed landscapes and traditions.

As we learn more about sustainability, Green Revolutions will occur in various guises. It is all within reach: more and better food for everyone through higher productivity, in ways that do not harm the environment, humans, or animals. But it will not happen unless we make it.

FIFTEEN

Food: Irresistible and Emotionally Charged

Do you mean to kill everybody? And has your master invited people in order to destroy them with over-feeding? MOLIÈRE, *The Miser*

In the pursuit of a utopian paradise, everything was collectivized.... People in the countryside were robbed of their work, their homes, their land.... Food, distributed by the spoonful in collective canteens according to merit, became a weapon to force people to follow the party's every dictate.
FRANK DINKÖTTER, *Mao's Great Famine*

Hunger and Scarcity

For anyone suffering from hunger, everything that can serve as food becomes irresistible. Acute hunger can drive people insane. Rotting meat, tulip bulbs, tree bark, soil, leather—in times of war or famine when there's no food at all, people eat anything that might make their stomachs feel just a little less empty. The despair that accompanies hunger can lead to selfishness, aggression, and extremes of behavior. Countless stories tell of people who secretly ate the few supplies remaining or became dangerously ill from gobbling food after a period of starvation. Reports by eyewitnesses to the many great famines of the twentieth century—as in the Soviet Union, Bihar, China, Biafra, the Sahel, and North Korea—are heart-rending, because they show how a lack of food robs people of their humanity. It's dehumanizing to eat food unworthy of the name, or to scrabble and fight to survive—acts that are at odds with the fundamentally civilized behavior distinguishing humans from almost all other species: the sharing of food outside our own family group. There are also reports of astonishing altruism. In the most deplorable circumstances, in concentration camps, for example, people have been known to give away their last crust.

Many, if not all, famines of the twentieth century—some as recent as a generation or two ago—are characterized by the fact that they took place in totalitarian or dysfunctional states that did nothing about them, or acted far too late, and the situation was made worse by ethnic conflict. The classic example is the Ethiopian famine of the 1980s. Famines in colonial states were sometimes the result of other priorities taking precedence; during the acute food shortage in Bengal in 1943, food was still being shipped to the rest of India. In China and the Soviet Union food was deliberately deployed as an instrument of totalitarian repression. In China as many as 45 million people may have died of hunger and mistreatment in less than four years, between 1958 and 1962. In Europe the Second World War was the last time that widespread famine struck. (Worldwide, during 1939–1945, the number of people who died of hunger and malnutrition was comparable to the number of deaths among those in uniform, at almost 20 million.) This was not because of scarcity stemming from low yields. It was a consequence of the hostilities and blockades.

Acute hunger today is almost exclusively confined to a few areas hit by civil war and lacking a central government, such as the Horn of Africa and the Great Lakes region of Central Africa, or it may sometimes be the result of a natural disaster, as in Burma. Chronic hunger is most common in the countryside. About 15 percent of the world's population suffers from incidental or structural hunger. That is still far too many, but it is noticeable that the risk of famine has declined considerably since borders and markets opened after the fall of the Soviet Union.

No clear relationship exists between hunger and food production. Local scarcity does not have to lead to acute famine, because food can be brought in from elsewhere. Famine is rarely the result of acute scarcity (in other words, of an absolute lack of food, except in wartime). Instead it almost always results from a relative lack of buying power among a large group of people, which arises suddenly from joblessness, sharply falling incomes, rising food prices, or other disturbances to the market and to relative prices, while production remains steady. Local consumers find themselves unable to compete with buyers elsewhere. In no case has a higher percentage of the population died than during the Irish famine of the mid-nineteenth century. At its height, food was still being exported to Britain. The custom at the time was to pay the wages of agricultural workers partly in food, which proved disastrous, because low wages combined with high food prices lead to very low payments in kind.

In the past famines could rage without any significant measures being taken, because little was known about supplies elsewhere and the governing class was not forced to act. That's impossible today, mainly because in democracies the authorities can be called to account. So it's significant that after the dissolution of the colonial government in India and the founding of a democratic state, no acute, widespread famine has occurred there—the famine in Bihar in 1966 was nothing like that of Bengal in 1943–1945, when 2 million people died—although millions of very poor people in India still lack enough money or land to feed themselves and so suffer from chronic hunger. The belief that state authorities can in principle be held to account for failing to feed their people—because basic human rights include the right to food—is a recent advance that we can hope will made acute and chronic hunger increasingly rare.

The fear of scarcity is hard to shake, however, even for those who no longer suffer from a lack of food but remember hunger, or even those who have heard about hunger from others. This remains true of a large proportion of the world's population. Although 85 percent of people now consume more or less sufficient calories, I would estimate that a quarter of them did not have a hunger-free childhood, and far more are children or grandchildren of those who did suffer from hunger. The experience of famine, whether direct or through the stories of eyewitnesses, is therefore still very close.

We are all descended from ancestors for whom food scarcity was the rule rather than the exception. Among hunters the total number of calories is the limiting factor. On average they consume more proteins but have fewer carbohydrates available. Thus, high protein consumption among hunters is mainly a by-product of their having to eat a great deal of meat to have a sufficient intake of calories. This leads to the preference hunters have for fatty and therefore high-calorie sources of protein, such as beavers in North America or the larvae of *Coleoptera* beetles in the tropics. In arable farming, calories come from diverse sources, so they are less of a limitation than the amount of protein. The quality of those calories depends on the combination of legumes and cereals. In the early years of agriculture, starchy plants were dominant, so for a while the protein intake and life expectancy of the population fell in comparison to that of hunter-gatherers. With the rise of domesticated animals, several thousand years later, the availability of protein for farmers gradually increased.

Although the invention of farming slowly brought an end to the uncertainties of the hunt and of gathering wild plants, food supplies were unpredictable for centuries because of failed harvests, poorly functioning markets, wars, and social disturbances. Hunger was often seasonal.

Farmers suffered most at the end of the winter, when hard work had to be done in the fields and supplies were running out; this seasonal pattern persists today in poor areas, such as the Sahel. Even if there was no acute hunger, most people consumed insufficient nutrients in the winter or the dry season.

For most of humankind for most of history, food was and is a monotonous business, with little variation aside from the occasional religious or social festival, or stroke of luck when large prey is caught or a bountiful harvest brought in. No ordinary farmer or citizen could make too many demands concerning flavor. A rotting or otherwise bad taste was masked with salt, spices, and roasting. Spices and different methods of preparation were necessary to bring a little variety. This is the origin of the Indian curry, for example, which is simply more of the same limited range of food variously spiced. Only the rich could eat things from far away, or foods that required elaborate preparation or were scarce and varied enough to show off. All kinds of striking similarities exist among the food of the higher classes all over the world in all eras. English aristocrats, like the Mongolian emperors, ate swan flesh and drank honey wine, as did the pharaohs and the Ethiopian kings.

The most fundamental changes in human evolution have been in modern agriculture and the modern food processing industry, abolishing the limitations of place and season and drastically reducing the unit price of food. As modern, pampered urbanites, we barely know the value of what it means to have a guarantee of permanent and continual food security. The current situation of an unlimited availability for many people of starch (and sugar), protein, and fat has never occurred before in all of human evolution. In Europe and the United States hardly anyone any longer has to give a thought to whether there will be anything to eat today or tomorrow. Just how extraordinary our food situation is becomes clear when we look at the variety of our food. In the past most people may have eaten the same things for most of their lives, although collectively their diet was more varied than that of any other species on earth.

This is clear from two major differences between our diet and that of our closest evolutionary relatives, the great apes. We can fetch food from a long way outside the area where we live, from all over the planet in fact, and unlike other primates, who do not prepare their food but use only their alimentary canal to made nutrients available, we can make our food easier to digest or to store and remove any undesirable characteristics through the correct methods of preparation. Heating makes almost all nutrients easier to absorb, including those in vegetables, such as the vitamins and minerals found in tomatoes—tomato soup is more nutritious than raw tomato salad. We can dry our food, or salt or ferment it, so that it can be kept—as with fish (dried fish, fermented fish sauce), milk (cheese, yogurt), grapes (wine, raisins, currants)—and we can remove toxins, as with cassava or soy (in the latter case to eliminate the bitter taste and the trypsin-inhibiting factor). As a consequence of agriculture and global trade, which has opened up the world to our food supplies and our clever methods of preparation, our diets are now a good deal more varied than those of any other species and than at any other time in history.

The long line of ancestors who experienced scarcity has left its physiological and psychological traces. Physiologically, we are programmed to eat too much, just in case, as soon as food becomes available; psychologically we find it hard to stop eating. The tendency toward excess, to eat as much as possible straight away, is logical if you don't expect there will be enough for long.

Delaying consumption was an unwise strategy for most of our history, because you never knew when food would be available again or whether it could be stored successfully. Keeping food is a secondary and complicated step, which (unlike immediate consumption) is not taken instinctively. Delay demands consultation, oversight, and trust among people. It generally goes against our first impulse. This applies not just to food but also to many other consumer items, hence the temptations and dangers of cheap consumer credit. The experience with hunger and fear of scarcity are important phenomena if we are looking for a general understanding of our evolution and the current situation, in which being overweight and indulging in overconsumption are common. Even if scarcity is no longer with us, or is very rare, it remains a determining factor for our behavior.

Beyond Paradise: The Distribution of Scarcity

In our conception of the mythical paradise, the distribution of food is not an issue. The promise is simply one of eternal plenty, and anyhow no real eating goes on. The only documented mouthful in the paradise story is out of the ordinary. When things finally reach that point, Eve eats first, then Adam, an order that goes against virtually every religious and moral rule of practically every era. The writers of Genesis probably couldn't help blaming Eve—the weaker flesh—for breaking the divine command. In any case the Fall marks an end to the "egalitarian" sharing of paradise. The sharing of scarcity begins at the same time and with it inequality among humans. For millennia scarcity and abundance were two sides of the same coin. Where scarcity reigned, the sharing out of food had to be regulated to ensure the survival of the group. In episodes of abundance—for example, in a year with a good harvest or when the enemy's food stocks were plundered—restraints had to be imposed. Abundance might otherwise lead to short-sighted behavior or the overthrow of existing power structures. Many if not all our etiquette and institutions have their roots in the need to regulate the sharing of food.

In almost all cultures it is the custom to put a large amount of food in front of guests, as a sign of status and hospitality and sometimes as a way of evening out differences in wealth, or indeed of emphasising those differences. In this hospitable abundance a deep incantation resonates at least as powerfully: never fear, the plates piled high with couscous or rice with three kinds of meat are a signal that there's enough for everyone; we don't need to fight over food, we can be friends. Even in rich countries this kind of behavior persists, not only at laden tables but when shopping. Almost everyone has more food in the fridge than they need and is therefore forced to throw away more than would be sensible.

Abundance is accompanied by a dual sense of guilt. The host feels guilty if all the food is eaten, and the guest feels guilty if he or she doesn't manage to eat it all. To offer too little food is to insult the guest, with a new undertone of threat. (Is the guest worthy of my food?) To fail to finish everything on your plate, let alone to refuse food, is to insult the host. (Was it not offered hospitably enough, or do we not trust each other after all?) Offering a lot of food and eating it is not just a biological adjustment to times of scarcity, it has social and moral significance.

The sharing or redistribution of scarcity and abundance takes many forms. Among Native Americans on the West Coast of the United States and Canada, the phenomenon of the potlatch survived well into the twentieth century. The term refers to the giving of gifts. The aim of the ritual was the redistribution of wealth. Although it was primarily a matter of expensive objects, such as sheets of beaten copper or blankets, potlatch also involved food, such as dried fish and oil. Sometimes the valuables were collectively destroyed. A comparable ritual existed among inhabitants of islands in the South Pacific in various forms, the Kula ring of the Trobriand Islanders being the best known. Shells, chains, and women were exchanged there in a complex manner between many partners, whereas in the highlands of Papua New Guinea food was the main gift, usually sweet potatoes and pigs, likewise evidence of wealth. In all cases the ritual concerns competition among tribal leaders and the need to limit differences in wealth. Such competition for power almost always expresses itself in the sharing of food.

Almost everywhere in the world, in more or less egalitarian communities as well as in hierarchical societies, social inequality is accompanied by an unequal distribution of food and nutritional status. This holds true for Europe and North America, where balanced diets and health largely coincide with social class. Still today, people eat differently in the countryside, and diets are less varied there than in the city. Although great poverty exists in the cities, the majority of the poor live in rural areas (about 70 percent). Acute poverty in poor countries correlates strongly with quantitatively and qualitatively inadequate food consumption, high child mortality, low birth weight, low weight during childhood, and limited height. Relative poverty in developed societies, among the lower social classes and those with little education, is now an indicator for the opposite: overweight.

One of the most common ways in which societies regulate food scarcity is by systematically disadvantaging women. In almost all cultures, women and children eat later than men. This was the case in Western countries until the nineteenth century, when, hand in hand with abundance, etiquette made its appearance, and women were invited to serve themselves first. In many contemporary societies with chronic food shortages and in earlier societies, to judge from the archaeological evidence, it seems that women, girls, and young children often had a lower feeding status than that of men and boys. At first sight this might seem unsurprising, because men and boys do the work that requires the greatest muscular strength and protect the group. But this is not really a good explanation, because depriving women of food means endangering reproduction and the survival of infants. Perhaps the limiting of food given to women is an indirect and implicit way of regulating the number of children born.

Moreover, it might increase the survival chances of relatively rich families, because their womenfolk, and therefore their infants, will be comparatively well fed. However that may be, young underfed women have children who are small and malnourished. This is the hidden face of hunger, caused in part by a shortage of micronutrients, such as zinc and vitamin A. Tragically, there are strong indications that the poor nutritional condition of the mother causes the fetus to save energy, so the child later has a significantly greater likelihood of becoming overweight or obese.

Slowly, and more rapidly from the nineteenth century on, worldwide scarcity declined. This is beautifully illustrated by the gradual increase in the amount of food shown in depictions of the Last Supper through the centuries. The trend toward larger portions and more meat is not a product of modern times alone. The longing for abundance has always existed. Although the twentieth century had notoriously disruptive famines, in the past hundred years abundance has been increasingly the norm. True, old cookbooks for the higher classes describe huge banquets with many courses, different kinds of meat and fish as the main course, puddings of dozens of eggs and liters of cream, but these feasts were always the exception.

The past century has been characterized by a gradual increase in portions and in the number of calories in each dish, as well as the number of snacks. The most emblematic example is the launch in the late 1960s of the Big Mac, the double hamburger in which twice as much beef, cheese, greens, and sauce could be fitted because of the extra layer of bread in the middle, which absorbs the sauce and makes the stack more stable. The Big Mac contains a quarter to a fifth of a person's daily caloric requirement, almost twice as much as the original hamburger. Variations on it include the Big Big Mac, the Bigger Mac, the Mega Mac, and the Double Big Mac. It was quickly followed by the extra-large portion of fries, extra-large ("tall") soft drinks, and so on. The promotion of abundance, even when unnecessary, is a response to historical scarcity.

The Obesogenic Environment

With only slight exaggeration, you could say that the poor used to eat to live while the rich lived to eat. Today it's if anything the other way around: the rich live to work and develop themselves, and those who lack satisfying work, or work altogether, live to eat (because they have little to distract them other than television, that perfect decor for mindless eating). After millennia of scarcity we now find ourselves in the kingdom of plenty. But the abundance that has satisfied our hunger comes at a high price.

As a symbol of our current abundance I know no sadder sight than that of a lone person chewing while wandering past shops with interchangeable objects and items of clothing they don't need. This is the crucial change in modern eating behavior: at all times and everywhere, at home and in public, people eat, even while walking, working, and driving. The day seems to be one continual meal. The eating human has grown to become a new phenomenon, a dependent subspecies of the genus *Homo* whose individuals need constant satisfaction. With a bottle of water or fruit juice to suck on, or a large cup of latte and a straw, the shopping and working eaters are reminiscent of overgrown babies.

In rich countries food consumption is no longer limited by anything, neither by money nor by scarcity—and barely by opening times or distance. Even in the town centers of poor and emerging economies we see the same constant availability. Junk food is everywhere, always in reach of the growing urban middle class. To be able to eat as much as you like whenever you like is the temptation behind the epidemic of obesity. The word "epidemic" is misleading in many ways, because unhealthy food and overweight are a stubborn and complex problem. Calling it an "epidemic" suggests that a few well-judged measures will save us, something along the lines of washing hands, vaccination, or wearing a mask. In a biological sense this is not an epidemic of obesity, because there is no source of infection, nor is there a mechanism (a vector, such as an insect) that transmits the disease. It is not bubonic plague, 'flu, or tuberculosis, an infection that affects everyone, whoever they may be. You don't get overweight by being close to overweight people.

Or do you? Psychologically there does seem to be an effect that is transmitted from one person to the next. Heavy girls tend to be friends with other overweight girls rather than thin contemporaries, in whose company they feel ill at ease. Children of overweight parents are more often heavy themselves. In classes with lots of overweight children, newcomers quickly gain weight. Of course, it is always a matter of individual decisions by eaters. All food goes in through the mouth. On average we make 200 decisions a day that have to do with buying, preparing, and consuming food. But you might wonder to what degree those individual decisions are determined by the conscious or unconscious copying of the behavior of parents or contemporaries and the influence of advertising and information. That "infectious" influence has its effects despite other information that consumers also have: anyone with a modicum of nutritional insight knows there are risks attached to being overweight and eating unhealthy food, and that fries, hot dogs, chocolate bars, and soft drinks contribute to those risks.

———

We now live in an obesogenic environment, which encourages us to eat through continual stimuli and gives us no reason to stop or to moderate our intake. Supermarkets that are open all hours of the day and night; advertisements for calorie bombs; tempting flavors created by combinations of fat, sugar, and salt; enormous portions; more easily absorbed liquid calories in fizzy drinks and fruit juices; laziness; low prices—anyone who chooses to can stuff themselves continually. Those who don't really want to may nevertheless be tempted. Food has become irresistible. Even if those same supermarkets have plenty of vegetables and healthy or low-calorie foods on offer, even if labels point us to the healthy, "good" options, even if help to lose weight can be found everywhere on the Internet—it's all simply further proof that we live in an obesogenic environment.

Our lifestyle is part of that environment. Our eating too much is a consequence of the falling away of strong family ties and the casualness and haste with which we eat. Anyone who snacks in front of the computer or in the car is distracted and is not paying attention to how much he or she is consuming. Working parents (rather than a parent who stays at home to safeguard the regularity and quality of the family meals), whether in broken families or not, have no time to cook elaborately. Many small but significant changes have contributed to the obesogenic environment: "latchkey kids" who arrive home from school alone and feel like a nice snack, life in suburbs with the car right outside, the disappearance of the local shop you could walk to, more dangerous traffic, and less walking and cycling. Being unemployed or underemployed is not the problem, incidentally, because it is known that individuals in these circumstances also fail to find the time and energy to cook.

Social pressure also prompts us to eat too much. People want to eat the same things as other people do, even in the case of unhealthy food that they don't particularly enjoy. Eating behavior is mimicked, just like other forms of behavior – think of risky conduct on the roads. Like everyone in my generation with parents who remembered life during the Second World War, I learned always to finish what was on my plate—in fact, almost everyone who came before me learned to eat what they were served. Throwing food away was "a shame." So you soon found yourself eating more than you wanted. Social pressure also explains why a child in the playground surrounded by chocolate bars and snacks doesn't want to be the only one eating an apple. If a whole family or group of friends goes to get pizza, it's hard to opt out. In fact there's a good chance you'll go the next time too, because eating pizza or a hamburger is part of the social event. Young people find it hard to withdraw from the food norms of their subculture. Hence the continued success of the hamburger and modern forms of convenience food, such as the wrap and the frozen pizza, or those Asian instant noodles that are now taking off all over the world.

There is something else that reinforces the obesogenic environment. Because being slim is so hard to achieve for most people, self-control in itself is put in a bad light. "See? I just wasn't meant to be thin," we think. Self-control is something for those successful people, not a virtue in itself. Collectively there are now fewer brakes on our impulses rather than more. Self-control is not a virtue of the responsible citizen but instead is just old-fashioned. The current mentality is one in which everyone has a right to their emotions and should—no, must—express them immediately and without restraint. Self-control in consumption, whether of food or other things, is hardly encouraged. People are all too happy to ignore the demands of society. Driving too fast, running a red light, putting in a false insurance claim, trying to dodge taxes—all behaviors that go against moral standards but are nonetheless generally tolerated, which makes it hard to be strict with ourselves when it comes to moderating our intake of food. It's a reversal of the process of controlling our impulses that until recently we saw as proof of advancing civilization.

In the end body weight is all about the balance between the absorption of energy from food and the use of that energy. Lifestyle in the sense of sitting in the car more and moving around less is certainly of relevance, but the trend toward obesity, in the past fifteen years at least, is largely attributable to higher food consumption, in turn inspired in part by lifestyle and family composition. Energy use per person has not reduced appreciably over that period, although it has if you look further back. In the 1950s and 1960s more people were engaged in manual labor, whether in the form of housework or in farming and industry. Nowadays more and more people move around by car.

Fat or Lean

Overweight has existed for a long time to a limited extent, but the scale on which we see it now is unprecedented. In 2006 the number of overweight people exceeded the number suffering from hunger for the first time in human history. That increase was so rapid that just eight years later the number of overweight people was more than half as large again as the number of hungry people on earth. Some estimates suggest that in 2015 the number of people carrying too much weight stands at 2.3 billion.

We should be less concerned about overweight than about obesity, but the former can be a preliminary stage to the latter. Obesity in children may be one of the greatest public health challenges today. In 2010 the total number of children younger than five who were overweight or obese was 46 million, an increase of 60 percent in twenty years. In contrast to what many think, this is not primarily a problem of rich countries. Most of the children concerned, more than 35 million, live in emerging economies, such as Brazil, China, and India, and belong to the middle class. In the United States a third of children are overweight, half of them obese. The number of children with weight problems has grown more quickly than has the number of adults with such problems. There are now around half a billion obese adults worldwide, so 10 percent of men and 15 percent of women are obese, defined as a body mass index (BMI, measured in kilograms per meter of height squared) of more than 30. Another billion adults are too heavy, with a BMI of more than 25. In OECD countries they amount to half the adult population, in Russia and Brazil likewise, in China almost a third, in India less than a fifth. In Europe the figures for the southern countries are slightly lower than those for the north, but developments in Italy and Spain are exactly the same as in the rest of Europe. In the Netherlands around 11 percent of adults are obese, a relatively low figure that can be explained in part by the national cycling habit. The lowest score is for Japan, the highest for the United States and Mexico, where almost 70 percent of adults are overweight. Excess weight and obesity in children seems still to be increasing, while among adults the situation is stabilizing in some countries, especially in the United States.

Determining precise figures is not easy because of problems of measurement and differences in definition, but the trend is clear: too much and too little often exist side by side. This is the double burden of overfeeding and underfeeding. In both cases people absorb too few nutrients in the right proportions. In China, for example, illnesses related to eating too much are now the most important cause of death, along with infectious diseases, but at the same time 8 percent of Chinese schoolchildren are not getting enough to eat. In India the situation is comparable: the number of patients with type 2 diabetes (which correlates strongly with overweight and overconsumption) has doubled, while 40 percent of children are underweight. Even Africa is not being spared. Estimates suggest that almost 40 percent of African women and 30 percent of African men are too heavy. Overweight in Africa is particularly complicated, because loss of weight is associated with HIV/AIDS, and in the marriage market corpulence is still an important sign of prosperity and is regarded as beautiful.

It remains to be seen whether excess weight (a BMI of between 25 and 30) really is a threat to public health, as long as diets are healthy and people are active. We do not know for certain whether being overweight is a prelude to morbid obesity. Obesity is the tip of an iceberg made up of a series of problems that come under the heading of "metabolic syndromes." Those who suffer from morbid obesity are statistically more likely to develop a whole series of chronic diseases associated with prosperity that are partly the consequence of an excessively rich diet. They include type 2 diabetes, some forms of cancer, and cardiovascular disease. The risks are not evenly spread. In South Asia and East Asia the figures for overweight are lower than elsewhere, but genetic susceptibility to insulin resistance means the chances of diabetes are far higher than in Europe. In children, obesity causes a shortage of essential nutrients, with serious consequences for growth and cognitive development. So we are not talking simply about a few extra kilograms, as in the early stages of putting on too much weight, but an endocrinological and physiological problem.

Around 40 percent of Europeans feel they are too fat. Waist measurements of British women have increased by 15 centimeters in the past half century (although this figure is not corrected to take account of the increase in height). It seems bra cups in northwestern Europe have increased by two sizes. The problem of poor diets concerns far more than overweight and obesity, although the two are often equated. Thin people may have an unhealthy fat and vitamin balance, while slightly heavy people may be extremely healthy. Parents who are overweight, or have eating disorders, are more likely to have overweight children. Parents who are overweight and have overweight children think other people's children are thin rather than normal. So the norm shifts. The fashion, film, and entertainment industries serve up super-slim or even skeletal models, and the media recommend new diets every day, but this is above all confirmation of how unattainable the ideal type is—it is certainly not a helping hand for the average consumer.

A direct connection links waist measurement and social class, although it doesn't always point in the same direction. Until well into the twentieth century, wealth was associated with a degree of plumpness. Mummies have been found in Egyptian graves with extensive skin folds that suggest they suffered from obesity, perhaps as a result of consuming too many honey cakes and alcoholic drinks. In cartoons by famous nineteenth-century artist Honoré Daumier, we see absurdly fat capitalists and emaciated workers. Those who didn't need to work much if at all— in other words, the rich—were overweight, while those who performed hard labor didn't eat enough to become plump. Overweight is undoubtedly an ideal in societies where an abundance of food is the exception. So chubbiness or even corpulence was once regarded as an attractive feature, not just in non-Western countries but in Europe too—think of Rubens' paintings of voluptuous young women, who were associated with abundance and fertility. We still see such women—and indeed men—in the work of the contemporary Columbian painter Fernando Botero. Of particular relevance in this connection is his wonderful "Adan y Eva," in which, beneath the nocturnal skies of paradise, Adam stretches out his hand for the forbidden fruit and an equally chubby Eve lays her hand on his shoulder, in a reversal of the paradise story in which Eve takes the initiative in plucking the apple. In West Africa the size of the "Mama Benz," rich market traders, is a sign of their power and prosperity. Chinese boys, most of whom have no brothers or sisters, are sometimes corpulent and spoiled, because they are the living treasures that have to make up for all the deprivation suffered by their parents and grandparents. Their weight and their poor prospects for future health may also be explained by the fact that in the womb they were exposed to food scarcity.

For the first time in history, thinness is becoming a broadly accepted status symbol, even in developing countries where obesity, hunger, and extreme slimness in young middle-class girls all exist side by side. Slimness is now associated with a better education and a higher income. The richer girls are, the slimmer and healthier they appear. This may not apply to female students in America who, with a slight delay and certainly not to the same degree, seem to be following after their less privileged contemporaries as far as waist measurement goes. In contrast, middle-class women in India are dieting furiously, a heart-rending development in a country where millions are "slim," because they have too little to eat.

Until a few decades ago, lower income groups suffered above all from shortages and a lack of buying power; now a low income is associated with poorer health and a diet in which fats are dominant and vegetables and fruit are lacking. Corpulence seems more objectionable in women these days than in men, a reversal of the earlier ideal. Chinese girls, too, seem to suffer more as a result of chubbiness than do Chinese boys. This is partly because of the stress placed on youthfulness, which causes women the world over to want to look like girls, and the story of the weakness of Eve may have a part to play as well. Women, the thinking goes, are simply less able than men to resist temptation.

The ubiquity of the ideal of slimness—as opposed to the slimness of nineteenth-century women in a time when the wealthy citizenry felt it proved women were fragile creatures who didn't need to work—is truly recent. Only now, in the twenty-first century, can we permit ourselves to be slim or even skinny, because we live in the certainty that there will always be sufficient food and our bodies don't need to have their own reserves. For modern men and women, slimness is the result of a combination of constant control of the impulse to eat and self-imposed physical effort. The spectacular increase in the use of gyms and jogging paths by the middle classes all over the world is proof that the human species now has access to so much food, and therefore energy, that it can be used for nonproductive activities. For all other species on earth, the use of energy has to be optimized. Even mammals that appear to play in order to learn, such as young bears or dolphins, or who "play" as part of their mating rituals do not do so to lose weight. In evolutionary terms, the way that people now systematically expend energy to control their weight, by voluntarily running or participating in sport, is unique. Most astonishing of all in this connection is that we have set up clinics where the human species can have fat sucked out by liposuction. The slimness that results could be seen as the ultimate decadence of a species that can afford to waste abundance.

––––––––

Our eating behavior and sense of hunger are the results of complex biochemical processes; learned habits; and associations (grandmother's irresistible apple tart!) and perception, such as our responses to smell, taste, and visual attractiveness. Some hormones have a short-term effect based on their presence in the blood, such as the "hunger hormone" ghrelin, whereas others, such as insulin, are linked to the amount of fatty tissue and in theory ought to prompt us to eat less. Our evolutionary history has made this regulatory system sensitive to shortages, whereas excesses (too many calories and eventually too much fatty tissue) do not quickly lead to compensatory behavior, such as moderation or fasting. We also have a tendency to value most highly the foods that offer the most energy most quickly: fats and sugars, preferably in combination. Dopamine and opiates affect both desire and its satisfaction. It seems as if in more and more people the biochemical signals that tell us we have eaten enough are working inadequately or not at all, so they continue eating. Experiments show that stress encourages us to opt for carbohydrates and fatty foods.

Our instinctive preferences for high-calorie foods that are easily digested, and therefore sugars followed by fats and proteins, can be attributed to hundreds of thousands of years of scarcity. If you introduce a sugarlike substance into the amniotic fluid of primates (including pregnant women), the fetus starts to make sucking movements. The preference for sugar is therefore probably part of our neurobiological structure. Similarly, people are averse to bitter tastes, which may indicate toxins, as in cassava (which in turn may be an evolutionary adaptation by plants and insects to protect themselves against being eaten). The human digestive system is designed to absorb quickly high-value, protein-rich, and low-fiber foods.

People who systematically eat more than they can expend through metabolic and physical effort develop extra fatty tissue, which in turn requires extra calories to maintain it. So weigh gain slows down after a while; we don't go on getting endlessly heavier. Conversely, weight loss leads to lower maintenance costs in energy terms, which explains why people soon start bulking up again after reaching their target weight, unless they stick to the diet permanently or have replaced a great deal of their fatty tissue with muscle, which again requires more energy to maintain. The fact that it is so hard to control the desire to eat by using willpower alone is attributable to the slowness of the satisfaction response. The body reacts to what is being eaten and how much, but only after an hour do we feel satisfied. In people who eat too much the stomach wall gradually expands, and the sense that the stomach is full comes a little later each time. The absorption of calories is regulated by the central nervous system in which the hormone leptin ensures that body weight remains more or less stable.

You might think that the number of calories a person needs on average is more or less constant, so that if we just stick to a steady food intake all will be well. But it's not that simple. Anyone who does physical work, lives in a cold climate, or is outside in winter needs to eat more. The average adult man in the Western world who leads a sedentary life needs 20 percent fewer calories than a far lighter Inuit hunter. This is purely because he is less active than the hunter—even though in theory a person who is larger or heavier needs more calories than someone who is carrying less weight. Now that in richer countries, and in the middle classes the world over, people are taller and weigh more, our calorie needs are increasing somewhat, but this is more than offset by the fact that it takes us less and less effort to feed ourselves. African farmers who still do everything by hand manage to consume only 2,000 calories a day, mainly in the form of carbohydrates, and they barely achieve a BMI of 20. The urban population consumes an increasing proportion of its calories as fat rather than carbohydrates. The population of Mexico, the country with the highest percentage of overweight people, consumes almost 40 percent of its calories in the form of fat.

Because weight gain happens gradually, sometimes over several decades, it's hard to get a grip on it. It's not usually caused by any radical change in behavior, such as suddenly starting to eat whole boxes of chocolates or large portions of French fries. Instead the process occurs in small, almost invisible steps: an extra sweet or sandwich, walking or engaging in sport a little less, and so on. Unfortunately the reverse is not the case; reducing excess weight demands a far more drastic approach than refusing a sweet once in a while or occasionally playing tennis. One telling and rather sad example is the case of a manager of a Brazilian hamburger restaurant who gained thirty kilograms during his twelve years on the job, because he believed he had to keep tasting the food as a quality check. Moreover, lunches were free for staff. He sued McDonald's and received compensation, based on the argument that his weight gain was unavoidable.

Emotionally Charged Food

Food is not just a source of pleasure and a way of affirming a social network. In times of scarcity food is a source of daily anxiety, but in the current era of plenty it's emotionally charged and problematic in a different way. Food can be a source of danger to our health and, to a far lesser degree, the environment. There's no other subject about which we so often say that we've transgressed. We may have "fallen" for a chocolate muffin—surely a reference to Eve and the Fall of Man. Something that's so essential to survival is of course never neutral, but while the emotional charge once related to religious rules and taboos that were overseen by a clearly defined group of authorities, such as the church or village elders, reality is now far more complicated. Almost everyone regards him- or herself as more or less an expert on food, and we all have an opinion about it. We are all confused, too. No one acts as an uncontroversial authority; each authority replaces the one before it. We are just as sceptical about official sources of information on food as we are about information put out by companies, the discoveries made by food science, or the latest diet book. Old and new media are an inexhaustible source of opinions, doubts, research, groundbreaking insights, ancient preconceptions, and stubborn old wives' tales that bring our confusion to the boil.

That food is the determining factor in many aspects of health is no recent insight. Food has always been a medicine. This was true in the time of the ancient Greeks and of the emperors of fourteenth-century Mongolia, as well as in nineteenth-century Britain. We now know far more about the relationship between food and public health than ever before, but epidemiological insights do not point to causal connections from which lifestyle rules for individuals can be derived. That fact too is a source of uncertainty. If a researcher finds evidence of a link between liver cancer and peanut butter, do you then have to give up your favorite sandwich with peanut butter and jam? The jam, incidentally, with all its E numbers for flavoring and coloring, cannot be assumed innocent either.

Uncertainty about food is not just the result of the great mass of products with unclear labels, promoted by suggestive advertisements, but also of shifting perceptions in the food sciences. Relationships that seemed straightforward, such as between fat consumption and some forms of cancer—or the reverse, the protective effect of fiber against intestinal cancer—turn out on closer inspection to be less than clear. Cholesterol used to be the great enemy, so eggs were downright dangerous. No longer. Chocolate was to be avoided but is now recommended again—in moderation, of course. Scientific knowledge about food and cooking increases with time, and so does public confusion. That foods have a moral charge to them is gratefully exploited by diet gurus and culinary journalists, who are forever making "great discoveries" about foods that help us sleep at night, or that "melt" fat cells or restore energy balance.

There is little reason to give a stamp of moral approval to individual foods. Apples, steak, bread rolls, or endive are not good or bad in any absolute sense. Only ingredients or meals that are tainted or that were created in circumstances harmful to humans or animals are bad. What seems good to us now may be seen quite differently in another few decades. Think of the shifting assessment of milk, once regarded as good for all, then criticized for containing too much saturated fat, but recently in favor again as a source of calcium for the elderly and children and an alternative to sugary soft drinks. This is the domain of urban legends, passed on by journalists who spend little time checking facts or nuances. Fructose is ultimately no better or worse than sucrose, although it has a different effect on insulin levels. You don't lose weight by eating proteins, even though the burning off of proteins takes more energy per calorie than the burning off of other nutrients. And so on. Fruit is healthy, but that doesn't mean there are no calories in it; too much fruit, especially in the form of easily absorbed fruit juice, will not help you stay slim despite all that promising fiber.

So the sources of confusion swell to a flood. Our food is said to be getting unhealthier than ever, with too much industrial processing, too little that is "natural." It's also seen as potentially dangerous. In an objective sense this is rarely the case, because possible sources of contamination in the food chain have been largely banished in rich countries. But as our food has become safer, the fears, misunderstandings, and superstitions surrounding it have grown. This is undoubtedly connected with the declining acceptance of risk and a failure to understand probability and orders of magnitude. Precisely because we no longer have much to fear, the odd occasion when food does pose a risk tends to be exaggerated. The perception that food is getting worse can easily be dismissed. Even correcting for the absence of medical services in the past, it is clear that differences in life expectancy, from no more than thirty years over millennia to more than seventy worldwide today, are closely connected to the current availability of sufficient and safe food. That some of the diseases of affluence may have to do with diets that are too lavish and contain too much fat is a completely new development, which in a number of countries may serve to limit further increases in life expectancy. But the trend is clear: our food is better and more diverse, and it is raising the quality and the length of our lives. Yet gurus still recommend diets designed to take us back to a pre-agrarian past, with a great deal of meat, few carbohydrates, and above all no bread.

———

There was some truth in the saying "an apple a day keeps the doctor away" in a time when hardly any fruit or vegetables were being eaten. But nowadays that dimension too is the subject of intensive research. Foodstuffs are being improved continually to contribute to the health of the consumer. To counter criticism that industrial production is in fact obesogenic, the composition of countless products has been revised over the past decade: fewer and different salts (of potassium rather than sodium, for instance); less sugar and fat; more vitamins, such as folic acid; and more calcium and other minerals. There are advantages as well as disadvantages to these revisions. The replacement of sodium chloride with potassium chloride for use as salt does lead to the removal of sodium and moisture from the blood, reducing blood pressure, but potassium chloride tastes bitter, so all kinds of technological tricks are needed to mask or eliminate that aspect of the flavor.

The food industry is increasingly adding substances that were not originally part of the food item concerned but provide an extra health dimension by reducing blood pressure or cholesterol levels, as well as those that offer other kinds of protection against cardiovascular disease, such as plant sterols. Some of the new generation of health-promoting foods are referred to as "novel foods" because of their ingredients or their methods of production. They include products of biotechnology, and they are coming close to being medicines. Great play is made of the collective fear of fat and of unhealthy food. The growing market for healthy products means businesses have much to gain by being able to make claims about nutrition and health.

Such claims indicate what the product contains, such as vitamin C, and if levels are unusually high, then comparisons with the standard product are deployed. Health claims substantiate the workings of a product based on recognized scientific research, perhaps stating that it helps with the avoidance of illness and generally strengthens resistance. It's too early to judge the results of this shift toward inherently healthier foods. Critics say that the reduction of fat or salt content is too slight to have any effects on the population and that the biological uptake of the new nutrients is limited.

The most pressing problem of additives is that the dose can't be controlled, so people may eat too much of them. This is less likely with foods that are used by consumers in fairly consistent quantities (such as oil, butter, or margarine), as opposed to sugar, snacks, or bread. The idea that individual food items can make a significant contribution to health also directly contradicts the axiom that the diet as a whole determines a person's health. At the same time the stress on individual foods does meet the confused consumer's need for a magic ingredient that will make everything right. If you just eat one artichoke a day or six walnuts or two spoonfuls of olive oil, or an improved yogurt, you'll no longer have to worry about anything. It's understandable wishful thinking, but no such miracle ingredient exists, and chances are it never will.

Food Choice and Moderation

That we are what we eat is an idea expressed many times in history, for example, by sixteenth-century painter Giuseppe Arcimboldo, who composed portraits out of plants and fruit. Plenty of people are happy to assert that what we eat determines our character. Meat eaters are said to be aggressive and vegetarians peace loving. There is no evidence whatsoever for this claim.

All the same, from an evolutionary point of view, we really are what we eat and have eaten. Even long before the invention of agriculture, in the East African savannah, people turn out to have been very flexible eaters. They adapted to changes in the availability of food and to the successful transition to cooking and the eating of meat. Some food choices seem surprising but are functional, like the clay soil eaten by pregnant women in West Africa (the clay is a source of minerals, including calcium, magnesium, zinc, and potassium), or the rotten wood with honey eaten on the Indian subcontinent (the wood-devouring bacteria produce B-group vitamins, and the honey serves to mask the taste). Such flexibility continues to this day. When we're exposed to new foods, there turns out to be a great deal we like, familiar or unfamiliar. As a result, we eat very differently now from the way our grandparents ate.

─────────

It's not true, however, that we have an inherent preference or instinct for healthy foods or sensible quantities. We probably have a powerful tendency to choose food we can obtain with the least effort. We have this in common with other primates. Even if they live in environments that are extremely biologically diverse, they feed themselves with only a small number of species, just as humans do. When hunter-gatherers settle down in temporary dwellings, they develop a preference for food that can be stored, perhaps because it has a hard shell, such as nuts and seeds, or can be left in the ground like some tubers and roots. Research among groups of hunter-gatherers still active today shows that the relatively limited range of foods available is optimal: more variety involves more effort.

In contrast to what is sometimes claimed, it is not true that people used to have a more varied diet or that to search for variety is a natural tendency. Diversity is also difficult to connect with healthy eating. Certainly, if you eat only bread and peanut butter or only rice with palm oil sauce, you will not get all the nutrients you need, but how diverse does a diet have to be? Anyone who eats two vegetables, a source of carbohydrate (such as rice or pasta), and from time to time some protein from soy or fish or meat is on the right track, even though this would be a diet of very few foods. There is no objective measure for the degree of diversity other than the number of different foods over a specified period. That measure is difficult enough to determine, because reconstructing diets based on what people recall generally results in distortion: we rarely can remember accurately what we have eaten across a whole year or even a couple of seasons. Those who eat without thinking will not remember the food. In any case, is yellow corn the same as white corn? Not from a nutritional point of view. In much of the research into diversity, both would not only be thrown together but combined with other foods under the heading of "grains."

———

Moderation is the exception throughout history. Born of need (which is to say, scarcity rather than a choice), moderation became an ideal to be emulated. Now we think of moderation as a solution to problems of health and the environment. In the past moderation was above all of moral significance. People who are moderate govern their instincts and conquer biological determinism. No wonder almost all religions approve of it as something to be achieved through fasting or by adherence to dietary laws. Slimness is presently one of the expressions of civilization, because it proves an individual can control his or her urges. Conversely, being overweight is now generally regarded as a sign of moral weakness, no matter how stigmatizing that may be.

Historically, fasting was a means of limiting food intake the world over. A side effect of fasting is that food scarcity becomes more manageable. It's no accident that the most important period of fasting in the Catholic and Orthodox Churches falls just before Easter and therefore in the spring. It coincides with that critical period between the depletion of winter food stocks and the start of the first harvest. This period is of greatest scarcity, at least in temperate climates, where it can be many weeks before anything edible is to be found on the land again. Scarcity is rarely given as a justification for religious fasting, however, instead the emphasis is on such ideals as "purity," asceticism, and concentration on the higher things to come. These then become a goal in themselves, and sometimes an obsession in the form of anorexia and other eating disorders. Miraculous qualities were attributed to women like Catherine of Siena and many others after her, until well into the nineteenth century, because of their fasting.

Fasting can lead to an enhanced consciousness of what you are eating. A comparable effect is seen with rules about what is edible and what not, which exist in almost all societies alongside fasting. Even in the paradise story it's clear that food is both a temptation and a danger, and it must therefore be regulated by prohibitions. Specialist knowledge of what you can or cannot eat when and where exists in all cultures; some of it we have now lost, some has become irrelevant, and some has been replaced by new taboos and new sins, the impetus behind them perhaps coming from a new type of businessperson who has replaced the church minister.

In Victorian Britain, for example, girls and boys from good backgrounds were expected to limit themselves to light food, as meat and heavy foods were reserved for men because of the association of such foods with physicality and sex. Now we say that we have transgressed if we eat a chocolate muffin, whereas our real transgression, if we want to keep using that word, is our ignorance, not the food itself.

The modern variants of fasting and moderation can be found in all kinds of diets, some of which forbid bread and carbohydrates, or even, in the case of juice diets, all solid foods. The aim is not to redistribute scarce resources but to avoid individual excess. What is new is the stress on vegetarian food, such as the call for Meatless Mondays, a campaign that associates itself with the saving of polar bears, suggesting a relationship between eating behavior and both the scarcity of raw materials and the production of greenhouse gases by livestock, rather than referring to any scarcity of food. Fasting for a short or long period is a drastic form of moderation, and few stay the course.

Moderation in itself is complicated. What is moderate eating? Never a hamburger again? Or one per month? Or would one a week be all right, as long as you eat lots of vegetables the rest of the week? Not so much as a bite of bread because of those feared carbohydrates but still a piece of fruit every day? In contrast to other transgressions and other forms of problematic behavior, food is all about the pattern as a whole, the long term. Stealing and deceiving are always morally wrong, even in small amounts, even on a single occasion, but a healthy diet can include foods that are less healthy, as long as the entire diet is in balance and in the right proportion to energy use. This reasonableness and weighing up is what makes it so difficult, because strict rules that leave no room for doubt or individual decisionmaking tend to offer firmer guidelines.

If it's so difficult to moderate our behavior and adhere to rules, then we must contract morality out, so that individual consumers no longer need to be held responsible in an almost impossible situation with so many incentives to eat. Instead society as a whole, made up of governments, consumers, and producers, should bear the burden. This idea is increasingly finding a ready reception with regard to traffic, for example, which is moderated by speed bumps, and now food. Perhaps we must be continually protected against ourselves, although no one is keen on a police state with a camera in every kitchen and a tracking chip on the fridge door and the garbage bag. After millennia in which we have regulated food because of the need to share out scarce goods—and after a century or so of regulation aimed at preventing decay and guaranteeing quality—we are now starting, hesitantly and awkwardly, on a new phase: the regulation of abundance.

From Abundance to a Healthy Balance

Healthy eating isn't really so complicated. Eat a variety of foods, not too much fat, include fiber, vegetables and fruit, occasionally oily fish and an egg, and less salt than most of us are used to. Eat meat and fish in moderation. Saturated fat is the enemy, but unsaturated fats are necessary, from dairy products and above all from vegetable oils. Carbohydrates should not be avoided, but neither should they be used to replace unsaturated fats, because then the balance between total cholesterol and good cholesterol will be adversely affected. Healthy eating is not just a question of calories, of course, but of a balance between sugars and proteins, fatty acids, minerals, vitamins, and salt. Other than that, move around sufficiently, don't count calories but weigh yourself regularly or measure your waist. The reduction and prevention of overweight and obesity can be achieved only through the reduction of the total intake of calories, or rather by bringing caloric intake into balance with caloric use through physical movement in individuals. The hormonal balance plays a role as well, but it is harder to influence.

However simple it may be to eat a balanced diet, collectively we do not manage to do so, and it seems we're getting worse. No other species on earth suffers from such a skewed balance between consumption and energy use. That overweight and obesity are increasing so rapidly while hunger continues to exist is the astonishing paradox of our time. In a sense we are the victims of our own evolutionary success. Many factors have contributed, from the enormous growth in agricultural production and in industrialization up to an including today's freedom-of-choice mentality. Because undernourishment, poor food, and corpulence are systemically connected with social class, and because plenty leads to waste and to pressure on nature and the environment, measures need to be taken. Tackling obesity and overweight is complicated, because healthy eating is connected with everything. It will all have to be coordinated through new agreements: agriculture and horticulture, including farm subsidies, the processing industry, international trade, distribution, urban planning, schools, family doctors, parents, advertising, laws, and taxes. The farmer, the food industry, and the supermarket are probably easier to influence than consumer behavior, but the market will not produce a balanced diet by itself, any more than will a call for people to take responsibility or the introduction of stringent government policy. For the regulation of abundance we lack institutions, mechanisms, and norms that can collectively ensure a balanced diet for all.

Although a huge difference exists between smoking and eating (smoking is not a daily necessity; it involves a single product with recognized medical consequences; the tobacco industry is not at all like the food industry), we can learn something from campaigns against smoking. The first lesson is that behavior and preferences are not unchangeable but change can take a long time, perhaps a generation or more. It also turns out that individual measures have no effect; they work only as part of a broad approach that includes both legislation and advertising, schools and family doctors, the workplace and public space. Because of focused information provision, excise duties and policy, not only is the rate of smoking declining in the Western world, smoking is becoming a target of moral disapproval, in rich countries at least, which suggests that a change in attitudes is achievable.

———

For food it would seem logical to start with supply, with agriculture and the food industry. But there the complications start. The reason for our abundance of food is the degree to which production has grown. As well as research (better cultivars) and technology (tractors, refrigeration), agricultural policy has contributed to a growth in supply. Because of the fear of shortages, production has been stimulated on a large scale by subsidies, in the United States since 1930 and in Europe and several other countries since the mid-twentieth century. As a result, never before has so much diverse and healthy food been available to so many people for such low prices. The recent fluctuations in food prices do not alter this fact. Except for the very poorest countries with the highest food imports, food is relatively cheap even in periods when prices are at their highest.

Currently the EU health sector is campaigning against subsidies, because they are said to have an obesogenic effect. On the face of it this seems correct. The majority of farming subsidies are allocated to the production of grain, edible oils, dairy produce, or meat, with only 6 percent of EU subsidies going to horticulture. The claim is that this emphasis leads to low prices for unhealthy products and to the neglect of vegetable and fruit cultivation. But on further examination the causal connection with obesity is hard to demonstrate.

First of all, subsidies have no real effect on the price the consumer ultimately pays. The price the farmer receives represents only a fraction— sometimes just a few percent—of the price in the shops. If the subsidy were abolished, the consumer would pay only a tiny percentage more. Anyhow, no one buys a kilogram of soy or corn. We eat those products in processed foods, such as cookies or bread rolls, so the ultimate effect on price is negligible. Secondly, subsidies have no influence on the decision whether to grow vegetables or corn, for example, because these very different products require quite different kinds of businesses and means of production. Horticulture is highly intensive and small scale, and it increasingly takes place in greenhouses, usually close to cities or to transportation links because of the limited life of the produce, whereas corn is grown on a large scale, often in more remote areas. A farmer does not simply switch from corn cultivation to horticulture. Anyhow, in the Netherlands at least, horticulture receives more subsidy than appears from the figures for EU support, because the price of energy is kept artificially low for growers. Also, for some years now, EU subsidies have not been aimed purely at stimulating production but as income support and as compensation for difficult production conditions in relatively remote areas—in the case of hill farmers, for instance.

In the United States criticism of subsidies is focused in particular on price support for corn that makes cheap—and, according to some, unhealthy— high fructose corn syrup available, which is then used in the food industry as a source of sugars. In the EU a similar argument is used against subsidies for sugar beet. Sugar is indeed a relatively cheap raw material, but it is by no means certain that the abolition of subsidies would help the consumer. It might actually lead to a growth in total sugar production worldwide, because subsidies keep inefficient farmers going, whereas high production costs would force the remaining farmers to be more efficient and therefore to produce more. The stimulation by subsidies of corn and soybean cultivation forms the basis of the meat industry the world over, and it has made meat cheaper for many poor population groups.

The stimulation of food production is in itself a blessing for the world's poor. Animal proteins are a great boon to anyone who is underfed, and sugar is still an easily absorbed source of calories (although naturally this does nothing to counter worries about the high sugar content of many food items). Subsidies are extremely unwise for many reasons, and incompatible with agreements about international trade because of geopolitical considerations. It is more sensible to work toward the complete abolition of support for production than to try to manipulate relative prices of "healthy" and "unhealthy" foods. That a portion of sweets can be cheaper than a piece of fruit is a fact. This is not a question of subsidies but of the cost of labor. Mechanization is probably the only way to reduce the price of fruit.

In these debates two things play a role: the relative price of "healthy" and "unhealthy" products and the price sensitivity of the consumer. The healthy–unhealthy distinction is tricky, because few foods are inherently unhealthy (with the exception of trans fats, which are increasingly being banned). You can't simply make all products that are high in calories more expensive—just think of olive oil or honey. Influencing the relative price assumes that healthy food is now consistently more expensive. But is it? Most junk food isn't cheap at all. That's not the reason people buy it, either. Studies show that lower income groups buy expensive convenience foods rather than cheap vegetables, and that the price is by no means always decisive; convenience often makes the difference. Poor, dysfunctional, and one-parent families have a tendency to buy unhealthy, high-calorie fast food, because they just don't get around to preparing a meal. If you are jobless and bored, treating yourself to food you enjoy is one of the few sources of comfort, and of course you don't want an apple but something that fills and fulfils you, which means something with fat and sugar. The problem of unhealthy diets among people in straitened economic circumstances is bound up with the fact that the poor have the feeling they are losing all control over their lives, including their eating behavior. Unfortunately there is little to indicate that making "unhealthy" products more expensive will lead to an improvement in eating habits.

And "healthy" doesn't always mean more expensive by any means. Often healthy foods have a lower unit price than snacks and junk food. In urban areas in rich countries at least, wholegrain bread, vegetables, fruit, and dairy products are cheap as a result of efficient and reliable distribution systems. The most important exception is the case of poor districts that have no decent supermarkets, known as food deserts, where no fresh vegetables and fruit are available. There comparisons have been made between, for example, sugar and cucumber, to show how expensive vegetables are. Based on calories, the cucumber comes out as many times more expensive than snacks, but the comparison is ridiculous. A cucumber is 95 percent water and has hardly any calories. No one eats lettuce or cucumber to get enough calories.

Even if we accept that price (and not convenience) is the most important consideration when buying food, we are still left wondering how governments should intervene in markets. If subsidies, for agriculture or other sectors, are shown to be obesogenic, then they should be abolished. But the only other tools available to governments attempting to stimulate healthy eating are taxes and legislation. Duties and taxes are not unambiguously effective instruments either. Experiments with adjusted tax rates may be worthwhile. Countries including Denmark and Finland have reduced the rate of value-added tax (sales tax) for vegetables, fruit, and other supposedly healthy foods, such as wholegrain bread and skimmed or semi-skimmed dairy products. It's not yet clear whether such tax reductions will have any effect on shopping behavior or public health.

The reverse is also possible, namely, raising taxes on unhealthy products. There is talk of a "fat tax." It's far from clear how it would work: based on fat content or type of fat? Would marbled meat be more expensive than steak? The degree of price elasticity—in other words, how buying behavior changes in response to price—is unclear. It seems unlikely that a higher price for butter or margarine would lead to it being spread more thinly. Denmark and Hungary have recently introduced a fat tax. In Denmark it amounts to a little over €2 per kilogram of fat, which will not make a huge difference to the price of a sandwich or a portion of French fries. In Hungary savory snacks and soft drinks are subject to higher taxation as well, but not the famous Hungarian sausage, which makes the fat tax look more like an instrument for increasing national tax revenue. The mistake is to think that individual food items and ingredients are at fault. Food is never one dimensional. A hamburger in its place is not potentially deadly or addictive (unlike cigarettes). What matters is the diet as a whole and the way of life. Demonizing fat as if it were a threatening virus does not help individuals to improve their nutrition. A tax on "bad" substances, such as fat or sugar, is too blunt an instrument and will probably have only a marginal effect.

—————

The most radical and, given current international relationships, most improbable form of governmental intervention is the reduction of production and imports in countries of plenty. In the United States and some European countries (Italy, France, and Portugal), the number of calories available amounts to more than 3,600 per person per day, between one- and two-thirds more than the average requirement. This excess inevitably leads to waste and to overeating. But we know from the past, including the recent past of huge price fluctuations in the first decade of the twenty-first century, that restricting production and free trade can have disastrous consequences. Import duties based on dietary considerations have little chance in an international context.

So we are left mainly with indirect measures that governments can introduce in cooperation with businesses, schools, and other institutions. This approach turns its back on individual responsibility in favor of more rules and control over all areas that have to do with food. We might consider the regulation, by law or otherwise, of packaging, including portion size, composition, sales outlets, information on labels, and advertising. As an extension of the ban on alcohol, it seems obvious to think of imposing stricter controls on the sale of soft drinks with added sugars, which are an important source of calories for young people.

The question is whether governments should forbid the sale of entire categories of food, such as sweets and snacks. They represent a profitable industry, because they consist of cheap raw materials (fat, salt, and sugar), but they provide the consumer with empty calories—in other words, they have little or no nutritional value. A legal ban on potato chips, for example, would be a major challenge to introduce internationally and might create a black market (the great chip-smuggling operation!), so improving the composition of the snack might be of more value.

Governments can require producers to put better information on labels. We now have ingredients listed on most foods (though not all), including the number of calories per serving and the size of a serving. Restaurants are now starting to make this information available on menus; fast food restaurants, such as McDonald's, already do so, in some countries in response to public pressure, in others because it is required by law. Low-calorie options in restaurants and on airplanes are increasing but are not yet commonplace. It turns out that information usually reaches those who are already conscious of what they are eating, rather than those who need it. Information in fast food restaurants about calorific content leads initially to a small number of consumers choosing the less high-calorie options, but they also buy more portions, so the total number of calories consumed is not reduced. Information may also be misunderstood: "contains no saturated fatty acids" does not mean that the product has fewer calories than one with saturated fatty acids. To make things easier for the consumer, additional labels and logos have been introduced by producers, such as traffic lights, clover leaves, and other indications of the healthy option. The number of them is now causing confusion; governments should make agreements about minimal information that does not require customers to have trained as biochemists.

Advertising is seen as one of the most underhanded and sometimes downright misleading ways of influencing consumers, who are thought to be unable to resist. The abolition of advertisements for snacks and other foods targeted at children seems an obvious step, and one already taken in some countries. Others are considering banning discounts along the lines of "two for the price of one" in the case of fast food and sweets. Limiting advertising that encourages overeating would seem to be against the interests of the food industry, but in the long term it is in no one's interest to see a large number of unhealthy consumers, so in food industry circles increasing efforts are being made to support ethically responsible advertising and voluntary codes of behavior.

More research is needed if we are to increase our understanding of how the brain processes information about food through smell, taste, and texture. How, for example, does the decision to eat yet another sandwich come about? How can food with a lower fat and sugar content nevertheless give a sense of being full? If we had more clarity on matters like these, food technologists and governments would have instruments that enable them to adjust products to fit more balanced eating habits. There is still insufficient proof that the composition of food plays a role—a reduction in carbohydrates, for example, or an increased percentage of protein. If a person is already overweight, a high fat percentage in his or her food quickly leads to an increase in excess calories. The same goes for the sugar content, which should be limited irrespective of the type of sugar (monosaccharide or polysaccharide). Liquid sugars in fruit juices in particular can lead to a considerable increase in the number of calories in a diet that goes completely unnoticed. Research in all these fields must be undertaken not just by businesses but also by public institutions.

Over the past decade the industry has taken a fair number of steps, usually in close cooperation with governments. Trans fats have been banned almost everywhere, and saturated fats are on the wane. At the same time the assortment of products associated with health has expanded: vegetable and fruit drinks, yogurts with extra minerals and bacteria, and low-fat products (including cheeses). The composition of products has been improved by the replacement of salt with spices, and by reducing the fat and sugar contents. Yet we find an endless variation on the high-fat, high-sugar theme in shops.

Products could also contain, in part, nondigestible calories, such as fat globules that give a feeling of being full and therefore reduce the desire to eat. This solution is highly praised in some diet products, but it does not exclude the possibility of a return to old habits. A reduction in portion size has potential, and it has already been introduced in the United States for the largest servings of soft drinks. But even with "healthy" alternatives there always remains a risk of overconsumption, or of misleading or confusing the consumer. A good example is the difference between an apple and an apple drink. Does the latter count as meeting the recommendation to eat more vegetables and fruit? Or does that recommendation only apply to the whole fruit, which is harder to digest and possibly contains different bioactive substances than the drink? Can you continue drinking apple juice with no ill effects?

Along with composition and ingredients, a broader policy is needed for vulnerable groups and neighborhoods: space for physical exercise and sports fields; after-school activities; safe bicycle routes; and a policy to encourage supermarkets to open where there are too few shops selling vegetables, fruit, and other foods that are not simply snacks. Vending machines selling soft drinks and sweets should be banned from schools, even though schools will lose revenue as a result. In their place, vegetables and to a lesser extent fruit could be sold for eating at break times, perhaps as sweets in the form of small carrots or tiny red peppers. Attractive alternatives work better than bans. One open question concerns the position of children who are obese. Putting them under special supervision if their parents cannot offer them good nutrition is a drastic measure that I feel goes too far. Advocates point to the need to protect children against damaging treatment by their parents, even if no crime has taken place, such as neglect, and children are being spoiled out of love (which can sometimes take the form of being unable to deny the loved one's demands, however misconceived).

Another issue is whether opening times in places where food is sold—supermarkets and also train stations and gas stations—should be limited to prevent the temptation of the quick snack. I don't know whether that would have much effect, although as a late supermarket shopper, I do see a remarkable number of ready meals in people's shopping baskets. Surely those items might simply be bought elsewhere.

Governments are actually the last ones to talk. The food on show at official meetings and receptions, and in congressional canteens, is still appalling, featuring carelessly thrown together fatty filled rolls. They could themselves set an example by serving non-obesogenic food, including vegetarian options. Or by providing prominent, safe, and well-lit staircases in office buildings; free or cheap sports facilities; bicycle parking; and so on. Who knows? Perhaps stand-up consultations, or even progress meetings held while out for a walk will become the rule rather than the exception.

———

At the root of the increase in weight problems and obesity lies the fact that our entire behavioral evolution and our technological progress have been aimed at getting hold of food that is as energy-rich and varied as possible, while the effort required to obtain food has been drastically reduced. Our lifestyle has changed to such an extent that many of us in developed countries barely need to make any physical effort any longer to work and to live. This development is so recent that our impulse to eat as much as possible and make as little effort as possible in the process has not been adjusted. Most symbolic of this in my view is the development of "finger food," ready treats you can eat with one hand while driving, telephoning, or at the computer. They tempt us to eat between meals.

After so many generations that experienced scarcity as a daily reality, those of us who live in the time and places of abundance don't seem to be able to stop stuffing ourselves. Yet we cannot and will not go back to a situation in which every consumer makes appropriate efforts to be able to eat. Individual food choices can be influenced only by a combination of all the measures suggested here, large and small. Many will have only a limited effect. As with the reduction of water or energy use, much depends on the development of a new consciousness on the part of the consumer. If you sell smaller portions, the consumer may simply eat two. If your food contains less fat or salt, the consumer may add those items to compensate, or buy a competing product. At the same time we need to realize that hammering on about healthy eating and declaring overweight morally wrong bears out, in a bizarre way, the paradise story. We like to look for confirmation of our own sinfulness. Ultimately the healthy choice should be the easiest option. Instead of the temptation being to sin, the sensible must become irresistible.

SIXTEEN

In Conclusion: Eve's Paradise

The optimist sees the rose and not its thorns; the pessimist stares at the thorns, oblivious of the rose. KHALIL GIBRAN

Question: How do we know for sure that Adam and Eve weren't Chinese? Answer: Because then they wouldn't have eaten the apple but the snake instead. *Chinese joke*

The Hamburgerization of the World

The hamburgerization of the world is a fact, literally and figuratively. In most countries you can get hamburgers as well as all sorts of other fast food. It embodies the aspiration of a growing world population to live a Western, free, and carefree way of life. There's a germ of truth in the joke that countries that have succeeded in getting McDonald's to operate on their territory don't fight one another, because they're full of contented middle-class citizens. It's impossible to imagine Europe and the United States without hamburgers and fast food, or for that matter, the new metropolises of Asia, Latin America, Africa, and the former Soviet Union.

Such Western foods as the hamburger seem to penetrate far more quickly to all layers of the world's population than do cars or Western bathrooms. This penetration is not just a matter of imitating Western norms. It's mainly a consequence of the move to the city and the industrialization of what were until recently agrarian societies. Adjustments need to be made to traditional food, which takes a long time to prepare and isn't easy to carry and eat during long working days in factories and offices. Rapid meals, such as sandwiches, wraps, and hamburgers, are replacing the customary gruel made with cassava, millet, or corn. The same applies to rice and chapatis, which are also difficult to transport with their accompanying sauce. The middle classes eat the genuine McDonald's and its cousins, while the low-income groups buy cheaper versions.

At the same time, to some at least, hamburgers have developed into ideological evidence of Western domination and unnecessary, even dangerous excess. Dangerous for cultural diversity, which succumbs to an imported product and an inability to taste food properly, and dangerous for our health, because fast food prompts us to eat too much fat. Hamburgers have been called the fourth meal, the extra 400–500 calories that have caused the current wave of obesity. They're dangerous for the environment, too, many would say, because to provide the beef, land is brought into cultivation on a huge scale for the growing of genetically modified feed crops, which are then shipped all over the world, and because cows contribute to greenhouse gas emissions. The health argument is valid to some extent, the cultivation aspect is not nearly as bad as is feared, and the large-scale growing of cattle feed ought not to be a source of anxiety. The primary significance of the hamburger, however, lies in the fact that it and other types of fast food are signs of a historical shift to an unprecedentedly high consumption of cheap animal proteins. This type of consumption is less and less an exception and reason for celebration; such foods are more and more often eaten by lone individuals, as a substitute for the traditional family meal, not at the table but on the road. Per kilogram, we pay far less for chicken than for wholegrain bread.

No less significant is the fact that the globalization of the hamburger and other fast food has prompted reflection and active opposition. The recognition of the health impacts of food and the importance of the cultural dimensions of cooking and food traditions, and the call for production to be more local, small-scale, and animal-friendly—all these things are direct or indirect responses to the hamburger and what it stands for. Even preexisting ideas have been given a new impulse by it, such as organic farming; the protection of farmed landscapes; and the retention of traditional breeds and varieties of domestic animals, vegetables, and fruit. An agglomeration of loosely related, diverse, and sometimes mutually contradictory movements has arisen, from slow food to the restitution of *la cucina povera* to healthy snacks and the breeding of health-promoting properties into plants and animals. Supermarkets and the food industry are increasingly helping to spread healthy and organic food all over the world.

These improvements are erratic. A great deal of unnecessary spraying and fertilizing is going on, and too much water is being wasted and pharmaceuticals used—in other words, too much inefficient food production happens, so we are using too much land to feed ourselves. Shocking amounts are unnecessarily lost during harvest, in factories, and in households. But the fact that we notice these problems and are collectively in a position to correct our ways of producing food is definitely a reason to remain optimistic, even if this process is endless and every improvement raises new questions.

That the hamburger itself has been aligned with many of these countermoves is typical. Despite what some critics think, hamburgerization has not created uniformity with a single greasy snack for everyone. Reactions to hamburgerization have led not to the abolition of the hamburger or of fast food but to a differentiation into other forms of fast food and changes to the hamburger itself. This differentiation expresses itself in what I would call the "gentrification of fast food." Or its pimping up, to use an even more fashionable term. Old types of food take over the function of fast food, and their authenticity gives them charisma and makes them chic. Aside from sushi, the best example is Spanish tapas, now popular worldwide, a snack once used to cover a glass of wine or a drink in a bar to protect it from flies.

The extraordinary thing about the hamburger in comparison with other foods is that it is continually evolving and yet remains itself (this is true to a lesser extent of pizza). From Seattle to Shanghai and Santiago, from Atlanta to Alma Ata and Abidjan: the geography and the clientele changes, but the attractiveness and the image remains. The hamburger is a sign of the modernization of the rising middle class, but it also demonstrates our ability to adapt and, in its luxury form, it is evidence of worldwide culinary literacy. Even the famous French chef Escoffier wrote a hamburger recipe, which is now back in vogue in top restaurants.

The hamburger is making a comeback. Even in hamburger chains, everything is evolving: locally bought milk, less fat, veggie burgers, more salad, recyclable packaging, even, just occasionally, books instead of games for children. Greener, with more customer-, animal-, and environmentally friendly products is the new mantra. This is undoubtedly mere sales talk up to a point, but the goals are measurable, and they answer to a general trend toward more conscious eating, even of fast food. This has been proven by a former director of McDonald's, who is setting up a chain of sustainable and healthy fast food restaurants under the name Lyfe Kitchen, where food without cream, refined sugar, genetically modified products, and artificial additives is served, but which in every other way resembles the original hamburger company.

No other food embodies so many dimensions of the modern world at once: the fast food of urbanization, the trendy snack of the young generation, finger food for eating at the computer, and (for those with a different perspective) the inedible and perverse product of a generation of indiscriminate pleasure seekers. All the technological developments and controversies of modern society come together in the hamburger and its little brothers the pizza, hot dog, and chicken in a box. The hamburger is the symbol of everything that causes friction. A French fast food chain, Quick, came under fire for wanting to serve only halal burgers in its restaurants. That would make it easier to attract a new group of consumers, and for everyone else it would make no difference, was the reasoning. The company was accused of being disloyal to the French identity and of discrimination. It's a bizarre twist in the history of the hamburger: once the objectionable export product of a depraved America that would corrupt French taste; now apparently a symbol of that same French culture. Short-sighted, too, because of the 2 billion people that will make up the additional numbers on earth by 2050, half will eat halal.

Contradictions flourish. In the Louvre, the heart of French culture, a McDonald's opened in 2009. As if that were not enough, there was horror in France at an advertisement for McDonald's in which the comicbook characters Asterix and Obelix joyfully ate hamburgers while the tone-deaf bard Cacofonix sat outside tied to a tree, pining as he watched. The motto was "Come as you are!" The horror was not a response to the brutal maltreatment of a member of a minority group (the musically challenged, the Americans might call them), but to the disloyalty of the notoriously intransigent Asterix, the Breton hero who stood up to the Romans, thereby embodying French resistance to American cultural domination. There was no way Asterix would eat a hamburger! In its own reaction the publisher of Asterix let it be known that "Come as you are!" did not mean that Asterix was defending bad food (*malbouffe*).

Should we deplore the onward march of the hamburger? After all, the use of meat that would otherwise be thrown away is ecologically responsible. As long as foods are still eaten that are not hamburgers, or do not resemble them, and as long as the hamburger's composition is sensible, with a good balance between nutrients and calories and a price appropriate to income, there is little objection to be made to fast food in its place. It does become a problem, however, if children want to eat only fast food because of the advertisements and the toys given out with hamburgers, and parents are unable to cook. Or if the hamburger leads to a higher daily intake of calories, to sloppy eating, to an inability to appreciate the taste of simple foods (without sauces and additives) and culinary traditions, and to the neglect of family relationships. Already an urban generation is growing up both in rich countries and in emerging economies that has not learned to cook and so can only heat up ready meals. Young people sometimes have no idea what kind of food their grandparents ate or what was produced in their own part of the world.

Paradise Lost and Found

The ambiguous response to the hamburger amounts to more than enthusiasm and unease about a dominant form of fast food. It's a reaction to modernization and capitalism. Modernization is a source of hope and anxiety. All progress builds on the past, but it changes the present and our view of the future. This makes many people feel insecure. In almost all developing countries and emerging economies, progress weighs more heavily than tradition. Tradition and social ties have to give way to the opportunity to produce more, to feed the poor, and to develop the country, and sometimes it's a crude and violent process, symbolized by the building of dams that disrupt the countryside. Where modernization is more subtle, it still all too often comes at the expense of valuable knowledge of herbs and spices, of ways of collaborating, of traditional landscape and architecture.

Changes now under way in poor countries and emerging economies are of the same order as the first changes in Europe and The United States as a result of urbanization, population growth, industrialization, and the depopulation of the countryside—in short, a consequence of the opening up of societies to the rest of the world. These are unavoidable historical steps, even if their imposition by central authorities has led to excesses in some countries. Nowadays the dominant vision (with the notorious exceptions of North Korea and Zimbabwe) is that development cannot happen unless it is accompanied by modern technology and an open market. Moreover, for national leaders, access to markets and modern technology are a right, demanded in international negotiations, which can guarantee their autonomy and which must not be limited by any Western power. They feel perfectly capable of judging for themselves what they need from the West.

This is not to say that poor societies have no sense of loss. It's a feeling expressed by many artists and writers, such as Arundhati Roy in India.

Yet almost always the sense of irrevocable loss is tempered by the knowledge that progress is necessary. Modernization is ambivalence, but it is also a search for balance.

One of the artists who have been most successful at making this visible is Cuban painter Julio Breff Guilarte. His striking 1993 painting "Llegan Mutantes Extraterrestres con la Ayuda Alimentaria de la ONU" ("Extraterrestrial Mutants Arrive with UN Food Aid) shows, in a colorful, naive style, two huge creatures, a cross between pin-ups and chickens, one blue and one pink. A camera crew and a peasant family are examining their giant eggs. It's a scene that, with its reference to the chicken that laid the golden eggs, contains a fear of genetic modification and of hybrids of humans and animals. Anxiety, then, but curiosity as well. This painting is not apocalyptic, serving up the hell of modern times.

By various strange routes, word reached Julio Breff Guilarte, who lives a solitary life in a Cuban village, that I had lectured about his painting. In 2011 I met him during his first visit to Europe. He'd brought with him a series of images of his paintings about the modernization of the countryside, including the appropriately named "El Tiempo Moderno" of 2009. We see an idyllic rural scene with ploughed fields surrounded by green hills that on closer inspection turn out to be giant squashes. In front of them is a forest of white and red trees: tree-sized impatiens. The painting is populated by twenty or so well-dressed people, mostly men, with in the foreground two women in floral-patterned dresses, each of them off to one side so that they frame the scene. Almost without exception, everyone is looking intently, though not anxiously, at the central part of the painting, where a traditional plough is being drawn by a blue ox and a red ox, steered by a farmer with clothes in the same colors, making it clear that they belong together. On top of the plough, a computer is affixed to a wooden duckboard. With his left hand the farmer is typing, with his right he holds the reins to steer the oxen. The computer screen shows the Cuban flag, or a mirror image of it. The plough with its computer refers to the new agricultural techniques—not genetic modification alone in this case but computer-guided zero tillage, a technique at which Brazil is a world leader and that is combined with genetic modification in the form of herbicide-resistant soy. The computer steers the oxen, and the left hand steers the right, in an earnest, fertile symbiosis.

Because of the isolation in which Cuba finds itself, you might expect the country to reject modern technology, but the opposite is the case.

Cuba is very progressive in the scientific field and has had an extensive biotechnology program for many years. It works closely with South American countries and China in that respect. When he was asked what his thoughts were about "El Tiempo Moderno," Breff Guilarte said: "The development of the Cuban farmer." I find the painting so inspiring because it shows that developing countries have ideas of their own about technology, which in this case connect the traditional, in the form of the plough, with the modern. His painting says: let us carve our own path, make our own choices, and find our own combination of the traditional and the modern.

—————

To many in the rich West, however, the market and technology have gone too far. Distrust is growing, toward wavering governments, big companies, and modern science, which makes us more vulnerable rather than less. Our perceived distance from the physical production of food; the lack of transparency of international food markets; stories about unsafe food; our inability to stem the growth of obesity; the complexities of climate change, pathogens, and other threats; and the specter of hordes of hungry immigrants: all these things create an atmosphere of doom and despondency. Close to powerlessness lies self-chastisement, the notion that modern humans are sinful because of their greed. The hamburger is seen as evidence of poor eating habits that we, the tainted West, have imposed on the rest of the world. Not only is the world a mess, we are to blame, because we are responsible for the loss of paradise. Swedish cartoonist Riber Hansson portrays this pessimism perfectly in his 2012 variation on Michelangelo's "The Creation of Adam," with a gray-haired Adam on a burning garbage dump being handed a noose by God.

For some there is only one answer to such misery: the dream of the paradise of the past, the praise of the small-scale and handmade, a less complex society, and less dependence on the world market, on industry, and on chemicals. The closer to nature the better. There is something hypocritical in the ode to simplicity in food production sung by the middle and upper classes. They want *la cucina povera*, but in a luxury version; they drive to the slow food restaurant, where they've made a reservation by mobile phone. Only when you have everything is it easy to limit yourself, voluntarily, selectively, and temporarily. Anyone who shrugs at the concept of a "middle class" is ignoring the fact that by 2030 it will be made up of three billion people.

The sense of unease about food that comes from far away or is produced by large-scale, "artificial" means is grist to the mill of local and national groups who campaign against centralization and lack of consultation, against national and international authorities, for instance. So a political agenda has emerged that brings together diverse groups on the left and right of the political spectrum. Their ideas are sometimes close to utopian, sometimes of the "no massive cattle sheds in my back yard" variety, often antitechnology and antimarket, but they can also be realistic and innovative, like the ideas of farmers keen to help preserve the landscape. For the truly radical reformers, however, resistance inevitably leads to autarchy, a complete rejection of the anonymous market. Smouldering or active discontent is a poor basis for decisions about the future of our food.

All over the world in recent decades we've seen that globalization and the prosperity that flows from it lead to more consumption among all social classes. When their incomes grow, the poorest families invest in the education of their children to a significant degree, while in rich countries, beyond a certain level the relationship between consumption and disposable income is not linear. It flattens out. There are many reasons to be concerned about the huge growth of consumption in the world, but it is wrong to dismiss it simply as the consequence of the imposition of Western norms. The desire to consume is a universal human tendency, not specifically Western or capitalist. Neither in China nor elsewhere has local culture simply collapsed under Western domination, or under external capitalist consumption patterns. Instead it has shaped itself to fit the new abundance that is in the reach of the rapidly growing middle class.

Those who deplore this do so from the comfortable position of a twenty-first century in which women no longer die in childbirth, backward superstition no longer leads to the rejection of twins, individual freedom is accepted everywhere, and life can be varied and satisfying almost no matter who you are. Anyone who knows the reality of the countryside or primitive factories—the long evenings without electricity or with inadequate lighting, the lack of distraction, long working days in heat or cold, the risk of fatal accidents, the absence of medical care, the impossibility of stepping out of that world and experiencing something else—will be unable to idealize it by reference to time-honored customs and community spirit. Those who see only loss and excess in the modern era are forgetting that the apparent harmony of the past entailed suffocation, poverty, and undernourishment. What has been achieved is taken for granted by those who have never known hunger or poverty. Hope is a hard fact; the past half century has given us a quarter more calories for twice as many people and a doubling of life expectancy. This applies everywhere. Africa is the only continent that still has an absolute shortage of food.

Although in parts of the United States, especially California and the East Coast, rejection of modernization is rampant, Europe is suffering most from the gloom. "The nineteenth century was a time of despair because it was no longer possible to have faith in God, the twentieth because it was no longer possible to have faith in man," said French Nobel Prize winner Roger Martin du Gard on the eve of the Second World War. I would add that the twenty-first century is a time of despair because it is no longer possible to have faith in the capacity of the earth. To put it crudely: God won't save us, nor will human empathy and cleverness, and now even our planet is letting us down. The lack of faith among a growing proportion of the Western population in the human ability to learn and the resilience of the earth may be the greatest barrier to future success.

The Great Stalemate

That food arouses strong feelings is logical, given how essential it is for our daily survival, and given that so many rituals have arisen around it throughout history. But now something more is going on than simply a continuation of those ancient fears and rules. Just as the present state of abundance for a large proportion of humanity is unique in history, so our anxiety about food seems to have reached an unprecedented peak. We experience food as both a blessing and a danger, a sin and a virtue, in a way that we have never defined so precisely before. This is because after thousands of years of chronic and acute scarcity—and the relatively short period of half a century in which an abundance of food and unbridled growth of food production suddenly came to seem natural—the recent dawn of a new century marked a transition to a period of increasing uncertainty, which has its roots primarily in psychology and politics.

The twenty-first century began with wildly fluctuating and rising food prices; increasing international and regional tensions; a dislocating financial and economic crisis of confidence; growing discontent among demanding, risk-averse citizens; and political shilly-shallying tipping over into micromanagement. In such a situation a minor event can give rise to fierce reactions and yet people can lose sight of the true proportions and seriousness of the situation. That is what is happening now with food and agriculture, as it is in the labor market and in medical and social care. More even than those fields of activity, food is truly international, and reactions have immediate global consequences: a poor corn harvest because of drought in Kansas affects the daily food supply of the residents of African cities through increased prices on the world market; corruption in China, leading to the deaths of babies from contaminated milk, improves prospects for dairy farmers in the Dutch province of Friesland; the demand by the middle classes for healthier fast food increases the world catch of tuna for sushi but at the same time stimulates research into the farming of tuna; careless use of antibiotics in livestock farming can cause resistance in bacteria affecting humans to emerge all over the world.

The predominantly European fascination with ruin and calamity reflects a fin de siècle feeling, a sense that the era in which Europe was in command of ideas and technology is ending. It will indeed end unless sufficient support exists for innovative and sustainable solutions that do not shy away from high-tech methods and at the same time are flexible and democratic. The former is a challenge for Europe, the latter mainly for Asia, several African and South American countries, and the states of the former Soviet Union. In the contrast between non-Western and Western countries, between poor and rich (and therefore between modernization and growth on one side and nostalgia for the past on the other), between central control and local initiatives, lies a stalemate that increasingly gets in the way of both sides. Put simply: the West, especially Europe, is hesitating and vacillating about the application of modern technology, whereas emerging economies are moving ahead at full steam with little consultation. The results are worrying in both cases: in the West because improvements are being blocked and people are looking to techniques that promise improvements but do not deliver; and in the emerging economies because there the mechanisms are not in place to keep a critical eye on modern technology and implement corrections where necessary. Countries are increasingly hostile to one other's viewpoints, so exchange and cooperation are hard to achieve, as we see from the stagnation of negotiations on climate change. Moralizing by rich countries is not simply innocent or morally neutral. It explains the polarization between the developed world and the Asian, South American, and African countries that want to move forward, using their resources, and that do not want limits placed on their progress.

————

This stalemate between emerging and poor economies on one side and the rich, Western, or OECD countries on the other is also a stalemate between the world of researchers and that of campaigners, between industry and nongovernmental organizations. People are eager to express it as an antithesis between economics and nature. Nostalgia is not just a longing that can degenerate into sentimentality and projection (for example, human loneliness projected onto animals). In its original meaning it has a pathological side. Politicians in the rich countries anxiously follow the high-profile middle class and public opinion in their resistance to modernization. They hesitate, or delay decisionmaking. This is clearest of all on the issues of the genetic modification of plants and animals, with Europe still not daring to take the decision to permit it and the United States expressing increasing doubts, while all the large former developing countries are introducing genetically modified varieties at a rapid pace.

The stalemate places restraints on our creativity and cooperation, which worries me for three reasons. First, because it makes us lose sight of the real threats to our food supply, such as unexpected weather conditions, or the potential for speculation and the fierce fluctuations in food and energy prices that would result. These threats cannot be solved by a nostalgic longing for a paradise that never existed, in which everything was still "good." Nor indeed can they be solved by technology forced through without criticism, nor by the accentuating of false antitheses. As far as those antitheses are concerned, modernization does not mean monotony (on the contrary, our diets have become endlessly more varied), genetic technology does not automatically lead to increases in scale, and animal husbandry can take place in closed or semiclosed stalls and still be environmentally friendly and meet all the requirements of animal welfare.

Second, the stalemate worries me because evolution in humans does not work exclusively at the level of the individual, in fact it does so less and less. It works at the level of the group. The driving force is the urge for survival not of the individual but of the collective. It's only because we cooperate and share knowledge and goods that we survive as a group and as a species. This is only possible if we share our knowledge, and we will not do so if we're diametrically opposed to one another. And third, in the stalemate lies the assumption that there are limits to growth, that the prosperity of one comes at the expense of another, that the cake will eventually be eaten up. Yet there is little reason to think so. Where there is waste, we can work more efficiently; where resources run out, they can almost always be replaced by something else, or production methods can be adapted. We have managed to adapt throughout human history.

Economic growth creates job opportunities and buying power. That a large proportion of the world's population still has little to spend does not mean they have no ambition to consume more, and patterns of consumption can be predicted. All over the world, people are waiting impatiently to fulfil their dreams of fridges, medicines, and televisions. Technology is the key to a better life. The historically unprecedented growth of the middle class in poor countries is as much evidence of the accessibility of prosperity and abundance for children of poor families as it is an assault on the environment and healthcare.

Consumer spending follows Western patterns to some extent—hamburgers and expensive cars, for example—but this does not mean that the Western model has won. These preferences are more an expression of a stage of consumption than the final victory of something as abstract as Western capitalism. For instance, the newest rich—the worldwide class of people for whom money is no object, who are remarkably well represented in the elites of poor countries—do eventually go in search of their roots, of what they regard as authentic in their native cultures. This is why Chinese art, ancient and modern, is so much in demand among Chinese millionaires and is breaking records at international auction houses. China is not alone in this development. In other poor countries something similar is happening. In contrast, almost everywhere (although least of all in Africa), a class just below that of the powerful elite is growing, and it borrows its identity at least in part from the consumption of products that can be seen as signs of progress. Everywhere, despite all the religious examples of asceticism, higher incomes lead to higher consumption. Everyone likes to forget that there are no roses without thorns. The longing for plenty is universal.

"Are you optimistic about the future?" I'm fairly regularly asked in interviews. That question recurs, in a rather less neutral version, at almost every talk I give in rich countries. There is usually someone who stands up and explains that there's no reason at all for optimism, that the speaker is forgetting about population growth, climate change, erosion, neocolonialism, big capital, and other forces that inevitably lead to hunger and malnutrition. In short, there's no light at the end of the tunnel and never will be unless we change our way of life drastically and permanently, preferably in the direction of as much self-sufficiency as possible. My simple answer is that we cannot permit ourselves to be pessimistic, that Western pessimism is not shared by the majority of the world's population, and that there is reason enough to face the future with confidence, despite everything. Yes, after 10,000 years of farming the influence of human food supplies can be seen all over the earth's surface. In remote tropical forests we find open spaces, in protected swamps we find fish and birds that have been in contact with manufactured chemicals. Even large parts of the polar regions and the atmosphere have not escaped fossil fuel emissions. Species of plant and animal have disappeared, and others have changed for good.

The other side of the coin is that for most human societies, centuries of scarcity have ended. Unless disasters of unprecedented magnitude take place, increasing and more equally shared prosperity for more people is possible in the long term. This can be achieved while at the same time the natural cycles of the earth are preserved as far as possible and fewer negative consequences are seen, certainly per ton of product or per thousand people fed. There is no fundamental technological reason to doubt the fact that sufficient food of reasonable quality can be made available to all.

"The other side of the coin" is actually the wrong way to put it, because it implies that the benefits justify the costs—as if for each lost plant species, hundreds of children have been spared. This suggests a plan, a weighing up of costs and benefits that no one has performed. Never before in history have we added up what our existence has done to the earth, let alone reached a political consensus about it. Only now are we hesitantly starting to realize, despite confusion and stalemate, that humanity as a species bears a shared responsibility for the future.

Dietary Laws, Again

We must find ways of channeling our abundance and where necessary reining it in, while ensuring that food supplies grow sustainably. We must make choices, because growth in production always brings undesirable effects with it: a landscape lost, a business bankrupt, a spring polluted. In that sense there are limits to growth—not in the Malthusian sense that raw materials are irreplaceable and will be exhausted, but because all production has ecological, economic, social, and ethical costs. We are the dominant species, and we dominate all the earth's ecosystems.

———————

It's essential that food production, from farm to fork, is viewed as the responsibility of us all. A sustainable food supply is a public good, created by millions of people for billions elsewhere, in a framework of national and international agreements. Responsibility is fostered by allowing people to participate in decisionmaking about where and how food is produced, thereby avoiding the "not in my backyard" effect. Responsibility is created by not saddling the individual or community with a sense of guilt, which only leads to doom-mongering and apathy. Punishment of human greed means giving a license to ideologues and preachers; it's no basis for political decisionmaking.

People are perhaps afraid of the anonymity of the global food supply network, but they also want to do something themselves, in neighborhoods and streets: allotments, cooking lessons, joint or shared possession of cars and equipment, barter, and support for local farmers and neighborhood meals. In quantitative terms these are rarely solutions, but initiatives of this kind do form the basis for change. People don't want to be merely passive consumers, they are usually eager to be responsible citizens. The huge amount of activity by communities on the Internet reflects tremendous potential. There are apparently more than four billion recipes on the Internet. After children and other relatives, food is said to be the most photographed subject online. If for only a tiny fraction of those recipes and pictures a connection can be made between cooking, sustainable modernization in the food supply chain, and poverty reduction, there will be a world to win.

Change and moderation don't arise by themselves. Improvements are needed all along the line, from farmer or fisherman to the final consumer. I've already used the term "new dietary laws" for this process to introduce not a new legal straitjacket but a broad mass of rules, a consciousness that will guide the production and consumption of food in the right direction. Again, food is consciousness and conscience. Although a great deal of legislation is already in place, in almost all countries it's divided up among agriculture, the environment, and public health. This division becomes clear when problems arise, for instance, with Q fever, which exists on the boundaries of all three and to which civil servants at the different Dutch ministries reacted in markedly different ways. There is room for a framework of law covering sustainable agriculture and food, one in which such principles as "the polluter pays" are made to count and that enables the sensible use of resources for which no market exists.

Is it possible to stimulate sustainability and thrift or moderation? Can we permanently adjust to a world in which recycling and the sparing use of resources is the norm? The market promotes reckless borrowing and spending, or at least fails to correct them adequately, and therefore has a negative effect on sustainability. If something is cheap, the market does nothing to prevent waste. In theory the market is neutral, and it doesn't matter whether money is spent on windmills or on fur coats. The market therefore offers no guarantee that sustainable intensification will be achieved, not just because some things have no monetary value but also because there is a big gap between individual decisions and the final result.

If I buy an apple tart, what do I know about the route it has taken to get to the shop? Even if I do know a little about it—such as whether it comes from a small bakery or a factory, which apples have been used, and where they were harvested—what choices do I have as an individual consumer? Moreover, most people assume that their individual choice makes little difference. If your neighbor doesn't make the effort to consume sustainably, why should you? However we look at it, it's also a matter of changing consumption patterns and reducing doom-mongering. It may take another generation before moderation is internalized and equipped with moral beacons.

The social anchoring of new dietary laws cannot happen without a far better understanding of who we are and what we eat. It seems to me essential to introduce into public school curricula a subject that covers food, health, agriculture, and the environment. What gets in the way of any meaningful discussion more than anything else is the shocking lack of knowledge about how food gets to our plates. People are unaware that the food supply network involves far more than planting a few vegetables, drying them, and packaging them as soup. Knowledge of farming and food is part of the general knowledge everyone in a civilized country should have, just like knowledge of arithmetic and grammar.

That knowledge should also include what I would call the "big stories," which bind together the arts, sciences, and social sciences. They are stories about the origins of farming and cities, the perpetual scarcity that prevailed until the Industrial Revolution, the great changes brought about by artificial fertilizer, the Green Revolution, and the capacity of the earth. We need to understand that this knowledge has not arisen over the past decade. We are building on a long history, and indeed standing on the shoulders of many anonymous giants. It's far from simple, because we tend to have contradictory notions and values. Strong convictions are not changed simply because they are challenged by education; in fact, they may sometimes be reinforced by opposition.

Education, advice, and information are not enough. We need to create a society in which it's again self-evident that we must collectively learn from mistakes, in which faith that science lays the foundations for progress exists next to a preparedness to involve everyone in choices regarding the food supply. A sustainable food supply network will come into existence only in a climate of responsible citizenship, based on an open debate, with understanding for those who think differently and acceptance of the facts. Because only knowledge and insight, along with an awareness of their limits, can help us to move forward. A new attitude to food means, for example, that we must learn to understand that the complexity of world food issues is not a fashionable figure of speech or an excuse for smugness.

This approach involves learning to look at the details, at what causes complexity (prices or environmental impacts), at where we can afford to generalize and where not (grain prices don't rise, only the prices of certain grains), and at what is unpredictable and over what period of time (such as weather effects). We need to develop a sensitivity to things that don't fit the pattern and things that unsettle our thinking. For that we need a sense of perspective, an ability to see the situation as a whole, to zoom in on the details and then to zoom out again to the larger picture. That in turn means not thinking just of ourselves but of the effects on others. Only then do we become aware of our privileged position, the accident of being born a well-fed, well-educated American or European rather than a Thai chicken farmer or a Chinese factory worker. Distance is needed too, because food and sustainable agriculture always involve dilemmas. There are few situations in which all that's desirable is possible: we can't have a ban on artificial fertilizer in combination with nature conservation and feeding the world and using less labor and avoiding chemical preservatives. It is always a matter of choices, and in some cases time has to pass before we know whether they were the right ones, so we need both a sense of responsibility and a willingness to take risks.

Rules, markets, education, and government are facilitators that will not help if nothing changes in how we live and consume. For everyone who has money, consumption has become the most important form of self-expression. It's no longer a matter of what you eat but of what you buy and where. Saddest of all is the arrogance with which we consume, as if the world belonged to us, and our disillusion when it turns out that consumption offers little joy and harms the earth. What we can buy is the surrogate of authentic experience: the bramble jam from a factory in an old-fashioned preserving jar; the pasta machine that we'll use only once to make fresh pasta. The new dietary laws ultimately demand that we search our own consciences and reflect on our own buying behavior and consumption patterns. Perhaps the best place to start might be the dining table, that breeding ground of opinions, questions, and simple democracy.

And Paradise?

The metaphor of paradise is still very much alive, in advertising and in public discourse. There is a brand of tea that has never been touched by human hands, Blanc Sacré from Mariage Frères in Paris. Women wearing gloves clip off the buds with gold scissors, like a divine gift. Conversely, from the largely safe, comfortable existence of the population in rich countries, where the abundance of choice rather than the lack of it can lead to existential astonishment, the risk-free and the easy are becoming a new challenge—not effortless plenty but actually the exertion of more effort. Those whose daily physical activity is largely made up of using the microwave, typing at a keyboard, and walking to the car can become addicted to physical extremes, such as marathon running. When it comes to food, home-baked bread, pesto made in a mortar and pestle, or wild asparagus can be viewed as a challenge.

Those who have it good want more. And then more still, because we are insatiable. The universal desire for more and the inability to curb it could be regarded as remnants of the Palaeolithic and the Neolithic, carried with us down the centuries. Doom-mongering and gloom could be seen as remnants of the past too, as a form of incantation (if you imagine the worst possible, then maybe you'll be pleasantly surprised). Those emotions don't fit with the power of the knowledge by which we are able to control our food supply chain with increasing precision. Human history can be seen as a way of defeating scarcity and converting it into plenty. Agriculture combined with population growth are mutually reinforcing processes that have compelled us to come up with entirely new solutions that would never have emerged if we had remained hunter-gatherers.

Now that scarcity is being overcome in more and more places, the question is how we can control abundance. Time and again I'm frightened by the sight, in so many countries, in so many shopping streets and huge shopping malls, of products for which several generations ago people would have had to pay the equivalent of a month's salary, even a year's salary, things people used to save up for that are now increasingly seen as fashion items for instant consumption. Cars, interiors, appliances, and clothes are replaced long before they wear out, purely because they're no longer in vogue. They are sold in shops where the air conditioning is set far too cold, because that ridiculously low temperature is part of the pattern of encouraging rapid, carefree consumption. Shopping, the slogan goes, has to be fun, and it's by no means simply an expedition to fetch what's needed. Without noticing we have arrived in a new paradise, where everything we desire comes to us without any apparent effort. Those who have no money buy on credit, because gratification must be instant. Those who don't know what they want are tempted by advertising that anticipates desires not yet felt, promising us that because of a new bathroom/car/sofa/pair of shoes/television, happiness will be ours. Those who want something new can be served immediately in the 24-hour economy and, increasingly commonly, by means of the Internet. Nothing any longer stands in the way of consumption.

This consumer paradise is deeply perverse, but not primarily because of the obvious illusions about the automatic relationship between happiness and material objects. In a sense this relationship has always existed, although the current scale and urgency of the illusory message is unprecedented. Its true perversity lies in the fact that consumers are not conscious of how much their increasing consumption is using up scarce resources, nor of the working conditions and ecological circumstances in which those often unnecessary products are produced. Because of the geographical distance between consumption and production, consumers have been separated from the effort needed to produce goods. The turnover of goods is increasingly rapid, and they're becoming increasingly cheap in relative terms. Relative price reduction is a consequence of greater efficiency of production; more can be produced for the same amount of time and effort. We are blinded to the fact that other collective resources are being drawn on besides capital, such as raw materials that have little if any price. Like the emblematic paradise of Adam and Eve, the modern consumer paradise is an impossibly idealized ecosystem in which production seems to take place more or less for free. Just like the abundance of food (which came about by magical means) in the paradise of those monotheistic religions, the richer part of humanity now has at its disposal an abundance of things to eat that seem almost without any cost.

At the same time, today's abundance creates its own scarcity. Old types of pear have disappeared, as have the hedgerows between fields, the country roads with donkey carts, the larks, the silence, and time itself. That's what we want back, that paradise, no matter if it's impossible. What we can achieve, if we get things right, is a new version of paradise, in which there's enough food for everyone and people continually strive for improvement—including the restoration of old farming landscapes, the return to favor of traditional breeds, reductions in the use of chemicals, and an easing of manual labor. Paradise is a world in which we have the opportunity to do whatever we can do, as well as enjoying eating with friends and colleagues, and participating in technological and social modernization.

Ultimately every form of doom-mongering is a break with the long history of striving for knowledge and control that began with the Fall of Man. Eve's curiosity, the testing of the boundaries of the commandment and then, after the expulsion from paradise, the will to survive scarcity and the unending struggle with the limitations of nature are things that demonstrate our strength, our mistakes, and our ability to learn. It's not the mistakes we make but the solutions we have yet to find that should concern us. Fear of making mistakes brings paralysis. What counts is the search for an answer through science (that organized form of doubt), through the thinkers and artists who offer us views of what is possible, and through the openness of well-functioning markets that are continually being corrected.

What counts is faith in what we don't yet know. Nervous people lack the desire and the strength to learn. Doom-mongering can be defeated only by hope. Hope is about the future, about much that has not yet been done, about where we come from and how we can preserve what is good about it. Hope is about now, about what we do to justify being hopeful. Those who see only thorns forget the roses; those who see only roses are hurt by the thorns. But the roses of tomorrow, the wheat and the rice, are being planted today, even if we don't know where and how. As poet Khalil Gibran wrote, "doubt is a pain too lonely to know that faith is his twin brother."

Now that we realize paradise does not exist on this planet, and that the image of effortless food supply and the exploitation of natural ecosystems with impunity plays tricks on us, we can free ourselves to create a new paradise. A paradise in which knowledge and effort do matter. Ultimately we can hope to find there our true human nature, not as spoiled mortals for whom food falls out of the trees, not as greedy leeches who appropriate everything that comes within our grasp, nor as naive worshippers of an idyll, but in full consciousness of what a scientific understanding of the ecology of the earth can bring us in the light of our real needs. These will be things of which we know nothing, or at most have a vague notion, such as proteins from algae or single-celled organisms, or other organisms from the sea, and the complete recovery of nutrients from the human consumption cycle.

———

Without food there is no evolution and no civilization. We are what we eat, literally, through the molecules we absorb from nature. We are who we are because of what we eat, and with whom. What it means to be human is concentrated in food and in our understanding of it. Inevitably, part of that is a consciousness that many have too little to eat, or cannot choose to have the things that, according to their culture and preferences, are associated with a decent meal: the displaced and the poor. Eve's paradise is not the world in which everyone can hold out their hand or open their mouth and be fed, but a paradise that combines curiosity, courage, and a desire for knowledge with social responsibility.

BIBLIOGRAPHY

This book ought really to have an endless bibliography. So much has been written about food, and the literature is so diverse in nature—scientific, journalistic, literary, social media—that the bibliography could easily have been ten times as long as it is. The list below is merely a selection, but it does include the most important sources, by which I mean the most inspiring and in some fields most recent, in alphabetical order by author or institution, followed by a few of the websites I consulted. I have deliberately decided against adding footnotes in the main text, because almost every sentence would require one. It was also impossible to arrange the bibliography by chapter, as most of the sources are relevant to more than one. The title of the book or article usually indicates which chapter it pertains to. Almost all the international statistics about food production are from the United Nations—especially the Food and Agriculture Organization of the United Nations (FAO), the World Health Organization (WHO), the United Nations Environment Programme (UNEP), the Population Council, and the United Nations Development Programme (UNDP), which have put much of their statistical data online. The Rabobank has given a useful context to many of these official figures and supplemented them with material of its own. For the United States I mainly used figures from the U.S. Department of Agriculture and for the EU data from from Eurostat. And for the Netherlands I used Statistics Netherlands; the Netherlands Institute for Social Research; and the Agricultural Economics Institute, Wageningen University and Research Centre. All statistics have been interpreted by me and where necessary, further extrapolated according to my own estimates. For anyone who would like to read further, here are a few pointers to works of particular importance.

Paradise theory cannot be found anywhere as such, but indirectly I derived a great deal from Bartlett Giamatti's *The Earthly Paradise and the Renaissance Epic* and Delumeau's *History of Paradise*. The most inspiring book about the relationship between food and human development is Wrangham's *Catching Fire: How cooking made us human*. The early development of agriculture and the domestication of species is described in a scientifically sound manner in the now rather old standard work by Harlan, *Crops and Man*, and very accessibly in Curvers' *Dorpen en steden van klei*. For later developments around the Mediterranean Sea, Braudel is of course indispensable, but so are Hourani's *A History of the Arab Peoples*, Abulafia's *The Great Sea: A human history of the Mediterranean*, and Wright's *A Mediterranean Feast*. The books by Mann, especially *1493*, are a marvelous source for information on the distribution of food crops and techniques after the discovery of America. Anyone wanting to know more about historical food shortages would do best to begin with Slicher van Bath and with Montanari's *Honger en Overvloed*. Historical pictures of gardens are beautifully collected in Ave Appiano's *Il giardino dipinto*. Details about the breeding of crops, adjustments to drought, and the technical modernization of farming come from countless scientific publications by the institutions that fall under the Consultative Group on International Agricultural Research and are not named separately here. No one who is interested in food and cooking should be without *The Oxford Companion to Food* by Davidson (even if, like all encyclopedists, he is does not achieve completeness in every department), nor without McGee for the techniques of food preparation. The history of bread can be found in, for example, *Le Retour du bon pain* by Kaplan. For modern changes in dietary patterns, Belasco is an enjoyable, primarily American souce, and the same goes for *Edible Ideologies* by Lebesco and Naccarato. For the Netherlands, Anneke van Otterloo offers a good overview, along with the geographically broader *All Manners of Food* by Mennell. Smil and various FAO publications point to the technical consequences of the growth of the consumption of animal products. For food taboos I naturally turned to Douglas, but also to Rozin. A clear quantitive approach to sustainability can be found in *Sustainable Energy— Without the Hot Air* by MacKay. Nestlé offers a readable, critical approach to the contemporary food industry, with an emphasis on America. The connection between it and globalization can be found most quickly in Barber. A very comprehensive picture of the future pressure points in food production is provided by a recent themed issue of *The Economist* edited by Parker. Finally, the wonderful photographs by Menzel and D'Alusio in *Hungry Planet: What the world eats* will set everyone thinking. References that relate to works published only in Dutch have been omitted. They can be found in the original Dutch edition of this book.

Abdel-Aal, E. S., P. Hucl, F. W. Sosulski: Compositional and nutritional characteristics of spring einkorn and spelt wheats. *Cereal Chemistry*, vol. 72, 6, pp. 621–624, 1995.

Abulafia, D.: *The Great Sea: A human history of the Mediterranean*. Oxford University Press, New York, 2011.

Académie de l'agriculture de France: *Deux siècles de progrès pour l'agriculture et l'alimentation 1789–1989*. Technique et Documentation Lavoisier, Paris, 1990.

Adams, F.: *On Ancient Medicine: The genuine works of Hippocrates* (translated from the Greek by F. Adams). Robert E. Krueger Publishing, Huntington, New York, 1972.

Adrià, F., J. Soler: *A Day at elBulli: An insight into the ideas, methods and creativity of Ferran Adrià*. Phaidon Press, London, 2008.

Ahmed, A. U., R. Vargas Hill, L. C. Smith, D. M. Wiesmann, T. Frankenberger: *The World's Most Deprived: Characteristics and causes of extreme poverty and hunger*. Discussion Paper 43. International Food Policy Research Insititute, Washington, DC, 2007.

Ahold: *Corporate Responsibility Report 2012*. Amsterdam, 2013.

Aiking, H. (ed.): *Meat the Truth: Essays on livestock production, sustainability and climate change*. Nicolaas G. Pierson Foundation, Amsterdam, 2010.

Aiking, H., J. de Boer, J. Vereijken: *Sustainable Protein Production and Consumption: Pigs or peas?* Environment & Policy, vol. 45. Springer, Dordrecht, 2006.

Akiba, B. J.: *The Book of Formation (or Sepher Yetzirah)*. William Rider & Son, London, 1923.

Alcock, J. P.: *Food in the Ancient World*. Greenwood Press, Westport, Connecticut, 2005.

Ali, H. G.: Current status of date palm in the world development of date palm cultivation and its role in the sustainability of agriculture in Oman. *Acta Horticulturae*, vol. 882, 8, pp. 29–37, 2010.

Alsdorf, L.: *The History of Vegetarianism and Cow-Veneration in India*. Taylor & Francis, London, 2010.

Altschuler, G. C.: *Three Centuries of Bagels: The evolution of a "modest bread."* Yale University Press, New Haven, Connecticut, 2008.

Ames, B. N.: Low micronutrient intake may accelerate the degenerative diseases of aging through allocation of scarce micronutrients by triage. *Proceedings of the National Academy of Sciences of the USA*, vol. 103, 47, pp. 17589–17594, 2006.

Anderson, E. N.: *The Food of China*. Yale University Press, New Haven, Connecticut, 1988.

Andreassian, V.: Waters and forests: From historical controversy to scientific debate. *Journal of Hydrology*, vol. 291, 1–2, pp. 1–27, 2004.

Anson, N. M.: Bioactive Compounds in Whole Grain Wheat. Dissertation, University of Maastricht, May 2010.

Antonson, H., U. Jansson (eds.): *Agriculture and Forestry in Sweden Since 1900: Geographical and historical studies*. Unit for Forest and Agricultural History, Royal Swedish Academy of Agriculture and Forestry, Stockholm, 2011.

Archibald, S., A. C. Staver, S. A. Levin: Evolution of human-driven fire regimes in Africa. *Proceedings of the National Academy of Sciences of the USA*, vol. 109, 3, pp. 847–852, 2012.

Argenti, O.: *Achieving Urban Food and Nutrition Security in the Developing World. Feeding Cities: Food supply and distribution*. International Food Policy Institute, Washington, DC, 2000.

Ashbridge, I.: McDonald's milk goes organic. *Farmers Weekly*, July 3, 2007.

Attenborough, D.: *The First Eden: The Mediterranean world and man*. Collins/BBC Books, London, 1987.

Ave Appiano, A.: *Il giardino dipinto: Dagli affreschi egizi a Botero*. Ananke Editore, Turin, Italy, 2002.

Bailey, G.: World prehistory from the margins: The role of coastlines in human evolution. *Journal of Interdisciplinary Studies in History and Archaeology*, vol. 1, 1, pp. 39–50, 2004.

Bala Ravi, S., I. Hoeschle-Zeledon, M. S. Swaminathan, E. Frison: Hunger and Poverty: The role of biodiversity. Report of an International Consultation on the Role of Biodiversity in Achieving the UN Millennium Development Goal of

Freedom from Hunger and Poverty. M. S. Swaminathan Research Foundation, Chennai, India, 2005.

Balfour, E. B.: *The Living Soil: Evidence of the importance to human health of soil vitality, with special reference to national planning*. Faber and Faber, London, 1943.

Balter, M.: Ancient DNA says Europe's first farmers came from afar. *Science*, vol. 325, 5945, p. 1189, 2009.

Barber, B. R.: *Jihad vs. McWorld*. Ballantine Books, Westminster, Maryland, 1996.

————: *Consumed: How markets corrupt children, infantilize adults, and swallow citizens whole*. W. W. Norton and Company, New York, 2007.

Barles, S.: Feeding the City: Food consumption and flow of nitrogen, Paris, 1801–1914. *Science of the Total Environment*, vol. 375, 1–3, pp. 48–58, 2007.

Barnes, P.: Capitalism, the commons, and divine right. Twenty-Third Annual E. F. Schumacher Lectures. Stockbridge, Massachusetts, October 2003.

Basho, B.: *The Penguin Book of Zen Poetry*. Penguin, London, 1988.

Battisti, D., R. L. Naylor: Historical warnings of future food insecurity with unprecedented seasonal heat. *Science*, vol. 323, 5911, pp. 240–244, 2009.

Begossi, A.: Food taboos at Buzios island (Brazil): Their significance and relation to folk medicine. *Journal of Ethnobiology and Ethnomedicine* vol. 12, pp. 117–139, 1992.

Begossi, A., N. Hanazaki, R. M. Ramos: Food chain and the reasons for fish food taboos among Amazonian and Atlantic forest fishers (Brazil). *Ecological Applications*, vol. 14, 5, pp. 1334–1343, 2004.

Beinhocker, E. D.: *The Origin of Wealth: Evolution, complexity and the radical remaking of economics*. Harvard Business School Press, Boston, 2006.

Belasco, W. J.: *Appetite for Change: How the counterculture took on the food industry 1966–1988*. Pantheon Books, New York, 1989.

————: *Meals to Come: A history of the future of food*. University of California Press, Berkeley, 2006.

Belasco, W. J., R. Horowitz: *Food Chains: From farmyard to shopping cart*. University of Pennsylvania Press, Philadelphia, 2009.

Belt, H. van den: Enclosing the genetic commons: Biopatenting on a global scale. In C. Baumgartner, D. Mieth (eds.), *Patente am Leben? Ethische, rechtliche und politische Aspekte der Biopatentierung*, pp. 229–244. Mentis-Verlag, Paderborn, Germany, 2003.

Bender, B.: Gatherer-hunter to farmer: A social perspective. *World Archaeology*, vol. 10, 2, Archaeology and Religion issue, pp. 204–222, 1978.

Bergen, H. van: *Snèk Book Curaçao*. Mon Art Gallery, Otrobanda, Curaçao, 2008.

Berger, J.: *Pig Earth*. Bloomsbury, London, 1999. (First published 1979.)

Berlin, A. M., T. Ball, R. Thompson, C. Herbert: Ptolemaic agriculture, "Syrian wheat," and *Tricticum aestivum*. *Journal of Archaeological Science*, vol. 30, 1, pp. 115–121, 2003.

Bernstein, W. J.: *A Splendid Exchange: How trade shaped the world*. Grove Press, New York, 2008.

Bezemer, M. T., W. H. van der Putten: Ecology: Diversity and stability in plant communities. *Nature*, vol. 446, pp. E6–E7, 2007.

Biblica: *New International Version Bible*, 2011.

Bjerga, A.: *Endless Appetites: How the commodities casino creates hunger and unrest.* Bloomberg Press, Hoboken, New Jersey, 2011.

Blixen, K.: *Out of Africa.* Modern Library, New York, 1992.

Bok, D.: *The Politics of Happiness: What government can learn from the new research on well-being.* Princeton University Press, Princeton, New Jersey, 2010.

Boniolo, G.: *Il pulpito e la piazza. Democrazia, deliberazione e scienza della vita.* Raffaello Cortina Ed., Milan, 2011.

Boonekamp, P., A. Haverkort, R. Hutten, E. Jacobsen, G. Kessel, B. Lotz, R. Visser, J. Vossen: *Durable Resistance against Pytophthora in Potato through Cisgenic Marker-free Modification.* Wageningen University, Wageningen, 2010.

Born, J. M., S.G.T. Lemmens, F. Rutters, A. G. Nieuwenhuizen, E. Fermisano, R. Goebel, M. S. Westerterp-Plantenga: Acute stress and food-related reward activation in the brain during food choice during eating in the absence of hunger. *International Journal of Obesity,* vol. 34, pp. 172–181, 2009.

Bottéro, J.: *Everyday Life in Ancient Mesopotamia* (translated by A. Nevill). Johns Hopkins University Press, Baltimore, Maryland, 2001.

Boutonnet, J. P., M. Griffon, D. Viallet: *Compétitivité des productions animales en Afrique subsaharienne et à Madagascar: Synthèse générale. Direction génerale de la coopération internationale et du dévelopment.* Ministere des affaires étrangeres, 2000.

Bowlby, R.: *Shopping with Freud.* Routledge, London, 1993.

Boyarin, D.: Jesus kept kosher: The Jewish Christ of the Gospel of Mark. *Tikkun* vol. 27, 2, p. 43, 2012.

Bramanti, B.: Genetic discontinuity between local hunter-gatherers and Central Europe's first farmers. *Science,* vol. 326, 5949, pp. 137–140, 2009.

Braudel, F.: *Capitalism and Material Life.* Harper and Row, New York, 1973.

———: *Afterthoughts on Material Civilization and Capitalism.* Johns Hopkins University Press, Baltimore, Maryland, 1979.

———: *La Méditerranée et le monde méditarranéen à l'epoque de Philippe II.* Livre de poche, Paris, 1993.

———: *Les mémoires de la Méditerranée: Préhistoire et Antiquité.* Éd de Fallois, Paris, 1998.

Braun, J. von: *The World Food Situation: New driving forces and required actions.* International Food Policy Research Institute, Washington, DC, 2007.

———: *Food Security and the Futures of Farms: 2020 toward 2050. Report from the Bertebos Conference.* Royal Swedish Academy of Agriculture and Forestry in cooperation with the Bertebos Foundation, Falkenberg, Sweden, August 2010.

———: Food Security and Economic Change: What to do about the food crisis. Dick de Zeeuw Lecture, The Hague, April 14, 2011.

Breton, D. le: *La saveur du monde: Une anthropologie des sens.* Editions Métailié, Paris, 2006.

Brillat-Savarin, J. A.: *Physiologie du Goût.* Sautelet, Paris, 1825.

Broadhurst, C. L., S. C. Cunnane, M. A. Crawford: Rift Valley lake fish and shellfish provided brain-specific nutrition for early *Homo. British Journal of Nutrition,* vol. 79, pp. 3–21, 1997.

Broadhurst, C. L., Y. Wang, M. A. Crawford, S. C. Cunnane, J. E. Parkington, W. F. Schmidt: Brain-specific lipids from marine, lacustrine, or terrestrial food resources, potential impact on early African *Homo sapiens*. *Comparative Biochemistry and Physiology* B, vol. 131, pp. 653–673, 2002.

Brookes, G., P. Barfoot: GM crops: Global socio-economic and environmental impacts 1996–2006. *Agbioforum*, vol. 11, 1, pp. 21–38, 2007.

Brown, J.: *The Pursuit of Paradise: A social history of gardens and gardening*. Harper Collins, New York, 2000.

Brown, L. R.: *Who Will Feed China?: Wake-up call for a small planet*. W. W. Norton and Company, New York, 1995.

———: The new geopolitics of food: From the Middle East to Madagascar, high prices are spawning land grabs and ousting dictators. Welcome to the 21st-century food wars. *Foreign Policy: The food issue*, June 2011.

Browning, F.: *Apples: The story of the fruit of temptation*. Penguin, London, 1998.

Brundtland Commission: *Our Common Future*. Oxford University Press, Oxford, 1987.

Bruno, N.: *Proverbi Siciliani: Straordinaria summa della secolare saggezza del popolo e della sua capacitá di adattamento*. Flaccovio Editore, Palermo, Italy, 2011.

Brussaard, L., P. Caron, B. Campbell, L. Lipper, S. Mainka, R. Rabbinge, D. Babin, M. Pulleman: Reconciling biodiversity conservation and food security: Scientific challenges for a new agriculture. *Current Opinion in Environmental Sustainability*, vol. 1, 1–2, pp. 34–42, 2010.

Bucx, T., M. Marchand, A. Makaske, C. van de Guchte: Comparative Assessment of the Vulnerability and Resilience of 10 Deltas: Synthesis report. *Delta Alliance Report* 1. Delta Alliance International, Delft-Wageningen, 2010.

Buell, P. D., E. N. Anderson: *A Soup for the Qan: Chinese dietary medicine of the Mongol era as seen in Hu Szu-Hui's Yin-shan Cheng-yao, introduction, translation, commentary and Chinese text*. Sir Henry Welcome Asian Series, Kegan Paul International, London and New York, 2000.

Buford, B.: TV dinners. *The New Yorker*, pp. 42–47, October 2006.

Burnett, J.: *Liquid Pleasures: A social history of drinks in modern Britain*. Routledge, London, 1999.

Burney, J. A., S. J. Davis, D. B. Lobell: Greenhouse gas mitigation by agricultural intensification. *Proceedings of the National Academy of Sciences of the USA*, vol. 107, 26, pp. 12052–12057, 2010.

Buruma, I., A. Margalit: *Occidentalism: The West in the eyes of its enemies*. Penguin, London, 2004.

Butzer, K. W.: Collapse, environment, and society. *Proceedings of the National Academy of Sciences of the USA*, vol. 109, 10, pp. 3632–3639, 2012.

Byron, G. G.: *Don Juan*. Penguin, London, 1973.

Canetti, E.: Die Stimmen von Marrakesch sind Aufzeichnungen nach einer Reise von Elias Canetti. *Süddeutsche Zeitung*, Munich, Germany, 1968.

Carrubba, R. W.: Englebert Kaempfer and the myth of the Scythian lamb. *Classical World*, vol. 87, p. 417, 1993.

Carter, S. E., L. O. Fresco, P. G. Jones, J. N. Fairbairn: *An Atlas of Cassava in Africa: Historical, agroecological and demographic aspects of crop distribution*. CIAT Publication 206. Centro Internacional de Agricultura Tropical, Cali, Colombia, June 1992.

CBS News: Counting calories at McDonald's, fast food chain to post nutrition information on packaging next year. Bootie Cosgrove-Mather. Chicago, October 25, 2005.

CCLJ (Centre Communautaire Laïc Juif): L'oeuvre de Papa Maistriau revit au Congo. Géraldine Kamps, April 3, 2012.

Cecchini, M., F. Sassi, J. A. Lauer, Y. Y. Lee, V. Guajardo-Barron, D. Chisholm: Tackling of unhealthy diets, physical inactivity, and obesity: Health effects and cost-effectiveness. *Lancet*, vol. 376, 9754, pp. 1795–1874, 2010.

Chandler, R., Jr.: *An Adventure in Applied Science: A history of the International Rice Research Institute*. International Rice Research Institute, Los Baños, the Philippines, 1982.

Chigateri, S.: Glory to the cow: Cultural difference and social justice in the food hierarchy in India. *South Asia: Journal of South Asian Studies*, vol. 31, 1, pp. 10–35, April 2008.

Childe, V. G.; *The Most Ancient East: The oriental prelude to European prehistory*. Kegan Paul, London, 1928.

Choudhary, B., K. Gaur: The Development and Regulation of Bt Brinjal in India (Eggplant/ Aubergine) *ISAAA Brief* 38. International Service for the Acquisition of Agri-biotech Applications, Ithaca, New York, 2009.

Clay, J.: *Exploring the Links between International Business and Poverty Reduction: A case study of Unilever in Indonesia*. Oxfam GB, Novib, Unilever, and Unilever Indonesia joint research project. Information Press, Eynsham, UK, 2005.

Clutton-Brock, J.: *A Natural History of Domesticated Mammals*. Cambridge University Press, Cambridge, 1999.

Coe, M. D.: *The Jaguar's Children: Pre-classic central Mexico*. Museum of Primitive Art, New York, 1965.

Collier, P.: The politics of hunger: How illusion and greed fan the food crisis. *Foreign Affairs*, December 2008. Available at https://www.foreignaffairs.com/articles/2008-11-01/politics-hunger.

Collingham, L.: *The Taste of War: World War Two and the battle for food*. Allen Lane (Penguin), London, 2011.

Compassion in World Farming: *Beyond Factory Farming: Sustainable solutions for animals, people and the planet*. Surrey, UK, 2009.

Conway, G.: *The Doubly Green Revolution: Food for all in the 21st century*. Penguin, London, 1997.

Cordain, L., S. B. Eaton, J. Brand Miller, N. Mann, K. Hill: The paradoxical nature of hunter-gatherer diets: Meat-based, yet non-atherogenic. *European Journal of Clinical Nutrition*, vol. 56, suppl. 1, pp. 42–52, 2002.

Corradin, R., P. Rancati: *Taste and Tradition. A culinary journey through southern Italy*, vol. 2. Silvana Editoriale Spa, Milan, 2011.

Corradin, R., J. Huizenga, P. Rancati: *Taste and Tradition. A culinary journey through northern and central Italy*, vol. 1. Silvana Editoriale Spa, Milan, 2010.

Cousteau, J.: *The Ocean World*. Harry N. Abrams, New York, 1985.

CPB (Netherlands Bureau for Economic Policy Analysis), PBL (Netherlands Environmental Assessment Agency), Netherlands Institute for Social Research: *Sustainability Monitor for the Netherlands 2011*. Statistics Netherlands, The Hague, September 2011.

Crawford, M. A.: The role of the dietary fatty acids in biology, their place in the evolution of the human brain. *Nutrition Reviews*, vol. 50, pp. 3–11, 1992.

Crews, T. E., M. B. Peoples: Can the synchrony of nitrogen supply and crop demand be improved in legume and fertilizer-based agroecosystems? *Nutrient Cycling in Agroecosystems*, vol. 72, 2, pp. 101–120, 2005.

Crick, M.: *Kafka's Soup: A complete history of literature in 17 recipes*. Granta Books, London, 2005.

Dalrymple, W.: *The Age of Kali, Indian Travels and Encounters*. Flamingo Harper Collins, London, 1999.

Damania, A. B., J. Valkoun, G. Willcox, C. O. Qualset: *The Origins of Agriculture and Crop Domestication: The Harlan Symposium*. International Center for Agricultural Research in Dry Areas, Aleppo, Syria,1998.

Davidson, A.: *The Oxford Companion to Food*. Oxford University Press, Oxford, 1999.

Davis, D. R., M. D. Epp, H. D. Riordan: Changes in USDA food composition data, 43 garden crops. *Journal of the American College of Nutrition*, vol. 23, pp. 669–682, 2004.

Deininger, K., D. Byerlee: *Rising Global Interest in Farmland: Can it yield sustainable and equitable benefits?* World Bank, Washington, DC, 2010.

Delumeau, J.: *History of Paradise: The garden of Eden in myth and tradition*. Continuum, New York, 1995.

Diamond, J. M.: *Guns, Germs, and Steel*. W. W. Norton and Company, New York, 1997.

———: *Collapse: How societies choose to fail or succeed*. Penguin Group, New York, 2005.

Dickinson, E.: *Complete Poems of Emily Dickinson*, Poem: 1377; Forbidden Fruit a Flavor Has. Harvard University Press, Cambridge, Massachusetts, 1955.

Diehl, J. F.: Food irradiation: Past, present and future. *Radiation Physics and Chemistry*, vol. 16, 3–6, pp. 211–215, 2002.

Dikötter, F.: *Mao's Great Famine: The history of China's most devastating catastrophe, 1958–1962*. Walker and Company, New York, 2010.

Dirmeyer, P.: Modeling the effects of vegetation on Mediterranean climate during the Roman Classical Period: Part I: Climate history and model sensitivity. *Global and Planetary Change*, vol. 25, 3–4, pp. 163–184, 2000.

Doniger, W.: *The Hindus: An alternative history*. Penguin, New York, 2009.

Donner, H.: New vegetarianism: Food, gender and neo-liberal regimes in Bengali middle-class families. *Journal of South Asia Studies*, vol. 31, 1, pp. 143–169, 2008.

Douglas, M.: *Purity and Danger: An analysis of the concepts of pollution and taboo*. ARK Paperbacks, London, 1984.

———: *Constructive Drinking: Perspectives on drink from anthropology*. Cambridge University Press, Cambridge, 1987.

————: *Risk and Blame: Essays in cultural theory*. Routledge, London and New York, 1992.

————: *Leviticus as Literature*. Oxford University Press, Oxford, 2000.

Drèze, J., A. Sen: *The Political Economy of Hunger*, vol. 1. Clarendon Press, Oxford, 1990.

Dror, D. K., L. H. Allen: Effect of vitamin B-12 deficiency on neurodevelopment in infants: Current knowledge and possible mechanisms. *Nutrition Reviews*, vol. 66, 5, pp. 250–255, 2008.

Dumanovsky, T., C. Y. Huang, C. A. Nonas, T. D. Matte, M. T. Bassett, L. D. Silver: Changes in energy content of lunchtime purchases from fast food restaurants after introduction of calorie labeling: Cross sectional customer surveys. *British Medical Journal*, vol. 343, p. 4464, 2011.

Edmeades, G. O.: Drought Tolerance in Maize: An emerging reality. Global Status of Commercialized Biotech/GM Crops, 2008. *ISAAA Brief 39*. International Service for the Acquisition of Agri-biotech Applications, Ithaca, New York, 2008.

Eetgerink, M.: Urban Agriculture. A quantitative assessment of urban food production. Dissertation, University of Amsterdam, Amsterdam, 2011.

Egmond, N. D. van, H.J.M. de Vries: Sustainability: The search for the integral worldview. Utrecht Centre for Earth and Sustainability. *Futures*, vol. 43, pp. 853–867, 2011.

Eppendorfer, W. H., B. O. Eggum: Dietary fiber, starch, amino-acids and nutritive-value of potatoes as affected by sulfur, nitrogen, phosphorus, potassium, calcium and water-stress. *Acta Agriculturae Scandinavica* B, vol. 44, 2, pp. 107–115, 1994.

European Commission: *Towards Sustainable Agriculture for Developing Countries: Options for life sciences and biotechnologies*. Brussels, 2009.

Evans, J. K.: Wheat production and its social consequences in the Roman world. *Classical Quarterly*, new series, vol. 31, 2, pp. 428–442, 1981.

FAO (Food and Agriculture Organization of the United Nations): World Fisheries and Aquaculture Atlas (cd-rom). Rome, 2001.

————: Human Vitamin and Mineral Requirements. Report of a joint FAO/WHO expert consultation. Bangkok, Thailand, 2001.

————: Report of the Committee on Food Security, 30th session. Rome, 2004.

————: *The State of Food and Agriculture 2003–2004*. Rome, 2004.

————: *Livestock's Long Shadow: Environmental issues and options*. Rome, 2006.

————: *The State of Food Insecurity in the World 2006: Eradicating world hunger—taking stock ten years after the World Food Summit*. Rome, 2006.

————: *The Double Burden of Malnutrition: Case studies from six developing countries*. Rome, 2006.

————: FAO Fisheries Circular 972/4, Part 1: Future prospects for fish and fishery products 4; 4. Fish consumption in the European Union in 2015 and 2030 Part 1. European overview. Rome, 2007.

————: International Conference on Organic Agriculture and Food Security. Rome, May 3–5, 2007.

FAO (Food and Agriculture Organization of the United Nations): Biotechnology in Food and Agriculture: Conference 14. E-mail conference: Coping with water scarcity in developing countries: What role for agricultural biotechnologies? March 5–April 1, 2007.

———: *How to Feed the World in 2050.* Rome, 2009.

———: *The State of Food and Agriculture 2010–11. Women in agriculture: Closing the gender gap for development.* Rome, 2011.

———: *Save and Grow: A policymaker's guide to the sustainable intensification of smallholder crop production.* Rome, 2011.

———: Histoire de la recherche agricole en Afrique tropicale francophone, vols. 1–6 (cd-rom). Rome, 2012.

FAO (Food and Agriculture Organization of the United Nations) and WHO (World Health Organization): Diet, Nutrition and Prevention of Chronic Diseases. *WHO Technical Report* 916. Geneva, 2003.

Farb, P., G. Armelagos: *Consuming Passions: The anthropology of eating.* Washington Square Press, New York, 1983.

Fereres, E., F. Orgaz, V. Gozalez-Dugo: Reflections on food security under water scarcity. *Journal of Experimental Botany Advance Access,* May 30, 2011.

Fery, R. L.: New opportunities in Vigna. In J. Janick, A. Whipkey (eds.), *Trends in New Crops and New Uses,* pp. 424–428. ASHS Press, Alexandria, Virginia, 2002.

Fiala, N.: Measuring sustainability: Why the ecological footprint is bad economics and bad environmental science. *Ecological Economics,* vol. 67, 4, pp. 519–525, 2008.

Finkelstein, J.: *Dining Out.* Polity Press, Oxford, 1989.

Fischer, G., M. Shah: *Farmland Investments and Food Security: Statistical annex.* International Institute for Applied Systems Analysis, Laxenburg, Austria, 2010.

Fischer, G., E. Hizsnyik, S. Prieler, M. Shah, H. van Velthuizen: *Biofuels and Food Security.* Land Use Change and Agriculture Program. International Institute for Applied Systems Analysis. OPEC Fund for International Development, Vienna, 2009.

Fischler, C.: Le consommateur partagé. In *Le mangeur et l'animal,* no. 172, pp. 135–148. Edition Autrement, Paris, 1997.

———: *Manger, Mode d'emploi? Entretiens avec Monique Nemer.* Fondation Nestlé France, 2011.

Flandrin, J. L., M. Montanari: *Histoire de l'alimentation.* Fayard, Paris, 1996.

———: *Food: A culinary history from antiquity to the present.* Columbia University Press, New York, 1999.

Fondation PROTA: *10 ans 2000–2010, Plantes africaines prometteuses.* Wageningen, 2010.

Fortanier, F.: *Multinational Enterprises, Institutions and Sustainable Development.* University of Amsterdam, Amsterdam, 2008.

Fowler, C., P. R. Mooney: *Shattering: Food, politics, and the loss of genetic diversity.* University of Arizona Press, Tucson, 1996.

France, A.: *Les opinions de M. Jérôme Coignard.* Calmann Lévy Language, Paris, 1910.

Franck, K. A.: Food + the city. *Architectural Design,* vol. 75, 3, pp. 78–85, 2005.

Frank, R. H.: *Luxury Fever: Money and happiness in an era of excess.* Princeton University Press, Princeton, New Jersey, 1999.

Frazer, J. G.: *The Golden Bough: A study in magic and religion* (abridged ed. R. Frazer). Oxford World's Classics. Oxford University Press, Oxford, 1994.

Freidberg, S.: *Fresh: A perishable history.* Belknap Press of Harvard University Press, Cambridge, Massachusetts, 2009.

Frenkel, S.: A pound of Kenya, please or a single short skinny mocha. In *The Taste of American Place. A Reader on Regional and Ethnic Foods.* pp. 57–64. Rowman & Littlefield, Lanham, Maryland, 1998.

Fresco, L. O.: *Schaduwdenkers en Lichtzoekers.* Huizinga Lecture, Prometheus, Amsterdam, 1998.

———: Fertilizer and the future. *Spotlight Magazine,* June 2003.

———: *Nieuwe spijswetten, Over voedsel en verantwoordelijkheid.* Bert Bakker, Amsterdam, 2006.

———: Sustainable agro-food chains; Challenges for research and development. In R. Ruben, M. Slingerland, H. Nijhoff (eds.), *Agro-food Chains and Networks for Development,* pp. 205–208. Springer, Wageningen, 2006.

———: A Landscape with a down-to-earth flavour. In H. van Os, H. Leeflang, J. Reynaerts (eds.), *The Discovery of the Netherlands. Four centuries of landscape painting by Dutch masters,* pp. 29–39. NAi Uitgevers, Rotterdam, 2008.

———: Challenges for food system adaptation today and tomorrow. *Environmental Science & Policy,* vol. 12, 4, pp. 378–385, 2009.

Fresco, L. O., W. O. Baudoin: Food and nutrition security. In P. Nath, P. B. Gaddagimath, O. P. Dutta (eds.), *Food Security and Vegetables: A global perspective,* pp. 7–42. Prem Nath Agricultural Science Foundation, Bangalore, India, 2004.

Fresco, L. O., B. Kroonenberg: Time and spatial scales in ecological sustainability. *Land Use Policy,* vol. 9, pp. 155–168, 1992.

Fresco, L. O., D. Dijk, W. de Ridder: Biomass, Food and Sustainability: Is there a dilemma? Updated version of the 2006 Duisenberg Lecture. Rabobank, Utrecht, 2006.

Friedman, T. L.: *The World Is Flat: The globalized world in the twenty-first century.* Penguin, London, 2006.

Friends of the Earth International: *Who Benefits from GM Crops? Feeding the biotech giants, not the world's poor.* Washington, DC, 2009.

Frijda, N.: *De Emoties: Een overzicht van onderzoek en theorie.* Prometheus/Bert Bakker, Amsterdam, 2005.

Frison, E. A., I. F. Smith, T. Johns, F. Cherfas, P. Eyzaguirre: Agricultural biodiversity, nutrition, and health: Making a difference to hunger and nutrition in the developing world. *Food and Nutrition Bulletin,* vol. 27, pp. 167–179, 2006.

Fukuoka, M.: *The One-Straw Revolution: An introduction to natural farming.* Rodale Press, Emmaus, Pennsylvania, 1978.

Fuller, D. Q.: Contrasting patterns in crop domestication and domestication rates: Recent archaeobotanical insights from the Old World. *Annals of Botany,* vol. 100, pp. 903–924, 2007.

Gabriel, D., S. M. Sait, J. A. Hodgson, U. Schmutz, W. E. Kunin, T. G. Benton: Scale matters: The impact of organic farming on biodiversity at different spatial scales. *Ecology Letters,* vol. 13, pp. 858–869, 2010.

Gadema, Z., D. Oglethorpe: The use and usefulness of carbon labelling food: A policy perspective from a survey of UK supermarket shoppers. *Food Policy,* vol. 36, 6, pp. 815–822, 2011.

Galloway, J. N., M. Burke, G. E. Bradford, R. Naylor, W. Falcon, A. K. Chapagain, J. C. Gaskell, E. McCullough, H. A. Mooney, K. L. Oleson, H. Steinfeld, T. Wassenaar, V. Smil: International trade in meat: The tip of the pork chop. *AMBIO: A Journal of the Human Environment,* vol. 36, 8, pp. 622–629, 2007.

Gallup, J. L., J. D. Sachs, A. D. Mellinger: Geography and economic development. *International Regional Science Review,* vol. 22, 2, pp. 179–232, 1999.

Gandhi, M.: *Young India,* p. 310, October 15, 1931.

Garabet, S., M. Wood, J. Ryan: Nitrogen and water effects on wheat yield in a Mediterranean-type climate I. Growth, water-use and nitrogen accumulation. *Field Crops Research,* vol. 57, 3, pp. 309–318, 1998.

Garrett, L.: *Food Failures and Futures.* Council on Foreign Relations, New York, 2008.

Garrity, D. P., F. K. Akinnifest, O. C. Ajayi, S. G. Weldesemayat, J. G. Mowo, A. Kalinganire, M. Larwanou, J. Bayala: Evergreen agriculture: A robust approach to sustainable food security in Africa. *Food Security,* vol. 2, 3, pp. 197–214, 2010.

Gauer, L. E., C. A. Grant, D. T. Gehl, L. D. Bailey: Effects of nitrogen-fertilization on grain protein-content, nitrogen uptake, and nitrogen use efficiency of 6 spring wheat (*triticum-aestivum* L) cultivars, in relation to estimated moisture supply. *Canadian Journal of Plant Science,* vol. 72, 1, pp. 235–241, 1992.

Gepts, P.: A comparison between crop domestication, classical plant breeding, and genetic engineering. *Crop Science,* vol. 42, pp. 1780–1790, 2002.

Gerbens-Leenes, P. W.: Natural Resource Use for Food: Land, Water and Energy in Production and Consumption Systems. Dissertation, University of Groningen, Groningen, 2006.

Gerber, P., H. A. Mooney, J. Dijkman, S. Tarawali, C. de Haan: *Livestock in a Changing Landscape. Experiences and Regional Perspectives,* vol. 2. Island Press, Washington, DC, 2010.

Giamatti, B. A.: *The Earthly Paradise and the Renaissance Epic.* Princeton University Press, Princeton, New Jersey, 1966.

Gibran, K.: *The Collected Works.* Alfred A. Knopf, New York, 2007.

Gide, A.: *Voyage en Congo, suivi du Retour du Tchad.* Aulard, Paris, 1928.

Giesecke, A. L.: *The Epic City: Urbanism, utopia, and the garden in ancient Greece and Rome.* Center for Hellenic Studies, Washington, DC, 2007.

Gilman, S. L.: *Fat: A cultural history of obesity.* Polity, Cambridge, 2008.

Giordano, M., K. G. Villholth: *The Agricultural Groundwater Revolution: Comprehensive assessment of water management in agriculture.* CABI, Wallingford, UK, 2007.

Giovannoni, J.: Harvesting the apple genome. *Nature Genetics,* vol. 42, pp. 822–823, 2010.

Glantz, M.: Guidelines for establishing audits of agricultural-environmental hotspots. Working Paper 15. Food and Agriculture Organization of the United Nations, Environmental and Societal Impacts Group, and National Center for Atmospheric Research, Boulder, Colorado, and Rome, 2003.

GM Soy Debate: Agro-ecological impacts of genetically modified soy production in Argentina and Brazil, an analysis of twelve claims about GM soy. 2009.

Goldschmidt, T.: *Darwin's Dreampond. Drama in Lake Victoria* (translated by Sherry Marx-Macdonald). MIT Press, Cambridge, Massachusetts, 1998.

Goldsmith, R. W.: An estimate of the size and structure of the national product of the early Roman Empire. *Review of Income and Wealth,* vol. 30, 3, pp. 263–288, 1984.

Goody, J.: *Cooking, Cuisine and Class: A study in comparative sociology.* Cambridge University Press, Cambridge, 1982.

Gorp, D. van: *Offshoring in the Service Sector: An empirical investigation on the off-shoring behavior of service firms.* Nyenrode Business University, Breukelen, the Netherlands, 2008.

Gothein, M.: *A History of Garden Art.* J. M. Dent and Sons, London, 1928.

Goudsblom, J.: *Fire and Civilization.* Allen Lane, London, 1992.

Goyan Kittler, P., K. P. Sucher, M. Nelms: *Food and Culture.* Wadsworth Publishing, Belmont, California, 2011.

Greenpeace: *Agriculture at a Crossroads: Food for survival.* Greenpeace, Amsterdam, 2009.

GRI (Global Reporting Initiative): *Earth Charter, Global Compact and GRI: Guidance to users on the synergies in application and reporting.* Amsterdam, 2008.

Griffioen-Roose, S.: The role of Sweet and Savoury Taste in Food Intake and Food Preferences. Dissertation, Wageningen University, Wageningen, January 2012.

Groningen, B. A. van: *Herodotus Historiën, met inleiding en commentaar. Commentaar op boek I–III, derde deel paragraaf 17, 18 en 19.* E. J. Brill, Leiden, 1946.

Guerrero, S., J. Cremades: *Acuicultura multitrófica integrada: Una alternativa sostenible y de futuro para los cultivos marinos en Galicia.* Xunta de Galicia, Consellería de Medio Rural e do Mar, Centro de Investigacións Marinas, Vilanova de Arousa (Pontevedra), Spain, 2012.

Gustavsson, J., C. L. Cederber, U. Sonesson, R. Otterdijk, A. Meybeck: *Global Food Losses and Food Waste: Extent, causes and prevention.* Food and Agriculture Organization of the United Nations, Rome, 2011.

Haan, C. de, H. Steinfeld, H. Blackburn: *Livestock and the Environment: Finding a balance.* Food and Agriculture Organization of the United Nations, Rome, 1996.

Harlan, J. R.: *Crops and Man,* second edition. American Society of Agronomy/Crop Science Society, Madison, Wisconsin, 1992.

Harris, M.: The myth of the sacred cow. In A. Leeds, A. P. Vayda (eds.), *Man, Culture and Animals. The role of animals in human ecological adjustments,* pp. 217–228. Publication 78. American Association for the Advancement of Science, Washington, DC, 1965.

Harris, M., E. B. Ross: *Food and Evolution: Toward a theory of human food habits.* Temple University Press, Philadelphia, Pennsylvania, 1987.

Hatziminaoglou, Y., J. Boyazoglu: The goat in ancient civilisations: From the Fertile Crescent to the Aegean Sea. *Small Ruminant Research,* vol. 51, 2, pp. 123–129, 2004.

Hawkes, J. G., J. Francisco-Ortega: The early history of the potato in Europe. *Euphytica,* vol. 70, pp. 1–7, 1993.

Health and Consumer Protection Directorate-General: *Labelling Competitiveness, Consumer Information and Better Regulation for the EU.* Brussels and Luxembourg, 2006.

Hein, L.: Optimising the Management of Complex Dynamic Ecosystems: An ecological economic modelling approach. Dissertation, Wageningen University, Wageningen, 2005.

Hemingway, E.: *The Old Man and the Sea.* Scribner's, New York, 1952.

Henrich, J., N. Henrich: The evolution of cultural adaptations: Fijian food taboos protect against dangerous marine toxins. *Proceedings of the Royal Society* B, vol. 277, pp. 3715–3724, 2010.

Henry, A. G., A. S. Brooks, D. R. Piperno: Microfossils in calculus demonstrate consumption of plants and cooked foods in Neanderthal diets. *Proceedings of the National Academy of Sciences of the USA,* vol. 108, 2, pp. 486–491, 2010.

Herodotus: *Histories, III:18, 450–420 BCE.* Oxford University Press, Oxford, 1998.

Hertwich, E., E. van der Voet, S. Suh, A. Tukker, M. Huijbregts, P. Kazmierczyk, M. Lenzen, J. McNeely, Y. Moriguchi: *Assessing the Environmental Impacts of Consumption and Production: Priority products and materials.* A report of the Working Group on the Environmental Impacts of Products and Materials to the International Panel for Sustainable Resource Management. United Nations Environmental Programme, Nairobi, 2010.

Hillocks, R. J., J. M. Thresh, A. Bellotti: *Cassava: Biology, production and utilization.* Oxford University Press, Oxford, 2002.

Ho, P.-T.: The introduction of American food plants into China. *American Anthropologist,* vol. 57, 2, pp. 191–201, 1955.

Hoffmann, R. C.: Environmental change and the culture of common carp in medieval Europe. *Guelph Ichthyology,* review 3, pp. 57–85, 1995.

Holling, C. S.: Resilence and stability of ecological systems. *Annual Review of Ecology and Systematics,* vol. 4, pp. 1–23, 1973.

Holmes, R.: *The Age of Wonder: How the romantic generation discovered the beauty and terror of science.* Harper Collins, London, 2008.

Hoogerbrugge, I., L. O. Fresco: *Homegarden Systems: Agricultural characteristics and challenges.* International Institute for Environment and Development, London, 1993.

Hoogland, C. T.: Feed Them Facts: Transparency of meat and fish production as a determinant of sustainability in food choices. Dissertation, VU University Amsterdam, Amsterdam, December 2006.

Hopkins, P. D.: Protecting God from Science and Technology: How religious criticisms of biotechnologies backfire. *Zygon,* vol. 37, pp. 317–344, 2003.

Hourani, A.: *A History of the Arab Peoples.* Faber and Faber, London, 1991.

Hrdy, S.: *Mothers and Others: The evolutionary origins of mutual understanding.* Harvard University Press, Cambridge, Massachusetts, 2009.

Huaman, Z., D. M. Spooner: Reclassification of landrace populations of cultivated potatoes (*Solanum* sect. Petota). *American Journal of Botany,* vol. 89, pp. 947–965, 2002.

Hudson, R.: Region and place: Rethinking regional development in the context of global environmental change. *Progress in Human Geography,* vol. 31, 6, pp. 827–836, 2007.

Huis, A. van: Potential of insects as food and feed in assuring food security. *Annual Review of Entomology* 58, pp. 563–583, 2013.

Huis, A. van, H. van Gurp, M. Dicke: *The Insect Cookbook. Food for a sustainable planet.* Columbia University Press, New York, 2014.

Hurvitz, A.: The historical quest for "ancient Israël" and the linguistic evidence of the Hebrew Bible: Some methodological observations. *Vetus Testamentum,* vol. 47, pp. 301–315, 1997.

Hyman, A.: A Note on Maimonides' Classification of Law. Koninklijke Brill, Leiden, 1977. *Proceedings of the American Academy for Jewish Research,* vol. 46/47 (Jubilee volume), pp. 323–343, 1978/1979.

IFAD (International Fund for Agricultural Development): *Enabling Poor Rural People to Overcome Poverty. Rural Poverty Report: New realities, new challenges: new opportunities for tomorrow's generation.* Rome, 2011.

IFPRI (International Food Policy Research Insititute): 2011 *Global Food Policy Report.* Washington, DC, 2012.

IFPRI (International Food Policy Research Insititute), Welthungerhilife, Concern Worldwide: 2011 *Global Hunger Index. The challenge of hunger: Taming price spikes and excessive food price volatility.* Washington, DC, 2011.

Impelluso, L.: *La natura e i suoi simboli. Piante, fiori e animali.* Mondadori Electa, Milan, 2003.

Ingram, J., P. Ericksen, D. Liverman: *Food Security and Global Environmental Change.* Earthscan, London and Washington, DC, 2010.

INRA-CIRAD (Institut National de Recherche Agronomique–Centre Internationale de la Recherche Agronomique pour le Développement): Agrimonde, Scenarios and Challenges for Feeding the World in 2050. Summary report. Paris, 2009.

Inter Academic Council: *Realizing the Promise and Potential of African Agriculture.* Inter Academic Council/Royal Netherlands Academy of Arts and Sciences, Amsterdam, 2004.

Jacob, H. E.: *Zes duizend jaren brood: De geschiedenis van ons dagelijks brood van de Egyptenaren tot in de twintigste eeuw.* W. De Haan, Utrecht, 1955.

Jacobs, Jr., D. R., L. Marquart, J. Slavin, L. H. Kushi: Wholegrain intake and cancer: An expanded review and meta analysis, *Nutrition and Cancer,* vol. 30, 2, pp. 85–96, 1998.

Jain, P.: *Dharma and Ecology of Hindu Communities: Sustenance and sustainability.* Ashgate New Critical Thinking in Religion, Theology, and Biblical Studies. Ashgate, London, 2011.

James, C.: Global Status of Commercialized Biotech/GM Crops, 2008. *ISAAA Brief* 39. International Service for the Acquisition of Agri-biotech Applications, Ithaca, New York, 2008.

———: Global Status of Commercialized Biotech/GM Crops, 2009. *ISAAA Brief* 41. International Service for the Acquisition of Agri-biotech Applications, Ithaca, New York, 2009.

———: Global Status of Commercialized Biotech/GM Crops, 2012. *ISAAA Brief* 42. International Service for the Acquisition of Agri-biotech Applications, Ithaca, New York, 2012.

Jansen, D. M., C.P.J. Burger, P.M.F. Quist-Wessel, B. Rutgers: *Responses of the EU Feed and Livestock System to Shocks in Trade and Production.* Wageningen University, Plant Research International, Wageningen, 2010.

Jansma, J. E., A.J.G. Dekking, G. Mighels, A. J. de Buck, M.N.A. Ruijs, P. J. Galama, A. J. Visser: *Stadslandbouw in Almere: Van toekomstbeelden naar het ontwerp.* Agromere, praktijkonderzoek Plant & Omgeving B.V. Sector Akkerbouw, Groene ruimte en Vollegrondsgroenten, Wageningen, 2010.

Jepson, P. C.: Challenges to the design and implementation of effective monitoring for GM crop impacts: Lessons from conventional agriculture. Paper for the Expert Consultation *GMOs in Crop Production and Their Effects on the Environment: Methodologies for Monitoring and the Way Ahead.* Food and Agriculture Organization of the United Nations, Rome, 2005.

Jones, V.: Review: How the Internet is being used to hijack medical science for fear and profit. *Scientific American* Blog Network, February 23, 2011.

Jonge, B. de: Plants, Genes and Justice: An inquiry into fair & equitable benefit-sharing. Dissertation, Wageningen University, Wageningen, 2009.

Judt, T.: *The Memory Chalet.* Penguin, New York, 2010.

Juniper, B. E., D. J. Mabberley: *The Story of the Apple.* Timber Press, London, 2006.

Kahneman, D., E. Diener, N. Schwarz: *Well-Being: The foundations of hedonic psychology: Scientific perspectives on enjoyment and suffering.* Russell Sage, New York, 1999.

Kaplan, S. L.: Bread, politics and political economy in the reign of Louis XV. *Persee Revues scientifiques,* vol. 35, pp. 1290–1296, 1980.

————: *Le Retour du bon pain: Une histoire contemporaine du pain, de ses techniques, et de ses hommes.* Perrin, Paris, 2002.

Kaplan, S. L., M. C. Fabiani-Kaplan: *Cherchez le pain: Guide des Meilleures Boulangeries de Paris.* Plon, Paris, 2004.

Karlen, D. L., G. E. Varvel, D. G. Bullock, R. M. Cruse: Crop rotations for the 21st century. *Advances in Agronomy,* vol. 53, pp. 1–45, 1994.

————: In Praise of Nutrients. Farewell address upon retiring as professor of nutrition, VU University Amsterdam, Amsterdam, January 28, 2011.

Kato, M.S.A., O. R. Kato, M. Denich, P.L.G. Vlek: Fire-free alternatives to slash-and-burn for shifting cultivation in the eastern Amazon region: The role of fertilizers. *Field Crops Research,* vol. 62, 2–3, pp. 225–237, 1999.

Kauwenbergh, S. J. van: *World Phosphate Rock Reserves and Resources.* International Fertilizer Development Center, Muscle Shoals, Alabama, 2010.

Kessler, D. A.: *The End of Overeating: Taking control of the insatiable American appetite.* Rodale, New York, 2009.

Kipury, N.: *Oral Literature of the Maasai.* Heinemann Educational Books, Nairobi, 1983.

Kiritani, K.: Predicting impacts of global warming on population dynamics and distribution of arthropods in Japan. *Population Ecology,* vol. 48, pp. 5–12, 2006.

Konstantinova, I., U. Vitiello: *Consigli e istruzioni del giardiniere di corte di Caterina la Grande.* Sellerio Editore, Palermo, Italy, 2003.

Kramer, K. J., S. Nonhebel, H. C. Wilting: Greenhouse gas emission related to Dutch food consumption. *Energy Policy,* vol. 27, pp. 203–216, 1999.

Krech, S., J. C. McNeill, C. Merchant: *Encyclopedia of World Environmental History*. Routledge, New York, 2004.

Kuijt, I., B. Finlayson: Evidence for food storage and predomestication granaries 11,000 years ago in the Jordan Valley. *Proceedings of the National Academy of Sciences of the USA*, vol. 106, 27, pp. 10966–10970, 2009.

Kurlansky, M.: *Edible Stories*. Penguin, New York, 2010.

Lair, A. V.: Les arts de la table: nourriture et classes sociales dans la littérature Française du dix-neuvième siècle. Dissertation, Ohio State University, Columbus, Ohio, 2003.

Lal, R.: Soil carbon sequestration to mitigate climate change. *Geoderma*, vol. 123, pp. 1–22, 2004.

Lal, R., B. A. Stewart: World soil resources and food security. In *Advances in Soil Science*. CRC Press and Taylor & Francis Group, New York, 2011.

Lambin, E. F., P. Meyfroidt: Global land use change, economic globalization, and the looming land scarcity. *Proceedings of the National Academy of Sciences of the USA*, vol. 108, 9, pp. 3465–3472, 2011.

Lander, N.: Fast Food Assignation. Restaurant insider: Nicholas Lander meets Steve Easterbrook, McDonald's UK chief executive. *The Financial Times*, p. 4, March 28, 2009.

Larson, G., U. Albarella, K. Dobney, P. Rowley-Conwy, J. Schibler, A. Tresset, J.-D. Vigne, C. J. Edwards, A. Schlumbaum, A. Dinu, A. Bălăçescu, G. Dolman, A. Tagliacozzo, N. Manaseryan, P. Miracle, L. Van Wijngaarden-Bakker, M. Masseti, D. G. Bradley, A. Cooper: Ancient DNA, pig domestication, and the spread of the Neolithic into Europe. *Proceedings of the National Academy of Sciences of the USA*, vol. 104, 39, pp. 15276–15281, 2007.

Lebesco, K., P. Naccarato: *Edible Ideologies: Representing food and meaning*. State University of New York Press, New York, 2008.

Lee, R. B.: *The !Kung San: Men, women and work in a foraging society*. Cambridge University Press, Cambridge, 1979.

Leeming, D. A.: *Creation Myths of the World: An encyclopedia*, vol. 1. ABC-CLIO, Santa Barbara, California, 2010.

Leonard, W. R.: Food for thought. Dietary change was a driving force in human evolution. *Scientific American*, pp. 106–115, June 2002.

Levi, P.: *Il sistema periódico*. Torino, Italy, 1975.

Levin, D.: Interview with Liao Yibai: The fantasies of a Cold War child. *International Herald Tribune*, New York, May 8, 2009.

Lévi-Strauss, C.: *Le cru et le cuit*. Plon, Paris, 1964.

Lev-Yadun, S., S. Abbo, J. Doebley: Wheat, rye, and barley on the cob? *Nature Biotechnology*, vol. 20, pp. 337–338, 2002.

Lewis, M.: *Boomerang: The biggest bust*. Penguin, London, 2012.

Lewis, M., J. M. Haviland: *Handbook of Emotions*, second edition. Guilford, New York, 2000.

Li, Y.: Obesitas bij kinderen in China: Prevalentie, determinanten en gezondheid. Dissertation, Wageningen University, Wageningen, December 2007.

Liebig, J. von: *Chemistry in Its Application to Agriculture and Physiology*, third edition. John Owen, Cambridge, 1842.

Lindhout, P., D. Meijer, T. Schotte, R.C.B. Hutten, R.C.F. Visser, H. J. van Eck: Towards F1 hybrid seed potato breeding. *Potato Research,* vol. 54, pp. 301–312, 2011.

Liu, H., L. Xu, H. Cui: Holocene history of desertification along the woodland-steppe border in northern China. *Quaternary Research,* vol. 57, 2, pp. 259–270, 2002.

Lobell, D. B., W. Schlenker, J. Costa-Roberts: Climate trends and global crop production since 1980. *Science,* vol. 333, pp. 616–620, 2011.

Lovelock, J.: *The Ages of Gaia: A biography of our living Earth.* Oxford University Press, Oxford, 1988.

Lubbers, R., W. van Genugten, T. Lambooy: *Inspiration for Global Governance: The Universal Declaration of Human Rights and the Earth Charter.* Robert Lückers, Wolters Kluwer, Alphen aan den Rijn, the Netherlands, 2008.

Lyons, M., U. Lyons (trans.): *The Arabian Nights: Tales of 1,001 Nights,* 3 vols. Penguin Classics, London, 2010.

MacKay, D.J.C.: *Sustainable Energy—Without the Hot Air.* UIT Cambridge, 2008.

Malakoff, D.: Did rumbling give rise to Rome? *ScienceNOW Daily News,* August 22, 2008.

Malthus, T.: *An Essay on the Principle of Population, as It Affects the Future Improvement of Society with Remarks on the Speculations of Mr. Godwin, M. Condorcet, and Other Writers.* J. Johnson, London, 1798.

Mann, C. C.: *1493: Uncovering the New World Columbus Created.* Alfred A. Knopf, New York, 2011.

Mansholt, S. L., J. Delaunay: *La Crise.* Stock, Eugene, Oregon, 1974.

Manu of Laws or "Manava Dharma Shastra" Ancient Hindu Code of Conduct for Domestic, Social, and Religious Life (author anonymous; translated by Wendy Doniger). Penguin Classics, New York, 1991.

Marris, E.: Ragamuffin earth. A small group of ecologists is looking beyond the pristine to study the scrubby, feral and untended. Emma Marris learns to appreciate "novel ecosystems." *Nature,* vol. 460, pp. 450–453, 2009.

McClintock, H. N.: Why farm the city? Theorizing urban agriculture through a lens of metabolic rift. *Urban Studies and Planning Faculty Publications and Presentations.* Paper 91. PDXScholar, Portland State University Library, 2010.

McDonough, W., M. Braungart: *Cradle to Cradle: Remaking the way we make things.* North Point Press, New York, 2002.

McEvedy, C., R. Jones: *Atlas of World Population History.* Viking, London, 1978.

McGee, H.: *On Food and Cooking: The science and lore of the kitchen,* updated edition. Scribner, New York, 2004.

McKibben, B.: *Deep Economy: The wealth of communities and the durable future.* Times Books, New York, 2007.

McManus, P., G. Haughton: Planning with ecological footprints: A sympathetic critique of theory and practice. *Environment and Urbanization,* vol. 18, pp. 113–127, 2006.

Meadows, D., L. Meadows, J. Randers, W. Behrens III: *The Limits to Growth.* New York: Universe Books, 1972.

Meindertsma, C.: *PIG05049*. Flocks Uitgeverij, the Netherlands, 2007.

Melanson, K. J., L. Zukley, J. Lowndes, V. Nguyen, T. J. Angelopoulos, J. M. Rippe: Effects of high-fructose corn syrup and sucrose consumption on circulating glucose, insulin, leptin, and ghrelin and on appetite in normal-weight women. *Nutrition*, vol. 23, 2, pp. 103–112, 2007.

Mennell, S.: *All Manners of Food: Eating and taste in England and France from the Middle Ages to the present*. University of Illinois Press, Champaign, 1995.

Mense, E.: *Hauptsache gesund? Subjektive Vorstellungen von Ernährung in der Kantine. Eine empirische Fallstudie*. Inaugural dissertation, Ruhr-Universität, Bochum, Germany, 2009.

Menzel, P., F. D'Alusio: *Hungry Planet: What the world eats*. Material World, Napa, California, 2005.

Merchant, C.: *Reinventing Eden: The fate of nature in Western culture*. Routledge, New York, 2004.

Meyer-Rochow, V. B.: Food taboos: Their origins and purposes. *Journal of Ethnobiology and Ethnomedicine*, vol. 5, pp. 1–39, 2009.

Millennium Ecosystem Assessment: *Living Beyond Our Means: Natural assets and human well-being. Statement from the board*. 2005.

———: *General Synthesis Report: Ecosystems and human well-being*. Island Press, Washington, DC, 2005.

———: *Ecosystems and well-being: Wetlands and water. Synthesis*. World Resources Institute, Washington, DC, 2005.

Millstone, E., T. Lang: *The Atlas of Food: Who eats what, where, and why*. University of California Press, Berkeley, 2008.

Milton, G.: *Nathaniel's Nutmeg: How one man's courage changed the course of history*. Hodder and Stoughton, London, 1999.

Milton, J.: *Paradise Lost*, third edition. S. Simmons, London, 1678.

———: *Paradise Regained*, first edition. J. Storky, London, 1671.

Ministerie van Economische Zaken, Landbouw en Innovatie: *The Vulnerability of the European Agriculture and Food System for Calamities and Geopolitics: A stress test*. Platform Landbouw, Innovatie en Samenleving, June 2011.

Ministerie van Landbouw, Natuur en Voedsel: *Biodiversiteit werkt voor natuur voor mensen voor altijd; beleidsprogramma biodiversiteit 2008–2011*. The Hague, 2008.

———: GMOs, European Agriculture and Food Production. Conference Report. The Hague, November 25–26, 2009.

Mintz, S. W.: *Sweetness and Power: The place of sugar in modern history*. Penguin, London, 1986.

Mintz, S. W., C. M. Du Bois: The anthropology of food and eating. *Annual Review of Anthropology*, vol. 31, pp. 99–119, 2002.

Mohammad, A., A. Munir, H. Rehman: *Fifty Years of Indian Agriculture*. Ashok Kumar Mittal, New Delhi, India, 2007.

Montanari, M.: *Honger en Overvloed*. Agon, Amsterdam, 1994.

Morris, I.: *Why the West Rules—For Now: The patterns of history, and what they reveal about the future*. Farrar, Straus and Giroux, New York, 2010.

Morris, M. L., D. Byerlee: Narrowing the wheat gap in Sub-Saharan Africa: A review of consumption and production issues. *Economic Development and Cultural Change*, vol. 41, 4, pp. 737–761, 1993.

Motz, G.: *Hamburger America: A state-by-state guide to 100 great burger joints. One man's cross-country odyssey to find the best burgers in the nation*. Running Press, Philadelphia and London, 2008.

Mulokozi, G., E. Hedrén, U. Svanberg: In vitro accessibility and intake of beta-carotene from cooked green leafy vegetables and their estimated contribution to vitamin A requirements. *Plant Foods for Human Nutrition* (formerly *Qualitas Plantarum*), vol. 59, 1, pp. 1–9, 2004.

Musselman, L. J.: *Figs, Dates, Laurel, Myrrh: Plants of the Bible and the Quran*. Timber Press, Portland, Oregon, 2011.

Nabhan, G. P.: *Where Our Food Comes From: Retracing Nikolay Vavilov's quest to end famine*. Island Press, Washington, DC, 2009.

Nath, P., P. B. Gaddagimath, O. P. Dutta, P. Nath: *Food Security and Vegetables: A global perspective*. Agricultural Science Foundation, Bangalore, India, 2004.

National Institute for Public Health and Environment, Ministry of Health, Welfare and Sport: *Dutch National Food Consumption Survey 2007–2010: Diet of children and adults aged 7 to 69 years*. National Institute for Public Health and the Environment, Bilthoven, the Netherlands, 2011.

Neruda, P.: *The Book of Questions* (translated by William O'Daly). Copper Canyon Press, Port Townsend, Washington, 1991.

———: *The Poetry of Pablo Neruda*. Farrar, Straus and Giroux, New York, 2003.

Nestlé, M.: *Safe Food: Bacteria, biotechnology, and bioterrorism*. University of California Press, Berkeley, 2003.

———: *What to Eat: An aisle-by-aisle guide to savvy food choices and good eating*. North Point Press, New York, 2006.

———: *Food Politics: How the food industry influences nutrition and health*. Second edition. University of California Press, Berkeley, 2007.

Netherlands Platform Rio+20: *Making Rio Work: 10 priorities for sustainable development & 10 best practices*. The Hague, 2012.

Newman, W. R.: *Promethean Ambitions: Alchemy and the quest to perfect nature*. University of Chicago Press, 2004.

Nugent, R.: *Bringing Agriculture to the Table: How agriculture and food can play a role in preventing chronic disease*. Chicago Council on Global Affairs, 2011.

OECD (Organisation for Economic Co-operation and Development): *OECD Environmental Outlook to 2050: The consequences of inaction*. Paris, 2012.

Okakura, K.: *The Book of Tea*. Alameda Press, Albuquerque, New Mexico, 2004.

Olivelle, J. P.: Food in India: A review essay. *Journal of Indian Philosophy*, vol. 23, pp. 367–380, 1995.

———: Food for Thought: Dietary regulations and social organization in ancient India. Gonda Lecture. Royal Netherlands Academy of Arts and Sciences, Amsterdam, 2001.

———: On meat-eaters and grass-eaters: An exploration of human nature in Kathâ and Dharma literature. In S. J. Rosen (ed.), *Holy War: Violence and the Bhagavadgîtâ*, pp. 99–116. Deepak Publishing, Hampton, Virginia, 2002.

Ovid, P.: *Artis Amatoria, Artis Amatoriae Libri Tres: Remediorum Amoris Liber, Medicaminum Faciei Fragmentum*. Nabu Press, Charleston, South Carolina, 2010.

Oxfam: Grow Campaign 2011: Global opinion research—Final Topline Report. Globescan, London, 2011.

Ozersky, J.: *The Hamburger: A history*. Yale University Press, New Haven, Connecticut, and London, 2008.

Paillard, S., S. Treyer, B. Dorin (coordinators): *Agrimonde: Scenarios and challenges for Feeding the World in 2050*. Paris, Éditions Quae, 2011.

Parker, J.: The 9 billion-people question: A special report on feeding the world. *The Economist*, February 24, 2011.

Parker-Pope, T.: How the food makers captured our brains. *New York Times*, p. D1, June 23, 2009.

Pearce, F.: *Confessions of an Eco Sinner: Travels to where my stuff comes from*. Transworld Publishers, London, 2008.

Pederson, R. M., A. Robertson: Food policies are essential for healthy cities. *Urban Agriculture Magazine*, pp. 9–11, March, 2001.

Persley, G. J.: *New Genetics, Food and Agriculture: Scientific discoveries–societal dilemmas*. International Council for Science, Paris, 2003.

Petrini, C.: *Terra Madre: Forging a new global network of sustainable food communities*. Chelsea Green Publishing, White River Junction, Vermont, 2010.

Pilcher, J. M.: *Food in World History*. Routledge, New York, 2006.

Pinstrup-Andersen, P.: Food security: Definition and measurement. *Food Security*, vol. 1, 1, pp. 5–7, 2009.

———: *The African Food System and Its Interaction with Human Health and Nutrition*. Cornell University Press, Ithaca, New York, and London, 2010.

Pistorius, R.: *Scientists, Plants and Politics: A history of the plant genetic resources movement*. International Plant Genetic Resources Institute, Rome, 1997.

———: *Rethinking Global Biodiversity Strategies: Exploring structural changes in production and consumption to reduce biodiversity loss. A contribution to the project on The Economics and Biodiversity (TEEB)*. Bilthoven, the Netherlands, 2010.

Plantum: Regulatory and legal affairs. Smarter rules for safer food. Available at www.plantum.nl.

Pleij, H.: *Dreaming of Cockaigne: Medieval fantasies of the perfect life* (translated by Diane Webb). Columbia University Press, New York, 2001.

Plinius Secundus, C.: *Naturalis Histori*. Athenaeum-Polak & Van Gennep, Amsterdam, 2004.

Ploeg, J. D. van der: *The New Peasantries: Struggles for autonomy and sustainability in an era of empire and globalisation*. Earthscan, London, 2010.

Plotz, D.: *Good Book*. HarperCollins, New York, 2009.

Polinger Foster, K.: Gardens of Eden: Flora and fauna in the ancient Near East. In *Transformations of Middle Eastern Natural Environments: Legacies and lessons*, pp. 320–329. Yale University, New Haven, Connecticut, 1998.

Pollan, M.: *The Omnivore's Dilemma: A natural history of four meals*. Penguin Press, New York, 2007.

———: *In Defense of Food: An eater's manifesto*. Penguin Press, New York, 2008.

Pollan, M.: Farmer in Chief. In *The Food Issue. New York Times,* October 12, 2008.

Polman, P.: Sustainability and Security of the Food Value Chain. Rabobank Duisenberg Lecture, Washington, DC, October 10, 2010.

Poole, G.: *Reel Meals, Set Meals: Food in film and theatre.* Currency Press, Sydney, 1999.

Popkin, B.: Dynamics of the global nutrition transition. In Proceedings of the 10th International Congress on Obesity, Sydney, September 3–8, 2006.

Popovski, V., K. C. Mundy: Defining climate-change victims. *Sustainability Science,* vol. 7, 1, pp. 5–16, 2012.

Potrykus, I.: Golden rice and other biofortified food crops for developing countries challenges and potential. Bertebos Conference, Falkenberg, Sweden, September 7–9. Royal Swedish Academy of Agriculture and Forestry, Stockholm, 2009.

Pretty, J. N., A. S. Ball, T. Lang, J.I.L. Morison: Farm costs and food miles: An assessment of the full cost of the UK weekly food basket. *Food Policy,* vol. 30, pp. 1–19, 2005.

Prince of Wales: On the Future of Food. Keynote speech to the Future of Food Conference at Georgetown University, Washington, DC, May 4, 2011. Rodale, New York, 2012.

Pringle, P.: *The Murder of Nikolai Vavilov: The story of Stalin's persecution of one of the great scientists of the twentieth century.* Simon & Schuster, New York, 2008.

Proust, M.: *À la recherche du temps perdu.* Gallimard, Paris, 2002.

Rabbinge, R.: Perspectives in Hindsight. Farewell address on departure as professor of sustainable development and food security. Wageningen University, Wageningen, November 24, 2011.

Rabobank Group: *Sustainability and Security of the Global Food Supply Chain.* Utrecht, 2010.

Raisson, V.: *2030 Atlas, les futurs du monde: Pour la première fois un atlas cartographie le futur.* Robert Laffont, Paris, 2010.

Randers, J.: *2052, A Global Forecast for the Next Forty Years.* Club of Rome, Winterthur, Switzerland, 2012.

Rees, W.: What's blocking sustainability? Human nature, cognition, and denial. *Sustainability: Science, Practice & Policy,* vol. 6, 2, pp. 13–25, 2010.

Regeer, B., S. Mager, Y. van Oorsouw: *Licence to Grow: Innovating sustainable development by connecting values.* VU University Amsterdam, Amsterdam, 2011.

Reijnders, L., S. Soret: Quantification of the environmental impact of different dietary protein choices. *American Journal of Clinical Nutrition,* vol. 78, 3, pp. 664S–668S, 2003.

Reynolds, R.: *On Guerrilla Gardening: A handbook for gardening without boundaries.* Bloomsbury Publishing, London, 2008.

Rifkin, J.: Leading the Way to the Third Industrial Revolution: A new energy agenda for the European Union in the 21st century—The next phase of European integration. TEDx Talk, Bethesda, Maryland, 2005.

Rijksinstituut voor Volksgezondheid en Milieu: *Dutch National Food Consumption Survey 2007–2010; Diets of children and adults aged 7 to 69 years.* Bilthoven, the Netherlands, 2011.

Rockström, J., W. Steffen, K. Noone, Å. Persson, F. S. Chapin III, E. Lambin, T. M. Lenton, M. Scheffer, C. Folke, H. Schellnhuber, B. Nykvist, C. A. De Wit, T. Hughes, S. van der Leeuw, H. Rodhe, S. Sörlin, P. K. Snyder, R. Costanza, U. Svedin, M. Falkenmark, L. Karlberg, R. W. Corell, V. J. Fabry, J. Hansen, B. Walker, D. Liverman, K. Richardson, P. Crutzen, J. Foley: Planetary boundaries: Exploring the safe operating space for humanity. *Ecology and Society*, vol. 14, 2, article 32, 2009.

Roebroeks, W., P. Villa: On the earliest evidence for habitual use of fire in Europe. *Proceedings of the National Academy of Sciences of the USA*, vol. 108, 13, pp. 5209–5214, 2011.

Rosegrant, M. W., N. Leach, R. V. Gerpacio: Alternative futures for world cereal and meat consumption: Meat or wheat for the next millennium? *Proceedings of the Nutrition Society*, vol. 58, pp. 219–234, 1999.

Rosenblum, M.: *Olives: The life and lore of a noble fruit*. North Point Press, New York, 1996.

Royal Swedish Academy of Agriculture and Forestry in cooperation with the Bertebo Foundation: *Golden Rice and Other Biofortified Food Crops for Developing Countries—Challenges and potential*. Ägerups Grafiska ab, Eskilstuna, Sweden, 2009.

Rozin, P.: *Psychobiological Perspectives on Food Preferences and Avoidances: Food and evolution*. Temple University Press, Philadelphia, Pennsylvania, 1987.

Rozin, P., S. Imada, J. Haidt: The CAD triad hypothesis: A mapping between three moral emotions (contempt, anger, disgust) and three moral codes (community, autonomy, divinity). *Journal of Personality and Social Psychology*, vol. 76, pp. 574–586, 1999.

Ruddiman, W. F., Z. Guo, X. Zhou, H. Wu, Y. Yu: Early rice farming and anomalous methane trends. *Quaternary Science Reviews*, vol. 27, 13–14, pp. 1291–1295, 2008.

Rudolph, H., F. Hillmann: How Turkish is the döner kebab? Turks in Berlin's food sector. *Scottish Geographical Magazine*, vol. 114, 3, pp. 138–147, 1998.

Rugebregt, P.: *Good Red Super Green: Slim bouwen voor beter groen*. Bouwfonds Ontwikkeling and NIROV, Hoevelaken, the Netherlands, 2009.

Rustomji, N.: *The Garden and the Fire: Heaven and Hell in Islamic culture*. Columbia University Press, New York, 2008.

Rybicki, E. P.: Plant-made vaccines for humans and animals. *Plant Biotechnology Journal*, special issue: Success Stories in Molecular Farming, vol. 8, 5, pp. 620–637, 2010.

Sabban, F.: Cuisine à la cour de l'empereur de Chine au xive siècle: les aspects culinaires du Yinshan zhengyao de Hu Sihui. *Médiévales* vol. 5, pp. 32–56, 1983.

Sabbe, S.: Consumer Perception and Behaviour towards Tropical Fruits in Belgium. Doctoral thesis, University of Ghent, Ghent, Belgium, 2009.

Safran Foer, J.: *Dieren eten*. Ambo/Manteau, Antwerp, Belgium, 2009.

Sasu, M. A., M. J. Ferrari, D. Du, J. A. Winsor, A. G. Stephenson: Indirect costs of a nontarget pathogen mitigate the direct benefits of a virus-resistant transgene in wild *Cucurbita*. *Proceedings of the National Academy of Sciences of the USA*, vol. 106, 45, pp. 19067–19071, 2009.

Satin, M.: *Food Alert. The ultimate sourcebook for food safety*. Facts on File, New York, 1999.

Sautoy, M. du: *Finding Moonshine: Mathematicians, Monsters and the Mysteries of Symmetry*. Harper Perennial, London, 2009.

Schama, S.: *The Embarrassment of Riches: An interpretation of Dutch culture in the Golden Age*. Alfred A. Knopf, New York, 1987.

————: *Landscape and Memory*. Alfred A. Knopf, New York, 1995.

Schlosser, E.: *Fast Food Nation: What the all-American meal is doing to the world*. Penguin Books, London, 2002.

Schouwenberg, L., M. Vogelzang: *Eat Love: Food concepts by eating-designer Marije Vogelzang*. BIS Publishers, Amsterdam, 2009.

Schwenke, K. D.: *Justus von Liebig und die Ernährungswissenschaft: Wissenschaftsgeschichtliche Betrachtungen zu seiner Tier-Chemie*, vol. 1. Übersicht, Teltow, Germany, 2003.

Senut, B., M. Pickford, L. Ségalen: Neogene desertification of Africa. *Comptes Rendus Geoscience*, vol. 341, 8–9, pp. 591–602, 2009.

Serventi, S., F. Sabban: *La Pasta; Storia e cultura di un cibo universale*. Editori Laterza, Rome, 2000.

Seufert, V., N. Ramankutty, J. A. Foley: Comparing the yields of organic and conventional agriculture. *Nature*, vol. 485, pp. 229–232, 2012.

Shafak, E.: *De Bastaard Van Istanbul*. Uitgeverij De Geus, Breda, the Netherlands, 2007.

Shelley, M.: *Frankenstein or The Modern Prometheus*. Tom Doherty Associates, New York, 1989.

Sherratt, A.: The secondary exploitation of animals in the Old World. *World Archaeology*, vol. 15, pp. 90–104, 1983.

Simmonds, N. W., J. Smartt: *Principles of Crop Improvement*. Longman Higher Education, London, 1979.

Simmons, I. G.: *Changing the Face of the Earth: Culture, environment, history*. Basil Blackwell, Oxford, 1989.

Simone, R.: *Il Mostro Mite, Perché l'Occidente non va a sinistra*. Gli Elefanti Saggi, Milan, 2008.

Singer, P.: *Animal Liberation*. HarperCollins, New York, 2002.

Singer, P., J. Mason: *The Ethics of What We Eat: Why our food choices matter*. Rodale, New York, and Random House, London, 2006.

Sitskoorn, M.: *Passies van het brein: Waarom zondigen zo verleidelijk is*. Bert Bakker, Amsterdam, 2010.

Slicher van Bath, B. H.: *De agrarische geschiedenis van West-Europa (500–1850)*. Het Spectrum, Utrecht and Antwerp, 1976.

Slow Food: *Formaggi d'Italia: Guida alla scoperta e alla conoscenza*. Agricola Editore, Bra, Italy, 1999.

Smaal, A. C.: Crying Cockles and Mussels … naar een schelpdiercultuur voor mens en natuur. Inaugural speech, Wageningen University, Wageningen, January 17, 2008.

Smil, V.: Nitrogen in crop production: An account of global flows. *Global Biogeochemical Cycles*, vol. 13, 2, pp. 647–662, 1999.

————: Nitrogen and food production: Proteins for human diets. *Ambio: A Journal of Human Environment*, vol. 31, 2, pp. 126–131, 2002.

————: Worldwide transformation of diets, burdens of meat production and opportunities for novel food proteins. *Enzyme and Microbial Technology*, vol. 30, 3, pp. 305–311, 2002.

Snyder, J.: Jan van Eyck and Adam's apple. *Art Bulletin*, vol. 58, 4, p. 511, December 1976.

Soler, J.: The dietary prohibitions of the Hebrews. *New York Review of Books*, pp. 14–17, June 14, 1979.

Spary, E., P. White: Food of paradise: Tahitian breadfruit and the autocritique of European consumption. *Endeavour*, vol. 28, 2, pp. 75–80, 2004.

Spielman, D. J., R. Pandya-Lorch: *Highlights from Millions Fed: Proven successes in agricultural development*. International Food Policy Research Institute, Washington, DC, 2009.

Sponheimer, M., J. A. Lee-Thorp: Isotopic evidence for the diet of an early hominid, *Australopithecus africanus*. *Science*, vol. 283, pp. 368–370, 1999.

Squier, S. M.: *Poultry Science, Chicken Culture: A partial alphabet*. Rutgers University Press, New Brunswick, New Jersey, 2011.

Stearns, S.: Biodiversity as natural capital. In *91st Dies Natalis: Darwin's Legacy: Biodiversity as natural capital*. Wageningen University, Wageningen, 2009.

Steekelenburg, M. van, H. C. van Latesteijn: *Metropolitane landbouw: Nieuwe ruimte voor de toekomst*. TransForum, Zoetermeer, the Netherlands, 2011.

Steel, C.: *Hungry City: How food shapes our lives*. Chatto and Windus, London, 2008.

Steele, T. E.: A unique Hominin Menu Dated to 1.95 Million Years Ago. Department of Antropology, University of California, Davis, 2010.

Steinbeck, J.: *Travels with Charley*. Pan Books, London, 1962.

Steinfeld, H., H. A. Mooney, F. Schneider, L. E. Neville: *Livestock in a Changing Landscape: Drivers, consequences, and responses*, vol. 1. Island Press, Washington, DC, 2010.

Summerhayes G. R., M. Leavesley, A. Fairbaim, H. Mandui, J. Field, A. Ford, R. Fullagar: Human adaptation and plant use in highland New Guinea 49,000 to 44,000 years ago. *Science*, vol. 330, pp. 78–81, 2010.

Swift, G., J. M. Coetzee, J. Lanchester: *Food: The vital stuff*. Granta, London, 1995.

Sylwan, P.: Return to Eden: Future paths to sustainable, natural resources management. Ake Barklund, Sweden. *Tidskrift Kungl. Skogs-Och Lantbruksakademiens*, vol. 149, 4, 2009.

TEEB (The Economics of Ecosystems and Biodiversity for National and International Policy Makers): *TEEB for Policy Makers. Summary: Responding to the value of nature*. Geneva, 2009.

Tennekes, H.: *The Systemic Insecticides: A disaster in the making*. Experimental Toxicology Services, Zutphen, the Netherlands, 2010.

Teubner, C.: *The Vegetable Bible*. Whitecap Books, North Vancouver, Canada, 2002.

Thaler, R. H., C. R. Sunstein: Libertarian paternalism: Behavioral economics, public policy and paternalism. *American Economic Review*, vol. 93, no. 2, pp. 175–179, 2003.

Thurow, R., S. Kilman: *Enough: Why the world's poorest starve in an age of plenty*. Public Affairs, New York, 2009.

Tilman, D., P. B. Reich, J.M.H. Knops: Diversity and stability in plant communities. *Nature*, vol. 441, pp. 629–632, 2006.

Tilson, J.: *A Tale of 12 Kitchens: Family cooking in four countries*. Artisan/Workman Publishing, New York, 2006.

Timmer, C. P.: *Agriculture and Pro-Poor Growth: An Asian perspective*. Center for Global Development, Washington, DC, 2005.

Tolstoj, L.: *Mijn Biecht*, Bijleveld, Utrecht, 2009.

Toussaint-Samat, M.: *History of Food*. Blackwell, Cambridge, 1994.

Trichopolon, A., T. Costabon, C. Bamia, D. Trichopoulos: Adherence to a Mediterranean diet and survival in a Greek population. *New England Journal of Medicine*, vol. 348, 26, pp. 2599–2608, 2003.

Turner, B. L., W. C. Clark, R. W. Kates: *The Great Transformation: The Earth as transformed by human action: Global and regional changes in the biosphere over the past 300 years*. Cambridge University Press, Cambridge, 1990.

Turney, C.S.M., H. Brown: Catastrophic early Holocene sea level rise, human migration and the Neolithic transition in Europe. *Quaternary Science Reviews*, vol. 26, 17–18, pp. 2036–2041, 2007.

UN Administrative Committee on Coordination/Subcommittee on Nutrition: Report of the 25th Session of the United Nations Sub-Committee on Nutrition, Oslo, Norway. ACC/SCN Symposium Report Nutrition Policy Paper 17. November. New York, United Nations, 1998.

UN Population Division: *World Population Prospects, the 2010 Revision*. New York, 2011.
———: *World Urbanization Prospects, the 2011 Revision*. New York, 2011.

U.S. Department of Agriculture, U.S. Department of Health and Human Services: *Dietary Guidelines for Americans 2010*. Washington, DC, 2010.

UTZ Certified Annual Report 2011. UTZ Certified Communications, the Netherlands, 2011.

Varisco, D. M.: Medieval agriculture and Islamic science. The almanac of a Yemeni sultan. Review by Lucie Bolens. *Journal of the Economic and Social History of the Orient*, vol. 41, 1, pp. 121–123, 1998.

Verhaegen, M., P. F. Puech: Hominid lifestyle and diet reconsidered: Paleo-environmental and comparative data. *Human Evolution*, vol. 15, 3–4, pp. 175–186, 2000.

Vidal, J.: Sustainable bio-plastic can damage the environment, corn-based material emits climate change gas in landfill and adds to food crisis. *Guardian*, UK, April 26, 2008.

Vietmeyer, N.: *Our Daily Bread: The essential Norman Borlaug*. Bracing Books, Lorton, Virginia, 2011.

Vondel, J. van den: *Lucifer* (translated by L. C. van Noppen). Continental, New York and London, 1898.

Vos, P.: *Scheppingsverhaal*. De Harmonie, Amsterdam, 1985.

Vos, W., H. Meekes: Trends in European cultural landscape development: Perspectives for a sustainable future. *Landscape and Urban Planning*, vol. 46, pp. 3–14, 1999.

Vrielynck S., C. Belpaire, A. Stabel, J. Breine, P. Quataert: *De visbestanden in Vlaanderen anno 1840–1950: Een historische schets van de referentietoestand van onze waterlopen aan de hand van de visstand, ingevoerd in een databank en vergeleken met de actuele toestand.* Wetenschappelijke instelling van de Vlaamse Gemeenschap, Brussels, 2003.

Wageningen University: *40 Years Theory and Model at Wageningen University.* Wageningen, 2008.

———: *Food or Fuel, Dies Natalis,* Wageningen, 2008.

Wagner, R.: *The Ring of the Nibelung.* W. W. Norton and Company, New York, 1977.

Waines, D.: Cereals, bread and society: An essay on the staff of life in medieval Iraq. *Journal of the Economic and Social History of the Orient,* vol. 30, 3, pp. 255–285, 1987.

Waite, A. E.: *The Holy Kabbalah.* Dover, Mineola, New York, 2003.

Walton, J. K.: *Fish & Chips and the British Working Class 1870–1940.* Leicester University Press, London, 1992.

Wang, Y. C., S. L. Gortmaker, A. M. Sobol, K. M. Kuntz: Estimating the energy gap among US children: A counterfactual approach. *Pediatrics,* vol. 118, pp. 1721–1733, 2006.

Wansink, B.: *Mindless Eating. Why we eat more than we think.* Bantam Dell, New York, 2006.

Webster, C. C., P. N. Wilson: *Agriculture in the Tropics.* Longman, London, 1966.

Wegner, L., G. Zwart: *Who Will Feed the World?* Oxfam Research Report. Oxfam, London, 2011.

Weijden, W. van der, P. Terwan, A. Guldemond: *Farmland Birds across the World.* Lynx Ediciones, Barcelona, Spain, 2010.

Wells, S.: *Pandora's Seed: The unforeseen cost of civilization.* Random House, New York, 2010.

Werckmeister, O. K.: The Lintel fragment representing Eve from Saint-Lazare, Autun. *Journal of the Warburg and Courtauld Institutes,* vol. 35, pp.1–30, 1972.

Werd, S. van der: *Isabel en Annabel in de sneeuw: Van een gekooid bestaan naar een vrij leven.* Red een legkip. Available at www.redeenlegkip.nl.

Westerman, F.: *De Graanrepubliek.* Uitgeverij Atlas, Amsterdam, 2008.

Westhoek, H. J., R. van Oostenbrugge, A. Faber, A. G. Prins, D. P. van Vuuren: *Voedsel, biodiversiteit en klimaatverandering: Mondiale opgaven en nationaal beleid.* Plan voor de Leefomgeving, The Hague and Bilthoven, the Netherlands, 2010.

Westhoek, H., T. Rood, M. van den Berg, J. Janse, D. Nijdam, M. Reudink, E. Stehfest: *The Protein Puzzle: The consumption and production of meat, dairy and fish in the European Union.* PBL Netherlands Environmental Assessment Agency, The Hague, 2011.

Whitfield, J.: Species spellchecker fixes plant glitches. *Nature,* vol. 474, p. 263, 2011.

WHO (World Health Organization) and FAO (Food and Agriculture Organization of the United Nations): Diet, Nutrition and the Prevention of Chronic Diseases: Report of a Joint WHO/FAO Expert Consultation. *WHO Technical Report* 916. Geneva, 2002.

Wijkstrom, U. N.: Short and long-term prospects for consumption of fish. *Veterinary Research Communications,* vol. 27, supplement 1, pp. 461–468, 2003.

Wit, C. T. de: Resource use efficiency in agriculture. *Agriculture Systems,* vol. 40, pp. 125–151, 1992.

Wit, C. T. de: Resource use analysis in agriculture: A struggle for interdisciplinarity. In L. O. Fresco, L. Stroosnijder, J. Bouma, H. van Keulen (eds.), *The Future of the Land: Mobilising and integrating knowledge for land use options*, pp. 41–55. John Wiley and Sons, New York, 1994.

Wolf, M.: Determinants and role of commodity prices. Rabobank Duisenberg Lecture, Washington, DC, September 25, 2011.

Wolman, A.: Metabolism of cities. *Scientific American,* pp. 179–188, March 1965.

World Bank: *World Development Report 2008.* Washington, DC, 2008.

World Business Council for Sustainable Development: *Changing Pace: Public policy options to scale and accelerate business action towards Vision 2050.* Geneva, Switzerland, 2012.

World Economic Forum: *Realizing a New Vision for Agriculture: A roadmap for stakeholders.* Geneva, Switzerland, 2010.

———: *Realizing a New Vision for Agriculture: A roadmap for stakeholders.* Davos, Switzerland, 2011.

World Food Program: Feed the world? We are fighting a losing battle, UN admits. Huge budget deficit means millions more face starvation. Interview with A. Seager. *Guardian,* UK, February 26, 2008.

World Resource Institute: *World Resources 2005. The wealth of the poor: Managing ecosystems to fight poverty,* Washington, DC, 2005.

———: *Water Scarcity: Private investment opportunities in agricultural water use efficiency.* Rabobank International, Utrecht, 2008.

Wrangham, R.: *Catching Fire: How cooking made us human.* Profile Books, London, 2009.

Wright, C. A.: *A Mediterranean Feast: The story of the birth of the celebrated cuisines of the Mediterranean, from the merchants of Venice to the Barbary Corsairs.* William Morrow and Company, New York, 1999.

WRR (Netherlands Scientific Council for Government Policy): Ground for choices: Four perspectives for the rural areas in the European Community. Report 42. Sdu Uitgevers, The Hague, 1992.

———: Sustained risks: A lasting phenomenon. Report 44. Sdu Uitgevers, The Hague, 1994.

Young, V. R., P. L. Pellett: Plant-proteins in relation to human protein and amino-acid nutrition. *American Journal of Clinical Nutrition,* vol. 59, 5, pp. S1203–S1212, 1994.

Zia-ur, R., A. M. Salariya: The effects of hydrothermal processing on antinutrients, protein and starch digestibility of food legumes. *International Journal of Food Science and Technology,* vol. 40, 7, pp. 695–700, 2005.

Zohar, I., T. Dayan, E. Galili, E. Spanier: Fish processing during the Early Holocene: A taphonomic case study from coastal Israel. *Journal of Archaeological Science,* vol. 28, pp. 1041–1053, 2001.

Zola, E.: *Le Ventre de Paris.* Charpentier, Paris, 1873.

Zuylen, G. van: *Tous les jardins du monde.* Gallimard, Paris, 1994.

bean sprouts, 221, 286, 288

beef: diseases, 39; Hindu taboo on, 40; production of, 116; steaks, 105, 112, 116, 122. *See also* cows; hamburgers; meat

beer, 89, 90, 348, 350, 360

bees, 234, 340, 395. *See also* insects

Beethoven, Ludwig von, 7, 252

Belgium, food markets in, 323

Bereshit, book of. *See* Genesis

Bern, 320

Bernini, Gian Lorenzo, "Apollo and Daphne," 173, plate 18

beta-carotene: in golden rice, 194–95; in vegetables, 270

Bible: agricultural images in, 49, 62, 70; bread symbolism in, 87; eating and cooking references in, 281–83; Ezekiel, 10; fishing in, 144; grasshoppers in, 134; Joseph in Egypt, 89; Noah and the flood, 60, 122, 244–45. *See also* Genesis

Bierstadt, Albert, 214

Big Mac index, 45–46

Big Macs, 44, 444

biocides. *See* pesticides

biodiversity: agriculture and, 65–66, 245–46, 255–61, 264–65, 273–74, 393; definition of, 245; food security and, 262–74; loss of, 132, 262, 267–68, 271; nutritional benefits of, 269–70; organic farming and, 232, 236; in paradise, 243–44; positive views of, 273, 274; preservation efforts, 255, 260–61, 269, 271–73

biodynamic agriculture, 224

biofuels, 47, 368, 378, 416, 432

bio-industry, 117. *See also* multinational corporations

biomass, 412

biotechnology: cloning, 176, 182, 188; in developing countries, 189–90, 191–94, 196–97, 203, 209, 210, 480–81; future of, 432; in organic farming, 201–2; regulations, 202–3; religions and, 209–10; in small-scale farming, 189, 198. *See also* genetic modification

bird 'flu, 131, 352, 404

birds, 110–11, 119, 131, 232. *See also* poultry

birds of paradise, 6

bison (buffalo), 381

Bligh, William, 84–85

Blixen, Karen, 375, 376

Boccaccio, Giovanni, 6

Bologna, 320

Borlang, Norman, 408

Bosch, Hieronymus, "The Garden of Earthly Delights," 3, 10, plate 3

Botero, Fernando, "Adan y Eva," 450

Bounty, HMS, 84–85

bovine spongiform encephalopathy (BSE), 131, 352, 363, 367

brackish areas, 160, 200, 400

brain: human, 35, 145; research on, 467

Brazil: cassava in, 64, 291; Cerrado, 186, 273, 357, 391; genetically modified crops in, 186, 187; organic farming in, 226; poverty in, 324

bread: baking, 83–84, 90, 94–95, 96; early types of, 89; factory-made, 95, 96; functional, 101–2; hamburger buns, 44, 101, 444; images of, 85–86; ingredients of, 84, 88, 89, 90–92, 99–100; low-carbohydrate, 97–98; multigrain, 99–100; nutrients in, 99, 100, 101–2, 194; old, 95, 329; political importance of, 91, 92; prices of, 91, 92, 95–97; rationing of, 91; regulations and taxes on, 91–92; sandwiches, 93, 94, 100; shortages of, 91, 92; as staple, 88–94, 97; symbolism of, 83–88, 102; traditional, 220; white, 91, 92, 94, 95–96, 99–102

breadfruit, 84–85, 98

breeder's rights, 204, 205, 206

breeding. *See* plant breeding

Breff Guilarte, Julio: "Llegan Mutantes Extraterrestres con la Ayuda Alimentaria de la ONU," 476; "El tiempo Moderno," 476–77, plate 24

Breughel, Jan, the Elder, "Earthly Paradise with the Fall of Adam and Eve," 10, 244, plate 1

Breughel, Pieter, the Elder, "The Land of Cockaigne," 23–24, 111, plate 10

Brillat-Savarin, Jean Anthelme, x

Britain: agriculture in, 80–81, 264; bread in, 95; city gardens in, 313; Corn Laws of, 80; curry in, 291; fish 'n' chips in, 154; garden cities in, 338; mad cow disease in, 352; McDonald's in, 47; overweight individuals in, 449–50; slaughtering regulations in, 128

broad beans, 67

Brown, Lester, xiii–xiv

Brundtland commission, 418, 420

BSE (bovine spongiform encephalopathy), 131, 352, 363, 367

Bt (*Bacillus thuringiensis*), 188, 196, 198, 200, 210

buckwheat, 90, 221

buffalo (bison), 381

bulgur, 221

Burger King, 43, 44, 46

burgers. *See* hamburgers

businesses, social responsibility of, 423–24. *See also* multinational corporations

Byzantine Empire, 109, 111

calcium, 102, 133, 455, 456, 458

Calcutta, 317

calories: in bread, 101; empty, 466; in fast food, 333, 466–67; in fats, 34; increased intake of, 444, 472; on menus, 466; in potatoes, 74; reducing intake of, 461; requirements, 453, 466; in restaurant meals, 466–67; sources of, 439

Canada: fish farming in, 164; McDonald's in, 48

cancer, 100, 115, 134, 219, 412, 449, 454–55

Canetti, Elias, 184

cannibalism, 104, 112

capitalism: critiques of, 301, 335, 376, 400, 422; democracy and, 422–23; globalization of, 422; hamburgers and fast food in, 43, 45, 475; market fail-

ures in, 421–22, 423; post-, 216, 241; time horizons of, 424

carbohydrates: avoiding, 97–98, 101; consumption of, 98–99, 461; creation of, 12

carbon dioxide (CO_2), 78, 132, 165, 326, 398, 407

cardiovascular disease, 100, 103, 115, 219, 412, 449, 456

Carnival, 37, 111

cassava: in Africa, 67, 291; in Brazil, 64, 291; cultivation of, 74; domestication of, 64, 65; in Europe, 269; genetically modified, 191–93; genome of, 192; global spread of, 98–99; growing conditions for, 190; nutrients in, 190; pests and diseases of, 190, 191, 192–93; processing, 190, 291; as staple, 190–91, 193; starch content of, 192; yields of, 193

catfish, 146

Catholic Church, fasting days of, 40, 111, 152, 459

cats, 120

cattle. *See* cows; livestock

Central Asia: agriculture in, 63; hybrid creatures in, 173

cereals. *See* grains

Ceres, 52, 244

Cerrado (Brazil), 186, 273, 357, 391

certification: of fish, 168–69; of food quality and sustainability, 368–69, 370–72; of organic farming, 370

Chagall, Marc, 8

Charles, Prince of Wales, 173–74

cheese, 114, 120, 140, 188, 300

chefs, xii, 297–99. *See also* cooking; restaurants

chemistry, molecular cuisine, 127, 297–99

chickens: diseases in, 287–88; domestication of, 109; feeds for, 227; products of, 335, 405; raising, 117, 404–5. *See also* eggs; poultry

chicken soup, 114

chickpeas, 64, 190, 221, 292

children, obese and overweight, 22, 448–49, 468–69

Chile: fish farming in, 164; organic farming in, 226; saltpeter in, 72

China: agriculture in, 63, 74, 76, 293–94; contaminated foods in, 349–50, 351; cooking in, 291–93; famine in, 438; fish consumption in, 146; fish farming in, 151, 162, 165; fish symbolism in, 142; genetically modified crops in, 196–97; genetic research in, 209; Goldfish Vase, plate 16; governance of, 423; hamburgers in, 45, 46–47; horticulture in, 55; imported crops in, 293–94; lactose intolerance in, 68; livestock in, 117, 196; millionaires in, 482; night soil in, 317; overweight and obese individuals in, 449, 450–51; restaurants in, 45; rice varieties in, 265; wheat in, 94

chocolate, 34, 35, 309, 360, 365–66, 455

cholesterol, 269, 455, 456, 461

Christianity: bread symbolism in, 87; Catholic fasting days, 40, 111, 152, 459; fish symbolism in, 142; mystics, 41; Protestantism, 40. See also paradise

chymosin, 188

cisgenesis, 182–83

cities: diets in, 271; early, 61, 315; entertainment zones in, 330–32; food chains in, 320–21; food markets in, 319–24; food riots in, 91; food supplies for, 91, 314, 315–16, 318–24, 343; food types in, 332; garbage in, 331, 400; gardens in, 311–14, 315–16, 335–36, 337, 338–41; green, 338–40; immigrant cultures in, 301, 323; local food in, 337–38; poverty in, 271, 312–13, 321, 324, 337; relationship to countryside, 316–18; smart, 341–42; waste from, 316–17, 342, 400; zoning, 342–43. See also urbanization

citrus fruit, 32, 73, 152–53, 302

city farms, 338–44

Claesz, Pieter, "Still Life with Herring, Wine and Bread," 85, plate 14

Clairvaux Abbey, 17

class differences, 443, 444–45, 450–51. See also middle class; poverty

Cleef & Arpels, 24

climate: agricultural development and, 65–66; droughts, 200–201, 395; fishing and, 149; rainfall, 60, 396, 397–98

climate change: adjusting to, 398; effects on agriculture, 396, 397–99, 412–13; end of Ice Age, 60; in Neolithic era, 58; sceptics of, 419; sea level rise, 413. See also greenhouse gas emissions

cloning, 176, 182, 188

CO_2, 78, 132, 165, 326, 398, 407

Coca-Cola, 48

Cockaigne, Land of, 18, 23–24, 111, 282

cocoa, 65, 226, 227, 371. See also chocolate

cod, 148, 150, 154, 165, 166

Code of Hammurabi, 80

Codex Alimentarius, 372

coffee, 65, 346, 348–49

colonialism, 375–76

Columbus, Christopher, 8, 73

community gardens, 337

Congo, 403–4

Congo River, 256, 396

conservation agriculture, 274

Constable, John: "The Glebe Farm," 80, plate 2; "Salisbury Cathedral from the Meadows," 253

consumers: choices by, 330, 359, 464–65, 469–70, 485–87; dilemmas faced by, ix–xiii, 307–10, 419; in food chain, 359; incomes of, 478; information for, 327, 368–69, 370–72, 466–67, 485–87; instant gratification for, 488; links to producers, 135–36, 239, 301, 302, 341; moral choices by, xi, 218, 327; preferences of, 482; price sensitivity of, 464, 465; separation from producers, xiii, 215, 239, 488–89. See also advertising

convenience foods, 321, 332, 335, 447, 464. See also fast food; finger food; ready-made meals

cookbooks, 297, 309, 444

cooking: with available ingredients, 280; constant change in, 295–96, 308–9; as construct and philosophy, 296–99; development of, 283–85; evolutionary advantages of, 284–85, 440–41; in food chain, 275–80; globalization of, 291–93, 295–96; kitchens, 307; as leisure activity, xii, 218–19, 221–22, 277, 309, 359, 487; local cuisines, 295; molecular cuisine, 127, 297–99; online recipes, 484; outside influences on, 295–96, 323–24, 333–35; rituals, 280; separation from eating, 276–77, 286, 309; skills, 221–22, 475; trust in, 36; worldviews and, 280, 296. *See also* dietary laws

Copia, 53

corn: in Africa, 63; as cattle feed, 74, 76, 99, 196; in China, 293–94; domestication of, 64, 178–79; genetically modified, 186–88, 195, 196, 201, 234; global spread of, 98–99; hybrids, 199

cornucopia, 53

Corsica, 66–67

cotton, Bt, 188, 189, 197, 202, 234. *See also* fiber products

counterculture, 335–36, 337

countryside: life in, 246–47, 249; population of, 390–91; poverty in, 246–47, 249–50; relationship to cities, 316–18; renaissance of, 247–49, 250–52; tourism in, 247–48, 428. *See also* landscapes

Cousteau, Jacques-Yves, 144

cows: domestication of, 64, 65, 115–16; draft animals, 108–9; genome of, 188; in India, 40, 112; mad cow disease, 131, 352, 363, 367; milk of, 40, 68, 75, 188; Sumerian sculpture of, 109, plate 8. *See also* beef; livestock

crabs. *See* seafood

Cranach, Lucas, the Elder, "Adam and Eve," 4, 10

creation stories: Laotian, 244; Masai, 7–8. *See also* Adam and Eve

Creutzfeldt-Jakob disease, 352, 363

crops. *See* agriculture; *specific crops*

cross-pollination, 62–63, 195, 198

Cuba, technology in, 476–77

cucina povera, 247, 309

cuisine. *See* cooking

curry, 291, 292, 293, 440

cycles. *See* ecosystems; food chains

dairy products: as by-product, 115–16; cheese, 114, 120, 140, 188, 300; consumption of, 123, 140; contaminated, 349–50; dietary laws, 40; genetic modification of, 136–37; ghee, 40; nutrients in, 113, 114–15, 455; production of, 75, 346–47; yogurt, 345, 346–47, 430. *See also* milk

Dante Aligheri, *Divine Comedy,* 6

date palms, 63

dates, 1, 86

Daumier, Honoré, "Le Banquier," 450, plate 22

Dead Sea, 59

deforestation, 66, 91, 132, 256–57, 259, 380–81, 396–97

deities: agricultural, 52–53, 88, 244, 282; bread and, 87–88; of nature, 215, 381

Demeter, 52, 244

democracy, capitalism and, 422–23

Denmark, fat tax in, 465

desertification, 398

deserts: Australian, 116; oases, 1–3, 58–59; Sahara, 1, 93. *See also* food deserts

developing countries: biotechnology in, 189–90, 191–94, 196–97, 203, 209, 210, 480–81; consumerism in, 482; cooking in, 19; countryside of, 249–50; economic growth in, 404, 415, 421, 422, 482; food chain in, 360; food demand in, 132; food in, 19–20, 323–24, 335, 348; Green Revolution in, 409–11; meals in, 306–7, 471; middle classes in, 94, 137, 156, 210, 391; modernization of, 475–77; obesity in, 448, 449; organic farming in, 226–27, 236; pesticides used in, 233–34; scarcities in, 19; school gardens in, 337; sustainability issues in, 421; urbanization in, 317–18, 471, 475

Dhaka, 317

diabetes, 100, 219, 449

dietary laws: changes in, 459–60; diversity of, 281; on fish, 152; genetic modification and, 209–10; Hindu, 40, 41, 288; ignoring, 37–38, 42; Islamic, 39, 122, 128, 210, 288, 474; Jewish, 38, 39, 40, 42, 121, 122, 128, 152, 209, 288; new, 484–85, 487; purity and, 288; purpose of, 38–39; reasons for, 37, 288; religious, 38–41, 121–22, 152

diets: balanced, 194, 460, 461–62; changes in, 220, 323–24, 333–35, 412, 458; flexitarian, 139, 157; healthy, 461–62; macrobiotic, 288; in past, 440; of poor, 451, 464; raw food, 122, 283–84, 285, 286, 287; restrictive, 460; traditional, 219–20, 291; variety in, 290–91, 440–41, 458–59; vegan, 113, 114, 223. *See also* vegetarianism

Dinant, Henri de, 4

diseases: bacterial, 233, 287–88, 349; cancer, 100, 115, 134, 219, 412, 449, 454–55; cardiovascular, 100, 103, 115, 219, 412, 449, 456; Creutzfeldt-Jakob disease, 352, 363; diabetes, 100, 219, 449; in fish farming, 164; malaria, 67–68; metabolic syndromes, 449; plant, 177, 190, 191, 192–93, 268–69, 272; zoonotic, 131, 352, 363, 397. *See also* livestock diseases

diversity, social, 243. *See also* biodiversity

dogs, 64, 120

domestication: of algae, 67; of animals, 52, 54, 61, 64–65, 108, 109, 115–17; of bacteria, 67; of fish, 151; of fruit, 67, 179; future of, 67; genetic modification and, 175, 176, 178–79; of grains, 59–60, 61–63, 66, 88, 89; of plants, 52, 54, 59–60, 61–64, 65, 66–67, 178–79; of vegetables, 64, 67

donkeys, 110, 184, 489

dopamine, 452

Doré, Gustave, 50–51

droughts, 200–201, 395. *See also* rainfall

drugs: genetically modified organisms and, 188; patents on, 203. *See also* antibiotics

ducks, 109, 117, 118. *See also* poultry

dumpster divers, 286–87, 336

durum wheat, 89

Dvořák, Antonin, 7

Earth Box, 340

Earth Summit (1992), 418–19

East Africa: agriculture in, 56, 93; food supplies in, 191, 456–57; human evolution in, 9, 107, 108, 145, 146. *See also* Kenya

eating: as connection to nature, 279–80; consciousness of, 277, 304–7; as dilemma, 307–10; emotional associations of, 304–5, 454; in food chain, 275–80; identity and, 303–4, 309; migration and, 323–24, 333–34; in moderation, 459, 460, 461; motives, 361–62; overconsumption, 37–38, 446–48; in paradise, 282–83, 362; in public, 330–32, 445; satisfaction, 453; separation from cooking, 276–77, 286, 309. *See also* diets; meals

ecological footprint, 364–65

The Economist, 45–46

ecosystems: agriculture and, 77–79, 412; change in, 11; critical thresholds in, 401; cycles of, 13, 279, 355; gardens as, 15–17; global, 14; human intervention in, 78, 175–78, 377, 380–82, 384, 385; independence from, 77–78; knowledge of, 29–30; paradise as, 8–10, 14, 22, 362; recovery of, 403–4; urban, 339. *See also* biodiversity; nature

education, 337, 485–87

eggplant, 73, 188, 210, 276, 313, 323

eggs: consumption of, 117, 119, 140; organic, 227; production of, 346

geese, 109. *See also* poultry

gender differences: in attitudes toward weight, 450–51; in meat eating, 120–21

gender roles: in fishing communities, 150; of hunter-gatherers, 222; mealtime norms and, 281, 443–44

gene banks, 267–68, 272, 273

Genesis, 8, 10, 18, 27–30, 49–51, 121–22, 144–45, 441–42

genetic diversity, 265–66, 271

genetic drift, 266

genetic material: as open source, 207; ownership of, 204–7, 208–9, 272; preservation efforts, 267–68, 272

genetic modification: of animals, 188; appropriate uses of, 185–86, 192–93, 194–95, 196, 202; biohackers and, 208; Bt crops, 188, 196, 198, 200, 210; concerns about, 180, 183–85, 195, 197–200, 203, 234, 354; continuity with past, 179–82, 185; debates on, 188–89, 209, 210, 481; for disease resistance, 272; domestication and, 175, 176, 178–79; for drought resistance, 200–201; errors made by industry, 186–87; expanded use of, 189; fears of, 42, 171–72, 173–74, 181, 186, 187–89, 208–9; of fish, 164–65; forms of, 182–83; fortified foods, 194–96; future possibilities for, 164–65, 200–202, 210–12; for herbicide resistance, 186–87; history of, 175–76, 178–79; labels, 171–72, 211, 372; of meat and dairy products, 136–37; misconceptions about, 198–200, 354; patents, 195, 203, 205–7; regulation of, 195–96, 202–3, 211; religious views of, 209–10; risks of, 189, 195, 197–98, 202; techniques of, 182

genetic resources. *See* genetic material

genomes: of apples, 179; of cassava, 192; of cows, 188; of pigs, 188; of rice, 195, 206, 267

Gerhardt, Ida, 102

Germany: animal rights laws in, 126; bread in, 95, 220; city gardens in, 313

Ghardaïa (Algeria), 1–2, 17

Ghiberti, Lorenzo, Florence Baptistery doors, 3–4

ghrelin, 452

Gibran, Khalil, 102, 490

Gilbert, Victor-Gabriel, "Le Carreau des Halles," plate 15

Gilgamesh epic, 5, 84

Giorgione, 214

globalization: of agriculture, 184–85, 186, 294; of capitalism, 422; concerns about, 364; of cooking, 291–93, 295–96; of crops, 293–94; of diets, 294–95; of food chain, xi–xii, 356, 435, 480; food safety and, 288. *See also* trade

gluten, 88, 89

GMOs. *See* genetic modification

goats: diseases in, 120, 131; domestication of, 64, 115; genetically modified, 185; meat of, 110; milk of, 114, 130, 185; raising, 130–31. *See also* livestock

Goes, Hugo van der, "The Fall of Adam," 24

golden rice, 194–96

Goldfish Vase, plate 16

golf courses, 250, 312, 377

Goyen, Jan van, "View of Haarlem and the Haarlem Lake," 253

grains: consumption of, 98; domestication of, 59–60, 61–63, 66, 88, 89; milling, 88–89; nutrients in, 63–64, 66, 101, 269–70; perennial, 431–32; varieties of, 221, 266; yields of, 75, 266, 394. *See also* *specific grains*

grapes, 4, 5, 32, 33, 272

Greece, ancient: Arcadia, 5, 22; bread in, 87, 90; deities of, 52, 53; vegetarians in, 123

greed, 30, 36, 184, 324, 382, 422

green cities, 338–40

greenhouse gas emissions: effects of, 377; genetic modification and, 201; from livestock farming, 131, 132, 136, 201, 405; from organic farming, 229, 236; reducing, 326, 398, 399. *See also* climate change

views of, 142–43; by prehistoric humans, 108, 177

Hu Szu-hui, *Yin-shan chengyao* ("Proper Essentials of Drink and Food"), 291–93

hybrids: crops, 179, 199; fears of, 172–74; human-plant, 171–72, 173–74, 208. *See also* plant breeding

hydrogen cyanide, 190–92, 289, 291

Ice Age, 58, 59, 60

immigrants, 301, 323, 334. *See also* migration

incomes: food choices and, 412; meat consumption and, 111–12

India: agriculture in, 57, 63, 76, 188, 226, 409; biotechnology in, 210; cities in, 61, 312–13, 317; countryside of, 249–50; deities in, 53; diabetes in, 449; famines in, 438–39; hamburgers in, 45, 46, 47; hunger in, 449; livestock in, 40; vegetarianism in, 112–13; wood eaten in, 458. *See also* Hinduism

Indonesia, 94

Industrial Revolution: agriculture and, 55, 74, 257; dietary changes, 91, 92; dietary changes and, 388; meat consumption and, 111

insecticides. *See* pesticides

insects: diversity of, 264–65; eating, 69, 105, 106, 134–35, 269; in food chain, 13; monarch butterfly, 198; natural controls of, 55, 61; on organic farms, 232; pests, 19, 49, 71, 73; pollinators, 10, 395; as protein source, 134–35, 391

insulin, 384, 432, 449, 452, 455

intellectual property, patents on genetic material, 195, 203, 205–7

intensification: of agriculture, 263, 264–65, 393; of fishing, 263–64; of horticulture, 366; of livestock production, 117, 404–5; sustainable, 263–64, 366, 429. *See also* fish farming

Inuit, 142, 149, 285

in vitro meat, 133–34

iodine, 152, 194

Iran (Persia), 15, 292, 400

Iraq: early cities in, 61; Shatt-al-Arab, 399–400; Tigris and Euphrates, 9, 50, 53, 60, 109, 315, 399. *See also* Sumeria

Ireland: bread superstitions in, 87; famine in, 74, 268, 438; meat consumption in, 118; potatoes in, 74, 177, 268

iron, 113, 194

irradiated food, 363, 366

irrigation: deficit, 429; development of, 16, 60–61; drip, 429; ponds, 159–60; water used, 159, 396

Islam: art, 4; dietary laws of, 39, 121; halal rules, 39, 122, 128, 210, 288, 474; Koran, 15, 51, 87; mystics, 41; paradise, 22, 25; ritual slaughter in, 128–29

isotopes, of carbon, 107–8

Israel, drip irrigation in, 408. *See also* Judaism

Italy: agriculture in, 21, 73, 74, 75, 248; bread in, 85, 86, 91; cities in, 73; cooking in, 293; deforestation in, 380–81; food culture of, 21, 278; food markets in, 316, 322; protests in, 46, 299; slow food movement in, 299–301; songbirds in, 110–11; Umbrian countryside, 246–47, 248, 250

Jack in the Box, 43

Japan: bread in, 94; *fugu*, 36; natural farming in, 217; rice goddess in, 52–53; sushi and sashimi, 155–56, 335

Jews. *See* Judaism

Jordan River, 53

Judaism: bread symbolism in, 87; dietary laws of, 38, 39, 40, 42, 121, 122, 152; food traditions and, 114; kosher rules, 38, 39, 40, 122, 128, 209, 288; ritual slaughter in, 128–29. *See also* Genesis; paradise

junk food, 445, 466. *See also* fast food; finger food

kangaroos, 119, 135

Karachi, 317

Mendel, Gregor, 180
Mesopotamia, 9, 303–4, 315, 399–400
metabolic syndromes, 449
methane, 11, 130, 132, 135, 136, 201
Mexico: cuisine of, 219–20; overweight individuals in, 453
Mexico City, 317
Michelangelo, Sistine Chapel, 50, 477
Middle Ages: agriculture in, 73, 75; fast days in, 40, 152; food laws in, 40, 80; food markets in, 320; food shortages in, 80; foods in, 73, 90–91; gardens in, 18; Land of Cockaigne, 18, 23–24, 111, 282
middle class: in developing countries, 94, 137, 156, 210, 391; diets of, 25, 95–96, 112, 137, 156, 445; growth of, 391, 477; obesity in, 448; slimness in, 451–52. *See also* consumers
Middle East: agriculture in, 50, 53–54, 57, 58–61, 63; apples in, 32; bread in, 86, 90; protein sources in, 110; soil fertility in, 29. *See also individual countries*
migration, eating patterns and, 323–24, 333–34
milk: by-products of, 432; of cows, 40, 68, 75, 188; fresh, 289; of goats, 114, 130, 185; of horses, 120; lactose intolerance, 68; nutrients in, 455; organic, 234; wasted, 329. *See also* dairy products
millet, 64, 294
Milton, John, *Paradise Lost* and *Paradise Regained*, 6, 9, 27, 32
moderation, 40, 459, 460, 461, 485
modernization, 181, 184, 237, 475–79, 481. *See also* intensification; technology
molds, 49, 56, 69, 73, 201, 233, 235, 268
molecular cuisine, 127, 297–99
Mongol Empire, 292–93
Mongolia, foods from, 292
monocultures, 259–60, 272, 406
Monsanto, 186, 187
morality: in consumer choices, xi, 218, 327; organic farming and, 217, 224–

25; self-control, 447; stigma of extra weight, 459; values, 296
More, Thomas, *Utopia*, 6
Morocco, immigrants from, 301, 323
Moses Bar Cephas, 23
mosquitoes, 67–68
MSC. *See* Marine Stewardship Council
muesli, 345, 346
multinational corporations, 117, 186, 187, 199, 203, 205, 423–24, 427
Mumbai, 312–13, 317
mushrooms, 133, 222
music, 7, 252

Nairobi, 313, 375–76
Native Americans: foods of, 323, 381; potlatch, 442–43; religions of, 41
natural farming, 217, 382–83
natural foods: appeal of, 217, 219, 289–90, 301, 364; myth of, 285–86; purity of, 223–24; use of term, 223–24
nature: dangers in, 215; eating as connection to, 279–80; humans' relationship with, 7–8, 15, 30, 213–17, 382–86; preservation efforts, 254–55, 258–59, 382, 383, 489; romanticized, 214–15, 239–40. *See also* ecosystems
Neanderthals, 146, 285, 286
Necropolis of Hermes, Sousse (Tunisia), floor mosaic, 149, plate 17
nectarines, 179–80, 270
Neolithic agricultural revolution, 55, 58, 59, 108
neo-Malthusianism, 380. *See also* shadow thinkers
Neruda, Pablo, 87
Netherlands: agriculture in, 76, 79, 81, 130, 399; bread in, 91–92, 95; cities in, 316, 338–39; city gardens in, 313, 314; dairy products in, 75, 116, 120, 130, 184, 216; debate on ritual slaughter in, 128–29; dietary changes in, 294–95; ethnic cuisines in, 334; fast food in, 47, 332; food markets in, 323; as garden, 17; horticulture in, 55, 355, 399,

organic farming (*continued*)
livestock, 230–32, 233, 235; markets for, 226, 237–39, 303; modern technology and, 240–41; moral connotations of, 217, 224–25; regulation of, 225, 226, 231; yields of, 226, 228, 230
Ottoman Empire, 90
overgrazing, 29, 71, 132, 397, 403
overweight individuals: cartoons of, 450; children, 22, 448–49; diseases of, 449; increased number of, 21–22, 448–50; influences on, 445–48, 450–51, 452–53; losing weight, 452–54; moral stigma and, 459; in Netherlands, 21–22; reducing number of, 461–70; wealthy, 450. *See also* obesity
Ovid, *Metamorphoses*, 5, 173
oxen, 109, 112
oxygen, 12

packaging, 47, 347, 430
Paleolithic Diet, 286, 287
palm oil, 69, 134, 368, 429
palm weevil, 134, 269
papaya, 188
Papua New Guinea. *See* New Guinea
paradise: Aztec myth of, 282; biodiversity in, 243–44; consumer, 488–89; as ecosystem, 8–10, 14, 22, 362; expulsion from, 3, 8, 22, 27–30, 49, 50–51, 68, 145, 283, 386; food supplies in, 4–5, 8, 10, 18, 31, 282–83, 362; in future, 489–90; as garden, 2–6, 9–10, 15, 17–18, 22–24, 52, 59; heaven as, 3; images of, 3–4, 8, 9, 10, 14, 17–18, 23–24, 244; in literature, 6; location of, 9; longing for, 477–78; loss of, 6–7, 375–80, 400; metaphors, xv, 23, 24, 36–37, 487; as natural order, 172, 213; oases as, 1–3; origin of word, 15; symbolism of, 8, 10; temptation in, 37; as utopia, 6–7, 8, 9. *See also* Adam and Eve
paradise fish, 6
paradise nut, 6
paradise theory, 24–26

Paris: chestnut vendors in, 322; Forum des Halles, 331; gardens in, 314; Les Halles, 319, plate 15; McDonald's in, 474
Partij voor de Dieren (Party for the Animals), 125–26, 128
pasta, 89, 94, 335
Pasteur, Louis, 92, 351
pasteurization, 351
pata negra pigs, 114, 123, 261
patents, 195, 203, 205–7
peaches, 293
peanuts, 65
pears, 171, 172, 176, 186, 208
peasants, 6, 7, 80, 141, 293–94, 410
perennial food crops, 431–32
Peru: deities in, 52–53; guano in, 72. *See also* Andes
pesticides: neonicotinoid, 395; reducing use of, 188, 196, 200, 234; residues of, 233–34, 372; resistance to, 198; use of, 411
pests: *Bacillus thuringiensis* and, 188; of cassava, 190, 191; insects, 19, 49, 71, 73; organic controls, 225, 232–33
pets, 120, 125
Philo, 23
Phoenicians, 148, 153, 158
phosphates, 70, 71, 75, 79, 136, 394–95
photosynthesis, 11–13, 14, 56, 201
phytase, 136, 196
Picasso, Pablo, 85
pigs: in China, 117; domestication of, 118; ecological impact of, 39; feeds for, 136; genome of, 188; products using, 123; raising, 117; swine fever in, 120, 352; truffles and, 66–67. *See also* pork
pineapple, 65, 327, 348, 429
pizza, 116, 335, 473
Pizza Hut, 46
plaggen manuring, 70, 72, 229
plant breeding: compared to genetic modification, 180–82, 185, 191–92; genetic diversity and, 265–66; in Green Revolution, 410; history of, 175, 178, 180; of new species, 178–80; objec-

tives of, 200, 269, 272, 407, 411. *See also*
domestication; genetic modification;
Green Revolution; hybrids
plants: co-evolution with humans,
67–68; domestication of, 52, 54, 59–60,
61–64, 65, 66–67, 178–79; genetic diversity of, 265–66; landraces, 61, 265–67,
268, 269, 271, 273; photosynthesis,
11–13, 14, 56, 201; proteins, 113, 133, 170,
391, 407, 432; wild, 222, 270, 273, 286–
87, 336, 352
Plato, *The Republic*, 5
Pliny the Elder, 381
ploughs, 53, 56, 61, 80. *See also* tillage
poetry, 6, 85, 102
Pol Pot, 318, 408
pomegranates, 1, 4, 9, 23, 32, 33, 41
population growth: in Africa, 375–76,
398; agriculture and, 55–56, 58, 73–74,
78, 82, 257–58, 293–94; economic
growth and, 390; food supplies and,
356–57, 387, 388–89, 391–92; in future,
263, 357, 390, 418; increased rate of, 78,
82; Malthusian view of, xiii–xiv, 380
pork: consumption of, 120; dietary laws
on, 39, 42, 105, 114, 121, 288. *See also*
meat; pigs
portion sizes, 44, 444, 468
Portugal: agriculture in, 76; food markets in, 320; traders from, 291
potassium, 70, 71, 394–95
potatoes: calories in, 74; diseases of, 177,
268–69; in Europe, 294; in fish 'n'
chips, 154; flour, 91; genetically modified, 182–83, 185; in Ireland, 74, 177,
268; Peruvian god of, 52–53; popularity of, 74, 98–99; starches in, 98; varieties of, 99, 265
potlatch, 442–43
poultry: domestication of, 109; eggs, 117,
119, 140, 227, 346; large-scale production of, 136, 404–5; meat, 110. *See also*
chickens; livestock
poverty: biodiversity and, 270–71, 273;
bread and, 85–86; in cities, 271, 312–13,

321, 324, 337; in countryside, 246–47,
249–50; *cucina povera*, 247, 309; diets
and, 451, 464; farming and, 191, 378–79,
410; food prices and, 308, 464; food
scarcity and, 443; reducing, 201
power, 37, 124
prices. *See* food prices
promethean ideas, 381, 384
proteins: human need for, 113; new
products, 132–35, 407; plant sources
of, 113, 133, 170, 391, 407, 432. *See also*
dairy products; fish; meat
public health, 131
purity: fasting and, 459; of foods, 287–
88, 289–90; in Hinduism, 112; longing
for, 214; of natural foods, 223–24; in
slow food, 300; spiritual, 288

Q fever, 120, 131, 352, 484–85
Quarter Pounders, 44, 121
Quick fast food chain, 474
quinoa, 98, 221, 269–70
quotas, fishing, 166–67

rabbits, 110, 177
radiation, of food, 363, 366
rainfall: amounts needed for agriculture, 60; climate change and, 396,
397–98. *See also* water
Ramayana, 112
Raphael, 144
raw food diets, 122, 283–84, 285, 286, 287
ready-made meals, 156, 276, 307, 309, 331
recycling: of shopping bags, 328–29; of
waste, 77, 369–70, 407, 428–29, 430
refrigeration, 166, 285, 326, 343, 347, 378
regulation: of abundance, 460–70; of
advertising, 467; of biotechnology,
202–3; of bread, 91–92; of fisheries, 166–
69; of food sales, 466–67; of genetic
modification, 195–96, 202–3, 211; of livestock production, 130; of markets, 80,
81, 82, 465–67; need for, 423; of organic
farming, 225, 226, 231; of slaughtering,
128. *See also* food safety

religions: agriculture and, 52–53, 381; biotechnology and, 209–10; bread symbolism in, 86–87; dietary laws of, 38–41, 121–22, 152; fasting in, 40, 41, 459; technological innovations and, 183–84. *See also* paradise

Renaissance paintings, 4, 214, 253

resources, sustainability of, 418

restaurants: chefs, xii, 297–99; Chinese, 45; as entertainment, 299, 330–31; ethnic, 333–34; fusion cooking, 45; low-calorie meals in, 466–67; molecular cuisine, 127, 297–99; number of, 333; outdoor, 330–31; status of, 297. *See also* fast food

retailers. *See* supermarkets

rice: cooking, 293; cultivation of, 63, 66, 70, 74, 159, 162, 293; eating, 64, 74; in Europe, 293; genetically modified, 190, 194–97; genome of, 195, 206, 267; global spread of, 98–99, 293; golden, 194–96; hybrid, 76; in sushi, 155; varieties of, 99, 265; yields of, 76, 409

rich countries. *See* OECD countries

Rio+20 summit (2012), 421

Rio Earth Summit (1992), 418–19

rituals: agricultural, 53; cooking, 280; at meals, 281, 304, 305–7; sharing food, 442–43; slaughtering, 128–30

rocket, 179

Roman Empire: agriculture in, 75, 380–81; bread in, 90, 99; decline of, 316; deities of, 52, 53; fish consumption in, 148–49; food supplies for, 316, 319, 347; garden images in, 18–19

Romanticism, 214–15, 253

Rome, food markets in, 316, 322

root crops. *See* cassava; potatoes; sweet potatoes; yams

Roth, Philip, 42

Royal Society, 189

Rubens, Peter Paul, 450; "Earthly Paradise with the Fall of Adam and Eve," 10, 244, plate 1

rules. *See* dietary laws; regulation

rural areas. *See* countryside; landscapes

Russia: Aral Sea, 159; bread riots in, 91; famine in, 438; gardens in, 314; McDonald's in, 45

rye, 88, 89, 90

saffron, 293

sago palm, 98

Sahara, 1, 93

Sahel, 51, 63, 395, 413, 437, 440

St. Lazarus Cathedral, Autun, 30–31

salad greens, 330

salinization, 54, 257, 315, 395

salmon: farmed, 153, 155, 163, 164; fishing for, 142; at McDonald's, 47; popularity of, 155

salmonella, 287–88, 349

salted fish, 148, 150, 154

saltpeter, 72, 75

salts, 333, 456, 468

sandwiches, 93, 94, 100

sashimi, 155–56, 335

savannahs, 56, 105, 107, 108, 145, 356, 383. *See also* Cerrado

scale, of food production, 433–36. *See also* intensification; small-scale farming

Scandinavian diet, 295

Schelfhout, Andreas, "The Farmstead," 254

Scheuermeier, Paul, 247

school gardens, 337

seafood, 134, 153, 156–57. *See also* fish; shellfish

sea vegetables, 170

seaweed, 114, 147, 156, 170

secularization, 24, 41, 106, 119, 209

selection. *See* plant breeding

self-control, 447

"Sennefer's Garden," 17–18, plate 7

shadow thinkers, xiii–xiv, 380, 382, 389, 390, 398–99

Shanghai, 276–77, 317

sheep: domestication of, 64, 115; meat of, 21, 47, 105, 110, 111, 115, 116, 127; wool of, 54, 115. *See also* livestock shellfish, 146, 147, 148, 154, 162, 406. *See also* fish

shopping. *See* consumers; markets; supermarkets

sickle-cell anemia, 68

silk potato, 185

Silk Roads, 32, 292, 293

Simpson's in the Strand, 36

sin, 30, 32, 35, 36, 48, 460. *See also* temptation

slaughtering: methods of, 128–29, 296; religious rules for, 121; rituals, 128–30

slave trade, 77–78

slimness, 451–52, 453, 459

slow food movement, 239, 299–301, 302, 303, 309

small-scale farming: biotechnology in, 189, 198; crops of, 260; disappearance of, 81–82, 426–27, 436; future of, 426–28, 432–33, 435–36; horticulture, 260; idealization of, 136, 426; livestock, 136; online sales by, 336–37; organic, 226; pressures on, 80–81; risks in, 426; slow food movement and, 300, 301; subsidies for, 248; sustainability of, 426

smart cities, 341–42

Smetana, Bedrich, 7, 252

smoking, 462

snacks. *See* convenience foods; finger food

snails, 119–20

Snijders, Frans, "Still Life with a Dead Stag," 126, plate 12

Snow White, 7

social responsibility, 326, 423–24, 490

soft drinks, 466, 468

soil erosion. *See* erosion, soil

soil fertility: declines in, 73; knowledge of, 29; law of the minimum, 70–71; legumes and, 66; loss of, 393; maintaining, 70–72, 228–29; in Middle East, 29. *See also* fertilizers

soil salinization, 54, 257, 315

solar energy, 12, 14, 68, 69, 78. *See also* photosynthesis

songbirds, 110–11, 119. *See also* birds

sorghum, 64

sourdough bread, 89, 95–96

Sousse (Tunisia), Necropolis of Hermes, 149, plate 17

South America. *See* Andes; *individual countries*

Soviet Union, famine in, 438. *See also* Russia

soy: as cattle feed, 76, 77, 406–7; as fertilizer, 79; genetically modified, 186–88, 202, 354, 406–7; products, 106, 133, 332; proteins in, 133

soy sauce, 133, 194

Spain: agriculture in, 260; conquistadores, 294; fishing in, 157–58; food markets in, 320; golf courses in, 312; landscapes in, 261; Neanderthals in, 146; restaurants in, 297; tapas, 473

spelt, 63, 88

spices: trade in, 292, 348; use of, 294, 440, 468

spiders, 185

spinach, 113

Spurlock, Morgan, *Super Size Me*, 43, 48

Sri Lanka, 9

Stalin, Josef, 318, 408

staple foods, 98–99, 190–91, 193. *See also* bread

starchy crops, 98, 192, 439

status, 46, 48

sterols, 412, 456

Stoppard, Tom, 6

strawberries, 9, 208, 221, 289, 294

street food, 21, 320, 321–22

Strik Bernard, "Suspended Blurr," 140, plate 13

sturgeon, 165, 166

subsidies: agricultural, 81, 82, 94, 248, 414, 462–64; for biodiversity preservation, 261; of biofuels, 416; of fishing, 167

suburbs: food supplies for, 321; gardens in, 18, 251; lifestyle of, 446, 447–48

Warhol, Andy, 43
wasps, 55, 188, 233, 259
waste: biomass, 412; from cities, 316–17,
    342, 400; food, 286–87, 317, 329–30,
    379, 394, 472; markets and, 485; pack-
    aging, 347; recycling, 77, 369–70, 407,
    428–29, 430; reducing, 429. *See also*
    manure
water: agricultural use of, 60–61, 70,
    395–96; bottled, 388; in ecosystems, 13;
    floods, 60, 122, 244–45, 377; footprint,
    365; irrigation, 16, 60–61, 159–60, 396,
    429; plant growth and, 13; pollution,
    159, 232, 264, 396; purity of, 289; rain-
    fall, 60, 396, 397–98; virtual, 365
watermelon, 73
weeds: in early agriculture, 61; edi-
    ble, 340; organic controls for, 225;
    in organic farming, 230. *See also*
    herbicides
West. *See* Europe; OECD countries;
    individual countries
West Africa: agriculture in, 64, 67, 334;
    bread in, 86; clay eaten in, 458; gar-
    dens in, 311–12; malaria in, 67–68;
    overweight individuals in, 450
western Asia. *See* Middle East
whales, 148
wheat: for bread, 89; durum, 89; global
    spread of, 294; gluten content of, 88,
    89; importance of, 88; milling, 88–89,
    92, 100; prices of, 96–97; primitive

forms of, 59, 62–63; trade in, 93–94;
    yields of, 75, 76, 97, 413. *See also* grains
White Castle, 43
Whole Earth Catalog, 301
whole food movement, 301–2, 303
Whole Foods Market, 302
wine, 85, 87, 272, 304. *See also* grapes
women: diets during pregnancy, 281,
    444; food for, 281, 443–44; household
    skills of, 222; slim, 451–52. *See also*
    gender differences
Wonder Bread, 92, 96
wool, 54, 115
work. *See* labor
World Heritage List, 219–20, 295
World Trade Organization (WTO), 129,
    202, 203, 308
wraps, 295–96
WTO. *See* World Trade Organization

Xochiquetzal, 282

yams, 64, 67
yogurt, 345, 346–47, 430

zero-tillage method, 54–55, 187, 217, 230,
    476
Zeus, 53, 381
zinc, 99, 192, 234, 458
Zohar, 28, 30
Zola, Émile, 319, 324
zoonotic diseases, 131, 352, 363, 397
Zuidam, Rob, 27